Mormon Midwife

The 1846–1888 Diaries of Patty Bartlett Sessions

Volume 2
LIFE WRITINGS OF FRONTIER WOMEN

A Series Edited by
Maureen Ursenbach Beecher

Volume 1
Winter Quarters
The 1846–1848 Life Writings of
Mary Haskin Parker Richards
Edited by Maurine Carr Ward

Volume 3
The History of Louisa Barnes Pratt
The Autobiography of
A Mormon Missionary Widow and Pioneer
Edited by S. George Ellsworth

Patty Bartlett Sessions. Courtesy of International Society, Daughters of Utah Pioneers.

Mormon Midwife

The 1846–1888 Diaries
of
Patty Bartlett Sessions

Edited by

Donna Toland Smart

UTAH STATE UNIVERSITY PRESS
Logan, Utah
1997

Copyright © 1997 Utah State University Press

Utah State University Press
Logan, Utah 84322-7800

Typography by WolfPack
  Dust jacket design by Michelle Sellers

Cover illustrations: Patty Sessions. Courtesy of International Society,
Daughters of Utah Pioneers. Patty Bartlett Sessions Academy in Bountiful,
Utah. Patty Sessions is on the left wearing a black hat and holding a child.
Courtesy of Kim Burningham.

10 9 8 7 6 5 4 3 2   99 01 02 03 04

Library of Congress Cataloging-in-Publication Data

Sessions, Patty Bartlett, 1795–1892.
    Mormon midwife : the 1846–1888 diaries of Patty Bartlett Sessions
/ edited by Donna T. Smart.
    p.   cm. – (Life writings of frontier women; v. 2)
Includes bibliographical references and index.
ISBN 0-87421-274-X
    1. Sessions, Patty Bartlett, 1795-1892–Diaries. 2. Women
pioneers–West (U.S.)–Diaries. 3. Midwives–West (U.S.)–Diaries.
4. Mormon women–West (U.S.)–Diaries. 5. Frontier and pioneer
life–West (U.S.) 6. Nauvoo (Ill.)–Biography. I. Smart, Donna T.
(Donna Toland), 1923–   . II. Title. III. Series.
F593.S45A3 1997
978'.02'092–dc21
    [B]   97–4785
                                                           CIP

CONTENTS

ILLUSTRATIONS

FOREWORD

Maureen Ursenbach Beecher

Reading the diary of a woman is like visiting across the back fence on a summer afternoon. While your wash dries on the line, and her garden awaits the seeds she is planting, you chat about the things that matter to each of you: your new carpet, her problem with the car, her daughter who is about to marry, your son who seems unable to find directions in his life, the neighbor whose husband recently died, and whether or not the town council will fix the potholes in the road this spring. Of just such topics is a woman's life filled; of such things she writes in her diary. The events and circumstances, the concerns and achievements of a woman's life are as worthy the attention of historians as are the doings of governments and corporations, generally the domain of men. Public and private and male and female worlds overlap, but as Laurel Thatcher Ulrich observed in the introduction to her Pulitzer Prize study, *A Midwife's Tale: The Life of Martha Ballard*, there are areas of both which have not in the past been deemed of interest—the details of the day to day activities of men and women, for example, but especially the domestic affairs of women. And, as Ulrich noted, "it is in the very dailiness, the exhaustive, repetitious dailiness, that the real power of Martha Ballard's book lies."[1]

Patty Bartlett Sessions, like Martha Ballard, was a Maine midwife. Two generations apart in lifespans, the two women shared many concerns, which each recorded in her notebook alongside the requisite notations of birthings attended. Characteristic of her time, Martha began and ended her life in Maine. Not untypical of her later time, Patty participated in the westward movement of eastern Americans, ending her life two thousand miles from Maine, in the valleys of the Rocky Mountains. What they shared was the world of women, a geography which knows no boundaries of time or space.

---

1. Laurel Thatcher Ulrich, *A Midwife's Tale: The Life of Martha Ballard, Based on Her Diary, 1785–1812* (New York: Alfred A. Knopf, 1990), 9.

The diaries of Patty Sessions have long enriched historians' views of the formation of the western Zion. As in her proud declaration, upon completing her 1847 hegira to the Valley of the Great Salt Lake, that she had driven her wagon "all the way but part of the two last mts [mountains]" and that she "broke nothing nor turned over," Patty speaks clearly of her important part in the move.[2] Accounts such as hers present evidence of women's involvement in commerce, education, government, and the courts, as well as the domestic and the religious worlds. Untold stories of the development of the American West are available in the life writings of women, and contemporary scholars are anxious to recover them for their value to historical analysis.

Women's life writings, though, are more than just the raw data that historians, sociologists, anthropologists, or economists may draw from them. They are literary texts in their own right. In each one a woman's life is revealed; each is as worthy of sympathetic reading as any more polished biography and is perhaps even more rewarding for coming from the subject's own pen. As such texts, they speak to the inner life of the reader.

Unmediated discourse of writer to reader is attempted here. Editorial background is provided where necessary but without modifying the author's own text. Only the form of print has changed; the reader may enjoy the lines without struggling to decipher sometimes tiny and confusing handwritten script. Approach this text, then, and those that follow in the series, with confidence in the veracity of its rendering. Read with interest, with forbearance, and with compassion—with reverence for the life disclosed.

Whether regarded as document or text, the life writing of a frontier woman can expand the lives of its readers. It is the hope of the editors that such will be the case with the present volume, *Mormon Midwife: The 1846–1888 Diaries of Patty Bartlett Sessions*, volume 2 of the series Life Writings of Frontier Women.

---

2. Patty Sessions, Diary One, 25 September 1847.

PREFACE

On 4 February 1995 the descendants of Patty Bartlett Sessions noted the two hundredth birthday of their pioneer ancestress. They are well acquainted with her since fragments of her diaries have been quoted in books such as *Guardians of the Hearth* by Claire Noall; *Women's Voices*, compiled and edited by Kenneth W. and Audrey M. Godfrey and Jill Mulvay Derr; volume one of *Covered Wagon Women*, edited and compiled by Kenneth L. Holmes; and other works, including volumes published by the Daughters of Utah Pioneers. One of Patty's descendants, Leroy W. Brown, edited segments of Patty's diaries, as he said in his dedication, for his children, "for whom this history was primarily written." He titled his version *History of Patty Bartlett Sessions: Mother of Mormon Midwifery*. Susan Sessions Rugh, who wrote a chapter for the book *Sister Saints*, edited by Vickey Burgess-Olson, is a great-great-great-granddaughter of Patty. Her essay presents a significant core of Patty's life experiences. All these sources have helped me know who Patty Sessions was. However, this is the first version of her diaries that is published in its entirety and that attempts to be faithful to the text as she wrote it.

Patty's life is so rich in historical byways that the editor is tempted to digress constantly and interrupt the tale of her meanderings from Maine to Missouri to Nauvoo to Winter Quarters to the Rocky Mountains. Willpower such as Patty demonstrated necessarily becomes a vital aspect of editing her diary.

THE DIARIES

The Historical Department of the Church of Jesus Christ of Latter-day Saints protects the originals of Patty's diaries. The Patty Sessions archival box contains five folders, each encasing one or more of her well-worn and fading diaries and a small book filled with her accounts. A sixth folder holds a few midwife records and other loose papers and scraps on which she wrote notes. She used a pen dipped in handmade ink on then-scarce paper and, for the most part, filled every fraction of every page. The first small leather diary, given to her by her daughter Sylvia at the beginning of the February exodus from Nauvoo, includes the period from 1846 through 1848; the second, relating experiences from 1849 through 1850, is homemade, sewn together with broken thread and held together with a very long straight pin; the years 1851 and 1852 make up the third volume; 1853 through 1855, the fourth; 1856 through February 1862, the fifth; and February 1862 through 1866, the sixth. A separate sheet includes entries for July and August 1880. All the diaries from 1849 on are homemade. Another larger, leather-bound volume was donated in recent years to the Historical Department. It contains reminiscences, minutes of the Relief Society over which she presided, and her journal entries until 4 May 1888, when, without explanation, the writing ceased. She died on 14 December 1892, less than two months before her ninety-eighth birthday.

TRANSCRIPTION AND RESEARCH

Mary-Jo Kline, author of the classic reference book on editing *A Guide to Documentary Editing*, warned in a workshop at Brigham Young University that a person working on original manuscripts must have a "tolerance for tedium." I can attest to the accuracy of that prophetic pronouncement.

The challenge was to prepare a manuscript faithful to the original, including spelling, punctuation, and grammar. That meant, first of all, enduring the eyestrain of typing all of the diaries from hard-to-read microfilm and then checking the transcription against the originals. It meant trying, often in vain, to identify the literally thousands of persons named in Patty's entries, including the babies she delivered, the way they *really* spelled their names, when they were born and when they died, and their importance in her time. It meant investigating and footnoting events she barely mentioned because *she* knew to what she referred. It meant repeating the redundant recitations of a workaholic who time and time again watered her garden, dried her fruit, wove her cloth, made clothes, tore rags for rugs, crocheted, knitted, washed, cleaned, and worried. A reader may figuratively gasp for air while trying to follow her frenetic pace. But an editor must, and a reader should, try to understand the compulsion to record such mundane events and what they say not only about her life but about a particular time and society. She was compulsive about writing down everything, scribbling notes and figures on the inside covers of her diaries—sometimes even upside down.

The rewards of studying Patty's diaries surpass her lists of wearisome, though informative, details about her daily activities that became, almost, rituals. Although she endured and recorded many significant personal and social transitions, the individuals who moved in and out of her world were more important to her. Although she was adept at hiding her feelings, occasionally her emotions spilled over onto the page, exposing her vulnerability. They surfaced, for example, when, instead of moving west with the pioneers, son David and daughter Sylvia opted to accompany her pharmacist husband to

Iowa City; when she dealt with her ambiguous feelings about polygamy; when she contemplated, and justified, her role during a medical emergency. In such instances a diary entry became almost a poetic prayer.

The next stage of editing involved comparing the corrected text against an enlarged photocopy of the microfilm that neither showed changes in ink color nor exposed penciled symbols and notes made by some hand other than her own. After necessary revisions, the thrice-corrected version was proofed again against the original diaries. At this crucial stage, some of Patty's descendants, great-granddaughters and great-great-granddaughters, checked the original text while I read aloud from my transcriptions.

The editing of Patty's diaries may never be finished. Every reading reveals new incidents that need research and explanation, dates and data that might be checked. It will be so with Patty Bartlett Sessions, I believe, as long as her journals are examined. There will always be corrections (despite human efforts to avoid errors) and additions.

Part of the research involved a trip to Patty's birthplace in Maine, cemeteries in the environs, and New England historical societies, all of which added variety and information to the project.

Editorial Methods

In an effort to help readers visualize Patty's additions and corrections to her writing or clarify references to individuals, the following methods have been employed:

1. To make reading the text easier, dates are highlighted, although Patty's entries were usually run together until her final diary, when she began using paper more generously.

2. Editorial insertions are enclosed in square brackets. Words in the editor's voice are italicized. Bracketed emendations, clarifications, and identifications, all extensions of Patty's text, are not.

3. Patty's insertions above lines are enclosed within carats: ^ ^. Her additions below lines are enclosed within angle brackets: < >.

4. The following procedures identify the numerous individuals who live on through Patty's diaries:

a. Descendants of David and Patty Sessions through their children are listed in Appendix 2.

b. The first time Patty names an individual, a full name (using the most common spelling) and the birth and death dates (when reasonably identifiable) are included within square brackets or footnotes, which provide further information about persons where the context indicates a need. At times even a reasonable guess at Patty's references was impossible. Such names remain unchanged. Toward the end of her diaries, as the popluation grew, duplications in names were common. Patty still often spelled phonetically, and checking adequately became impossible. Therefore, more persons are left without identification.

Attempting to pinpoint the scores of people whom Patty named has been time consuming and painstaking, sometimes painful. Trying is full of risks and opportunities for error. Nevertheless, in an effort to value individual persons, as Patty obviously did, I have dared to do so. Many of the works listed in the bibliography provided hints or specific information. Lyndon W. Cook, *The Revelations of the Prophet Joseph Smith*, offered special insights. Perhaps the most useful source was the fifty-volume work of Susan Ward Easton Black, *Membership of the Church of Jesus Christ of Latter-day Saints 1830–1848*. Although the complexity of Easton's project guarantees mistakes, these books provide a wealth of information. I also consulted lists of members of emigration companies, although most of those are incomplete. Census records and city directories sometimes provided useful information. Of course, the voluminous records in the Family History Library of the Church of Jesus Christ of Latter-day Saints were a valued source, as were genealogical records of the Sessions family, some of which Patty's own entries confirmed or corrected. As far as was humanly possible, names and dates were checked in more than one source. A conscientious reader will understand, however, that when Patty's own tombstone carries the wrong year of death, absolute certainty is elusive and, in some cases, unobtainable. In that spirit, I seek the reader's forbearance. The reader may also be frustrated trying to keep track of when, how, and if Patty had mentioned a certain individual before. I know the feeling from years of experience. At least you have an index to aid you.

5. Events and references requiring more explanation are discussed or cited in notes.

6. Patty's spelling and punctuation have been retained. No effort has been made to show her unusual line and word breaks, however. She depended entirely on available space. She punctuated dollars and cents differently at various places in her diaries (perhaps indicating how much she needed to hurry). Sometimes she separated dollars and cents with a colon, sometimes with a period, sometimes with a space, and sometimes not at all. The reader will experience no great problem in deciding what her intent was. One consistent habit of Patty's was to use a = when she abbreviated names, such as Wms= for Williams. A strikeout line through a word or passage represents Patty's scribbling over what she wrote. She did not neatly line through a passage. Patty often spelled phonetically, but her meaning is usually clear. Quite often—perhaps because of fatigue, or later, age—she confused days of the week and/or dates. But she always straightened herself out.

One symbol constantly used by Patty was a slanted line, like a slash with an attached curved line, which looks much like an italic leaning *h*. She especially employed the symbol to designate time or weight. Although several New England libraries and other historians were consulted, I could not find a definitive answer for its meaning. My best guess is that it stands for one-fourth, but that is not certain. That it might represent hecto or one hundred seems unlikely since it often follows the time of day, such as 2 *h*.

ACKNOWLEDGMENTS

A number of persons deserve credit for this important contribution to pioneer history. I begin with John R. Alley, executive editor of Utah State University Press, who provided invaluable assistance during the stages of preparing the manuscript for publication. Without his keen eye, the final product would be much less polished.

I express gratitude to all in the Historical Department of the Church of Jesus Christ of Latter-day Saints, but especially to James L. Kimball, who shared his extensive information on the inhabitants of Nauvoo, their names and dates, their residences and occupations, and other pertinent information. Jim was "on call" for other answers about research as well and welcomed all inquiries. Ronald O. Barney and W. Randall Dixon, both of whom have been efficient and effective directors of the archives division, made the diaries and other valuable records available. They were sensitive about the fragile nature of the original manuscripts and stressed the responsibility of preserving the diaries' material remains, as well as their internal integrity. Until the final stages of the project, Randy continued to make me aware of references to Patty that cropped up during his research. Ronald G. Watt was also encouraging and of great help. Veneese Nelson was always pleasant and helpful, as was Larry R. Skidmore who advised on the maps. Bill Slaughter's guidance on the photos was invaluable. I must include April Williamsen and Linda Haslam and Matthew Heiss and Jay Burrup. To all, thank you.

Patty's descendants were a delight. Her legacy courses through their veins, and they were pleased to participate and help in every possible way. The "Sessions" women who assisted with the final reading introduced me to other descendants. They clarified information about the family. They showed me artifacts I had not seen, some of which are reproduced in photos in this volume. We shared the profound realization that Patty's personal record books had been kept by one whose birth took place two hundred years ago. We shared a realization of both the nearness and the remoteness of history. These women who trace their ancestry back to Patty and David Sessions include Irene Poulson, Doris Rigby, Patty Hartley, all from the lines of Perrigrine, Patty and David's eldest son; Norma Earl, a descendant of Sylvia, who owns the medical book presumably used by Patty; Delilah Brown, who owns the sampler Patty began to embroider when she was a girl and was gracious in allowing us to photograph her treasured memento; and Ada Eddins, who provided family information and moral support. It was difficult to obtain exact information on David Sessions, Jr., but a chance encounter with Sarah Hale, who provided her records, was helpful. Two other brief acquaintances sent new information to the project: Clara H. Parry and Mary R Parry. A complete photocopy of Perrigrine's diaries provided by Irene Poulson proved an invaluable companion to the diaries of P.G.'s mother, Patty. All have my gratitude.

The following Sessions family members made financial contributions to support the publication of Patty's diaries: Marcella Allred and Arvella Beckley, Mrs. E. L. Ashton, LeRoy W. Brown, Truman H. Carver, Ada Eddins, Marcell Graham, Mrs. T. J. Green, Irena S. Hamilton, Nadine F. Harman, Kay Klaveano, Merrill Madsen, Vicki L. Martin, Marjorie S. Murdock, Marjorie A. Olsen, Irene S. Poulson, Sandra J. Preece, Robert A. Ramsey, Stephanie N. Stuart, Ila G. Winzenried, and Barry T. Wride. Thank you to all of them for their generosity and devotion to seeing their ancestor's writings in print.

With the concurrence of William W. Slaughter of the Historical Department of the Church of Jesus Christ of Latter-day Saints, J M Heslop, a professional photographer, historian, and writer, photographed, developed, and printed the pictures of the diaries and the sampler. Other photos were provided by family members.

Others deserve a rousing "thank you!" for helping when no one else could—or would: my husband, William B. Smart, an avid historian, astute editor, and unfailing support for the seven years I have worked on these diaries; and our daughters, Melinda Graves and Kristen Rogers, who provided hours of research and helpful encouragement. Jean Sorensen, a neighbor, spent time digging out some details. Blanche Miles, conservator at the Church Museum of History and Art, helped ferret out information on some of Patty's numerous cottage industries. I am most appreciative to all of them.

And of course, this volume would be delayed many more years had not Maureen Ursenbach Beecher dreamed of a published series of pioneer women's diaries and offered me the privilege of editing those of Patty Sessions.

The careful copyediting of Barbara Bannon pointed out inconsistencies. I'm appreciative of her scrutiny, which demanded preciseness. In some cases, conflicting records and Patty's own inconsistencies made precision impossible. For example, records showed at least four spellings for Patty's grandson: Fabian, Fabyan, Fabyon, and Fayben. Patty wrote 4 and 7 in a very similar style. It is easy to misread those numbers, and often Patty spelled phonetically—or was in such a hurry that she omitted letters and committed other inconsistent errors.

Every effort was made to present the diaries as accurately and properly as possible. To do less would be an affront to Patty's numerous posterity, to historians who may enrich their research through her records, and, of course, to Patty herself. This may be, after all, only the beginning of discovering what a treasure trove of historical information she has left. Undoubtedly, there will be many who can and will correct mistakes and misconceptions. Such contributions will be appreciated by all who cherish these diaries.

INTRODUCTION

In May of 1888 Patty Bartlett Sessions wrote the words "it is now Friday the 4th," put down her pen as if for a temporary pause, and abruptly ended more than four decades of diary entries. The Mormon pioneer trek from Nauvoo, Illinois, to the Salt Lake Valley; the rise of Mormon cities in the western wilderness; the attempted invasion of Johnston's army; the coming of the railroad; and the building of Mormon temples represent only a few of the significant events mentioned in her annals. The domestic life of a people was the more continuous substance of her record. She lived on until 14 December 1892 and died less than two months before her ninety-eighth birthday.

Patty was a compulsive record keeper. Although diaries dating from the Nauvoo exodus of February 1846 compose this volume, evidence points to her having kept a journal much earlier–perhaps starting soon after she married David Sessions on 28 June 1812. Unfortunately, those records have disappeared. Evidence also suggests the esteem she earned among her peers throughout the years; between 1 September 1884 and 15 November 1885, the *Woman's Exponent*, a Utah magazine devoted to the cause of women, published a series of eight articles based on her life.[1] It recorded that Patty was then "in her ninetieth year, and in the enjoyment of excellent health, able to wait upon herself, transact her own business and her own accounts. In many respects she is a very remarkable woman."[2]

Although Patty must have been interviewed by the unidentified author (probably Emmeline B. Wells, who was then editor), diaries provided most of the substance of the *Exponent* sketches, since phrases such as "Mrs. Sessions in

---

1. The biographical sketches are found in eight *Woman's Exponent* issues: 13 (1 September 1884): 51; 13 (15 September 1884): 63; 13 (1 November 1884): 86; 13 (15 November 1884): 94–95; 13 (1 February 1885): 134–35; 13 (1 March 1885): 150–51; 14 (1 June 1885): 2; 14 (15 November 1885): 85–86, 94–95.

2. "Patty Sessions," *Woman's Exponent* 13 (1 September): 51.

her journal says" appear regularly. This volume is enriched by details gleaned from those articles.

The wonder of Patty's diaries is that, despite an extremely busy and often harried life, she wrote daily, except during one period of serious illness. She clung to this habit with resourcefulness and faithfulness until circumstance, probably infirmity from old age, prevented her continuing.

Her final diary entries graphically trace a gradual decline from an energetic, productive, pioneer woman to one still determined to follow habits of a lifetime and to write about her days and doings, but with little vigor, vanishing vitality, and much aimless repetition. Her words trail into nothingness, allowing no opportunity for closure and, regrettably, giving no account of her last years and last days. People generally die of something in addition to old age—stroke, heart attack, cancer. In the case of Patty Sessions, we do not know what it was. The newspaper obituary does not say. Patty's simple pause turned into permanent silence, but her historical contributions had already been fixed.

Her foremost legacy came through her role as a midwife. Midwifery was an important profession in Maine, where Patty Bartlett was born on 4 February 1795 to Enoch Bartlett and (Martha) Anna Hall. The country was sparsely settled, doctors scarce, and families large, if that of Enoch Bartlett provides a prototype. His first wife, Eliza Seager, bore ten children before she died when her youngest child was nine years old. Four years later, Patty became the firstborn of Enoch's second wife, Anna, who bore nine children and lived a few months past her one hundredth birthday.

When Patty's father brought her mother home, the country was so new that "they rode forty miles on horseback by a spotted line," where trees were blazed to mark the trail, and "then forty more where there was only a track, and took all she had on the same horse."[3]

Enoch and Anna Bartlett lie in a rural graveyard, visible from the front doorstep of a still-occupied house built by Enoch in the early 1790s to accommodate his large and growing family. A wooded hillside slopes down to the Sunday River Road, which skirts the cemetery. Today, from Bethel, Maine, Route 2, a meandering country road, follows the river north to a weathered covered bridge of 1872 vintage. Across today's more modern bridge, a dirt road turns right and up a hill to the large, two-story, colonial house where Patty was born and lived until she married.

The military service of one of Patty's ancestors—probably Joseph Bartlett of Middlesex, Massachusetts—during the 1690 Canadian campaign of the French and Indian Wars made her father, Enoch, a landholder; instead of wages, Massachusetts offered its soldiers or their survivors land grants. In

---

3. "Patty Sessions," *Woman's Exponent* 13 (1 September): 51.

1737 descendants of the servicemen of Sudbury, Massachusetts, and adjacent towns who had participated in the 1690 campaign petitioned the legislature for a township, which was not then awarded. Perhaps the conditions were too stringent. A certain number of settlers were required, as well as a house of public worship and an ordained minister.[4]

On 23 May 1768 Enoch's father, Ebenezer Bartlett, signed a new petition. In June a township known as Sudbury-Canada was granted on both sides of the Androscoggin River. Part of this original grant was incorporated as Bethel in 1796, and a township called Bostwick was then organized. In 1805 Bostwick citizens petitioned for incorporation under the name of Newry; the petition was granted. According to the 1790 census, 324 persons populated Sudbury-Canada Township, 60 of them heads of families, including Enoch Bartlett. In 1800, when Patty was five years old, the census showed Enoch Bartlett in Bostwick, also known as the Sunday River Plantation, where there were 12 heads of families and a total population of 102. So with some truthfulness, Patty could claim that she was born in Sudbury-Canada, in Bostwick, on the Sunday River Plantation, in Bethel, or in Newry, but she chose Bethel. Maps of 1858 locate the Enoch Bartlett home in Newry.

Whatever the name of the community where Patty spent her childhood, its primitive and harsh environment shaped her work ethic. Rearing a large family in such a new settlement required the labors of the whole family.

> They cut and fitted their firewood. . . . They raised sheep, sheared them, spun the wool, wove the cloth and made their garments. . . . They saved their tallow and dipped their candles. . . . They obtained their food from the soil and the forest. . . . They welcomed the traveler at their door because he broke the monotony and bore "news" that was months old. . . . They made their own music, travelling miles to gather around a hearth, for an evening's sing. . . . When the evening meal was finished the pioneers did something besides toast their feet on the hearth. The family circle was seldom idle. The women were busy spinning, weaving, sewing, knitting, candle dipping, soft soap mixing, while the men fashioned shoes, ax-handles, ox yokes, brooms, baskets, wooden bowls, spoons and such.[5]

Patty fit the pattern. Years later on 24 June 1863 in Salt Lake City, Patty recorded, "got my web [woven fabric] out for blanket & undergarments 28 yds I do feel thankful to my heavenly Father that he gives me health and strenth and a dispostion to work and make cloth and other things for my comfort

4. W. B. Lapham, *History of Bethel 1768–1890* (Augusta, Maine: 1891), 15–20.
5. "Bethel Then and Now," *The Bethel Citizen*, special edition, 10 July 1974, p. 18.

The house of Enoch and Anna Hall Bartlett, Newry, Maine, where Patty Bartlett was born in 1795. Courtesy of Irene S. Poulson.

A sampler Patty Bartlett began in Maine and finished in the Salt Lake Valley in 1848. Sampler courtesy of Delilah Brown; photograph by J M Heslop.

David Sessions (1790–1850), who married Patty Bartlett in 1812. Courtesy of International Society, Daughters of Utah Pioneers.

now in the sixty ninth year of my age. And I also feel thankful that I had a mother that put me to work when I was young and learned me how."

She learned more than domestic skills. Her diaries, including her copious financial records, testify to Patty's business acumen. She was more comfortable as an economic producer—even at times being an all-too-necessary means of support for her husbands and their polygamous wives—than a consumer. She was tightfisted, allowing no one, including family members, to bilk her out of hard-earned money; but she was also often magnanimous in supporting causes in which she believed.

She did not learn her financial or medical skills or her production abilities in a formal school setting. Particularly for females, schooling was limited—even seen as unnecessary—in her day. Patty did recall being carried in the arms of the schoolmistress into her father's shop when it was used for a classroom. There she was taught to read and write—skills that served her well but that neither of her parents acquired.[6]

At the age of seventeen, she married David Sessions, despite strong parental objections. The young couple moved ten miles away to his parents' home in Ketcham. With David's rheumatic mother needing constant care, Patty found herself in charge of the household. Here she stumbled into midwifery, quite by accident.

One day a young woman was taken suddenly ill, and sent for Mother Sessions [Patty's mother-in-law, Rachel Stevens/Stavens, b. 1767], who was in the habit of attending obstetrical cases in the vicinity; she was very feeble and had to be led, and before she had time to go any distance, another messenger came telling the young Mrs. Sessions to run as quickly as she could. She hurried on with all speed and when she arrived it was thought the young woman was dying; Mrs. Sessions, who was entirely unskilled in affairs of this kind, but had abundant nerve force and moral courage, took the child and put the mother in bed before Mother Sessions arrived. . . . A short time afterwards the doctor and some other help came, but all was over. The doctor examined the mother and child to see that all was right, and finding everything in a good condition, he was anxious to see the young and inexperienced woman who had so skilfully performed the work. The doctor called upon her and congratulated her upon her ability, and told her she must attend to that business, not to have any fear, for she would prosper in it, as it was a new country and there were many about to move in, it would be necessary to have more help of this kind. About four months after she attended another young woman in her confinement, and from that

6. "Patty Sessions," *Woman's Exponent* 13 (1 September): 51.

time she has followed the profession of a midwife until within a very recent date, when she felt that at her age she was no longer to be depended upon.[7]

It may have been Dr. Timothy Carter, the first permanent physician in Bethel, who encouraged Patty to practice midwifery. He came to Bethel in 1799 and for fourteen years was the sole practitioner, making fifty-mile rounds on horseback along the Androscoggin River. Three predecessors, Dr. Martin, Dr. N. T. True, and Dr. John Brickett, had lasted only briefly. The very earliest settlers had been ministered to by an Indian, Molly Ockett, who knew roots, barks, and herbs "from which she concocted salves, drinks, and poultices for the sick. She was often called upon as a midwife to attend women of the region at childbirth."[8] Conceivably, Molly Ockett could have attended Anna Bartlett when Patty was born, and Patty may have gained some of her extensive knowledge of herbs from the area's last resident Indian practitioner. Rachel Sessions undoubtedly also advised her daughter-in-law, as did the doctor who first urged Patty to take up midwifery.

Her skill in delivering babies would become critical to the well-being of fellow members of the Church of Jesus Christ of Latter-day Saints, which she joined in 1834. As a Mormon, Patty received stronger confirmation of her decision to follow an obstetrical career. In an obituary Phebe Carter Foss Sessions, wife of Patty's son David, remembered that "While at Nauvoo she [Patty] was set apart by Brigham Young [who became Mormon Church president in 1847] and Heber C. Kimball [who became a counselor to Brigham Young] as a doctor for women. Leaving Nauvoo she went to Winter Quarters where she was very efficient in waiting upon the sick, especially the women."[9]

Of course, neither Nauvoo, Illinois, nor Winter Quarters, Iowa, existed when Patty was midwifing in Maine. Brigham Young and Heber C. Kimball were only eleven or twelve years old when Patty and David were married. More about them later. Nevertheless, as Patty's life unfolded, she learned to value and celebrate spiritual reinforcement from church leaders and from women who belonged to her church. Beginning in 1846, when the saints were driven from Nauvoo and trekked across Iowa to what became their Winter Quarters and later crossed the plains to what became Utah, Patty wrote often in her diaries about an elite circle of women of the Church of Jesus Christ of Latter-day Saints. This select group met regularly to bless and be blessed, to

---

7. *Ibid.*

8. Joyce Wanger, "19th Century Medicine in Bethel, Maine," *The Bethel Courier* 14 (Fall 1990): 1–2.

9. Phebe C. Sessions, "Biographical Sketch: Patty Sessions," *Woman's Exponent* 27 (1 and 15 June 1898): 294.

testify in tongues, to heal and be healed. Patty was a central figure among them and obviously appreciated her prestige. Among others the group included many of Brigham Young's wives, such as Eliza R. Snow, and a number of the wives of Heber C. Kimball. On 26 September 1847, two days after arriving in the Salt Lake Valley, Patty rejoiced that she put Lorenzo Young's wife Harriet to bed with a son "the first male born in this valley it was said to me more than 5 months ago that my hands should be the first to handle the first born son in the place of rest for the saints even in the city of our God I have come more than one thousand miles to do it since it was spoken." The prophesy had been pronounced in a meeting with her "sisters" in Winter Quarters before the 1847 trek to the Great Basin.

Church founder Joseph Smith himself had approved of women's increasing spiritual powers. In early remarks to the Relief Society, he had instructed them that ". . . foolish things were circulating . . . against some sisters not doing right in laying hands on the sick. Said that if the people had common sympathies they would rejoice that the sick could be healed . . . these signs, such as healing the sick, casting out devils, etc., should follow all that believe, whether male or female."[10]

Patty's belief in and dedication to the spiritual gifts and powers of women motivated her to encourage young girls, including her granddaughter Martha Ann, to learn to speak in tongues and share other manifestations of the spirit. Her journal describes meetings with them, her instruction, and their shy efforts to partake of such spiritual fare.

Patty didn't depend alone on being set apart by her church leaders for midwifery or gaining practical knowledge. She studied. The Church of Jesus Christ of Latter-day Saints Museum of History and Art owns a rare 1840 book with the impressive title *Aristotle's Works: Containing the Master-piece, Direction for Midwives, and Counsel and Advice to Child-Bearing Women.* This book overflows with 320 pages of information and color illustrations of the fetus in various positions and stages of development. It was donated by a descendant who verifies that it belonged to Patty Bartlett Sessions, midwife, who has been credited with escorting 3,997 babies into the world.[11]

Whether or not the number is accurate (her extant diaries do not support that many), Patty recorded hundreds of deliveries, identifying one or both parents, the sex of the child, and the date and time of birth. She also recorded her prices and duly noted payments. She could be bone weary or in

---

10. Joseph Fielding Smith, comp., *The Teachings of the Prophet Joseph Smith* (Salt Lake City: Deseret Book Co., 1977), 224.

11. Quig Nielsen, "Patty Sessions delivered 3,977 babies as a midwife," *Davis County Clipper,* 2 March 1992, quoting Kate B. Carter, ed., *Our Pioneer Heritage* (Salt Lake City: Daughters of Utah Pioneers, 1959), 2:426.

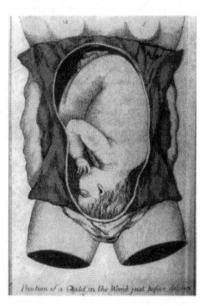

Title page, table of contents, and two illustrations from *Aristotle's Works*, an instructional manual for midwives that was owned by Patty Sessions. Courtesy of LDS Church Museum of History and Art.

a low mood but still be depended upon to answer a request for medical atten-tion—and later to write about it in her diary. The accumulating facts become indisputable.

Dependability is a by-product of necessity. As newlyweds, David and Patty used ingenuity and toil to get ahead. By the spring following their mar-riage, David had earned a cow and some cotton by working on his parents' farm. Patty had made butter, sold it, and bought a pail in which to milk. She spun the cotton and made a bed tick and sheets. She picked cattails and filled the tick so the couple might at least have their own bed. And before their first anniversary, David procured land and built a log house in nearby Ketcham.

"In the Spring we moved into our own house," Mrs. Sessions in her jour-nal says. "An old acquaintance of mine told me she was going back to where she came from and wanted me to buy her loom for four dollars. Mr. Sessions earned the money and purchased the loom, and I soon had all the weaving I could do fetched to me from ten to twelve miles." Mrs. Sessions earned quite a reputation as a weaver both for good work and promptitude; her work was always ready for her patrons at the time specified.[12]

When opportunity arose for Patty, she not only grasped but expanded it. From her weaving skills, she created a lasting home industry, one that pro-vided a lifelong means of income and self-fulfillment. She kept at handwork of one kind or another until she left off writing her narration, augmenting weav-ing with sewing, knitting, braiding straw, and making rags into rugs for herself and others. She persisted in knitting socks to the very end. Family tradition tells of so many dropped stitches and other errors in the stockings she made in her declining years that they were unraveled each evening (without her knowl-edge, of course) and the yarn given back to her for the next day's session with the knitting needles. Throughout her years she taught her skills to family members, neighbors, and friends.

She was a gardener with extraordinary tenacity and ability. She sowed and planted and watered and weeded and reaped her vegetables and fruit, which she dried and sold, selling seeds and starts as well. She generally paid her tithing, the ten percent donation required from worthy Mormon church members, in fruit. Overpayments she collected back in money. She was an industrious member of her community's workforce, harder working, more productive, and more successful than many of her male contemporaries. Although she was doggedly independent, others were often dependent upon her for assistance with money, produce, or employment as laborers. For her

---

12. "Patty Sessions," *Woman's Exponent*, 13 (1 September): 51.

A pioneer loom much like those Patty Sessions used. Loom on display at the Daughters of Utah Pioneers Museum; photograph courtesy of LDS Church Museum of History and Art.

times she was certainly a liberated woman, who, out of training, habit, and circumstances, increasingly valued economic self-sufficiency.

The will to be self-sustaining must have developed early in her marriage,
as undoubtedly the progress the newlyweds experienced in Ketcham (a town
marked today only by crumbling foundations) was as much a product of Patty's
industry as of David's. But the land was hilly and rocky, and they decided they
could farm more successfully elsewhere. They took their new son, Perrigrine
(born 15 June 1814), and moved northeast about nine miles to Andover West
Surplus on Bear River, which would be annexed to Newry in 1837.

> . . . the conveniences were not very great, for Mrs. Sessions in her jour-
> nal says, "we moved into an old cabin where they had made salt, and
> lived there until we built a new house which we moved into in the night,
> lest the old, rickety cabin should fall down upon us. . . . As soon as my
> husband's father learned that we had moved into a new house he came
> and wanted us to take them (his wife and himself) to live with us. The
> old lady was not able to stand on her feet, but had to be moved in a
> chair on wheels; she remained with us while she lived, four or five years;
> during all that time never straightened nor turned herself in bed once.
> She was a very large, heavy woman, and I had to lift and move her
> around or wheel her from room to room. One day I was moving her
> and my arm slipped from the chair and caught my elbow between the
> slats, which pulled the elbow cap out of place. The pain was very great,
> but when mother Sessions asked if she had hurt me, I said I guessed not;
> with help I seated the old lady and then went into my front room where
> I had a girl sewing for me, told her to take hold of my hand and hold it
> still, and let me pull back and straighten my arm; she did so and I
> pushed it into place, and put my arm in a sling, in which I had to keep it
> for some weeks. When father came home he wished to know what ailed
> my arm, I told him rheumatism or something else."[13]

Courage and willpower helped her handle many of her trials and
challenges.

David and Patty had bought two hundred acres of land, on which,
according to Perrigrine, "my Father lived untill 1837 . . . and built a large
house and two large barnes with severil sheds bought more land joining and
a sawmill and built a grist mill and had a large farm of four hundred Acres
of land all in one piece."[14] And Patty continued her practice of midwifery

---

13. "Patty Sessions," *Woman's Exponent* 13 (15 September): 63.

14. Perrigrine Sessions, "Diaries," 3 February to 19 March 1886, pp. B-4, 5 (here-
     after cited as DPG), holograph, Archives of the Historical Department, Church

regularly, day or night, rain or shine, sometimes going twenty miles on horseback in the night over those lonely roads."[15]

During the ensuing years, their worldly good fortune continued, and the number of children increased to seven. But they were beset by tribulation, as Perrigrine's diary describes:

> May the ninth, 1823 my brother David jun was born and the sixteenth of September following my Sister Anna was taken with the colery morbus and died the twentieth being three years and six months old at her death and the twenty-second my GrandMother [Rachel] was taken with the same complaint and died Oct 1 and September 23 1824 my Grand Father [David Sessions, b. 1749] being as well as common at his dinner and went to a neighbours hou[se] set down on a chair and died instantly did not know as any thing ailed him untill he could not speak . . . March the 16 1825 my Sister Anna B the second was born and the first day of September 1825 my Grand Father Enoch Bartlett died with a fever August the first 1827 my brother Bartlett was born and February the 15–1828 he died being six months and fifteen days died with the hooping cough and in 1832 were all sick with the typhus fever and my sister Anna died August tenth aged seven years and four months and twenty four days at this time my Mother could not raise her hand to her head and lay in the same room whare my sister died my Father and brother Sylvanus lay in an other room and did not see her after she was taken sick My Aunt Apphia and her daughter lay in an other room they were all helpless I had had the fever and had got so that I could set up some my brother David was just comeing down with the fever and my Sister Sylvia being the second time deprived of her only sister she morned and wept untill she had to go to bed at this time my fealings I could not discribe . . . September 15 my brother Sylvanus died being sixteen years and three months and twelve days old . . . at this time my Father and Mother had got some better but my Grandmother Bartlett was there and she and David were so sick that they did not know when Sylvanus died altho they were in the same room. After my Grandmother got better she was carried home on a bed six miles betwene two horses . . . there was Eleven that had the fever at my Fathers that summer and many others in the neighbourhood.[16]

---

of Jesus Christ of Latter-day Saints, Salt Lake City; photocopy of holograph in possession of Donna T. Smart, courtesy of Irene Sessions Poulson.

15. "Patty Sessions," *Woman's Exponent* 13(15 September): 63.

16. DPG, 3 February 1845, p. B-7.

So David and Patty buried four of their eight children in Maine: Sylvanus (3 June 1816–15 September 1832); Anna B. (21 March 1820–20 September 1823); Anna B., the second (16 March 1825–10 August 1832); and Bartlett (1 August 1827–15 February 1828). Where these Sessions children are buried is not known for certain, although as early as 4 April 1814, two committees had been chosen to lay out a burying place, obtain the land, and fence it; and on 1 April 1816 the deeds for Bear River and Sunday River cemeteries were recorded. That location would be the most likely. Surviving such dreadful circumstances and childhood diseases were Perrigrine (15 June 1814–3 June 1893), the firstborn; Sylvia (31 July 1818–13 April 1882), the first daughter; and David, Jr. (9 May 1823–19 April 1896). Amanda, who was born later on 14 November 1837 in Far West, Missouri, died on 15 May 1841 in Nauvoo, Illinois.

In August 1833 occurred an event of such significance for the David Sessions family that it cancelled any prospects of their living and dying near their birthplace, as their parents had, and of being buried next to those already planted in the ground.

The Americas had been settled by immigrants who had left their native roots and the graves of their dead to seek a place to worship in their own fashion. Their quest continues to this day, but the first half of the nineteenth century spawned a particularly significant number of seekers after religious freedom and community, including such well-known figures as Bronson Alcott, Ralph Waldo Emerson, Margaret Fuller, Albert Brisbane, George Ripley—and Joseph Smith (born 1805).

According to his own account, when he was fifteen years old, Smith felt, as he described it, "confused" by the religious frenzy in New England. His family had accepted the Presbyterian faith, but the youthful Joseph felt inclined toward Methodism. However, he could not reach "any certain conclusion who was right and who was wrong." Joseph felt a prompting when he read the Epistle of James, first chapter and fifth verse: "If any of you lack wisdom, let him ask of God, that giveth to all men liberally, and upbraideth not; and it shall be given him." The boy retired to a grove near the Smith farm in upstate New York (now known by Mormons as the Sacred Grove) and prayed for enlightenment on which church was right. He reported that he saw a vision of God the Father and Jesus Christ, during which he was told that all churches were wrong. On a single night in 1823, a personage appeared three times at Joseph's bedside and taught him from the scriptures and about other religious matters, particularly emphasizing the location of ancient records that were buried near Palmyra, New York, in the Hill Cumorah. The angel, called Moroni, had been the last keeper of the records that he later showed to Joseph Smith with the caution that he must wait to obtain and transcribe the plates.

Joseph had to mature through such tutorial visitations for four years. Finally, the plates were delivered to him, and, after overcoming considerable

Sylvia Sessions Lyon (Clark). Courtesy of
Ardell Backman.

Perrigrine Sessions. Courtesy of Irene S.
Poulson.

David Sessions, Jr. Courtesy of
International Society, Daughters of
Utah Pioneers.

obstacles and persecution, he began the transcription on 5 April 1829. The result was the Book of Mormon, the translation of which took about sixty working days. The Book of Mormon chronicles the immigration of three separate bands of people to the Americas, predating the birth of Jesus Christ.

According to Joseph, it was because of the contents of this book and heavenly instruction that the Church of Jesus Christ of Latter-day Saints was born on 6 April 1830. To Joseph Smith and his followers, this new church was a restoration of the one established by Jesus Christ before his crucifixion. Priesthood authority as it had existed in the primitive church was also restored. As Jesus had instructed his apostles to go into all the world and preach the gospel, so also the Mormons, as they came to be known, sent missionaries forth almost immediately.[17]

In August of 1833 Mormon missionaries came preaching in Andover West Surplus. Their message altered the Sessions family's lives dramatically and permanently since they had been prepared for the new religion by Patty's spiritual yearnings. According to Perrigrine, their neighbors were all Methodists, and ". . . my Mother by reading the Bible began to think that baptism was necessary and October the first 1816 she was baptized [as a Methodist] my Father made no pretentions to religion as yet but did not appose her . . . [later] my Father made a profession of Methodism and in january he was baptised by immersion in 1820."[18]

Patty at once accepted the message of the Mormon missionaries, but her husband needed to study longer. To appease him, she waited until July 1834, when, with David's consent, she was baptized and confirmed a member by missionary Daniel Bean. Perrigrine wrote

> she stood firm steming all oposition and she received much of it from her neighbours and some of her brothers & sisters she remained alone in the Church almost one year before any of the rest of us joined the church & six miles from any other member. I will here say that we had severil visits from the Twelve [Apostles, of the governing body of the Mormon Church] and other traviling Elders which gave us much joy the Twelve held a conference to my Fathers on the 12 of August, 1835. Brigham Yongs and Lymon Johnson two of the Twelve were present and the blessing of God atendid the meating. . . . here the gathering of the saints was taught and preparations began to be made to remove to Zion this looked like a great sacrifise to make as the distance was so far but we began to dispose of property as my Father and I had considerable—

---

17.   For more complete information as given by Joseph Smith, see his *History of the Church of Jesus Christ of Latter-day Saints*, vol. 1 (Salt Lake City: Deseret Book Co., 1976).

18.   DPG, p. B-6.

times were hard and money scarce but after a continual persevevervince [*sic*] we all started. . . . we took leave of our neighbours and friends on the fifth of June 1837–when many a tear was shed.[19]

As Perrigrine implied, one of the principles that the fledlging church taught was the gathering of Israel and its adoptees. From the earliest days of church history, the people of upper New York and its environs openly showed apprehension and suspicion toward the newly founded religion. Members began to search for a safe place to practice their religion freely, and Kirtland, Ohio, became an early location for Mormons. In fact, their first temple, dedicated on 27 March 1836, is still an impressive edifice in Kirtland but now belongs to the Reorganized Church of Jesus Christ of Latter Day Saints, a splinter group that declined to follow the leadership of Brigham Young. But in Kirtland financial woes plagued Joseph Smith and other church leaders, and at the time the Sessions family departed from Maine, fledgling Mormons were turning toward a new Zion in Far West, Missouri. After an arduous journey, Patty and David's family arrived there in November 1837, having traveled by land and water, by self-made trail, and by well-used road. They had been delayed in Kirtland, Ohio, for seven weeks while family members suffered through the measles. It was in Kirtland that they saw their prophet for the first time, when they heard Joseph Smith speak in the Kirtland Temple. Meeting the prophet must have strengthened their resolve, a boost they needed, because the last part of the journey would be particularly difficult for Patty, who gave birth on 14 November 1837 to a daughter, Amanda, shortly after reaching Far West.

With customary diligence, the Sessions family wasted no time getting established once they had reached Missouri. They bought property in Far West, including two block houses and five acres of fenced land. During the winter they fenced one hundred more acres.

Details of their days in Missouri are sketchy as only fragmentary quotations from Patty's earliest diary exist. The *Exponent* mentions more than a few visits from and to Joseph Smith, one occurring when he married Patty's daughter Sylvia to Windsor P. Lyon.

> During all this time we find Sister Sessions performing daily household duties and attending obstetrical cases regularly. Very frequently one sees in her diary entries like this: "Rode twelve miles last night, put Sister ＿＿＿ to bed, fine boy, etc.–rode six miles and put Sister ＿＿＿ to bed with a pair of twins, difficult case, severe labor, but the Lord blessed us and we got through all right, patient safe, etc."[20]

---

19. *Ibid.*, pp. B-9, 10.

20. "Patty Sessions," *Woman's Exponent* 13 (1 November): 86.

In spring 1838 the Sessions men planted corn, potatoes, and grain on forty acres, after which Perrigrine left for Maine to collect debts. While he was gone, armed and angry Missourians, perhaps fearing being overrun by these strange, religious "fanatics," turned to violence to force the growing Mormon colony from their state. At his return Perrigrine found that "twenty or twenty five of the Saints had been murtered and fifty or sixty in Prison among whome was the Prophet and his brother Hirum with chaines on in a cold wet Dunjeon with horse beef to eat . . . the Prison being garded by those that swore they should never come out and the whole Church under the exterminating order of Libern W. Boggs Governor of the State."[21] Boggs had ordered that "the Mormons must be treated as enemies, and must be exterminated or driven from the State if necessary for the public peace–their outrages are beyond all description."[22] Perrigrine described the mob's killing cattle, hogs, and sheep and stealing horses. And he reported the relief and joy all the Sessions family felt when a letter from the Prophet Joseph instructed them to head for Illinois.[23]

Again they were on the move. From 15 February 1839 until early in April, through mud and cold and ice-clogged rivers, the Sessions family struggled toward Illinois. They occasionally found lodging but usually had no shelter but a tent. On 26 February Patty recorded, "still muddy, and we have to tent out, cold, wet and inclement, no shelter but a tent, a sick babe and no comforts. Trust in God and pray for courage and endurance."[24] Perrigrine's wife Julia and Patty were both ill with what Patty called ague (probably malaria) during the journey, and Patty carried the ailing eighteen-month-old Amanda in her arms the whole distance. A temporary house of their own in Carthage, Illinois, must have seemed like the promised land. Perrigrine recorded

About the first of May . . . brother Joseph the Prophet got liberated from prison and met with the saints in Qincy [*sic*] in conference This gave us much joy to see his face among the Saints and here the voice of inspiration that floed from his lips this caused our drooping spirits to revive as we were like sheap with out a shepherd that had been scatered in a cloudy and dark day here a commity was apointed to search out a location whare the Saints could gather togather to and the place caled Nauvoo now was the place[25]

21. DPG, 3 February 1845, p. B-14.
22. Dale A. Whitman, "Extermination Order," in *Encyclopedia of Mormonism*, 5 vols, ed., Daniel H. Ludlow (New York: Macmillan, 1992), 2:480.
23. DPG, 3 February 1845, pp. B-14, 15, 16.
24. "Patty Sessions," *Woman's Exponent* 13 (1 September): 86.
25. DPG, p. B-16.

On 27 June 1839 Perrigrine left for a mission to Maine, from which he would not return until 2 June 1840. In the meantime, a month earlier the family had moved from Carthage to Nauvoo, and Mr. Sessions, as Patty always called David, began—once again—to build a house, which was completed the following September.

The Woman's Exponent is silent on events during that first winter in Nauvoo. Since one account reports that the Sessions family lost twelve hundred dollars in land and four hundred dollars in livestock and corn when they were driven from Missouri, survival must have been their major worry.[26] Not all of them did survive; Amanda, at the age of three years, six months, and one day, died on 15 May 1841 of croup. She was buried in Nauvoo.

In 1842 Patty participated in a Mormon ceremony that was of overwhelming importance to her. She wrote about it in her later diary: "I was sealed to Joseph Smith by Willard Richards March 9 1842 in Newel K Whitneys chamber Nauvoo for time and all eternity. . . . Sylvia my daughter was presant when I was sealed to Joseph Smith."

One of the major doctrines of the Church of Jesus Christ of Latter-day Saints centers around the eternity of family relationships. How this belief translated into practice in the early years is difficult to explain. Todd Compton notes

Because of the complexity of Mormon marriage practice and experimentation, there is a great deal of ambiguity concerning what constituted marriage in early Mormonism, and Mormon theological terms for marriage and plural marriage can be confusing. I define as marriage any relationship solemnized by a marriage ceremony of some sort. "Sealing" as used in early Mormonism is a complex term that deserves extensive study, but as it developed in Nauvoo Mormonism, it often meant the linking of man and woman for eternity as well as for time, i.e., eternal marriage. . . . when a man and a woman (not siblings or parent-child) were "sealed," the sealing was always a marriage.[27]

To Mormons many of the sealings could be termed "spiritual marriages." There were non-marital sealings as well, through which members were "adopted" into the eternal families of other, usually leading Mormons. Both of these were religious rituals intended to assure one a place in eternity. Sealings were also performed to guarantee single or widowed women temporal support. Still

26. Clark Johnson, *Mormon Redress Petitions: Documents of the 1833–1838 Missouri Conflict* (Provo, Utah: Religious Studies Center, Brigham Young University, 1992), 335–36.

27. Todd Compton, "A Trajectory of Plurality: An Overview of Joseph Smith's Thirty-three Plural Wives," *Dialogue* (Summer 1996), 1.

others were marriages meant to be consummated here and endure hereafter. Some sealed marriages were polygamous, and some in the early years of the church involved polyandry as well as polygyny. Then and now, one holding priesthood authority must perform the sealing ordinance for worthy recipients for it to be valid.

How Patty regarded her sealing to Joseph Smith is problematic. But being sealed to the Prophet Joseph Smith was so important to Patty that some years later, on 3 July 1867, she personally saw to it that the ordinance was further validated. Joseph F. Smith stood in for his uncle.

The Woodruff Manifesto of 1890 ostensibly put an end to polygamous sealings, and the practice of sealings to church authorities changed in 1894, when Mormon president Wilford Woodruff presented a revelation stating that children should be sealed "to their parents and they to their parents as far back as the records can be obtained."[28] Until Woodruff's pronouncement, as Patty's diary confirms, it was common for individuals to be sealed to revered church leaders. Since Woodruff's revelation, however, emphasis, focus, and practice have centered on church members completing accurate genealogical research and performing temple ordinances by proxy for their deceased ancestors. Of course, Patty's copious genealogical records (omitted from this volume) indicate that she began to fulfill that responsibility even before Woodruff's dictate, as soon as the Logan Temple was completed and dedicated in 1884.

Sylvia Sessions was also sealed to Joseph Smith. She confided to her daughter, Josephine, that the ceremony had taken place at about the same time as Zina D. Huntington and Eliza R. Snow were sealed to the prophet as plural wives. According to Fawn M. Brodie in *No Man Knows My History*, Zina Huntington was sealed to Joseph on 27 October 1841 and Eliza R. Snow on 29 June 1842.[29] If, as Brodie implies, the Nauvoo Temple records of sealings were available for research when she wrote her biography of Joseph Smith, they lacked information about Sylvia since Brodie left question marks following both her age and the date of her sealing to the prophet. The life summaries Brodie wrote for Sylvia and Patty are both flawed, so her research appears to be suspect. At present Nauvoo Temple endowment dates are available, but sealing dates for Joseph Smith are not in the Nauvoo Temple records for 1845 and 1846.[30] A personal history of Sylvia written by one of her descendants

---

28. Thomas G. Alexander, *Things in Heaven and Earth* (Salt Lake City: Signature Books, 1991), 322.

29. Fawn M. Brodie, *No Man Knows My History* (New York: Alred A. Knopf, 1963), 335.

30. "Nauvoo Temple Endowment Register," 10 December 1845 to 8 February 1846 (Salt Lake City: Temple Index Bureau, 1974). Sealings did not begin in the temple until 1845.

reports that Sylvia was sealed to Joseph Smith 26 January 1846, long after the martyrdom. Heber C. Kimball stood as proxy. This is the date she reportedly also married Kimball for time.[31]

It seems uncharacteristic of Patty not to mention Sylvia's sealing to Joseph Smith, particularly since some studies indicate that Sylvia's daughter, Josephine Rosetta Lyon, was Joseph Smith's child. Danel W. Bachman quotes from a 24 February 1915 affidavit sworn by Josephine Lyon Fisher in the presence of Andrew Jenson, Joseph H. Grant, and her son, Irvin Frederick Fisher. Josephine states that her mother Sylvia on her deathbed "told me that I was the daughter of the Prophet Smith, she having been sealed to the Prophet at the time that her husband Mr Lyon was out of fellowship with the Church."[32]

According to family tradition, Windsor P. Lyon was excommunicated for suing Thomas B. Marsh for an unpaid loan. This was in 1842, according to church records. Lyon was rebaptized in his own kitchen in Nauvoo on 1 February 1846 by Heber C. Kimball and received his endowment (personal sacred ordinance) in the Nauvoo Temple on 3 February. Plans for the flight from Nauvoo were well along at this time. Family tradition also records that during the administration of Wilford Woodruff, Sylvia had the sealing to Joseph Smith canceled and was sealed to Windsor P. Lyon. There is no evidence that Heber C. Kimball and Sylvia had a marital relationship either before or after she came west.

Despite the strange fact that Patty wrote nothing linking Sylvia with Joseph Smith, evidently she also believed that Josephine was the prophet's daughter. In 1905 Angus M. Cannon met with Joseph Smith III (1832-1914), son of the martyred prophet and president of the Reorganized Church of Jesus Christ of Latter Day Saints, the splinter group that claimed authority through Joseph Smith's posterity. Steadfastly, the Reorganized Church had maintained that there was no practice of polygamy during Joseph Smith's lifetime. As Cannon tried to convince him, the younger Smith asked why there were no children to prove it. Cannon responded, "I will now refer you to one case where it was said by the girl's grandmother that your father has a daughter born of a plural wife. The girl's grandmother was Mother Sessions, who lived in Nauvoo and died here in the valley. . . . Aunt Patty Sessions asserts that the girl was born within the time after your father was said to have taken the mother."[33]

---

31. Stanley B. Kimball, *Heber C. Kimball Mormon Patriarch and Pioneer* (Chicago: University of Illinois, 1981), 313.

32. Danel W. Bachman, "Plural Marriage before the Death of Joseph Smith" (master's thesis, Purdue University, 1975), 141.

33. Angus M. Cannon, "Interview with Joseph Smith III," pp. 25–26, 1905, typescript, Archives of the Historical Department, Church of Jesus Christ of Latter-day Saints, Salt Lake City.

Josephine Rosetta Lyon was born on 8 February 1844. Patty was indeed very circumspect in what she revealed.

Although Patty's husband, David, would have been in Nauvoo when her own sealing to Joseph Smith took place, his reaction is an imponderable. But on 11 June 1842 he started for Maine with a "Bro. Pack." Patty regretted his leaving: "He left me alone, and I am very lonesome."[34] During her husband's absence, Patty apparently concentrated even more diligently on her profession as midwife. She also recorded in her diaries, as always, the names of familiar church figures with whom she associated, such as Joseph Smith, Willard Richards, and Joseph's mother, Lucy Mack, or "Mother Smith."[35]

On 24 July 1842 she "went to the Relief Society and signed a petition to send to the governor of the state." The *Exponent* writer continued with the information, "This was the first petition of the Relief Society, and it was then quite an event in the history of women."[36] The petition was sent in tandem with one from the Nauvoo city council. Both requested the Illinois governor, Thomas Carlin, to protect Joseph Smith at a time when Missouri officials were seeking his extradition. The Relief Society petition purportedly contained about one thousand signatures.[37]

The years between 1840 and 1846 stayed busy and productive for Patty as she moved among the sick and treated them; she helped to lay out the dead; she officiated in her calling as a midwife. On one occasion she froze her hands and toes as she went through severe weather to attend to a sick woman. In August of 1842 she attended the birth of a stillborn baby, her first such event, she indicated, "in thirty years of midwifery."[38]

---

34. "Patty Sessions," *Woman's Exponent* 13 (1 November): 86.

35. In those days, "Mother" seemed to be an honorific title bestowed upon older, experienced women. Patty referred to her mother-in-law as Mother Sessions. Other women, as they gained stature and years in the church, were called Mother, as was Patty herself later.

36. "Patty Sessions," *Woman's Exponent* 13 (1 November): 86, 94. The Relief Society was organized on 17 March 1842 by Joseph Smith for the women of the Mormon Church. Its purpose was to fulfill the "natural" inclinations of women to minister charity to those who were needy or cast down in spirit. Although its goals have expanded, it still operates in much the same way. Emma Smith, Joseph's wife, was the first president. During the exodus and early years of colonization, the formal organization was suspended although the women continued their charitable activities wherever they were. The churchwide organization was reestablished by Brigham Young in the late 1860s with Eliza R. Snow at the helm. Patty wrote a good deal about Relief Society activities in the Salt Lake Valley.

37. Jill Mulvay Derr, Janeth Russell Cannon, Maureen Ursenbach Beecher, *Women of Covenant* (Salt Lake City: Deseret Book Co., 1992), 38.

38. "Patty Sessions," *Woman's Exponent* 13 (15 November): 94.

In her record keeping she specifically named the individuals whose paths crossed hers, many of them to appear in later entries. But the most poignant accounts refer to relationships with Joseph Smith, his mother, and his wife Emma. For example, between 6 August 1842 and 8 February 1844, when Sylvia gave birth to Josephine Rosetta, the *Exponent* biography quotes twenty-six references Patty made to the prophet or members of his family, twenty-one of them concerning "Brother Joseph." In one she said she was making shirts for Brother Joseph. In another he laid hands on her and healed her when she was sick. "From that time she speaks of Joseph having visited at her house almost daily." And "on the 12th of February she says Brother Joseph was at her house, and Mr. Lyons, Sylvia's husband, lent him five hundred dollars."[39] This was four days after Josephine was born.

Unfortunately, the *Exponent* admits that it has chosen to leave out the "trying scenes of the people in Nauvoo before and after the death of the prophet and his brother. Suffice it to say that Sister Sessions suffered with the people in sacrificing her home, etc., and also mourned much in her own breast, for she had the most profound admiration and respect for him as a Prophet of God."[40] Patty and David received their endowments in the newly completed Nauvoo Temple in 1846.

Although Patty's extant diaries begin in February 1846, many details leading up to the exodus must be drawn from other sources. For a multiplicity of reasons, the Mormons were forced once again to abandon their safe haven, their "City Beautiful." Nauvoo had risen from the swamps in the bend of the Mississippi River at what was then Commerce, Illinois. Converts from the United States, Canada, and Europe had poured into the city in such numbers that by 1845 the population was estimated to be fifteen thousand. To other residents of the states where they lived, Mormon doctrines were strange, their numbers were threatening, and their influence was frightening. The Nauvoo Legion, the Mormon militia with Joseph Smith at its head, was intimidating. Detracters and apostates spread rumors, particularly about polygamy. They established a new press to print the *Nauvoo Expositor*, a paper that denounced Smith and the church. In retaliation the Nauvoo city council authorized its destruction—an event that precipitated the arrest and assassination of Joseph Smith and his brother Hyrum and the eventual flight of the saints from Nauvoo.

Perrigrine's diary casts little light on the events surrounding his parents' departure. He helped to outfit them for the journey, which left him and his family without money or means to go themselves, and he described officiating in temple ordinances (many of the Mormons stayed behind to finish the temple,

39. *Ibid.*, 95.
40. "Patty Sessions," *Woman's Exponent* 13 (1 February): 135.

despite their abandonment of the city), as well as early attempts to burn the temple. Then without further explanation, he attributed his being able to leave on 20 May 1846 to "the wagon and team that the Lord had Blessed me with."[41]

Resettlement requires preparation and planning. Like all pioneer women, before the trek began, Patty had to determine what to take and what to leave and how to pack in the most orderly way. She drove a team for virtually the entire distance, an achievement in itself, but she also cooked meals. And she never ceased to be a midwife. On 30 April 1846 she was called to attend Adeline Benson (a false alarm) and "came home could hardly reach the waggon. I went to bed rested me but could not eat. . . . about noon I thought I could eat some peach pie I had a kettle of coals in the waggon I cooked my peaches on them and by laying down and resting several times I made me a pie went to the stove and baked it have eat some and feel better."

Patty did not discuss particulars about being female in the wagon train. Cleanliness of person and belongings must have been a constant consideration. At least she fretted enough about washing, sometimes recruiting help for that chore. Almost once a month, she also mentioned ironing with what we recognize today as awkward, heavy irons during the journey from Nauvoo to Winter Quarters and from Winter Quarters to the Salt Lake Valley. Personal hygiene had to be a constant challenge, not to mention the implications and complications of exhaustion from dealing with illness and death and delivering babies day after day or night after night. Dust and insects, mud and wind, scorching sun and pelting rain, and swollen rivers had to be confronted daily. Still Patty wrote regularly during both reasonably good and difficult days for the following forty-one years, a time when her continuing story and the central focus of her life—socially and economically—reflected the growth of Salt Lake City and the Mormon Church.

The value of the diaries of Patty Bartlett Sessions cannot be exaggerated. Patty told her tale while she was living it, shifting attention from one scenario to another with little or no elaboration. She was too busy to explain fully what she already knew, writing, as it were, only reminders for herself. Yet she must have had some intuitive sense that her life and activities were historically important. Occasionally she assumed a more literary tone. She freely, fully, and dramatically discussed her ambiguous feelings as her husband David took polygamous wives. Obviously she resented not being consulted the way she would have liked, but she was convinced she *ought* to accept the principle of plural marriage. Rosilla, David Sessions's first plural wife, remained behind at the time of the exodus from Nauvoo, but in June caught up with the company in Iowa, probably traveling with Perrigrine and his family. On 22 June 1846 Patty wrote, "caled to sister Martha Reeves put

---

41. DPG, 3 February 1845, p. B-45.

her to bed with a son when I came home found Perrigrine and family and Rosilla there we was glad to see each other once more it has been 4 months & 10 days since I started and left my children if David Windsor Sylvia and her babe [Josephine] was here I feel as if I should be happy but alas they are not and sorrow fills my heart."

By July 31 she felt abandoned: "rains some fair in the afternoon I have seen many a lonsome hour this week Mr Sessions has found some fault with me and we are here alone almost, only three tents Holmans Everets and ours I do want to see the rest of our co so much that I am quite disconted. . . . August 1 I still feel very lonsome. . . . Sunday 2 Mr Sessions took Rosilla and asked me to go to the river then took her and waided across the river left me on this side was gone 2 or 3 hours got a few grapes P G [Perrigrine] and Mary [one of Perrigrine's wives] went with them I went back to the waggons. . . ." Although such outbursts of emotional distress were infrequent, they surfaced when she could not disguise her feelings. Her journals on such occasions chart her individual inward journey as well as the outward historical record of a people.

She must have been relieved when Rosilla turned back to Illinois—without persuading David to go with her, a relief that was relatively short-lived. In the spring of 1849, David consulted Brigham and then married nineteen-year-old Harriet Teeples Wixom. He was fifty-nine, Patty was fifty-four. David died on 11 August 1850, leaving behind Harriet's young son by an earlier marriage, Harriet pregnant, and, of course, Patty. The diaries reveal the sometimes reluctant responsibility Patty assumed for Harriet and her children.

In 1851 Patty married John Parry (1789–1868), a Welsh convert, whose wife had died as they were crossing the plains. Although she always spoke of him with respect and affection, she bemoaned the interruption of their relationship when he took a plural wife in 1854. Harriet (1822–1901), known only by the surname of Parry, bore twins, Joseph Hyrum and Bernard Llewelyn, in 1855; a daughter, Louisa Ellen, in 1857; a son, Edwin Francis, in 1860; and a son, Henry Edward, in 1862. In Wales between the years 1809 and 1824, John had fathered four sons and three daughters by his first wife. Patty delivered some of the former, and several of the latter featured prominently in her writings. Both of Patty's husbands died at her home, where they seemed to gravitate when they were ill.

Actually Patty probably gained more from polygamy than she realized. Always of a strong nature, she became even more astute in her business dealings as she took control of her own affairs. Forced independence helped Patty to establish her success in various ventures.

For the most part, however, Patty's writing is restrained. She seems to want to report the facts objectively. Usually she does. But sometimes her objectivity is tinged with self-justification. She wants to feel good about herself and to present her best side. She justifies her role in situations requiring emergency medical decisions. She excuses herself for not going to Sunday meetings. She defends herself for wanting a refund on her tithing or for fees charged for her services, produce, or properties.

In order to be absolutely fair—and in her mind she was fair—Patty kept copious records of business dealings. She reported with legitimate pride that she entered the valley with one five-cent piece that she "picked up on the red Bute and since Mr Sessions died I have took care of myself and have laid up considerable."[42] She "laid up considerable" because she worked hard as a midwife and as a consultant on other medical matters; she toiled at cultivating her gardens and orchards and in selling and preserving their fruits; and she wisely invested in other properties, saving what she made in all her endeavors. She bought stock in Zions Cooperative Mercantile Association, and by 1883 owned shares worth sixteen thousand dollars. She was as compulsive about her financial accounting as about recording her daily activities. Thus her financial ledgers become veritable repositories of information about the pioneer economy. She recorded the costs of delivering babies, of purchases she and others made at the cooperative store she operated for a while, and of items she acquired for her home; the charges for properties she purchased, the rent received from them, and construction expenses; and the value of in-kind payments for tithing. She never made a loan without noting it and crossing it out when paid. She made a record of all her business dealings with her family, including her two husbands. Patty Sessions was a formidable business woman, often seeming just plain miserly. She was not miserly, but she was frugal. She worked hard for what she accumulated. She took care of her belongings and her property. She expected the same of others and a fair accounting—such as she offered—for business dealings. Although her system is sometimes hard to decipher, it is fascinating in its content and comprehensiveness (only small samples could be included here).

Many of Patty's transactions evolved out of her social contacts. As mentioned earlier, she was a charter member of a group of women sealed to Joseph Smith during his lifetime, and this close-knit group supported each other materially and spiritually. Since life often revolves around births and illness, Patty was a central figure in an extremely high percentage of the growing number of households in the community of Salt Lake City and later Bountiful, as she had been in Nauvoo, in Winter Quarters, and in the wagons of the pioneer parties of 1847. Obviously she was respected enough to be trusted in emergencies and to be in demand for parties and important social occasions. On 23 December 1881 an anniversary celebration of the birth of Joseph Smith was held in Salt Lake City. Patty sat at the table with President John Taylor, Apostle and later President Wilford Woodruff, Apostle and later

---

42. From the first page of the final of Patty's diaries included in this publication.

John Parry, who married Patty Sessions in 1852 and was the first leader of the choir that became the Mormon Tabernacle Choir. From J. Spencer Cornwall, *A Century of Singing: The Salt Lake Mormon Tabernacle Choir* (Salt Lake City: Deseret Book Co., 1958), 348.

The Patty Sessions Academy, which she built in 1884 for her grandchildren and other Bountiful children. Patty is on the left wearing a black bonnet and holding a child. Her son Perrigrine, in vest and hat, stands in front of the doorway with four of his wives to his left. Courtesy of Kim Burningham.

President Joseph F. Smith, Patriarch John Smith, and many other illustrious citizens of the area.[43] As she was important to others, they were also important to her. Names of friends and associates take up a substantial amount of the paper to which she applied her pen.

She was influential within the spiritual economy of the community, especially for the women, but in some ways for the men, too. Though the spiritual occasions when the sisters met to strengthen each other took on a celebratory air, there was no hint of usurping or infringing on male priesthood authority. The women merely exercised the spiritual gifts and powers to which they knew they were entitled. Without a doubt their gatherings strengthened all to face the hardships and obstacles of their forced settlement of a strange land. The men also recognized, approved of, sometimes participated in, and encouraged the women's activities. Patty wrote on 22 November 1847, in the evening prayed for Heber [Kimball] with Elen and Mary Elen [Kimball's wives] I anointed Elen acording to Hebers request when he met me on the road."

Since Patty was vitally interested in education, her diaries provide information about that aspect of early life in the Salt Lake Valley. She herself took advantage of whatever learning experiences arose. She availed herself of public lectures, was a participating member and leader of the Council of Health established by Willard Richards, and studied the Deseret Alphabet (the Mormon attempt to invent a universal language). Among some loose papers, a small scrap contains a list of dates and two words, "Dancing school." She enjoyed that dancing school and bragged that she could dance with her grandchildren and have fun. She recognized the worth of schools and teachers and even paid to build a school in Bountiful, the Patty Sessions Academy, for her grandchildren and the children of those who could not afford the cost of education. Phebe Sessions wrote, "She left money enough in the Parent Co-op so that the dividend will run the school continuously ten months in the year and pay all the expenses pertaining to it."[44]

Her public spiritedness embraced more than education. She gladly donated to the Perpetual Emigration Fund, established to support the migration west of poorer Mormons. As president of the Indian Relief Society, she was a key contributor to the Mormon efforts to clothe the Indians. She made rugs for the Salt Lake Tabernacle, collected donations for the poor from members of the Relief Society, and donated generously to the building of temples.

She took in boarders for pay and hosted various visitors for nothing, sometimes doggedly, other times willingly. One overnight "guest" did not pay her any money, she said, but left enough bedbugs to make her wish they were coins. When she wrote those lines, she did not mean to be funny. Her

43. "Anniversary Gathering," *Woman's Exponent* 9 (1 January 1881): 116.

44. Phebe C. Sessions, "Biographical Sketch," 6.

observations always seem deadly serious. So her small snatches of humor—of which she appears to be completely oblivious—elicit unexpected chuckles. On 6 December 1851 she wrote, "I have cut all my wood since Monday." Then, on December 14, after she had married John Parry, she noted, "I was married to John Parry and I feel to thank the Lord that I have some one to cut my wood for me." She was unconsciously very funny sometimes.

Her photograph shows just how serious she was. She called it a "likeness," so what is it like? Most apparent are the chiseled and determined jawline, the wide, unflinching eyes that stare into the camera without a hint of a smile, the prominent nose. Her face is framed by one of the caps she sewed from time to time; her slender hands that worked at so many tasks hold her needles and something she is knitting. She wears a dress of dark brocade, with a long, pointed collar and a round, hand-crocheted one. Of course, people who sat for photographs in those days had to remain absolutely still, but her stern character is still permanently etched. Patty's photograph shows one view only, however, whereas her writings leave a trail of information, beckoning the reader to explore all kinds of inexhaustible byways and hidden paths.

Patty, as time passed by, as she became deaf, as the population grew and her faculties diminished, withdrew more and more into the bosom of family and very close associates. She still wanted to maintain the work ethic accumulated over decades, but her faculties began to fail, which diminished the accomplishments that she had recounted in all those earlier diaries. Her writing eventually slows to a plod, gives little information, and even seems boring in its habitual repetitions.

But such a statement reflects a shortsighted value judgment. To be obsessed with deciphering all the intricacies of her diaries; to witness the gradual aging and decline of a great pioneer woman; to see her entries fade into words such as "the same" and later a mere recital of dates; to read "it is now friday the 4th" and then find the rest of the page—and all other pages—blank is to feel a sense of profound loss, but also to understand a fraction more about the fleeting nature of human experience and to develop respect for the enduring value of personal records.

Further, to read the diaries of Patty Sessions is to gain an exceptional insight into one human psyche and the dynamics of early Mormon women and to participate vicariously in building western society. Patty's diaries unveil the mindset of a woman whose story underscores the historical importance of the dailiness, the ordinariness, the dullness, and the constant vitality of human endeavor.

Patty Bartlett Sessions. Courtesy of Irene S. Poulson.

Diary One, 1846–1848

Beginning a diary signifies faith that one's life is going somewhere for some reason. When Patty Sessions began her trail diary, she knew she was on the move to an unknown destination. She had faith in God's intervention in the affairs of the church that held her unswerving allegiance. She trusted her leaders. She had faith in the body of Latter-day Saints and particularly in the spiritual powers of the women who were her counterparts. She believed that the migration was necessary. She had confidence in her ability not only to endure to the end of the journey but also to use her considerable abilities to help others endure. In the following pages, Patty gives her perspective of the journey to the valley of the Great Salt Lake with matter-of-factness but enough poignancy to awaken us to her complexity.

"The form [of diary keeping] has been an important outlet for women partly because it is an analogue to their lives: emotional, fragmentary, interrupted, modest, not to be taken seriously, private, restricted, daily, trivial, formless, concerned with self, as endless as their tasks," wrote Mary Jane Moffat and Charlotte Painter, the editors of Revelations: Diaries of Women.[1] *Although directly referring to the diaries of more celebrated women, Moffat and Painter precisely delineate the tenor of Patty's diary entries.*

---

1. Mary Jane Moffat and Charlotte Painter, *Revelations: Diaries of Women* (New York: Vintage Books, 1975), 5.

A Day Book given
to me
Patty Sessions by
Sylvia P Lyon this
10th day of Feb.
1846
Patty Sessions
her Book
I am now fifty one
years six [six *is written on top of* old] days old
Feb 10 1846 City of
Joseph Hancock Co Ill

1846

the sun came out dried my bed and clothes
but my tears will not dry up

FEBRUARY 1846

Feb 10th 1846 Nauvoo or City of Joseph My things are now packed ready for
the west have been and put Richards ^Bird^ Wife [Emeline Crandall] to bed
with a daughter [Amanda Fidelia]. in the afternoon put sister Hariet Young to
bed with a son [Oscar Brigham][2] **11th** mad[e] me a cap and in the evening
went to the [Masonic] Hall to see the scenery of the massacree of Joseph and
Hyram Smith[3] **12** this morning Br [Philo] Dib[b]le gave me a ticket to go in to
^the^ scenery any time[4] we then bade our childre^n^ and friends good by

---

2. Harriet Elizabeth Cook (1824–1898) was the fourth wife of Brigham Young
   (1801–1877).

3. A display of oil paintings and relics, probably including the death masks of the
   prophet Joseph Smith (1805–1844), who was the founder of the Church of Jesus
   Christ of Latter-day Saints, and his brother Hyrum (1800–1844), church patriarch. Joseph and Hyrum were martyred at Carthage Jail, Illinois, on 27 June
   1844. The chief duty of a church patriarch was to confer blessings on church
   members.

4. Dibble (1806–1895) was a bodyguard of Joseph Smith at the time of the martyrdom. According to Dibble family history, he made the death masks of the brothers two days after their death (Ogden W. Kraut, "Pioneer Journals: Life History
   of Philo Dibble, Sr.," p. 2., typescript, Archives of the Historical Department,
   Church of Jesus Christ of Latter-day Saints, Salt Lake City [hereafter cited as
   CHD]). Edwin S. Dibble collected information on his grandfather under the title

and started for the west crosed the river about noon Mr. Sessions and I with manny other Brethren[5] I nit almost a mittin for Mr Sessions while he went back to get some things we left **13** we have had a goo^d^ nights rest attended prayrs in our waggon and have eat our breakfast ^noon^ made me two red night caps out of some flannel Sylvia sent me[6] Mr Sessions has gone over the river to get his plow handles has got back with them **14** this morning it snows Sister Oakly has set up all night because her waggon did not get across the river I gave her and Mariann and carlos Mur[r]ay some breakfast[7] we are now ready to leave the bank of the river to go to the other camp 3 oclock we have arived to the other camp it ^on shugar Creek^[8] has just done storming the ground coverd with sno^w^ and water and is verry bad under foot attended prayers in Father John Smiths tent[9] **sunday 15** day I have wrote a letter to send to Perrigrine[10] and visited many of the sisters **monday 16** President B

"Genealogy of Philo Dibble," 1973, p. 8. (Typescript copy in possession of Donna T. Smart). Dibble brought the masks to Utah in 1851. They were sold to Harrie Brown of Logan in 1855 and later passed to Wilford Wood of Woods Cross, then to the Mormon Church for the church museum. Dibble also created two paintings of what he envisioned as a series—one of Joseph Smith addressing the Nauvoo Legion three days before the Carthage imprisonment and one depicting the murder. They were brought to Utah later. He traveled around the area lecturing and showing his pictures and relics. The Church Museum of History and Art, which now displays the plaster impressions of the death masks, attributes the originals to George Cannon.

5. David Sessions, Patty's husband, was born on 4 April 1790 in Farley, Orange County, Vermont. They were married on 28 June 1812 in Maine. She refers to him as "Mr." Sessions, a custom in her day. Emily Thornwell's *The Lady's Guide to Perfect Gentility* (duplicated copy of 1856 original, n.p., Huntington Library, San Marino, Calif.) describes "How a lady should speak of her husband," saying that "A lady should not say, 'my husband,' except among intimates; in every other case she should address him by his name, calling him 'Mr.'"

6. Sylvia Porter Sessions, third child of David and Patty, born on 31 July 1818 in Andover West Surplus, Oxford County, Maine.

7. Elizabeth DeGroat (1795/6–1885) and her husband, Ezra Hemstead Nassau Oakley (1788–1879), were later members of the Big Company that left Winter Quarters in June 1847. By October of 1847 more than fifteen hundred persons and 556 wagons had arrived in the Salt Lake Valley. Carlos Murray (1829–1855) entered the Salt Lake Valley in July 1847 with the Pioneer Company.

8. Sugar Creek, situated nine miles west of Nauvoo, was a temporary gathering place for the fleeing Mormons.

9. Following the martyrdom of Hyrum, John Smith (1781–1854), an uncle of Joseph and Hyrum, became church patriarch. He had been ordained a patriarch by Joseph Smith in 1844. His first wife was Clarissa Lyman.

10. Usually Patty refers to Perrigrine as P G. He was born on 15 June 1814, in Newry, Oxford County, Maine, the first child of David and Patty Sessions. Perrigrine remained in Nauvoo when his parents left in February of 1846.

Young came into camp this morning[11] it is very cold the wind blows we can
hardly get to the fire for smoke and we have no tent but our waggon Brother
Taylor has got here this eveing[12] he had one team that got frightened ran
down hill upset the waggon hurt a lady and a boy some I helped dress her
wounds and made her some tea **17 tuesday** dresed the boys legs hear from
home By Wm= Kimbal[13] they have Began to organise and we go first hundred second ten Pr Youngs company Capt. Holman[14] **Wendseday 18** David
^Sessions^ and Enoch Tripp came into the camp[15] took dinner with us ^I^
wrote a a letter to Sylvia another to Rosilla[16] send them by Enoch David has
gone to Farmington [Iowa] **19 thursday** it snows hard the wind blows no tent

11. Brigham Young (1801–1877) was president of the Quorum (or Council) of the
    Twelve Apostles. When Joseph Smith was assassinated, church leadership
    passed to the Quorum. Brigham Young was sustained as president of the
    Church of Jesus Christ of Latter-day Saints on 27 December 1847 in Iowa,
    where, after the initial trek to the Salt Lake Valley, he had returned with other
    leaders to bring families and additional settlers to Zion.

12. John Taylor (1808–1887), with Willard Richards, was a voluntary companion to
    the prisoners in Carthage Jail when the martyrdom took place. During the late
    afternoon, Taylor twice sang all fourteen verses of "A Poor Wayfaring Man of
    Grief" when requested by Joseph Smith. He was saved from martyrdom when
    ammunition struck a gold watch in his pocket. He did, however, suffer severe
    wounds to his left thigh, knee, hip, and arm. Since all the rest of the Quorum
    were on missions, keeping order and directing the church in the early weeks
    after the martyrdom devolved to Taylor and Richards. John Taylor was presi-
    dent of the Quorum of the Twelve Apostles from 1877 to 1887 and president of
    the church from October of 1880 until his death on 25 July 1887.

13. William Henry Kimball (1826–1907) was the first surviving son of Heber Chase
    Kimball and Vilate Murray. Much later he built Kimball Junction in Parley's
    Canyon, east of Salt Lake City.

14. John Greenleaf Holman (1828–1888) came to Utah in 1847 with the Pioneer
    Company.

15. David Sessions, born on 9 May 1823 in Newry, Oxford County, Maine, was the
    fifth child of Patty and David Sessions. Enoch Bartlett Tripp (1823–1909) was a
    nephew of Patty's whose name appears often in the diaries. Patty's sister,
    Namah Hall Bartlett, married William Tripp, who was an Episcopal-Methodist
    preacher and a member of the Maine legislature. William taught his son the
    trade of boot- and shoemaking. According to the diaries of Perrigrine Sessions
    (hereafter cited as DPG), p. B-43, CHD, Enoch and the husband of Sylvia
    Sessions, Windsor P. Lyon, were baptized on 18 January 1846 by Heber C.
    Kimball. It was a rebaptism for Lyon (see page 16 in the introduction and note
    41 of this diary).

16. Rosilla Cowen (b. 1813) became a plural wife of Patty's husband David on 3
    October 1845 and received her temple endowment on 1 January 1846, accord-
    ing to the "Nauvoo Temple Endowment Register," 10 December 1845 to 8
    February 1846 (Salt Lake City: Temple Index Bureau, 1974).

yet Mr Sessions sent a dollar yestarday for cloth to make the ends it has come but no twine to sew it with David has come back it storms fast he takes dinner with us again and starts for home it has stormed and ~~the~~ wind has blew all day **20 Friday** it does not storm but the wind blows and it is very cold **21 saturday** it is clear warm sun but cold air **22 sunday** I ^visited^ Loisa ^Beman^ and Eliza Snow[17] **23 monday** we got canvas for a tent sewed some on it **24 tuesday** ^stormed all day^ finished sewing it together Mr Sessions went ho^me^ to get tent poles and other things **25 wednesday** lie very cold this morning put Jackson Redings wife [Martha] to bed with a son [Joseph C.][18] **thursday 26** lie so cold I co^u^ld hardly stir. Sylvia David and the girls came over to see us Mr Sessions came home the girls got into the river **Friday 27** Mr Sessions and I went over to Nauvoo to get the stove and cow **saturday 28** came back put our stove in the tent we put John Scot[t]s wife [Elizabeth Menerey, 1815–1886] to bed mis cary are comfortable[19] **sunday** have a meeting and start along ^travel 5 miles^

MARCH 1846

March the first picth our tents **monday 2** travel on ^12 miles^ one of our horses has the thumps[20] I go a foot up and down the hills pitch our tents **tuesday 3** ready to start again travel 8 miles go through Farmington up the

---

17. Louisa Beman or Beaman (1815–1850) may have been the first plural wife of Joseph Smith, married on 5 April 1841 by Joseph H. Noble (see Andrew Jenson, *Historical Record* [Salt Lake City: Church of Jesus Christ of Latter-day Saints, 1886], 6:232). The women who were sealed to Joseph Smith appear to have bonded in friendship. Patty was also one of them. To members of the church, a sealing was binding in heaven and on earth. It solemnized a marriage covenant and family relationship for eternity. By this time Beaman was probably a plural wife of Brigham Young. Eliza Roxcy Snow (1804–1887) was an innovative leader of women in the early church. She acted as secretary to the women's organization, the Relief Society, when it was first organized in 1842 in Nauvoo. On 29 June 1842 she became a plural wife of Joseph Smith in a ceremony performed by Brigham Young. For the purpose of support and in name only, she also became a plural wife of Brigham Young. She crossed the plains to Utah with the Big Company. Eliza R. Snow shouldered important responsibilities in the organization and administration of church auxiliaries in the West.

18. Return Jackson Redden or Redding (1817–1890/1) was a member of the Pioneer Company. His wife Marthy M. (according to Conrey Bryson, *Winter Quarters* [Salt Lake City: Deseret Book Co., 1986], 155) died on 15 March 1847 at Winter Quarters. Their son died on 17 August 1847 "of bowel complaint." Some accounts state that Redden was the first person to see the Salt Lake Valley when he was hunting for lost cattle.

19. John Scott (1811–1876) was captain of the artillery at this time.

20. A throbbing movement of the sides of the chest, caused by spasmodic contractions of the diaphragm; similar to hiccups.

Desmoine river over take Br Miller he has gone a head all the way[21] **Wednesday 4** we stop and rest finish our tent Br Miller starts along [from Bonaparte, Iowa] again **thursday 5** ^put John Joens [Jones] wife to bed [*in margin*] mis cariage^ we start along Mr Sessions has lost sight of the cow I have to drive while he goes to hunt for her we go up the river Mr Sessions over takes us has not found the cow. cross the river ford it below the mill damm up hill bad road I go a foot get on to the prairie stop and feed go across the priarie it is so late we do not pitch our tent ^travel 13 miles Indian^ ^creek^ **Friday 6** I go back ten miles this morning to see Sarah Ann [Whitney (Smith Kimball)][22] she is ^sick^ sent for me I rode horse back she was beter when I got there. and I drove her carriage in to the camp in the after noon with her and her mother [Elizabeth Ann Smith Whitney, 1800–1882] the camp did no^t^ start to day. our horse was sick last night but they laid hands on him and he is beter to day **Saturday 7** Br Holdman [John Greenleaf Holman] and the rest of his ten starts along we stop Br Brigum says we must not start with our horse he will send a team back for us the other teams begin to come along Brigums Co has taken a thousand dollar jobb 7 miles on a head ^but did not do it^ do not send a team back to day, we stay alone here to night ^I have the ague^[23] **sunday 8** Sarah ann sends back 9 miles for me she has a son, born before I get there calls it David Kimball Smith born in the ~~valy~~ valley of David.[24] Br Whitney sends back for

---

21. George Miller (1794–1856), the second bishop in the church, had been a faithful member. The "Journal History of the Church of Jesus Christ of Latter-day Saints" (hereafter cited as JH), 26 March 1846, CHD, records that President Young censured Parley P. Pratt (1807–1857) and George Miller for "drawing off from . . . the main body of the camp and going ahead. . ." and that Bishop Miller "has since left us and gone his own way, having refused to be led by the counsels of the Presidency, and removed to Texas." Miller was disfellowshipped in 1848.

22. Sarah Ann Whitney had been married to Joseph Smith in 1842. She became the fourteenth wife of Heber C. Kimball as of 17 March 1845.

23. An acute fever, sometimes accompanied by paroxysms of chill, fever, and sweating. Ague often meant malaria.

24. Patty and David had left Sugar Creek on 17 February in the first hundred, President Young's company, and had passed Farmington, which is approximately twenty-five miles from Nauvoo, and gone on to Indian Creek, probably the Des Moines river crossing. Whether Sarah Ann was in a valley called David or called it David because of the birth of her child cannot be determined. The child died on 18 August 1847 of cholera. Conrey Bryson gives a different birth date and records the death as "Smith, David Kimball (1 yr.) Son of Heber and Sarah Kimble Smith" (*Winter Quarters*, 156). Whether both Patty and Bryson transposed the middle and last names, or Smith became the last name out of deference to Sarah Ann's earlier marriage to Joseph Smith is not clear. The baby David was the son of Heber C. Kimball.

Mr Sessions[25] ^I go on 3 miles to our tent^ met him he had exchanged his mare for a yoke of oxen **monday 9th** Mr Sessions overtakes me to day. ^at Richersons point^ [26] yesterday I felt bad I was not well and I and our things were scatured on acount of our heavy load and bad roads and were in nine different places we are all together now but our cow we are now about sixty miles from Nauvoo Br Ezra Benson came after me nine oclock in the evening I went and put his wife [Pamelia Andrus, 1809–1870] to bed with a daughter at ten oclock in the tent[27] came back found Mr Sessions a bed without his supper no one to get it for him when I went away he was gone to trade his horse for oxen but did not **10th** ^**tuesday**^ this morning I feel very bad, here we are we was counseled to come, our team cannot draw our load and unless we can get some more team we must stop and some of our tens says we must give up all our provision and then we can go along. I now expect the brethren to go along and leave us my feelings I cannot express but my disire is that they may not lea^ve^ me, after breakfast I went to Br Kimbals tent[28] he was praying after he had done he says Mother Sessions what is the matter you dont feel right I know. I told him we could not go along. he said I shall

---

25. Newel Kimball Whitney (1795–1850), the first bishop in the church, had been pledged to assist the families in every possible way in their removal from Nauvoo. His wife was Elizabeth Ann Smith; their daughter was Sarah Ann.

26. Richardson's Point was about fifty-five miles from Nauvoo, a second resting place.

27. Bryson (*Winter Quarters*, 32) quotes Benson's own account of the birth. "After the cold weather abated a little, the different camps took up their line of march through the rain, sleet and mud; the nights were very cold and frosty. My wife Pamelia gave birth to a daughter, about eleven o'clock on the 9th of March. It rained hard. We had nothing but a tent to cover her and had to raise her bed on brush to keep her from the water. . . . We named our child Isabella." Pamelia was the first wife of Ezra Benson (1811–1869); her sister, Adaline Brooks Andrus (1813–1898), was Benson's plural wife. Adaline became the great-grandmother of Ezra Taft Benson, thirteenth president of the church, through George T., the son Patty would deliver on May 1. Benson, later on the trek between Winter Quarters and the Salt Lake Valley, became captain of the second ten of the Pioneer Company. He was a member of the Quorum of the Twelve Apostles from 1846 until his death. Pamelia was married to Benson on 1 January 1831.

28. Heber Chase Kimball (1801–1868) became first counselor to Brigham Young when Young was sustained as church president in December 1847 at Winter Quarters. During the trek westward from Winter Quarters, he was one of the division leaders of the Pioneer Company. At this time he was a member of the Quorum of the Twelve Apostles. The Sessionses and Kimballs had lived near each other in Nauvoo and were good friends. For a list of equipment and supplies required for trail travel, see Stanley B. Kimball, *Historic Resource Study Mormon Pioneer National Historic Trail* (Washington, D.C.: Department of Interior/National Park Service, 1991), 129.

not go to day and I will plan for you ^and^ said many other things that comforted me and it began to rain and I huried back to the tent. Br Charles Rich brings our cow along to us[29] we are glad to see her Br Brigum came in to see us told me we should not be left behind for he wanted me along and I should go soo^n^ Mr Sessions came in said he had put off the hors [*page torn*] for a yoke of four year old stears and twenty bushels of oats sold two halters for 4 bushels of wheat I feel now as if we can go along we are in Chequess [Chequest Creek] **wen^d^sday 11th** it still rains caled to Sister Rockwood[30] she miscarried **thursday 12** it rains wrote back to P G by Br Carns Father[31] John Smith came into our tent made us quite a visit said much on the resurrection **Friday 13th** clouday cold & squaly **Saturday 14th** wrote a letter to Rosilla **sunday 15** Fair but the wind blows hard visited Br Chase[32] he is sick Brs Holman & Rocklin started back for the family **Monday 16th** got Loenza Pond to wash for me[33] visited Zina with Eliza Snow[34] it has been a fine day **tuesday 17th** Tanners child died I ironed windy sent 4 bushels of wheat to mill. **Wednesday^** flour divided^ **18** Edwin Little died this morning ^broug^ht^ back into the camp to ^be^ buried[35] he was caried out to a

---

29. Charles Coulson Rich (1809–1893) became a member of the Quorum of the Twelve Apostles on 12 February 1849. He was captain of the guard and in charge of artillery of the Big Company (see Leonard Arrington, *Charles C. Rich* [Provo, Utah: Brigham Young University Press, 1974]).

30. Nancy Haven (1805–1876), was the wife of Albert Parry Rockwood (1805–1879), one of two division commanders for the Pioneer Company.

31. Daniel Carn/Garn (1802–1872) had been at Far West and served as bishop in Nauvoo in 1842 as well as at Winter Quarters in 1846. He became a captain in Brigham's fifty in the emigration company of 1848. His father was John Carn or Garn.

32. Isaac Chase (1791–1861), and his wife, Phoebe Ogden (1794–1872), went west in the Big Company that left Winter Quarters in June of 1847.

33. Loenza Pond, then sixteen years old, was probably the daughter of Stillman Pond. Keeping the washing done must have been a constant challenge. One more-than-a-century-old anonymous Kentucky "receipt" for washday included: "1. bild a fire . . . to heet kettle of rain water. 2. set tubs so smoke won't blow in eyes if wind is pert. 3. shave one hold cake soap in bilin water. 4. sort things, make three piles, one pile white, one pile cullord, one pile work britches and rags. 5. stur flour in cold water to smooth then thin down with bilin water. 6. rub dirty spots on bord, scrub hard, then bile, rub cullord but don't bile just rench and starch . . ." etc.

34. Zina Diantha Huntington Jacobs (1821–1901) was the wife of Henry Bailey Jacobs, from whom she was later separated. She had been married by her brother, Dimick Huntington, to Joseph Smith in October 1841 (according to the Record of Marriages, Hancock County, Book A, p. 40). In 1846 she was sealed to Brigham Young for time and Joseph Smith for eternity.

35. Edwin Sobieski Little, son of Brigham Young's sister, Susannah Young, and James Little, was helping his uncle Brigham across the river with the wagons

house in his sickness he is this evening ^buried^ I have baked some pies
thursday 19 the camp starts we go leave the tent for Br Holman goods as he
has not got back yet we travel 12 miles camp on Chequess Creak Davis Co
new purchase Ioway cold and no tent **Friday 20th** cold morning but fair
weather travel on ten miles low bottom muddy have to double teams cross fox
river double up the hill yesterday we put some of our load into Wests waggon
put the stears on to it Amos Davis drives it,[36] it has been very cold to day I
have been very cold untill now. the anxiety of mind to get through the mud
has warmed me so that I can write while they are gone back after the other
teams to come up I now travel 3 miles on foot to the camp & have traveled 3
more in the forenoon to keep warm we have come 15 miles to day **saturday
21** good roads come 11 miles to day camp on the head of Chariton waters
some on one side and some on the other **sunday 22** we have put stove in Br
[George Barton] Wicks [1803–1885] tent 2 nights we go through the bottoms
cross the Shariton river by leting our waggons down by ropes and drawing
them up the same way Zina had a son [Henry Chariton] at the river[37] comfortable we traveled 4 miles doubled teams up hills and camped it rains to
night John Young came in[to] the camp[38] we saw him **monday^23^** we do
not start to day he came to see us tells us much about Nauvoo Br Clark killd
a turkey ^and others killed deer^ David [Varner] Davis [1823–1896] got lost
hunting was gone all day it rains all night **tuesday 24th** rains and snows very
cold and muddy stay in the waggon wrote a letter to Sylvia yesterday
wednesday 25 snows cold nothing for our teams to eat yesterday nor this
morning but brows[39] and snow and mud over shoes get a little corn to night
thursday ^26^ cold wind blows hard blows our tent down every little while

---

when the ice broke and he fell into the icy waters. He contracted pneumonia and
later died (see Golden L. Jackman and Teton Hanks, comps., "Descendants of
Ephraim Knowlton Hanks and his Wives," typescript, CHD). Juanita Brooks
(editor of *Diary of Hosea Stout*, 2 vols., [Salt Lake City: University of Utah Press,
1964], 1:139, n. 14) describes the place where Little was buried.

36. Alva West (b. 1834) was in the company over which Perrigrine Sessions was
captain on the trek from Winter Quarters to the Salt Lake Valley. Amos Davis
(b. 1811) was a merchant and landowner in Nauvoo.

37. Henry after his father, Henry Bailey Jacobs, and Chariton after the river (see
Janet Peterson and LaRene Gaunt, *Elect Ladies* [1946; reprint, Salt Lake City:
Deseret Book Co., 1990], 49–51).

38. John Young, Jr., (1791–1870) was Brigham's eldest brother. In 1846 an estimated
ten thousand Mormons stayed in Nauvoo, so when John came the next day and
"tells us much about Nauvoo," he probably had much to report. Most of the
Mormons who had remained in Nauvoo moved west by the following
September. John Young was part of the Big Company, leaving Winter Quarters
at the same time as the Sessions family.

39. Browse refers to the tender shoots and twigs of trees and shrubs.

Friday 27 the wind bl[o]ws very hard Br J Young goes home this morning I
send Sylvias letter by him I have coals in the waggon to keep me warm **satturday 28** Br Sherwood came to board with us[40] more moderate **sunday 29**
very cold requested to cut no wood nor leave the camp, but to keep the
sabath day **monday^30^** Brs Holman and Locklin has returned & brough
me some letters from my children warm and pleasant ^weather^ **Tuesday
31** I have read my letters with joy and gratitude to God for the privilige of
hearing from them, have read Perrigrines letter to Brigham he says they will
all get away soon and if Windsor and David [Sessions] dont come now they
will be glad to follow after and come crouching[41] Porter Rocwel has come
into the camp[42] brought us a letter from P G & Rosilla

APRIL 1846

wednesday April 1st wrote a letter to PeGrine it is warm and pleasant we
have been here ten days ^12 oclock^ we start along go seven miles I walk 5
camp on the ^burnt^ prairie east fork of ^shoal Creek^ [near present-day
Cincinnati, Iowa] take the stove out of Br Wiks tent and go in to Br
Rockwoo^ds^ tent **thursday 2** stop here to day change our waggon put our
load all into one waggon I am almost ^~~we put~~^ tired out cooking loading &
unloading we put our oxen all on one waggon and let [Amos] Davis go **friday
3** start before breakfast go 7 miles ^came up with Br Millers camp^ stop and
eat I went into several tents it thundered and lightened and rained all the ater-
noon we traveled 11 miles more through mud and rain ^Mr Sessions went all
the way a foot^ and then camped rained all night ^here we took [William]
Richmond [b. 1821; d. during Civil War] to team & board^ **saturday 4** mud

40. Henry Garlie Sherwood (1785–1862) was commissary general for the Pioneer
     Company and drew up the first survey of Salt Lake City.

41. Windsor Palmer Lyon ws born on 8 February 1809 in Orwell, Addison County,
     Vermont; he died in 1849 in Iowa City, Johnson County, Iowa. He was a
     colonel, an army surgeon, and proprietor of a drugstore in Nauvoo. Married to
     Sylvia Porter Sessions at Far West, Caldwell County, Missouri, in 1838, he had
     been baptized in 1832 in New York. According to "A Record of the Names of the
     Members of the Church of Jesus Christ of Latter-day Saints as Taken by the
     Lesser Priesthood in the Spring of the Year 1842," he was cut off (see Lyman De
     Platt, comp., *Nauvoo 1839–1845* [Highland, Utah, 1980], 1:298). Family tradi-
     tion attributes the 17 March 1839 excommunication to a suit against Thomas B.
     Marsh, who would not repay money loaned to him by Lyon. Perrigrine's diary
     and the autobiography of Enoch Bartlett Tripp both record the baptism of Tripp
     and Lyon on 1 February 1846.

42. Orrin Porter Rockwell (1813–1878) was a member of the Pioneer Company and
     acted as a scout and hunter during 1846–47. On his own authority, he had acted
     as a bodyguard for Joseph Smith and later for Brigham Young as well. He is well
     known as one of the colorful figures of Mormondom.

aplenty the worst time we have had yet we shall have to stay here untill the
mud is dried up Mr Sessions is so lame he can hardly go he lays in the waggon
half of the time today ^as it still rains^ I went a foot some when it was up hill
and we had to double teams I got wet but I feel well

*[On 25 February 1846, when Patty delivered Martha Redding of a son, she likely flipped
ahead some pages to record her earnings as a midwife. The days slipped by, and she found
herself finishing her 4 April entry just ahead of the pages for her accounts, shown in the table
below. Presumably she again left blank pages before beginning her account of 5 April, shuf-
fling back and forth between her textual and financial accounts until 1 April 1847, when
Parley P. Pratt gave her a dollar on a two-dollar charge. His wife, Sarah Huston, bore a
daughter, Julia. The advance pioneer party left Winter Quarters on 7 April 1847.]*

sunday 5 I rose this morning the sun shines with splendor which gladens our
hearts our waggon cover is froze hard and mud and watter a little froze over-
shoes to the tent Br [John] Taylor and family came within 3 miles of the camp
and staid all night without fire the ground is so wet that many could not lie
down without lying in the water Mr Sessions is better to day, we are now
1=35 miles from Nauvoo ^we are^ in Missouria on a branch of lones creek
wrote a line to P G by Br Corah [perhaps George W. Coray, b. 1819] **Monday
6** the chur^ch^ 16 years old to day it rains hard Br Rocwood came to our
waggon told us the word was get out of this mud as soon as possible we move
before breakfast go 3 miles cross the creek on new bridges that our men had
made had to double team all the way through mud and rain eat in our wag
while the team goes back after Br Rockwoods waggon nothing but brows for
teams to eat Br Brigham came up with his company driving his ^team^ in the
rain and mud to his knes as happy as a king here we camped the men went
some to browsing the cattle some to cutting wood & burning coal we got supper went to bed and it soon began to thunder and lighten and the ^rain^
came faster than ever about 2 oclock in the morning I was caled for to go back
two miles it then snowed I rode behind the man [Rufus P. Steward] through
mud and water some of the way belly deep to the house I found the sister that
I was caled to in an old log cabin her child was born before I got there she had
rode 13 miles after she was in travail crosed the creek on a log after dark her
husband carried over such things as was nessesary left his waggons and teams
on the other side as the water had carried of the bridge, **tuesday 7** the ground
froze some I got on to the horse on a mans sadle rode home to our waggon the
creeks had raised ^6 feet^ the mud froze the man went on foot with me I got
home safe it came of fair Br Rocwood brought in some wild ionions and priari
flowers **wednesday 8** the water has fell so that men have gone to making
bridges and some after corn for the teams sister Horn washed a little for me[43]
a little corn for the teams two ears apeice Mr Sessions has made two yokes to

---

43. Mary Isabelle Hales (1818–1905) married Joseph Horne (1812–1897) in 1836.

Dr to Patty Sessions for Attendance Feb: 25–1846

Feb 25	Jackson Reding	paid	x2:00
28	John Scott	paid	2X00
March 4	John Gean		0 50
8	Sarah ann		2-00
9	Ezra Benson	cr100100	x200x
11	A P Rockwood	^ cr 25	0x5025
April 7	Rufus P Steward	paid	x1:50
22	Hosea Stout		1:50
May 1	^ Ezra ^ Benson		^ cr 50 ^ 1 50
June 1	P P Pratt	paid	x1:00x
	Joseph Horn	paid	x1:50
10	black Jane	paid	1:x00 ^ crx50 ^
16	Alvah Tibets		2:00x ^ crx50 ^
17	Jacob Hutchinson		2 00 ·
July 3	John Freeman	paidx	2:00x
14	Amasa Lyman	paid	1:00x
14	Janvrin Dame x	^ paid cr ^	200x85-175
Sept 14	James ^ W ^ Cumming x	200 ^ cr82 ^	paid
17	Sealey Owens x	x200	paid
23	Wm= Wordsworth	cr 45	paid x2x00
^ Oct ^ 1	Erastus Snow	paid	x2x00x
4	John Bills	crx12 ^ cr ^ (84x	100xpaid 2x0x0
7	[Joseph] Bates Nobles	^ given to the poor ^	paid 2x00
9	Phineas Cook	^ cr100 ^	paidx200x
12	Welcome Chatman	^ cr 44 ^	2 00
16	Edward Hunter	paid	2x00x
18	Samuel Russell	^ crx100.13x ^	84x2x0x0x
19	John S Fulmer		2..00
19	Daniel Clark	paid	2x00x
19	Charles Pucket		2x00x
19	Wm=Pitt	paid	2x00x
Nov:	Wm=Spears		2 00
3	James M Flake	^ paid ^	2 00x
6	Brigham H Young	x2x00	^ paid ^ x
16	Jon=C Wright	paid	x2 00x
19	Aviah Browor	paid	x2 00x
19	Norman Bliss	^ cr25-25 ^	-25 2 00
19	Isaac Hate	paid	x2x00x

24	Elis Sanders	paid	2x00x
27	Wm= G Young	cr 182	2 00
^Dec^ 3	Lucinda Calihan	paid	x2:00X
4	George Grant	^cr 100	cr 100^ paid 2x00x
8	Wil: Woodruff	paid	x2 00X
16	Meltiar Hatch	-x2x00 paid	
21	^Sis^ Vannorton	paid	2x00x
23	Tarlton Lewis	paid 2x0x0 paid	
23	Lorenzo Brown	x1x00 paid	
25	Isaac Busenbark	200 ^cr 62 3*h*^	
26	Elijah F Sheets	x200xcr^paid^100	
31	Joseph Hart	x200 paidx	
Jan 4	Erastus Snow paid	x2x00xcr 100x	
5	Horace Alexander		x2x00x
7	Cyntha Dikes	paid	2x00xx
8	Loisa Beamon		2 00
8	Gilbert Belnap	2 00 ^cr^135	
8	George B Wollace	x2x00 paid	
13	Newton D Hall	x2 00 paid	
14	sister Haight	200	
15	Solomon Wicksom	200	
16	Samuel Egleston	x20x0 paid	
17	George Langley	x200x^cr100^paid	
18	Charles E Avery	200 ^cr123^	
28	Wm= Wicks	x2x00 paid	
^Feb^ 2	Alvin Clements		2 00
4	James Bullock	x2 00x^cr100^ paid	
5	Gilbert Morse		2 00
6	Newel K Whitney	2x00x paid	
11	Benjamin R Lamb	x2x00 paid	
12	Simeon A Dunn	x1 00x paid	
15	John Oakley	x2x00 paid	
26	Wm= Kimbal	x2x00 paid	
27	Bates Nobles	x150xpaid	
^March^ 1	John Thomas	1 00	
8	Wm= Dykes	2 00^cr37cts^	
10	Wm= Davies	2 00 ^cr102^	
11	[James]Davenport	x150x paid	
14	Stilman	x1x50 paid	
^April^ 1	P P Pratt	2 00 ^cr 100^	

day one for Rocwood and one for Holman a general time for washing to day
thursday 9th Jane Glen [n, b. 1805] washes the rest of my clothes it rains
again she cannot get them dry it has rained hard all night **Friday** ^10^ the
water is ^as^ high as before and keeps rising still raining 2 oclock the sun
came out our brethren have gone to ^look^ an other camping place for fear
we shall get flowed out here have all the teams got up ready to move 4 oclock
came up a dreadful storm of wind and rain but soon over 8 oclock the creek
ceased to rise we remained where we were the teams turned out again, **saturday 11** cloudy mud so deep that we can hardly stir men go over their boots
in the road in mud the bridge that the pioneers built has gone off ^some of^
our men have gone to build it [a]gain Brigham and others have gone back to
see the other part of the camp 4 oclock return Br Kimball with them he said
that it took 7 men to hold his tent down monday night in the rain and hail
and that the most part of the camp was within 3 miles of us we were glad to
see him and hear from the rest Jane has got my clothes dry would take nothing for washing said I visited her when she was sick and thought she was
dying and prescribe^d^ for her and she lived and had not forgot it **sunday
12** two months to day since I left my home I have been in the cold in the
snow and rain with out a tent but now we are blockaded with mud and no
feed for teams but brows I never have felt so bad as now but I am not dis-
couraged yet the counsel have met to devise means and ways for our salvation many have met in the tents for meetings I in the waggon alone have
prayed and wept before the Lord in behalf of this people and my children
praying God to spare our lives untill we all shall meet again, my health is
poor my mind weighed down but my trust is in God the counsil returned 4
oclock Br Willy said he was going to Nauvoo[44] I wrote a letter to P G **monday 13** Br Rockwood said we were caled upon to divide out our goods said
that Brigham thought we had store goods we told him we had but litle but
was willing to divide that even to our clothing I told what we had and that
16 dollars in money was all we had and store goods none of much acount
but when it was called for it was all ready we divided one bag of flour at
Richersons point another at Charidon and some more at the east fork of
shoal creak and have enoug^h^ to divide again if caled for it was fair
weather and we overhaled our load to dry our rusk ^and^ things that was
wet at 4 oclock we moved half mile onto the hill piched our tents Br
Brigham ^and wife^ came in he said he was sick I made him some tea he
drank it said he felt better **tuesday 14** fair but windy Br Canada [probably
Charles Kennedy, 1807–1890] came in said Br [Samuel] Tomas was sick and

44. Whether this is James Grey Willey (b. 1814), who, with his wife Elizabeth (b.
     1818), crossed the plains with the Big Company, is not clear. Later in her diary,
     Patty mentions Jeremiah Willey (1804–1868), who was married to Samantha
     Call (1814–1905), a sister to Perrigrine's wives, Lucina and Mary.

had been for some time[45] I enquired the cause he said he wanted nursing wished me to go and see him I went found him on the ground in the tent wind blowing under the tent onto him I fixed bed clothes round him went back got some porrige caried to him ordered some other things ^and to wash him^ for him went home some one said Mother Sessions you are always doing good I said I wished I could do good sister Rockwood said come here I will comfort you I went she said I had done her a great deal of good she never had anything do her so much good as the medicine I gave her yesterday as she was very sick then and is quite well to day noon Charles Decker has returned from Nauvoo[46] he has brought me some letters from P G Sylvia & Rosila stating that David will not come with the rest my heart is pained & filed with greif where shall I go to get releif I will go to God and pray to him that my heart may be comforted Sarah Laramee came to the waggon it comforted my heart [to] see and hear her words wrote some more in my letter was sent for to go back 2 miles to a sick woman sister [Rufus P.] Steward I asked her no pay **wednesday 15** finished my letter sent it by Br Willey visited Br Tomas again found him better Loiza Beman came to see me I read my letters to her and she read one to me I then went and visited Eliza Snow I took comfort ^the camp is mostly together^ **thursday 16** we move along 6 miles I have not been well today since I stoped visited Br Tomas and a sister at Dr Rich<ards>[47] both some better we are camped on the head watters of Locus[t] creek[48] **Friday 17** move on 6 miles one oclock stop and make a bridge over madison creek then go two miles encamp on Pleasant Point I rode on Br Sherwoods Pony from the br^i^dge to the camp, I had traveled on foot about 5 miles and ^should^ have gone a foot to the camp (for our teams were very weak having but little to eat) had he not made me ride his Pony **Saturday 18th** ^Br Sherwod has

---

45. Samuel Thomas was helped by many of the pioneers. For example, Hosea Stout reported on 1 April, "Br Samuel Thomas was at my tent sick & I had him to move" (Brooks, *Hosea Stout*, 1:146).

46. Charles Franklin Decker (1824–1901) was married on 5 February 1847 to Vilate Young (1830–1902), daughter of Brigham Young and Miriam Works. He and Vilate traveled west with the Big Company.

47. Willard Richards (1804–1854) reputedly practiced medicine near Boston. He was a member of the Quorum of the Twelve Apostles and a personal secretary to Joseph Smith, as well as general church historian, an office he held until he died. A cousin of Brigham Young, he became second counselor in the First Presidency when it was reorganized. Willard was with Joseph and Hyrum in Carthage Jail at the time of the murders. Richards would become a member of the Pioneer Company.

48. Here William Clayton heard the good news that his wife had safely delivered a son in Nauvoo. He withdrew to a spot where he could be alone and wrote the words to the optimistic hymn, "Come, Come, Ye Saints" (see Kimball, *Mormon Pioneer Trail*, 77).

gone out^ pleasant and warm I feel very tired and feeble was so tired last night that I could not sleep I have been this morning ^and^ visited Br Tomas made him some bitters ^and food^ and ^put^ my brandy into it and I have found all the sugar and many other things & milk and crackers &c that he has had I ordered his feet washed and left him the camp all met decided that those that could fit themselves out to go over the mountains could go and those that could not would locate about 30 miles from this and make a ^big^ farm & so get means to move on & also to serve as a kind of tavern for those that are behind to refres^h^ themselves as they come along Mr Sessions feels very bad we have divided out our provision ^when caled to^ and he hardly knows how to fit ourselves again but I think we can by selling off ^some of^ our things and I had rather do that than stay behind **Sunday 19** a publick meeting is appointed to day went to meeting it was good as it was the first meeting we have had since we left Nauvoo [*name smeared*] has arrived from Nauvoo brought me a letter from Windsor and Sylvia I read them with joy **monday 20th** have wrote a letter to David cleaned my stove to sell Br Spencers co arived last night[49] the camp has now all got up again **tuesday 21** we move on 7 miles stop and make a bridge kill a wild hog we eat supper move over the bridge for fear the grass will get a fire here we camp for the night ^I traved a foot 3 miles^ **Wednesday 22** I have slept but little got my breakfast went and put Hosea Stouts wife to bed with a daughter [Louisa][50] finished my letter sent it by Porter prepared food and drink for Tomas packed up my things and ^ready to [go]^ started at half past nine oclock A M let Dr Richards have some brandy to wash his wife with traveled 10 miles I went foot 7 miles rode 2 with Wm= Young [1806–1875] saw many snakes **Thursday 23** a very heavy thunderstorm last night we are on the the grand river waters pleasant grove, two horses bit last night by snakes, the men have built a bridge Br Brigham has gone to look the best way to go gave orders not to have a team cross the bridge untill he came back he came half past 4 oclock P M we started he went forward traveled 1 2h mile camped ^in a valley^ for the night it came ^up^

---

49. Daniel Spencer (1794–1868) became captain of the first hundred of the Big Company, organized on 15–17 June 1847, which included the first fifty over which Perrigrine Sessions was captain.

50. Hosea Stout (1810–1889) married Samantha Peck on 7 January 1838. She died, according to Stout's diary, in 1839 since he described visiting her grave in February of 1846 and mentioned having buried her seven years earlier. Later Stout married Louisa Taylor. On the day of his daughter's birth, Stout writes, "The weather was warm, sultry with a damp heavy air & broken clouds Earley this morning the camp commenced moving. At 8 o'clock and just as we were going to start Louisa was taken sick and delivered of a daughter and we called its name Louisa. This was my first born in the wilderness" (Brooks, *Hosea Stout*, 1:155). The child died on 5 August , 1847.

a thunder shower my ^gold^ beads broke off my neck in the afternoon droped into my bosom I did not miss them untill I went to bed as I undresed I found one of them I made search found some of them on the bed in the waggon and some of them the next morning on the ground I found them all but one **Friday 24th** ^made a bridge this morning^ 1 oclock we start travel 6 miles ^stoped to bait^ arived to the camping ground [Garden Grove] 3 oclock I went a foot 5 miles the camp organised themselves some went to diging wells some to spliting rails some to hi^r^ding cattle & to making a farm on the Weldons fork of Grand river **saturday 25** Br Sherwood ^& Tomas^ goes to board with Br Holman the work is to hard for me to board him any longer the men have gone to their work Mr Sessions to making axe handles and yokes as h^e^ is sick this afternoon cannot work **Sunday 26** I was sick all night have worked to hard overdone my self I go to meeting it is close to the waggon we had a good time and when Br Brigham blesed the people I felt his blessing even to the healing of my body have been better ever since Mr Sessions is no better **Monday 27** it rains they meet to decide what each one should do Mr Sessions [works] at axe handles yokes & ploughs &c it has rained all night & still rains **tuesday 28** raining I have been sick all night Mr Sessions is better I cannot set up **Wednesday 29** rains & is very mudy I lay here in the waggon my bed and pillows wet & I cannot set up but a few minutes at a time 2 oclock Br Brigham came and laid hands on me I felt better but could not set up 7 oclock ^at night^ Br Benson came after me Adline was sick I got up but could hardly stir he took me out of the waggon & helped me to his tent I could not set up but went to bed, as my labours was not needed for the presant, **thursday 30** I came home could hardly reach the waggon. I went to bed rested me but could not eat Mr Sessions has cooked for him and Wm= [Richmond], about noon I thought I could eat some peach pie I had a kettle of coals in the waggon I cooked my peaches on them and by laying down and resting several times I made me a pie went to the stove and baked it have eat some and feel better sister Rockwood ^made me some^ porrig yestarday & some barley coffee today,

May 1846

Friday May 1st Br Benson came after last night again I went found Adline sick I came home got some medicine went back and staid all night 4 ^A M^ oclock she had a son [George T.] Wm= Richmond has gone to Grand river to work we have no one to board now, I am quite sick again to day **Saturday 2** fair weather this morning, it has rained for six days my bed has been wet all the time and has not been made I have got it out to dry to day Br Brigham told me yesterday we beter not sell the stove nor my sadle, he gave ^me^ some counsel about many things, said we had ^better^ buy another cow I let him have ten Dollars in money to send and buy one with his it has clouded up again ^this after noon^ **sunday 3** still cloudy Br Sam= Tomas died last night in Br Holmans tent next to ours I feel better to day think I shall go to meeting as it is close to the waggon it rains hard this afternoon thunders clears of **mon-day 4** is fair weather I am not so well had a sick night **tuesday 5** feel quite well to day ^bake meat & fig cakes^ make some ink[51] wrote a few lines to David **wednesday** ^**6**^ sister Lathrop sent for me[52] ^she was^ very sick went the second time she is some better come up a thunder storm of wind and rain many trees blew down some fell on horses and cattle none kiled as I have heard several horses bit by the snakes **thursday 7** sist<er> Lathrop sent for me again she is bet<ter> **Friday** ^**8**^ overhould our waggon and sent of his sadle and harnesses to sell weigh our load it weighed 1221 and 4:51 is provision and we have been dividing out ^provisions^ ever since we starte^d^ **saturday 9** commence a letter to mother[53] Hosea Stouts child died with fits[54] I went and laid it out **Sunday 10** it is a fine day go to meeting partake of the sacrement finish my letter to mother write another to David go and see

---

51. Along with her considerable other abilities, Patty knew how to mix medicines and herbs. Her son-in-law, Windsor P. Lyon, was a pharmacist. She may have taken along some of the chemicals required for making ink. One early recipe for ink instructs, "Beat up well together in an iron mortar the following ingredients in a dry state; viz. 8 oz. of best blue gall-nuts, 4 oz. of copperas, or sulphate of iron, 2 oz. of clear gum arabic, and 3 pints of clear rain water. When properly powdered, put to the above; let the whole be shaken in a stone bottle three or four times a day, for seven days, and at the end of that time, pour the liquid off gently into another stone bottle, which place in an airy situation to prevent it from becoming foul or mothery. When used put the liquid into the ink-stand as required" (David N. Carvalho, *Forty Centuries of Ink* [New York: Burt Franklin, 1971], 195–96). Evidently black ink was considered the ideal but sometimes faded to brown. Patty's diaries are written almost entirely in brown ink—knowing whether black ink faded to brown or she made it brown would require an expert opinion. Gallnuts, along with other plants and barks, are one source of tannin, used for centuries in ink mixtures. Perhaps Patty had her own method of making tannin.

52. Jane Peacock (b. 1820) was the wife of Asahel Albert Lathrop (1810–1871).

53. Patty's mother, Anna Hall, was born on 28 April 1768 and died on 27 August 1868.

54. According to Patty's medical book, "When fits or convulsions arise from teething or any other cause, the feet must be immediately bathed in warm ley [meadow or lea] water, and an anodyne administered, such as syrup or poppy or paregoric. Garlic should be bruised and applied to the stomach; and if there is heat of the head, spirits, rain water, and vinegar may be applied. These means must be repeated as often as fits occur; in obstinate cases, it may be necessary to use a warm bath" (under "Diseases of Children" in W. Beach, *The Family Physician* [New York: by author, 1842], 629–30). Fits were sometimes attributed to a stroke of some disease such as epilepsy or apoplexy, and usually produced convulsions or unconsciousness. In severe cases, as Patty remarks, death could and did occur.

Hosea Stout recorded in his diary of 8 May 1846, "I went out in company with Benjn Jones . . . when I was sent for and informed that my little son Hyrum was dying. I returned immediately home and found the poor little afflicted child in the last agonies of death. He died in my arms about four o'clock. This was the

Andrew Calhoon[55] he told some things about the children that Windsor had sold his place &c **monday 11** I have been and tried to get some one to wash for me but I cannot even of those that have got their pay 1 oclock Brs Dustan and wives came from Nauvoo to our waggon said they must wash for themselves the next day and would wash for me[56] **tuesday 12** this morning Br Finatus Dustan came and got my clothes their wives washed them for me said I was welcome to what they had done I was very glad as I was not able to wash myself 4 oclock I visited sister Horn she was sick and sent for me I also visited sister Taylor[57] she was lame **Wednesday 13** I have ironed my clothes packed our load ready to move along. they have made a big field got it fenced it and built some houses will leave some to take care of it and put in the crop the ^rest^ of us will go on to another place we start along ^leave^ Br Rockwood he cannot find his oxen 12 [o' clock] ^travel 6 miles^ stop and bait go on 6 miles more camp on the prairie no wood or fire came up a dreadful shower of wind and rain scarcely one in the camp but what got wet **Thursday 14** the ground is full of water and it is cold we start along go 2 miles double teams all the way come up with George A Smiths Co[58] then we stop eat breakfast about 12 oclock draw wood a mile to cook with dry our clothes stay all night Zina visited me we hear from Br Rockwood ^6 miles back^ **Friday 15** we all go on, some Brethren from Nauvoo overtake us they have been on the road but 3 weeks we 3 months we have traveled 6 miles to day and camped to build a bridge across a prairia sleug^h^ half mile to the timber 12 oclock this afternoon Daniel Davis come up[59] **Saturday 16** Br Rockwood came up this

---

second child which I had lost both dying in my arms. He died with the hooping cough & black canker" (Brooks, *Hosea Stout*, 1:160).

55. Andrew Cahoon (1824–1900); the *Manuscript History of Brigham Young 1846–1847* (ed. Elden J. Watson [Salt Lake City: by editor, 1971], 158) reports Cahoon as "starting for Nauvoo . . . with a mail of twelve letters."

56. There were seven Dustan brothers: David (b. 1818); Fortunatus (b. 1820); Buchias (b. 1822); Seth (b. 1825); Joseph (b. 1827); Franklin (b. 1835); and Christopher (b. 1837).

57. Leonora Cannon (1796–1868) was the first wife of John Taylor, having married him on 28 January 1833. In early entries Patty usually uses the term "sister" with the husband's surname when referring to the first wife and calls plural wives by their maiden names—at least until the pioneers reached the Salt Lake Valley and the doctrine of plural marriage was announced publicly. Leonora emigrated with the Big Company.

58. George Albert Smith (1817–1875) was a cousin of Joseph Smith. He was a member of the Pioneer Company and the Quorum of the Twelve Apostles when he made the journey. He was a counselor to Brigham Young from 1868 to 1875.

59. Daniel Coon Davis (1804–1850) later joined the Mormon Battalion. His wife, Susanna Moses, accompanied him.

morning we were glad to see him 8 oclock we all take up our line of march
travel 12 miles I go a foot 5 and ride the most of the rest of the way with
Henry Jacobs and wife and had a good visit with them[60] 7 oclock we stop and
camp and make a bridge across a prairia slugh ^**sunday 17**^ Brs Kimbal
Richards and Whitney came up have no meeting move on 3 miles camp on
another slugh ^**monday 18**^ make a bridge move along ^3 miles^ make
another bridge I let sister [Susanna Moses] Davis have some tea she gave me
ten ^cts^ cross over I pick up some clamb shulls go 2 miles turn go south 1
mile stop and make a bridge I go and see a big rock it was split in peaces I
broke of some of it and kept it Brs Brigham and Heber went on hear from
Parleys camp by Br Snow[61] they return we all go on come up with Parleys co
here we camp we have traveled 12 miles I went a foot 5 **tuesday 19** they have
concluded to make a farm here I have made Mr Sessions an under garment
two Indians came into the camp after a ^stray^ horse we had caught it for
them they tell us we are on their land two men go to see about it **Wednesday
20** it rains 1 oclock the sun came out very warm 7 oclock came up a thunder
shower **Thursday 21** I was caled to see sister Tibits[62] she was sick came
home and went to the creek and washed a little few weeks ago I sent a book
out to sell with Br Rockwoods things it was the Taylors guide worrth fifty
cents as he aprised it his things and that, he apprised at 9 dollars he got a rifle
worth 10 dollars for them all. he wo^u^ld not give me but 10 lb of corn meal
^at^ fifty cents per bushel for the book I weighed the meal there was but 7
lb 6 ounces of it and he was so unwiling to let me have ^any^ that Mr
Sessions would not let me say any thing more to him **Friday 22** made Mr
Sessions two frocks **Saturday 23** many brethren have come up from Nauvoo
Br [John] Taylor came home from Nauvoo we went to see him but can hear
nothing from our children by any one I fear they will not get here untill we
shall leave. I know nothing when they will come. my feelings I cannot dis-
cribe but my trust is in God **Sunday 24** it rains the me^n^ that went to see
the Indians have returned last night bring favourable news. I have been to
meeting to day the word was 1:00 waggons 4 able men to a waggon must be

60. Henry Bailey Jacobs (1817–1886) was at this time the husband of Zina Diantha
     Huntington, who, as stated in note 34, married Brigham Young.

61. Parley P. Pratt (1807–1857) was a member of the Quorum of the Twelve
     Apostles, was a zealous missionary, and had spent time in jail for his beliefs. A
     prolific writer, he left many hymns and other contributions to Mormon litera-
     ture. Lorenzo Snow (1814–1901) was at this time clerk of the fourth fifty of the
     Mormons on the way from Nauvoo to Winter Quarters. He became a member
     of the Quorum of the Twelve Apostles in 1849 and president of the Mormon
     Church from 1898 to 1901.

62. Caroline Beard (1826–1906) was the wife of Alvah Lewis Tippets (1809–1847).

fitted out for the mountains I have wrote a letter to the children send it by
Holbrook[63] **monday 25** ^Br Sherwood goes on with Millers camp to make
bridges^ rains this morning again Br Kimb^al^ came to the waggon said I
must not feel bad I was crying when he come I could hardly tell for what for I
had many things to hurt my feelings I told him some things he said all would
be right and not to give way to my feelings in the afternoon Sister Eliza Snow
and Markum came up to the waggon[64] said ^they^ was glad to see me once
more it gave me joy for I had cryed the most of the day **Tuesday 26** saw some
friends from Nauvoo Milan Andrews and wife [Abigail Jane Dailey,
1805/15–1894] made me quite a visit[65] hear nothing definate from the children
Br Kimbal saw Mr Sessions told him things that made him feel better when he
feels well It does me good told him we must go along with the church and if
our waggon did not come to keep the one we had ours being off to Grand river
as we had changed waggons some time ago and it is said this belongs to the
church Br Whitney said we must give it up Br Rockwood said if he went after
his he could have it and many other things that made us feel bad, but Br
Kimball found it out he made all right ^he said we should keep this one^
Wednesday 27 I have washed got very tired could not sleep **Thursday 28**
ironed and visited Eliza Snow & Parley Pratts folks &c **Friday 29** Br Kimbal
came to the waggon counseled us and spoke comforting words ^said we must
have waggon fixed^ Sister Rockwood gave me some tallow I ran 17 candles[66]
I thought it quite a presant sister Ceneth Davis gave me a peice of butter[67]

63. Joseph Holbrook (1806–1885) and Elders Mikesell and Newel K. Knight were
to preside over the first fifty to leave Nauvoo. Holbrook was supposed to examine every family's provisions to ascertain that they had plenty to make the journey (see Young, *Manuscript History*, 271).

64. Dinah Merry Markham was the mother of Stephen Markham, who was to take
about a hundred pioneers to prepare a road in advance of the main body. He
was in charge of the second fifty of the first hundred between Nauvoo and
Winter Quarters (Young, *Manuscript History*, 55, 100).

65. She must mean Milo Andrus (1814–1893), who had been with the Latter-day
Saints who were driven out of Missouri and a policeman in Nauvoo and assisted in moving the pioneers to Utah. He was also one of the great early Mormon
missionaries and a dedicated leader.

66. "Candles were made from the tallow of the sheep. The candlewax was poured
into molds made by the tinsmiths, pioneer craftsmen, who also made pots, pans,
buckets, cups, eating and cooking utensils, as well as other items" (Shirley B.
Paxman, "Early Mormon Family Life and Home Production," [lecture delivered
at Harold B. Lee Library, Brigham Young University, Provo, Utah, 7 December
1979], 10).

67. Cynthia Davis was married to George Washington Clyde on 30 October 1824.
He was a policeman in Nauvoo, where he died in 1844. She died in 1874 at
Springville, Utah County, Utah.

thank the Lord for friends Lucy Walker arived here to day[68] said the children were coming **Saturday 30** Mary Elen Haris arived to day[69] we were glad to see each other she said they shurely were coming my heart was glad, but alas Joseph Young arived 4 oclock[70] he said Lyon Sylvia & David were not coming untill next year I feel as though this was a trick of the Devil he said Perigrene was coming <u>but</u> Lyon his teams tent crackers and all and was not a coming shure my feelings I cannot describe as I fear they will never come my heart is full but I feel so bad I cannot shed tears **Sunday 31** I was caled to P P Pratts 1 oclock this morning Delivered Mary Pratt of a son [Helaman] at 5[71] then went to meeting it was a conferance it came up a thunder shower rained very hard we got wet some it still rains and when ^I^ think that Sylvia and David and Josephine is not coming[72] tears fall from my eyes as fast as the drops of rain from the skies for I can now give vent to my feelings by weeping Oh Lord Comfort my poor wounded heart wrote a letter to Lyon

JUNE 1846

monday 1st have sent my letter by Henry Jacobs Mary Pratt paid me one dollar it is very cold I got wet to my skin last night ^milking^ went to bed with my clothes wet 12 oclock the sun came out dried my bed and clothes but my tears will not dry up Horrace Rockwell [b. 1825, brother of Orrin Porter Rockwell] got home brought me a letter from Lyon stating that he was not

68. Lucy Walker (1826–1910) was married to Joseph Smith on 1 May 1843. After the martyrdom she married Heber C. Kimball on 8 February 1845. Patty had close associations with many of Kimball's wives.

69. Mary Ellen Harris (c. 1818–1902) married Heber C. Kimball on 1 October 1844.

70. Joseph Young (1797–1881) was an elder brother of Brigham Young. He was placed in charge of the people remaining in Nauvoo after most of the Mormons had to flee.

71. Mary Wood (1819–1898) married P. P. Pratt on 9 September 1844. On 31 July of that year, Pratt was on his way to England to serve a mission (see his son Parley P. Pratt, ed., *Autobiography of Parley P. Pratt* [1938; reprint, Salt Lake City: Deseret Book Co., 1985], 312).

72. Patty's granddaughter, Josephine Rosetta Lyon, was born on 8 February 1844. The other Lyon children were deceased. Marian or Maryann died on 20 March 1842, age two; Philofreen died on 27 January 1844, age three; Asa Windsor died on 25 December 1842, age twelve hours. Joseph Smith wrote on 20 March 1842 (Sunday), "I preached to a large assembly in the grove, near the temple on the west. The body of a deceased child of Mr. Windsor P. Lyon being before the assembly, changed my design in the order of my remarks" ("The Prophet's Sermon on Life and Death, the Resurrection and the Salvation of Children," in *History of the Church of Jesus Christ of Latter-day Saints*, 2d ed., vol. 4, [Salt Lake City: Deseret News Press, 1949], 553–55).

coming but going to Iowa city[73] and ^P G on the road^ I then wrote a few lines more send it by John [Dickenson] Huntington [b. 1827] **tuesday 2** we are now ready to take up our line of march and leave this place we have been here ever since the 18 of May it is a prety place the saints call it Mount Pisgah here we leave many good Brethren Sisters Horn. ^E^ Snow. Zina. Emily.[74] and many more. Perrigrine is on the road and we think he will soon overtake us. we travel on 4 miles camp we crosed a branch of Grand river and another small branch both bridged **Wednesday 3** got our teams up to start Sister Horn sent for me I went back to Mount Pisgah put her to bed with a daughter [Elizabeth Ann] rode a horse back 4 miles each way got home to our waggon half past one oclock found our company all there except Hazen Kimbal[75] he was gone back to meet his folks 2 oclock all start on go six miles camp on the prairi **Thursday 4** take up our line of march Br Brigham took our stove to cary along wants to bye it. we travel 9 miles ^cross some of the Plat watters^ stop and bait then go 9 miles & camp here Elenor Jane Davis comes up[76] **Friday 5** take up our line of march soon strike the indian trace very cold rains a little 10 oclock the sun came out very warm travel 15 miles 2 oclock stop for Br Brigham he came up told us all to stop he went on ah^e^ad came back said we must camp he thought it 20 miles to timber and there was alitle brush here and good water we camped here ivy thick ^all around^ <I fear I shall

73. Two more children were born to Sylvia and Windsor in Iowa City: Byron Windsor on 4 September 1847, died on 13 December 1851; and David Charles or Carlos, born on 8 August 1848, died on 21 April 1850.

74. Perhaps this is Emily Trask Cutler (1825–1852), who married Heber C. Kimball in December 1845.

75. Hazen Kimball (1812–1886) was a captain in the Jedediah M. Grant contingent of the Big Company. Kimball did not stay long in the Salt Lake Valley. On Monday, 15 August 1848, Henry W. Bigler noted in his diary that they were camped on the sink of the Humbolt. He writes, "This evening 18 emigrants wagons rolled into our camp and encamped for the night. They were from the States bound for California. . . . We got but little news about Salt Lake matters as they did not come by way of Salt Lake Valley. I however met with one man and his wife that I knew and was at the time members of the church in good standing but now it appeared to me they were disaffected and was on the eve of apostasy. He had wintered last winter in Salt Lake Valley but left in March and went to Fort Hall and came on with this emigration, indeed he said he was dissatisfied with the situation of the place (Salt Lake) and with the people and had left. He said the people was plowing and sowing wheat all last fall and all winter that they had put in about eight thousand acres in grain. His name is Hazen Kimball. To me Sister K. Did not seem to be so bad as her husband in relation to Mormonism. . . ." ("Diary of Henry W. Bigler 1846–1850" pp. 93–94. Copy of 1937 Brigham Young University typescript in CHD.)

76. Eleanor Jane Davis (1824–1896) was married to William Summerville on 4 February 1844. He had four wives so Eleanor was probably a plural wife.

get poisoned> **Saturday 6** our cow & ox and some others is not found we are
waiting for them go on meet them they had been six miles a head where some
brethren Hucthinson [Jacob Flynn Hutchinson, 1816–1867] camped I milked
then moved on again go 9 miles overtake Br Heber form a circle with our waggons pitch the tents ^and build our fires^ out side put the catle inside the circle this is the first time we have camped this way it is pleasant valley on the
ottoway [Nodoway] river **Sunday 7th** had a meeting a company of indians
came in to the camp 4 oclock move on cross a bad place mow and gather grass
to put in to the mud instead of timber al over safe travel 8 miles cross the
north fork camp on pleasant priaria valley splended place form a line a quarter of a mile in length **Monday 8** move on pass an indian town ^here we cross
one bridge built on flat wood^ many came to the camp as we were fording the
river in another place both caled nationey boteny [Nishnabotna] travel 15
miles come up with Lovelys [Loveless?] and Wm= Young camped on the bank
of the creek we are now in the 3d ten Br Dikes capt=[77] go there to wait on sister Hutchinson [Constantia Elizabeth Clementina Langdon, 1818–1867] **tuesday 9** travel 12 miles come up with Brs Millers and Pratts ^company^ they
were sent on from the Pisgah farm to make bridges here we camp to make a
bridge **Wednesday 10** put black Jane to bed with a son [Silas F. James][78] paid
me 24 pounds of flour Br Dikes asked 4 cts per pound others asked but 2 Jane
and Isaac lives with him **Thursday 11** have got the bridge done it is a long
bad place watter 10 feet deep 4 rods wide ^bridge built on flood wood^ be
side low wet ground to bridge on each side ^these waters caled nationey
botany^ all got over safe soon passed an indian grave travel 8 miles Mr
Sessions sick vomited could hardly sit up untill we camped Br Comions
[James Cummings] has returned from Emits co[79] **Friday 12** Mr Sessions is

77. George Parker Dykes (1814–1888) became adjutant to the Mormon Battalion.

78. Jane Elizabeth Manning (1813–1908), a black pioneer, learned about the church
before 1840 and was baptized. In the fall of 1840, she started for Nauvoo with
eight other relatives. She recalled her journey in 1893, giving an account of
walking until shoes were so worn out that they could see the print of their feet in
blood. "We stopped," she said, "and united in prayer to the Lord, we asked God
the Eternal Father to heal our feet and our prayers were answered and our feet
were healed forthwith" (qtd. in Henry J. Wolfinger, "A Test of Faith: Jane
Elizabeth James and the Origins of the Utah Black Community," p. 20, typescript, CHD). Jane had married Isaac James (b. 1822), a black Latter-day Saint,
before they left Nauvoo. She had worked in the household of Joseph Smith until
shortly before he was killed.

79. James Emmett (1803–1852/3) had been recruited by Joseph Smith to take a company and explore westward in preparation for an exodus from Nauvoo. After
the martyrdom Emmett and followers set out on their own. Brigham tried to dis-
suade them, even giving George Miller and Emmett assignments together.
Although both turned dissident, most of Emmett's followers returned to the

better stop to build another bridge here Br sherwood came to the waggon on horseback gave me the names of the waters that we had pased said it was 20 miles to the bluffs and he was going on 12 oclock stoped to bait[80] our cow calved we stoped an hour or more after the rest moved on then took the calf in the waggon and overtook the camp ^traveled 10 miles^ **Saturday 13** built a bridge then traveled 8 miles got to the ^counsel^ bluffs camped plenty of strawberys but I being not well I could not pick any **Sunday 14** I have no appitite to eat but Sister E. Elsworth brought me some strawbery sauce[81] it did taste good I thanked the Lord for puting it in her heart to bring me some 2 oclock move to the river the first camp ^any^ mostly all to gather here we camp on the bank of Missouri river **Monday 15** ^let Brigham have $9.65 cash to get bread stuff^ I have washed got so tiered I am truly sick can neither eat nor sleep **Tuesday 16** irned picked up my iron ware that was lent out and sold the teaketle ^for 75 cts^ let Jacob Hutchinson have the Pot and spider to cary on for the use of them[82] if I want them to return them again when caled for if not returned to be paid for 2 oclock moved ^back 6 miles^ onto the bluff the camp all went 10 oclock Sister car[o]line Tibbets sent for me I went put her to bed with a son paid me 50 cts **Wednesday 17** put sister Constantia Hutchinson to bed with a son [Jacob Flynn] **Thursday 18** Br Hide came in to the camp[83] many have been Strawberying Br Hutchinson gave me some **Friday 19** received a letter from Perigrine and Sylvia by Sister Hyde **Saturday 20** visited Sister Hyde and Elizabeth Buchanan Coolage [1815–1913, wife of

main body of pioneers (see Richard E. Bennett, "Mormon Renegade: James Emmett at the Vermillion, 1846," *South Dakota History* 15, no. 3 [Fall 1985]: 217–33. See also Gerald E. Jones, "Some Forgotten Pioneers: The Emmett Company of 1844," [paper presented at the Sidney B. Sperry Symposium, Brigham Young University, Provo, Utah, 26 January 1980], 193–209, typescript in CHD). James Willard Cummings (1819–1883) had left on 26 March with James Butler to notify Emmett's company to proceed to Ft. Laramie. Cummings and Butler decided the six-hundred-mile trip was not feasible so they started back to the main body on 19 April.

80. When folks on the road stopped "to bait," they gave a portion of food and drink to their animals.

81. Elizabeth Young Ellsworth (1825–1903) was the oldest child of Brigham Young and Miriam Works. She was married to Edmund Lovell Ellsworth (1819–1893), who emigrated with the Pioneer Company.

82. A spider was a trivet or tripod to support pans over a fire.

83. Orson Hyde (1805–1878) was at this time a member of the Quorum of the Twelve Apostles. He had served from 25 February to 4 May 1839, when he was dropped. He was reinstated on 27 June 1839 and served until his death. Nancy Marinda Johnson (1815–1886) married Orson Hyde on 4 September 1834. She was sealed to Joseph Smith in 1843. Orson Hyde had plural wives at this time, but Nancy Johnson was his first wife.

Joseph Wellington Collidge] and Francis S there has been a consert to day
down to the French town[84] many went came back with the musick in the
Omnibuss the rest of the cariages fol^low^ing after it was splended I did not
go my self **sunday 21** go to a meeting then visit sister Taylor **Monday 22**
caled to sister Martha Reeves put her to bed with a son when I came home
found Perrigrine and family and Rosilla there[85] we was glad to see each other
once more it has been 4 months & 10 days since I started and left my children
if David Windsor Sylvia and her babe [Josephine] was here I feel as if I should
be happy but alas they are not and sorrow fills my heart **tuesday ^23^** it
rains some it was very cold ~~night~~ last night ^I slept alone^ and is to day we
put the stove in the tent **Wednesday 24** cold rains some to day got letter from
Sylvia Dated June 3d said she was going to Iowa in a week I ^**Thursday 25**^
wrote to her Br Kimball ~~wrote &~~ made us a visit ^rained very hard^ **Friday
26** put the letter in the office the girls washed P G overhaled his load
Saturday 27 it is two years to day since the Prophets Joseph and Hyrum was
massacreed in Carthage Jail. Rosilla looked over her things gave me some
things that Sylvia sent me **Sunday 28** went to meeting Dr Richards at the
close of the meeting spoke very feeling said it was two years this ^time^ he
came into Nauvoo with the bodys of the Prophets how changed the scene the
people then were in tears howling and lamenting their loss. now they were
with out a house in tents and waggons clothed with a spirit of rejoiceing and a
smile upon every face. it rains this after noon at 5 oclock the men meet together the Twelve conclude to take a hundred men and go to the mountains[86]
monday 29 Perigrine is going I cut some undergarments for him ^we^

---

84. She is probably referring to Point aux Poules, a village located on the east bank
    of the Missouri, approximately fifteen miles downstream from where the
    Mormons were camped.

85. Two of Perrigrine's family were Martha Ann, age eleven, and Carlos Lyon, age
    four, born to Perrigrine and Julia Ann Kilgore (1815–1845), who had died at
    Nauvoo. Perrigrine also brought his plural sister wives, Lucina and Mary Call.
    Patty often refers to these family members. Perrigrine recorded that there were
    twelve hundred wagons at Council Bluffs (DPG, p. B-45).

86. By "the Twelve" Patty means members of the Quorum of the Twelve Apostles,
    who were at this time, in order of seniority, Brigham Young, Heber C. Kimball,
    Parley P. Pratt, Orson Hyde, John Taylor, John Page, Wilford Woodruff, George
    A. Smith, Willard Richards, Lyman Wight, Amasa M. Lyman, and Orson Pratt
    (see *1993–1994 Church Almanac* [Salt Lake City: Deseret News Press, 1992]).
    There had been considerable discussion about forming an advance company to
    go to the Great Basin to prepare for the onslaught of emigrants. At the meeting
    mentioned, forty men, including the Twelve, volunteered to leave their families;
    take swift livestock, grain, and corn; and make "a dash for the mountains"
    (Brigham H. Roberts, *A Comprehensive History of the Church*, 6 vols. [Provo, Utah:
    Brigham Young University Press, 1965] 3:63 and n. 12).

almost made them **Tuesday 30** finished them cut 2 more helped make them Hazen Kimbals wife came to see me they have got up again gone into Br Hydes Co Rosilla and I went up there

July 1846

Wednesday July 1st Brighams ten moved down to the river ^last night^ the boat is done ready to cross 8 oclock the ^word^ is to us be ready to go to the river at 10 oclock when ten oclock came the word was put the teams to the waggons and start in 10 minnites before that time was out the men were caled to a public counsel. some of the troops had come in to enlist men ^for one year^ to go to Collifonia[87] the twelve had a private counsel after and Brigham is going back to Mount Pisgah and sent word to us to stay where we were if we chose **Thursday 2** ^I slept alone^ I went up on the Bluffs looking for the cattle ^I traveled 3 or 4 miles^ 9 oclock Mr Sessions found them. I visited Sisters Taylor & Horn. **Friday 3** Br Brigham came took dinner with us told to go to the river the girls were washing we packed up our load ready to start Br [? John] Freeman came after me I went back 3 miles where Br Parley camped put his wife ^[Nancy B.?] Freeman^ to bed with a daughter ^[Rosaline?]^[88] returne^d^ to the camp found Mr Sessions and P G were gone we rode after them found them camp^ed^ on the bottom about 10 oclock 4 miles from where they left **Saturday 4** we move to the camp near the river had our bread stuff weighed out that was got with the money that we let Brigham have to send off to buy with, we got 9=83 pounds 1:75 wheat the rest corn, no flour, it being independance [day] the Indians rode out in style came to our camp danced the war dance were painted dresed in their fashion, in the evening we had a hard shower of wind hail and rain, it blew our tent down got many things wet **Sunday 5** dried our things loaded up ready to go over the river any time **Monday 6** went down to the setlement Rosilla sold her teaset for two dollars twelve oclock word came to go to the river the oxen was gone and we could not find them I traveled three or four miles after them Elbrige had

---

87. President James K. Polk had been petitioned by the Mormons for help in removing to the Great Basin. Although denying formal requests, Polk's secretary of war worked with Jesse C. Little, the Mormon representative, to arrange for five hundred Mormon men to form a battalion to serve in the Mexican War. These men would receive food and pay, which would aid the migration process. Patty refers to Captain James Allen's arrival to recruit the Mormon Battalion (Roberts, *Comprehensive History*, 3:64–84, and Carl V. Larson, ed. and comp., *A Data Base of the Mormon Battalion* [Providence, Utah: Keith W. Watkins, 1987]; also see Leonard Arrington, *Great Basin Kingdom* [Lincoln: University of Nebraska Press, 1958], 21).

88. The Freeman and Pratt names with question marks were written into Patty's diary in pencil by other hands than hers. The brackets have been added.

let them go while he was gone in the river swiming[89] Mr Sessions traveled 6 or 8 PG 2 or 3 at last we found them went to the river got a cross ready to go to sleep at half past 2 oclock in the morning **Tuesday 7** here we are in between two mountains the road not cut through but men are at work making it as fast as they can it is so warm here in the valey no air it does seem as if we should melt 4 oclock word came that the road was done we were glad to hear it as our cattle had neither eat nor drank since yestarday we started along I drove the cows part of the way and then drove a team where the bushes were higher than the waggon the road only wide enough for the wagon to pass ^and as thick as they could stand^ with one hand I held on to the stearsbow for fear I should fall down and the wheel run over me and the whip in the other no air could circulate and I sometimes felt as though I should melt but thank the Lord he caried us safe through **Wednesday 8** the team gone back to draw up Br [Anson] Call [1810–1890] they have come we start along I drive our team to the camp 4 miles Mr Sessions drives P Gs he is at work on the boat I got very tiered it was very warm ^a good spring here^ **Thursday ^9^** I have slept but little [*blotted out:* Mr Sessions has said many hard things to me] I feel as though my heart woul^d^ break ^I^ cannot eat I wash my clothes it rains a litle before they are dry I see many warm hearted friends yet I feel as though my heart would burst with grief **Friday 10** sorrow of heart has made me sick I lay in the waggon all the forenoon have many more hard things said to me but the Lord supports me it is sh[o]wry all day **Saturday 11** ^I [*blotted out:* slept alone]^ eat my breakfast but I am so full of grief that there is no room for food and I soon threw it up I can only say I feel bad [*blotted out:* lay alone part of the night] **Sunday 12** I feel some better he has promised to treat me well [*several entries stricken out and ink changes color:* I lay alone] **Monday 13** wash visit the Sister Davis she is sick I have visited her several times ^I talk with her awhile^ **Tuesday 14** I have put Eliza wife of Amasa Lyman to bed with a son[90] and also Sophia wife of Jonvrin Dame with a daughter [Sarah Elsie][91] **Wednesday 15** cut a pair of pants for Elbrige and help make them is going into the army they have been enlisting soldiers several days **Thursday 16** have a meeting this morning the word is all that is ready go on to Grand Iland and over the mountains others to stay here we have bought 200 of flour of

---

89. Probably Elbridge J. Cowin, whose name was listed on the original muster-in rolls for the Mormon Battalion but had a line drawn through it (see Larson, *Mormon Battalion*, 55–56). Elbridge was most likely a relative of Rosilla.

90. Eliza Marie Partridge (1820–1886) was married to Joseph Smith on 4 March 1843. She married Amasa Mason Lyman (1813–1877), a member of the Quorum of the Twelve Apostles, on 28 September 1845.

91. Sophia Andrews (1818–1847) was the wife of Jonvrin Hayes Dame (1808–1885).

Lorenzo Young[92] gave $5 00 for it ^Rosilla let him have the 2 dollars she got for her teaset^ P G has put projection on to his waggon **Friday 17** visited sister Hyde got some things that she brought on **Saturday 18** killed our calves sold them at the Indian town $2:40 ^each^ **Sunday 19** had a meeting in the after noon for buisness Brigham and Heber came from over the river and went back again after meeting **Monday 20** we washed and P G put a projection on to our ^new^ waggon ^put our bed into it^ then went and bought a yoke of oxen gave 35 dollars for them I let him have $7:37 ^cts^ cash to help pay for them **Tuesday 21** it rains 10 oclock the sun came out ~~move our bed in to the other~~ very warm we are now ready to move on do not go **Wednesday 22** it rains a little Brigham came home is going to the Elkhorn he told ^Mr Sessions^ he could not advise us to go over the mountains I have wrote a letter to Sylvia **Thursday 23** Orson Pratt and wife and children came over the river[93] took dinner with us I visited Lorenzo Youngs wife [Harriet Page Wheeler, 1803–1871] **Friday 24** I leave my letter at the Office and start along ^and leave the cold spring & camp^ to go to Grand Island go 9 miles ^I go a foot 6 miles^ camp find goose beries and choak cheries **Saturday 25** go on 11 miles to the Elkhorn I go a foot 5 miles ^here we are to build a bridge^ **Sunday 26** 4 waggons have returned from Millers co they have had some trouble with the Indians have lost some catle fish are plenty here no water but the river **Monday 27** the men have gone to work on the bridge **Tuesday 28** we wash came up a heavy shower of wind and rain after dinner we got wet P G was out in whole shower **Wednesday 29** they still work on the bridge **Thursday 30** the girls go and pick some grapes I make some wine out of them **Friday 31** rains some fair in the afternoon I have seen many a lonsome hour

---

92. Lorenzo Young (1807–1895) was a brother of Brigham Young. He was one of the members of the Pioneer Company. He is reputed to have cultivated the first garden flowers in the Salt Lake Valley.

93. Orson Pratt (1811–1881) was an older brother of Parley P. Pratt. Orson was a member of the Quorum of the Twelve Apostles and one of the Pioneer Company. He led the advance company into the valley on 22 July 1847. Pratt had been excommunicated in 1842 because he differed with some of the ideas and practices of Joseph Smith, but after reflection and study, he changed his mind and in 1843 was reinstated as a member of the Quorum. Orson Pratt's scientific interest and knowledge enriched the knowledge of the pioneers. He also wrote and presented important theological treatises for the church. In 1852 Brigham Young assigned Orson to preach the first public sermon on plural marriage. At the time of the migration, Orson's wife, Sarah (Sally) Marinda Bates (1817–1888), had given birth to five children: Orson Jr., Lydia, Celestia Larissa, Sarah Marinda, and Vanson. She bore twelve children in all, six of whom died by their second year. By July 1846, though Pratt had objected to plural marriage, in addition to Sally, he had been sealed to Charlotte Bishop (1844), Adelia Ann Bishop (1844), Mary Ann Merrill (1845), and Louise Chandler (1846).

this week Mr Sessions has found some fault with me and we are here alone almost, only three tents Holmans Everets and ours[94] I do want to see the rest of our co so much that I am quite disconted

AUGUST 1846

^**August**^ **1** I still feel very lonsome the girls go and get some more grapes **Sunday 2** Mr Sessions took Rosilla and ^asked^ me to go to the river then took her and waided across the river left me on this side was gone 2 or 3 hours got a few grapes P G and Mary went with them[95] ^I went back to the waggons^ **Monday 3** we washed and ironed I helped **Tuesday 4** we have got word from Brigham to go up the Missouri river in stead of going to Grand Island we start this morning ^**Wendnesday 5**^ leave the bridge no stringers on six butments built come up with some others that started last night stop to bait I miss my knife would go back if and find it if I had a horse we traveled 16 miles camped I found my knife in the bed **Thursday 6** P G and Holman and Averett go to find a good way to go[96] P G found a good spring Averett Holman go again and P G ^and^ a few of the co go to the spring half a mile camp it is good watter and cold **Friday 7** we stay here to the spring Holman and Averett have gone again mean to see Brigham before they return Br Boice [George Boyes, 1827–1874] came and camped with us to day the men have gone to hunt for game they return no game Holman and Everet return say we must go and meet the camp I have not been well to day I have lain in the waggon most all day

SEPTEMBER 1846

Sept 2d I have been very sick have not wrote any since the 7 of August to day I have wrote a few lines to Sylvia I did not have my clothes on for 20 days I vomited 4 days and nights all the time got to the camp on tuesday Brs Brigham and Heber laid hands on me Sister young gave me some tonic on Wednesday that seemed to reach my disease the Doctor said I had the inflamation in the stomach and it would be a miricle if I got well when they told me I was almost gone I felt calm and composed told them where my garments

---

94. Probably Addison Everett (1805–1866), who entered the valley with the Pioneer Company.

95. Mary Call (1824–1865) married Perrigrine on 28 June 1845, as did her sister Lucina (1819–1904).

96. Obviously Patty is using Everett and Averett interchangeably. Other possiblilties besides Addison Everett include John Everett (b. 1803), who was in the first fifty, over which Perrigrine was captain; and Elisha Averett (1810–1890), a twin to Elijah Averett, who joined the Mormon Battalion and had been a member of the Nauvoo band. According to Brigham Young (*Manuscript History*, 6), a Br. Hanson and E. Averett played violin and flute in the Nauvoo Temple.

were and all things nessesary for my buriel[97] and requested to have the lati-
tude and longitude taken where I was lain and also to have cedar posts put
down to my grave with my name cut on them so that I could be found when
cal^e^d for many thought I was dying and the news went out that I was dead
but the saints held on to me by faith and prair and through their faith and the
power of the priesthood I was raised I got so low that a tea spoon full of
^cold^ watter or ice water at a time was all I could take for two days Brigham
said they must all hold onto me as long as I breathed and 15 minutes after I
had done breathing I had the best of care took of me and friends from almost
every part of the camp to visit me and to set up with me and I feel thankfull to
God that I got in to the camp for I think I must have died had I been any
where else but with the main body of the church, **Sunday 6** Elbridg has gone
back to Nauvoo I have rode out with sister young and others several times I
am geting better as fast as I can I have muc^h^ sorrow of heart but I hope the
Lord will comfort me I have set up but little to day **Monday 7** I feel better Mr
Sessions is more kind to me **Tuesday 8** I feel bad again he has been and talked
with Rosilla and she filed his ears full and when he came to my bed I was also
quite chled he was gone so long and I was so cold I had been crying he began
to talk hard to me before he got into bed and thretens me very hard of leaving
me Oh m^a^y the Lord open his eyes and show him where he is deceived by
lisening to her false tales Per G woman washed Lucina had the chils[98] it rains
Rosilla went away told nobody where she was going **Wednesday 9** rains all
day **Thursday 10** we have dried our clothes I have slept in the tent ever since
I was sick Rosilla came back this afternoon **Friday 11** Lucina and Mary both
have the augue **Saturday ^12^** I went to see sister Woodrooff[99] and then
went to see sister W Snow[100] **Sunday 13** wait on the girls ^they^ still have
the ague **Monday 14** Rosilla took hold and did ^part of^ the work I went
and put James Cumings [1819–1883] wife [Aura Annette Atwood, 1827–1905]

97. By "garment" Patty meant sacred underclothing faithful Mormons wore, in
which she wished to be buried.

98. Perrigrine recorded the death of his wife, "Juliann," as 25 January 1845. He and
two children lived with his parents until May, when "I began to look for a companion when I fell in with Lucina Call. . . ." He reports later that he received his
"indewments in the house of the Lord with Lucina my Wife . . ." (DPG, pp. B-
35, 39, 43).

99. Phoebe Whittemore Carter (1807–1885) married Wilford Woodruff (1807–1898)
on 13 April 1837. He was a member of the Quorum of the Twelve Apostles at this
time and became the fourth president of the church from 1880 to 1898.

100. Melvina Harvey (1811–1882), wife of Willard Trowbridge Snow (1811–1852)
gave birth to her daughter Almira on 10 September 1846. The results of Patty's illness and her emotional distress become very evident at this point. She fails for a
time to state the sex of children she delivers and even fails to record some births.

to bed [with a son, James Willard, Jr.] **Tuesday 15^** [Rosilla] said she had a chill laid a bed most of the day **Wednesday 16** P G brought home a watter mellon ^and^ some apples came into camp I bought a ^14^ dozen gave a cent a peice the first vegatable I have tasted this year it was good **Thursday 17** visited sister ^Snow^ put Oens [Seeley Owens] wife to bed[101] **Friday 18** Lucina mised the ague **Saturday 19** I lay alone felt bad **Sunday ^20^** visited sister Wordsworth[102] **Monday ^21^** I still feel bad Rosilla wants to cook and eat by herself I will not let her when she can eat with the rest of us and is well **Tuesday 22** she will not eat with us nor receive any counsel from him to do right **Wednesday 23** I put Wm Wordsworths wife to bed ~~Thursday 24~~ caled to B Youngs wife[103] packed up to move but did not many have gone **Thur^s^day 24** we leave Cutlers Park and move to the ^Mo^ river 4 miles **Friday 25** P G goes to the ox herd Mr Sessions and I have a long talk with Rosilla he has talked with her many times alone but she will not hear to either of us nor receive any counsel from him but persists in her own way **Saturday 26** I look over some cookeys bake some pies **Sunday 27** do not go to meetting **Monday 28** look over the rest of the cookeys **Tuesday 29** cooked a turkey baked pies we have had another talk with Rosilla she says she will not receive any advice from me she will do as she pleases & she will not come into the tent nor eat with us again **Wednesday 30** Mr Sessions has gone to the ox heard ^came back^

OCTOBER 1846

Thursday Oct. 1 put Minerva to bed [with a daughter, Mary Minerva][104] **Friday 2** get Jane Glen to wash **Satturday 3** iron Mr Sessions took all the Saliratus I had[105] gave it to Rosilla told her to lock it up from me and keep it ^he also abused me very much^ for she had told him many things that were

---

101. Seeley Owen[s] (1805–1881), according to Patty's account book, paid two dollars on 17 September. He was a member of the Pioneer Company. His wife, Lydia Ann Pickle, died at age thirty-five on 19 September 1846 "of fever" (Bryson, *Winter Quarters*, 151).

102. William Shin Wordsworth or Wardsworth (1819–1888), husband of Ann Fogg, was one of the Pioneer Company.

103. Louisa Beaman (Young) gave birth to twins, Joseph and Hyrum, in 1846. According to Leonard Arrington (*Brigham Young: American Moses* [New York: Alfred A. Knopf, 1985], Appendix C), they may have died in 1846 as well.

104. Minerva White (1822–1896) was the first plural wife of Erastus Snow. They were married on 2 April 1844. Again it is significant that Patty does not designate her as Snow's wife. Erastus Snow (1818–1888) became a member of the Quorum of the Twelve Apostles on 12 February 1849. The child, Mary Minerva, died on 1 August 1847 at Winter Quarers. Erastus was in the Pioneer Company.

105. Saleratus, a type of baking powder or soda, was scooped from the ground where it rose like alkali from soda springs. The pioneer would pour water on to dissolve it, let the dirt settle, and then use the liquid—often to make soda biscuits.

untrue and when he found out the truth he took ^the most of it^ back again
and gave it to me **Sunday 4** I feel bad I am in trouble **Monday 5** I make her
many ofers and so did he but she said she would not except of any for she
would not come in to the tent nor go to work any where else he then told her
she must suffer the consequence for he was not able to maintain her in idle-
ness and he should say no more to her I put Almina Bills [wife of John Bills] to
bed **Tuesday 6** Mr Sessions gone to cut house logs **Wednesday 7** got a letter
from Windsor [Lyon] **Thursday 8** wrote a letter to Sylvia **Friday 9** I put sister
cook [Ann Eliza Howland, wife of Phineas Wolcott Cook] to bed with a
daughter [Eliza Hall] last night went horse back 5 miles baked some pies visited Sister Kimbal **Saturday 10** went to A Lymons to see Dionethia[106] visited
the sick most of the day **Sunday 11** it rains we have had another talk with
Rosilla tried to have her come in and eat but she is still stuborn and rebelious
~~she washed a large was for herself~~ ^she^ is able to walk miles but says she
will not work. I heard her tell him she was able to do all our work and knew
it would be better for her to do it but she had said she would not work and she
would not ~~Monday 12~~ put Welcome Chatmons wife to bed [with a daughter,
Fidelia][107] **Monday 12** worked so hard I had a chill went to Bishop Hunters to
see the sick[108] **Tuesday 13** sent for to go to sister Coolage [Collidge] sent medicine visited sister Pitt[109] she is sick **Wednesday 14** took the rusk and put it in
the other waggon **Thursday 15** fix down the carpit **Friday 16** put Br
^Edwards^ Hunters wife [Laura Alvina Shimer] to bed [with a daughter,
Carolina Roccaly][110] very cold **Saturday 17** frose last night the first ice we
have had **Sunday 18** put Abigail wife Samuel Russell [Mary Abigail Thorn,
1821–1904] to bed [with a child, Francis Marier] **Monday 19** put Sister
Fullmer [Olive Amanda, wife of John Solomon Fullmer, 1807–1883, to bed
with a daughter, Mary Ann] sister clark [with a son, David W.][111] sister

(See Kate B. Carter, ed., *Heart Throbs of the West*, vol. 2 [Salt Lake City: Daughters
of Utah Pioneers, 1940], 499.)

106. Amasa Mason Lyman (1813–1877) was a member of the Pioneer Company.
Dionethia Walker was his fifth wife; they were married in July 1845.

107. Welcome Chapman (b. 1805) was married to Susan Amelia Ridely (1807–1888).

108. Edward Hunter (1793–1883) had been bishop of Nauvoo's fifth ward, became
bishop of Salt Lake City's thirteenth ward, and was presiding bishop of the
church from 1851 to 1883.

109. Cornelia Melvina Devine (1824–1860) was married to William Pitt (b. 1813).
She was his second wife; his first, Caroline Smith, had died in 1844.

110. The daughter died on 22 October 1846 at Winter Quarters, age six days (see
Bryson, *Winter Quarters*, 146).

111. Although Patty credits Daniel Clark in her accounts, a son, David W., was born
to David and Sarah E. Clark on 19 October 1846. He died on 9 November 1846
at Winter Quarters (see Bryson, *Winter Quarters*, 136).

[Charles] Pucket sister Pitt to bed [with a son, William Heber Pitt][112] this fourenoon Rosilla left here to day 19 **Tuesday 20** baked ~~Mr. Sessions fell from a load of hay~~ **Wednesday 21** wrote a letter to Sylvia Mr Sessions was turned off of a load of hay got hur^t^ is better to day it was done yesturday **Thursday 22** made me an undergarment **Friday 23** bought some stuff to make me a hood **Saturday 24** Clarisa Decker made it[113] gave me the making of it Rosilla came back I went and tried to talk with her but she was very abusive to me untill P G told her to hold her tounge or he would roll the waggon away with her in it if he went to the counsel for help **Sunday 25** went to meeting then Mr Sessions and I had a talk with Rosilla she was very willful and obstinate he told her to come into the tent and if she did right she should be used well I told her it was a big cud for me to swallow to let her come in after she had abused me so shamefuly he said they had abused me a great deal worse than she had been abused he knew he had done wrong and abused me bad and he was sorry and ashamed of it and if I would forgive him ^and let her come in^ he would do it no more and would sleep with me when I was at home and use me well and he knew she had abused me worse than I had her I said if she come in I should be boss over the work and she must be ^carefull^ how she twisted and flung at me for with out more humility in her than I see there I could bear but little from her we left her and went to bed **Monday 26** she came in and eat breakfast **Tuesday 27** she washed ^sister calahans child died^[114] **Wednesday 28** Ironed but little said between she and I **Thursday 29** I cook still she does not ofer to **Friday 30** she mends ~~a little~~ some clothes asked me for some sewing I gave her an old vest to mend **Saturday 31** P G killed a beaf I visited the sick and did the work

NOVEMBER 1846

Sunday Nov 1st went to meeting then went to see Br Holman he is dead[115] **Monday 2** put Wm Spears wife [Genet] to bed [with a daughter, Mary][116] Mr

112. William Pitt, with E. Averett, performed musical numbers in the Nauvoo Temple on 2 January 1846. At the time of the organization for the exodus, Pitt called out the musicians. The Pitt daughter, who had been born on 12 September 1845, died on 17 April 1847 at Winter Quarters (Bryson, *Winter Quarters*, 153).

113. Clarissa Decker (1828–1889) was a plural wife of Brigham Young and one of only three women to enter the valley with the Pioneer Company.

114. Lyman Caleyham, age one year, died on 27 October 1846 at Winter Quarters (Bryson, *Winter Quarters*, 135). His parents were probably Lucinda Shipman (1822–1906) and Thomas William Callahan (1812–1889).

115. Joshua S. Holman, husband of Rebecca W. Holman, died at Winter Quarters on 1 November 1846 at the age of fifty-two (Bryson, *Winter Quarters*, 145).

116. Mary Spears, age five days, died on 7 November 1846 at Winter Quarters (Bryson, *Winter Quarters*, 157).

Sessions told her last night she must go to work and favour me for I was not able to do so much she said she would do what I told her to and no more he said well you must do right for she has bore so much she will bear but little more I got but about 2 hours sleep last night and I have cut the meet of the bones of the beaf and salted it I have to work all the time and notwithstanding all he has said to her about helping me she never ^has^ to favo^ur^ me in the least but before supper gave me the lie ^many times^ and talked very saucy to me and when I could bear it no longer I told her to hold her toungue and if she gave me the lie again I would throug the tongs at her she then talk^ed^ very saucy to me I told her there was the tent door and she might walk out if she could not cary a better toungue in her head about a half hour after she got up and went into the waggon then told Mr Sessions I drove her out doors with the tongs they all know to the contrary **Tuesday 3** she came into the tent but will not work I cook she eats I put James M Flakes wife [Agnes Hailey Love] to bed [with a son, Frederick][117] ^**Wednesday 4**^ he has lain with her three nights she has told him many falsehoods and is trying to have him take ^her^ to Nauvoo and then to Maine and leave me for good I have not spoke to her to day yet she says I have quarrel^ed^ with her all day I go to bed know not what to do **Thursday 5** she came into the tent Mr Sessions told ^her^ to go to work ^she said^ if she did I would not let her I had forbid her a dozen times doing anything which was false for she had not touched the first thing to help me she then said if I would ask her I then asked her to clean the dishes I waited 3 hours she then went over the river and never touched them ^I baked some pies^ when she came back she was very saucy to me said she would eat but she would not ^work^ for me **Friday 6** he Mr Sessions told her to go to work and help me to clean the dishes as I had asked her she said she would not if we wanted it done we might do it our selves I did not speak P G said he had seen me abused long enough and she had cause^d^ it she gave him the lie he said she must take that back or leave the tent he had seen me cook and she set and do nothing and then come to the table and croud me away long enough she left ^and went to the waggon^ saying she had nothing to do with him nor the old woman I then went put Brigham H Youngs wife [Cedenia O. Clark, b. 1828] to bed [with a daughter, Sarah][118] **Saturday 7** Sarah Lawrence and Emily Haws [b. 1827]

---

117. James Madison Flake (1815–1850) was the master of Green Flake, a slave, whom he gave to Brigham Young (Bryson, *Winter Quarters*, 99). Snowflake, Arizona, was named for William Jordan Flake, son of James and Agnes.

118. Brigham Hamilton Young (1824–1898) was the son of Phineas Young, brother of Brigham Young. Phineas and Brigham H., Richard Ballantyne, and James Standing were held hostage and abused for more than a week in retaliation for the arrest of some of the lynching party in Nauvoo. All were subsequently released (see Young, *Manuscript History*, 277–85).

was here[119] **Sunday 8** I did not go to meeting **Monday^9^** he went and talked with her last night then wanted me to find provition for her to live some where else ^I said^ I could do it but I thought it was hard as old as I was to have to maintain her without work he was mad turned his back said he could do it himself she must have a living if she would not work **Tuesday 10** ^I baked mince pies^ she goes away some where every day **Wednesday 11** she told him she wanted him to cary her things to the river he talked with her some and she went away we moved some of our things into our house[120] when she came back he invited her in she made him no answer did not come in **Thursday 12** he invited her in again she came in did not speak to any of us but him he told ^her^ she had better go to work there was a woman close by that wanted her to work for her she said well she wont have me for I wont work for her he did not tell her who it was he told her he was sory to have her go to such a poor place as she was going for they had nothing to do nor eat she said she should go and if he was going she wanted him to go quick he went ha[u]led her things to the river and left her there **Friday 13** we have movd the rest of our things into the house **Saturday 14** put down a carpet ^and baked mince pies^ **Sunday 15** sister Shumway died[121] **Monday 16** put Jon= C. Wrights wife to bed [with a son, Enoch][122] **Tuesday 17** visited ^Zina and^ the girls in the Market **Wednesday 18** made more canker medicine **Thursday 19** put sisters Brower [to bed with a son, Ariah Hussey] & Bliss [to bed with a daughter, Mary Ann] & Hate to bed [with a son, Isaac Chauncey][123] ^Lydia Cook washed we had let her have a peticoat^ **Friday**

119. Sarah Lawrence (b. 1826) was sealed to Joseph Smith on 11 May 1843. She married Heber C. Kimball on 12 October 1844. They were divorced in 1851.

120. Perrigrine writes in his journal, "I built a house to winter in altho not a bit of lumber and timber scarse but each family set to work to prepare for winter this was a tedious job as many families had no man to build or take care of them but all done what they could for themselves and others and it would astonish the world to see how quick there was about twelve hundred houses built with a good flouring mill altho we had but little grain to grind I got a house sixteen by twenty redy and moved into it the 13 of Dec . . ." (DPG, pp. B-46–47).

121. Julia Ann Hooker (1807–1846) was the wife of Charles Shumway, who became one of the Pioneer Company. Shumway was the first to cross the Mississippi in the exodus from Nauvoo.

122. Jonathan Calkins Wright (1808–1880) married Rebecca Wheeler (1813–1850) on 1 March 1838. He came to Utah in October 1850 and became a judge, educator, farmer, county clerk, recorder, and prosecuting attorney. Enoch, their child, died at eighteen days of spasms.

123. Margaret Elizabeth Hussey (1817–1885) was the wife of Ariah Coates Brower (1817–1884). Mary Eliza Cole was married to Norman Ingles Bliss. Eliza Ann Snyder (1815–1888) was the wife of Isaac Chauncey Haight (1813–1888).

20 Mr Sessions went over the river to see Rosilla **Saturday 21** he staid all
night he talks much since about leaving camp **Sunday 22** P G has killed a
wild goose big and fat Mr Sessions went to meeting ~~the men~~ Brs Lee & Egan
that went to the Army have returned safe[124] **Monday 23** sister Wiley helped
us eat ^part of^ the goose **Tuesday 24** sister [Lucinda?] Wilson helped eat
the rest I went and put sister Sanders to bed [with a daughter, Ellen C.][125]
Wednesday ^25 washed^ **Thursday 26** ^caled to Wm Youngs^ put his
wife [Adalia Clark] to bed [with a daughter, Delecta][126] **Friday ^27 Saturday
28^** visited the sick Rosilla came back ^here^ sais she is going back to the
Missisipi river she left word for Mr Sessions to come over and see her **Sunday
29** he went over at night and staid with her **Monday 30** did not speak to me
when he came home

DECEMBER 1846

Tuesday Dec= 1st sister Horn came ^on^ here **Wednesday 2** washed
Thursday 3 ^Rosilla started for Nauvoo^[127] put sister Calihan [Lucinda
Shipman Callahan] to bed [with a daughter, Agnes Ann] **Friday 4** ^baked
pies^ put George Grants wife to bed[128] **Saturday 5** made my muff **Sunday 6**
they butchered an ox **monday 7** rendered the tallow ^and baked mince pies^
Tuesday 8 put sister Woodruff to bed [with a son, Ezra][129] ~~W~~ and run candles
Wednesday 9 nit on P G mittens **Thursday 10** visited the sick **Friday 11** fin-

---

124. John Doyle Lee (1812–1877) at this time was returning from the Mormon
     Battalion, where he had been sent to bring back funds from the volunteers to
     their families. Howard Egan (1815–1878) accompanied Lee on his trip. Egan
     had been a member of the Nauvoo police and Nauvoo Legion and was part of
     the Pioneer Company.

125. Rachel Broom Roberts (1807–1892) was the wife of Ellis Mendenhall Sanders
     (1808–1873).

126. Delecta Adalia Young (age unknown), daughter of William and Adalia Young,
     died on 28 November 1846 (Bryson, *Winter Quarters*, 163).

127. In September 1852 Perrigrine received a mission call to New England and
     retraced much of the original Mormon Trail. On 3 November he recorded in his
     diary, "in the morning visited her that was Rosiley Cowin. She had bin married
     to my Father but had apostitised and maried a man by the name of Baley . . ."
     (DPG, p. B-63).

128. According to Bryson (*Winter Quarters*, 143), Loisa M., age twenty-three, wife of
     George D. Grant, died on 30 December 1846. It is unclear whether Patty refers
     to George D. Grant or George Roberts Grant, who was one of the Pioneer
     Company—but it's probably the former.

129. The son of Phoebe Whittemore Carter and Wilford Woodruff was six weeks
     early and died on 10 December (Francis M. Gibbons, *Wilford Woodruff, Wondrous
     Worker, Prophet of God* [Salt Lake City: Deseret Book Co., 1988]).

ished P G mittens baked mince pies **Saturday 12** visited the sick wrote a letter
to Sylvia **Sunday 13** the Mohakgh Indians shot here in our camp last Tuesday
night kiled none ^3 wounded^ Friday night kiled 40 that were hunting news
came here last night and such a howling I never herd before[130] did ^not^ go to
meeting **Monday 14** mended Mr Sessions coat **Tuesday 15** P G has gone to
the ox herd after Br Grovers oxen[131] **Wednesday 16** put Meltiar Hatch wife to
bed [with a son, Meltiar][132] P G has got home **Thursday 17** he has gone to
Missouri after provision I sent $18-50 money by him to get provision got a win-
dow put in **Friday 18** fixed my cloak the Mohaws Indians move from here
Saturday 19 received a letter from David dated Nov 14 **Sunday 20** went to
meeting to Br Kimbals **Monday 21** ^baked pies^ put sister Vannorton to
bed[133] **Tuesday 22** visite^d^ the sick **Wednesday 23** put sister Brown to bed
miscariage also wife [Melinda Gimble, 1811–1894] of Tarlton Lewis with a son
[Tarlton, Jr.] **Thursday 24** went over the river to see sister Morse then a visiting to sister Gean to celibrate her birthday[134] **Friday 25** Christmas day went to
Br Woolleys to a party then went and put sister Busenbark to bed [with a son,
William][135] Eliza Snow came home with me **Saturday 26** I had a party Mary
came home she has been gone 3 weeks almost will be next Tuesday ^baked
pies^ put sister Sheets to bed [with a daughter, Margaret] this evening[136]

---

130. According to Brigham Young, "About three A.M., the report of six guns was
heard in camp in rapid succession followed by a terrible outcry of Indians and
the barking of dogs. Big Head, an Omaha chief, with his family and relatives
had encamped in their lodges a little north of Winter Quarters, and were fired
upon while in sleep; Big Head and two others were severely wounded. The
Indians came into camp immediately and were attended by Drs Cannon,
Sprague and Levi Richards" (*Manuscript History*, 471).

131. Thomas Grover's oxen had been drowned on the 9th, and John Goal loaned
him a span of horses and wagon to be returned at journey's end. John Goal's
wife demanded them back and could not be persuaded otherwise. Brigham told
Brother Grover to trust in the Lord (Young, *Manuscript History*, 51). Whether
Perrigrine is loaning oxen to Brother Grover is not clear from Patty's entry.
Thomas Grover became a member of the Pioneer Company.

132. Permelia Snyder (1827–1917) was the wife of Meltiar Hatch (1825–1895).

133. Julia Ann Van Orden (1810/11–1869) was the wife of Hector Horton Haight
(1810–1870).

134. Cynthia Ann Bevans (b. 1823) was the wife of Gilbert Morse (b. 1815). Esther
Ann Pierce (b. 1801) was the widow of William Atkin Gheen (1798–1845).

135. Abigail Manning (1807–1852) was the wife of Isaac Busenbark (1801–1876).

136. Margaret Hutchinson (1818–1847) was the wife of Elijah Funk Sheets
(1821–1904), who traveled to Utah with the Big Company in Perrigrine's fifty.
Margaret died of canker at twenty-seven on 1 February 1847. The child died on
4 April 1847 (see Bryson, *Winter Quarters*, 156).

Sunday 27 went to meeting Monday 28 Sarah Alley died.[137] Tuesday 29
Wednesday 30 visited the sick Thursday 31 baked mince pies went and put
Joseph Harts wife [Clarissa] to bed [with a daughter, Harriet A.][138]

1847

we have got home all safe . . . I have drove my waggon all the way

JANUARY 1847

Jan=1: ^Friday^ I had a new years party Eliza Snow Loiza Beaman Zina
Jacobs &c were here enjoyed myself well opened and read the sixtyeth chapter
of Isiah P G came home from Mo brought 30 bushels corn meal 8:00 lb pork
16 shugar 4 gallons molases Saturday 2 tried my lard went to a party to Br
Winchesters Sunday 3 wrote a letter to David Monday 4 put Erastus Snows
wife [Artemesia Beaman, 1819–1893] to bed [with a son, Mahonri
Moriancumr],[139] helped take care of the meat Tuesday 5 I have been out all
night had no sleep put sister Alexander to bed[140] came home wrote a letter to
Mother sent both to st Joes by Br Scott P G has started off to go to the rush
bottoms hunting broke down the waggon Elsworth came back got another
Wednesday 6 I have baked some mince pies caled to sister Cyntha sealed G
P Dikes[141] Thursday 7 put her to bed ^with her 20th child^ I have visited
the sick Friday 8 put Loiza [Beaman (Young)][142] Adaline [Knight, with a son,
Gilbert Rosel] & Melissa [King, with a daughter, Mary McMurphy] all to bed

137. Sarah B. Alley (1819–1846) was the wife of Joseph Bates Noble (1810–1900).
Sarah was a plural wife, which is probably the reason for Patty's calling her by
her maiden name. Sarah died of childbed fever. Two deaths occurred in the
Noble family in 1846. Hyrum B., the one-year-old son of Joseph and Mary
Adeline Noble, died on 5 November 1846 (Bryson, *Winter Quarters*, 151).

138. The child died at thirteen days on 12 January 1847 (Bryson, *Winter Quarters*,
144).

139. Erastus Snow and Orson Pratt were the first Mormons to see the Salt lake
Valley. Mahonri Moriancumr is a character in the Book of Mormon.

140. Nancy Reeder Walker (1817–1847) was the wife of Horace Martin Alexander
(1812–1881). The child born at this time was Horace Martin. Nancy died on 28
January 1847.

141. George Parker Dykes and Cynthia Soles (1801–1847) had been married earlier
and were sealed at this time. Cynthia died on 11 January 1847 of childbed fever,
and the baby, Rachel, died on 13 January 1847. George joined the Mormon
Battalion.

142. Moroni Young was born on 8 January 1847 and died on 10 August 1847 of
"teething and canker" (see Bryson, *Winter Quarters*, 163).

in 6 hours and a half[143] **Saturday 9** ^I came home^ visited the sick **Sunday 10** visited the sick **Monday 11** caled to sister Empy staid all night she got better **Tuesday 12** Brigham Heber & wives were here on a visit **Wednesday 13** put sister Hall to bed [with a son, Newton Daniel][144] visited many sick P-G **Thursday 14** put sister Knight to bed[145] miscariage yesterday visited the sick today spun some yarn for a comforter **Friday 15** put Harriet T–Wicksome to bed [with a son, Seth James][146] **Saturday 16** put sister Egleston to bed [with a son, Samuel E.][147] **Sunday ^17^** had a good meeting at the Markee put sister [*blurred:* G] Passy to bed **monday 18** put sister Avery [wife of Charles E. Avery] to bed **Tuesday 19** visited the sick ^we were^ chose ^into Br Hebers^ co **Wednesday 20** visited the sick Eliza Snow was here made me a cap **Thursday 21** went to Br Leonards to a party[148] I visited the sick ^**Friday 22^** Eliza snow was here again **Saturday 23** visited the sick **Sunday 24** went to meeting heard a revelation read[149] then visited the sick **Monday 25** niting Mr Sessions a comforter **Tuesday 26** caled to sister Hannah Jones talked to her for her bad conduct[150] then I went to the Bishops to have a bedstead fixed up for her and to make her comfortable although I thought she was a bad woman yet she lay on the ground and about to be confined and I pited her **Wednesday 27** visited her again set her son to fix her bed sted **Thursday <28>** put William Wicks wife to to bed caled on for counsel by Sabre Grible [Gribble, b. 1794] caled on again to visit Hannah **Friday 29** Sabre came again ^for me^ I went to see sister Whiteney and others that were sick **Saturday 30** visited the sick **Sunday 31** went to meeting

143. Adaline Knight (1832–1919) was the wife of Gilbert Belnap (1821–1899). Melissa King (b. 1832) was married to George Benjamin Wallace (1817–1900).

144. Sarah Jane Busenbark (1825–1905) was the wife of Newton Daniel Hall (1819–1889).

145. Martha McBride (1805–1891) had been married to Vinson Knight, who died in 1842. She married Joseph Smith in 1842 and Heber C. Kimball on 12 October 1844.

146. Harriet Elvira Teeples or Teaples (1830–1881) was at this time the wife of Solomon Wicksome/Wixom.

147. Lurania Powers Burgess (1808–1870) was the wife of Samuel Eggleston (1804–1884).

148. Lyman Leonard (1793–1877) and his wife, Abigail Calkins (b. 1795), are mentioned frequently in Patty's diary.

149. *The Doctrine and Covenants*, Section 136, given through President Brigham Young on 14 January 1847, contains instructions on how the camp is to be organized for the westward journey, as well as defining certain commandments and standards of behavior.

150. There is no explanation of her "bad conduct," but Hannah Jones, wife of Alonzo Jones, died at Cutler Park; dates are unknown (see Bryson, *Winter Quarters*, 146).

FEBRUARY 1847

Monday Feb 1st wet the down the Leach[151] and visited the sick **Tuesday 2** out all night put Alvin clements wife to bed [with a son, Alpheus G][152] **Wednesday 3** visited the sick and baked mince pies **Thursday 4** my birthday fifty two years old Feb 4–1847 in the camp of Isriel Winter quarters we had brandy and drank a toast to each other desireing and wishing the blesings of God to be with us all and that ^we^ might live and do all that we came here into this world to do. Eliza Snow came here after me to go to a litle party in the evening I was glad to see her told ^her^ it was my birth day and she must bless me she said if I would go to the party they all would bless me I then went and put James Bulloch wife to bed [with a daughter, Mary Catherine][153] then went to the party had a good time singing praying speaking in toungues before we broke up I was caled away to sister Morse [Cynthia Ann Bevans] then to sister Whitney then back to sister Morse put her to bed 2 oclo^ck^ [with a son, William A.][154] **Friday 5** this morning I have been to see sister Whitney she is better I then went to Joanna Rounda she said it was the last time I should see her in this world she was going to see my children[155] I sent word by her to them I then went to the Silver Grey party[156] Eliza Snow went with us I danced with Br Knolton Mr Sessions not being well ^Joanna died

151. Presumably Patty was extracting lye by filtering or leaching water through wood ashes. Often a leach was built of a hollowed out log, with boards at a slant to form sides. Ashes were placed inside the log and water poured over them and the lye caught in buckets as it trickled over the end of the log. She would use the lye to make soap, which she mentions on February 6. (See Kate B. Carter, ed., *Heart Throbs of the West*, vol. 1 [Salt Lake City: Daughters of Utah Pioneers, 1939] 293–94.)

152. The child of Alvin Clements (1822–1855) and Rhoda Gifford (1827–1904) died on 26 February 1847 of canker (Bryson, *Winter Quarters*, 137).

153. James Bullock (b. 1806) is mentioned in Hosea Stout's diary as an interpreter (see Brooks, *Hosea Stout*, 2:516). His wife was Mary Hill (1812–1850).

154. William A. Morse died on 7 March 1847 at Winter Quarters (Bryson, *Winter Quarters*, 150).

155. Patty and David had buried five children prior to this time: Sylvanus, Anna B., a second Anna B., and Bartlett in Maine; and Amanda in Nauvoo (see the introduction, p. 10, for their dates).

156. "Silver Greys" was a term used for older folks. According to Mary Haskins Parker Richards, ". . . there is a company called the Silver Grays . . . Fathers [Isaac] Morly, & John Smith the Patriarch. are appointed to Manage & Conduct the affairs of the same" (see Maurine Carr Ward, ed., *Winter Quarters: The 1846–1848 Life Writings of Mary Haskin Parker Richards* [Logan, Utah: Utah State University Press, 1996], 130). There were also Silver Greys mentioned in connection with the Nauvoo Legion.

this evening^ 157 **Saturday 6** made soap visited some that were sick then went put sister Whitney to bed she had a son [Newel Melchizedek] born Eleven oclock P M **Sunday 7** warm and pleasant I went to meeting then visited the sick Br Hathaway came here **Monday 8** finished making soap[158] **Tuesday 9** visited the sick ^P G gone hunting^ **Wednesday 10** visited the sick did me up some caps **Thursday 11** ^caled to see sister^ Lamb[159] put sister Lamb to bed came home eat breakfast then went to get some one to take care of sister Knight traveled around till afternoon Eliza Mitchel said she would take care of her I came home very tired Br Kimbal said he ^would^ say for himself and in behalf of Joseph that I had done my part for her **Friday** ^**12 oclock**^ caled to sister Dun child born before I got there[160] I then visited the sick Br John Young and wife [Theodosia Kimball] visited us had a good time **Saturday 13** visited sisters Buel and Rockwell[161] had the wild hairs puled out of my eyelids my eyes very sore **Sunday 14** Went to meeting then in the evening collected Zina ^Jacobs^ Eliza Snow sister Marcum [Markham][162] ^at^ sister Buels to pray for Sylvia and child that they might be delivered from bondage and Windsor and David come here with them we prayed sung in toungues spoke in toungues and had a good time then went ^to^ put sister Oakley to bed[163]

---

157. Johannah Carter (1824–1847) and Lauren Hotchkiss Roundy (1815/16–1900) had two sons, Byron Donalvin, born in 1844 in Nauvoo, and William Heber, born according to one source on 8 February 1846 and another on 5 February 1847. If William Heber was newborn in 1847, it is strange Patty did not say so. The two children accompanied their father westward with the Big Company.

158. Patty would save every scrap of fat and drippings for months. Then ashes were saved and stored in a barrel with added water and stirred and skimmed until the waste ashes settled to the bottom and clear lye water was left over. This was heated with the grease in a large kettle outside the house. As the lye consumed the grease during hours of slow cooking, a syrup formed. The experienced soap maker tested the syrup in clear water and lye water until she knew it was just right. She perfumed it, if desired, and poured it into molds to dry. (See Carter, *Heart Throbs*, 1: 293–94.)

159. Elizabeth DuBois (b. 1823) was the wife of Benjamin R. Lamb (b. 1821).

160. Jane Caldwell (b. 1808) was the third wife of Simeon Adams Dunn, whom she married in May 1846. They were later divorced. This child was named Joseph Moroni Dunn.

161. Presendia Lathrop Huntington (1810–1892) had previously been married to Normal Buell. She was sealed to Joseph Smith on 11 December 1841 and to Heber C. Kimball on 4 February 1846. She was also a midwife.

162. Sister "Marcum" could have been Hannah Hogaboon (1803–1892), who ws married to Stephen Markham (1800–1878), later a member of the Pioneer Company. Or she could have been his mother.

163. Mary McCormall Patterson (b. 1824) was the wife of John Degroat Oakley (1818–1890).

child [Mary Elizabeth] born 4 oclock A M **Monday 15** I have been out all
night had no sleep visited the sick all day **Tuesday 16** we wash visited the
sick sister Young died 15 at sister Holmans[164] **Wednesday 17** visited the sick
then carded some wool **Thursday 18** visited the sick **Friday 19** visited with
sister Hyde at Loizas she is making me a dress **Saturday 20** visited the sick
it snows P G came home from hunting **Sunday 21** there is more snow than
I have seen at once since I left Maine dont go to meeting caled to sister
Davenport **Monday 22** stay ^ed^ all night visited the sick **Tuesday 23** visited the sick yestarday I cooked for the widow orphan and poor that they
might feast and have thier hearts made glad today in the counsel house
Wednesday 24 spun 2 skeins then visited the sick **Thursday ^25^** to sister
^Mary Ann^ Nobles[165] she was sick all day **Friday 26** wrote to Sylvia send
two letters to her by Perrigrine put Mary Kimbal [Mary Davenport,
1824–1905, wife of William H. Kimball] to bed ^out all night^ **Saturday
27** put Mary Ann Nobles to bed [with a daughter, Mary Elizabeth] P G
starts this morning for Sylvia I visited the sick **Sunday 28** Br and sister
Leonard and sister Buel was here last night we spoke in toungues and had a
good time

MARCH 1847

Monday March 1st spun went to Br Tomases [John Thomas] put his wife
[Ann Jarvis] to bed [with a daughter, Sarah Ann] **Tuesday 2** carded and spun
some wool strained some honey I went to bed sick **Wednesday 3** not well to
day **Thursday 4** visited the sick **Friday 5** not well **Saturday 6** not well picked
some wool **Sunday 7** did not go to meeting I visited the sick Precinda and
Zina was was here **Monday 8** put sister Mary Dykes to bed Fornatus Duston
Josiah call and wives came here **Tuesday 9** fixed the cards set over some of the
teeth[166] **Wednesday 10** put Wm= Davies wife to bed[167] then visited the sick
Thursday 11 visited the sick all day got a wheel [spinning wheel] at night put

164. Bryson (*Winter Quarters*, 163) records that Jane Young, age twenty-seven and the wife of George W. Young, died of consumption. She was born in 1819 in Canada.

165. Mary Ann Washburn (1827–1882) was a plural wife of Joseph Bates Nobles (1810–1900). He was bishop of the thirteenth ward at Winter Quarters. Three of his children and his first wife, Mary Adeline Beman, became part of the Big Company of 1847.

166. She probably referred to carding tools. They were two wooden paddles with narrow rows of sharply pointed metal "teeth." The wool was stuck on one tool and the other drawn against it to create long fibers that could then be spun into yarn.

167. Franklin J. and Ann Davis had a daughter, Lydia, who was born on 10 March 1847 at Winter Quarters and died on 26 March. Instead of William, this could be the "Davies" to whom Patty refers.

Almira Davenport to bed [with a daughter, Almira][168] **Friday 12** carded spun and visited the sick **Saturday 13** carded spun visited Sister Gean with E R Snow sister Chase[169] **Sunday 14** to meeting to Br J Wolace Br Kimball preached **Monday 15** put sister Stilman to bed[170] visited the sick sister E R Snow came here last night she has done me up a cap and wrote me some poetry which she composed which I shall write here

Composed for Mrs Patty Sessions By Miss E R Snow [*in right margin, sideways:* March 15 1847]

> Truth and holiness and love
> Wisdom honor, joy and peace
> That which cometh from above
> In your pathway shall increase
>
> Thus the spirit of the Lord
> In your bosom shall abide:
> And produce a rich reward,
> While the still small voice, shall ^ (guide ^
>
> Faith and holy confidence,
> That will bear your spirit up,
> Shall henceforward recompence
> All the bitter of your cup
>
> Righteous are your hearts desires,
> And they will not be denied;
> But our Father oft requires
> That our patience shall be tried.
> Though he should at times withhold
> Longer than your hopes expect:
> You'll receive a double fold
> When his wisdom shall direct.

---

168. Almira Phelps (1805–1881) was the wife of James Davenport (1802–1883), who would be a member of the Pioneer Company. He ferried pioneers over the Platte River.

169. Ann Alice Gheen (1827–1879) married Heber C. Kimball on 10 September 1844.

170. Barbara S. Redfield (b. 1808) was married to Dexter Stillman (1804–1852). They had a son, Dexter, who was born on 16 March 1847 at Winter Quarters. He died on 28 July 1847 of consumption. Dexter Stillman joined the Mormon Battalion.

Therefore let your spirit rest–
God will order all things well;
And ere long you will be blest
More than human spe^e^ch can tell.

And the Lord himself will spread
Thro' your heart a holy pride
Of your chosen earthly head,
Your companion by your side.

Mutual shall your blessings be
Mutual joys shall crown your ^(way:^
Then in time:–Eternity
Opens to a brighter day.

Tuesday 16 Eliza Snow left here I visited the sick and also Mary Pearce she died to day[171] **Wednesday 17** she was buried I went to the funeral Brigham preached I then visited the sick Mr Sessions and I went and laid hands on the widow Holmons ^step^ daughter[172] she was healed I was sent for to go to a private meeting with Brighams family did not go Mr Sessions wished me to go another way I went **Thursday 18** I visited the sick **Friday 19** Eliza Snow came here to dinner we then went and visited sister Whitney **Saturday 20** scoured yarn[173] **Sunday 21** went to meeting Br Brigham told his dream of seeing Joseph the charge he had to this people from him to keep the spirit of the

---

171. Mary Harvey Pearce or Pierce or Peirce (1821–1847) died of pneumonia. Brigham Young recorded, "I buried my wife, Mary H. Pierce, aged twenty-five years, daughter of Robt. and Hannah Pierce. She died of consumption" (*Manuscript History*, 538).

172. The "widow Holmon" to whom Patty referred logically would be Rebecca Whitcomb Greenleaf (1793–1849), married to Joshua Sawyer Holman (1794–1846), who had died on 1 November 1846 at Winter Quarters. Rebecca died in July of 1849 in Coonville, Iowa. Why Patty first wrote "daughter" and then inserted the word "step" above the line is problematical. The Holmans had four daughters: Mary (1822–1822), Rebecca (1824–1849), Parmelia (1827–1881), and Abigail Elizabeth (1836–1912). One must also wonder if the daughter Rebecca is confused with the mother Rebecca since the death dates are the same.

173. There were two processes for cleansing wool. When the sheep was sheared, the wool was put in large willow baskets and then suspended over a stream and dipped up and down until loose sand and dirt were removed, then spread out to dry. After it was spun into skeins of yarn, it was "scoured" by being washed with soap and the softest water, usually rainwater or water softened with a plant called oose (see Carter, *Heart Throbs*, 2: 179).

Lord[174] I then visited the sick **Monday ^22^** I commenced niting a comforter Harvy [Harvey] Call [1808–1849] came down from Punchaw **Tuesday 23** visited sister Martindale [Mahalia Stigleman, wife of William Addington Martindale, 1814–1873] she is very sick then visited sisters Buel Jacobs and Leonard Mr Sessions came in the evening

[The next page is written upside down.]

for salve for old sores the bark of indigo ^weed^ root boiled down beas wax a very little rosin

for jaundice take one tablespoonful of casteel soap shavings mixed with shugar three mor^n^ings then miss three until it is taken nine mornings shure cure

for bowel complaint take tea one spoonful of rubarb one forth carbnet soda one table spoonful brandy one tea spoonful peperment essence half tea cup ful warm water take a table spoonful once an hour untill it opporates ~~take one tea spoonful of rubarb one forth of soda table spoonful brandy teaspoonful pepperment half teacup warm water~~

for vomiting six drops ladnum the sise of a pea of soda 2*h* tea spoon pepperment 2*h* tea cups water take a tablespoon ful at a time till it stops it if the first dose dont repeat it

harts horn–laudnum–carb^i^nate amonia–sweet oil–camphor for milk leg or inflamation or sweling

Wednesday 24 visited the sick **Thursday 25** ^finished comforter^ visited the sick **Friday 26** Br [Gilbert] Belnap [1821–1899] sent me quarter of dear meat I divided it with sisters Kimbal and Buel then went to a special meeting Brigham preached **Saturday 27** visited the sick **Sunday 28** went to meeting all the twelve preached that was here my leg is lame and I rode with Br Snows family

---

174. The JH (23 February 1847) quotes Brigham Young's account of the dream to the "brethren of the Twelve." Joseph stood near a lighted window while Brigham stood in the twilight. Brigham asked Joseph to comment on the law of adoption or sealing principles, but Joseph answered, "Tell the people to be humble and faithful, and be sure to keep the spirit of the Lord . . . keep their hearts open to conviction, so that when the Holy Ghost comes . . . their hearts will be ready. . . . They can tell the spirit of the Lord . . . it will whisper peace and joy to their souls; it will take malice, hatred, strife and all evil from their hearts; and their whole desire will be to do good, bring forth righteousness and build the kingdom of God . . ."

Monday 29 I bought 5 cents worth horse redish set some of it out, sowed some garden seeds in trays of dirt and put some more into the ground **Tuesday 30** nit on another comforter I was sent for to go to sister Leonards I went, in the evening they sent for Mr Sessions we prayed spoke in toungues interpreted prophesied and had a good visit **Wednesday 31** ^I^ nit ^and visited the sick^

APRIL 1847

~~March~~ **Thursday** <April> **1st** put Sarah [Huston, 1845–1886] wife of P P Pratt to bed [with a daughter, Julia] visited with sister Knight at sister Buels Mr Sessions and I then visited the sick ^anointed^ and laid hands and had a blessing **Friday 2** took up our beaf sold 75 lb to Br Litle[175] I have finished the comfortors one for Mr Sessions the other for Perigrine we have let the Pioneers have 24 pounds of pork ^let them have it March 31^ & 2 bushels of corn meal **Saturday 3** visited the sick sisters Buel & Knight were here visiting I was caled to Br Waggoners wife in the evening **Sunday 4** went to meeting ^then^ visited the sick **Monday 5** commenced ^to nit^ Marys mits visited the sick **Tuesday 6** went to conference 12 ocl^(ock^ ajorned sinedi [*the following is spread out and written above three lines:*] ^received a letter from Windsor & Sylvia dated 7 of Feb^ I then visited the sick **wednesday 7** the Pioneers mostly started[176] sister Holmon was here on a visit **Thursday 8** Parley P Pratt has returned from England[177] **Friday 9** the most of the twelve have started as pioneers expecting to come back ^next^ monday ^I visited the sick^ **Saturday 10** opened a chest aired the things mended some finished Marys mits **Sunday** ^11^ went to meeting Parley preach gave us a history of his journey to England I then visited the sick **Monday 12** I visited the sick sister Horn gave me 75 cents for the Doctoring her when sick **Tuesday 13** visited sister E R Snow with sister Leonard had a good time spoke in toung^ues^ and prophesied the spirit of the Lord was with us I visited others that was sick also **Wednesday 14** the twelve came back on monday as they expected and have

175. Probably Jesse Carter Little (1815–1893), who acted as liaison with President Polk on the mistreatment of the Mormons and the organization of the Mormon Battalion. Jesse Little was a member of the Pioneer Company.

176. The party consisted of 144 men, 3 women, and 2 children. The men were chosen for skills that would be useful in preparing the way for the thousands to follow (for a concise history of the Pioneer Company, see Hal Knight and Stanley B. Kimball, *111 Days to Zion* [Salt Lake City: Deseret News Press, 1978]).

177. On 15 July 1846, "Lots were cast between Elders O. Hyde, P. P. Pratt and J. Taylor, which two should go to England; the lot fell on Elders Hyde and Taylor to go." However, on 25 July, Hyde, Pratt, and Taylor were authorized to "take into their management . . . all . . . of a temporal and spiritual nature pertaining to . . . the Church in the British Empire . . ." (Young, *Manuscript History*, 274). Pratt was returning from this assignment.

started again this morning for the mountains Br Taylor came home from England last night he and Parley has not gone to the mountains **Thursday 15** Lewis Robinson and family arived last night brought me a letter from W P Lyon Sisters Leonard Lamb & Miller visited me to day Mr Sessions and I were caled to ^anoint and^ lay hands on sister Holmon we then went to sister Leonards had a feast of the spirit of the Lord ^nit Lucina a pair of mits^ **Friday 16** I have been to a number of places to collect pay that was due me but got but got but one half bushel meal Mary Elen [Harris Kimball] is here cuting Carlos [Perrigrine's son] some clothes this evening visited sister Pitts [Cornelia Melvina Devine] child [Cornelia M., age one] it was dying **Saturday 17** it is dead I nit me a pair of mits brewed some beer **Sunday 18** it is quite cool this morning Porter [Rockwell] ^and others) ^ starts to go ^on with^ to the pioneers I visited E R Snow & sister Leonard they are not well **Monday 19** looked over my chests **Tuesday 20** sisters Leonard & Buel were here on a visit **Wednesday 21** 1 oclock P G and Sylvia and child come I was almost over come with joy and gratitude to God for our preservation to see each other again David could not get the team over the river and it raind and I could not go and see him his Father went and caried him some vituals and see him **Thursday 22** 1 oclock David came I was almost overcome again my children were soon ^all that were living^ seated around the table with their Father and Mother we rejoiced together and thanked the Lord I then was caled to see the sick **Friday 25** we visited the sisters and brethrun all day in the evening ^David^ went to a party they prayed and danced and prayed again Sylvia her Father and I with a few more sisters met at Br Leonards he was gone but Mr Sessions presided and we had a good time we prayed propesied and spoke in toungues and interpreted and were refreshed **Saturday 24** we visited and were visited all day **Sunday 25** went to meeting Br Taylor preached we then visited sisters Nobles ^&^ Ashba [probably Martha Ellen Ashby, 1832–1873] **Monday 26** went to several places Br Mager is taking our portraits[178] visited ^at^ sister Pearces[179] ^with^ sisters Young Kimbal Whitney & E R Snow and others in the evening we all went to the girls house had a meeting it was good **Tuesday 27** visited sister Kimbal and others ^and^ rode out to the bur[y]ing ground **Wednesday ^28** visited^ Lucy [Walker (Kimball)] & Francis & Laura

---

178. William Warner Major (1804–1854) joined the church shortly before the martyrdom. Hosea Stout writes on 7 March 1845, ". . . went . . . to see Br Major who was painting the scenery of the murder of Joseph and Hyrum . . ." (Brooks, *Hosea Stout*, 1:25). According to Brooks, he made sketches along the way to Utah which were later exhibited. He died while fulfilling a mission to England. The portrait the Daughters of the Utah Pioneers owns of David Sessions, Sr., looks very much like a sketch touched up with paint. This could be one of the "portraits" Patty mentions.

179. Sister Pearce was probably Hannah Pearce (1802–1872), mother of Mary Pearce who had died.

Pitkin and many others[180] put sister Van waggoner to bed **Thursday 29** visited
Sary Ann [Whitney (Kimball)] and sister Whitney [Elizabeth Ann Smith]
Sylvia had a chill at sister Buels as we visited her in the forenoon we prayed
and laid hands on her she was better **Friday 30** we visited the girls at Brighams
E R Snow and myself made arangement to have the Mothers in Isriel meet at
sister Leonards[181] and have a ^prayer^ meeting Saturday

MAY 1847

May 1st Sylvia and I went to a meeting to Sister Leonards none but females
there we had a good metting I presided it was got up by E R Snow they spoke in
toungues I interpreted some prophesied it was a feast[182] **Sunday 2** went to meeting in the forenoon in the afternoon visited ^sister^ Taylor took dinner then
took supper with sister Noon [Sarah Peak Noon] ^then^ had a meeting to sister Kimbals there we had a feast of the good spirit **Monday 3** have been writing
a letter to mother then went to sister Youngs visited in the afternoon had a meeting in the evening **Tuesday 4** Sylvia packed up her things to go home Br Call
came from Punckaw[183] **Wednesday 5** they are here yet David drove to the river

---

180. Frances Jessie Swan (b. 1822) married Heber C. Kimball on 30 September 1844.
    They were separated in 1851, and she later married a Mr. Clark. Laura Pitkin
    (1790–1866) married Kimball on 3 February 1846. She was a midwife for the
    Kimballs.

181. According to Carol Cornwall Madsen, "Though Joseph Smith had explained to
    the Relief Society that 'elect lady' meant 'to preside,' the term, along with
    'daughter of God,' 'priestess,' and 'Mother in Israel' carried deep significance to
    an earlier generation of Mormon women, for these titles were most frequently
    applied to those women who had received the fullness of the sealing power"
    ("Mormon Women and the Temple," in *Sisters in Spirit,* ed. Maureen Ursenbach
    Beecher and Lavina Fielding Anderson [Urbana and Chicago: University of
    Illinois Press, 1987], 103).

182. Eliza R. Snow records in her diary: "May 1st. This afternoon had a most glorious
    time at br. Sessions. Sis. Sessions presided—present Moth. Chase Cutler Cahoon
    sis. Whit. Kim. Pitkins, Lyon, Basil, Knight &c—spoken by the spirit of prophecy
    that the Pioneers are well, happy, and in council—that tomorrow they will have a
    greater time of rejoicing than they have ever had" ("Journal. Winter Quarters of
    the Camp of Israel," 1 vol., n.p., original holograph, HM 27522, Huntington
    Library, San Marino, Calif.).

183. With ten wagons in his charge, Anson Call had accompanied George Miller's
    Company of sixty-two wagons to where Miller had set up an advance camp at the
    junction of Running Water [the Niobara River] and the Missouri River. Brigham
    Young sent word for Miller's group to return to the main company. Miller came to
    confer with Brigham in April, leaving his camp 134 miles north. Afterward Miller
    convinced his followers to depart from the leadership of Brigham Young. Obvi-
    ously Call decided otherwise, although he did not emigrate to Utah until 1848.
    "Punckaw" undoubtedly referred to Ponca, still a community today, and the Indi-
    ans of the same name, with whom Miller and his company had friendly dealings.

the wind blew so they could not cross came back Sylvia and I visited Loiza E. R
Snow has composed some poetry for Sylvia I will write it here in my book
To Mrs Sylvia P Lyon by Miss E R Snow

Go thou loved one, God is with thee
He will be thy ^stay^ and shield,
And fulfill each precious promise
Which his spirit will direct,

From thy Father and thy mother
Who are twined around thy heart
Also from thy Elder Brother,
Thou art call'd awhile to part,

But thy husband will caress the[e],
And thy sweet angelic child,
With her groing charms will bless thee
Thus the hours will be beguiled,

And thy younger Brother David,
With his harmless cocial glee—
With the heart and hand of kindness
Often times will comfort thee

And the saints of God who're banished
From their country and their home,
Who for Jesus testimony
In the wilderness now roam,

Will with prayer and suplication
Plead thy cause before the throne
Of the great Eternal Father
Where thy works of love are known.

Guardian angels will protect thee
And the spirits still small voice,
Will from day to day direct the[e]
Therefore let thy heart rejoice.

O my Father though that dweleth
In the upper courts of light;
Open thou the way before her
Guide, O guide her feet aright.

May Thursday 6 put Helen Kimbal [Whitney] to bed[184] the child still born David could not get over the river **Friday 7** could not get over the river we washed **Saturday 8** got the waggon over but concluded to wait for W W Phelps[185] **Sunday 9** it is Davids birth^day^ 23 years old and the same time of day that he was born he and Sylvia left me on the bank of Missouri river started for home Mr Sessions went over and saw them leave the river may the Lord speed them in all safty home may they keep the spirit of gathering and with all their connections gather up their substance and come to us again as soon as the Lord will is my prayer Mr Sessions an I returned to the house went to meeting counsel was given for the safty of our catle and also for raising a crop in the evening I was sent for to go and lay hands on Zinas child we had a prayer meeting **Monday 10** we have over ha[u]led our chests **Tuesday 11** Sister Leonard & Buel were here on a visit sister Buel had the toothache bad we laid hands on her **Wednesday 12** I have mended some visited the sick **Thursday 13** E R Snow is here making me some caps **Friday 14** visited with E R Snow Loiza Beaman & sister Pearce at sister Taylors had a good visit **Saturday 15** E R Snow here again finished my caps made me three **Sunday 16** she staid all night it rained I went up to the girls with her we had a meeting **Monday 17** I was caled to George Grants child last night it was sick visited the sick to day saw Amos Davis heard from Sylvia & David he met them 50 miles this side Mt Pisgah **Tuesday 18** visited the sick in several places anointed and laid hands on sister Murrys son **Wednesday 19** visited the sick then put Jedidiah Gra^nts^ wife [Carolyn Van Dyke, 1818–1847] to bed[186] then went to sister Levets to meeting[187] 18 sisters met we spoke in toungues interpreted & had a good time **Thursday 20** put sister ^Isaac^ Brown to bed [with a daughter, Emley Jane][188] and visited the sick in the rain **Friday 21** fair weather visited the sick and tacked a comforter got 4 lb coffee of sister Benson **Saturday 22** fixed the waggon cover visited the sick **Sunday 23** Jed= Grant

---

184. Helen Mar Kimball (1828–1896) was a daughter of Heber Chase Kimball and Vilate Marray. She was a plural wife of Joseph Smith and later married Horace Kimball Whitney.

185. William Wines Phelps (1792–1878) filled important roles in the church as schoolteacher, printer, justice of the peace, editor, and composer of hymns. He helped explore for the church as well.

186. Jedediah Grant's wife was Carolyn Van Dyke. She was born on 16 June 1818 and married Grant on 2 July 1844. On 29 September 1847 Patty mentions her death on the 26th. For an account of her death see Gene A. Sessions, *Mormon Thunder* (Chicago: University of Illinois Press, 1982), 62-69

187. The meeting was probably held at the home of Phoebe Levett (b. 1795), who, with a daughter Emeline, a son George, and a daughter Louisa, emigrated with the Big Company.

188. Hannah Jane Davies (1823–1905) was the wife of Isaac Brown (1818–1851/2).

got home[189] I went to meeting **Monday 24** visited the sick a steamboat
^name Archer^ came up to day a man fell off of the boat and was drowned
this afternoon **Tuesday 25** went on to the steam boat Archer found the wife of
the man that fell of the boat took her to meeting to sister Buels there we comforted her I visited the sick before and after meeting **Wednesday 26** visited
the sick Isaac Browns child [Emley Jane] died while I was there **Thursday 27**
Made soap visited sister cutler with E R Snow and others[190] had a good [meet-
ing] prayed and sung and spoke as the Lord directed **Friday 28** made more
soap have got over 50 pound hand soap let a kind of a Br Lewis have 25
pounds of ^good^ grease I have not got only soap to do a part of one washing and that was poor stuff for all the grease **Satturday 29** packed 1:86
pounds of pork for the mountains I then went to collect some debts got nothing then went to a meeting to Eliza Beamans with many of the sisters, sisters
Young and Whitney laid their hands upon my head and predicted many
things that I should be blesed with that I should live to stand in ~~the~~ a temple
yet to be built and Joseph would be there I should see him and then I should
officiate for my labours should then be done in order and they should be great
and I should be blessd and by many and there I should bless many and many
should be brought unto me saying your hands were the first that handled me
bless me and after I had blesed them their mothers would rise up and bless me
for they would be brought to me by Joseph himself for he loved litle children
and he would bring my litle ones to me &c &c my heart was fild with joy and
rejoicing–**Sunday 30** sister E R Snow and others had a good time at sister
Buels with a few then all went to sister Tomsons[191] many more came had a
feast of good things of ^the^ kingdom there in the evening we went to sister
Kimbans [Kimball?] had a glories feast of feeling and hearing **Monday 31**
pack and loaded our waggon and slept in it

189. Jedediah Morgan Grant (1816–1856) had left Winter Quarters for a mission in
the East during the winter of 1846–1847. He returned with materials to make a
flag that was used for several years in the Salt Lake Valley. It was called the
"mammoth flag" (Andrew Jensen, *Latter-day Saint Biographical Encyclopedia*, 4 vols.
[1901; reprint, Salt Lake City: Western Epics, 1971], 1:58.

190. Clarissa Cutler (1824–1852) married Heber C. Kimball on 29 February 1845.
They were separated in 1848, and she married Calvin Fletcher in 1849. Of
course, Patty could have been referring to Emily Trask Cutler (see note 74).

191. Mercy Rachel Fielding (1807–1893) married Robert Blashel Thompson
(1807–1841) in 1837. He acted as clerk and editor for the church. He died on 27
August 1841 in Nauvoo. In 1843 Joseph Smith performed the marriage of
Mercy as a plural wife to Hyrum Smith, who was husband to her sister Mary.
Mary Fielding (Smith) and her family and Mercy and her daughter Mary Jane
accompanied their brother, Joseph Fielding, to the valley of the Great Salt Lake
as members of the hundred of Daniel Spencer (also called Parley P. Pratt's
Company).

JUNE 1847

Tuesday June 1 sister E R Snow is here the girls wash some for her she lines Carlos hat [Perrigrine's and Julia Ann Kilgore's four-year-old son, 1842–1926] ^we^ had a feast in the afternoon at sister Millers

[She inserts]
Iowa City Jonson Co Iowa Teritory
Mr S Huntsuckers fery
Austin Post ofice—Atchison
county Missouri to be:
forwarded to the camp of
Isriel

[crosswise at bottom of page, followed by a big ink smear:]
Indian hemp root cure for
gravel, for dropsy & for fits
for stifle that is out the white
of an egg beat to a froth the oil
s[et]tles to the bottom put it all on
bathe it in with hot iron

1 oz gumgabba rum
2 do megunda pitch)
1 lb rosin) 2*h* oz hartshorn ^last put <in>
heat it together like cookeing wax this for
stren[g]thing plaster

then we blessed and got blessed & blesed sister Christeen by laying my hands upon her head[192] and the Lord spoke through me to her great and marvelous things—at the close I thought I must ask a blessing at sister Kimbals hand but it came to me that I must first bless her and show Herber [probably Heber's] girl the order that duty caled them to perform to get any blessings from him upon them I obeyed layed my hands upon her head although it was a great cross and the power of God came upon me I prope I spoke great and marvelous things to her she was filed to the overflowing she arose and blesed the Lord and caled down a blessing on us and all that pertained to her sister Hess fell on her knees and claimed a blessing at my hands I then blesed her sister Chase claimed a blessing of sister Kimbal she blesed her with me, she spoke great things to her the power of God was poured out upon us E R Snow was

---

192. Christeen Golden (1822–1896) married Heber C. Kimball on 3 February 1846.

there and many others thank the Lord **Wednesday 2** it rains **Thursday 3** fair weather we expect to start to morrow for the mountains I caled to Sarah Ann this evening with E R Snow sisters Whitney and Kimbal came in we had a good time things were given to us that we were not to tell of but to ponder them in our hearts and proffit thereby[193] before we went down there E Beamon E Patrige Zina Jacobs came here[194] laid their han^ds^ on my head blesed me, and so did E Snow thank the Lord **Friday 4** we do not go to day Mr Sessions and I went to Br Leonards to a party we had a feast of good things both temporal and spirutal when going there I caled to sister Kimbals and with E R Snow blesed Helen and Genette[195] then in the gift of toungues E R Snow sung a blesing to all the rest of the girls then we went to Br leonards **Saturday 5** we start for the ^mount^ains^ and leave winter Quarters [for the] mountains or a resting place ten years to day since we left our home and friends in Maine we now leave many good friends here and I hope they will soon follow on to us I drive one four ox team go 4 miles camp **Sunday 6** go 15 miles camp on the pappy [Papillion Creek] 51 waggons **Monday 7** a heavy thunder shower last night we go 7 miles get to the horn [Elkhorn River] camp have a lameness through my chest caused by driving the team **Tuesday 8** I am better we wash and iron **Wednesday 9** go up the horn one mile cross over one of our waggons coming off of the raft droped the nigh wheels into the watter and we had to unload every thing then draw the waggon out then load up again and drive up the bank and all safe nothing broke or wet or lost of 26 hndred weight the rest of our co is on the other side one waggon of Br Singles sunk the raft and went overboard[196] wet all the load they got it out again **Thursday 10** they have dried the meal and grain and sustain but little loss more Brethren have come into the camp I have commenced a letter to Sylvia and David the men build a fence to yard the catle **Friday 11** 55 waggons more came up all crossd the river safe the Patriarch John Smith came **Saturday 12** it rains we hull some corn the men have gone fishing with a sceine–have come home got none the Brethren keep coming Sister Pratt [Mary Ann Frost] we hear has come to winter quarters **Sunday 13** he has gone back to see her we have a meeting I then visit sister Tomson many of the Brethren have come to

193. Eliza R. Snow writes of this occasion, ". . . had a powerful time deep things were brought forth which were not to be spoken . . ." ("Journal," June 1847).

194. Eliza Maria Partridge (1820–1886) and Emily Dow Partridge (1824–1899) were both plural wives of Joseph Smith, married in 1843. After the martyrdom Eliza married Amasa M. Lyman and Emily married Brigham Young.

195. The husband of Helen Mar Kimball, Horace Kimball Whitney (1823–1884), had accompanied the Pioneer Company, as had Hosea Cushing (1826–1854), the husband of Helen Jeanett or Genet Murray (1826–1901).

196. Nicholas Singley (b. 1791) was a member of the fourth ten of Perrigrine's first fifty of the Big Company.

day **Monday 14** we wash many more have come Br Pratt has returned says she is going back to Maine[197] sister Snow and a great many others have come to day we had a good time in Br Pearces cariage where E R snow rides she came home with me we had a good time in our tent Mary and Lucinia both spoke in the gift of toungues the first time they ever spoke in the gift Br Taylor has come his teams are on the other side **Tuesday 15** the men are caled together to organise I have made several small cheses since we started ~~Wednesday 16~~ ^we have had a good meeting to day^ I presided it was on the prairia we have good times times every time we meet **Wednesday 16** I am happy all the time **Thursday 17** the Brethren keep coming **Friday** ^**18**^ they still keep coming they sent the Marshals back after the cannon last night we have had a meeting at Br [Rufus] Beaches [1795/6–1850] **Saturday 19** I have sent a letter to Sylvia expecting to start along soon 12 oclock we start along leave waggons on the banks and crossing go to the Platt river 15 miles pass a dead body suppoesd to be killed by the Indians the wolves had eat him considerably his buttons were cut of and the legs of his pantaloos here we camp **Sunday 20** go to meeting before we went heard that Jacob Weatherbee [Weatherby] was shot by the Indians he was a teamster to drive one of Grangers teams he started ^yestarday^ to go back ^yestarday^ to Winter Quarters with a Br Lamson [Alfred Boaz Lambson, 1820–1905] and sisters Jonson and Chamberlain[198] got near eight miles back and three naked Indians rose out of the grass walked by the waggon drew their guns ^cocked^ Weatherbee and Lamson jumped out of the waggon clinched two of the Indians to get their guns ^and the third one shot^ Weatherbee through the hip and bowels he fell the Indians then ran off as soon as the scuffle began the oxen were frightened turned round and sister Chamberlain put the whip on to them to run them back to the Horn sister Jonson staid with Weatherbee Lamson ran toward Winter Quarters met Brs Lot Cutler and Whitney with cariages coming to the camp they took Weatherbee and brought him and all the rest back to the Elk Horn where a number of brethren were yet camped. he died this morning 9 oclock was ^calculated^ to be caried back to

---

197. Later, in Salt Lake City, on 8 October 1852 Pratt recorded, "On my arrival home [from a mission to the Pacific] I found my wife, Mary Ann Frost, and my two children, Olivia and Moroni, who had arrived from Maine, where they had been for several years. The two children were glad to see me, but their mother had for several years been alienated from me. I however, supported her until the following spring, when she applied for and obtained a bill of divorce; after which, with the two children, she removed to Utah County" (*Autobiography*, 374). In her defense it should be noted that Mary Ann Frost (1837–1891) had endured many hardships while Pratt was away serving missions.

198. For Almira Johnson's sworn testimony and the account of Alfred Lambson, see the JH (19 June 1847). Nancy Chamberlain was being sent back to Winter Quarters because she had no means of support on the journey.

Winter Quarters to burry him but he mortified and smelt so bad they buried him in a buffaloe robe near the liberty pole. this liberty pole was raised the 14 day of [*left blank*] and a white flag [flew from it][199]

[The birth of babies had slowed down considerably, or else Patty stopped recording her obstetrical visits so diligently. After the April 1 entry, Patty recorded only four births before their departure for the Great Basin: April 28, VanWaggoner; May 6, Whitney; May 19, Morgan; May 20, Brown. The records that interrupt her diary here were begun on the plains. Each birth is separated by a pencil line. She listed these deliveries formally but later added others to her daily entries.]

I Patty Sessions delivered Sylvira wife of Samuel Turnbow of a daughter name Margaret Ann born June 25 9 oclock P M [Sylvira Caroline Hart (1818–1853) was the wife of Samuel Turnbow (1804/14–1876).]

I also delivered Laura A wife of James B. Shaw of a daughter name Laura Almira born June 29–9 oclock A M [Laura Ann Gibbs (b. 1829) and James B. Shaw (b. 1824)]

I also delivered Elizabeth wife of Robert D Covington of a son name Robert L[aBorius] born August the 1–15 minutes past 8 oclock P M *[see note 212]*

I also delivered Lucy L a wife of John Van Cott of a son name Losee born August 23 half past 12 oclock P M *[see note 205]*

I also delivered Harriet Page wife of Lorenzo Dow Young of a son born Sept 26 7 oclock P M the first male born in this valley[200]

---

199. Stanley B. Kimball writes, "Once across the Elkhorn, the pioneers headed for the broad and gentle valley or floodplain of the Platte River. This staging ground, later named the Liberty Pole Camp (from a large cottonwood pole erected there July 4, 1847, by the Second Company of pioneers), was located approximately one-quarter of a mile from the Platte River, southwest of Fremont and west of U.S. 77. The pole remained until at least 1857 . . ." (*Mormon Pioneer Trail*, 84). Patty recorded the pole as raised on the 14th instead of the 4th.

200. Harriet Page Wheeler (1803–1871) traveled in the Pioneer Company, "occasioned by the insistence of Young's younger brother, Lorenzo, that he be allowed to take his asthmatic wife . . . and her two children. This, of course, necessitated including at least one or two other females to keep Harriet company. Fortuitously, Brigham had married Harriet's daughter, Clara Decker, so he took her. Kimball took Ellen Sanders, one of his [then] sixteen wives . . ." (Kimball, *Mormon Pioneer Trail*, 48. Also see notes 228 and 287 below).

I Patty Sesions delivered Sally Ann wife of James Brinkerhoff of a son name Levi born Nov 5–8 oclock A M <1847> *[see note 242]*

I also delivered Elizabeth M wife of Simson D Huffacre of a son name David S born Nov 6 haff past 12 oclock P M 1847 *[see note 243]*

I als[o] delivered Ann wife of Daniel M Thomas of a daughter name Nancy C born Nov 6 half past 1 oclock P M 1847 [Ann Crosby and Daniel Monroe Thomas (b. 1809)]

I also delivered Mary wife of James Brown of a daughter name Mary Eliza born Nov 8 half past 12 A M 1847[201]

I also delivered Lydia Ordelia C Elendon wife of Gilbert Hunt of a daughter name Mary Elen born Nov 17 2 oclock A M 1847 *[see note 245]*

I also delivered Dorcas A wife of Joseph C Kingsbery of a daughter name Bathsheba [Dorcas] born Nov 19 7 oclock A M 1847 *[see note 247]*

I also delivered Emily wife of A O Smoot of a son name [Abraham] Albert [Ether] born Nov 22 7 oclock A M 1847 [Emily Hill Harris and Abraham Owen Smoot]

I also delivered Rhoda wife of Albert Carrington of a son name Young Brigham born Dec 13 1/4 11 A M *[see note 251]*

I also delivered Sophia wife of John Taylor of a daughter name Hariet Ann born Dec 14 6 oclock A M 1847 [Sophia Whittaker]

[Patty then repeats the information that was on the fragment before she began listing her deliveries:]
morning 9 oclock was ^calculated to be^ caried back to Winter Quarters to burry him but he mortified and smelt so bad they buried him in a buffaloe robe near the liberty pole. this liberty pole was raised the 14 day of June 1847

---

201. Mary McCree Black Brown (1820/1–1906) accompanied James Brown (1801–1869) with the Mormon Battalion. She is said to have been the first cheese maker in Utah, and he reputedly established Ogden. His death came from an injury sustained when he caught his arm in a cider press, leading to gangrene. On 3 June 1847 Brigham had dispatched four men to travel to Pueblo, Colorado, to direct the sick detachment that had dropped out of the battalion. They were to join the Pioneer Company. That group, which included the Browns, arrived in the Salt Lake Valley a few days after the original company.

and a white flag put on it another raised here with white flag the 18 day they have had a meeting under it to day I went I then went and had a meeting with a few sisters at Br Pearses

[From this date on, an earlier reader of the diary has inserted a bracket in pencil immediately before Patty's dates. These have not been included here.]

Monday 21 we wash the cannon and temple bell has come and sciff we are all ready now to go in the morning we have been waiting almost two weeks for the cannon[202] **Tuesday 22** on the banks of the platt river ready packed to move on start 8 oclock A M we are organised to move five a breast the two cannons sciff and temple bell heading the midle line go 15 miles camp near the platt river **Wednesday 23** start 9 oclock travel two a breast cannons heading one line sciff and the temple bell the other travel 15 miles camp on the prairie 2 miles from the river on a place looking some like our old place in Maine **Thursday 24** start 8 oclock A M go 10 miles stop 1 oclock waiting for the rest of the co to come up as some of the camp had feelings they caled a meeting made all things right received good instructions and had good feelings **Friday 25** 10 oclock move on go 10 miles camp a company of traders came along Dr Bartlett was one had been to Pawnee I then was sent for to [go] back 3 or 4 miles I went back put sister Turnbow [Sylvira Caroline Hart] to bed she had a daughter [Margaret Ann] come home 12 oclock at night–**Saturday 26** start 8 oclock go 20 miles camp on beaver creek I have got the toothache bad it rains to night **Sunday 27** cloudy I feel bad my face sweled bad can hardly set up its quite hard on me to drive the team all the way but the Lord will give me strength acording to my day[203] 11 oclock I feel impresed upon to go and see sister Snow I went and found her sick we had a litle meetting she and I were both healed by the power of God I then went to a publick meeting it was good I then went to visit Sister Elbrige[204] she was lame I laid hands on her she blesed me and I

---

202. The bell was from the Nauvoo Temple. It had been cast in England, shipped across the Atlantic by sailing vessel, and hauled up the Mississippi by flatboat. It weighed fifteen hundred pounds. The skiff was evidently used to explore rivers and lighten loads (see Gertrude R. Lobrot, "Bell, boat and cannons trekked west together," *Church News*, 14 July 1985, pp. 5,13). Brigham Young had sent for the bell in a letter to Babbitt, Heywood & Fullmer, Trustees, on 27 September 1846 (see *Manuscript History*, 397–99).

203. Perrigrine writes in his diary, "Organised in my company was eighty seven Wagons and fifty men over fourteen and four hundred souls in all and four hundred head of stock here we had some thirty wagons with out a Man to drive them but the females volunteered to drive them my Mother was one of them they looked hard as we had no road there was six hundred and sixty wagons in all . . ." (DPG, p. B-51).

204. There were a number of Eldredges in the Big Company. This may have been Nancy Black (1812–1895), who was married to Ira Eldredge (1810–1866), the

blesed her I then came home had a litle meeting in our waggon it was good my grand daughter Martha Ann had the gift of toungues but through fear did not speak after the sisters had gone she aked me to let her and Martha Van Cott have a little meetting[205] and wished me to attend we went into our waggon she she spoke in toungues and prayed I gave the interpretation and then told them to spend their time in that way and they would be blessed she is eleven years old **Monday 28** we wash the men are caled out to drill we have prayers night and morning at the ringing of the bell we start 1 oclock go 6 miles camp ~~we travel in the rear~~ the cannons go in the rear of our co we are still at the front of Parleys division his division goes in the rear this week 12 oclock at night I was sent for to go on two miles to put sister Shaw [Laura Ann Gibbs] to bed she had a daughter [Laura Almira] born 9 oclock A M ^29^ she traveled on when our co came up 10 oclock we traveled 10 miles camp on the loop [Loup] fork of Plat river [near present-day Columbus] we pass the Pawnee vilage to day it has been burnt by the Sues [Sioux] ^we then^ crosed a creek [Cedar River] chalk in the bottom so that it stuck to the waggon wheels we camp on the bank of the loop drive our cattle all together into the river to drink it was a pretty sight **Wednesday 30** start 8 oclock wait for Abraham Owen Smoots co to start along and get out of our way one hour go 10 miles come up with the whole camp the men go to find a place to cross we have pased another ^old^ Indian vilage today we do not cross to night camp

July 1847

Thursday July <1> Br Taylors [William Taylor, 1823–1910] co cross first P G and some few others have gone hunting returned saw some cantalopes [antelopes] got nothing this afternoon we cross the Loop camp on the bank our co have all got over safe go 1 mile to day **Friday July 2** we start half past 7 oclock go 20 miles camp on the prairia without wood or watter only what rain fell from the clouds we had a heavy shower of wind and rain it beat into the waggons a good deal **Saturday 3** start 7 oclock go 16 miles strike The Pioneer trail near the Platt river camp P G shot an Antelope today we crosed the sleiugh on a bridge made of grass where we watered at noon Br Sheets [Elijah Funk Sheets] cals this creek Muskeetoe bend here we took out our stove found old indian wickeups to burn in it **Sunday 4** I took some of the things out of the waggons found some wet a litle it rains a litle a man broke his arm last night in our co rasling his name is Martin De Witt [b. 1826] the sun

captain of the second fifty of the first hundred, also known as the Parley P. Pratt Company.

205. Martha Van Cott (1838–1908) was the daughter of John Van Cott (1814–1883) and Lucy Lavinia Sackett (1815–1902). On 23 August Patty delivered a new baby boy, Losee, to Lucy and John.

comes out we go to meeting have good instruction I had a meeting at sister Tomsons tent at 6 oclock P M we had a good time **Monday 5** we have made a bridge to cross the creek last night there was an indian seen creeping up to the camp when hailed he ran through the creek and fled we have ^to^ get more team to put onto the cannon at ten oclock they fire both cannons and start go 15 miles they held a counsel last night Parleys co was to go in the front we have traveled all day on the Pioneer track camp on their camp ground find a guide board 2:17 miles from winter Quarters the way we have come 1:90 miles **Tuesday 6** start 8 oclock go 18 miles camp on the bank of a stream from the platt river where the Indians had camped we burnt their wickeups for wood some waided the river to get wood brought it over on their backs the camp did not all get up last night neither have they to night Smoots co have not been heard from since Monday [Jedediah M.] Grants co did not get up to night **Wednesday 7** start 8 oclock go 15 miles camp where the Pioneers did found another guide board it said they had kiled 11 buffaloe the 2 of may P G had the waggon wheel run over his foot lamed him so that he cannot drive his team the Dr boy drives for him we have passed a great many of these litle dogs that live in the ground in holes **Thursday 8** start half past 8 oclo^ck^ ~~go on to~~ cross a sleiugh go 2 miles come to where the Pioneers camped 3 days found another guide board then we went up the creek 3 miles found two horses P G was the first that saw them Br Pratt was with him Brs Pratt and Taylor caught them and kept them ^we^ make a bridge cross over go 2 miles make another bridge cross go 5 miles camp see some buffaloe **Friday 9** some of the men have gone ^to^ kill the buffaloe we start half past 7 the men return see no buffaloe past the Pioneers camp ground when we first start but the sleiughs are so high we cannot follow their trail ^go up^ make a bridge of grass cros go 12 miles ^to day^ strike their trail camp on the bank of the platt river Br Crosby waided it[206] the girls wash it is very warm we find a pine tree floated down the river **Saturday 10** start 8 oclock go 5 miles camp 11 oclock we are now 252 miles from Winter Quarters to burn coal and fix waggons and wash &c &c six men went out to hunt went horse back they do not return to night **Sunday 11** the hunters have sent for a waggon to bring their game I have a meeting in our waggon with the litle girls sister Tomson was with us I then went to a public meeting then to sister Snows she sent for me we had a meeting there I then went ~~hold~~ had a meeting to sister Tomson the hunters came in got 18.00 cwt of buffaloe meat **Monday 12** divide it out among the 50 ~~they~~ the men went out of our co P G went they went out of other cos but did not get so much meat any of them as our 50 that sent out six men there was one

---

206. Jesse Wentworth Crosby (1820–1893), his wife, Hannah Elida Baldwin (1820–1907), and their son George Henry (1846–1916) were all members of Perrigrine Sessions's fifty.

dead ^buffaloe^ in the willows where we camped we start 9 oclock pass buffaloe rings where they lay it looks like our camp ground we go 12 miles camp
on the river they smoke the meat waid on to the island to get wood Br [Daniel]
Spencers 50 goes in the front this week he is capt over the first hundred
Tuesday 13 start 9 oclock go 15 miles camp on the river waid to the to the
~~river~~ island to get wood it has been a complete pasture for buffaloe the grass is
fed short some men went out hunting this afternoon kiled 4 bufaloe left the
meat for ~~the others~~ Grants co to bring in their herd broke out of the yard last
night and broke waggons killed a cow broke of[f] several horns one horses leg
and they have got to stop and repair waggons **Wednesday 14** go 6 miles stop
for the rest of the camp to come up see two herd of buffaloe near the camp
ground find a guide board with a letter in it stating it to be 3-60 miles from
winter quarters we call it 2:84 it is very warm some men have gone out to kill
a buffaloe kiled 1 divide it out in our 50 **Thursday 15** start 8 oclock go 15
miles camp at a spring we put milk in it to cool P Gs black ox was sick to day
Br Singley let him have a pair **Friday 16** he is a going to yoke the well ox and
put it on forward we start 8 oclock go 12 miles get along first rate to see thousands of buffaloe camp on the North fork of Platt river 14 miles from the
mouth after we had camped a herd of buffaloe ran in among our cattle we shot
one wounded three more took oxen and drew him in to camp before he was
dresed he was kiled in full view of the camp went after the others but did not
get them **Saturday 17** start 8 oclock go 16 at noon kill another buffaloe and
draw it into camp dress it while the teams are baiting hear that leters have
come from pioneers [*two indecipherable words scratched out*] I g[a]ther a few dry
weeds built a litle fire on a buffaloe dung broiled some meat for my diner
drank sweeten ginger and water I have seen many thousands of buffaloe to
day one crosed our track just forward of us we had a fair view of him camp on
the river no wood get news that Br Grants co had lost 75 head of catle by their
breaking out of the yard we take out our stove burnt buffaloe dung **Sunday
18** bake mince pies bread and meat over buffaloe dung 11 oclock go to public
meeting hear that Grants co had not found their catle some of our men went
this morning to look for them 4 oclock caled together to hear leters read from
the pioneers they were from some individuals that were left at the fery which
they had made they had ferried over four hundred Oregon waggons[207] they

---

207. Brigham Young had left nine men with a leather boat called the Revenue Cutter to
operate a ferry across the Platte River in Wyoming: Thomas Grover (1807–1886),
Captain John S. Higbee (1804–1877), Luke S. Johnson (1808–1861), Appleton
Milo Harmon (1820–1877), Edmund Lovell Ellsworth (1819–1893), Francis
Martin Pomeroy (1822–1882), William Adam Empey (1808–1890), James
Davenport (1802–1883), and Benjamin Franklin Stewart (1817–1885). Emigrants
paid $1.50 per wagon and load or used flour for payment at $2.50 per hundred
pounds (see Arrington, *American Moses*, 119).

had heard from the rest of the pioneers the 28 of June they were well and in the south pass of the mountains I then had a meeting at sister Tomsons P G is not well I gave him some medicine **Monday 19** he is some better he has met for counsel sent men out of each co to hunt for Grants catle he is 20 miles back we cannot go on untill he comes up with his co we must get them along some way 10 oclock I meet with the litle girls in my waggon have a good time the Lord is pouring his spirit out on the youth they spoke in toungues and rejoiced in God my heart was made glad 2 oclock had a meeting at sister Tomsons we had a good time I blesed and was blesed the men that went to hunt for Br Grants catle some of them have come in found 3 three oxen of the Oregon co,s loosing the rest kiled a buffaloe they kiled an Antalope P G is worse **Tuesday 20** he is no better start 8 oclock go 10 miles camp on the river find some flood wood to wash with they have sent word from Br Grants co that they have found none of their catle 20 yoke of oxen gone we have caled a meeting saying ^4^ hundred must make out 5 yoke out of each hundred we have made out the 5 yoke ~~Tues~~ **Wednesday 21** sent Br Gustan back with them[208] we start 8 oclock get 5 miles where we watered at noon they kiled 6 buffaloe gave Br Taylors co 3 of them divided the other 3 in our co we did not camp untill dark the catle was very uneasy I went into the waggon looked out saw them go round and round like a whirlpool the ^men^ saying they would break and runaway. I knelt down and prayed for the Lord to quiet them I arose they were quite still we went to bed heard no more from them **Thursday 22** heard this morning that the Indians killed 13 buffaloe close by us yesterday but none seen by us only the carcases of the buffaloe found warm the men are commanded to sleep with one hand on the lock of his gun last night we saw more than two thousand buffaloe at one time yesterday we go on 10 miles ^pass many dead buffaloe^ saw an encampment of Indians ^and^ as soon as we were camped there was more than 1:00 came to our camp it is the first I have seen since we left Winter quarters we have fiered the cannon and one six shooter for them to see and hear gave them some bread and they feasted rode round the camp and then we rang the bell our men paraded and motioned to them to go away they went we sent word back to Br Taylors and Smoots co that were back to come up they have not come we made safeguard P G is better so he got out of the waggon walked round gave some orders **Friday 23** it rains and has all night the Indians have come in sight ^this morning^ the guard was caled orders gave to not let them come near the waggons but they went another way 10 oclock they begin to come we stay here to day many Squaws came today they appear friendly they ^sing^ dance and ride round we dance and have music fire two cannons Parley and Taylor feast and smoke with the Cheif. Br Grants co came in sight

---

208. Thomas Gustin (1801–1849) was traveling with his wife and seven children in the group over which Perrigrine Sessions was captain.

to night Mr Sessions stands on guard **Saturday 24** we are at Ceder Bluffs start go 10 miles pass see and trade with many Indians pass their Lodges on the other side of the river P G went over and many others camp on the river Grants co came up this morning but do not get up to night **Sunday 25** 7 oclock some of the Pioneers came into the camp we have stoped to repair waggons and wash and have a meeting I go hear leters read from the Pioneers I send a leter to Sylvia by Pugmire as he is from the Pioneers and going back to Winter Quarters[209] **Monday 24[6]** start 7 oclock go 20 miles at noon water and bait a grove of ceder on the other side saw the Indians on the other side they stoped unloaded their Ponys in the cedar ^we^ pased over the hardest sand hill we have found I drove my team was not well went a foot untill I could scarce stand. crosed many small creeks camp on a large one two rods wide Br Spencer is a head he started last night went five miles Br Rich came up **Tuesday 27** start 7 oclock go 18 miles in the forenoon the Indians came some we have not seen before a big chief among them when we stoped to bait they came like bees their loges were across the river I drove into a mudhole got stuck put on more team came out camp near the river kill a ratlesnake close to the waggon thunders and lightens hard rained some **Wednesday 28** go 18 miles cross many water places mudy holes pased over ground that was over flowed by the rain last night but litle rain where we were at noon baited on the last grass we found till night in the afternoon came up a dreadful wind thunder lightning a very litle rain where we were on the other side of the river the ground was all aflood we pased over sand bluffs in the wind the sand and gravel flew in our eyes so we could not see at times we had to hold our waggon cover to keep them from bloing off this is ruin bluffs [Ancient Bluff Ruins][210] we camp on the Pioneers camp ground **Thursday 29** go 20 miles at noon bait and water at the river good feed we are in sight of chimney rock cliff of sand looking like a tome on the other side the river or an old coarthouse [Courthouse Rock] go over the blufs camp on the river go and lay hands on Mary jane Tomson we have traveled to day behind Br Spencer we came up with him last night **Friday 30** go 20 miles pass the chimney rock[211] ^&^

---

209. Jonathan Pugmire, Jr. (1823–1888) had been with the Mormon Battalion and among the sick who were sent under Captain James Brown to spend the winter at Pueblo, Colorado. Having started for the valley of the Great Salt Lake earlier, on 11 June 1847, they were met by Amasa Lyman and others who brought letters from Winter Quarters and counsel from Brigham Young. Pugmire had been married to Elizabeth McKay.

210. These were named by English Mormon emigrants, according to Stanley B. Kimball. But why, then, did Patty call them ruin bluffs, when the Big Company followed the Pioneer Company by only a couple of months? (See *Mormon Pioneer Trail,* 86.)

211. Courthouse Rock and Chimney Rock are approximately twenty miles apart.

many places that looked like ancient buildings camp on the river find good feed kill a ratle snake save the gall and greace **Saturday 31** go 15 miles camp on the river no wood and poor feed the bluff on the other side looks like the temple last night [Isaac] Brown & others went over the river on to the bluff kiled 3 antalopes a very curious looking place the bluffs look like ancient edifices some have gone over to night we met Br Devenport [James Davenport] this morning from the Pioneers it gladened my heart to see him he was in co with men that had been to Oregon two women with them

AUGUST 1847

Sunday August 1 I was caled to sister Covington[212] I went back 5 miles she came back with me I put her to bed this evening with a daughter P G Mary & Martha went over on the Bluffs got 6 quarts of black curants two catle died to day by eat ^ ing ^ a white substance that lay on the ground we are at Scots Bluffs **Monday 2** go 22 miles travel over dry priaria no feed only one place come to that 1 oclock but a small place there do not get to feed to camp till dark leave the catle out but litle feed here two catle died in Spencers co **Tuesday 3** go 12 meet men from the Army Br Willey [Jeremiah Willey, 1814–1868] came here at night half mile from the river poor feed **Wednesday 4** wrote a letter to sister Kimble[213] sent it by Willey this morning start 8 oclock go 10 miles find black currants get 6 quarts camp the Indians came into the camp spred their flag we fed them they went off plenty of wood here we pased some yesterday 15 days since we have had any wood except a very litle flood wood we have picked that up and carried it along **Thursday 5** go 7 miles pass fort Larrimee [Laramie] see many Indians fear them but litle feed yesterday or today I have fixed my waggon cover the girls bake currant pies **Friday 6** go 5 miles pick more currants about 12 quarts and choak cherry a plenty we stop to burn coal and fix waggons and make yokes we have came over a very bad hill especialy to come down camp near the foot of it **Saturday 7** the men set waggon tires women wash we bake pies hull corn **Sunday 8** we wash iron &c start 2 oclock go 3 miles camp **Monday 9** go 15 miles we have had bad hills come over one when we first started very rough went a mile turned to the left went a mile turned back went up a hard rough hill over a high prairia one dry river no feed broke two axeltrees some spokes out we camp where there is but litle feed **Tuesday 10** get the waggons fixed all ready to start one of Mores oxen were

---

212. Elizabeth Thomas (1820–1847) married Robert Dockery Covington (1820–1902). This child was Robert LaBorius, a son, as earlier recorded—a rare mistake for Patty.

213. Probably Vilate Kimball, who did not emigrate until 1848 and had a baby in February 1847.

gone[214] we went on and left them he found it come up at night we go 17 miles pass no feed and find but litle at night go over a high hill and low beds of gravel camp at a good spring ^ on horse shew creek ^ **Wednesday 11** go 3 miles over the worst hills we have found broke some waggons stop to repair but litle feed have to go back down the hill to a spring to get water buffaloe seen here **Thursday 12** go 17 miles over hills and valeys all the way hard and dry cross ^ big timber ^ creek go apeice through a deep gulley camp on the bank but litle feed **Friday 13** go 18 miles pass over the red Butes Br [Rufus] Beach got a wild horse broke to waggons crosing creek do not get camped untill after dark today is the first day since last friday that I have been able to drive yet I have drove with Martha to help me I have been sick toothache and fever no appetite to eat **Saturday 14** stop to mend waggon good feed 3*h* of a mile to the south kill 4 buffaloe some of the hunters did not get into camp till after dark ^ they ^ could not find the camp hollored P G and others went to them and piloted them in sister Brown got lost when she went to milk[215] she hollored and was piloted in **Sunday 15** I jirk the buffaloe meat one of the Pioneers came in to the camp with news from the twelve say we are 4:58 miles from salt lake where they have located we had a ^ confession ^ meeting partook of the sacrament &c **Monday 16** Br Benson Porter & Bindley came into camp[216] Porter eat breakfast with us bring good news from the Pioneers and their location they go back to meet the other cos we go 13 miles camp on the platt river Br Church met us[217] camped with us Br Parleys litle waggon broke down the lock chain broke on my waggon as we came down the hill to camp good feed over the river stone coal in the bend of the river ^ bank ^ ten rods from the road east **Tuesday 17** go 15 miles camp on the river crosed dear [Deer] creek this forenoon met John Higbee Joseph Young Phineous Young and E Elsworth come to us eat with

214. Samuel Moore (1804–1883), his wife, Eunice Sibley Bliss (1807–1890), and their three children were in the group over which Perrigrine was captain.

215. Probably Hannah Jane Richards (1823–1905), who, with her husband, Isaac Brown (1818–1851/2), was in the group that included the Sessions family.

216. Orrin Porter Rockwell and John Wesley Binley (b. 1814) had both served as bodyguards to Joseph Smith. Binley was a member of the Mormon Battalion. Jenson's *Biographical Encyclopedia* (4:733) says ". . . he met the Pioneers on the North Platte; afterwards he was sent back to hurry up the companies and then returned to the 'Valley' with John Neff in Jos. B. Noble's Fifty." On 12 May 1846 Hosea Stout wrote that ". . . Binley was acting the rascall in everything he went about . . ." (Brooks, *Hosea Stout* 1:161). By July of 1847 he must have been vindicated. The other men were of course members of the Pioneer Company.

217. Haden Wells Church (1817–1875) was a member of the Mormon Battalion who was probably on his way to rejoin his family. His wife, Sarah Ann Arterbury (1824–1889), and their child Hyrum S. (1846–1885) were traveling with the Abraham O. Smoot Company.

us[218] **Wednesday 18** wrote a letter to Br Kimbal go 18 miles camp at the old fery but litle feed have come down and up some bad places **Thursday 19** it rains some of the catle are mising I have have wrote a leter to Sylvia to send by Phineas Young start and go 5 miles P g ~~turned over his waggon got his things wet~~ had his waggon turned over with carlos in it into the water got his things wet carlos not hurt although he was under water all but his face and sacks of grain and trunks a top of him he cut the cover and got him out and all the rest of the things loaded up again forded the river camped opened the things it rained we could not dry them **Friday 20** go 12 miles a big bull came down the hill in the road to us we caught him yoked him turned one out of my team that had a sore neck put him in we then went on killed two buffaloe camped on a flat the water poison 2 catle died there after we crosed the river last night Mathews litle girl went down to the river[219] found a ten dollar gold peice at the edge of the water **Saturday 21** go 13 miles ^killed 3 buffaloe^ camp on a ^willow^ spring no stream Brs Benson Porter & Bindley left us to go back to the Pioneers ^we^ found another bull he is lame **Sunday 22** go 13 Br Pratt kiled a buffaloe Brown kiled ^an^ antalope camp on a small stream that runs into the sweet water good feed and water **Monday 23** we stop to recruit our teams I put sister VanCott to bed with a son [Losee] it has been a good day to dry our things that got wet when the waggon turned over we have got them all dry up till late giving the catle new milk they had eat or drank something that made them sick two died **Tuesday 24** go 10 miles start before breakfast camp on sweet water at Independence Rock I went up on the Rock got a peice off of the top to carry along we have got sallaratus plenty just before we come to this Rock the lake that had the best was at the left when we came **Wednesday 25** go 15 miles camp a mile from water we are in the pass very cold I wanted mitens to drive with **Thursday 26** kiled an indian dog last night in the camp good feed here frost here this morning have a very warm day go 10 miles camp on the sweet wate[r] good feed ^Parley went after the catle^ **Friday 27** frost again but a warm day go 10 miles camp

---

218. John Somers Higbee (1804–1877), Phineas Howe Young (1799–1879), brother of Brigham Young, and Edmund Ellsworth, son-in-law of Brigham Young, all started west with the Pioneer Company. However on 18 June 1847, Higbee and Ellsworth were two of the nine men left to operate the ferry at the Platte River. Higbee's wife and children were in the Abraham O. Smoot Company. On 3 July, just short of Fort Bridger, a packet of papers including distances was compiled and sent back to the companies on the trail. Five men were chosen to go back and act as guides for the next company. Phineas Young was one of the five. Joseph Watson Young (1829–1855) was traveling with the Jedediah M. Grant Company. His father was Lorenzo Dow Young, a brother of Brigham; his mother was Persis Goodall.

219. Probably Nancy Melissa (b. 24 June 1842), daughter of Wiliam Matthews (1808–1888) and Elizabeth Adeline Henderson (1807–1875).

Saturday 28 ^where we left carlos^ go 11 miles cross sweet water 4 times once in the mountains where they shut close together camp on it Br Gustins last cow died here **Sunday 29** go 16 miles camp on the river again meet some more Pioneers going back to meet thier families **Thursday [Monday] 30** go 10 miles camp on the river hull corn with some of the saliratus Br Pratt went upon the mountain cut black birch sticks **Tuesday 31** go 7 miles camp ^on a rig=^ had up hill and rocky roads the worst we have found here we meet more Pioneers Br Rounday Lovlin Gleason & others[220] they bring us good news from the valley

SEPTEMBER 1847

Wednesday Sept 1 go 12 miles camp on sweet water in sight of table Rock **Thursday 2** go 14 miles camp on the Pacific spring see indians here trade some with them get some skins **Friday 3** go 25 miles camp on litle Sandy drive till after dark before we get to feed **Saturday 4** go 1 mile stop good feed here the Pioneers come to us it mad our hearts glad to see them they staid all night with us eat and drank with us had a good meeting **Sunday 5** they bid us good by with their blessing and left us to go to their families they gave a good report of the valley said it was the place for us we start 12 oclock go 8 miles camp in the big sandy but litle feed **Monday 6** go 16 miles camp on big sandy with traders lent one of them some shugar & coffee ^name^ Miller it rained in the night and snowed **Tuesday 7** snow on the ground this morning go 16 miles cross green river hail and rained go down the river camp very cold gather a peck of black currants **Wednesday 8** lay still ^& rest^ warm and pleasant to day we hull corn Sister Tomson and I went down on the river bank had prayers alone **Thursday 9** go 13 miles then had to go 1 mile to camp ^out of the road^ and find feed camp on mudy fork **Friday 10** go 7 miles camp on hams fork on a branch of green river got a peck of currants last night spread them to dry to day Fuller and Loffingwell had a meeting to setle difficulty[221] all go a berying this afternoon get one bushel of currants and bull berys **Saturday 11** go 15 miles camp on blacks fork spread our berys pass rocks very high on the left close to the road looks like some old monument clay coulor the bull lay down as we went into camp **Sunday 12** go 9 miles camp on black fork picked beans put them to soak this morning cook them

---

220. Shadrach/Shadrack Roundy (1788–1872) was one of three men who plowed the first land in the Salt Lake Valley on 23 July 1847. Patty mentions Chauncey Loveland (1797–1876) often in her diary. John Streater Gleason (1819–1904) was one of the company of pioneers who entered the valley with Orson Pratt a few days ahead of Brigham Young.

221. Elijah Knapp Fuller (b. 1811) was captain of the third ten of the first fifty under Perigrine Sessions; William Leffingwell (b. 1805) was captain and clerk of the fourth ten.

this afternoon go to meeting Parley told us some items of the law of the valley **Monday 13** go 10 miles camp at fort Bridger **Tuesday 14** go 13 miles over mountains and down steep places one [on] the new road round and down the valley camped where the water stood but did not run Br Pratt did not get into camp till near dark Br Lawson [James Lawson, b. 1820] broke his wagon coming down the ^hill in^ the valey **Wednesday 15** stop mend the waggon start 11 oclock go 10 miles camp on a mountain see a big bear track near where we camped drove the catle into the valey we drove on a mountain go 5 miles new road cut of 3 miles **Thursday 16** go 10 miles camp on Bear river pass the tar spring 30 miles from fort Bridger between the tar spring and the river a bad hill doubled teams to come up steep to come down droped the teaketle bed coming down get some strawbery vines to cary on we have some curant bushes also[222] Br Sherwood come from the valley to us here **Friday 17** bad finding catle this morning get them start 11 oclock go 5 miles camp good feed but no wood had a meeting to setle a quarel cut 3 off from the church[223] **Saturday 18** had a fuss with Sister Hunter and family this morning[224] go 10 miles camp at cave Rock those that were cut off would not come along with us, sister Hunter would not come we took the children along she has come up to night very much enraged sais she will have revenge and Perrigrine shall be kiled for she has backers to back her up he and Br Pratt took her had her bound with a cord and put under guard Porter and John Green came into camp in the night[225] **Sunday 19** those that were cut off came up this morning

---

222. Patty's first allusion to what would become a passion with her—gardening. Apparently she had been collecting specimens along the way to plant in the valley.

223. On 17 September 1847 the JH records: "Capt. Sessions' company made a late start, having had much trouble in the morning to find their cattle. They traveled 5 miles and camped where the feed was good, but no wood. They held a meeting to settle a quarrel and three were disfellowshipped." The next day the JH reports, "John Smith writes: 'The three brethren who had been disfellowshipped made a request to leave the company, which was granted.'" Perhaps Fuller and Leffingwell's difficulty, a situation Patty recorded on September 10, had some connection to the action, perhaps not.

224. Undoubtedly this was Keziah Brown (b. 1808), whose husband, Jesse Devine Hunter (1804–1882), was a member of the Mormon Battalion. Another of Hunter's wives, Lydia Edmonds, accompanied him with the battalion. Keziah was traveling with her children: Asa (b. 1832), Mary B. (b. 1834), Jesse (b. 1839), Samuel (b. 1841), and Martha (b. 1844). From all indications Mr. Hunter never came to Utah but was appointed Indian agent in California, had a try at the gold mines, and then became Indian agent in southern California, where he died. His wife Lydia died at San Diego on 27 April 1847, leaving one son, James.

225. John Young Greene (1826–1880), with Porter Rockwell, was a part of the Pioneer Company.

while the men were hunting catle went on she went on with them we have found the catle go 10 miles camp a good spring came out of the hill ran by the head of our corall sister Hunter ^ stoped camped with us ^ met Joseph Young with teams going back to help on the rear of the camp Porter and Green has gone back to the valey left this morning I gave them some crackers lent them two tin cups the mountains here are very high on each side some small pines on the north side of us **Monday 20** go 12 miles camp on weaver [Weber] river we have pased through one canion I drove through safe red majestic rocks on the right all the way P G caught two trout **21** Br Shelton pased with two yoke of oxen[226] stay here till noon to mend Parleys waggon made a new box Br Losson [James Lawson] did not get up last night came this forenoon start 1 oclock go 8 miles camp on a willow stream set the wagons any way John Smith turned his waggon over down hill sister hunters exaltree broke we put a pole under drove into camp there was more broke I was caled to Dealia Beach [Cordelia Williams, wife of Rufus Beach] in the night **Wednesday 22** divide the co each ten go by themselves we go 10 miles camp on a fork of weaver [Weber] river our waggons stand in the road I have took up some goosbery bushes [to plant] the Doctor [Darwin Charles Richards] broke his waggon twice P G shot a duck saw where a grisly Bear pased [Martin] Dewitt saw him **Thursday 23** Br Wipple pased us[227] we lost the bull here P G found him overtook us after we got almost over the mountain I drove ^ up and down ^ till he come had to leave one of my oxen he was lame go 10 miles camp on willow spring **Friday 24** go 14 miles P G went back and got the ox we drove him into the cannion left him got into the valley it is a beautiful place my heart flows with gratitude to God that we have got home all safe lost nothing have been blesed with life and health I rejoice all the time **Saturday 25** P G went back to help up the rear of his camp they have all got here safe some broken waggons but no broken bones I have drove my waggon all the way ^ but ^ part of the two last mts P G drove a litle I broke nothing nor turned over had good luck I have cleaned my waggon and myself and visited some old friends **Sunday 26** go to meeting hear the epistle read from the twelve then went put Lorenzo Youngs wife Harriet [Harriet P. Wheeler] to bed with a son [Lorenzo Dow, Jr.][228] the first male born in this valley it was said to me more than 5 months ago that my hands should be the first to handle the first born son in the place of rest for the saints even in the city of our God I have come more than one thousand miles to do it since it was spoken **Monday 27** I went to the warm

226. Sebert C. Shelton (1793–1857) was a member of the Mormon Battalion.

227. Edson Whipple (1805–1894) was a member of the Pioneer Company–undoubtedly on his way back to Winter Quarters.

228. The child died on 22 March 1848. (See Jackman and Hanks, "Ephraim Knowlton Hanks." Also see notes 200 and 287 herein.)

spring and bathed in it[229] it is a splended place **Tuesday 28** helped wash Br Smoots co has come in **Wednesday 29** I went to the bowery saw the Patriarch John Smith seal James Lawson to Mercy R. Fielding in the evening went to the fort Br Grant had got in with his wife [Carolyn Van Dyke] she was dead died last Sunday Br and sister Leonard were with him **Thursday 30** she was buried in the afternoon I visited sister Elen Kimbal[230] I anointed ^her^ and prayed for her ^we^ had a good visit

OCTOBER 1847

Friday Oct 1 visited sister Taft with sister Hamlinton[231] I have visited the sick Br Beaches wives[232] both sick and Br Pratts wife Belinda [Belinda Marden, 1820–1894] **Saturday 2** mended my dress visited sister Leonard with sister More had prayers and a good visit in the evening visited E R Snow[233] she has just come in this week has been a good time to me my heart has been glad in seeing my sister **Sunday 3** wrote a letter to Sylvia went to meeting they organised the counsel[234] **Monday 4** washed visited capt. Browns wife **Tuesday 5** Mary went away to the herd[235] I visited sister Elen Kimbal Mr Sessions and I

---

229. Warm Springs was located at Second West and Eighth North. A public bathhouse was constructed there in 1850. In the 1900s the facility was expanded and called the Wasatch Springs Plunge. In 1981 the Children's Museum of Utah was established at the site.

230. Ellen Sanders (1823–1871) married Heber C. Kimball on 5 November 1844. She accompanied him in the Pioneer Company.

231. Harriet Ogden (1807–1888) was married to Seth Taft (1796–1863), who had been part of the Pioneer Company. Harriet and their fifteen-year-old daughter traveled in the first hundred of the Big Company. The husband of Chelnechia Smith (1818–1870), Madison Daniel Hambleton (1811–1870) was a clerk in the first hundred of the Big Company.

232. Rufus Beach (1795–1850), with wives Cordelia Williams (1830–1907) and Laura Ann Gibbs (1814–1894), was in the fourth ten of Perrigrine's fifty of the Big Company.

233. Eliza R. Snow traveled with the Jedediah M. Grant Company that arrived in the Salt Lake Valley on 2 October 1847.

234. Patty was referring to the organization of the Salt Lake stake of Zion. "Father" John Smith was made president with Charles C. Rich and John Young as counselors. Brigham Young and all the apostles, except Lyman Wight, who was in Texas, were sustained to preside over the church. And a high council was chosen for the Salt Lake stake: Henry G. Sherwood, Thomas Grover, Levi Jackson, John Murdock, Daniel Spencer, Lewis Abbott, Ira Eldridge, Edison Whipple, Shadrach Roundy, John Vance, Willard Snow, and Abraham O. Smoot, most of whom have been mentioned in Patty's entries.

235. Perrigrine writes in his journal, ". . . after a journey of all most four months we landid in Great Salt Lake Valey on the twenty fourth of September 1847 all well

eat mince pie with her **Wuesday 6** [W *is written over a* T] Br Shaw [James B. Shaw] let me have a dress[236] Thorn starts back for winter quarter[237] ~~Wednesday~~ [Tuesday *is written on top of* Wednesday] Sister Rich died yestarday 5 buried today 6[238] sister Elen K[imball] made me a visit also sister Leonard was here **Thursday 7** I visited E R Snow also I went to father Smiths **Friday 8** I nit P G came home from the herd **Saturday 9** Covington paid me let me have a dress patern yestarday P G and his father got a load of logs for a house **Sunday 10** went to meeting **Monday 11** washed bed quilts some soldiers came in Mr Sessions has gone up to the herd **Tuesday 12** E R Snow was here more soldiers came **Wednesday 13** wrote a letter to Mother Br Dikes paid me two dollars **Thursday 14** visited sister Kimbal had a meeting **Friday 15** caled to Eliza Steward [Eliza Jane Stewart][239] she is very sick I dont think she will live sister Choshe [Phoebe Ogden Chase] visited me **Saturday 16** Br Bronell

---

and not a death had been while on the journey in my company of four hundread Souls yet severil children were born on the way staid with the maine camp five days I then took a herd of cattle and my family and started North here I made the first wagon track past the Hot Spring that was ever made traviled ten miles and camped with the heard of cattle here I had my hands full to take care of the cattle lived in my wagon as before . . ." (DPG, p. B-54). His wife, Mary, according to Patty, accompanied him. "The community which grew in an area from what is now North Salt Lake to Centerville—and included a portion of Woods Cross and West Bountiful—was first named 'Sessions Settlement.' The name was later changed to North Canyon and the final name of Bountiful was not approved until Feb. 27, 1855. Bountiful was incorporated as a 'city' on Dec. 14, 1892" ("The Wanderer Who Founded Bountiful Community," *Bountiful Centennial Quarterly* (Winter 1990): 6).

236. No doubt James Shaw was paying Patty for the delivery of a daughter to him and his wife Laura on 29 June 1847.

237. Joseph Thorn (1811–1886) had arrived on 25 September with the Abraham O. Smoot Company. Lorena Thorn (b. 1814), Joseph C. Thorn (b. 1839), and Helen S. Thorn (b. 1846) were traveling with the same company. However, Hosea Stout, although tardily chosen to be captain of the guard on the trip west, had stayed in Nauvoo and with others met and escorted returning pioneers to Winter Quarters. On 17 December 1847 Stout wrote, "At home. Some 20 more of the brethren came in from the valley today. Jos Thorn had also moved back with his family. He got dissatisfied" (Brooks, *Hosea Stout*, 1:291).

238. Nancy O'Neal Rich (1782–1847) was the mother of Charles Coulson Rich. She had accompanied the first ten of her son's guard company. They reached Salt Lake on 2 October 1847.

239. This name is confusing, because of Patty's entry on 14 December Eliza Jane Stewart (1832–1909) had been in Abraham O. Smoot's Company. She was the daughter of Ruthinda or Ruth Baker and George Stewart. At this time she was fifteen years old. There was an Elvira Steward, b. 1813, and there was a Mary Eveline Stewart, b. 1834, daughter of George and Ruthinda who died on 15 December 1846. See 14 December.

[Russell Gideon Brownell, 1818–1895] came with many others of the battallion **Sunday 17** went to meeting Mr Sessions came home from the herd ^got timber^ **Monday 18** he went up again after timber I was caled to aniont and lay hands on Eliza Steward I have been mending one of the soldiers clothes Br Bronells I have given Br Lovlin a comforter and a pair of mitens Br Straten gave him two pound six ounces flour[240] sister Whitney gave him two pound of crackers that was all I could get for him all though I tried many for some I gave them 22 pounds of dried beaf and 23 pounds of crackers and a pint cup full of butter and some ginger they started for winter quarters after dark **Tuesday 19** I went to a party to Hector Hates [Haight] Mr Sessions come home with another load of timber **Wednesday 20** he went again we set up our tent **Thursday 21** finished my stockins he came home with a load of timber **Friday 22** he went again sister Neff was here[241] **Saturday 23** E R Snow staid with me last night I went visiting with her to day went to sister Nobles P G came home with his Father with two load of timber **Sunday 24** P G went back with both teams we went to meeting **Monday 25** quilted Marthas peticoat **Tuesday 26** visited E R Snow and Claricy [Clarissa Decker (Young)] **Wednesday 27** weighed seeds that Brownell left here peas 61 3h wheat 24=3h corn 42=2h oats 24 2h buck wheat 10-3h beans 7=5h flax seed 4-3h millet 1 3h **Thursday 28** visited sister More **Friday 29** finished a pair of socks **Saturday 30** sisters E R Snow & Claricy & Leonard were here on a visit **Sunday 31** went to meeting to Claricys so cold could not have a public meeting to day

November 1847

Monday Nov 1 the wind blew our tent down and tore it to peices I was sent for to go to sister Brown [Mary McCree Black] it snowed I staid all night I have been lame for some time am very lame this morning **Tuesday 2** it is cold we have our stove in Br Leonards tent **Wednesday 3** had a meeting to Elen Kimbals **Thursday 4** put sister Brinkerhoof to bed with a son [Levi] born 8 oclock A M[242] **Friday 5** had a meeting at Claricy Youngs **Saturday 6** put sister Huffacre to bed with a son [David] born half after 12 P M[243] then put sister Tomas [Ann Crosby, wife of Daniel Monroe Thomas] to bed with a daugher [Nancy C.] born 1 oclock P M **Sunday 7** had a meeting at Claricy Youngs with the litle girls **Monday 8** put sister Brown to bed with a daughter [Mary Eliza] born half past 12 A M in the evening went to meeting at sister

---

240. Joseph A. Stratton (b. 1821) and Mary Ann Stratton (b. 1815) were in the same company as the Sessionses.

241. Mary Barr (1801–1875) was the wife of John Neff II (1794–1869).

242. Sally Ann Snyder (1815–1891) was married to James Brinkerhoff (1816–1875).

243. Elizabeth Melvina Richardson (1829–1911) was the wife of Simpson David Huffaker (1811–1891).

Elen Kimbals with the young ladies **Tuesday 9** went to sister Pearces sisters Brown ^money^ and Tomas ^black cloth^ paid me **Wednesday 10** cut out a coat for a soldier name Spidle [John Spidle, b. 1819] **Thursday 11** sewed on the coat did the work **Friday 12** finished the coat gave the making to him **Saturday 13** the ground is geting bare it has been covered with snow nearly for ten days warm and pleasant yestarday and to day **Sunday 14** visited sisters E R Snow and E Kimbal **Monday 15** we had a meeting to sister Witneys last Saturday night P G came down to day **Tuesday 16** Goodgen and Br came here to day[244] **Wednesday 17** put sister Hunt [Lydia Ordelia C. Elendon, wife of Gilbert Hunt] to bed with a daughter [Mary Ellen][245] **Thursday 18** we moved into our house[246] the men start for California **Friday 19** put sister Kingsbury to bed with a daughter [Bathsheba][247] **Saturday 20** visited her **Sunday 21** had a meting at sister Whitneys where she was in the evening went to a prayer meeting at Br Eldrige **Monday 22** put sister Smoot [Emily Hill Harris, wife of Abraham Owen Smoot] to bed with a son born 7 oclock A M in the evening prayed for Heber with Elen and Mary Elen [Kimball's wives] I anointed Elen acording to Hebers request when he met me on the road **Tuesday 23** visited sister Smoot she paid me one dollar fifty cents **Wednesday 24** quilted with Lucinia on her peticoat **Thursday 25** visited sister Love[248] **Friday ^26^** I was baptised[249] **Saturday 27** put up my curtains Mary came down I have been to meeting 5 times this week female meetings **Sunday 29 8** went to ^female^ meeting in the evening to public prayer meeting **Monday 29** visited at Br Pearses had a meeting in the evening **Tuesday 30** visited sister Elen Kimbals had a meeting in the evening **Wednesday** [*blotted out*] I visited sister Tafts

---

244. Probably Andrew Goodwin (b. 1810), who was a member of the Mormon Battalion.

245. Gilbert Hunt (1825–1858) was a member of the Mormon Battalion. His parents were Jefferson Hunt and Celia Mount.

246. Perrigrine writes in his diary, "Father and I had built a house in Salt lake City or in the fort the first thing was to build a fort by joineing house to house the house was built of logs sixteen by twenty four with too rooms my Father and Mother and a part of my family moved in this seamed a little like home once more I will here say that my Father and I lived as one family all the days of our lives and had all thins common as what was ones intrust was the intrust of all the Family . . ." (DPG, p. B-54). The fort was located where Pioneer Park is today.

247. Dorcas Adelia Moore (1828–1869) was the wife of Joseph Corroden Kingsbury (1812–1898).

248. Nancy Maria Bigelow (1814–1852) was the wife of Andrew Love (1808–1890).

249. Patty had of course been baptized when she joined the church. In early days it was customary to rebaptize so that members could renew their covenants.

December 1847

Dec 1 Thursday I visited sister Higbee had a meeting in the evening **Friday 2** visited sister Chase had meeting **Saturday 3** visited sister Meeks [Sarah Mahurin, b. 1802, wife of Priddy Meeks, b. 1795] had a meeting in the afternoon visited sister Scofield had a meeting in the evenning **Sunday 5** went to a public meeting in the evening to a public prayer meeting **Monday 6** E R Snow was here cuting garments she staid all night **Tuesday 7** visited with her at Mager Rusells[250] went in a good time to comfort them **Wednesday 8** had a meeting at sister Leonards we went **Thursday 9** Mr Sessions came home from the herd with P G and a load of timber has been gone a week bucthered an ox **Friday 10** took care of the meat **Saturday 11** tried the tallow snowed and cold **Sunday 12** sister E R Snow here **Monday 13** put sister Carrington to bed with a son [Young Brigham] born 7 oclock A M[251] **Tuesday 14** put sister Sophi Taylor [Sophia Whittaker, 1825–1887, wife of John Taylor] to bed with daughter [Hariet Ann Whittaker] born 6 oclock A M Mr Ses has gone to the herd **Weday 14** Elvira Steward died the first one that has sickened and died in the valley I gave her a sroud to lay her out her mother a widow visited with E R Snow and others at sister Hickenloopers[252] to a prayer meeting in the evening **Thursday 16** visited sister Nobles [Mary Adeline Beaman, 1810–1851, wife of Bates Noble] with E R Snow Mr Sessions came home with P G with timber **Friday 17** I went to sister Browns to an evening meeting **Saturday 18** Jirked meat **Sunday 19** went to a family meeting at Br Whiples partook the sacrement in the evening to a public prayer meeting to Br Wilis **Monday 20** visited sister Higbee had a meeting there in the evening **Tuesday 21** visited sister Hunt had a meeting in the evening **Wednesday 22** visited sister Brown had a meeting in the evening **Thursday 23** visited sister Writer[253] Dined there had a meeting in the evening went to a public meeting to Br Browns **Friday ^24^** set my dishes up in my cupboard **Saturday 25** P G and Lucinia came home from the herd **Sunday 26** the Brethren met at Br Writers to hear Br Pratt he did not come & none of the men would open a meeting Br Writer gave the meeting unto his wife she caled in a few sisters had a good

250. Samuel Russell (b. 1813) was captain of the second fifty of the Abraham O. Smoot Company, and Amasa Russell (1793–1863) was captain of the second ten of the second fifty.
251. Rhoda Mariah Woods (1822–1886) was married to Albert Carrington (1813–1899), a member of the Pioneer Company. Albert Carrington had graduated from Dartmouth in 1833. He was an early editor of the *Deseret News* and held offices in the provisional and territorial government.
252. Sarah Hawkins (1804–1866) was the wife of William Haney Hickenlooper (1804–1888).
253. Rebecca Wallerton (1815–1894) was the wife of Levi Evans Riter (b. 1805).

meeting some of the men staid with us **Monday 27** the patriarch John Smith was caled with many of the sisters to Br Wilises so that he might understand our order [Mothers in Israel] I presided had a good meeting put sister Celea [Seely?] to bed with a daughter Saturday night Dec 26 1 oclock A M **Tuesday 28** visited sister Gates[254] Br Pratt and others were there **Wednesday 29** visited sister Crisman[255] had a meeting in the evening I was caled out went and put sister Spencer to bed with a son [Jared] born Dec 29 half past 8 P M[256] **Thursday 30** visited Mary with E R Snow and others **Friday 31** the last day of the year visited sisters Houd[257] and homes [Holmes?] with sisters Snow and many others blesed them and was blesed by them

1848

I have worked in the garden untill I am allmost done out

JANUARY 1848

Saturday Jan= 1–1848 Mr Sessions myself and sister Snow and a number of others spent new years at Br Millers Br Jackman was there[258] he said it was the best meeting he ever had it was the best new years I ever spent we feasted then blesed and was blesed **Sunday 2** had a family meeting at Br Kimbals partook of the sacrement went to a publick [meeting] at Br Wilises **Monday 3** visited sister Carington babe it is very sick **Tuesday 4** it died this morning **Wednesday 5** put sister Brown to bed with a son [William] born 1h past 1[259] I then went to meeting at sister Higbees **Thursday 6** caled to sister Hess[260] I was invited to visit sister Taylor but had to stay with sister Hess put her to bed

---

254. Elizabeth Wilson (b. 1812) and George Gates (1811–1896) had been in Perrigrine's fifty.

255. Mary Hill (1814–1892) was the wife of Charles Crisman (1807–1893).

256. Emily Shafter Thompson (1819–1895) was married to Daniel Spencer (1794–1868). He had captained the first hundred of the Big Company so Perrigrine had been under his leadership.

257. Mary Ann Hunt (b. 1824) was the wife of John Erick Forsgren (1816–1890). Lucinda Morgan (1820–1902) was married to Simeon Fuller Howd (1823–1878). Patty delivered their daughter Elmira Permelia on 23 September 1848.

258. Probably Josiah H. Miller (1795–1865), who was married to Amanda Morgan (1795–1879). Levi Jackman (1797–1876) had been a member of the Pioneer Company.

259. Phebe Narcissa Odell (d. 1852) was the wife of William Brown, Jr. (1816–1899).

260. Emeline Bigler (1824–1862) had accompanied her husband, John Wells Hess (1824–1903), with the Mormon Battalion.

with a son [Jacob] 2*h* 6 P M **Friday 7** put sister Fouts to bed with a daughter [Miranda] 2*h* 5 A M[261] I then went and blesed Helen Kimbal with sister Chase in the evening caled to sister Lathrop staid all night **Saturday 8** put her to bed with a daughter born 2*h* 4 A M then went to a young Ladys meet-ing to sister Houds had a good meeting **Sunday 9** went to a family meeting the litle girls had a good meeting at our house in the afternoon **Monday 10** visited sister Cotchner [Kartchner][262] took dinner then blesed her and had a meeting in the afternoon **Tuesday 11** I had a number with sister Snow to visit me they took dinner then blesed me we then had a good meeting, **Wenday 12** Helen, Mary Elen, Mary Forsgrin, Violate Decker [Vilate Young] were here on a visit **Thursday 13** took dinner then had a meeting with Br and sis-ter Gates **Friday 14** I went to sister Uens [probably Ewing] to dine and have a meeting but I was caled a way to Charels Deckers [husband of Vilate Young] staid all day and night **Saturday 15** put her to bed 2 oclock A M [with a daughter, Miriam Vilate] we went at 10 to Br Hickeloopers dined then had a meeting **Sunday 16** I am quite unwell do not go to meeting put sister Secrist to bed with a daughter [Mary Elizabeth] born 5 2*h* P M **Monday 17** put sister Ester Russell to bed with a son born 1 A M[263] to day visit my sis-ters that I have put to bed am not well yet **Tuesday 18** not well fringed a handkerchief **Wednesday 19** mended sox **Thursday 20** visited sister whit-ney **Friday 21** quilted my peticoat got very tired **Saturday 22** caled to vio-late[264] she was very sick in the afternoon I went to see sister Sheets with sister Snow and Mary[265] I was caled to Violate again left my visit **Sunday 23** do not feel well and do not go to meeting out door had a meeting in the after-noon at sister Crisman for the litle girls **Monday 24** I was not well in body or mind sister Snow made me a cup of tea I felt beter **Tuesday 25** she came and staid all day with me I feel beter I sift over two beryls of flour **Wednesday 26** visited sister Davis[266] and had a meeting in the afternoon **Thursday 27** P G has come down to go and lay of land for himself and his ten returned does

---

261. Margaret Mann (1803–1896) was married to Jacob Foutz (1800–1848). He died on 14 February 1848.

262. W. D. Kartchner, his wife, and their child arrived with the Mississippi saints on 29 July 1847.

263. Ann Eliza Logan (1822–1878) was the wife of Jacob Foutz Secrist (1818–1855). Esther Hill (b. 1816) was married to Samuel P. Russell (b. 1813).

264. Vilate Murray (1806–1867) was Heber C. Kimball's first wife; they were mar-ried on 22 November 1822.

265. Susanna Musser (1827–1861) was married to Elijah Funk Sheets (1821–1904). They traveled in the same pioneer company as the Sessionses.

266. Elizabeth Davis was born in 1794. There was also Mariah Davis (b. 1834), both in the Abraham O. Smoot Company.

not like the land goes home[267] **Friday** he came down again Sister Snow and I visited Adline Benson **Saturday 29** we with several others visited sister Hamlinton Thursday night put sister Horn to bed with a miscarriage **Sunday 30** I went to sister Snows we had a good time she spoke in toungues great things I interpreted **Monday 31** we visited sister Dilworth [Eliza Wollerton, 1793–1876, wife of Caleb Dilworth] took dinner then had a meeting

FEBRUARY 1848

Feb=Tuesday 1 visted sister Higbee with sister Snow and Mary **Wednesday 2** I was makeing me a dress. **Thursday 3** had a meeting at sister Savages[268] **Friday 4** my birth day 53 years old to day Father Abot and wife and sister Snow was here Father Smith and wives did not come[269] we had a good visit in the evening Br Jackman [Levi Jackman, 1797–1876] was here I enjoyed myself well I then went and put Jane Taylor to to bed with a son [Richard James] born 10 PM[270] **Saturday 5** went to meeting at sister Millers Lucinia came down here **Sunday 6** ^I^ did not go to meeting all the rest went **Monday 7** P G came down Lucinia went home with him **Tuesday 8** put sister Snow [Melvina Harvey, 1811–1882, wife of Willard T. Snow] to bed with a pair of twins daughters [Helen and Ellen] born one 2 3h the other 3 A M I then visited with sister Snow and others and dined with sister Pomeroy [Irene Ursula Haskell, 1825–1860] had a good meeting in the afternoon **Wednesday 9** had a meeting at sister Higbees to pray for the Patriarch Father Smith, Mr Sessions went up to the herd P G stays here **Thursday 10** we had a meeting at sister Savages **Friday 11** visited sister Ensign [Mary Bronson, 1806–1888, wife of Horace Datus Ensign] in the evening I went to Jane Taylors to the blesing meeting of her babe She made a feast **Saturday 12** we had a meeting at sister Hendricks[271] **Sunday 13** put Elen Kimbal [Ellen Sanders] to bed with a son

---

267. This date is earlier than the one given in the JH (24 September 1848) for the start of land distribution (see Arrington, *Great Basin Kingdom*, 51, for a discussion of the method of apportioning land).

268. Mary Abigail White (1823–1904) was the wife of David Leonard Savage (1812–1886).

269. Lewis Abbott (1795–1861) and Ann Marsh (1800–1849) were in the same pioneer company as the Sessionses. But Rufus Abbott (b. 1784) and Anna (b. 1787) were in the second fifty of the same company. Patty could have meant either one. John Smith had married Clarissa Lyman in 1815, and Ann Carr (b. 1790), Miranda Jones (b. 1784), Mary Aiken (b. 1797), Julia Hills (b. 1783), Asenath Hurlbert (b. 1780), and Rebecca Smith (b. 1788) all in January of 1846.

270. Jane Ballantyne (1813–1900) became John Taylor's third wife in 1844. Leonora Cannon was the first and Elizabeth Kaighin the second. At this time there were eight in all.

271. Drusilla Dorris (1810–1881) was the wife of James Hendricks (1808–1870).

[Samuel Chase] born 8 P M I was invited to sister Oens to tea and to meet-ing[272] but did not get through with Elen time to go **Monday 14** Sally brought the skins home that she smoked I then went to visit sister Taylor with sisters Snow and Gates in the forenoon in the after noon we went to a party at Br Horns **Tuesday 15** we had a meeting at sister Alens to pray for her she is sick and has been for some time **wednesday 16** went and anoint-ed and layed hands on sister Higbee she was healed **Thursday 17** we visited sister Riter and took dinner then had meeting in the after noon **Friday 18** Mr Sessions and I and sister Snow prepared a dinner and caried it to Father Smiths we eat he and his family eat with us he blesed us with a patriarchal blesing[273] I gave him two dollars in money for Mr Sessions and mine he gave E R Snows to her she came home with us staid all night in the night I was caled to sister Alens she was dead and her babe **Saturday 19** sister Snow staid all day made me a cap **Sunday 20** no public meeting snow and mud prevented **Monday 21** we had a meeting to Willard Snows his wife and child sick we visited at Br Leonards in the evening **Tuesday 22** Br Snows babe died his wife is beter but a young man that lived there ate some roots and it is supposed he was poisoned with the roots he died this afternoon ^and^ Mr Sessions and I visited at Hazen Kimbals this evening **Wednesday 23** I atended the funeral this afternoon Br Grant preached **Thursday 24** had a visit in the forenoon and then a meeting at sister Shockleys [Mary Shockley, b. 1799] Br Pedigrew and Hancock was there[274] Br Pratts wives Elizabeth and Agatha was here on a visit in the evening[275] Br Bringherst [William Bringhurst, 1818–1883] and wife [Ann Wollerton Dilworth, 1821–1898] also here **Friday 25** we had a meeting at sister Youngs we took dinner at Br Nebekers[276] first sister Hunt and Wilkey was here on a visit to day[277] **Saturday 26** I put Susan wife of David Fairbanks to bed with

272. Sister "Oens" was probably Elizabeth Pickle (b. 1826), the wife of Seeley Owen. His first wife, Lydia Ann or Adaline, had died on 19 September 1846. He mar-ried Elizabeth on 22 March 1847.

273. Patty records her patriarchal blessings in a later journal. They are not included in this book.

274. James Phineas Pettigrew (1825–1879) and George Washington Hancock (1826–1901) had both been members of the Mormon Battalion.

275. Elizabeth Brotherton (b. 1817) had married Parley P. Pratt on 24 July 1843, and Ann Agatha Walker (1829–1908) married him on 28 April 1847.

276. Probably John Nebeker (1813–1886), who was married to Lurenia Fitzgerald (1819–1898).

277. Most likely both Celia Mounts (1805–1897), wife of Captain Jefferson Hunt (1803–1879), and Isabella McMere Wilkey (b. 1821), wife of David Wilkey/Wilkie/Wilkin (1819–1891), accompanied their husbands with the Mormon Battalion.

a daughter born 4 1*h* A M[278] sisters Tomas and Nolan was here on a visit[279] **Sunday 27** I went to a female meeting to Br Smoots we took supper and visited in the evening there a boy was kiled instantly to day by a log roling from the saw his name John Oakey[280] put Eliza wife of James Alred to bed with a daugh^ter^ [Eliza Maria] born 12 P M[281] **Tuesday 29** put Ann wife of Henry Nebechar to bed with a son [Ammon] born at 4 *h* A M[282]

MARCH 1848

Wednesday March 1 visited those two sisters **Thursday 2** we had a meeting at sister Shockleys Delia Beach was here on a visit we sent 20 dollars off yestarday to bye a cow let Br Rogers have 13 lb of dried beaf to cary with him to Callifornia **Friday 3** went to Father Smiths got our blesings caried them some butter & milk **Saturday 4** caled to sister Mores [Eunice Sibley Bliss] then went & had a meeting to sister Wilcox **Sunday 5** I went to a public meeting then to sister Turnbows [Sylvira Caroline Hart] we had a meeting there **Monday 6** caled to sister More dined at sister Loves with sister E R Snow **Tuesday 4** put sister More to bed with a pair of daughters [Eunice and Ester] first born 2:2*h* second 3 A M sowed winter wheat last week by freesing it first before sprouting **Wednesday 8** I have sent Sylvia a letter dated March 5 **Thursday 9** put Hannahett [Hannahetta Snively, 1812–1898, wife of Parley P. Pratt] to bed with a daughter [Lucy] born 10: 1*h* A M **Friday 10** sent for to go to John Sessionses ^wife^ [Mary Emmeline][283] **Saturday 11** put her to bed with a daughter born 1 - A M Mary and I visited sister E R Snow I finished fringing my handkerchief **Sunday 12** went to meeting **Monday 13** mending **Tuesday 14** sewed **Wednesday 15** put Elizabeth wife of [*space left*] Grundy to bed with a daughter born 5 P M **Thursday 16** put Susan wife of Lorenzo Rounday to bed with a son [Wallace Wesley] born at 4 P M[284] **Friday**

278. Susan Mandeville (1819–1899) was married to David Fairbanks (1810–1895).

279. Amanda Thomas (1827/28–1909) was married to Jabus or Jabez Townsend Nowlin (1821–1893), who was in the Mormon Battalion.

280. John Oakey would have been almost six years old, having been born on 21 March 1842 in Hancock County, Illinois.

281. Elizabeth Bridget Manwaring (1821–1866) and James Tillman Sanford Allred (1825–1905) had both accompanied the Mormon Battalion and had arrived in the Salt Lake Valley just three days after the Pioneer Company.

282. Henry Nebeker (b. 1818) and Harriet Ann Van Wagoner (1817–1899) were married on 6 January 1847. She had formerly been married to John Havens.

283. John Sessions (1821–1896) and his wife had both been part of the Mormon Battalion. Apparently they were not related to David Sessions.

284. Elizabeth Hudson Hendricks (1827–1893) was the wife of Isaac Grundy (1813–1891). Susannah Wallace (b. 1818) was married to Lorenzo Wesley Rounday (1819–1876).

17 visited those that I have put to bed then put Lois wife of Leonard E Harrington of a daughter born 9 2*h* P M[285] **Saturday 18** sister Snow was here with sister Holmes[286] **Sunday 19** Br Wiple and Elen [Sanders] was here **Monday 20** commenced to finish my sampler that I began when I was a girl and went to school **Tuesday 21** sister Snow was here **Wednesday 22** put Letisha wife of Allen Smithson to bed with a son born 4 P M **Thursday 22** I went to the funeral of Lorenzo Youngs babe[287] it died with fits **Friday 24** snowed **Saturday 25** snowed **Sunday 26** P G and Lucina came home **Monday 27** snowed and melted on the house leaked bad **Tuesday 28** rained some ^the^ house leaked some Mary Elen [Harris] here cut Carlos a coat **Wednesday 29** it storms and the house leakes bad **Thursday 30** Storms snow and rain some the house leaks some this morning clears off **Friday 31** frose some last night fair weather to day we have had a wet bad time one night we sat up one night most all night it rained down through the house so I diped up much water in the house and caried out we had no floor and it was very mudy and our things wet to day we have got the most of our things dry not a house in the fort but what leaked but we feel to thank the Lord for the rain and snow for the land needed it very much

APRIL 1848

Saturday April 1 we washed our things up got them dry I then went and put Nancy wife of Laren Farr to bed with a daughter [Julia] born 9 1*h* P M[288] **Sunday** visited her and others that I had put to bed then see sister Snow had a good time with her in private conversation **Monday 3** made soap **Tuesday 4** worked at it again Sisters Chase and Richardson was here visiting[289] **Wednesday 5** finished my soap made over 1·00 lb best kind then went to a

---

285. Loise or Louise Russell (1822–1902) was the wife of Leonard E. Harrington (1816–1883).

286. Jonathan Harriman Holmes (1806–1880) had been a member of the Mormon Battalion. He had married Marietta Carter (1820–1840) on 13 April 1837 and then Elvira Annie Cowles (1813–1871) on 1 December 1842/44. Elvira was sealed to Joseph Smith on 1 June 1843. On 28 January 1972 approval was given by the First Presidency of the church for her first daughter, Lucy Elvira (b. 1845), to be sealed to Joseph Smith and Elvira. This would assure that Lucy Elvira and Elvira would be eternal members of Joseph Smith's family. Elvira appears often in Patty's diary.

287. This must have been the child Patty had delivered on 26 September 1847, the first male child born in the valley (see notes 200 and 228).

288. Lorin Freeman Farr (1820–1909) and Nancy Bailey Chase (1823–1892) would become key people in the settlement of Ogden, Weber County, Utah.

289. Olive Harnden Richardson (b. 1786) was the mother of Darwin Charles Richardson (1812–1860), who is usually referred to as Dr. Richardson by Patty.

^female^ meeting to sister Chases **Thursday 6** the church has been organ-
ised 18 years to day We females had a prayer meeting to day at sister Adline
Bensons to pray for the Brethren that were at winter quarters and elsewhere[290]
I then went and put sister Mary wife of Samuel Ensign to bed with a son born
April 6- 7 P M[291] **Friday 7** I was visiting at Susan Hunters [Susanna Wann,
1825–1885, wife of Bishop Edward Hunter] with sisters Taylor Snow Pearce
Hunter &c was caled a way to sister Love she was like like to miscary went
back and finished my visit **Saturday 8** caled to Peter Nebecchars [Nebeker,
1822–1883] wife [Elizabeth Davis, 1829–1851] **Saturday 9** put her to bed
with a daughter [Susannah Elizabeth] born 4 P M it has snowed nearly all day
Monday 10 I sewed all day making me a dress **Tuesday 11** put [*space left*] wife
of Tomas Benbo [Thomas Benbow] to bed with a daughter born 10 2*h* A M[292]
Wednesday 12 visited her she has consumtion do not think she will live long
I also went with sister Snow to see sister Love she is beter **Thursday 13** I was
with Elizabeth [Whittaker, 1828–1880] wife of Joseph Cane [Caine,
1822–1857] **Friday 14** put her to bed this morning with a daughter [probably
Elizabeth Turner] born 6 A M **Saturday 14** butchered an ox sister Shirtleifs
child died with fits[293] **Sunday 16** rained and slit yesterday lent Robinson 24
pounds beaf last Friday I was at Brother Ensigns to the blesing of his babe by
the Patriarch **Monday 17** took care of the beaf **Tuesday 18** sowed the garden
seeds **Wednesday 19** Mary Elen [Harris] and Elen [Sanders] was here cut a
coat for Mr Sessions I cut 2 pair pantaloons for him **Thursday 20** cut a pair
for Carlos baked mince pies **Friday 21** I helped Mr Sessions lay down a floor
the first floor that I could set my foot upon as my own for more than two years

290. Three weeks after the arrival of the Pioneer Company in the valley, two groups
turned back toward Winter Quarters to guide others westward. The first group
of 71 men and 33 wagons was led by Tunis Rappley and Shadrach Rounday;
the second group of 108 men was headed by Brigham Young and Heber C.
Kimball. Although the population increased with the arrival of the sick detachment of the Mormon Battalion and the Mississipi saints, this left fewer than 180
people in the valley until the arrival of the Big Company, since others had gone
to California to relay instructions to the remaining Mormon Battalion members
and those called the New York Mormons, who had sailed to California with
Sam Brannan. The two groups that went to Winter Quarters returned in late
September and October of 1848 with more than 2,000 people and 4,000 animals
(see Kimball, *Mormon Pioneer Trail*, 137; see also the epilogue in Knight and
Kimball, *111 Days to Zion*).

291. Mary Everett Gordon (1811–1868) and Samuel Ensign (1805–1885) had been
in the first hundred with the Sessionses.

292. Sarah Holmes (b. 1820) and Thomas Benbow (b. 1823) were both born in
England.

293. Elizabeth Loomis (b. 1816) and Vincent Shurliff (1814–1893) probably lost their
daughter Susan E., born on 28 March 1847 in Nebraska.

I have lived on the ground all the time and been moving in the evening I went to a meeting feast and the blessing of Br Canes babe **Saturday 22** visited with E R Snow at Br Abots I then was caled to see sister Molon[294] she was very sick **Sunday 23** I went to meeting **Monday 24** I put up my bed curtains visited sister Molon **Tuesday 25** put Mary my sons wife to bed with a daughter [Julia] born 5 2*h* P M **Wednesday 26** put Mary wife of [*space left*] Nolon to bed with a son born 1 A M Lucinia washed Mr Sessions went home to the farm with P G we sisters met to pray with and for sister Molon by her request I presided over the meeting we had a good meeting She said she was beter **Thursday 27** I hung up our beaf to smoke it rained and I had to take down my curtains and other things the house leaked **Friday 23** it still rains part of the time I was caled to sister Sheets [Susanna Musser Sheets] put her to bed with a daughter born 6 2*h* P M **Saturday 29** visited them that I have put to bed found them all doing well then went to the warm spring with sister Higbee and Kimbal and bathed in it **Sunday 30** rained the house leaked I visited sister Snow Mr Sessions and I laid hands on her she was beter

May 1848

Monday May 1 put Elizabeth [Young] wife of Edmond Elsworth to bed with a daughter born 1 A M it rained hard the house leaked bad **Tuesday 2** Lucinia went home and Agnes Sparks came here to take care of Mary for her board **Wednesday 3** it rained hard we got some more dirt on the house so that it does not leak to day **Thursday 4** but it has soaked through and it leakes now bad I was up nearly all night to keep Mary and the babe and things dry it rains and snows nearly all day **Friday 5** it has cleared of cold frose hard kiled many things in the garden **Saturday 6** frose again last night **Sunday 7** cold I did not go to meeting **Monday 8** put black Jane to bed with a daughter born 10 2*h* A M **Tuesday 9** I now have to take care of Mary and her babe and do the rest of the work her breasts very sore and her babe very troublesome I have been up 2 and 3 times a night with it ever since it was born **Wendsday 10** I cut out some pantaloes for P G and Carlos **Thursday 11** worked on my dress **Friday 12** much to do got very tired **Saturday 13** finished my dress Mr Sessions come home from the farm been gone a week goes again to morrow **Sunday 14** we went to meeting he then went to the farm **Monday 15** I worked the garden planting was then caled to Reuben Alreds wife[295] **Tuesday 16** she is still sick she will miscarry quite an excitement the ^Ute^ Indians have killed 2 of wanshops [Wanship] sons and the news came that they had killed 2 of our men but we sent and found out the thruth and fears ceased but

---

294. Laurany Huffaker (b. 1809) was the wife of Jesse Molen (1805–1852).

295. Reuben Warren Allred (1827–1916) and Elzadie Emeline Ford (1827–1887) had both accompanied the Mormon Battalion.

the most of our people left their farms and ran to the fort[296] **Wednesday 17** sister Alred miscaried this morning I have been there the most of the time since she was sick **Thursday 18** Br Braisier is diging a well for us[297] has got it done Mr Sessions came home **Friday 19** I worked in the garden **Saturday 20** P G came down drove down another cow Br Singley has herded one cow 25 days he takes the other tomorrow morning herds both for 3 cents per day **Sunday 21** she got away and was not herded we went to meeting partook of the sacrement **Monday 22** put sister Fouts to bed with a son born 10 A M[298] I wrote a letter to Sylvia ^windsor^ and David send it by Mc Bride[299] the cow is come back to the herd **Tuesday 23** worked in the garden **Wednesday 24** got a watter pot made paid 75 cents cash found all [cows] **Thursday 25** I dreamed that I saw David he said he was glad he was here he would stay that he was going to get maried to morrow but he must fight a duel for the girl he shoo^k^ hands with me and kissed me and I kised him I then awoke **Friday 26** sister [Phoebe] chase here on a visit I sold her a dress patern to pay for a floor **Saturday** I worked on my sampler we have letice and redishes **Sunday 28** a hard frost we went to meeting partook of the sacrement **Monday ^29^** sister E R Snow was here in the fore noon I then went to the feast and blesing of Br Houtz babe it was a great blesing by the Patriarch **Tuesday 30** Mr Sessions has gone to the farm to keep the crickets off of the crop they are taking all before them that they come to the frost kiled a good deal **Wednesday 31** I worked in the garden

---

296. *The Life Story of Brigham Young* records, "In the earliest days of the settlement a band of yelling savages came down to the fort in Salt Lake City. Wanship, their chief, who was at war with Little Wolf, had taken two Indian girls prisoners, had killed one and they were torturing the other . . ." (Susa Young Gates and Leah D. Widtsoe [New York: Macmillan, 1930], 136). Leonard Arrington gives different information: "The first important contact the Mormons had with any of these groups was in the fall of 1847, after Brigham, Heber, and others had gone back to pick up their families in the Missouri Valley. A group under the leadership of Wanship, a small Ute band, had fought the rival Little Wolf's band and, although losing two men, took two teenagers, a boy and a girl, as prisoners . . ." (*American Moses*, 210). Whether or not the stories are related, Patty confirms that the following spring, months before Brigham's return to the valley, Wanship created panic among the settlers.

297. Richard Brazier (1793–1871) had been with the Mormon Battalion.

298. Who this Foutz is cannot be determined. Jacob Foutz was captain of the second fifty of Edward Hunter's hundred. Foutz's group arrived on 1 October 1847. He was forty-seven. He had no sons old enough to be married, although his daughters were. There were no other Foutzes who emigrated in 1847.

299. Either Samuel McBride (1789–1874) or John McBride (b. 1788) must have been going back east. They had emigrated in the Edward Hunter Company.

JUNE 1848

Thursday June 1 put Olive wife of Erastus Bingum to bed with a daughter born 10 A M[300] **Friday 2** visited sister Richardson **Saturday 3** I visited Elen Kimbal and altered my silk dress **Sunday 4** went to meeting **Monday 5** put Elizabeth wife of William Laney to bed with a son born 11 P M[301] **Tuesday 6** visited at Bishop Hunters with sisters Taylor Snow and Pearce it rained P G it watering his wheet **Wednesday 7** I am making soap **Thursday 8** made some canker medicine for sister Nebechar **Friday 9** finished my soap Porter got home and many others from california **Saturday 10** put Hanna wife of Asel Lathrop to bed with a son born 5 2 *h* A M bought me an armed chair paid in soap **Sunday 11** went to meeting Porter spoke in his own defence[302] **Monday 12** put John Chase wife to bed with a daughter [Clarissa] born 4 A M at the saw mill[303] **Tuesday 13** put Clarisa wife of Lewis Robison to bed with a son born 11 1*h* A M[304] **Wednesday 14** worked in the garden **Thursday 15** Lucinia came down I worked in the garden every day nights and mornings **Friday 16** cut and fixed some ^3^ dreses **Saturday** put Lurenia wife of John Nebechar to bed with a son ^John^ born 3 -3*h* P M **Sunday 18** went to meeting **Monday 19** worked in the garden **Tuesday 20** worked in the garden **Wednesday 21** put Fanny wife of Dimic Huntington to bed with a daughter born 7 P M[305] **Thursday 22** put

---

300. Erastus Bingham, Jr. (1822–1906) was a member of the Mormon Battalion and married to Olive Hovey Freeman. His father, Erastus Willard Bingham, had been a captain in the Sessionses' pioneer group.

301. Elizabeth Scearce (1822–1908) was the wife of William Laney, Sr. (1815–1891).

302. The JH for 5 and 9 June 1848 says that Porter Rockwell had led some members of the Mormon Battalion back to Salt Lake and "Spoke in his own defence." According to Richard Lloyd Dewey, "In October [1847] a captain of the Mormon Battalion, Jefferson Hunt, returned from duty in California and offered to lead a company of hand picked men back to California to make necessary purchases for the Valley Saints' survival . . . Porter was one of those picked . . . Porter refused to make the return trip. Undoubtedly he felt taking the southern route again was suicide. . . . [Much later] He and James Shaw . . . rounded up 25 discharged veterans who needed to return to the valley. . . . Seven weeks later they arrived . . . in one-half the time of Hunt's disastrous trek. . . . Upon Porter's arrival in Great Salt Lake City he was asked to answer charges of deserting John Hunt's party. Porter pleaded his case before the High Council on June 11 and they dismissed it" (*Porter Rockwell: The Definitive Biography* [New York: Paramount Books, 1986], 147).

303. John Darwin Chase (1815–1902) and Almira Higgins (1830–1873) had both been with the Mormon Battalion.

304. Clarissa Minerva Duzett (1822–1891) was the wife of Lewis Robinson (1816–1883).

305. Dimic Baker Huntington (1808–1879) and his wife, Fanny Maria Allen (1810–1894), were both with the Mormon Battalion. They were parents of the

Susan wife of Job Sidwell to bed with a son [William] born 1 2*h* A M[306] Mr
Sessions came home sick **Friday 23** he is no better I gave him some medicine
Saturday 24 he is better I have worked in the garden untill I am allmost done
out **Sunday ^25^** went to meeting **Monday 26** worked on my sampler
Tuesday 27 worked on it again **Wednesday 28** got Carlos in to sister
Dilworths School[307] **Thursday 29** run the watter through our garden **Friday
30** watered the garden then put sister Holmes to bed with a miscarriage

JULY 1848

Saturday July 1 finished watering the garden Mr Sessions came home just as I
got it done **Sunday 2** I was so tired I could not sleep last night did not go to
meeting **Monday 3** we washed Mr Sessions went back to the farm **Tuesday 4**
put sister Gustan [Mary Peterson, 1805–1865, wife of Thomas Jefferson
Gustan] to bed with a son born 2 2*h* A M it has rained some to day
Wednesday 5 worked in the garden **Thursday 6** sister E R Snow was here
Friday 7 Mr Sessions has come home I have worked hard all the week to take

---

first child of American parents born in Colorado. The infant was born on 21
October 1846 and died on 9 November in Pueblo. Dimic Huntington was noted
as an Indian interpreter and drum major of the martial band.

306. Susan Robinson (1808–1891) was the wife of Job Sidwell (1801–1877).

307. Mary Jane Dilworth (1831–1877) was the first schoolteacher in Utah, according
to the JH. According to Gates and Widtsoe (*Brigham Young*, 283–84), she opened
her school in a tent on the west side of the fort in October of 1847. Later, meeting houses were used for schools until buildings could be constructed. Mary Jane
was the daughter of Eliza Wollerton and Caleb Dilworth. Speaking of the first
building used for a schoolhouse, Oliver B. Huntington, a schoolteacher at the
fort, wrote, "The houses were all built as a part of the fort wall, with portholes
for defense in case of an attack by Indians, and generally with a six-light window
opening to the inside of the fort. The roofs consisted of poles or split logs laid
close together and covered with cedar bark that grew about the marshes. Such
was the general makeup of the first schoolroom, with an immense quantity of
dirt piled on the flat roof as a probable protection from the rain. For a floor we
had a similar but more solid material than that of the roof—hardened clay. The
one window was just large enough for six panes of 8 x 10 glass; but we lacked
the glass; it was not to be had, for there was no store in all this territory.

And while I think of that matter, we did not need any glass, for we had no
sash; and there was no sawmill. . . . So we were wont to take some thin cotton
cloth, and oiling it, or rather greasing, we would then tack it to what primitive
window frames we had. . . .

For writing tables some man's wagon box was torn to pieces and laid on
trestles. Seats or benches were made in the same way. Our stove was a fireplace,
a real spacious liberal fireplace, in which we burned cedar or sagebrush. But we
were so healthy and warm-blooded then that we needed but little outside fire to
keep us warm . . ." (Kate B. Carter, ed. *An Enduring Legacy*, vol. 10 [Salt Lake
City: Daughters of Utah Pioneers, 1987], 385).

care of the cows calves and garden **Saturday 8** I bought a mare of a Spanyard gave him 5 dollars cash and 12 lb flour 25 cents per pound $800 I also bought a buffaloe robe gave 8 lb flour and an old tin bason caled the robe 2-50 **Sunday 9** did not go to meeting Mr Sessions is going back again **Monday 10** we washed **Tuesday 11** cut and made me some collars **Wednesday 12** put sister Elizabeth to bed with a son born 1-2h A M then helped get a bean out of Joseph Scofields nose[308] **Thursday 13** I have been sick all night E R Snow came here staid a day and night with me I am very sick all day the Elders came and adminestered to me the pain left me but I am very weak **Friday 14** do not set up much Mr Sessions came home to night **Saturday 15** I sit up but little to day **Sunday 16** hear from Winter Quarters do not go to meeting I am not able **Monday 17** P G and Robert is reaping wheet **Tuesday 18** I am some beter can walk out **Wednesday 19 Thursday 20** P G has done reaping and gone home **Friday 21** making me a collar **Saturday 22** visited sister Peirce with sister Bringherst and Snow **sunday 23** do not go to meeting have to watch the garden **Monday 24** worked so hard I could not sleep sister Snow was here **Tuesday 25** I went with her to sister Loves visiting **Wednesday 26** I have been around to get some flour that we have lent out untill I am tired allmost out and to get it sent to the farm[309] I then put Edward Hunters wife [Mary Ann Whitesides, 1825–1914] to bed with a daughter [Margaret] born 2 2h P M **Thursday 27** sister E R Snow was here **Friday 28** Sister Taylor I hear that Marth has left P P

308. Joseph Schofield (1809–1875) was married to Clarissa Aurelia Terry (b. 1820) and was a member of the Pioneer Company.

309. In 1882 Priddy Meeks wrote about the famine caused by crickets and other misfortunes. "The famine was so sore before I went in the mountains to hunt," he writes. "My wife went to Sister Cessions, a very prominent woman among the rich women, and a verry good woman, too. I think if it had not been for her husband, he was thought to be a great miser, they had an abundance of flour on hand and he burried it in the earth to hide it. My wife says, 'Sister Cessions, won't you let me have a few pounds of flour? I will try and pay you for it.' 'Yes,' she said, and appeared to be quite sorry for her destitution and seemed to pity her verry much. 'How much a pound will I have to pay you?' 'Oh, I think about ten cents a pound.' 'And I am verry thankful to get some and I am willing to pay that much.' After some more talk on the subject, she says, 'I think the flour should be about twelve and a half cents a pound, seeing it is so scarce and hard to get.' My wife said, 'If you think so, I will pay it.' And after a little more santemonious talk and pitying of my wife's situation, she says, 'I think I ought to have fifteen cents a pound.' I do not know the answer my wife made to this, but one thing I do know, she let her keep her flour, which being burried in the ground they lost the whole of it, and the old man lived but a year or two after and died. I do not know what became of the old woman, while my wife survived the hardships she had to suffer and is now in 1882 alive and well and enjoying a clear conscience, which is worth more than all their flour" ("Journal," p. 20, typescript, Utah State Historical Society, Salt Lake City).

Pratt[310] **Saturday 29** ^plenty of green corn cucumbers squash^ **Sunday 30** not able to go to meeting **Monday 31** we watered the garden

AUGUST 1848

Tuesday August 1 P G began to thrash **Wednesday 2** I worked on my sampler visited at sister Bringhirst with sisters Dilworth and Writer **Thursday 3** put Eliza Dewell to bed with a son [William Henry] born 7-2h A M **Friday 4** put sister Lucinda Smithson to bed with a daughter born 1 P M[311] **Saturday 5** ~~cut straw~~ ^cut straw^ **Sunday 6** I went to meeting heard from the cos back I got a letter my Br and one from Sylvia she is not coming this year I feel bad about it **Monday 7** wrote a letter to her **Tuesday 8** sister Houd was here on a visit **Wednesday 9** made preparation for a feast **Thursday 10** went to the bowry 9 A M[312] saw the liberty pole raised heard the cannon fired then between 12 and 2 feasted after 2 danced heard the music and the prayers and preaching **Friday ^11^** wrote a letter to my Br then put Loiza wife of Shumway to bed with a son [Charles M.] born 3 P M[313] **Saturday 12 Sunday 13** went to meeting finished my letters to Mother and Br and one to Sylvia send them by Br Standige[314] **Monday 14 Tuesday 15** sewed **Wednesday 16** mended Mr Sessions came home sais Lucinia is sick **Thursday 17 Friday 18** sister Benson was here on a visit **Saturday 19** Abigail Abbot here on a visit[315] **Sunday 20** did not go to meeting **Monday 21** sister E R Snow and Maryanet Pearce here on a visit **Tuesday 22** put sister Rice [Lucy Whitter Gear, d. 1913, wife of William K. Rice] to bed with a son [William Kelsey] born 3 2h A M I then caried a web to sister Gustan to weave then finished my Sampler that I commenced when I was young **August 22 1848 Wednesday 23** I visited to Dr Richardsons **Thursday 24** sisters Taylor Horn and Hunter was here on a

---

310. This would be Martha Monks (b. 1825), who married Parley P. Pratt on 28 April 1847. One child, Ether, was born on 30 January 1849 and died on 22 February. Martha leaving Pratt is not mentioned in his *Autobiography*. The dates do not fit together properly; whether Martha left Parley, returned, and left again is unclear.

311. Eliza Avery Whiting (1819–1872) was the wife of William Henry Deuel (1812–1891). Lucinda Wilson (b. 1813) was married to William Cox Smithson (1804–1889).

312. The Bowery, situated on the Temple block, was built of upright timbers, covered over with boughs and brush. The first public building in Salt Lake City, it was the meeting place for religious and community gatherings.

313. Louisa Minnerly was the second wife of Charles Shumway; his first, Julia Ann Hooker, had died at Winter Quarters.

314. Henry Standage (1818–1899) had been with the Mormon Battalion. He was probably on his way to his wife, Sophronia Armenia Scott, who had not yet come to the valley.

315. Abigail Abbott (1829–1854) had been in the second ten of Perrigrine's fifty. On 26 December 1850 she married Albert Tyler.

visit **Friday** ^25^ I flowered a collar **Saturday 26** Mary has gone to the farm **Sunday 27** I did not go to meeting **Monday 28** washed Elizabeth Hendricks was here on a visit[316] **Tuesday 29** I made shirts calico the first wagon came from winter Quarters Seth Dodge [1821–1882] **Wednesday** ^30^ frost this morning^ some more come inn **Thursday 31** they keep coming

SEPTEMBER 1848

Friday Sept 1 snow on the mountain the frost did no harm I put Martha wife of Sanford Bingham to bed with a son born 4- 2*h* P M[317] Mary came home again they brought down the rest of the wheet we had 1-00 bushel brought down mellons to sell **Saturday 2** Mary went back we took care of the wheet **Sunday** I visited sister Snow she is sick **Monday 4** Lucinia came home here **Tuesday 5** more waggons come in **Wednesday 6** put sister Badger to bed with a son[318] ~~Thursday 7~~ wrote a letter to Sylvia 6 of Sept **Thursday 7** put sister Church to bed with a son [Haden Wells][319] ^**Friday 8**^ **Saturday 9** visited sister Tomas **Sunday 10** Elen Kimballs babe sick **Monday 11** rode out 12 miles to sister [Agnes] Sparks **Tuesday 12** came home Mr Sessions got some new corn ground **Wednesday 13** Lucy and some others came in **Thursday 14** saw Clary Chase **Friday 14** more came in **Saturday 16** I was sent for to go back over the mountains to a sick woman I was not well and did not go she had twins both grown together **Sunday 17** not well did not go to meeting **Monday 18** washed sisters Dillworth and Writer here visiting **Tuesday 19** more came in **Wednesday 20** Brigham & family came in **Thurday 21** [Thurday *written on top of* Friday] he and wife here with her mother and his daughter and feasted on mellons Marthas birth day She has a party here **Friday 22** I have seen many of my friends **Saturday 23** put sister Howd [wife of Simeon Fuller Howd] to bed with a daughter [Elmira Permelia] born 2 2*h* P M **Sunday 24** went to meeting Brigham preached Heber and his co came in **Monday 25** washed sister Buel was here on a visit **Tuesday 26** put sister Tubs to bed with a daughter born 5 A M[320] **Wednesday 27** carded wool **Thursday 28** spun knit **Friday 29** I have had co every day this week **Saturday 30** Elen Sanders babe is dead & buried yestarday I went and had her come to our house to comfort her she said she had not felt so composed since it died

---

316. Elizabeth was a daughter of Drusilla Dorris and James Hendricks.

317. Martha Ann Lewis (1833–1898) and Sanford Bingham (1821–1910) were neighbors of Patty.

318. Nancy Garr (1822–1900) was married to Rodney Badger (1823–1853), who was a member of the Pioneer Company.

319. Sarah Ann Arterbury (1824–1889) was married to Haden Wells Church (1817–1875) of the Mormon Battalion.

320. Sophia and William Tubbs (b. 1824) had been with the Mormon Battalion.

OCTOBER 1848

Sunday Oct= 1 I went to meeting Adison Pratt was there[321] had returned from the sandwich Iland been gone more than 5 years Brigham & Heber took supper with us **Monday 2** I washed I am not well **Tuesday 3** ironed not well **Wednesday 4** some better **Thursday 5** to[day] is a feast day for the soldiers I have cooked for confrence it rained & the feast was put off **Friday 6** we met sung & prayed and ajourned the conference untill Sunday the soldiers had thier feast **Saturday 7** Mary Elen cut Mr Sessions a coat Br Kimbal was here **sunday 8** went to conference caled away put sister [Celia] Mount [wife of Jefferson Hunt] to bed **Monday 9** wrote a letter to Sylvia washed &c **Tuesday 10** Br Whitney wife Br Kimbal Sarah Ann [Whitney] Mary Elen [Harris] sister Buel [Precindia Lathrop Huntington] all here to dinner sister whitney staid all night **Wednesday 11** she staid till almost noon Loizas [Louisa Beaman (Young)] babe died this evening I was there laid it out **Thursday 12** Lucinia has been sick to day **Friday 13** she is sick to day **Saturday 14** I put her to bed with a son 5 A M sister Susan Hunter was here on a visit yestarday she set up with the [babe] to night the babe had a fit to day **Sunday 15** it is better P G and Mary came down to day and went back **Monday 16** I have to work hard **Tuesday 17** Mother [Elizabeth] Davis washed for me **Wednesday 18** Lucinia babe sick sister Mansfield set up with the babe left 11 oclock I then set up the rest of the night **Thursday 19** it died 5 oclock this morning buried it 5 P M its name Perrigrine **Friday 20** ^P G & Mary went home^ Mr Sessions came down **Saturday 21** sent the team back **Sunday 22** Lucinia not so well **Monday 23** she is better Mary Elen came here sick I laid hands on her **Tuesday 24** she is better the rest of the soldiers has come **Wednesday 25** I am quite sick **Thursday 26** no better Eliza Harriman [Elizabeth Jones] worked for [me] **Friday 27 Saturday 28** a little better **Sunday 29** put Fanny wife of Lanson Coleby to bed with a daughter born 2 2*h* P M[322] **Monday 30** nailed down my carpet Br Leonard got his shoulder broke **Tuesday 31** I am not well

321. Addison Pratt (1802–1872) had left Nauvoo on 1 June 1843 for a mission to the Society Islands. He and his companions arrived on the island of Taubai on 30 April 1844, where Addison began the first branch of the church organized on the Pacific islands. On his way home he met members of the Mormon Battalion and Samuel Brannan, who appointed Pratt to preside over the San Francisco branch. After he arrived in the valley on 28 September 1848, he reported on his mission to Brigham Young and stayed for about a year, during which he taught the Tahitian language at his home. He was sent on a second mission to the islands in 1850; his wife, Louisa Barnes (1802–1880), and four daughters followed in October. In 1852, when he was banished by the French, he returned with his family to San Francisco, became disaffected, and never returned to Utah (see Kathleen Perrin, "Year of Church in Tahiti," *Church News*, 7 May 1994, p. 12).

322. Fanny Knight (1829–1893) was the wife of Alanson Colby (1811/13–1880).

NOVEMBER 1848

Wednesday Nov 1 Thursday 2 Mr sessions came home Lucinia and I visited at Dr Richardsons he came took supper with us **Saturday 4 Sunday 5** went to meeting Father Kemton got whiped from the stand[323] **Monday 6** Eliza washed for us **Tuesday 7** ironed was at sister Buels in the evening **wednesday 8** sister Buel here all day **Thurs 9 Friday 10 Sat 11** [Almina] Bills has got Mr ^Ses^ and P G coats made P G had a trial concerning the man he found[324] **Sunday 12** did not go to meeting ^made a cow[l]^ **Monday 13** cut Mr Sessions a vest **Tuesday 14** Lucinia washed **wednesday 15 Thursday 16** cut 5 pair of pantaloons **Friday 17** put Emily Spery to bed with a [daughter, Philinda Amanda][325] **Saturday 18** sister snow here on a visit I went and looked at our lot **Sunday 19** went to meeting **Monday 20** Lucina and Carlos went up to the farm to live **Tuesday 21** here alone Martha went with them to is coming back to live with me **wednesday 22 Thursday 23** Harriet Young here on a visit **Friday 24** Martha Ann came home **Saturday 25 Sunday 26** I went to meeting **Monday 27** I washed and ironed **Tuesday 28** put Sarah Ann wife of Isaac Laney to bed with a daughter [Sarah Ann] born 10- 2h P M[326] **wednesday 29** made soap **Thursday 30** the mail come in from the states

DECEMBER 1848

Friday Dec -1 John Gean [1806–1859] came here I got a letter from Sylvia **Saturday 2** Mr Sessions came home **Sunday 3** went to meeting heard much news &c Lyman Whites pamphlet read and he cut of from the church[327] **Monday 4** twisted thred **Tuesday 5** wash **Wednesday 6** Loiza Zina Precinda and sister Ashba [Martha Ashby] here on a visit I went and put sister Litle to bed with a pair of twins son [Joseph] born 10- 2h daughter [Josephine] 11 2h

---

323. Wilford Woodruff's journal does not describe this specific incident but mentions a "Brother" Kempton, who several times was "whipped" by Brigham Young from the stand (see *Wilford Woodruff's Journal*, ed. Scott G. Kenney, 9 vols. [Midvale, Utah: Signature Books, 1983], 4:44, 47–48, 63, 113).

324. The JH does not mention the trial, nor does Perrigrine's diary. Eliza R. Snow adds this information: "sat. 16th Trial aginst Perrigreen Sess. Yest. & today—ajourned till tomorrow."

325. Emily Louisa Miller (1827–1908) was the wife of Charles Sperry (1829–1914).

326. Sarah Ann Howard (1822–1902) was the wife of Isaac Laney (1814/15–1873).

327. Lyman Wight was once a member of the Quorum of the Twelve Apostles, but he rebelled along with George Miller. His pamphlet was entitled, "An Address by way of an abridged account and journal of my life from February 1844, up to April 1848, with an appeal to the Latter-day Saints, scattered abroad in the earth." It disputed the leadership of the Quorum.

P M[328] **Thursday 7** snowed **Friday 8** went to see the twins then went to sister Loves **Saturday 9** worked on Marthas dress **Saturday 10** snowed **Monday 11** Dr Bernhizle moved into our house[329] P G kiled an ox sent us 2 quarters fore & hind **Tuesday 12** took ^care^ of it **wednesday 13** very cold the Dr man froze his feet **Thursday 14** very cold **Friday 15** more moderate thaws **Saturday 16 Sunday 17** cold and snows **Monday 18** melted snow to wash put Charlotte Snow [Charlotte Merrill, 1825–1850, wife of Lorenzo Snow] to bed with a daughter [Roxcy Armatha] born 8 - 2*h* P M **Tuesday 19** washed **wednesday 20** ironed **Thursday 21** old sister Huntington here on a visit[330] **Friday 22** Brigham here took dinner with us
[A big blotch appears at the top of a new page—as if she had spilled the ink; then there is the following entry:]
a daughter born–**Tuesday 18**––Mores babe died **Sunday 19 1848 Saturday 23** ^went to sister Holmes ^Mr Sessions went to Neffs Mill **Sunday 24 Monday 25** christmass[331] Martha Ann went to Br Pearses to dinner **Tuesday 26 wednesday 27** sisters Love and Miller was here on a visit **Thursday 28** sister Pearce was here on a visit **Friday 29** Lucinia came down **Saturday 30**
[She lines the following entry above and below:]
a week ago to day I went to sister Holmes to celebrate Joseph Smiths birthday[332] **sunday 31** Lucinia went home Marth Ann went with her Mr Sessions [went to meeting]

---

328. Hannah Hull (1816–1893) was married to Andrew Lytle (1812–1870), who was a member of the Mormon Battalion.

329. John Milton Bernhisel (1799–1882) described himself as a doctor of medicine. He had graduated from the University of Pennsylvania in 1820. Among many contributions to the church, Bernhisel had testified in behalf of Joseph Smith and visited him in jail prior to the martyrdom. He was the first elected representative from Utah Territory and a member of the board of regents of the University of Deseret; he also selected books for Utah's first library.

330. The first wife of William Huntington, Sr., Zina Baker Huntington (1786–1839), had died. He then married Lydia Clisbee (Partridge), widow of Edward Partridge. Patty may be referring to Lydia, who was born in 1793 (only two years before Patty) and died in 1878.

331. The Christmas holiday as we know it seems not to have been part of the Sessions lifestyle, although Patty mentions Christmas while they were in Winter Quarters. Evidently, in Nauvoo children attended school on 25 December (see Roger A. Hendrix, "I Have a Question," *Ensign* [December 1992]: 28).

332. Evidently Joseph's birthday was celebrated regularly. In 1881 the *Woman's Exponent* reported: "Thursday, December 23d ult. was the anniversary of the birth of the Prophet Joseph Smith, one of the grandest, noblest men, who ever lived. It was celebrated in the 16th Ward Assembly Rooms, with a gathering of his old friends and members of his family, and others who revere his memory, as the leader of the last dispensation. . . ." "Anniversary Gathering," *Woman's Exponent* 9 (1 January 1881) 116.

[Patty must have needed to clarify her entry of 4 February 1848. Father John Smith seems to have objected to the women's meetings. Since Patty respected him, she wanted to patch up any misunderstanding. The next entry—out of order—and a page with some figures and lines conclude her writing in the little leather book Sylvia had given her mother before the Nauvoo exodus.]

Feb 4 – 1848 my birth day Father Abot and wife was here and sister E R Snow I invited Brother John Smith and wives but Father Abot told me that Father Smith told him that I was trying to take the advantage of his weakness and get him here to one of my meetings he told me this at night after seeing it was nothing but a visit to celibrate my birth day sister Snow and I thought it best to go down there she took a cap that she had made she gave the making I gave the border and the ribin as we had promised when I gave them the invitation to come here I took some fried cakes and some sugar I gave that to Father Smith sister Snow gave Mother Smith the cap told him that she gave the making and that I gave the triming he blessed me and said many good things to me and we left with good feelings **Sunday 6** Father Abot caled again ^told me^ sister Leonard said that there was as good sisters as I was and she could have a meeting without me or sister Snow he also told that Mary Pratt had been misrepreting some of our words that we said at sister Cotchners caring the idea that we thought we stooped very low to visit her this we know was false

[The inside of the back cover reflects Patty's unique bookkeeping methods.]
July 1 crosed river   crackers
since

		money cts	flour lb	meal lb	corn lb	bush	meat 20
Dec	1st	2400	1 50	31	47	3 2h	
	9	1=00	50	10	10	1	
	12	2 00	29	6			
	13						
	16–			22		1	
	26–	1 00					
	28–	2:28					
	29–	1 00					
Jan	4–	1 00					
	9		28				
	26–				leather 3 dollars		
Feb		50					
	3	2 84	2 84				
	15	31	31				
	20	28	28				

                                25
                                388
                                10 04
                                284
                                115
[written at an angle alongside the above:]
fort John   550
ferry   125
independance   50
pass   51
[upside down on the back page:]
Dr domestic   silk
     cott   cloth   calico
Dec   yds
    12 –   13   –   2   10 fancy
    14   11   watch
                                twisst
                                caps
[On a folded piece of blue paper inserted into the diary is the following recipe (written in different handwriting):]
       "Teaples Eyewater"
           1 oz White Vitrol
           1 oz Sugar Sead
           The Whites 1 Doz Eggs
           2 Qarts Rain Watter
Put the watter in A pot
Boil the watter with whites of the Eggs
Steady til there is about 3 pts then
strain it of then put it into jar
or pitcher then stir it every 10
minutes for 2 hours keep it just a blood heat then stand still
keep it a stedy boil for 24 hours
then cork it up tite in a bottle
for use
[A note from David Sessions on the bottom reads]
Mar 4 I wis you to make some of this as soan as you can I. and Phebe would
have been down and took dinner with you but she is sick we must go home I
will call for some of this sunday David
[in Patty's writing:]
for eye water
I wrap two eggs in a wet cloth and roast them till quite hard then grate or
pound them fine then add half oz. of white vitrol mix it well together then add

one pint of warm rain or snow water and keep it warm for three hours often stiring or shaking it then strain it through a fine thick flanel and bottle it up for use

[On the opposite page, upside down, as if it had been folded:]
Cure for gravel wild rose berrys boiled long drink the tea

Diary one (1846–1848) has a very aged, dark tan leather binding and is 6 x 3¾ inches in size. Near the beginning of 1848 until the end, larger 6½ x 4 inch pages have been inserted. Almost as if she intended to notarize her record, Patty wrote the dates she began and ended the book in large ink figures on the front and back cover. She used brown ink, except for the months between July 1846 and June 1847, when she used blue. Evidently brown ink was easier to make and lasted longer. Courtesy of LDS Church Archives; photograph by J M Heslop.

DIARY TWO, 1849–1850

The Book of Mormon (Ether 2:3) records, "And they did also carry with them deseret, which, by interpretation, is honey bee. . . ." This symbol captured the imagination of the Mormons, as well it might. Their social ideal resembled a swarm of bees buzzing around the same hive. Indeed, the desert they settled came to be known as the State of Deseret. No one fit the image of honeybee better than Patty Sessions. Approximately a year and three months in the Salt Lake Valley had elapsed when she began her second diary, which reflects a flurry of activities in her personal life and in the settlement. Zion was proliferating as an influx of new persons—babies and emigrants—entered the scene. From the first moment any of the Latter-day Saints arrived, they were caught up in the building of the Mormon kingdom. They sought not only to provide for their families but to establish a stable economy for others who were treading the increasingly well-worn trail west.

Local government emerged during these years, but it was not very distinguishable from the church. The place was building, we can visualize, with a fervor akin to a frantic frenzy. Although the severity of the winters of 1848 and 1849 created trials, although hunger proved to be a major foe, the saints worked unitedly to solve their difficulties. Patty's racing entries reflect the energy expended in Zion. Virginia Woolf, a dedicated diarist herself, understood that mindset:

> *I have just re-read my year's diary and am much struck by the rapid haphazard gallop at which it swings along, sometimes indeed jerking almost intolerably over the cobbles. Still . . . if I stopped and took thought, it would never be written at all, and the advantage . . . is that it sweeps up accidentally several stray matters which I should exclude if I hesitated, but which are the diamonds of the dustheap.*[1]

In effect Woolf is describing the diaries of Patty Sessions.

---

1. Virginia Woolf, quoted in Mary Jane Moffat and Charlotte Painter, *Revelations: Diaries of Women* (New York: Vintage Books, 1975), 13.

1849

this day will be long remembered by thousands . . .
this is the begining of a new era with us

JANUARY 1849

Jan 1–1849 Monday I have staid at home made Artificials[2] had no co enjoyed myself well it has thawed rained a litle Mr Sessions gone to a prayr meeting this evening & Martha Ann to her Fathers [Perrigrine's] I alone **Tuesday 2** Martha came home rained some **Wednesday 3** we went to P Gs with Br Pearce and wife had a good ride and visit **Thursday 4** Mr Sessions and P G went to the bank ofice Mr Sessions had some talk with with Brigham about going back **Friday 5** I feel bad I went to Dr [Darwin Charles] Richardsons [1812–1860] with sister Bringhers [Ann Bringhurst, 1821–1898] on a visit the men came and spent the evening yestarday **Saturday 6** I still feel bad in my [*torn off*] is no better **Sunday 7** Br [Cornelius Peter] Lott came here talked with Mr Sessions[3] **Monday 8** I still feel bad **Tuesday 9** I was caled to sister

2. One decoration in pioneer homes was a glass globe, which covered wax fruit, flowers made from wool, cloth, or silk, or sometimes even preserved natural flowers. Also hair flowers and wreaths were created and framed to adorn the home. The wax fruit was made with plaster of paris, white wax, cardboard, and paint. The women would make a box from the cardboard, mix enough plaster of paris to cover one half of the chosen fruit, arrange the fruit, and allow the mixture to set. The fruit was then removed, the mold smoothed, and a hole cut on each side. The entire surface and the mold were greased, the fruit replaced, and plaster of paris poured over the entire arrangement to form a second mold. When it was set, the cardboard was removed and two perfect half-molds were left, into which melted white wax was poured. The two halves were fastened together and shaken to keep the wax in motion. When cooled, the fruit was removed and painted. If imperfections or unevenness occurred, the process was repeated. From the entry of 22 June, it would seem that Patty was making artificial flowers, but she could have been making fruit—or both. (See Kate B. Carter, ed., *Heart Throbs of the West*, vol. 2 [Salt Lake City: Daughters of Utah Pioneers, 1940], 473.)

3. Cornelius Peter Lott (1798–1850) had come west with the Pioneer Company. The "Journal History of the Church of Jesus Christ of Latter-day Saints" for 7 January 1849 records, ". . . In the evening President Brigham Young, Heber C. Kimball and Newel K. Whitney attended High priests Quorum meeting in the fort, at which David Sessions was disfellowshiped for breach of covenant, etc." The entry for 14 January 1849 reads, "President Brigham Young . . . attended a meeting of the High Priests' quorum in the evening where he spoke with great power on different subjects. David Sessions acknowledged his error and was restored to fellowship" (hereafter cited as JH, Archives of the Historical Department, Church of Jesus Christ of Latter-day Saints, Salt Lake City).

Buel her child was born but thought to die untill I got there Br Kimball and Elen came there to see us **wednesday 10 Thursday 11** I was caled to Willard Snows Susan was sick[4] I staid all day and all night she was a criple and was deformed so that her child could not be born with out instruments the Dr came ^Friday morning and^ delivered her with instruments the child alive but she died in a few minutes the case of the kind I never witnessed ^before^ although I have practised midwifery for 37 years and put thousands to bed I never saw a woman die in that situation before **Saturday 13** we have a cow sent down from the farm yestarday I have had co all day **Sunday 14** went to Susans funeral heard good preaching **Monday 15** Mr Sessions goes to the farm to stay all the week **Tuesday 16** Martha washed **Wednesday 17 Thursday 18** cut a dress for Martha Ann **Friday 19** Drs ^mother^ sister Richardson [Olive, b. 1786] here on a visit yestarday **Saturday 20** I made 2 wreaths for weding **Sunday 21 Monday 22 Tuesday 23** made artificials **wednesday 24** I went to sister Holmes **Thursday 25** it thaws a good deal **Friday 26** still thaws **Saturday 27** put Minerva White [Snow] to bed with a son [Erastus White Snow] born 2 A M ~~Sunday 28 went to meeting~~ I then visited sister Precinda with many more in the evening John Pack and wife here on a visit[5] **Sunday 28** I went to meeting to Br Mcbrides **Monday 29** we washed **Tuesday 30** ^visited Ruth[6] and Mary Elen [Harris]^ **Wednesday 31** worked on Martha Ann bonnet

FEBRUARY 1849

Thursday Feb=1st I made artificials for sisters Shirtlief Charlotte Cob & Edeth Pearce here on a visit[7] Martha has got a new pair of shews **Friday 2** making cap triming **Saturday 3** P G and Mary & Carlos came down I went to

---

4. Susan Harvey (1808–1849) had married Willard Trowbridge Snow on 14 May 1837. He was married to Melvina Harvey the same day and had a wife, Mary Bingham.

5. John Pack (1809–1885) had crossed the plains with the Pioneer Company. He had been married on 20 October 1832 to Julia Ives; on 21 January 1846 he married Nancy Amelia Boothe, Ruth Mosher, and Eliza Graham.

6. Heber C. Kimball had three wives named Ruth: one was Ruth L. Pierce (1818–1907), whom he married on 3 February 1846. She had been married to Monroe Cazier, with whom she bore six children. She separated from Kimball and on 14 August 1861 married John Harrington. Also on 3 February 1846 Heber married Ruth Amelia Reese (1817–1902). On 7 February 1846 Ruth Wellington (b. 1809) was married and sealed to Kimball; his biographer, Stanley B. Kimball, says that Ruth Wellington may actually have married Kimball on 23 July 1844.

7. These were probably Charlotte Cob(b?), who was married to Elijah Drake on 25 May 1815, and Edith Eveline Pierce (1836–1917), daughter of Robert and Hannah and sister of Margaret and Mary. She married James Madison Fisher on 12 February 1857.

sister Clarisa Hoit[8] she miscaried **Sunday 4** my birth day 54 years old **Monday 5** made a wreathe for wedeing **Tuesday 6** made artifils [artificials] **wednesday 4** made more **Thursday 8** ~~Friday~~ put Lois [Judd] to bed with a daughter wife of Benjamin T Mitchel [Benjamin Thomas Trotter Mitchell, 1816–1880] born 11 P M **Friday 9** worked on pantaloons **Saturday 10** visited some. **Sunday 11** I am lame with irisiplus in my foot[9] **Monday 12** made artificials **Tuesday 13** done the same had co **Wednesday 14** I am still lame **Thursday 15** worked on artificials **Friday 16** done the same **Saturday 17** finished my fringe for a bed dress **Sunday 18** went a meeting at Zinas **Monday 19** washed sent ten bushels of wheet to mill the bolt goes **Tuesday 20** put Adline to bed with a son [Oliver Goddard] born 2 - 2*h* A M she is wife of Lorenzo Snow[10] **wednesday 21** made a wrethe **Thursday 22** made and worked a peticoat **Friday 23** very warm the snow goes fast it is very mudy and has been for some days **Saturday 24** warm **Sunday 25** some cut of from the church for loose conduct **monday 26** we washed **Tuesday 27** sewed **wednesday** nit fringe I was with the Drs wife [Jane Cyrene Cobleigh (Richardson), 1817–1892] she had a son

March 1849

Thursday March 1 I visited Zina and Lora and laid hands on Loria Martha has gone to the farm today **Friday 2** I am doing many things **Saturday 3** made some bitters[11] and carried to Loria **Sunday 4** put Eliza wife of H Heriman to bed with a son born 10 P M[12] **Monday 5** I visited a sick babe willam Snows **Tuesday 6** warm and mudy ^martha came home^ **wednesday 7** Br Kimbals women here on a visit Ruth and Mary Elen **Thursday 8** **Friday 9** still mudy **Saturday 10** **Sunday 11** P G and Mary came down staid all night **Monday 12** Elected the officers[13] **Tuesday 13** I have had co all this

8. Clarissa Amanda Miller (1829–1904) was the wife of Israel Hoyt (1828–1883).

9. Erysipelas, an acute skin disease caused by streptococcus, claimed eight lives in 1850 (see Ralph T. Richards, *Of Medicine, Hospitals, and Doctors* [Salt Lake City: University of Utah Press, 1953], 21).

10. Mary Adaline Goddard (1812–1893) had been married first to George Washington Hendrickson. She married Lorenzo Snow in 1845.

11. A liquor having a bitter taste.

12. Henry Harriman (1804–1891) and Elizabeth (Eliza) Jones had come to the valley with the Heber C. Kimball Company of 1848. They had experienced a good deal of suffering in Missouri and Illinois and were called upon to colonize various places. In 1857 Henry Harriman, who was one of the first seven presidents of the Quorum of Seventy for more than fifty-three years, was asked at age fifty-two to take charge of a company of missionaries to Great Britain. This company pulled handcarts back across the plains.

13. The first election of political officers took place on this date. According to Juanita Brooks (*Diary of Hosea Stout*, 2 vols. [Salt Lake City: University of Utah

week **wednesday 14** co again Br Heber and Mary Ann[14] and Sarah Ann [Whitney] here on a visit Thursday too[k] Br Comton in to board few days[15] Agreed to take J Redings wife [Naomi Eliza Murray, 1830–1869] to board **Friday 16** co again **Saturday** very mudy it has stormed some almost every day for some time snow and rain **Sunday 18** we went to meeting **Monday 19** rained and snowed again **Tuesday 20** snow again **Wednesday 21** Jackson Redings wife came here to live **Thursday 22** he came here to board untill he goes away ~~mu~~ the mud dries up fast I went to visit sisters Ruth and Mary Elen Kimbal **Fridayday 23** I worked on artificials **Saturday 23 Sunday 24** went to meeting **Monday 25** ^Dr Bernhisel moved away^ commenced making soap worked at it **Tuesday 27 wednesday 28** and **Thursday 29** finished sister [Judith Hughes] Higbee here on a visit **Friday 30** made artificials and visited sister Laura Pitkins **Saturday 31** ~~I went to meeting~~

APRIL 1849

Sunday March [April] 1 I went to meeting **Monday 2** washed **Tuesday 3** commenced a letter to Sylvia **Wednesday 4** brade straw **Thursday 5** caled to sister Briant sent for to come home put Noama wife of Jackson [Redding] to bed with a son [William Carlos] born 6 P M **Friday 6** conference commence I did not go **Saturday 7** I sewed a straw hat **Sunday 8** went to meeting conference ajourned till Oct 6 the weather has been wet and very cold weighed ^gold dust $^ 65 - 35 to send to the states for goods **Monday 9** ^Redin left^ finished my letter to Sylvia ^Reedon left^ washed **Tuesday 10** had co sisters [Vilate] Murr[a]y & Frances [Jessie Swan] Kimball put Caroline wife of Benjamin T Mitchel [Caroline Conrad, b. 1828] to bed with a daughter born 7 2*h* P M **Wednes 11** put my letter in the mail **Thursday 12** I baked bread for Br Cumton [Compton] to carry with him as he caries the mail back **Friday 13**

Press, 1964], 2:348), 655 votes were cast for Brigham Young for governor, Willard Richards for secretary, Heber C. Kimball for chief justice, and Newel K. Whitney and John Taylor for associate justices. Also elected were a marshal, attorney general, treasurer, assessor, road supervisor, and twenty justices of the peace, most of whom were also bishops of their respective areas.

14. Mary Ann Shefflin (1815–1869) married Heber C. Kimball on 4 February 1846. They were separated in 1850, and she married Alfred Walton. She is buried in the Kimball cemetery.

15. Allen Compton joined the Mormon Battalion, leaving a sick family behind in little shelter after their home was burned by a mob. He became ill himself and was left to winter at Pueblo, Colorado. In the spring of 1847, he was sent to Ft. Laramie, overtook the Pioneer Company on Green River, and entered the valley on 22 July 1847. He started back on 14 August and joined his family on 18 November 1847. He returned to the valley with the first mail to come to Utah, arriving on 30 November. After April conference he was sent back to Council Bluffs to build boats and ferry the saints across the Missouri.

made out a bill of goods to send back for ^goods^ send one hundred & eight dollars gold dust **Satturday 14** Br Cunton starts with the mail **Sunday 15** did not go to meeting put sister Lemon to bed with a son [William McLure] born 6 P M[16] **Monday 16** washed **Tuesday 17** worked at artificials **Wednesday 18** worked in the garden sewed ionions **Thursday 19** sewed Beats **Friday 20** visited [Willard Glover] McMullins babe it is sick[17] **Saturday 21 Sunday 22** went to meeting **Monday 23** washed **Tuesday 24** visited the sick **wednesday 25** made a hat **Thursday 26** put sister Baker to bed[18] **Friday 27** McMullens babe died I have visited the sick **Saturday 28** P G and Mary came down Organised the [Nauvoo] Legion[19] **Sunday 29** do not go to meeting take care of Marys babe **Monday 30** make artificials

May 1849

Tuesday May 1 washed **Wednesday 2d** Martha Ann commenced going to school **Thursday 3** sewed more garden seeds it rained yestarday and last night wet the ground well and we feel thankful for it **Friday 4** sewed Peas **Saturday 5** planted the first corn here P G planted last week on the farm **Sunday 6** I went to meeting **Monday 7** washed **Tuesday 8** E R Snow was here on a visit **Wednesday 9** sisters Kimbal whitney & cushon[20] ^& Snow^ were here on a visit **Thursday 10** Christeen here cut me a dress **Friday 11** McMullen wife and sister Dodge [Lovina Braden, b. 1822] here on a visit **Saturday 12** sisters Clerks here Naoma gone to see her mother **Sunday 13** I put Alzada wife of Reuben Alred to bed with a daughter born 6 P M **Monday 14** washed **Tuesday 15** I went up to Br Kimbals & Whitneys & Youngs **Wednesday 16** sewed on my dress **Thursday 17** visited ^with^ Naoma sisters E R Snow & Holmes at [*smeared:* Br Kimbals, *and replaced by*] Wolices [George Benjamin Wallace, 1817–1900] House Hebers wives live there I also got some tins made for

---

16. Catherine Mayer (b. 1808) was the wife of William McClure Lemmon (b. 1808).

17. Probably Willard Glover McMullin, born on 2 June 1848 in Winter Quarters.

18. This would almost certainly be Charlotte Wiear Leavitt (1820–1906), who was married to Simon Baker (1811–1863) on 8 April 1843. Simon was a widower with eight children. He and Charlotte had a daughter, Abigail Leavitt, born on 7 January 1846 in Nauvoo, and also an infant Benjamin, who was in the emigrating company. A daughter Charlotte reportedly was born on 5 April 1849, but Patty's date is more likely correct.

19. The Nauvoo Legion, organized in 1840, was a militia of between three and four thousand volunteers and an important organization in Nauvoo. It was reorganized in Salt Lake City. On the same date as Patty's entry, 28 April 1849, Hosea Stout wrote, ". . . To day the Legion was organized according to the appointment last Sunday . . ." (Brooks, *Hosea Stout*, 2:351).

20. Helen Janette Murray (1826–1901) was married to Hosea Cushing (1826–1857), a member of the Pioneer Company.

Alzadas babe it is a criple I think it can be cured it is reel footed **Friday 18** I
have been droping corn this morning **Saturday 19** P G & Mary came down
here Mary & I went to Br Peirces on a visit **Sunday 20** Mr Sessions & I went up
to P Gs it rained **Monday 21** we came home **Tuesday 22** Mr Sessions went to
mill it rained & hails very cold **Wednesday 23** the house leaked bad it still rains
& snows the snow covers the ground all white Martha pushed it off of the roof
of the house with a rake corn up six inches peas in bloom all under snow 12
oclock the sun came out and cleared off but not very warm **Thursday 24**
rained & snowed very cold the ground frose this morning **Friday 25** more moderate the cold has killed but litle **Saturday 26** quite warm we have sewed some
may peas to day the widow [Mary Fielding] smith here on a visit[21] we let her
have some flour **Sunday 27** we went to meeting **Monday 28** washed **Tuesday
29** ironed **wednesday 30** braided straw **Thursday 31** visited Sister Buel

JUNE 1849

Friday June 1 [*smeared:* go] split straw **Saturday 2** it raining we got water on
the garden **Sunday 3** went to meeting a foot **Monday 4** washed **Tuesday 5**
ironed **wednesday 6** sewed a hat **Thursday 7** fixed my dress **Friday 8** fixed
another **Saturday 9** P G and Lucinia & Carlos down here we went to sister
Smoots a litle while **Sunday 10** went to meeting **Monday 11** we washed there
is many here every day after bread stuff and we keep letting it go they say they
have none and ours still holds out **Tuesday 12** set out beet and cabage plants
old Br Baldin died last night[22] I have had co all day sisters Wm= Young [Leah
Smith] McMilen & Spaldin[23] **Wednesday 13 Thursday 14** sisters Pearce and
Bringherst here on a visit the Boys come down to plow among the corn **Friday
15** P G birthday he is [*space left*] years old today [Perrigrine would have been
thirty-five] he is here with Mary and child he is having a trial before the counsel ajourned untill to morrow 3 oclock **Saturday 16** the counsel set again
ajourned again utill 3 oclock tomorrow **Sunday 17** Mr Sessions and Martha
has gone up to P Gs with Mary I stay alone my spirits cast down I feel bad yet
my trust is in God he is my all and on his holy name I call for his spirit to direct

21. The widow of the martyred patriarch, Hyrum Smith, had arrived in the valley
    in September 1848 (see Ivan Barrett, *Mary Fielding Smith* [n.p.: RIC Publishing
    Co., 1984]).

22. Caleb Baldwin (1791–1849) was arrested with Joseph Smith and they shared a
    cell at Liberty, Clay County, Missouri, during the winter of 1838–1839. He had
    been driven out of Jackson County in 1833 and was involved in the Battle of the
    Big Blue. Previously he had served as an ensign in the War of 1812. He emi-
    grated to Utah in 1848. He died of "chill fever" (see the JH, 11 June 1849).

23. Martha and Mary Richards (b. 1820) were wives of William Glover McMullin.
    Ann Eliza Drake (1817–1872) was married to Ira Newton Spaulding (1809–
    1882).

me through my life and for wisdom in all things O Lord give ^me^ thy spirit
that it may be a light to my path give me knoledge that I may know thy will and
how to do it give me wisdom that I judge between truth and eror for I desire to
do good and not evil make the path of duty plain before me and give me grace
to walk therein and do give me patience to endure all that I may be caled to
pass through Marthann and Mr Sessions has come home again **Monday 18** we
washed, some emigrants came in we hear from winter quarters **tuesday 19**
some more came in[24] **wednesday 20 Thursday 21** I have co almost every day
Friday 22 I make artificial flowers **Saturday 29** P Gs trial cloesed to day he
came off better than when he began[25] **Sunday 24** I went to meeting heard
much good many emigrants there the past week I have been called on to lay
hands on the sick they have been healed Mary Ann Nobles was one she had a
visit from Sarah Nobles who has been Dead over two years conversed with her
over one hour **Monday 25** I have washed Martha Ann is not well I picked my
garden strawberys carried some to sister Abbot she is very sick with consumtion **Tuesday 26** very warm **wednesday 27** visited at sister Holmes with sisters
E R Snow and Love and many others it being 5 years this day since the
Prophets were martyred **Thursday 28** it being 37 years to day since we were
maried **Friday 29** I am sent for to Br Lewises his child very sick died soon after
I got there[26] sick only about 8 hours I then went to see sister Abot with
Precinda and Zina **Saturday 30** the Emigrants are still coming in

July 1849

Sunday July 1 we have green peas did not go to meeting **Monday 2** we are
washing Naoma washes with us for the first time we had all our green peas
stole last Friday night we followed the tracks to Wm= Burtins [William Burton,
1809–1851] waggon and picked up peas near his waggon where he slept in the
morning he was gone to trade with the emigrants we think the peas was carried
there and sold **Tuesday 3** we have received a letter from Mother stating she

---

24. Emigrant records are incomplete, but there were groups that arrived on 18 and
19 June and 21 July, as Patty indicates. According to Leonard Arrington, by the
spring of 1849, the population of the Great Basin was "some 6000 persons"
(*Great Basin Kingdom* [Lincoln: University of Nebraska Press, 1958], 97).

25. The JH does not mention the trial, nor does Perrigrine's diary. Eliza R. Snow
wrote only, "sat. 16th Trial against Perrigreen Sess. yest. & today—adjourned till
tomorrow" ("Journal. Winter Quarters of the Camp of Israel," holograph, HM
27522, Huntington Library, San Marino, Calif.). Hosea Stout wrote on 23 June
1849, "The trial of P. Sessions was ended after some three or four settings. The
charge sustained against him. He had been guilty of taking advantage of the
people in the sale of his corn &c. and is now to make restitution to all he has
injured" (Brooks, *Hosea Stout*, 2:353).

26. This could be Tarleton Lewis, Jr., born on 23 December 1846.

and all the rest are well [*in the margin:* dated Jan 30] and one from Sylvia stating Windsors death all the rest well **Wednesday 4** a man right from there the 13 of April here to day gave me some coffee and told me many things about Windsor and all the rest **Thursday 5** bought a ten gallon keg **Friday 6** very warm and dry **Saturday 7 Sunday 8** went to meeting **Monday 9** washed **Tuesday 10** Judge Warner came here sick **Wednesday 11** bought a dress pattern and some hand kercheifs shawl **Thursday 12** Cooked for some emigrants gave me 3 dollars **Friday 13** traded more Caled to Hariet Taylor [Harriet Whittaker, d. 1882, a plural wife of John Taylor] **Saturday 14** put her to bed with a daughter [Sophia Elizabeth] born 6 A M **Sunday 15** wrote one letter to Mother & one to Sylvia sent it by the United S mail went to meeting set under the bowry or shade **Monday 16** watered the garden **Tuesday 17** put sister Holmes [Elvira Annie Cowles] to bed with a daughter [Marietta] born 6 A M **Wednesday 18** Judge Warner left to go on to the mines **Thursday 19** finished Marthas dress cut mine **Friday 20** Mr Sessions bought a waggon yestarday and a can a set of harness and many other things **Saturday 21** put Ann Halley [probably Hawley] to bed with a daughter born 8 2*h* A M a great many emigrants came in to day **Sunday 22** I did not go to meeting **Monday 23** cooked for the feast **Tuesday 24** this day 2 years ago the Pioneers arived in this valley and we celibrate this day instead of the 4th this day will be ^long^ remembered by thousands who were presant at the dinner good order was preserved & every thing went off well this is the begining of a new era with us[27] Richard wilton staid here last night gave $[*inkblot*]: 25 cts ~~Tuesday 25~~ ^**wednesday 25**^ I have been up to see Loiza and many others went to Frosts to the store got

---

27. The JH account of the celebration on 24 July 1849 is worth reading. Beginning before 7:00 A.M. with artillery fire, martial music, the unfurling of a 65-foot-long national flag atop a 104-foot-high Liberty Pole, a six-gun salute, ringing of the Nauvoo bell, and "spirit-stirring airs from the band," the occasion glowed with pomp. At 8:00 white-clad bishops and their respective ward banners were situated; at 8:15 the stake presidency and the Quorum arrived, and the bands went to escort other dignitaries to their places in the Bowery. Respectful attention was paid to the Declaration of Independence and the Constitution. After music and several addresses, ". . . the bishops of each ward [went] to collect the inhabitants of their respective wards together, and march with them to the dinner tables, when several thousands of the Saints dined sumptuously on the fruits of the earth, produced by their own hands, who invited several hundreds of the emigrants, even all who were in the Valley to join in; and a [emigration] company who came in during the dinner were stopped, dismounted, placed at one of the tables, and were astonished by the warmth of their reception; two or three scores of Indians also partook of the repast; indeed such a feast of the body, coupled with a feast of the soul, has not been experienced for a length of time." After a description of more addresses and many toasts, the *Journal History* concludes, "Not an oath was uttered, not a man intoxicated, not a disturbance or jar occurred to mar the union, peace, and harmony of the day."

some apron cloth ~~Wednesday 26~~ got letters by [Howard] Egan from Sylvia & windsor writen before he died got them at the feast **Thursday 26 Friday 27** wattered the corn all day got very tired **Saturday 28 Sunday 29** went to meeting forenoon **Monday 30** washed **Tuesday 31** wheeler came here lame ^ and John williams with^ by a fall from a mule

AUGUST 1849

wendsday August 1 poultesed his leg all day ~~W~~ [*written over* Tues: Wed] **2** he is beter Mr Sessions went to the farm ~~yestarday~~ Tuesday ~~Thursday~~ **3** still beter Bery & Rice came here **Friday 3** Blackwell brought his cousin here I have quite a family to wait on **Saturday 4** I work hard **Sunday 10** do not go to meeting Mr Sessions came home a number to supper **Monday 6 Tuesday 7** they all go away bound for the gold mines they gave me as good as 30 dollars for waiting on them Mr Sessions gone to the farm **Wednesday 8** I went up to Hebers & Brighams to see Loiza B and Eliza Snow **Thursday 9** had company of Emigrants from Iowa city one name Comic the other name ~~Downing~~ Downor **Friday 10** they staid all night gave me 2 dollars and informed me concerning my children there **Saturday 11** had many here from Iowa brought me letters from David & Carlos **Sunday 12** went to meeting hear a trial on Pomroy[28] **Monday 13** get another letter water the garden **Tuesday 14** go to the store to get some thing got some coffee then went and washed and an anointed Sister Gates & laid hands on her caled last night to sister Clarrisa Hait[29] she had a miscarrige **Wednesday 15 Thursday ^16^** go the [store] again could get nothing I wanted cut me a dress **Friday 17** caught Tom gates & Sam Lance steeling mellons[30] then went and put Marian to bed with a son

---

28. Pomeroy, a merchant, had joined Howard Egan's Company on 20 July 1849. Hosea Stout records, "Thurs. 9th. Mr Pomroy came in with a train of 34 waggons loaded with goods & groceries. He started for the mines but fell short. Sat. 11th . . . The council to day appointed a committee to notify Mr. Pomeroy to pack up his goods & leave here as 'he had found us in peace to leave us so.' This was because he was said to be one who had assisted to drive us from Missouri. He demanded a hearing which was granted. . . . Sund 12th . . . at 4 o'clock Mr Pomroy's trial came off He was tried before the people. Some 5 or six of our people came forward and testified that they knew Mr Pomroy in Missouri during the time of our difficulties and that he was our warm friend and had to send off his family & property to keep them from mob violence such was the antipathy against him because he took such an active part in our favor. Suffice it to say he was honorably acquitted" (Brooks, *Hosea Stout*, 2:355).

29. Clarissa Richtmyer or Buckmyre (1815–1868) was the wife of David Bateman Haight (1807–1870).

30. This probably was more than a teenage prank. Thomas Gates, Sr. (1776–1851) and Samuel Lance (b. 1785) were older than Patty. A son of Thomas Gates, Thomas Gates, Jr., was born on 5 June 1829.

born 9 P M[31] ^she was comfortable^ **Saturday 18** she has had fits near 30 **Sunday 19** she is beter put John Murdocks wife [Sarah Zufelt, 1804–1871] to bed with a son [Brigham] born 11 1*h* P M **Monday 20** washed **Tuesday 21** went to some waggons bought some shoes &c sister Gates here on a visit went to a tent bought some linen clothes of a ducth Lady **wednesday 22** went again **Thursday 23** worked on my dress **Friday** ^**24**^ dito **Saturday 25** finished it **Sunday** went to meeting then caled to Mary Ann Nobles there near all night **Monday** washed gave 10 lb flour to go back and meet the the co **Tuesday 28** a public sale of some boys that had been steeling ~~Wednesday 29~~ put Metilda Hunt to bed with a daughter born 11 - 2*h* P M[32] **wednesday 29** not well **Thursday 30** I am sick all day Mr Sessions sewed ionions **Friday 31** put Mary Ann Nobles to bed with a daughter born 6 1*h* A M I am beter

SEPTEMBER 1849

Saturday Sept 1 visited sister washburn[33] with sisters [Martha Ellen] Ashba [Ashby] & [Jane Anne] Twist [b. 1804] had a good supper plumb cake &c &c I went to the store bought one lb candy two lb peaches Mr Sessions bought 12 lb Aples[34] **Sunday 2** I do not go to meeting Naomi has gone to eat mellons I went up to P Gs to see a man there sick **Monday 3** he is very sick Carlos has hurt his head it is cut very bad by a fall one week ago I dresed it **Tuesday 4** had a doctor to the emigrant he said he had the tyfus fever I then came home **wednesday 5** went to the office to get paper money changed **Thursday 6** went again did not get it done **Friday 7** visited at sister Baldwins with Naomi that night an emigrant came here drunk Br Andrews took him away[35] **Saturday**

---

31. Mary Ann Fisk (1815–1862) was the wife of Charles Nelson Baldwin (b. 1815).
32. Matilda Nease (1828–1865) was a plural wife of Jefferson Hunt. She and Celia Mounts had accompanied him during his duty with the Mormon Battalion.
33. Probably Tamer Washburn (b. 1805), mother of Mary Ann Washburn Noble. She and her husband, Abraham Washburn (1805–1886), had lived near Patty in Nauvoo.
34. Arrington (*Great Basin Kingdom*, 81–82) discusses merchandising in 1849 in Salt Lake City. He names as merchants the Pomeroy brothers; Louis Vasquez, partner of Jim Bridger; Mormons John and Enoch Reese; and highly successful non-Mormons Holladay, Warner, Livingston, and Kinkead. Further, Arrington quotes John Taylor (in *Frontier Guardian*, 9 January 1850) as writing, "You would have thought the ladies were bees and their stores the hives–though unlike in one respect, for the bee goes in full and comes out empty, but in this case it was reversed." Edward W. Tullidge writes that in 1849 Livingston and Kinkead brought in the first regular stock of goods, valued at twenty thousand dollars (*History of Salt Lake City and Its Founders* [Salt Lake City: Star Printing, 1883], 379).
35. Since Milo Andrus and his wife were in England on a mission and didn't return until 1850, Patty is probably referring here to Simeon Andrews (b. 1898) who had come west in the Big Company.

Mr Sessions came home **Sunday 9** do not go to meeting Mr Sessions went back again **Monday 10** washed rained and hailed house leaked **Tuesday 11** P G sent down for a sroud the man is dying **Wednesday 12** P G & Daniel brought the man down to bury him **Thursday 13** I must go and see sister Holmes babe it is sick **Friday 14 Saturdday** Francis here on a visit put Martha Mcmullin to bed with a daughter born 1 P M **Sunday 16** I went to meeting **Monday 17** summoned as a witness on a trial before Bishop Smoot **Tuesday 18** I am doctering sister Lance [Mary Alhor, b. 1794, wife of Samuel Lance] **Wednesday 19** Dr Mc comic was here bid me good bye he is going to the gold mines **Thursday 20** bought a chest paid 250 cent Elen K[imball] here **Friday 21** Mr Sessions came home ~~Saturday 15~~ I visited sister Ad Pratt he is going to the Islands[36] **Saturday 22** P G & Mary came down here **sunday 23** went to meeting Brigham preached like Joseph plain and to the point Mary Elen [Kimball] went home with P G we got a bill of goods that we sent for by cumton [Allen Compton] **Monday 29** we washed sisters Bernhisell here on a visit[37] staid all night **Tuesday 25** Martha Ann went home with her I was caled to sister Messer last night staid till midnight many emigrants start to day to go the south route **Wednesday 26** we went to Br Andrews on a visit **Thursday 27** the mail from California arived Writer come I went to [Newton Daniel] Halls put his wife [Sarah Jane Busenbark] to bed with a daughter [Mary Elizabeth] born Friday 28 12 3*h* A M **Saturday 29** went to the store got cups plates tea pot &c **Sunday 30** went to meeting in the fore noon to Br Riches after

OCTOBER 1849

Monday ^Oct^ 1 I went to the store again I have traded 30 dollars Naomi got 64 dollars from Jackson **Tuesday 2** she let us have 26 dollars of it her Mother is here they have wrote a letter to Jackson I wrote some in it **Wednesday 3** she went home **Thursday 4** I went to the store Martha Ann is sick **Friday 5** I have cooked for the confrence all day **Saturday 6** I am sick cannot go to confrence I worked to hard yestarday Mr Sessions went **Sunday 7** I went to meeting many of the Elders are to be sent to the nations **Monday 8** Martha is gone to her fathers [Perrigrine] **Tuesday 9** she came **Wednesday 10** I went up to P Gs came home **Friday 12 Saturday 13** cooked for P G to go to the East[38] Sarah &

---

36. This was the second mission of Addison Pratt to the Society Islands. He left on 8 October 1849 and arrived in Tahiti on 24 May 1850. His wife, Louisa Barnes (1802–1880), and four daughters followed him six months later.

37. John Milton Bernhisel was married to Julia Ann Haight (1805–1865) and Elizabeth Barker (b. 1830).

38. Perrigrine writes in his diary, ". . . on the fifteenth of October I started back acrost the plaines to the States after my sister Sylvia and her family, this was a hard journey as I had some six hundred miles of snow and the wether cold wether all the way to the State of Ioway I arived in Iowa City the first day of Jan 1850 here I

Eliza Gibs was here[39] wrote a letter to Sylvia & another to my Mother & Br Jon=^th^[40] do not go to meeting to day **Sunday 14 Monday 15** P G has started to day for the states I sent $1-25 by him to get things he caried 5 or 6 hundred dollars may the Lord prosper and bless him and all that he has gone after with a safe arival to this place and we all live and be prospered & blessed to meet them and enjoy their society a long time **Tuesday 16** we went to Br [John] Taylors to a splended party of about three hundred we had a splended feast P P Pratt prophesied that when Br Taylor returned from France we should meet again 4 times as large a Co **wednesday 17** dug our pottoes **Thursday 18** Mr Sessions & Col husked corn &c **Friday 19** ~~Sister~~ I visited at Jedidiah Grants **Saturday 20** I mended **Sunday 21** put Jane Taylor to bed with a daughter [Annie Maria] born 4 A M then went to Cottenwood **Monday 22** put Mahola Hollyday to bed with a daughter born 7 - 3*h* A M **Tuesday 22** sisters Buel & Genettee [were here] Mr Sessions came home brought 4 cheeses home **Wednesday 24** Charlotte Snow [Charlotte Merrill Squires, b. 1825, wife of Lorenzo Snow] here on a visit the california boys came in[41] **Thursday 25** Mr Sessions is going to the farm **Friday 26 Saturday 27** went up to see about our goods that Br Rockwood brought to us from cum-ton did not get them I was thrown from a horse coming home hurt but litle **Sunday 28** put Edward Wades wife to bed with a son [Edward William] born

---

found my Sister and Brother David well and glad to see me yet the Object of my journey looked stark to acomplish & in a short time after I arived I found that my Sister was on the back ground and it was doubtful if she left for the Valey at length she told me that I must not feal bad for she was agoing to get maried that night this was as hard a trial as I ever met with to think that I had traveled thirteen hundred miles after her and then I was disapointed but finaly I succeedid to persuade my Brother to return home with me acordingly we fited out and started for home on the eleventh of April with a company of men that were going to California to dig Gold . . ." (p. B-55 [hereafter cited as DPG], Archives of The Historical Department, Church of Jesus Christ of Latter-day Saints, Salt Lake City).

39. Sarah Waterous Gibbs (1827–1903) and Eliza Jerusha Gibbs (1831–1889) were sisters, daughters of Aaron and Prudence Carter Gibbs.

40. Jonathan Bartlett, Patty's brother, was born on 31 July 1800, the fourth of the nine children, according to Perregrine's diary (DPG, p. B-3).

41. Eighty members of the Mormon Battalion reenlisted for six months in the fall of 1847. Some of these were present when gold was discovered at Sutter's Mill. Some returned to the body of the Church in 1847, others in the fall of 1848. Brigham H. Roberts wrote, "The company that reenlisted at Los Angeles for six months . . . served eight and then were mustured out of service. Some of these . . . went by way of the coast to the mines or engaged in other industries in California for a time, but most of them finally made their way to the Salt Lake valley in the course of one or two years, though a few remained permanently in California" (*A Comprehensive History of the Church*, 6 vols. [Provo, Utah: Brigham Young University Press, 1965], 3:369). Some of these may be the "boys" to whom Patty is referring.

10 A M[42] I then went to Rockwoods got the goods [*sideways in margin:* Naomi got a letter] **Monday 29** visited at Harriet Taylors with her sisters[43] & Naomi **Tuesday** visited at Br Bringhersts with sister Pearce **wednesday 31** Naomi [Redding] let Mr sessions have one hundred Dollars her letter said 2:00 but Heber took the [gold] dust to change and that was all he could let her have then

NOVEMBER 1849

Nov 1 Thursday Br Tylor [Albert Peck Tyler, 1826–1889] broke his leg ^I gave him some rice & 2 bits more^ I was at Father Pedigrews **Friday 2** put Betsey Ann to bed with a daughter [Rosana] born 1 P M[44] **Saturday 3** I have been with Naomi to the store got nuts & screws to hang my cupboard doors Br Benson has been here **Sunday 4** it rains I was caled to Br Taylors got wet **Monday 5** had co sisters **Tuesday 6** put Wm Browns wife [Phebe Narcissa Odell] to bed with a daughter [Margaret] born 3 2*h* P M Naomi paid 74 dollars making in all 2:00 **wednesday 7** had co sisters Mary Elen Kimbal Gates & clothier[45] caled to Elizabeth Taylor [Elizabeth Kaighin, 1811–1895, wife of John Taylor] & left my co put her to bed with a son [Thomas Edward] born 10 P M **Thursday 8** visited her and others sister Loiza she is very low **Friday 9** I washed baked sweet cake got very tired **Saturday 10** my back is very lame Mr Sessions is to work on the farm & I have had to cut wood all this week for the stove I hope he will get home soon he gets home to night **Sunday 11** put Benj= Jonson wife Melissa to bed with a daughter [Delcinea Alvera] born 7 A M[46] I went to meeting **Monday 12** caled to Elias Gardner ^wife^ [Betsey Elizabeth Markham] **Tuesday 13** baked **wednesday 14** caled to sister Bringherst **Thursday 15** it rains Mr sessions is at home and carlos is with him **Friday 16** they go back **Saturday 17** saw Simeon Carter put his wife Lydia out door &

42. Edward Davis Wade (1825–1880) had been a member of the Mormon Battalion. His wife, Belinda Hickenlooper (1832–1894), had been with her parents in the second fifty of the first hundred of the Big Company; the Sessionses were in the first fifty. Edward and Belinda were married on 2 January 1849.

43. Harriet Ann Whitaker (b. 1824) and Sophia Whitaker (b. 1825) were plural wives of John Taylor. Elizabeth Whitaker (b. 1818) was married to Joseph Cain, and another sister, Mary Ann Whitaker (b. 1811), was married to Richard Harrison.

44. It was not uncommon for Patty to stay overnight when a birth was imminent. Betsey Ann (1823–1901) was the daughter of David Pettigrew (1791–1863) and Elizabeth Arden/Alden. Betsey Ann was married to John Richard Gilbert, Jr. (1822–1902).

45. Probably the wife of Andrew Jackson Clothier (1823–1876).

46. Benjamin Franklin Johnson (1818–1905) was a member of the Pioneer Company. His wife was Melissa Bloomfield (1820–1860).

pushed her down into the mud[47] **Sunday 18** put Betsey wife of Elias Gardner to bed with a son born 1 P M ^heard from P G^ then came home went to see Mrs Messors [Musser] twins both dead heard from P G to day **Monday 19** put Sophronia Martin wife of Jesse B to bed with a son [Jesse Bigler] born 8 2*h* P M[48] paid 50 cent cash 37 tallow **Tuesday 20** Syrus Canfield Maried over again[49] **wednesday 21** put Moriah Balintine to bed with a daughter [Delecta Annie] born 9 2*h* P M[50] **Thursday 22** Br Corbit here making shoz[51] the white cow came yestarday **Friday 23** Br Cobit here again **Saturday 24** the ward cut a ditch to cary of the water Sister [Howard] Egans here on a visit & sister Corbit I was caled to sister Goodell[52] **Sunday 25** ^Mr Sessions asked Brigham^ snows I came home went right back again **Monday 26** put her to bed with a daughter born 2 A M **Tuesday 27** nit on Mr Sessions mitens Simeon carter Maried Last night **Wendney 28** it rained hard last night houses leaked bad I gave the Bishop $200 for Maryett Gates yesterday[53] **Thursday 29** I have been to see the sick a sister Lee and others **Friday 30** Mr Sessions and Lucinia came down

DECEMBER 1849

Saturday Dec: 1 I feel bad Mr Sessions has told me his plans and contracts that he has made with Hariet[54] also what Brigham said about it I go with Lucinia see Loiza and to the store Mr Sessions rather cold towards me

---

47. Simeon Daggett Carter (1794–1869) married Lydia Kenyon (b. 1794) on 2 December 1818. He married Hannah Dunham on 19 January 1846 and Louise Gibbons on 14 November 1849, according to some records; but according to Patty, he married Louise on 26 November.

48. Sophronia Moore (1832–1915) was the wife of Jesse Bigler Martin (1825–1908).

49. Syrus Culver Canfield (1817–1889) was married to Louisa Janes or Jones in 1841; to Clarissa Lora Jones in 1844, and to Laura Albina Allen (date unknown). Perhaps Patty is referring to this last marriage.

50. Hulda Meriah Clark (1823–1883) was the wife of Richard Ballantyne (1817–1898).

51. Daniel Dewey Corbett (1809–1892) was listed in the 1850 census as a shoemaker and in 1870 as a farmer. His first wife was Almira Bangs Wright (1811–1859).

52. Isaac N. Goodell is listed among the pioneer companies of 1847. Isaac Newton Goodale is listed as having four children in the 1850 census, but there was also a Jackson Goodale, and the name Goodall is present in pioneer records as well.

53. Maryetta Rowe (b. 1831) was the plural wife of Hiram Gates (b. 1802).

54. At age sixteen, Harriet Teeples married thirty-six-year-old Solomon Wixom on 18 January 1846. Although the Teeples and Wixom families left Nauvoo with the exodus of pioneers, they settled in Garden Grove, where, on 15 January 1847, Patty delivered Seth James Wixom. In the spring of 1848, the Teeples family left for Utah, and Harriet came with them because her husband's first wife

Sunday 2 they go back again Martha goes with them Mr Sessions denies me a small favour I feel very bad **Monday 3** I slept but litle last night I got up and read to pass away time snows all day I have to take care of the cow and fire my feet is wet all day I have been to see Abigail Abot on special buisiness she denied **Tuesday 4** I have to clean the snow off of the house wet my leach make soap my feet wet all the time Mr Sessions comes down brings Adline B[enson] and Martha I feel very bad **Wednesday 5** [*blotted out:* he is cross to me sais many hard things Naomi heard a few] **Thursday 6** he went back caried Adline left me crying I feel very bad see that I must live alone I commence familly prayer **Friday 7** I feel some beter Martha slept with me cryed much told me her dreams it has snowed all day I have fixed the cow pen and hen coop **Saturday 8** nit Andrew a pair of mitens helped Naomi quilt she prayed with us to night caled to Mary Shirtlief put her to bed[55] **Sunday 9** 2 oclock A M with a son [Luther Gorham] in the afternoon caled to Hariet Snow [Harriet Amelia Squires, b. 1819, plural wife of Lorenzo Snow] put her to bed with [a son, Lucius Aaron] born a few minutes before 12 at night **Monday 10** I came home I caled and see Loizas breast Clarisa had a babe this morning[56] **Tuesday 11** very cold has been for some time Naomi went to see her sister her babe frose his cheeks Mr Sessions came down and brought half an ox **wednesday 12** he went home again **Thursday 13** I was caled to Elizabeth Taylor she had a broken breast thawed some **Friday 14** I have got the beaf took care of we have washed it is geting cold again I have felt bad for some time but as I canot help it and beleiving all will be right in the end I feel better **Saturday 15** Mr Sessions came home **Sunday 16** he goes back again ^finished my dress^ **Monday 17** I go with sister Carter and with several others at Dr Sprgues[57] she there by us was examined and found inocent **Tuesday 18** cut carpet rags **Wednesday 19** put Rachel wife of Miles Miller to bed with a son [Samuel Miles] born 4 A M[58] came here from sand pitch snowed

---

was too ill to travel. They arrived on 24 September 1848; a year later, Harriet met David Sessions, who was fifty-nine. Brigham Young granted her a divorce from Solomon Wixom, and when she married David, her son's name was changed to James Monroe Sessions.

55. Mary Elizabeth Hadlock (1820–1907) was the wife of Vincent Shirtlief/Shurtlief/Shurtliff.

56. Clarissa Decker (Young)'s daughter, Jeannette Richards, was born this date.

57. Samuel Lindsey Sprague (1805–1870) was one of the first doctors to emigrate to the valley, arriving in 1848. The accusations against Mrs. Carter were not disclosed. Perhaps they have something to do with Simeon Carter's putting his wife out on 17 November and his subsequent new marriage.

58. Miles Miller (1818–1900), the husband of Rachel Ewing (1829–1898), was a member of the Mormon Battalion. They had been called in November to settle an area in north-central Utah, San Pete.

Thursday 20 wind blows hard came down **Friday 21** thaws Mr Sessions here Sisters Mary Hate [Haight] & Mary Mur[ra]y Hate [Haight][59] & Charles Hyde [1814–1891] here we blessd and was blesed I feel very bad with a numbness in my hip and side do not sleep much **Saturday 22** I feel worse mend Mr Sessions clothes for him to go back my hand is very numb I can hardly hold my pen to write or needles to sew **Sunday 23** he goes back I feel some better **Monday 24** cut me a dress **Tuesday 25** Christmas Naomi and Martha go to see Naomis Mother I stay a lone Cambell came here wished me to do an erand to Martha for him I feel very lonesome my health is poor the numbnes is not much better I make sweet cake have mince pie I am so lonesome I can eat but litle **wednesday 26** put James Lewis's wife to bed with a daughter [Emily] born 4 A M[60] then put Mary Ann wife of John Taylor [Mary Ann Oakley, 1826–1911] to bed with a son [Henry Edgar] born 10 P M **Thursday 27** work on my dress **Friday 28** Mr Sessions came down with a load of wood Colonel here is going back **Saturday 29** Mr Sessions goes back I feel bad he said things to me that make me feel bad **Sunday 30** I slept but litle I wish to do right but I fear I shall fail through sorrow Oh Lord give me thy spirit to guide me safe in the right way **Monday 31** Mr Sessions came home I was glad he is kind

1850

*my husband is gone and left me
and I feel that my loss is his gain*

JANUARY 1850

Tuesday January 1, 1850 I feel well in body he is kind Martha Ann goes to a party with Jackson Clothyer **wednesday 2** I go and see Brigham He told me what to do Lucy Smith here[61] **Thursday 3** she staid all night [Vincent] Shirtlief brought the beaf for Baker I salt it I see sister wheeler **Friday 4** I talk with Adline B[enson] she told me some things **Saturday 5** put Diantha Gardner to bed with a daughter [Betsy Ann] born 12 P M[62] I expect Mr Sessions he said he

---

59. Mary Adelia Haight (1830–1890) was a daughter of Hector Caleb and Julia Van Orden Haight. Mary Murray Haight was a plural wife of Isaac Chauncey Haight, who was Hector's brother.
60. Emily Jennison Holman (1832–1911) was the wife of James Lewis (1814–1898).
61. A plural wife of Joseph Smith, Lucy Walker Smith married Heber C. Kimball in 1845. Lucy Meserve Smith (1817–1890) was a wife of George A. Smith. This was probably Lucy Walker Smith.
62. Diantha Hanchett (1833–1902) was a plural wife of Elias Gardener (1807–1890), who was a member of the Pioneer Company.

would come **Sunday 6** he did not come I have slept but litle for the last week snowed yestarday & to day not very cold he came to day very kind to me **Monday 7** he goes back **Tuesday 8** I bye a mare of Barna [Barney] Ward gave 75 Dollars for her Mr sessions brings me a load of hay **wednesday 9** he goes back Naomi goes to her sisters **Thursday 10** I am here all alone **Friday 11** put Margaret wife of Alfred Randle to bed with a son [probably Orrin H.] born 2 2*h* P M[63] the Sessions came do[wn] to go to Mill brought Mary & Harriet down **Saturday 12** he goes to mill **Sunday 13** Hariet sealed to Mr Sessions **Monday 14** he takes her to the farm with him leaves me here alone I feel as well as I can Rosilla Cowin was sealed to him Oct th[e] 3d four year last Oct= left him ^1846^ three years ago last Dec- 23 went back to Nauvoo we have not seen her since[64] **Tuesday 15** it snows and is cold I am all alone feel very lone some sister Smith and sister Snyder came here just at night spend the evening it is cleared of warm **Wednesday 16** sister Smith staid all night Naomi come home I went and put Sarah [Sarah Ann Prichard, b. 1826] wife of Lorenzo Snow to bed with a daughter born 4 2*h* P M snows **Thursday 17** it snowed last night it is bad for me to get out sister Messer sent her boys over to clen the snow off of the house I am very glad **Friday 18** snows all day I have to cut my wood yestarday and to day **Saturday 19** Mr sessions came down snows all day brought me a load of wood I have been sick all day **Sunday 20** I am some better snow 14 inches deep he goes back **Monday 21** very cold wind blows hard snows **Tuesday 22** more warm snows some grows cold **wednesday 23** south wind wind blows snows and cold **Thursday 24** still blows snow flies drifts cold the worst storm I have ever seen in the west **Friday 25** the cow is drifted all in the hay all under snow 3 feet deep I have shoveled snow 2 [*blotted out:* house] hours before I could feed the cow and mare, then I shoveled out the wood I am tired out it has thawed to day **Saturday 26** put Oens wife [probably Elizabeth Pickle, b. 1826] to bed with a son born 1 2*h* P M **Sunday** Mr Sessions came down with hay and beaf 1/3 of an ox **Monday** ^28^ went back Robert went to work for him **Tuesday 29** quite pleasant **wednesday 30** pleasant **Thursday 31** good weather Mr Sessions came brought a load of wood and Hariet to her Fathers to live

FEBRUARY 1850

Friday Feb= 1 he went back sisters [Leonora Cannon] Taylor [Margaret Thompson McMeans] Smoot & [Hannah Harvey] Peirce here on a visit sister Carter came Martha went to speling school **Saturday 2** wash get very tired

---

63. Margaret Harley (1823–1919) was married to Alfred Randall (1811–1891).

64. In his journal entry of 3 November 1850, Perrigrine spoke of seeing Rosilla and added, ". . . saw many of my Old acquintancies but cold in their spirits and it seamed as tho a cloud of Darkness hung over those that once wer Saints . . ." (DPG, p. B-63).

Hariet and sister Snyder came here **Sunday 3** Mr Sessions came down brought Harriet here again **Monday 4** my birth day our horses both took from us to go to Utah without leave[65] he and I go and visit sister Pearce **Tuesday 5** he goes back a foot **wednesday 6** had co sister Abot & Gardner **Thursday 7** we have fine weather **Friday 8** colder **Saturday 9** put Sarah Louce to bed with a son born 2 1h P M[66] Mr Sessions came down foot **Sunday 10** yestarday and to day we hear from Utah [Valley] Joseph Higbee kiled[67] 7 more wounded **Monday 11** Mr Sessions wishes to have Hariet come here to live I consent **Tuesday 12** he goes home she comes when he comes down again she has been here to day I went up to see our lot with him **wednesday 13** Mary Ann [Pierce Cazier (Kimball)] Ruth [Shefflin (Kimball)] & Nancy [Maria Winchester (Kimball)] here on a visit **Thursday 14** put Reuben Millers wife to bed with a daughter [Ellen Elizabeth] born 1 P M[68] Russell Mary & Jenet here on a visit Jenet staid all night **Friday 15** Baldwin girls here in a visit[69] **Saturday 16** Mr Sessions came home **Sunday 17** Nate & wife here all day[70] **Monday 18** Hariet moved here I went back with Mr Sessions **Tuesday 19 Wednesday 20 Thursday 21** kiled the hog weighed 4-25 lbs **Friday 22** we came home I was sick all night **Saturday 23 Sunday 24** he goes back caryes Rebecka Hawk with him[71] **Monday 25** pleasant Dr Bernhisels wife here **Tuesday** [25 *corrected to*] **26** she staid all night **Wednesday** [26 *corrected to*] **27** snowed the horse ~~Wednesday 27~~ came home from Utah

65. According to Brigham H. Roberts, in Utah Valley during the winter of 1850, an Indian known as Old Bishop was accused of wearing the shirt of a Mormon from Fort Utah (Provo). Ordered to remove the shirt and hand it over, Old Bishop refused to do so, protesting that he had purchased the shirt. During the ensuing skirmish, one of the whites shot the Indian, disemboweled and filled his body with stones, and threw it into the Provo River. The Indian desire for revenge precipitated a nasty war between Indians and whites. The Sessions horses were evidently "recruited" for the war (*Comprehensive History*, 3:467–76).

66. Sarah Elizabeth Luce (b. 1829) was a plural wife of William Adams Hickman; later she married William Albert Beebee. The child mentioned here was William Adams Hickman, Jr. Some sources say he was born on 14 February 1850.

67. Higbee was a casualty in a battle fought against Old Elk and his Indian warriors on the Provo River near Fort Utah. Higbee was the son of Isaac Higbee, president of the settlements in Utah Valley.

68. Orice or Orace Burnham (b. 1813) was the wife of Reuben Miller (1811–1882).

69. She may have meant Ann Eliza Robinson and Mary Robinson (possibly sisters), wives of Caleb Clarke Baldwin, who had been imprisoned with Joseph Smith in Liberty Jail. Caleb, as earlier recorded, was deceased (see note 22).

70. Nathan Hawk (1823–1910) and his wife, Elizabeth Conrad. Hawk was a member of the Mormon Battalion.

71. Rebecca Hannah Hawk (1835–1905) was Nate Hawk's sister.

looks very bad ^my mare^ is left could not get her home she has lost her colt and tore her back very bad some thinks she will die **Thursday** [26 *corrected to*] **27** I send the horse North by Br Kilburn [Ozias Kilbourne, Jr., 1810–1901] **Friday 28** Naomi gone to her Mothers I get Nate to move her to her house

MARCH 1850

March 1 Saturday March 2 put Sophia Taylor [Sophia Whitaker (Taylor)] to bed with a son [James Whitaker] born 2 1*h* A M Mr Sessions came down **Sunday 3** Naomi moved away from here into her own house **Mond** Mr Ses= went back I rode with him to see Sophia warm and mudy Hariet gone to Ja= Wolseys [Jacob C. Woolsey] **Tuesday 5** I went to see [Daniel Hammer] Wells about my mare[72] she is left at cotten wood she lost her colt while in the war at Utah [Valley] and had her back tore very bad Wells said she should be brought to me as soon as she can be got here without riding her and Capt Grant is to colect the damage for me of Rolin for abusing the mare **Wednesday 6** sisters [Permelia Snyder] Hatch & [Laurany Huffaker] Mullin [Molen] here on a visit Hariet gone to ~~move or~~ help her aunt to move into another house she has been gone some where every day since she came here **Thursday 7 Friday 8** we have washed **Saturday 9** Mr Sessions came down horse back **Sunday 10** he went back again I then went put sister Mitchel to bed with a son born 11 3*h* P M **Monday 11** I have not been well for some time Charles Hyde here **Tuesday 12** Marth ann went to a party with Wm= Smoot last night[73] **Wednesday 13** she and Hariet went to see Lucinda Wolsey [Lucinda Jameson, 1826–1896, wife of Hyrum Woolsey] **Thursday 14** they wash it has snowed the house leakes I have been to see a sick child and also sister Mitchel Aunt Ann here **Friday 15** snow 5 inches deep snowes some now ~~Lucinda Ann maried~~ **Saturday 16** Mr Sessions came down with hay **Sunday 17** ^Aunt Ann maried^ he went home **Monday 18** put Elizabeth wife of Beriel cawinton [Berrill Covington, b. 1794] to bed with a daughter born 7 1*h* A M **Tuesday 19** Hariet went to the Eeast part of the City to look in a peep stone for a stranger **Wednesday 20** she came home ^sister Prat here visit^ **Thursday 21** I visited Abgial Abot **Friday 22** Marthaann has been sick but she is better Mr Sessions has come down with some hay and wood heard that my mare died last Tuesday night **Sat 23** he went back again **Sun 24** rained last night **Mond 25** rained house leaked **Tuesday 26** rains we have took down the bacon that was smoking **Wednesday** [26 *corrected to*] **27** put caroline wife of

---

72. Daniel Hammer Wells (1814–1891), major-general in the Nauvoo Legion (the state militia) and field commander at the time of the later Utah War in 1857–1858. From 1857 to 1877 he served as second counselor to Brigham Young.

73. William Cochran Adkinson Smoot (1828–1920) was the only child (adopted) of Abraham Owen and Margaret Thompson. He was a member of the Pioneer Company and the last of that group to reach the valley.

Wm= Huntington to bed with a daughter born 3 A M[74] then went to see Naomi **Thursday** [27 *corrected to*] **28** we have washed to day sister carter is here **Frid** [28 *corrected to*] **29** I visited with sisters Pratt & Holmes at sister Loves Mr Sessions came down horse back carlos came down **Sat** [29 *corrected to*] **30** we took out our potatoes **sunday 31** they went back

APRIL 1850

Monday April 1 in the evening caled to sister [Ann] Bringherst she got better I staid all night **Tuesday 2** put Pegga Ann wife of Wm= Sperry [Margaret Ann Sidwell, 1830-1910/16, wife of William Lamont Sperry, 1824-1901] to bed with a son [William Sidwell] born 12 1 *h* P M **Wednesday 3** put Mary wife of Isaac Hatch to bed with a son [John] born 7 A M[75] **Thursday 4** visited Alzada [Elzadie Emeline Ford, wife of Reuben Warren Allred] Alreds babe **Friday 5** saw it again made medicine for it and others Mr Sessions and Mary came down **Saturday 6** we went to confrence had a good meeting **Sunday 7** we went again he went back to the farm I went put sister Bringherst to bed with a pair of twins son and daughter she born 10 P M son 11 P M **Monday 8** rains confrence adjorned **Tuesday 9** Mary went home and Martha with her **Wednesday 10** we washed Baret moved away I worked burning straw and raken it up in the garden **Thursday 11 Friday 12** I have made Mr Sessions a hat this week to day I have been to get sister Writer to make Martha a bonnet **Sat 13** went to cary my bonnet to her Mr Sessions came down and Martha I rode to with him in the waggon part way we came back he plowed a litle in the garden **Sunday 14** do not go to meeting he went home Hariet and Martha went to meeting when he went home **Monday 15** washed I worked in the garden **Tuesday 16** worked in the garden the wind blew over our stove pipes down rained **Wed 17** snowed last night I went and put Mary Sealey to bed with a son born 8 A M[76] then wrote a letter to Elisha [Bartlett] my Br and one to P G **Thursday 18** put sister Love to bed with a daughter [Mary Ellen] born 12 - *h* P M **Friday 19** I have been put my letter in the [*blurred:* office] mail and to other places then went and put Elen wife of Lorenzo Snow [Eleanor Houtz, 1831–1896] to bed with a daughter [Amanda Eleanor Snow] born 5 2*h* P M **Saturday 20 Sunday 21** Mr Sessions came down we went to meeting he went home left Lucinia **Monday ^ 22 Tues^ 23** he came down John Squires with him plowed the garden she and I visited at Dr Richardsons **Tuesday 23** Mr Sessions came down John with him plowed the garden **Wednesday 24** I put Eliza Ostrander [b. 1818, wife of Walter Ostrander] to bed with a daughter

---

74. Caroline Clark (1819–1901) was the wife of William Dresser Huntington (1818–1891).

75. Jane Garlic (1822–1900) was the wife of Isaac Burres Hatch (b. 1823).

76. Mary Pettit (1822–1911) was the wife of David Randolf Seely (1819–1892).

born 5 A M Br Hanks and wife started to day for the Islands Russel and others[77] Mr Sessions went home I have set up my leach **Thursday 25** rained **Friday 26** rained till noon I then sowed ionions and Beats **Satday** (26 *corrected to*) **27** Mr Sessions came down **Sunday 28** did not go to meeting **Monday 29** Mr Sessions went to mill **Tuesday 30** he went home

May 1850

wednes May 1 I have planted potatoes making soap **Thursday 2** made soap **Friday 3** washed **Saturday 4** Mr Sessions & Mary came down **sunday 5** did not go to meeting he had to hunt the cow found her she had been gone 6 days **Monday 6** I have been to get the lot fenced I got the poles drawed there paid 1:25 cts for it cut James [Harriet's son] some clothes **Tuesday 7** I went to see Loiza got some brown linen to make James some aprons **wednesday 8** I have sowed the last garden seeds I have sowed ~~that field~~ & planted the most of the lot I then went to Dr Richards to a medical meeting[78] **Thursday 9** worked on Marthas dress **Friday 10** finished it **Saturday 11** Mr Sessions came down **Sunday 12** went to meeting then went home sister Buels [Kimball] child drowned yestarday[79] **Monday 13** he came down again to see Brigham

---

77. Sidney Alvarus Hanks (1820–1870) crossed the plains in the Brigham Young Company of 1847. Patty's words, "Brother Hanks and wife," are confusing because, according to Andrew Jenson, Sidney Alvarus Hanks went to the Society Islands in 1852, returned in 1860, and married Mary Ann Cook on 1 June 1862 (*Latter-day Saint Biographical Encyclopedia*, [1901; reprint, Salt Lake City: Western Epics, 1971], 4:706. Hanks was one of the "adopted" sons of Brigham Young (see Brooks, *Hosea Stout*, 1:242).

78. *Medicine in the Beehive State* relates that the Society of Health was formed "to give information to the masses of the people, to lessen their burdens, and to enable them to help themselves" (Henry Plenk, ed. [Salt Lake City: University of Utah Press, 1992], 546). The society was organized in the spring of 1849, twenty years before the nation's first state board of health was founded in Massachusetts. Next a Council of Health was organized, which met weekly at the home of Willard Richards. The first issue of the *Deseret News*, edited by Willard Richards, ran an announcement on the Council of Health and continued, "Though we may fail to convince some of the superiority of botanic practice we feel confident that our exertions under this head will shake the faith of many in the propriety of swallowing, as they've long done with confidence, the most dilaterious drugs, believing in the goodness of the Creator that he placed in most lands medicinal plants for the cure of all diseases incident to that climate, especially so in relation [to] that in which we live" (quoted in Norman Lee Smith, "Why Are Mormons So Susceptible to Medical and Nutritional Quackery?" *The Journal of Collegium Aesculapium* 1, no. 1, [December 1983]: 37–38).

79. Presendia Celestia Kimball was born on 9 January 1849 and drowned on 9 May 1850, according to Stanley B. Kimball, *Heber C. Kimball: Mormon Patriarch and Pioneer* [Urbana and Chicago: University of Illionois Press, 1981], 310). Patty's date is 11 May 1850.

Tuesday 14 went home again I went and put sister Cain to bed with a son born 5 2*h* A M[80] **Wednesday 15 Thursday 16** he came down again ^Dimic [Huntington] and wife here.^ **Friday 17** went home **Satd 18** he came down again **Sunday 19** we do not go to meeting Martha & Hariet went noon he went home I staid alone with her child [Harriet's son, James Monroe] **Monday 20** I washed a big wash **Tuesday 21** made curtains **wedns 22** I went to the medical meeting **Thursday 23** good groing weather **Friday 24** Mr Sessions came down ~~it is training day~~ **Saturday 25** it is training day Mr Sessions went home **Sunday 26** we all went to meeting Hariets boy went for the first time **Monday 27** I washed some emigrants came in [*written vertically in margin:* Emigrants 27] I a frost last night kiled some things **Tuesday 28** I have planted over again more emigrants came in **Wednesday 29** cut my gingham dress **Thursday 30** Mr Sessions came down I went put sister Willie [Elizabeth Ann Pettit, wife of James Grey Willey, 1814–1895] to bed with a daughter [Mary Sutton] born 9 P M ^ sister Teaples here first time ^ [81] **Friday 31** Mr Sessions went home

JUNE 1850

Saturday June 1 finish my dress **Sunday 2** ~~Mr~~ we all went to meeting Mr Sessions came down staid allone **Monday 3** he went back again I watered the garden **Tuesday 4** I hoed the garden then helped wash Harriets Aunt fany here **Wenday 5** she is here still I go to the medical meeting **Thursday 6** they all go to the fast meeting I stay at home take care of her boy **Friday 7 Satday 8** Fany here still Mr Sessions came down **Sunday 9** he went to mill we all went to meeting [*illegible blot*] I got three letters from Sylvia P G & David she is not coming she has got maried therefore she cannot come[82] **Monday 10** I am much disapointed but I try to thint all will be right in the end Mr Sessions goes home I go and see Naomi **Tuesday 11** Eliza Fox here on a visit she sais Sylvia has maried a good man ~~Wed~~ I have wattered the lot here **Wednes 12** got an emigrant to hoe it I have hoed the garden **Thursday 13** I have set out plants an hoed till I am tired almost out **Friday 14** I have seen a man from Iowa city well acquainted with Sylvia and David also with Mr Cleark I [*smudged:* Frid] went to Pearces to see him **Saturday 15** Mr Sessions & Mary came down **Sund 16** we all went to meeting they went home **Monday 17** I went and contracted for ten thoasand dobys to build a house [*smudged:* Did] made me a cap

---

80. Elizabeth Whitaker (1828–1880) was married to Joseph Cain (1822–1857). Joseph was associated with the *Deseret News*, and the *Pioneers of 1847* calls Elizabeth a diligent Relief Society worker. The child was Joseph Moore.

81. This would be Huldah Clarinda Colby (1812–1881), the mother of Harriet, David Sessions's plural wife. Harriet's father was George Bentley Teeples (1803–1884).

82. Sylvia married Ezekiel Clark in Iowa City on 1 January 1850. Windsor P. Lyon had died in Iowa City in January 1849.

Tuesday [Tuesday *written on top of* Wednesday] put down my carpet we had a hard frost last night kiled a good deal **wednasday 19** bought a horse gave 37 dollars for it to B Ward **Thursday 20** made two pair mocasons one for Martha the other for James **Friday 21** made a truss for Clineman[83] it is quite warm it has been very cold in the low land almost all the corn and vines kiled by the frost **Saturday 22** he came down fell from his horse hurt him bad **Sunday 23** he went home felt bad from his fall I was caled to Philip Lewis put his wife to bed with a son born 9 3*h* P M[84] **Monday 24** wash and work in the garden **Tuesday 25** here alone Mr Sessions came down went back again setled for damage done in sister Clarks garde[n] David came. **Wednes 26** P G came I went up to his house with him **Thursday 27** came home David and his Father came home with me **Friday 28** Mr Sessions went to mill sold 50 lb flour 50 cents per pound bought two dress paterns one for Hariet $10 one mine $11-82 cts **Saturday 29** I have setled with some men to board took $9 - 76 **Sunday 30** did not go to meeting ^put sister Turnbow [Sylvira Carolyn Hart] to bed with a son [Samuel Joseph] born 2 A M^

JULY 1850

Monday July 1 Mr sessions put up the fence on P Gs lot sis. wilson here **Tuesday 2** hoed the garden David and Martha came down from P Gs **Wednesday 3** Mr sessions & David has gone to Mill I have sold 61 lb flour 21 lb meal for 25 - 84 **Thursday 4** Mr Sessions went to the farm **Friday 5** washed forenoon then took Julia Baldwin[85] through a course of medicine[86] **Saturday 6** visited the sick **Sunday 7** went to meeting Mr Sessions came down with a load of wood **Monday 8** we washed sister Call here to have me

83. Conrad George Kleinman (1815–1883) was a member of the Pioneer Company.
84. Philip Bessom Lewis (1804–1877) had four plural wives. The one who delivered on this day was probably Jane Amanda Stevens; the child would have been Philip Edmund or William Henry.
85. Julia Murdock Baldwin (1831–1880) was the daughter of Caleb and Nancy Kingsbury Baldwin. In 1855 she married George Washington Boyd.
86. Priddy Meeks wrote of a woman he treated, "Nothing more or less than gave her a thorough course of Thomsonian Medicines each time. I had nothing but Kayenne pepper and ginger for my composition power and lobelia, and as I went along, gathered green Sumac leaves off the bush, which answered well for kanker medicine and to make a tea to put the medicine in for her to drink. . . . And with five (5) regular courses of Thomsonian medicine, she was made a sound woman, much to the joy of all her friends" (see "Journal," pp. 5–6, typescript, Utah State Historical Society, Salt Lake City). Samuel Thomson of Boston had organized herbal remedies into a system that came to be known as "puke 'em, purge 'em, sweat 'em." He emphasized lobelia for almost everything—and he marketed his method by selling licenses to use his system for twenty dollars and guidebooks for two dollars. Willard Richards studied with

doctor her babe took it through a course of medicine **Tuesday 9** David went home took a boy home with him to herd **wednesday 10** put sister Harrison to bed with a daughter [Mary Ann] born 5 A M[87] **Thursday 11** visited her again Sisters Lemon [Catherine Mayer] & Covington [Elizabeth Thomas] here on a visit ^cut Hariet a dress^ **Friday 12** Merill Bartlett here staid all night **Saturday 13** cut Marthann a dress she and Hariet has gone to see Lucy Jane on a visit I take care of her babe **Sunday** P G & Lucinia & David came down to meeting I did not go Martha went **Monday 15** cut her a new ^white^ dress **Tuesday 16** sister carter helped to make W̶ Mr Sessions went to the farm **Wednes. 17** he came back we finished Marthas white dress **Thurs 18** Mr Sessions went to the farm again I visited sister Smoot **friday 19** I visited sister Pearce he has got home **Saturday 20** Naomi here wishes to come back here to live again we have concluded to let her come but Hariet sais if she does she will go away there will be so much more work to do **sunday 21** I have sent a line to Naomi not to come she did not get it **Monday 22** she came here ^to live^ I was caled to sister Mitchel **Tuesday 23** put her to bed with a son born 3 2h P M **Wednesday 24** put Mary Egan [Mary Ann Tuttle, 1830–1910, plural wife of Howard Egan] to bed with a son 2 2h P M went to the Aniversiry all day **Thursday 25** I have worked so hard I am so tired I am almost sick **Friday 26** work hard **Saturday 27 Sunday 28** I wrote a letter to Br Jon= [her brother, Jonathan Bartlett] **Monday 29** I washed a large wash ^Mr Sessions went to the farm^ **Tuesday 30** H̶e̶ Elijah Ward brought me eighty dollars for my mare that was lost or died by hard ussage in the war with the Utah Indians last February Ward leaves here to day to go back and meet the morman emigration I paid [*one scratched-out word, illegible*] $1:25 dolollars last week for dobies and halling them to the spot **wednesday 31** Mr Sessions came home last night sick is quite sick to day I have been and put sister Woodbury [Kathrine R. Haskell, wife of Thomas Hobart Woodbury, b. 1822] to bed with a daughter [Catherine Marie Haskell] born 9 A M I then went to the medical meeeting saw a Dr [*two words scratched out, illegible*] Vaun[88] heard him and Br Benson talk came home Mr Sessions no better

Thomson and purchased a license, so undoubtedly Thomsonian medicine was taught at the Council of Health (see Smith, "Why Are Mormons So Susceptible," 35–36). But Patty's 1840 medical book also instructed the reader on a course of medicine for "1st. The Course in Chronic Diseases" and "2d. Painful and Inflammatory Diseases" (W. Beach, *The Family Physician* [New York: by author, 1842], 636–38).

87. Mary Ann Whittaker (1811–1898) was the wife of Richard Harrison (1808–1882).

88. The *Deseret News* of 13 July 1850 carried an advertisement for Doctor J. M. Vaughn, physician and oculist, a graduate of the "Old School," with offices at the house of Timothy B. Foote, Block 138 near the Bath House.

AUGUST 1850

Thursday August 1 he is no better but grows worse I go and get medicine for him give him ametic **Friday 2** worse **Saturday 3** worse I send for the children think he will not live at night he apears better the children came ^Dr Vaun came to see him^ **Sunday 4** he holds better the P G and wife goes home David stays **Monday 5** the Dr came again he apears full as favourable to day we think it is numb palsey that he has as he has no use of his lower limbs and is almost sence less **Tuesday 6** complains of aching in his back ^Dr came again^ we think he is better **Wednesday 7** about the same no use of his legs David is here **Thursday 8** ~~Thursd~~ I think he is worse more senceles **Friday 9** I know he is worse David goes for P G and Mary they came down did not know P G when he came nor Mary or David knew me just before and kissed me we sent for Br Mager he came to take his portrait **Sat day 10** he is still senceless no better P G & Mary goes home he & Lucinia came down at night he is worse snores very hard we have him administered to and turn him over he breathes esier apears to sleep quiet the most of the night **Sunday 11** groes worse has not spoke since Friday but I think he knows what we say ten oclock he died very easy[89] lost the use of his hands yesterday morning we are quite shure it was numb palsey came on gradualy **Monday 12** we buired him I ~~know~~ feel my loss but do not mourn as one that has no hope for I do feel that my loss is his gain yet I cannot help weeping and feeling bad P G and family went home David staid with me **Tuesday 13** Oh how lonesome I am David goes up to the farm **Wednesday 14** I put Jacob F Cecrist wife [Ann Eliza Logan] to bed with a son [Jacob Moroni] born 5 1*h* A M I then went to the medical meeting to[ok] Hariets boy with me Br Brigham was there **Thursday 15** I went on a visit with sisters Smoot & Hunters to Presd Youngs to see his women **Frid 16** altered my dresses Sister Collins here and C Hide **Sat 17** I ~~went to~~ was t[o] sister Secrist she had took cold found her very sick **Sund 18** it looks like heavy rain but does not I went to meeting then went home with P G **Mond 19 Tuesd 20** David and I went to see sister Roads and her 3 babys **Wednsd 21** I came home went to the store **Thursd 22** went again **Frid 23** put Mrs Sweet to bed with a daughter born 4 1*h* A M then put sister Robinson [Selina/Celina Hayward Chaffee, b. 1820, wife of Peter Robinson] to bed with a son [Charles Robinson] born 8 1*h* P M **Satday 24 Sunday 25** did not go to meeting **Monday 26** David & P G came down David went t[o] mill **Tuesd 27** P G went home **Wed 28** David came back went home Naomi with him went

---

89. Perrigrine wrote in his diary, "Father died the August 11th/1851 [*really 1850*] with a Paraletick Strock altho he lived a bout a week after he was struck he died and was Buried in Great Salt Lake City this left Mother alone . . ." (DPG, p. B-57). Patty mentioned in one of her diaries that Perrigrine was checking dates with her. Undoubtedly, some of his entries were written in retrospect.

to see Rolfs house then to the medical meeting then to the store **Thursd 29** then to sister Smoots in the forenoon in the Afternoon I had co. sisters Smoots Dimic wife [Fanny Maria Allen Huntington] and his sister [Diantha Huntington Jacobs (Young)] & Abigail Abot **Friday ^30^** did up caps **Satday 31** Hariet gone to Cotten wood I have had tow men here to get boarded Drs Vaugh & [*blank space*] here to see us I then went to a quilting at sisters Smoots it rains quite cool

SEPTEMBER 1850

Sund Sept 1 the men returned staid all night **Mond 2** I worked on Marthas black dress **Tuesd 3** put sister Canida to bed with a son born 11 2*h* P M **wed 4** put Wm= Langs wife to bed with a daughter born 11 3*h* P M Thurs 5 **Thurs 5** I went visiting at Father Abots and went to the bath house **Frid 6** Confrence I went **Satd 7** I went again **Sunday ^8^** I went again ajourned **Mond 9** sewing Davids pants **Tuesd 10** we [we *written on top of* I] washed **Wed 11** I went to the medical meeting **Thursd 12** sewed **Frid 13** I visited sister drown[90] sister Ensign then came here in the afternoon **Satd 14** wrote a letter to Sylvia and one to my Br Jon= David finishe hauling the wheet **Sunday 15** I went to meeting **Mond 16** I went to the store **Tuesd 17** I washed **Wed 18** We hear of the Indians fuss the men gone to [Capt. John] Browns to see to it David came down **Thurd 19** he went to mill came hear again **Friday** he went home we hear that the Indians have fled I have doubled my carpet yarn made sister Drown a cap **Sat 21 Sund 22** did not go to meeting **Mond 23** ^washed^ Br [Newel K.] Whitney died[91] **Tuesd 24** ~~we washed~~ Martha went to the farm **wed 25** I was caled to sist McConols she had fits put in a quilt **Thusd 26** quilted **Frid 27** got my quilt out P G and Martha came home P G Caught a grisley Bear ~~Thusday 28~~ hear that Charlotte Snow died last Tuesd [*two words scratched out, illegible*] **Saturd 28** I went up to P G **Sund 29** they caught another Grisley Bear I came home the california boys came in Amisa [Lyman] &c **Mond 30** I went to the store bought 20 lb coffee

OCTOBER 1850

Tuesd Oct 1st David came got the carriage yestarday **Wed 2 Thurs 3** I put on a quilt **Frid 4** Hariet went up north **Satd 5** I got my quilt out I went last night to see Br Lenard he has his leg broke in two places **Sunday 6** I went to meeting P G caught another grisley Bear **Mond 7** Hariet has come [*letter scratched out, illegible*] back to her mothers sent for her things by her mother I did not let them go untill she came herself I told her she was going away from home and

---

90. Probably Mary Ann Sweazy, plural wife of Charles Madison Drown (b. 1815).
91. Newel K. Whitney, presiding bishop of the church, died of "Billious Pleurisy," according to the *Deseret News* (28 September 1850).

she would be sorry for it for she never had as good a home before she said she had had a good home here she knew I asked her if I had not used her well and her child she said yes in the presence of Naomi and Martha Ann her Mother and aunt was here I told her I should not let her come back again if she went away nor I should not board her away from here ~~Tuesday 8~~ I have been to get me a ring made with David ~~and~~ **Tuesd 8 Wed 9 Thurs 10** finished Marthas dress **Frid 11** sewed carpet rags **Satd 12** made a cusheon cover **Sund 13** P G sent me 50 lb sugar I did not go to meeting P G caught another Bear **Mond 14** I washed **Tuesd 15** put Emily Sperry [wife of Charles Sperry] to bed with a son [Charles Henry] born 1 2h P M very cold **Wed 16** put Claricy Hoit to bed with a daughter [Harriet Amanda] born 4 A M then put Martha Straten to bed with a daughter [Gav/brilla] born 9 P M[92] **Thurs 17** David down here dug my ionions yestarday Martha went ~~to~~ with Naomi to her Mothers **Frid 18** I have been to the office and saw Heber he talked with me about my lot at E R Snows **Satd 19** I went to settle with Hariet P G ofered to give her $1:50;00 a year to be paid quarterly P G and Lucinia staid all night **Sund 20** I did not go to meeting went put sister Clark to bed with a daughter born 11 P M **Mond 21** Harrison Walton started for the States **Tuesd 22** I went to see Lorenzo Snows child **Wed 23** I bated [batted] wool by carding it and tied my comforter P G & his men came down brought Harriet 12 bushels wheet and a quarter of beaf and dut [dug] my potatoes **Thurs 24** they finished diging and buried them took a waggon bed full for tithing to the office I have visited sister Straten twice she is sick **Frid 25** made my comforter **Satd 26** I went to the office to get P Gs land put on record **Sund 27** did not go to meeting **Mond 28** put sister Empy to bed with a daughter born 6 A M I then went to Br Woodruffs bought me some crocry ware bowls cups &c Br Joseph Straten [Joseph Albert Stratton, b. 1821] died **Tuesd 29** ^David brought the white cow down^ quilted a peticoat **Wed 30** ^took the others home^ put sister Judd to bed with a miss cariage dug my beets **Thursd 31** I twisted carpet yarn it rains P G came here hired Charles Foster[93] David and Brian staid here night before last

NOVEMBER 1850

Frid Nov= 1 doubled and twisted more put Aaron Farrs wife to bed with a son born 7 2h P M [*two letters scratched out, illegible*] Mrs Clothen Hate Stewart here visiting rained **Satd 2** snow 8 inches deep Martha cleanes it of the house ground not froze the first snow we have had this faul to lay on the ground

---

92. Clarissa Amanda Miller (1829–1904) was married to Israel Hoyt. Martha Jane Layne (b. 1824) was the wife of Anthony Johnson Stratton (1824–1887).

93. Charles Adams Foster (b. 1822), a farmer and doctor. His wife was Elizabeth McElray.

Sund 3 rains & snows all day **Mond 4** rains some snow **Tuesd 5** fair **Wed 6** Briant and carlos came down brought me a load of wood and caried me to the medical meeting and took my cow home to P Gs to winter **Thursd 7** charles Hyde & Dr Morse here to Dinner fine weather **Frid 8 Satd 9** took Kite into my house he is to pay 3 dollars per month **Sund 10** I went & laid Br Shirtliefs child out [Luther Gorham] 11 months old born Dec 9 ^1849^ 2 A M ^Barney ward here^ **Mond 11** warm Martha & Naomi gone visiting sister Beach **Tuesd 12** I went up to P Gs Lucinia sick **Wed 13** she is beter the young man is better **Thursd 14** ^Naomi went away^ both better **Friday 15** Mary sick I came home Martha went up **Satd 16** I am all alone Naomi moved away last Thursd the 14 **Sund 17** put Emerett Louisa [Emerett Louisa Davis, b. 1811] wife of Alfred Randall to bed with a son [Levi Leander] born 10 2*h* A M **Mond 18** put sister Smith to bed with a son born 12 2*h* P M **Tuesd 19** set up my leach run out the lye **wednsd 20** Briant staid here last night the mail has come in I have wrote a letter to Sylvia then go to the medical meeting P G gone to mill **Thursd 21** he came back I have made 77 lb soft soup [soap] **Frid. 22** made mince pies **Satd 23** picked up some of my things to move into my house **Sund 24** Martha came home got some clothes went back again David started for Utah [Valley] yesterday **Monday 25** I went and see Br Leanard and sister Bringherst **Tuesd 26** caried my carpet rags to the weaver then washed **Wed 27** I have been and cleaned out my new house am very tired **Thursd 28** did ironed and did up caps **Friday 29** baked mince pies **Satd 30** visited at Br Andrews he was sick came home Br Hill spent the evening here

DECEMBER 1850

Sund Dec 1 put sister Carter to bed with a son born 7 2*h* A M I then went and see Harriet James got his lip cut I am alone this evening no one in the house I now think of days gone by when I had a husband Oh Lord comfort my heart and give me thy spirit and to do right at all times **Monday 2** David and Charles came down to move me into my house **Tuesday 3** I move into my house[94] Marthann came down she David & Charles stay with me **Wed 4** Charles went home rented my house 2 months David stays here he got ~~the~~ my new carpet gave $3-50 cts for weaving I feel very lone some Oh if my husband was with me as he was onece how happy I could be but I must now be as happy as I can **Thursd 5** I regulate my things **Friday 6** David got me some window curtains ^4 his boots^ I put them up **Sat 7** made my carpet **Sund 8** Briant & charles came down brought me a load of wood David gone home &

---

94. Perrigrine writes, "I helped mother to build her a house in the City and fence her city lot and set out some fruit trees the City improved very fast this year and health and prosperity seamed to smile upon the later day saints in the Valies of the Mountains . . ." (DPG, p. B-57). Her house stood at North Temple and Fourth West on property later purchased by Union Pacific.

Charles Briant stays Martha gone to the fort I am here alone it has been very cold ever since I moved **Mond 9** I have been to the fort to see sister Taylors child it has a scalt head I shall charge two dollars for visit and medicine Briant has cut up my wood **Tuesd 10** he has gone home we cleaned the house **Wed 11** fixed my toilet **Thurd 12** put sister Elizabeth [Loomis] Shirtleif to bed with daughter [Mary Elizabeth] born 10 *2h* P M **Frid 13** put Elizabeth Walker to bed with a daughter [Victoreen Elizabeth] born 9 *2h* [*smudged:* P M] A M[95] P G & Mary came down here **Satday** I went to see sister [Margaret] Lawrence or Buterfield[96] **Sund 15** pleasant weather P G and Mary went home & Briant and charles Smoot here **Mond 16** I put sister Camkin to bed with a daughter born 5 A M[97] came home went to sister walker gave her ametic **Tuesd 17** cut me a dress **Wed 18** put Harriet Sessions to bed with a son born 5 A M [David, d. 1851] it snowed **Thursd 19** we washed **Friday 20** sewed on my dress **Satd 21** David here I put down my carpet **Sund 22** Mary Ann Drown here **Mond 23** fixed Marthas things for christmas **Tuesd 24** she went to the bath house gone all night Dimic & Zina here a while **Wed 25** I made a chicken pie sisters Giles & Fox here eat supper[98] **Thursd 26** Martha is going to the infare of Abigail Abots weding she is Married to day[99] **Friday 27** P G and Lucinia came down we went to the Exebition at the bowry **Satd 28** P G setled up his and his Fathers tithing also for building my house $7-70 **Sund ^29^** they went home Martha and I went down to see Hariette **Mond 30** I washed **Tuesd 31** Martha at school yesd and to day I baked mince pies this is the last day of the year and I feel to thank the Lord that I am alive and well and my children my husband is gone and left me and I feel that my loss is his gain David ^Sessions^ and Moses Dailey [Moses Daley, Jr., 1827–1881] here to dinner

[The last page is written upside down:]
March 5 1850 sister Hatch told me many things by cards that I should loos mony ~~away~~ and hunt for it long time but I would find it a man would owe me money and I would be troubled to get it that I would go to a feast see a man there I had not seen for a long time and would be glad to see him that Mr Sessions would be sick but would get well that I would go to a funeral of a

95. Elizabeth Foutz (1827–1910) was the plural wife of Henson Walker, Jr. (b. 1820).

96. Margaret Lawrence (b. 1801) was probably the widow of Edward Lawrence when she became the plural wife of Josiah Butterfield (b. 1795). Butterfield was later excommunicated. Margaret came west in 1850.

97. Elizabeth Bell (1815–1886) was the wife of George Campkin (1815–1892).

98. Mariah Giles was sixty-eight in 1860 according to the census. Eliza Jerusha Gibbs (1831–1889) was married to Jesse Williams Fox (1819–1894). Probably Patty was alluding to them.

99. An infare was a feast and reception for a newly married couple, usually held at the home of the groom a day or two after the wedding.

young man I should feel bad that a dark complected man and ^dark^ wife would come on here no children that a light complected woman would cause me a good deal of trouble and feelings that I would have a long talk with a light comted ^large^ man she thought Brigham that a dark com= woman would tell many things about me false but after a while she would come and ask my forgiveness and be a good friend that Mr sessions would be presant at the arival of the man and wife when they came on that I would get a large sum of money

my husband	1849			
came	Jan		23	
			21	1
			27	
			31	
Feb = came	2=5		[*torn off*]	
			3	
			4	0
Jackson Reding			9	0
Naomi here			11	0
come March 21⌉	w d d		16	0
went do 2⏐	weeks 16 6-3		17	0
come July 22⏐	5		19 -	0
went Nov 14⌋	330		20	0
	200		21	1
	due 130		22	0
			29	
March			1	0
			9	(
			16	0
			22	(
			31	1
April			5	1
			13	(
			20	0
			27	1
			29	0
May			4	(

Patty Sessions
1849

[*upside down:*]

Dr	Milk to Abot	2:55
	Cr 1 chair	1.50
	Another chair	1 00

[By these records it would appear that Patty charged Jackson Redding $330 for his wife Naomi's board and room and that Naomi stayed for sixteen weeks and six days. Of the total charge, $200 had been paid. She appears to show a rate of $5, but for how long a period is unclear; $5 a day would add up to $590, and $5 a week would equal between $80 and $85. More significantly, Patty kept careful track of the days when her husband stayed with her. What the list of zeros and ones means is a puzzle.]

[On the front outside cover of this diary is written January 1 1849 *at the top and* Patty Sessions 1849 *halfway down. Crosswise are the following records:]*

Teaples took the cow	April	9	1850
returned her		19	
Mercer took the cow	April	21	
lost her		28	
		& 30	
herded no more			
Hickenlooper took her	May	6	
gave her up again	May	24	
Shirtlief took her	May	27	
gave her up	Sept—30		
he kept her			
18 weeks		450	
Drown took her	Oct	1	
gave her up the	Oct	29	

[upside down:]
Sary Ann C
. . . gs   33 2*h*

[upside down on the other side of the page:]
June 30 milk
to Tomas to March 19
96 quarts
      600
paid   400
paid   200

Mrs Messer
took the cow
April 23
gave her up
the 9 of August
wich came to
108
we paid her

Diary two (1849–1850) has no binding. It was handmade of pages folded from 7½ x 6½ inches into a book that is 6½ inches long and 3¾ inches wide. The paper has darkened from what probably was beige. The book was sewn with thread and patched later with an inch-long straight pin. The front and back (the diary is coverless) contain financial notes, written every which way. All entries are in brown ink. Courtesy of LDS Church Archives; photograph by J M Heslop.

Diary three (titled 1851–1853, but ending at the start of 1853), more aptly
described as a handmade notebook, is composed of 7½ x 5 inch folded pages
sewn together with three long stitches of brown and black thread. The finished
size in 5 inches long and 3¾ inches wide. The paper is faded blue or gray
except for a few white pages sewn in at the end. There are no covers. The ink
is brown. Courtesy of LDS Church Archives; photograph by J M Heslop.

DIARY THREE, 1851–1852

The years 1851 to 1852 were a time of settling in. Patty, always involved in taking care of those around her, provided more than obstetrical services; she also plunged into general health care. The women began a health council of their own, perhaps because of Brigham Young's diatribe against male doctors given in December 1851. He said, "A doctor, if He had good sens would not wish to visit women in child birth. And if a woman had good sense she would not wish a man to doctor them on such an occasion"[1]

Patty herself was sick more often than usual during this period. She tended to dramatize her illnesses but placed great faith in the power of the priesthood and the support of friends to heal her. And she took little or no time off from work to be sick. She continued to plant and expand her garden. She had her portrait painted and her "likeness" taken. For her, life became more normal, though for the reader, it still seems frantic and too busy. Being busy made up her life and her diary.

Gertrude Stein wrote, "A diary should be instantly in recording a telegram. Also in recording embroidery also in recording having wished to buy a basket. That is it."[2] Impulsively, subconsciously, the diaries of Patty Sessions follow Stein's dictates.

---

1. Brigham Young, quoted in *Wilford Woodruff's Journal*, ed. Scott G. Kenney, 9 vols. (Midvale, Utah: Signature Books, 1983), 4: 84.

2. Gertrude Stein, quoted in Mary Jane Moffat and Charlotte Painter, *Revelations: Diaries of Women* (New York: Vintage Books, 1975), 18.

1851

I feel to thank the Lord that I have some one to cut my wood for me

JANUARY 1851

Jan=1 1851 new year **Wed 1** Martha Ann and I went down to Br Drowns [Charles Madison Drown?] had a good visit spent the day much more pleasant than I did a year ago **Thurs 2** sewed **Friday 3** sewed again **Satd 4** sewed again Charles and Bunty came down Bunty staid all night[3] cut me some wood **Sund 5** David came down I went home with him he brought me down some pork **Mond 6** I went in the evening with Lucina to see sister Collins **Tues 7** Bucland brought me home **Wed 8** Mclennel cut wood half day for me[4] he moved in to my house last Satd 4 is to pay four dollars per month rent to me for it Bickman Briant Charles Hamman staid here last night[5] **Thur 9** Mclellen cut more wood charged one dollar 25 cents for it we have had quite a snow ^**Fri 10**^ the sleighs were runing in every direction last night and again to day Martha [Ann] has gone to night to writing school I am here alone **Sat 11** Br [John] Taylor and wife here to get medicine for their babes sore head I paid eleven dollars ^$11-20^ and 20 cts to [*left blank*] Eldrige it being the amount of my tax on the school house ^$11-20^ Martha Ann presant it has stormed the most of the day rained and thawed ~~my~~ it leakes round my stove pipe bad **Sund 12** David came down staid all night John Barnard here in the evening[6] **Mon 13** I let David have cloth for a pair of fine shirts he went home I visited at Br Gibses with sisters Buel Jackman Banke Fouts sister Buel came home with me **Tues 14** I had a party sisters Jackman Bouke[7] Gibs [Abigail E.] Zina [D. H. Young] Caroline & Buel [Precinda H. Buel (Kimball)] & Clark all here we had a good time **Wed 15** sister Buel went home I put in a quilt for Mary **Thurs 16** quilted

3. Probably George Bundy, listed in the 1850 census as a laborer.

4. This may be William Carol McClellan (1829–1916), who had been a member of the Mormon Battalion.

5. These men may have been members of the Mormon Battalion. Patty lodged many of the battalion men. The men were possibly Gilbert Bickmore (1823 or 1827–1896), a wheelwright; John Strange Bryant; and Ebenezer, Lorenzo, or Oliver Harmon, all of whom had been battalion members. The identity of Charles is unknown.

6. John Porter Barnard (1804–1874) was a blacksmith and farmer, and, according to Susan Ward Easton Black, a leader of the squatter government of 1851 (*Membership of The Church of Jesus Christ of Latter-day Saints 1830–1848*, 50 vols. [Provo, Utah: Brigham Young University Religious Studies Center, 1984]).

7. Lucinda Harmon (1822–1894) was the wife of Levi Jackman (1797–1876). Euphamia E. Dibble (1799–1847) was married to John Adams Bouck (b. 1796/7).

all day it is cold **Fri 17** got the quilt out Martha has been sick all the time since Mond has set up but litle she is beter to day the weather is more moderate **Saturday** ^**18**^ conference of the seventies P G Lucinia & Mary came down I did not go **Sunday 19** I went Brigham preached told a temple must be built I was taken sick at the forenoon meeting they brought me home in great distress **Mon 20** I got eiseir the children went home in the night I grew worse it was thought I could not live they sent for the children but by the faith of the saints and the power of the priesthood I have recovered it is now **Feb= 2**

FEBRUARY 1851

Sunday I have not been out doors yet but can set up and work some Lucinia staid with me 9 days and I do thank the Lord for good children and that I live amo^n^g the saints and that the saints are my friends I wrote a letter to Sylvia yestarday David is here came down yestarday many of the sisters has been to see me since I was sick Sister Smoot Whitney Buel Zina Young she was here when I was at the worst si[s]ter Pulzipher Clark & Francis [Jessie Swan] Kimbal &c &c **Monday 3d** Martha Ann is taken sick and I have to work and take care of her David has gone home after doing all the chores he could **Tuesd 4** my birthday she is better sisters Drown Lorette Zina & Persis Richards were here on a visit[8] Lorette got the supper Zina & Persis staid all night we had a good visit we prayed & blesed and was blesed spoke in toungues &c **wed 5** Zina and Persis went home. Francis and sister Gibs was here **Thursd 6** sister Abot was here P G and Br [John] Stoker [1817–1881] came and got dinner **Friday 7** Bunty came staid all night I have been peiceing up a quilt finish it to day **8 of Feb Sun**, David came down took Martha and me in the buggy to see Naomi he took Sarah Lawrence [Kimball] home with him **Mon 10** snowed a litle last night clear this morning Martha has gone to school[9] **Tues 11** Brs C. [Charles] Foster & [Shadrach] Roundy here **wed 12** it snowed hard all day **Thursd 13** Br Leonard & wife here on a visit **Frid 14** Martha & I went to Br Leonards Br Kimbal and wife there we had a good sleigh ride and a good visit **Sat 15** David & Mary & Susan Duncan [1829–1921] here to Dinner I rode in the sleigh with them to Dr Hotchcase[10] herd

---

8. Persis Goodall (1801/6–1894) was married in 1826 to Lorenzo Dow Young (1807–1895), Brigham's youngest brother. According to genealogical records, they were the parents of eleven offspring.

9. Martha Ann probably attended a ward school, since several wards began building schools in the fall of 1850. Such buildings were used for day school, church meetings, and social events. The first school in the valley was conducted by Mary Jane Dilworth in the Old Fort in a military tent (see note 307 in Diary 1).

10. Sternes Hoskiss was listed in the census of 1850 as a physician who was thirty-four years old.

there of the death of Dr Vaughn he was shot last Sunday by Hamlinton[11] David & M & S has gone home Peck here wishes to have me board him a while[12] **Sun 16** I do go to meeting sister Nobles [Mary Adeline Beman] buried her funeral sermon preached **Mond 17** I washed **Tues 18** ironed P G came down to mill brought me a meal chest **Wed 19** it snowed last night P G has returned from mill left flour here to sell has gone home Mernervy Empy [Empey] & Jane R & linzy here Mary has gone to day to see about the Indians steeling catle & horses **Thurs 20** more gone today Naomi came here with P G yestarday & has gone home to day **Frid 21** a party to the Bath house to night Martha A was a going but her Partner has gone to hunt the Indians ~~Satu 22~~ P G & Mary Susan D[uncan] came down ~~Sat~~ I went with them to see Hariet **Sat 22** very cold and snowy **sunday 23** more moderate they go home Peck goes away Paid me six dolars for his board **Mond 24 Tues 25** I worked on a hearth rug **Wed 26** put Lois wife of B T Mitchel to bed with a daughter born 3 2*h* P M the boys came back from hunting the Indians **Thurs 27** finished my hearth rug bought me a bedsted gave ten Dollars **Frid 28** set it up put up my curtains the rest of the boys came in

MARCH 1851

Sat Mar th 1 more gone out **Sund 2** do not go to meeting **Mond 3** David has come down been to the store I sent by him got me 9 2*h* yards of linen gave $1=25 per yard **Tuesd 4** he went home I cut my linen up **wed 5** Martha went to a picnic party to Packs **Thursd 6** I went to the Counsel house to see & hear them give their endowment **Fri 7** I went down to see sister Drown Hariet came here staid all night **satd 8** P G & Mary came down and went home she

---

11. Juanita Brooks writes, "Thurs Oct 3–1850. Instituted a suit for Foot vs Vaughan in damage $10000 in the County Court & had him arrested and held in custody for adultery with his wife which occupied most of the day. . . . Monday Oct 7th 1850 The case of Dr Vaughan had been stopped by the Gov" (*Diary of Hosea Stout*, 2 vols. [Salt Lake City: University of Utah Press, 1964], 2:381). Vaughan must have moved to San Pete County, where the killing took place, because Stout records later, "Saturday 15th February 1851. Last evening Charles Shumway and M. D. Hambleton came in from San Pete They bring news that M. D. Hambleton on last Sunday killed Dr. J. M. Vaughan for similar conduct with Mrs. H. as took place with Dr. & Foots wife last summer" (p. 393). And "Monday, 17th March 1851 Hambleton did deliberately shot Vaughan on one Sabbath at meeting or just as the meeting was dismissed. His seduction & illicit conversation with Mrs Hambleton was sufficiently proven insomuch that I was well satisfied of his justification. . . . He was acquitted by the Court and also by the Voice of the people present. The court was not a trial but a Court of Inquiry" (p. 396).

12. Four men named Peck had been with the Mormon Battalion: Edwin M. Peck (1828–1903), Isaac Peck (1828–1904), Thomas Peck (only on muster-in rolls), and Thorit Peck (1826–1858).

got her teeth fixed **Sund 9** I went to see Naomi she is sick Hariet went home
to night Peck came here **Mond 10** he and I went down to the fort got some
vegatables Carlos came down last Frid is here yet Br Smoot moves away to
day Br Andrews went last Frid we have washed to day **Tues 11** Peck went
home & Carlos with him **wed 12** David came down **Thurs 13** he and I went
and took out the Potatoes Charles foster helped Rodney ^& wife^ started
away **Frid 14** Drown went David went home ~~Sat 15~~ got some letters from
Sylvia David and the gibs Girls Davids datet Nov= **Sat 15** I doubled yarn for
Eliza Fox **Sund 16** I went to meeting **Mond 17** P G came down I went to see
Naomi **Tues 18** paid Major for taking my Portrait sisters Smith and Knights
here on a visit sister Knights staid all night **wed 19** she is here **Thurs 20** she is
here yet yestarday we visited at Br Risers [George Christian Reiser,
1818–1892] I have been and put Lucinda wife of Levi Jackman to bed with a
daughter born 10 - 2h A M **Friday 21** finished Doubling Elizas yarn caried it
home she paid me one dollar and half for it **Satd 22** I went to the medical
meeting I have staid alone night and day the most of the time this week **Sund
23** I am alone yet I expect Martha home to day she does not come **Mond 24**
the mail has come in Br Major is here painting my Portrait **Tues 25** I go over
to Br Pulziphers [Zerah Pulsipher, 1789–1872] come home sister Higbee here
on a visit **Wed 26** Martha Ann has not got home yet Br Pulzipher came in this
morning to see if I had any wood it snowed and rained last night a bad storm
but very pleasant this morning **Thursd 27** Martha Ann came home David
with her P G came last night we sold the potatoes and beets David brought me
some boards to put up my fence they then went home ^**Frid 28**^ I got a Bro
to put up the pole fence inside Peck was here ^& B S^ **Sat 29** he went home
Sun 30 David came down brought the school teacher [Phebe, later his wife]
~~Mond~~ I did not get to meeting the wind blew hard ^B S^ **Mond 31** snowed
last night B S here staid all night Horace put up the rest of the inside fence

APRIL 1851

Tuesd April 1 finished Major came here painting my portrait Martha and I
went over to Br Roundys **wed 2** I have pick up the vines and burnt them off
of my lot then Martha and I went see Zina had a good visit I then went and
put sister [*left blank*] Barnum to bed with a daughter Born 11 PM[13] **Thurs 3**
Charles Foster staid here last night Martha Ann is sick had some rose bushes
set out the wind blows hard **Friday 4** P G & David came down to plow and
fence my lot **Satd 5** they go home the fence not done all of it **Sun 6** it rains

---

13. Probably Polly Beach (1831–1894), who was married to Charles Davis Barnum
(b. 1800). Barnum had accompanied the Pioneer Company, after having used
his skills at carpentry to prepare the wagons for the trip. He returned to Winter
Quarters that same year for his family. They all came west in 1850.

and snows a bad time for conferrence I do not know as I shall go to day 9 oclock clears off but it was so damp and cold the conference was ajourned till Mond P G Sessions & Mary came down Bonna [Barney?] Ward here **Mond 7** we all went to conference it was a good time the church 21 years old yestarday much buisines done[14] Brigham was so unwell he did not go onto the stand Heber presided conference ajourned untill Sept Graham & wife staid here all night **Tuesd 8** I worked in the garden ^put in ionions & beets^ Wash= Jones came here staid all night helped some in the garden **wed 9** he went away I worked very hard ^sowed ionions^ **Thursd 10** P G and a man came down brought Naomi here we went to the fort got Peach trees and roots & vines set them out **Frid 11** got some more set them out they went home I have sowed my peas letice redishes sold Lemons widow 10 Dollars worth of Peach trees **Satd 12** watered the peach trees and planted my potatoes **Sund 13** P G Lu– David came down I went to meeting with them. They all went home B S here **Mond 14** worked in the darden [garden] **Tues 15** I visited Barna Ward he was very sick I let Esq Wells have 4 doz Peach trees I then visited sister Buel she anointed me and sister Jackman and blesed us both. **Wed 16** sewed posy seeds Br Major came finished my Portrait McBride took my sensus **Thursd 17** I have been to look at a feather abed at Br Jerimis **Frid P G** David & Charles came down brought lumber to finish my fence **Sat 19** finished it David went home Br Ward came here sick yestarday is here yet Charles stays I go to a medical meeting the wind blew hard got me a dress patern of sister Smith **Sund 20** it has rained the most of the night rains untill near noon cl[e]ars of Br Ward goes away **Mond 21** Charles finished the fence went home ^I plant^ after seting 12 locus trees I gave $1:50 for them I then commenced making soap **Tuesday ^22^** I went down to my old place sold 28 peach trees to Br Major ^$700^ and four to sister Smith $100 both due then finished making soap filed my trough full **wed 23** cut me a dress **thurs 24** worked on it planted corn cucumbers &c **Frid 25 Sat 26** finished my dress **Sund 27** went to neeting P G Mary David here **Mond 28** caled to Mary Robison cut me a dress **Tues 29** put Mary Robison [wife of Caleb Baldwin] to bed with a girl born 1 -2*h* P M **Wed 30** cut Martha a dress Brs Roundy & Jackman with their wives here on a visit

MAY 1851

Thursd May 1 worked on my dress **Frid 2** watered my garden **Sat 3** went washed and anointed br Coltrins babe then went paid my tithing then to a medical meeting I have a sore throat **Sund 4** do not go to meeting ^go give sister Brunson Emitic^ David Lucinia down **Mon 5** wash ^bought a looking

---

14. At this conference it was voted to build a temple, and Edward Hunter was appointed presiding bishop of the church, succeeding the deceased Newel K. Whitney.

glass ^ **Tuesd 6** P G and Lucinia down the wind blew very hard a part of sister Buterfields [Caroline Sprout, b. 1800] house blew down **Wed 7** put Caroline Mitchel [Caroline Conrad, wife of Benjamin Trotter Mitchell] to bed with a son born 6 2*h* A M as they were bring me home one of the horses droped down died in a minute I came home a foot then went and see sister Brunson again staid and nursed her all the afternoon **Thursd 8** visited her again **Frid 9** rained all day and night and night again the house leaked I have to go to bed to keep warm as I have no wood cut and I can not cut it I am so unwell **Sat 10** fair weather I cut my wood and then set out cabage plants **Sund 11** do not go to meeting **Mond 12** P G came down I went home with him **Tuesd ^13^** I came home again with David **wed 14** ~~Thursd 15 visited Br Roundys Frid 15 visited at Zinas Satd 16 went~~ I visited at Br Roundys **Thurs 15** visited at Zinas with sisters Branch and Atwood[15] **Frid ^16^** went to sister Jackmans found Precinda and Lora K [Laura Pitkin (Kimball)] there Precinda came here staid all night **Satd 17** we all went to medical meeting Penneno caried us **Sund 18** put Samuel Mores wife [Eunice Sibley Bliss, b. 1807] to bed with a son born 10 - 1*h* A M **Mond 19** I was taken very violent sick for 3 hours I was not thought to live doubts remained for 24 hours **Mond 25** until to day I have not had my clothes on the childlren have been down to see me often I am geting well I hope but I feel bad still 2 oclock P M I was taken worse again had a very sick night **Tuesd 26** still worse send for a doctor and for the children **Wed 27** a litle easier but did not get so as to set up untill

JUNE 1851

Tuesd June 3 I set up a litle **Sat 7** I feel much better have walked out Hariet is here this is the first I have wrote since the 25 of May and only a litle then when I was taken sick on the 19 of May I was sewing as well as ever as far as any thing that I knew when I took the last stich I tried to take another stich but could not I was instantly siesed with trembling cold and pain and vomiting very soon followed & cramping. but by the faith and prayers and good nursing and medical asistance by the hands of the saints and the power of the priesthood I have so far recovered as to walk out I thank the Lord for a place among the saints **Sund 8** P G & Mary & David down to meeting **Mond 9** I still feel beter **Tuesd 10** I walk down to Br [Levi] Jackmans **Wed 11** have my potatoes plowed I visited at sisters Bouks **Thursd 12** have my potatoes hoed **Frid 13** I work in the garden a litle **Sat 14** Charles Lucinia & Carlos came down we went to medical meeting Carlos watered my garden **Sund 15** David came

---

15. Probably Relief Cram (1820–1909) wife of Millen Atwood (1817–1890), who was a member of the Pioneer Company. Emily Cornelia Atwood (1819–1869) was a sister to Millen Atwood. She was married to William Henry Branch (1820–1890).

down I do not go to meeting but rode up to the ~~warm~~ hot spring with Br Brunson and wife **Mond 16 Tuesd 17** I visited sister Cook she is sick **wed 18 Thurs 19** sister Violate [Murray (Kimball)] Sarah L[awrence (Kimball)] Mary Elen [Harris (Kimball)] here on a visit Br Kimbal & Wm [Kimball] here to Dinner & Supper **Frid 20** I have watered my garden all over except the oats this week **Satd ^21^** got Davids watch fixed then was caled to sister Eldridge[16] she is sick with Erisipless & baby is sick **Sund 22** I have visited them again P G & David down Frid last to get the wagon & carriage fixed **Mon 23** put sister Riser [Sophia Christiana Kull, 1821–1871, wife of George Christian Riser] to bed with a son [Richard] born 9 - 2h A M Dimic and wife here stay all night **Tuesd 24** we all went on a visit to Br Jackmans **Wed 25** made me a cap **Thursd ^26^** work in the garden **Frid 27** David gone to mill the boys come home from the indians fuss **Sat 28** David gone home I g[o] t[o] the medical meeting give four dollars [–] to the tithing ofice for the tabernacle **Sund 29** finished a letter to Sylvia ^Br Parry here for it^ **Mond** sent it worked in the garden

July 1851

Tuesd ^July 1^ Martha fixed her white dress **Wed 2** visited at Br Foxes **Thursd 3** put sister Cannon to bed with a son born 3 2h A M Martha went up to her Fathers **Frid 4** I went to a picnic party at Br Cannons in the grove [Memory Grove] **Sat 5** Saw them come home from the Salt lake **Sund 6** did not go to meeting David came down with Martha he staid all night **Mond 7** I worked in the garden **Tuesd 8** I went to a sisters medical meeting[17] **wed 9** finished Davids pants **Thursd 10** went to a prayer meeting **Frid 11** had a quilting **Sat 12** took sister Clary through a course of medicine I am not well have a bowel complaint sister Cob here **Sund 13** ^took a child through a c[ourse in] medicine^ do not go to meeting **Mond** sister Fany K here I was caled to Caroline [Conrad] Mitchel **Tuesd 15** took her through a course of medicine **wed 16** she is better **Thursd 17** put on a quilt went and took sister Clary

---

16. This is probably Ruth Baker, a plural wife of Elnathan Eldridge (b. 1811). The child would be William Nelson, born on 21 December 1850.

17. Significantly, Patty uses the phrase, "sisters medical meeting." By this time, the Council of Health, as established by Willard Richards in 1849, had given birth to a Female Council of Health. The auxiliary council was introduced and expanded to include women interested in health care. Phoebe Angell was appointed president, with Patty Sessions and Susannah Lippincott Richards as counselors. They heard lectures by local physicians, "discussed faith and herbs in healing, attempted to design more healthful female fashions, spoke and sang in tongues, and enjoyed a social and spiritual interchange" (see Richard L. Jensen, "Forgotten Relief Societies, 1844–67," *Dialogue* 16, no. 1 [Spring 1983]: 107). Patty mentions Angell's appointment and her own on 17 September 1851.

through a cours of medicine then went and put sister Houtz to bed with a son [Frederick Mease] born 11 P M[18] **Frid 18** got my quilt out **Sat 19 Sund 20** went to meeting **Mond 21** Martha went to a Party to the bath house **Tuesd 22 Wed 23** went to the concert **Thursd 24** went to the aniversirary of our coming into the valley had a great and good time **Frid 25** watered my garden **Sat 26** Br P[arry] visited me **Sund 27** went to meeting A M got a letter from my Br Jon= wrote one to him P G & I **Mod 28** took sister Clary through a course of steeming **Tuesd 29** washed **wed 30** went to the store got Martha & I a new dress cut them out **Thursd 31** worked on them

AUGUST 1851

Frid August 1 went and took sister Houts through a course of medicine **Sat 2** went to sister Branches then to the medical meeting Br P[arry] here **Sund 3** went to meeting P G L & David down David staid all night with Ph[ebe] **Mond 4** put sister Kite to bed with a daughter born 11 -3h A M[19] **Tuesd** cleaned garden seeds **Wed 6** finished my dress **Thurd 7** sewed carpet rags very warm **Frid 8** put sophrona [Moore] wife of Jessee Martin to bed with a daughter [Isabell] born 4 - 3h A M then took sister Riser through a course of medicine Dr Bernhisel here to see me **Satd 9** I gave sister Nortons child Emetic & Caroline Mitchel one **Sund 10** went to meeting then visited sister Martin gave her Emetic **Mond 11** visited the sick **Tuesd 12** washed my bed commenced a fine shirt for Br Parry **wed 13** visited the sick **Thursd 14** visited the sick again found Caroline [*blotted word*] worse **Frid 15** found her dying she died 11 A M the rest better finished the shirt washed it out he came here brought a water mellon the first ripe one I have have had Jackman here **Saturday 16** had co S[arah] Lawrence [Kimball] L[aura] Gibs P G has been to Tooelee to get lumber got none **Sund 17** watered my garden it soon began to rain and I did not go to meeting **Mond 18** I went up to P G with David **Tuesd 19** had a pic nic party there **wed 20** came home with P G **Thursd 21** put sister Lewis to bed with a daughter born 6 P M **Frid 22** Martha and I went to Dimics **Sat 23** put sister Branch to bed with a son [William Henry] born 11 A M **Sund 24** went to meeting **Mond 25 Tuesd 26 wed 27 Thursd 28 Frid 29** got stone halled for my well **Satd 30** Bought 5 lb coffee 25 sugar 1 tea 1 pitcher a pair candle sticks **Sund 31** went to meeting

SEPTEMBER 1851

Mond Sept 1 put sister Butterfield [Caroline Sprout, wife of Abel Butterfield, 1812–1886] to bed with a daughter [Caroline] born 8 P M **Tuesd 2** visited at sister Butterfield with sister Snider Br & sister Cluff staid here all night **Wed 3**

---

18. Lydia Mease (1817–1888) was the wife of Jacob Miller Houtz (1814–1896).
19. Julia Ann Carr (1809–1881) was the wife of Joseph W. Kyte (b. 1809).

I went to the medical meeting **Thursd 4** got my well dug **Frid 5 Satd 6** made a flannel shirt for Br Parry **Sund 7** went to confrence **mond 8** go again **Tuesd 9** go again **Wed 10** again it ajorned till the 6 of Oct P G has stoned my well almost out **Thursd 11 Frid 12** C Foster hauled me some stone **Sat 13** he finished my well **Sund 14** I went to meeting **mon 15** sewed on skirt for Lucinia **Tuesd 16** took sister Blair through a course of medicine[20] **wed 17** cut up my corn & shocked it went to medical meeting was chose ~~second~~ first counselor to sister Angel **Thursd 18** sewed on shirts **Frid 19 Sat 20** put sister Grant to bed with a daughter born 10 $2h$ A M **Sund 21** went to meeting **Mond 22** took sister Grant through a course of medicine **Tuesd 23** took sister Fulmer through a course of medicine **wed 24** went to a female meeting **Thursd 25** put sister Foresight to bed with a daughter [Savilla Delira] born 9 A M[21] **Frid 26** commenced my hen house **Sat 27 Sun 28** took sister Norton through a course of medicine then went and took sister Higbee through a course of medicine **Mond 29** visited the sick **Tuesd 30** took sister Simson through a course of medicine

OCTOBER 1851

wed Oct 1 went to a medical meeting **Thursd 2** sister Foresyth worse have a hard time to save her life she took cold **Frid 3** took sister Boyd through a course of medicine **Satd 4** caled to sister Fulmer[22] **Sund 5** put her to bed with a son [Don Peter Marvin] born 5 A M then went to meeting Lucinia & Francis walton staid here all night **Mond 6** confrence we all went **Tuesd 7** training rained **Wed 8** rained they dismissed training David lost his horse staid here all night with Jo[seph] Henry [1829–1907] **Thursd 9** he went home came back again hunting for his horse the california boys came in brought news Moses Lenards being shot by the indians[23] I put Br [Albert] Pettys daughter to bed with a daughter born 10 - $2h$ P M[24] **Frid 10** I picked up 32 bushels of potatoes Simson dug them out **Sat 11** I went to Br Lenards they feel bad about their son they brought me home visited Br Foresyths boy he is very sick **Sund 12** visited him again then went to meeting was introduced to Br Tomson then came home Br [Parley P.] Pratts wives came here to supper Belinda [Marden]

20. Probably Cornelia Jane Empy (b. 1820), married in 1837 to Seth Millington Blair. She died on 2 September 1852.
21. Isabella Donald (1819–1852) was married to Thomas R. Forsyth (1813–1898).
22. Rhoda Ann Marvin (1813–1892) was the wife of David Fullmer (1803–1879).
23. Moses Calkin Leonard was born on 26 July 1827 and was the son of Lyman Leonard and Abigail Calkins.
24. Albert and Isabella McClure Petty had two daughters, Eliza Jane, born on 26 June 1830, and Sarah Geraldine, born on 17 March 1833. Sarah married Newman Brown in 1851. The daughter was named Sarah Brown.

& Mary [Wood] I then went and gave Foresiyths boy emetic **Mond 13** caled to Pettys **Tuesd 14** went to george Boids [George Washington Boyd, 1825–1903] **wed 15** went to the medical meeting cut Dr Clinton off[25] **Thursd 16** been Boids again **Frid 17** there again **Satd 18** put her [Julia Murdock Baldwin, 1831–1851] to bed with a daughter [Julia Ann] born 5 A M dug potatoes 11 bushels **Sunday 19** went to meeting Mr Tomson Stephen Hale and wife here to supper **Mond 20** dug potatoes Mr Tomson helped me **Tuesd 21** he worked for me again dug potatoes and beets and buried them **wed 22** had a female meeting I was caled to Br Stowels put her to bed with a daughter born 7 P M **Thursd 23** Julia Boyd sick staid there and to Br Wms all day took Br Wms through a course of medicine **Frid 24** there again staid all day with Julia had the Dr there **Sat 25** there again all day **Sund 26** she died I went to meeting sisters Smoot & Bernhisel staid here last night Mary came here last Tuesday is here yet will stay here longer **Mond 27** I went to Julia Boids funeral **Tuesd 28** wrote a letter to Sylvia and one to Sister Pratt **Wed 29** put them in the Office then went to the medical meeting trial of sister Cob David and Mary staid here last night P G brought me two load of wood **Thursd 30** I am spining Davids rolls **Frid 31** and

NOVEMBER 1851

Satd Nov 1 spining **Sund 2** I went to meeting **Mond 3** spun again in the forenoon ^P G & Lucinia here^ in the afternoon cut Davids bucskin pants he is here **Tuesd** sewed on them cut 2 shirts for Wm Bears[26] Martha sewed on one **Wed 5** went to the female meeting had a good time sister Angel sung a song in toungues I interpreted have wrote it off **Thursd 6** worked on the pants finished Wms shirt **frid 7** Mary sick I send for P G & Lucinia they came I cut Charles pants then put Mary to bed with a son [Byron] born 11 2*h* P M **Sat 8** P G & Lucinia went home I finished both pair of pants Br Leonard & wife here **Sun 9** all comfortable I went to meeting ^P G Lucinia^ came home found her not so well **Mond 10** she is better **Tuesd 11** remains so **Wed 12** I went to the counsel of health cut sister Cob off from the counsel came home found Mary worse Br Pary and I administered to her **Thursd 19** she is better **Frid 14** I spun **Satd 15** spun **sund 16** I went to meeting P G & Lucinia & Carlos down in the night she was taken worse **mond 17** remains worse **Tuesd ^18^** no beter **Wed 19** worse I gave her Emetic **Thursd 20** she is better the Dr

---

25. Dr. Jeter Clinton (b. 1813) came to Utah in 1850 and was listed as a physician in the 1850 census. He became a member of the first city council, and according to Juanita Brooks, was always prominent in public affairs (*Hosea Stout*, 2:437). During the 1860s, he was listed as a coroner.

26. William Beere or Beers (1827–1859) had been a member of the Mormon Battalion.

came said her fever was gone **Frid 21** she is better **Satd 22** gave her another emetic brought the flegm off of her stomac I then went and put Eliza Shurtlief [Elizabeth Topham, 1833–1919, wife of Vincent Shurtliff] to bed with a daughter [Sarah Jane] born 10 1*h* P M **Sund 23** Mary is still better David is down Br P[arry] saw Brigham last Mond **Mond 24** spun, finished **Tuesd 25** sent it up to be couloured **wed 26** went to the counsel of health P G and Lucinia down Ruth Carter staid here all night **Thursd 27** commenced charles Harts mittens[27] **Frid 28** nitting **Satd 29** Finished them P G & David down Wash Jones here **Sund ^30^** got a letter from Syvia wrote one to her P G & David staid all night gone home Marys breast has broke she is better Jones has burried up my potatoes

December 1851

Mond Dec 1 he made a bridge across the ~~dich~~ ditch he then went up north **Tuesd 2** I have to cut wood for two fires **wed 3** niting Davids fringed mittens **Thursd 4** finished them Mary is worse taken lame **Frid 5** [*illegible words scratched out*] up with her good part of the night covered up my pink roots **Sat 9** [*illegible word*] she is no better I have been to a female meeting it snowed very hard when I came home Br P had his indowment to day I have cut all my wood since Monday **Sund 7** David and Lucinia down **Mond 8** Mary is better **Tuesd 9** I have to cut my wood it is very hard **Wed 10** I went to the counsel of health Br Brigham us a lecture in the counsel house **Thursd 11** I am niting David another pair of fringed mittins **Frid ^12^** feel almost wore out cuting wood **Satd 13** they dedicate the school house up north **Sund 14** I was married to John Parry[28] and I feel to thank the Lord that I have some one to cut my wood for me **Mond 15** P G is down here **Tues 15**[29] mended clothes **Wed 17** [*written over* 16] nit on Davids mittens. **Thursd 18** [*written over* 17] I feel first rate **Fri 19** [*written over* 18] finished David mittens **Satd 20** [*written over* 19] went to the counsel of health Dr [Priddy] Meeks there it was caled a female meeting **Sund 21** snowed so we did not go to meeting Br Clarks moved away gave Mary Emetic she sets up but litle **Mond 22** went to the 2d Lecture of Orson Pratt on astronomy **Tuesd 23 Wed 24** David down here Martha went home with him and Phebe to a party **Thursd 25** Christmas she came home Mr

---

27. Charles Hart, born in 1836 in Quebec, Canada, was in the Abraham O. Smoot Company of 1847.

28. John Parry (1789–1868) was born in Wales. He emigrated with one wagon in 1849 with the George A. Smith Company. His wife, Mary Williams, died en route. Parry was a master mason and a musician/composer. He introduced lucerne, a type of alfalfa, to the Great Salt Lake Valley.

29. Some degree of stress, unhappiness, or confusion arises here since Patty writes the wrong date from Tuesday, 16 December, through Saturday, 20 December, and corrects herself by writing the correct dates on top of the wrong date.

Parry ^and I went^ to a party to the Cabinet shop picnic for those that worked on the public works we had a good time it lasted two days we were there both days it was the best party I ever was to **Sat 27 Sund 28** David here staid all night **Mond 29** he was very sick but went home after he got better **Tuesd 30** wrote a letter to Sylvia and another to Br Jon= **Wed 31** cooked for thanksgiving prayed and thanked the Lord for the preservation of our lives[30]

1852

the heavens gave me light over bad places . . . as my candle went out when I first started

January 1852

Jan 1 1852 Thursday I got up this morning washed us attend to our prayers feasted on the best we had which was fresh pork vegatables mince pye and custard sweet cake &c. for supper we had a variety of good things **Friday 2 Sat 3 Sund 4** we went to meeting P G came for Mary he come to meeting brought us home took dinner carried Mary home David was here went home in the evening we went to meeting Wm Smoot here staid all night **Mond 5** Martha Ann went up to her fathers I cut out some quilt linens for her **Tuesd 6** I cleaned took up the carpet in the kitchen put it down again **wed 7** scoured some **Thurd 8** made soap **Frid 9** finished **Sat 10** stewed squash mended &c David & Jo Henry here stay all night Mr Pary took sick very sick all night **Sund 11** he is no better David & Joe went home David came down with ^his ox again^ staid all night **Mond 12** went and see Brigham took Mr Parrys ox home to keep Mr Parry is sick yet **Tuesd 13** he is a little better **Wed 14** he is so he goes out **Thursd 15** I wash **Frid 16** go up in town to setle up my tithing

---

30. Governor Brigham Young proclaimed a day of thanksgiving and prayer to be observed on 1 January 1852. Wilford Woodruff records part of the proclamation in his journal: "I recommend to all good citizens of Utah that they abstain from evry thing that is calculated to mar or grieve the spirit of their Heavenly Father . . . rise Early . . . and wash . . . with pure water . . . see that no creature . . . is Hungry thirsty or Cold while the women are preparing the best of food for their Housholds & their Children ready to receive it in Cleanliness & with cheerfulness . . . let the Head of Each family with his family bow down . . . and acknowledge all his sins & the sins of his household call upon the Father in the name of Jesus for evry blessing . . . for himself his kindred the Israel of God the univers of man praying with full purpose & heart & united faith that the union of the United States may be preserved inviolate against all the devises of wicked men . . . in the name of Jesus ask the Father to Bless your food . . . if you feel to make merry . . . sing a song of thanksgiving and lift up your hearts continually in praise & acknowledgement of the unbounded mercies you are momentarily receiving" (*Woodruff's Journal*, 4:89, 92).

did not quite bought some cloth 30 yards 2-3*h* ginam **Sat** went to councel of
health David Wm= & Martha came down **Sund 18** they went home I went to
meeting afternoon & evening **Mond 19** washed in the evening went to the
Lectures **Tuesd 20** snowed last night **wed 21** sister Smoot here wm= David
here P G & David stay all night P G gave me 89 lb flour **Thursd 22** I have
made two bed ticks **Frid 23** put the feathers in to them ironed **Satd 34** ~~Sunday~~
~~we~~ went to female meeting **Sund 25** we went to meeting **Mond 26** I washed
then went up to P Gs **Tuesd** gave Mary Emetic **wed 28** she is better **Thursd
29** Martha Ann married to William Smoot [1828–1920], Joseph Henry &
Susan Duncan [1829–1921] married the same time a good weding **Frid 30** we
all went to Willims Mothers had a great infare **Sat 31** came home got a letter
from Mother written by E S Bartlett I wrote one to Sylvy

February 1852

Sund Feb 1 we went to meeting **Mond 2** went to the Lecture **Tuesd 3** I went
put sister Murry to bed with a son born 1 - 3*h* P M **Wed 4** David staid here
last night P G and Lucinia came down I went down to Taylors to get some
tallow it is my birthday 57 years old to day Feb= 4 1852 **Thursd 5 Friday 6
Sat 7** went to the Female meeting **Sun 8** went to meeting David down here
Mond 9 I washed **Tuesd ^10^** cut out my dress Mr Perry bought marino
one **wed 11** went to the counsel of health **Thursd 12** Wm= & Martha &
Harriet Ses= here staid all night **Frid 13** P G & Lucinia came down all went
home **Sat <16> [14]** Sisters Pearce & Bringherst here on a visit **Sund 15** went
to meeting caled out went and put sister Wade [Belinda Hickenlooper] to bed
with a son [James Monroe] born 10 m before <4> P M **Mond 16** put sister
Pettit to bed with a son born 10 minutes before 7 A M **Tuesd 17** David P G
down staid all night **Wed 18** been to see sist wade **Thurs 19** Mr Perry
^paved^ round the door **Frid 20** we went up to P Gs with Wm= & Mother
& Martha Ann **Sat 21** Martha Baptised had a meeting to P Gs her Father
gave her a fathers blessing we had a good meeting **Sund 22** we came home
Harriet was married[31] David staid here **Mond 23** he went home **Tuesd 24** P
G came down staid here all night I got a letter from Sylvia **Wed 25** I have
setled up my tithing in full & got receipts then went to the councel of health at
Br Thomases we have got 14 quarts of beet molasses for Mr Parrys beets &
carrots **Thursd 26** made soap **Frid 27** ~~got a letter from Mother writen~~ commenced a letter to mother direct it to E S Bartlett[32] **Satd 26** Mr Parry gone to
the counsel **Sund 29** did not go to meeting

---

31. Harriet, plural widow of Patty's deceased husband David, married Nathaniel
Worden (1826–1907).

32. Early in Perrigrine's journal, as he lists his ancesters, he mentions that his grandmother Bartlett is living with Patty's brother Elisha (b. 1796).

MARCH 1852

Mond March 1 put Caleb Parrys wife to bed with a son [Bernard Evans] born 16 ^m^ [be]fore 10 P M[33] **Tuesd 2** carried my beets to get them made into molasses **wed 3** washed went to see calebs wife found her comfortable **Thursd 4** baked pies **Frid 5** ironed Mr Parry set out some choak cherry trees **Sat 6** he went to the High Counsel it did not set Wm & Martha came here staid all night **Sund 7** they went home We went to the counsel house in the forenoon I went to the school house in the afternoon **Mond 8** David staid here last night went home today P G came down & went home we went to the fort got some peach trees I cut my alapacka dress bought 3 lbs butter of Tomas wife **Tuesd 9** fine weather ^set the trees out^ D[avid] Fulmer paid 4 dollars for me yestarday at the tithing office **Wed 10** I went to the counsel of health Heber gave us a lecture Dr Sprague spoke in toungues I interpreted it was great[34] **Thursday 11** it snowed last night I gathered snow washed and have snow water to wash with again **Frid 12** Mr Parry fixed the hen coop **Satd 13** he went to the high counsel I got John Edwards to cut some wood **Sund 14** we went to meeting had a good preach from Heber John Edwards & wife here in the evening **Mond 15** I went to see old sister Pack[35] caled to see many more it

33. Caleb Parry (b. 1824) was a son of John Parry, Patty's husband. His wife was Catherine Vaughn Evans (b. 1826). They came to Utah in 1849 in the George A. Smith Company.

34. In 1852 Benjamin G. Ferris, secretary of the Territory of Utah, and his wife visited Utah. Each wrote a book. In *Mormons at Home*, Mrs. Ferris scornfully describes a meeting ". . . This Council of Health . . . is a sort of female society . . . whose members have meetings to talk over their occasional various aches and pains. . . . The meeting was in one of the ward school-houses. There were from forty to fifty present, old and young, and, judging from physiognomical indications, they all, with two or three exceptions, belonged to the lowest class of ignorance. . . ." Chronicling some of the proceedings and people in deprecating terms, Mrs. Ferris describes Dr. Sprague as having a "look of vulgar dissipation" and says he was "moved by the spirit to bless the patient in an unknown tongue, pronouncing, in a blatant tone, words something like these: 'Vavi, vava, vavum–sere, seri, sera, serum.'" She continues: "They proved to be the invocation of great blessings, both temporal and spiritual; she was to have everything that heart could desire; her seed was to outnumber the hosts of Abraham, Isaac, and Jacob. Poor thing, she looked as though she needed some better guaranty for temporal comforts than these empty sounds. She could not have been over eighteen; had a large baby in her lap and another child at home; was poorly clad, and undoubtedly half fed" (B. G. Ferris, *Mormons at Home* [New York: AMS Press, n.d.], 199–204; also quoted in William Mulder and A. Russell Mortensen, eds., *Among the Mormons: Historic Accounts by Contemporary Observers* [New York: Alfred A. Knopf, 1958], 262–65).

35. Probably Phylotte Green Pack (1774/6–1866), mother of John Pack (1809–1885), member of the Pioneer Company. John returned to Winter Quarters and moved his family to the Salt Lake Valley in 1848.

is very cold and snows this afternoon **Tues 16** warm again **Wed 17 Thursd 18** sister Edwards sewed for me on my black dress **Frid** I washed ironed **Sat 19** I went to the female meeting it was good **Sund 20** went to meeting in the forenoon then P G and Mary came from Smoots they ^smoots^ came with them Martha was sick brought on a bed she had 3 spasms after she got here I gave her lobelia till she vomited she had no more of them but got better **Mond 22** she [Martha] went through the ordinances in the counsel house for her indowment then went home David staid here last night went to the counsel house with her Martha Ann saw her go through[36] **Tuesd 23** I have cleaned parsnips for molasses Mr Parry has now been in the high counsel 3 days ~~Tuesd 2~~ **Wed 24** I went to the female meeting 53 gave in thier names to join the counsel we had a good meeting spoke much on the subject of taking care of our health to avoid tight laceing cold or wet feet to take care of our infants and how to train up our children that they may be prepared to be saints and fill the measure of thier creation in ritcheousness **Thursd 25** I am boiling away my parsnip juice for molasses **Frid 26** sister Higbee here spoke in toungues said she should have a child finished my black dress **Satd 27 of March** ^1852^ I was sealed to Mr John Parry. I was married to him the 14th of Dec= 1851 **Satd 27** I have been in ^to see^ the indowments again to day **Sund 28** did not go to meeting went to see sister Jackman ^wrote to Sylvia^ **Mond 29** worked in the garden **Tuesday 30** sewed **Wed 31** washed & finished my letter to Sylvia

April 1852

Thursd April 1 went to Ed Wades got a pound of butter had a load of wood paid in seeds and potatoes had 4 lb butter of sister Tomas went to Br [Ira V.] Ameses daughter she had a child[37] **Frid 2** put Mary Shurtlief to bed with a

---

36. The upper floor of the Counsel House, the first public building in Salt Lake City, was serving as a temporary endowment house. In 1855 an endowment house was built on the northwest corner of Temple Square, where it stood until 1899, when it was torn down to make way for the Salt Lake Temple. An endowment consists of ceremonial cleansing and clothing; instruction beginning with the Garden of Eden through mortality and an eventual reunion with God; covenant making, including promises to obey moral, charitable, and consecration laws; and being in communion with God as a presence in his holy house (see Daniel H. Ludlow, ed., *Encyclopedia of Mormonism*, 5 vols. [New York: Macmillan, 1992], 2:454–57).

37. Ira Ames (1804–1869) and Charity Carter (1807–1839) had two daughters, Clarissa, born in 1827, and Rebecca, born in 1830. Clarissa married Thomas Munjar on 16 July 1843; she was rebaptized on 14 July 1852 and married again on 1 August to John Williams. Ira's second wife was Sarah Johnston; they were married in August 1849.

daughter [Martha Maria] born 20 mi before 9 A M **Satd 3** went to the female meeting got a letter from Sylvia She has lost Byron[38] **Sund 4** David Wm Smoot and Martha came here gone to P Gs **Mond 5** I have cooked for confrence **Tuesd 6** it commenced it lasted **Sund 11** we have had the best confrence I ever went to the new tabernacle was dedicated and the Lord poured out his spirit on the people they spoke in toungues and praised the Lord and prophesied Mr Parry and I have been all the time he has gone now this evening to a meeting I am here alone I am happy and feel thankfull for what I enjoy it is said there was 2-500 people at this confrence[39] **Mond 12** I work in the garden **Tuesd 13 Wed 14** I went to the counsel of health **Thursd 15** David came down **Frid 16** he went to Smoots **Sat 17** we met at the school house to devise a fashion for female clothing for health and beauty went to Isaac Hills wife[40] **Sund 18** s[h]e got to bed this morning 5 A M a daughter we went to meeting Brigham & Heber preached yestarday I had my likeness taken with a deguaratipe by [Marsena] Cannon[41] ^Heber told us to go the exploring route with him^ **Mond 19** I have worked in the garden some every day set ionions & sowed other seeds **Tuesd 20** still work there **Wed 21** went to sister Smiths to see about the fashion sister Smoot Wm= & Martha staid here last night **Thursd 22** David here staid all night **Frid 23** he has gone to Smoots the ground covered with snow cleared off warm **Satd 24** I went to sister Smiths to help form a fashion for the females that will be more conducive to health than the long ^tight^ waisted dress filed with whale bone & hickery that they ware now **Sund 25** we went to meeting went to see M[illen] Atwoods child it was burnt bad by its clothes taking fire **mond 26** Cate here & P G & David ^he^ staid all night **Tuesd 27** P G & Lucinia here **wed 28** to the councel of health 1:73 have joined the two last meetings **Thursd 29** rains & snows I wash **Frid 30** still storms

---

38. Byron Windsor Lyon was born in 1847 in Iowa. He died on 13 December 1851 in Iowa City.

39. On 21 May 1851 construction of a tabernacle had begun on the southwest corner of Temple Square. Truman O. Angell was the architect. Audiences had overflowed the capacity of the bowery, and the weather often hindered religious meetings. But the Tabernacle, too, was outgrown before it was completed, and by 1854 seating space for seven thousand had to be found outside the building (Stewart L. Grow, *A Tabernacle in the Desert* [Salt Lake City: Deseret Book Co., 1958], 20–26).

40. Isaac Hill (1806–1879) had five wives and numerous children. The LDS Family History Library has no listing for a child born on this date.

41. Juanita Brooks records, "Marsena Cannon, the first photographer in Utah, was born August 3, 1812, in Rochester, New York, and came to Utah in 1849. The first issue of the *Deseret News* (June 15, 1850) carried his advertisement for taking pictures . . ." (*Hosea Stout*, 2:410).

MAY 1852

Sat May 1 storms snow & rains **Sund 2** I do not go to meeting **Mond 3 Tuesd 4** work on his lot I drop corn **wed 5** we work on my lot plant potatoes **Thursd 6** I bake and go to fast meeting ^I planted mellons and cucumbers^ **Frid 7** David came down ^& brought some batting^ **Satd 8** he went to smoots I went & put Harriet [Sanders] Kimball to bed with a daughter born 4 P M ^babe died^ **Sund 9** went & see her then went to meeting in the fore noon got counsel of Willard Richards & went back gave her an Emetic came home David Wm & Marthann here **Mond 10** they ~~stay~~ go to P Gs I buy some gimp of Needom[42] sell him some garden seeds cut Davids pants **Tuesd 11** wash P G & Lucinia Wm= & Martha here to dinner I go with P G up to see Harriet ^Kimball^ up to the bath house **wed 12** go to the counsel of health set in counsel with sisters [Phoebe Ann Morton, 1786–1853] Angel & Susannah [Lippincott] R[ichards] before & after meeting **Thursd 13** go and see Harriet again found her still on the gain it rained **Frid 14** a rainy day **Sat. 15** still rains I fix me some dresses **Sund** go to meeting in the forenoon in the afternoon go to Br Tomases wash and anoint his wife **Mond 17** sow beet seed **Tuesd 18** go and see Br Mason he has a bad burn had a fit fell in the fire sister Higbee came home with me made me a sack **Wed 19** went to sister Armstrongs to get a bonnet made[43] **Thursd 20** visit Br Mason again his leg looks better took away large peices of dead flesh **Friday 21** finished my skirt and sack **Sat 22** went to see about my bonnet then visited sister Purkins gave her counsel & told her I thought she opporated upon Harriet Kimbal to soon & gave black pepper to her hurt I then went to see susannah found her sick on bed told her to quit going among the sick or she would never get well I then went to the female counsel had a good meeting **Sund 28** went to meeting Brigham has got back from the exploring expedition he preached visited Br Mason again he is geting better **Mond 24** David staid here last night P G has come down to hunt for Davids colt I have cut me a sack, last Friday Mr Parry and myself visited at old sister Taylors with Br Rich wife and Chase & wife sister E R Snow &c &c had a good visit ~~Sat~~ **Tuesd 25** I worked in the garden **Wed 26** I went to the counsel of health had a good meeting **Thursd 27** I washed sister mason helped me we took ^up^ the carpet cleaned put it down again **Frid 28** visited Br Mason he gets better **Satd 29** sister Carter sewed for me I have got me a new hat wore it to the course last wed **Sund 30** wrote a letter to Sylvia went to meeting got a letter from her **Mond** finished my letter send it David Lucinia Carlos down to meeting yesterday

---

42. Gimp is narrow braid or cord for trimming.
43. Probably Mary Kirkbride (1815–1895), a pioneer of 1847 with the Big Company. Her husband was John Christopher Armstrong (1813–1857).

JUNE 1852

Tuesd May [June] 1 wed 2 Thursd 3 I have worked in the garden to day is
fastd[ay] We go to meeting **Frid 4** work in the garden **Satd 5** go to the female
meeting had ^one of^ the best meetings I ever had sister granger spoke
toungues beautiful **Sund 6** we went to meeting **Mond 7** put sister Walton to
bed with a son born 25 minutes past eight A M **Tuesd 8** Sister Mason helped
me wash Br Sprague & wife here on a visit **wed 9** I went to the counsel of
health **Thursd 10** worked in the garden **Frid 11** the same ^gave sister Moss
emetic^ **Satd 12** put sister Lund to bed with a son [Wilson William] born ten
minutes after nine[44] came home worked in the garden P G Lucinia David
Carlos here to dinner Br Leonard & wife here on a visit **Sund 13** we went to
meeting **Mond** gave Br Brunson emetic **tuesd 15** cooked to carry to the picnic
on Ensign peak to morrow **Wed 16** went on to the Peak three or four hundred
had a good time President John Young President J[ames Willard] Cummings
Judge E[rastus] Snow Judge [William Wines] Phelps gave lectures it truly was
an intrestering day[45] **thursd 17** worked in the garden **Frid 18** the same **Sat 19**
went to a female meeting **Sund 20** went to meeting **Mond** worked in the garden **Tuesd 22** went to the church farm[46] ^gave the same^ **Wed 23** went to
the counsel of health **Thursd 24 & Frid 25** worked in the garden **Satd 26** did
the same **Sund 27** went to meeting **Mond 28** commenced a letter to Sylvia
Tuesd 29 washed sister Mason helped me **Wed 30** finished my letter put it in
the ofice mail not come in then went to the counsel house to see about the 24
of July 48 Fathers & 48 Mothers are requested to walk in prosesion on that day
with their litle boys and girls boys follow the aged fathers the girls follow the
aged mothers

JULY 1852

Thursd July 1 Ann Mason is weeding my garden **Frid 2** water the garden a
little I go up to P Gs Julya is sick with the hooping cough[47] I rode a horse back
Sat 3 I gave her emetic came home she is better Harriet Dunn [Harriet

---

44. Eliza Ann Brace (1821–1907) was the wife of Wilson Lund (1815–1889).
45. Ensign Peak, north of the Temple block, in the earliest days of the settlement
   was used as an outdoor endowment house and must have continued to be a
   gathering place. John Young became first counselor to Charles C. Rich when the
   first stake was organized in the Salt Lake Valley. Erastus Snow was also a counselor. W. W. Phelps served as justice of the peace.
46. The Church Farm was proposed at the October conference in 1848. Eight hundred acres were to be cleared and planted to produce food for the poor. It was
   located south of the city (Leonard Arrington, *Great Basin Kingdom* [Lincoln:
   University of Nebraska Press, 1958], 54).
47. Julia was the oldest child of Perrigrine Sessions and Mary Call.

Atwood Silver, plural wife of Simeon Adams Dunn] here **Sund 4** go to meeting **Mond 5** the forth celibrated I sold beets carrots beans lettice for the dinner Mr Parry went I staid at home baked and sewed **Tuesd 6** I went up to P Gs Julia worse rained **wed 7** she is better **Thursd 8** I came home David came after me that night again I rode horseback she laid in a fit 5 hours I gave her lobelia injections she came out of the fit **Frid 9** she is better **Sat 10** I came home **Sund 11** went to meeting David down **Mond 12** I was over to see sister Elmira Burges[48] she is sick **Tuesd 13** caled to sister Tomson she had a bad breast **wed 14** went to the counsel of health **Thursd 15** met for the 24th to organise **Frid 16** sister Higbee here sewed for me **Satd 17** she is here again **Sund 18** went to meeting Wm= & Martha gone up to P Gs **mond 19** worked in the garden **Tuesd 20** in the [*On the back of the page, she has finished the sentence:* garden again. *Then she added new pages and continued on them. She also repeated a few entries, adding the words in italics*]

garden again **wed 21** went to the counsel *on health* **Thursd 22 Frid 23** cooked *prepared* for the 24th **Sat 24** *I went to the tabernacle to celibrate* met at the tabernacle at 7 A M celibrted the day it was grand and sublime **Sund 25** went to meeting **mond 26** worked in the garden **Tuesd 27** [*written over* Wesd 28] went to the church Farm to see a sick child Cate came home with me sick for me to take care of she was ~~sick~~ better **Thursd 29** gave her medicine **Frid ^30^** gave her emetic got a letter from Sylvia I wrote one to her **Satd 31** closed my letter went to the female meeting it rained I got my feet wet coming home **Sund ^31^** Cate went home a great deal better

AUGUST 1852

August 1 David came after me to go and see a Mrs Winn I staid all night **Mond 2** gave her Emetic come home **Tuesd 3** went down to see Cate again she is worse staid all day left her better **Wed 4** went to see her again then went to the counsel of health **Thursday 5** I washed **Frid 6** ironed baked worked in the garden Mr Parry went to Brighams Mill yestarday again to day **Satd 7 Sund 8** went to meeting Brigham preached on the spirits going to prison **Mond 9** I went to the counsel house did not stay Wm. & Martha here **Tuesd 10** Dr Sprague Br Nebecar & wife here performed a painful opporation **Wed 11** Mr Parry got up the oatts stacked them **Thursd 12** he work for walker **Frid 13** I picked my onions **Sat 14** went to the female meeting **Sund 15** went to meeting **Mond 16** had Co Dr Pearson here told me about Sylvia his wife had a babe two weeks old **Tuesd 17** went to the counsel of health **Wed 18** visited sister Duncan she was sick took her through a course of medicine **Thurs 19** I visited her again she was better P G & Winn here Winn paid

---

48. Iona Almira Pulsipher (1817–1868) was the wife of Horace Burgess (1816–1849).

me three Dollars **Frid 20** scalded my pickels paid Ann Tomas all for the
wood sister Carter making my bonnet **Sat 21** went to see Sister Duncan she
is not so well I then went and put sister Mcentire to bed with a son [Brigham
Patterson] born 9 & 10 minutes P M[49] **Sund** took sister Duncan through a
course on medicine Br Taylor has got home & Benson Snow & Richard Mr
Parry had a friend come from Wales **Mond 23 Tues 24** worked on my bonet
Wed 25 bought medicine and other things of Dr Pearson they left for the
gold mines I went to Father Gibs to see Duncan Susannah there with me
Thursd 26 Mr More & wife came here to board I went to Br Hunters gave
his son Emetic washed **Frid 27** ironed Sister Fooss [Sarah Brackett Carter
Foss, 1800–1894] & 3 of her daughers here E [Sarah Elizabeth] -Ph=[oebe]
R[h]o[da] **Satd 28** special confrence P G caled to go to England to preach
Sund 29 Orson Pratt preached on the plurality of wives the first that it has
been made public[50] **Mond 30** William & Martha staid here last night & David
he got a letter from Sylvia P G and sister Duncan here to dinner he went in
where they were giving endowments Br Smoot has got home[51] Wm= & his

---

49. Anna Patterson (1811–1880) was married to William McIntyre (1813–1882).

50. With more detail Hosea Stout notes the same event (Brooks, *Hosea Stout*,
2:449–50). Today the practice is called "plural marriage," the more accurate
term; the word "polygamy" is rarely used. Reports of plural marriage in the
1830s and 1840s led to persecution, and the public pronouncement on 29
August 1852 provided the excuse for full-scale attempts to punish the Mormons
in whatever way possible (Danel Bachman and Ronald K. Esplin, "Plural
Marriage," in Ludlow, *Encyclopedia of Mormonism*, 3:1091–95). Joseph Smith dictat-
ed the formal revelation in 1843. Wilford Woodruff issued the manifesto prohibiting the practice in 1890. Patty, as her diaries reveal, struggled personally
with the principle but accepted it in theory and shielded her associates by referring to marital status in veiled allusions.

51. According to Brigham Young's journal, "Capt. Abraham O Smoot with the first
company of emigrants by the perpetual emigrating fund from England arrived
on the afternoon of the 3rd inst" ("Journal History of the Church of Jesus Christ
of Latter-day Saints," 3 September 1852, Archives of the Historical Department,
Church of Jesus Christ of Latter-day Saints, Salt Lake City). The Perpetual
Emigrating Fund was established in 1849 to assist the poor in coming to Zion.
Voluntary donations, to be replenished by the emigrants, made up the fund. On
New Years Day in 1852, Abraham Owen Smoot arrived in England on a mission. The mission president, Franklin D. Richards, however, gave Smoot the
assignment to lead emigrants to Salt Lake City. Surviving a harrowing storm
between Liverpool and New York, Smoot traveled to St. Louis and purchased
supplies for the overland journey. Narrowly escaping an explosion on a flimsy
freighter that killed twenty saints, he went on to Kansas City to begin the journey. There fifteen died from cholera. At the end of the epidemic, Smoot himself
contracted the disease. His recovery was miraculous, although he lost seventy-
five pounds in a few days. Toward the end of the journey, the animals suffered
from lack of food, as did the emigrants; one young man drowned; and a woman

mother has gone back with him to meet the company Martha is here **Tues 31** she & I are going to ^the^ counsel of health we went ~~wed Sept~~ [Albert] Carington delivered a lecture[52] we went to the store Martha got her a new dress

SEPTEMBER 1852

wed Sept 1 she cut it out **thursd 2** got it almost done P G and his woman down Martha went home with them **Frid 3** Br Smoot wife and Wm= came back with the company here to supper Wm staid all night **Satd 4** they went home ^we^ went to see the camp carried some mellons **Sund 5** went to meeting **Mond 6** P G and all his folks down went in to the counsel house wm= came carried Mr Parry and me up to P Gs staid all night **Tuesd 7** had a blessing meeting P G blessed all his family he blessed me I blessed him he and I blessed David. Mary spoke in toungues I interpreted it rained but we had a good time it cleared off in the afternoon and we came home wm= and Martha went home [Mo]re and wife left here yestarday **Wed 8** I washed sister Knight here **Thursd** I ironed & schilded my bed stead[53] **Friday 10** P G and Mary here ^we went.^ ^Fosses^ staid ^here^ all night sister Pratt got in came here[54] **Sat 11** P G and Mary went home **Sund 12** we all went to meeting **Mond 13** P G and family came down we all had our likenesses taken P G went home got Emorett came back Wm= & Martha came got their likenesses taken then we all went in to the counsel house saw Emorett sealed to P G[55] they all went home Wm and Marth stay all night David staid here last night **Tuesd 14** Wm= & Martha went home I rode up to the tabernacle with

---

wandered away, never to be seen again. Captain Smoot arrived in the valley on 30 August, but at the time noted, he returned to lead the company's descent from the mountains. Unknown to members of the company, the bodies of two missionaries who had died in England were brought with them (see C. Elliott Berlin, "Abraham Owen Smoot, Pioneer Mormon Leader" [master's thesis, Brigham Young University, 1955]).

52. On 10 April 1852 Hosea Stout noted ". . . Conference . . . Carrington spoke on the subject of Doctors & their practices" (Brooks, *Hosea Stout*, 2:435.

53. Patty may have had a brass bed that she "schilded" with a protective coat or polished to bring out the luster; the word "schill" is used with shiny metal.

54. Elizabeth Brotherton (1817–1897), the first plural wife of Parley Parker Pratt, and Phoebe Sopher (1823–1887), his sixth plural wife, had accompanied him on his mission to the Pacific. Phoebe had recently lost a one-month-old child but was pregnant again. Elizabeth was left in San Francisco in poor health as Pratt went on to Chile. According to Reva Stanley, he returned on 18 October 1852, a month later than Patty's entry. Perhaps either Elizabeth or Phoebe traveled ahead (see *The Archer of Paradise* [Caldwell, Idaho: Caxton Printers, 1937], 244, 278).

55. Fanny Emorett Loveland (1838–1917) would have been Perrigrine's third living wife.

them went to the counsel of health **wed 15** P G and all his family came down he and Emorett had their likenesses taken came here to dinner then I rode out with them through town P G left to go to Eurrope and we came back they went home it rained & wind blew hard **Thursd 16** sister Pratt moved in to a house **Frid 17** I have cut my sage gathered seeds I feel to pray for P G by night and day and all those that are with him I often think when shall we all meet again but all is well whether in this or the next world if we do the will of our master keep his commands and obey counsel **Satd 18** Butterfield brought a quarter of bearmeat here last night I have sold and took care of it got a part of the cellar dug to day **Sund 19** went to meeting **Mond** sick I took emetic sold one bushel 2*h* onions for three dollars **Tuesd 21** not well sister Brunson here **wed 22** I am better **Thursd 23** coloured David here **Frid 24** sister Brunson sewed for me **Sat 25** went to the female meeting **Sund 26** went to meeting David Lucinia down Mr Parry went to meet Joseph Parry [1825–1911, his younger brother] he came home with him **Mond 27** I went with sister Angel Susanah and sister Bradock to wash anoint sister Hickenlooper and fox then I went and see sister Hyde sister Parry [probably Eliza Tunks, 1824–1866?] got in came here **Tuesd 28** she & Joseph both here went to the counsel of health **wed 29 Thursd 30**

OCTOBER 1852

Frid Oct 1 sister Parry altered my dreses I wrote a letter to P G yesterday sister Huff here with two children came day before yestarday **Sat 2** I keep them all yet another child came to day **Sund 3** they go away to day I go to meeting **Mond 4** sister Hutchins came here to stay awhile **Tuesd 5** I bake and prepare for confrence **Wensd 6** confrence commenced lasted till **Sund eve 10 Mond 11** I have been to all the conference had a good meeting I wash **Tuesd 12** iron and go to the counsel of health Br Benson spoke to us **wed 13** went with sisters Mumford [Hannah Cann Crosby, b. 1808] &c Angel to carry some things to Sister Abbot that had donated by the counsel of health for her releif found her helpless but neat and cl[e]an possessing a good spirit **Thursd 14 Frid 15 Sat 16** met with the females Joseph Parry & wife moved away from here **Sund 17** went to meeting David down staid all night **Mond 18** Mr Parry worked on the cellar **Tuesd 19** he is very sick **Wed 20** I have been up the most of the night **Thursd ^21^** very sick yet gave him emetic **Frid 22** he is better we have a man here diging potatoes **Sat Satd ^23^** he has dug 50 bushels ^wm= Martha here staid all night^ **sun 24** go to meeting Br Parley ~~got home~~ preached **Mond 25** washed **Tuesd 26** went to the counsel of health sister Angel gone to Utah some things given for the good of the poor some money $260 **Wed 27** Susannah and I visited the sick **Thursd 28** got two letters from Sylvia **Friday 29** wrote a letter to P G and one to Sylvia **Satd 30** went to the female meeting received many things for the poor I gave them all to sister Angel she is Treasureer I and Susannah counseler **Sun 31** went to meeting

David here sister Hutchins went home with wm= her son the two Marys came here just got in two Marys husband and Roberts[56]

NOVEMBER 1852

Mond Nov= 1 the men went back to the waggons the woman staid here **Tuesd 2** they have gone to Calebs come back to night I am molding candles Mr Parry has sold his ox had 8 d out of it. cold the wind blows hard **Wed 3** they go to Ann Parrys [1818–1882, sister to John and Joseph] **Thursd 4** I was caled to see Forsiths boy very sick last night[57] been again to day then went to Br Taylors he gave me an order on Livingsteans store $5 he owes me $5 more **Frid 5** I went took up the order got me a new dress rode with Br Leonard left my glasses went back **Sat 6** the waggons came in Marys both gone to calebs to the waggons Mr Parry had some things & seeds sent him I took care of them then worked diging carrots &c very hard all day visited the sick boy last night again to night all alone the heavens gave me light over bad places where the road was good it was very dark as my candle went out when I first started home **Sund 7** rains hard I stay at home sister Hutchins came back **Mond 8** I wash **Tuesd 9** rains ~~dig the beets~~ two men diging beats sister Hutchins moves away I do not go to the counsel of health **wed 10** the ground covered with snow sewed fixed my clothes **Thursd 11** very cold beet not all dug froze very hard last night **Frid 12** mended my carpet **Satd 13** went to the female meeting voted in one in each ward except 1st & 5th to look after the poor after the meeting was dismised those presant that had been voted in tarried we gave them some instructions how to procede blesed them and came home **Sunday 14** do not go to meeting visited sister Forsith and children gave one emetic last night made canker medicine to day for them Mr Parry gone to meeting **Mond 15** mendid Mr Parrys coat **Tuesd** baked visited sister Forsith she is sick **wed 17** snowed David & Br Lasley [John Welton Lasley, 1812–1858] came down to bury Lasleys daughter **Thursd 18** Phebe here making my dress **Frid 19** we work on the same rains ~~Satd 20 she went home~~ & snows I went to Joseph Parrys to put his wife to bed sister there put her to bed child [a boy, Edward, born] a few minutes after I got there

[The next page is upside down and has a blank space between **Sat 27** *and* Mr Parry heard a very remarkable noise last night. . . . *The latter entry appears to be out of order and*

---

56. One Mary was undoubtedly Mary Parry (1813–1893), daughter of John Parry, Patty's husband. Mary Parry was married to John Williams in 1836. John also had a sister Mary, born in 1804 in Wales. An older sister, also named Mary, had died in 1802.

57. Thomas R. Forsyth and Isabella Donald (1819–1852) had seven children, ranging in age from twelve to one: Thomas Robert (b. 1840), Jennett Agnes (b. 1842), George James (b. 1844), Isabella Jane (b. 1846), Marianne (Minnie) (b. 1848), Neil Donald (b. 1849), and Savilla Delina (b. 1851).

has been moved. Saturday 20 to and including Thursday 25 have been transferred here to
November where they seem to belong. She repeated a few words from the preceding entry.]
in a few minutes after I got there **Sat 20** Phebe went home **Sund 21** I went to
Forsiths staid all day took care of them left them better Mr Parry went to meeting David here **Mond 22** he went to Tooelee after lumber **Tuesd 23** snows &
blows very hard Mr Parry had to work very hard to keep the cow calf & mare
from perishing **wed 24** more moderate I went to Forsith they are very sick five
of them **Thursd 25** I went again found them some better David has come
back from Tooelee Mr Parry has paid him $45 cash for a mare he is to get her
shod & in the spring if we choose he will take her back and give us $50 for her
^**Dec**^ **Frid** ^3^ ~~2~~
[She next attempts to describe an event that she wrote both in her diary and on an inserted
page as follows:]
Dr P Richards came after me to go and [see them]
Thursd 25 I went again found them some better forsith came home with me I
told him I thought his babe would die wished him to have a doctor least I
should be blamed the road was so bad snow and mud that I could not go
again unless he came after me with a horse he said he would **Friday 26** very
mudy **Satd 27** no better rains **Sat 27** put Mrs Akans to bed with a [*space left*]
born 5 10 minutes A M [*large space left*] **Sund** ^28^ rains **Mond 29** Forsith
sent for me I went the babe was dead she was worse & Genette very sick I left
them more comfortable **Tuesd 30** I went again they thought they were better

DECEMBER 1852

wed Dec 1 I went again found them about the same I wished them to send for
some Dr that belonged to the counsel she said no she did not want any body
else to know what a fix they were in four sick then all lying on one bed I told
her they were badly situated but I did not know how it could be helped then
Thursd 2 I went again found them some better but the weather being very
unfavorable I was afraid they would take cold again and get wors again I
wished them to have somebody else and liberate me told them the next day I
would go and see Dr Richards or Sprague **Friday 3d** as I was preparing to go
Dr P Richards came after me to g go with him and see a woman he had been
attening we caled as we went along and sister Forsith and girl found them better he thought they would get well if they took no cold: said I had give them
all he could think of then
[This is the end of the information. She must have thought it important that her involvement
be clear. In the second version, she repeated the same explanation.]
^**Dec**^ **Frid** ^3^ Dr P Richards came after me to go and [see] a woman he
has been tending upon I got him to go and see Forsiths wife and children
before I went to see the woman we found them better setting up we then went
and see the woman found her very low I told him I thought she was dying and
told her husband the same she died that night her name was Clemons I then

went and saw Susannah was gone all day **Satd** [*number scratched out*] **Satd 4**
Lorenzo Snow sent for me to go and see one of his wives Harriet [Amelia
Squires, b. 1819] a misscarriage as I came home went and see Forsiths folks
found them better gone all day I was sent for yestarday & to day to to go up
north ten miles to see a sick woman Martha & Wm has gone up to P Gs **Sund
~~28~~ 5** I went to meeting **Mond 6** I went to Forsiths again still better sent for
again to go up North I went found the woman sister Walton very sick staid
with her all night took her through a course of medicine left her better came
home on **Tuesd 7** went to Forsiths again still better **Wed Dec 8** Wm and
Martha came here got dinner went home I rode in a carriage with Ann Barrat
to Forsiths found them much better but it was a very stormy snowy day the
floor very wet I told them I was afraid they would take cold for I was very
cold could not keep my feet warm I soon began to feel sick and wished for the
carriage to bring me home but it did not come I got so bad that Br Forsith got
an ox waggon brought me home I was very sick I was administered to took
cayanne & lobelia got easier **Thursd 9** I am better very weak & sore all over
Ann came soon after I got home is here still **Frid 10** very weak **Satd 11 Sund
12** some better Br Forsith came here to know what to do for his wife she is
worse says Genette is much better I sent her some compasition & lobelia told
him to get sister Judd to to make an injection and put that in and give it his
wife as he said she had nothing passed her since Thursd and her cough was
worse and she had a good deal of fever I told him she had taken cold & to give
her the tincture of lobelia for her cough and to pay strict atention to her for if
she had taken cold I was affraid he would loose her for she was consumptive
anyhow David & Carlos came here staid all night **Mond 13** they went home I
got into the kitchen **Tuesd 14** Ann washed for herself and some for me Mr
Parry went t[o] Forsiths said they were very bad **Wed 15** he went again they
told him she was worse **Thursd 16** he went again she was dead Ann left here
I do my work alone have got quite well **Frid 17** thaws little it has been very
cold for a long time **Satd 18** still thawing the wind blows hard and has for
some time **Sund 19** I do not go to meeting the south wind has blown for some
days hard turned and blew from the north and snowed fast
*[The following entries for the 18th and 19th have been moved here. She mixed up her dates
and added the November 25–December 3 entries on loose pages, as well as the following:]*
Mr Parry heard a very remarkable noise last night do not know what it was
Dec 18 1852 Dec 19 I dreamed of seeing P G & A Barot swiming last night **20**
Dreamed last night of P G wishing me to sow some root abago seed for him I
sowed it saw wheat coming up ~~Sat~~ **Tuesd 21** I go to see susannah sister Angel
was there snowed again **Satd 25** christmas day it has snowed the most of the
past week very cold to day David down yesterday and Lovlin wished me to go
up there next Mond he is going to get Married **Sund 26** I do not go to meeting David down **Mond** he staid all night carried me home with him we met
Jack Reding & Naomi from california **Tued 28** I baked pies **Wed 29** I baked

more David came down **Thursd 30** he was married brought his wife [Phebe Carter Foss, b. 1832] home with him had a splended party or infair **Frid 31** rained I do not get home

JANUARY 1853
Sat Jan 1–1853 I came home

[On the front outside page is written]

Wade	1 lb butter	1851
Lund	x13 lb beef	
do	1 lb 5 oz butter 20 cts ?	
do	1 lb half	do
	1 - 13 oz do	
	1 - 13 oz do	
	0 1	
	<u>1 18</u>	
	<u>936x</u>	
	1 1*h* 55	Patty Sessions
		1851-1853

[upside down:]
H
May 15
Oct 22

Samples of Patty Sessions's midwife records. Courtesy of LDS Church Archives; photograph by J M Heslop.

DIARY FOUR, 1853–1855

During the years 1853 through 1855, as always, Patty's days were full of domestic and medical activities. But these years invited her into new avenues as well. She went to dancing school. She attended lectures given by Dr. William France, a convert to Mormonism in England and a doctor of fine reputation. She joined a "theological society." She participated in community concerns, such as petitioning for a transcontinental railroad to pass through the territory. She continued to try to name every person with whom she had contact, although, as the population increased, people became increasingly harder to identify. And she wholeheartedly used her energy to be "presidentess" of a society to aid the poor.

> *If I should not live long enough to become famous, this journal will be interesting to the psychologist. The record of a woman's life, written down day by day, without any attempt at concealment, as if no one in the world were ever to read it, yet with the purpose of being read, is always interesting . . . and I write down everything, everything, everything. Otherewise why should I write?[1]*

These words were written by Marie Bashkirtseff in the preface to her journal. Patty didn't exactly write "everything, everything, everything." But she mentioned what we could call everything in passing. What she didn't reveal should fascinate a reader and amateur psychologist as much as what she did.

---

1. Marie Bashkirtseff, quoted in Mary Moffat and Charlotte Painter, *Revelations: Diaries of Women* (New York: Vintage Books, 1975), 48.

1853

he left lice enough to pay me for my trouble had they all been coppers and cents

JANUARY 1853

Jan 1 1853 Saturday I have been up to P Gs to Davids infair he was Married last thursday Dec- 30 I came home found all well have been gone ever since last monday **Sund 2** I went to meeting then went & see Naomi went to Br Jacobs in the evening **Mond 3** washed & baked **Tuesd 4** ironed & baked pies David down **wed 5** split husks to put in a bed **Thursd 6** moved the corn **Frid 7** mended & churned then went and put Mathew Castows wife to bed with a daughter [Elizabeth Mary] born 11 P M[2] **Satd 8** went to the counsel of health ^then to see sister Tylor [Abigail Abbott, 1829–1854]^ **Sund 9** went to O Conners wife on Br Taylors farm Dr Wms= came[3] I gave her up to him **Mond 10** David Phebe & Mary came down he went to mill **Tuesd 11** we went to sister Fosses I then went and gave sister Moss an Emetic in the evening **Wed 12** Cadwaliday brought us a load of wood yestarday[4] to day he is cuting it up **Thursd 13** sister Pratt & Mary Ann was here **Frid** put in a quilt for Martha Ann [her granddaughter] Ann Barrot [Barrett?] helped quilt it **Satd 15** I got it out David took the calf home yestarday **Sund 16** we went to meeting David & Phebee & Mary down we are going out to Smoots **Monday** we went to Smoots Sister sick **Tuesd 18** we came home **wed 19 Thursd ^20^** I baked pies went to sister Angels she was not at home got some nails at the store **Frid 21** Dixon staid here last night left live vermin in the bed but did not so much as thank us for his loging supper and breakfast I do not know but he left lice enough to pay me for my trouble had they all been coppers and cents for there was two kinds of them **Satd 22** went to the counsel of health **Sund 23** went to meeting stoped at sister Fosse David and Phebe were there David brought me

---

2. Mary Elizabeth Daniels (1824–1903) was the wife of Matthew Galland Casto (b. 1822).

3. Ezra Granger Williams (1823–1905) was listed in the 1860 census as a physician. He had come to the valley in 1849 and established a hospital in 1852. Williams's wife Henrietta wrote in her journal, "We gave up our new home for a hospital when the gold rush of '52 was on. . . ." The home, a seven-room adobe structure, stood at 44 East North Temple (see Howard D. Wilcox, "Deseret's First Hospital," *Utah Medical Bulletin* [December 1976]: 3, photocopy, Archives of the Historical Department, Church of Jesus Christ of Latter-day Saints, Salt Lake City.

4. This possibly could be Matthew Caldwell (1822–1912), a member of the Mormon Battalion. Many of the battalion members boarded at Patty's home temporarily, and some of them worked for her (see note 5 for Diary 3).

home **Mond 24** I washed **Tuesd 25** visited at Dr Richards **wed 26** ironed
sewed carpet rags **Thursd 27** commenced a letter to Sylvia **Friday 28 Satd 29**
David & Judge Childs here[5] **Sund 30** went to meeting **Mond 31** finished my
letters one to P G and one to Sylvia and put them in the office Mr Parry has
commenced Browns House to day

February 1853

Tuesd Feb-1 sewed carpet rags **wed 2** the same **Thursd 3** the same Naomi
came here **Frid 4** my birthday 58 years old to day I feel well and happy praise
the Lord **Sat 5** Naomi goes away Phebe here Mary Parry came here with
Calebs child to wean[6] I go to the counsel of health had much good instruction **Sund 6** Wordon came here staid all night[7] I do not go to meeting he and
Mr Parry goes Mary and child here yet **Mond 7** I comence a pair of mittens
for Mr Parry **Tuesd 8** nitting **wed 9** I was called to sister Roads [Rhodes?]
she was dangerously sick Susannah was there I soon found we could do
nothing for her we sent for sister Shearer she could do nothing for her we
then perposed to her to have a Dr but she said she had been butchered once
by Dr Vaughn and she would not have a Dr neither would she take any
lobelia the childs arm was born before I was sent for and her pains had left
her we all staid all night **Thurs 10** we all stay she had no pains appeard
chearful conversed about many things sometimes would say she should die
then we would tell her she had better take somthing she would then say she
was just so easy when her twins were born thus the day pased off we washed
her and changed her clothes about 5 oclock P M eat her supper after and
commenced having pains the childs arm still in the birth place could not be
put back about 9 we became alarmed sent for the Elders again and for a Dr
he was not at home the Elders came Br Woodruff staid by her[8] Br Willard

---

5. Probably John S. Child, the probate judge of Carson County (see Juanita
   Brooks, ed., *Diary of Hosea Stout*, 2 vols. [Salt Lake City: University of Utah
   Press, 1964], 1:681).

6. Caleb Parry and Catherine Vaughn Evans had a son, Bernard Evans, born on 3
   March 1852. Mary Parry was Caleb's older sister.

7. Patty is probably referring to Nathaniel P. Worden, who in 1852 married
   Harriet, the other widow of David Sessions. They moved to Provo, then to what
   is now Eden in Ogden Canyon. Worden later moved to southern Utah, and in
   1867 Harriet married Francis Clarke.

8. Wilford Woodruff writes in his diary: "This was a painful day. I was called at
   about 1 oclok this morning to administer to sister Rhodes who had been labour-
   ing in Child birth for two days. She was nearly worn out as she Could not be
   deliverd. Brothr Franklin Richards with myself administered to her but she died
   at 2 oclock amid the greatest Agony. I closed her eyes. At 3 oclock PM. there
   was a Post mortem examination. The Presidency and several of the Twelve were

[Richards] could not come Dr Sprague was sick Brigham was not to be found and we got no Dr untill she was dead sometime after between 10 and 11 the child gave a strong move while her pain was on her she instantly put her hand on her left side and said she was dying told sister Shearer she could do no more for her at 2 oclock A M she fell asleep the child died but a few minutes before she did the next day she was opened found that the child had made a rupture through the womb in her left side where she put her hand and said she was dying the child was taken out she sowed up again the child laid in her arms and **Sat 12** she was buried Br Brigham preached a great discourse[9] als[o] told the people that he had searched into the whole of the affair and there was no blame to be laid on any one and he did not wish to hear stories about it. I know she would not have anything done for her that was not done neither would she take any medicine **Sund 13** I went to meeting **Mond 14** [4 *written over* 5] we went to see and hear the ground dedicated to the Lord where the temple is to be built and they commenced diging it out[10]

----

present. The surgical operation was performed by Dr Andrews. And no blame was attached to the mid wives who officiated. <The following is the result of the examination: The child lay across the womb with own hand oblong, the head lay on the right side the feet on the left. The child had torn the womb to bits with this feet and the [afterbirth?] so if the child had been born the woman could not live. The doctor gave the following instructing to the woman: If the child presents feet first put the hand into the womb and bring out the child feet first. And if the child's face is turned so the chin would hook under the [-] bone turn the child with the face towaards the backbone. Then it can be born. If the child's feet come doubled up put up the hand and bring down one limb at a time in the womb and turn the child. He said a [−] should not be consulted at such times but the midwife should use her own judgement>" (ed. Scott G. Kenney, *Wilford Woodruff's Journal,* 9 vols. [Midvale, Utah: Signature Books, 1983], 4:190.

9. Wilford Woodruff reports the discourse of Brigham Young in detail: ". . . When we loose our Friends we mourn. . . . Women were not made to die in child bed as sister Rhodes has done. . . . But what would really be a cases of mourning? It would be to follow a person to the grave who had not improved their day of salvation. . . . I would say to the children dont mourn for your mother. I would to God you was as sure of salvation as your mother is. . . . [Sister Rhodes] lives now more than she did before. . . . I request the children to do as well as your mother has done according to the light you have & I will warrant you salvation & Eternal life. . . . I want to say to all present there is no blame to be attached to any of the sisters who waited upon Sister Rhodes. They have all done as well as they could for I have enquired into the whole affair & her time had Come to die & so will [yours] in its turn" (*Woodruff's Journal,* 4:191–92).

10. Willard Richards wrote an account, which was published in the *Deseret News.* "Monday, February 14th, 1853 [was] as clear and lovely a day as the sun ever shone on G. S. L. City. . . . While the people were assembling, they were cheered with the sweetest strains from the Brass, and capt. Ballo's Bands." A survey of the Temple was taken by Jesse W. Fox, supervised by Truman O. Angell, the

tuesd 15 the seventies [Quorum of Seventy] meet to day Mr Parry has gone I am baking I hear that my grand daughter Martha Ann has got a son [William Cochran Adkinson Smoot] one week old to day I am now great grand Mother **Wed 16** I go to meeting to day David down to day **Thursd 17** I finish Mr Parrys mittens it snowed and rained some I have saved watter enough to wash sister James here to get counsel what to do for her side she has a sweling on her side I gave her counsel what to do **Frid 18** sewed carpet rags Ann Barrat here brought a letter to me to read that she had got from her Br **Satd 19** I went to the counsel of health much good instruction given **Sund 20** we have been to meeting had a good meeting I feel first rate in body and mind the Lord blesses me with his spirit and I have enough of this worlds goods to make me comfortable and I feel happy praise the Lord for his goodness **Mond 21** I sewed **Tuesd 22** I washed Susannah was here Mr Parry to work on the public works after she went away I made a pig pen **wed 23** he brought a pig home put it in the pen sister More came here **Thursd 24** Mary here & David in the evening all went home **Frid 25** Elizabeth Foss here in the forenoon in the after noon we went to visit sister Kesler [Emeline Parker, b. 1816] **Sat 26** went to Br Miloms funeral **Sund 27** we went to meeting **Mond 28** Mr Parry has gone to the high counsel since sister Roads was opened I have done but little work I touched some of the clothes that was under her when she was opened got my fingers [*scratched out:* ––] bloody on my right hand they have been very sore every since one is not well yet those that opened her have had very bad hands and also the one that washe^d^ her they seem to be mortification sores Mary Parry and Joseph & wife here Mary has come to stay

MARCH 1853

Tuesday she cleans my house some **wed March 2d Thursd 3** Fast I go to meeting **Frid 4** we have Co sisters Hyde, Pratt Kimbal and others Br Hyde came in the evening David & wife staid all night **Sat 5** I went to the counsel

---

architect. Brigham Young addressed the assembly, describing some of the vicissitudes the church had endured. Heber C. Kimball offered the consecrating prayer: "it seemed he knew not when to stop, till his lungs failed him, and he said Amen, and all the people with joyful hearts shouted AMEN." At the southeast corner of the site, the church presidency picked around a piece of earth about one foot square, assisted by the Quorum of the Twelve Apostles, the mayor, Jedediah M. Grant, and others. Its origin unknown, a one-dollar silver piece fell on the site, and Heber C. Kimball prophesied "that it was a good token, and means would not be wanted to build the Temple." President Young declared the ground broken and dismissed the people, but some had their tools ready, and "much earth was removed that afternoon . . ." ("The Temple" [*Deseret News*, 19 February 1853], 3:26).

of health much good instruction given David went to Smoots came back they stay all night again here I go to Br Campkins she is sick **Sunday 6** I stay with her I put her to bed with a daughter [Sarah] born 9 P M I then came home **Mond 7** Mr Parry has gone to hunt for the mare he came back did not find her **Tuesd 8** I went to see sister Kampkin she is smart **wed 9** Mary [Parry] & I dug the parsnips snows and rains cleared of at dark **Thursd 10** rains after noon ground covered with snow my thumb is not well yet and I do not know when it will be well **Friday 11 Sat 12 Sund 13** we go to meeting sister Shearer came home with us then I went with her to see Susannah **Mond 14** made a leach **Tuesd 15** ^Mary^ washed **wed 16** cannot make soap for the want of wood sew carpet rags **Thursd 17 Frid** the same **Sat 19** go to the counsel of health then up to Hary Waltons 10 miles to see his wife found her very sick **Sund 20** staid all day and night left her better then visited his mother found her quite sick prescribed for her then to Br Lovlins to see her babe its thumbs one weak and bids fair to be a criple I prescribed for that then came home found Wm & Martha here they staid all night **Tuesd 22** he caried Martha & I up to see John Smith & family we had a good visit he brought us back left Martha here and ^babe^ he went home **Wed 23 Thursd 24 Frid 25** she is here yet we have got the mare home last monday the ground covered with snow this morning **Sat** ~~go to the counsel had a good meeting~~ **Sund 27** go to meeting Martha goes home with David **Mond 28** Mary washed **Tuesd 29** ironed **Wed 30** sewed ionions **Thursd 31** the same

April 1853

Frid April 1 worked in the garden **Sat 2** went to the counsel of health Mary Parry went with me **Sund 3** went to meeting Martha and Wm came here & went home **Mond** washed baked & cleaned **Tuesd** ironed baked pies **Wed 6** went to confrence saw the corner stones laid for a temple conference held till sund **Thursd 7** Marry was Maried by Mr Parry to Job Rolin [Job Rolland/Rowland, 1813–1879] **Frid 8 Sat 9 Sund 10** the conference closed **Mond <11>** we washed made soap **Tuesd <12>** ironed & finished my soap sowed peas last tuesd ^& potatoes^ **wed 13** worked in the garden **Thursd 14 Frid 15** the same **Sat 16** go to the counsel I have been at Eldridge [Eldredge] his babe is sick two days **Sund** Mary & Job leave to day to go to Iron County we go to meeting **Mond 8** plant potatoes Mr Parry has not been well since conference he took cold then **Tuesd 19 Wed 20 Thursd 21 Frid 22 Satd 23** I have worked in the garden all this week and visited Eldridges boy he is better **Sund 24** I went out to Cannadas [Cannaday?] last night get home to night find the boy worse a sore coming on his neck **Mond** wash **Tuesd 26** work in the garden **Wend 27** the same **Thd 28 Frid 29** wind blows so hard we do not work much in the garden I fear we shall not finish puting in all the potatoes **Satd 30** go to the counsel

MAY 1853

Sund May 1 go to meet. **Mond 2 Tuesd 3d Wed 4 Thursd 5** I go to fast meeting in the tabernacle I go to sister Keeler[11] she miscarried **Frid** visited her again as the after birth did not come away then went took sister Kamkin through a course of medicine Br Eldrige boy died Dr Wms tended on him the last two weeks last Tuesd put sister Cannada to bed with a pair of twins **Sat 7 Sund 8** went and took sister Keeler through a course of medicine **Mond 9** got a letter from Sylvia & more from P G **Tuesd ^10^** worked in the garden **Wed 11** took sister Kamkin through another cours of medicine **Thursd 12** the afterbirth came away from sister Keeler **Frid 13** visited her again found her better **Sat 14** went to the counsel we meet next wed in the tabernacle **Sund 15** went to meeting **Mond 16** Sarah Ann came here to live awhile I wash **Tuesd 17** we work in the garden **wed 18** the same ^& attended counse^l^ **Thursd 19** the same ~~our cow has~~ I then went put sister Miller to bed with a pair of twins miscarriage **Frid 20** took two children through a course of medicine **Sat 21** set out cabbage plants **Sund 22** went to meeting Wm & Martha came told about Br Smoot getting burnt with powder[12] Br Sister Georges boy has been very sick with scarlet fever rash & throat got distemper I attended him he has got well **Mond 23** work in the garden **Tuesd** the same, **wed 25** the same, we have got our cow home she has been lost for four weeks she has dryed up her milk **Thursd 26** work very hard in the garden **Frid 27** the cow has got away again I have been up to the store and see Susanah Sarah Ann has gone to a party **Satd 28 Sund 29** we go to meeting Brigham preached on the lack of confidence **Mond 30** the mail came in got two letters from P G **Tuesd 3[1]**

JUNE 1853

May [June] 1 Wed [4 *marked out* and 1 *written over it*] **1** I have worked hard in the garden sold $2 50 form [from] the garden for the national Party then went to the counsel of healt[h] **Thursd 2** I washed and ironed Sarah went home her

---

11. Probably Ann Brown (b. 1818), who married Daniel Hutchins Keeler (b. 1811) in January 1853.

12. Abraham Owen Smoot described the experience: "I was emptying a small keg of powder and standing in a stooping position right over it, and as it did not run out very freely I shook the keg, when it exploded. The staves and pieces of hoops were scattered in every direction, some pieces being afterwards found at least eight rods distant. I was blown into the air and my face and hands most terribly burned. It was a marvel that the staves of the keg were not driven through my body, but it did not appear that a single one had struck me. The whole of the skin came from my face and hands, yet, wonderful to relate, there is not now a mark of powder about my face, and my eyesight, the loss of which I was most fearful of, was not impaired by it" (G. Elliott Berlin, "Abraham Owen Smoot, Pioneer Mormon Pioneer Leader." [master's thesis, Brigham Young University, 1955], 65).

Mother is sick **Frid 3** sew turnip seed Mr Parry is replanting corn **Sat 4** weed garden **Sund** ^5^ do not go to meeting Martha came here ^staid all night^ **Mond 6 Tuesd 7** and so on to **Sat 11** I worked hard in the garden **Sund** went to meeting **Mond 13** Br Smiths son dro[w]ned in the creek brought in to our house we tried to bring too but failed **Tues 15** I went to the funeral **Wed 16** went to the counsel **Thursd 17 Frid 18 Sat 19** I worked in the garden Sary came back **Sund 20** all went to meeting I have worked all this week in the garden **Satd 26 Sund 27** [*the 6 is written on top* of 7 *and the 7 on top of* 8] put sister Harper to bed with a son born 6*h* P M **Mond 27** worked and **Tuesd 28** [8 *written on top of* 9] **wed 29** went to the counsel Phebe came home with me **Thursd 30** she is making me a dress Cottoms boy killed last tuesd by falig from a waggon[13] **Thursd 30** I wrote a letter to Sylvia got one from P G

JULY 1853

Frid July 1 Phebe finished my dress then went home **Satd 2** I baked **Sund 3** went to meeting Wm and Martha here and sister Smoot took supper went up to P Gs **Mond 11** [4] we all went to celibrrate the day Wm Martha, Mary & Emorett Lasley & 5 others all here to dinner **Tuesd 5** I went to the store bought 10 lb sugar & carried my hat to get it alterd went again got 10 lb more **wed 6** Harriet came here **Thursd** I gave her cloth to make James a coat and got Mcentire to cut it gave her some bed valances and gimuim [gingham] to make the babe an apron ~~Frid 8~~ put Sarah Snow [Ann Prichard, b. 1826] wife of Lorenzo to bed with a son [Lorenzo Dow] born 11 *h* P M **July 7 Frid 8** baked & brewed **Satd** washed and ironed **Sund 10** went to meeting Hariet went up to P Gs **Mond 11** ~~watered the garden~~ **Tuesd 12** I was caled to sister Winegar [Mary Judd, wife of John Winegar] **weds** [14 *smeared; should be*] **13** to the counsel of health ^Last^ Mond 11 sisters Angel & I & Susannah washed and anointed sister Hunter **Thursd** I put sister Winegar to bed last night with a daughter born 1 *h* A M **Frid 15** watered the garden **Sat 16** Cate here yestarday **Sund 17** went to meeting **Mond 18** washed irond made preserves of currents **Tuesd 19** go and wash and anoint sister Higbee **wed 20** worked in the garden **Thursd 21** commenced a letter to P G and one to Sylvia **Frid 22** took care of the peas **Sat 23** the mail came in **Sund 24** go to meeting got two letters from P G & one from Sylvia **Mond 25** went & washed & anointed Franklin Richards wife, quite a fuss with the indians[14] **Tuesd 26** put sister Eldred to bed

---

13. The *Deseret News* for 30 July 1853 reported, "June 1853, killed instantly by falling off a wagon in this city, JOHN ALMA, son of Thomas and Ann [Smith] Cottam, aged 10 years 11 months and 19 days . . ." ("Died," 3:67).

14. On 25 July 1853, an entry in the "Journal History of the Church of Jesus Christ of Latter-day Saints" stated that "An express arrived in Salt Lake City at 3 A.M. bringing report of the Indians who had shot two men, who were riding through Summit Creek, Utah County; one was shot in the right wrist and the other

with a son born 4 P M **wed 27** went to the counsel of health **Thursd 28** David Lucinia Mary Carlos Julia here **Frid 29** made Sarah Ann sack & skirt **Sat 30** I have finished a letter to P G and one to Sylvia put them in the office **Sund 31** we went to meeting Mr Parry was taken sick in the forenoon meeting we brought him home Enoch Tripp and family came here from the states[15]

AUGUST 1853

Mond August 1 Mr Parry no better **Tuesday 2** no better Hariet went away **wed 3** Enoch went away up North Mr Parry no better we have the Dr **Thursd 4** no better **Frid 5** we thought last night & this morning that he must die we sent for Brigham about the time his son Caleb got to Brigham he exclaimed that the destroyer had let go his hold and that he should get well Brigham came but he was quite easy when he got here he laid hands on him and said he would soon be about his son staid with him two nights & 3 days the most of the time **Sat 6** he is still better Hariet went home **Sund 7 Mond 8**

---

through the left shoulder. The Indians took one horse." The report further stated that the Indians had driven out the families and taken possession of their houses. On 30 July 1853, another report explained that Chief Walker (Wakara) had been difficult for more than a year, despite the "mild" course of action Governor Young had advised the citizens to take toward him and his tribe. On 18 July, it said, many of the tribe, including Walker and his two brothers, Arrapia (Arapene) and Ammon, were camped on the Peteetneet River just above Payson. ". . . as Arrapia was riding from the town to his camp he passed close by Alexander Keele, who was on guard, and though another Indian was near by, as near as the spectators could judge, it was Arrapia shot Keele dead on the spot, and this too, after having partaken of a hospitable meal in the fort with all apparent friendliness . . ." ([hereafter cited as JH], Archives of The Historical Department, Church of Jesus Christ of Latter-day Saints, Salt Lake City).

15. Enoch Bartlett Tripp (b. 1823) was the eldest son of William Tripp, Jr.(b. 1794), a Methodist preacher and shoemaker, and Namah Hall Bartlett (b. 1798) was Patty's sister. He arrived in the Salt Lake Valley on 27 July, 1853. He had first come to Nauvoo because of a rumor that one could profit through speculation as the Mormons prepared to flee their city. However, Tripp visited his cousin Sylvia at Lyons Drug Store–a part of which served as her home. She sent for her mother, Patty, who was happy to greet her nephew. Although Enoch was prejudiced against the Mormons, he observed what he felt were good qualities and later inquired of Patty to see the "Mormon Golden Bible." Patty showed him a Bible that he recognized as similar to the one his father used. "Aunt Patty said they had another book that the Mormons held as sacred as the bible and brought it forward saying it was called the Book of Mormon . . ." Heber C. Kimball came to the home of Windsor P. Lyon to rebaptize him on 1 February 1846 and baptized Enoch as well. Enoch was asked to stay in Nauvoo to aid in the removal of the saints since as a newcomer, he would arouse less suspicion (see Enoch Bartlett Tripp, "Autobiography," 8–10, microfilm, #ms 8795, Archives of the Historical Department, Church of Jesus Christ of Latter-day Saints, Salt Lake City).

he is getting better **Tuesd 9 wed** he is so that I went Mond 3 and put Jane [Ballantyne] Taylor to bed to day [with a son, David John] go ~~and~~ to the counsel of health **Thursd 11 Frid 12** he is still better **Satd 13** a special confrence I went **Sund 14** he and I both went in Enoch Tripps carriage in the forenoon went home with Enoch & David that night it has done him good riding **Mond 15** I took a man through a course of medicine up there **Tuesd 16** we came home **wed 17** I washed **Thursd 18** ironed commenced to make Sarah Anns dress I got her and me a dress and other things of Enoch **Frid 19** cut her a bonnet we have had a fine shower her mother is here making her dress Mr Parry has got so he works a little in the garden **Sat 20 Sund 21** we went to meeting in the afternoon went & helped wash & anoint sister Reece **Mond 22** Sarah Ann went home **Tuesd** I was called to Jane Orman[d] [Jane Lloyd Jones, 1831–1853] she had Dr William sister Daniels &c since last Thursday I took her through a course of medicine she was better **Thursd 24** she is worse and but little hopes of her I am sent for counsel Dr Sprague came said the child must be taken away by force I told him somebody else must do it he went and came again with Dr Andrew he said perhaps she would get through herself with without force told us to wait and he would stay at home and if we needed him he would come any time Susannah came before Andrews she staid with me both Dr went home about 3 oclock in the morning the childs head was born but we could not get the body with force we sent for Br Andrews he came put a towel around it neck he puled on that I steaded the child and kept from making any inscision on the Mother as soon as the child was born we had to burn rags and sugar to cleanse the house as we had done it many times before when I first went there I then took the afterbirth we put her to bed she soon appeared as comfortable as we could expect she had her sences we staid with her the most of the day but felt that she could not live she said she was well satisfied with what we had done and could meet me in another world and hail me with joy she died about nine oclock P M ~~Thur~~ **Frid 26** she was buried with her babe in her arms **Sat 27** ~~Sun~~ I commenced a letter to ~~P G~~ Sylvia and one to Mother **Sund 28** ^got letters^ we went to meeting **Mond 29** finished my letter **wed 30** put them in the office Phebe & David came here staid all night **Thursd 31** David went to Smoots she staid here made me a dress her Mother was here David came took her [the mother] home & Phebe staid here

SEPTEMBER 1853

Frid Sept 1 she and I went to her Mothers **Sat** <Mr> Parry & I went to the singing exebition at the tabernacle[16] **Sund 3** we went to meeting **Mond 4** we went to E Tripps **Tuesd 5** cut and shocked the corn & made Sarah a sack **wed**

---

16. This would have been the "old" Tabernacle, completed for conference in 1852. Made of adobe brick, as Patty mentions, the building was dedicated during the

6 I go to the counsel of health ^got a load of wood from Woolcot^ **Thursd
^8 Frid 9^** washed & ironed **Satday 10** baked pies **Sunday 11** put Harriet
Taylor [Harriet Whitaker, b. 1825] to bed with a son [William Whitaker or
John] born 7 P M **Mond 12** went to see her **Tues 13** I went again **wed 14** went
up to town **Thursd 15** made preserves of mellons **Frid 16 Satd 17 Sund 18**
went to meeting Enoch Tripp & wife here **Mond 19** made preserves &
couloured black **Tuesd 20** Mr Parry commenced work last Thursd on Littles
house he has been sick a long time **wed 21** I went to the counsel had a good
meeting **Thursd 22** visited Abigail Tylor she is very sick **Frid 23** Martha came
here **Sat 24** we went to see Abigail again Phebe came here both staid all night
Sund 25 rains I do not go to meeting Martha commenced a letter to P G her
Father I commenced one to Sylvia Br Smoot & wife came took Martha home
David came took Phebe home Mr Parry came from meeting is writing in
Sylvias letter the first he has ever wrote to her **Monday 26** I put in Marthas
quilt **Tuesd 27** washed sister Higbee here helped me quilt in the afternoon
Wed 28 she came helped me get the quilt out staid all night **Thursd 29**
starched & ironed gathered my peaches had 1:40 ~~carried~~ **Frid 30** finished my
letters put them in the office the mail came in

OCTOBER 1853

Sat Oct 1 went to the Office got a letter from P G I carried sister Abigail Tylor
3 pies **Sund 2** went to meeting **Mond 3** paid 14 peaches for tithing bought me
a bonnet gave 3 dollars for it got it done up **Tuesd 4** quilted my peticoat **wed
5** baked went to the counsel got my bonnet **Thursd 6** went to conference last
Mond I got the things P G sent by Br Forsgreen[17] Lucinia & Mary came & got
them today he sent me a cravat very nice one **Frid 7** went to confrence **Sund
9** put Elizabeth [Kaighin] Taylor to bed with a son [Arthur Bruce] born 10
minutes past three A M was with her all day yesterday **Mond 10** Wm Parry &
wife came here[18] and others sister Taylor Lee John Morris & wife Joseph Parry
& wife &c **Tuesd 11** I put Wms wife to bed here with a son born 2 oclock & 16
minutes P M **wed 12** washed Br Migley [Joshua Midgley, 1832–1912] here

first session of conference on 6 April 1852. For the first time, three thousand
saints could meet indoors at any time of year. This Tabernacle, with its triangle-
shaped frame enclosing a carved pine sun and rays beneath the apex of the roof,
was used until 1867, when the present Tabernacle was completed. As early as
1854, however, seating did not accommodate the crowds, forcing congregations
outside again (see Stewart L. Grow, *A Tabernacle in the Desert* [Salt Lake City:
Deseret Book Co., 1958], 20–27).

17. John Erick Forsgren (1816–1890) had been a member of the Mormon Battalion.
His wife was Mary Ann Hunt.

18. William Parry (1820–1891) was another son of John, Patty's husband. His wife
was Jane Vaughn (b. 1820).

told me much about P G **Thursd 13** Mary ^ Morgan^ here from the camp
^ washed^ **Frid 14** ironed Sister ^ Agnes^ Moss here I wrote for her she
ironed for me **Satd 15 Sund 16** do not go to meeting **Mond 17 Tuesd 18** Eliza
Morgan washed **wed 19** ironed went to the counsel of health **Thursd 20 Frid
21 Sat 22** I have a hard time to take care of Wms wife and do my work **Sund
23** do not go to meeting **Mond 24** sent for to go to David Tubmens
[Tubman?] Jane his daughter sick thought she was dying **wed 26 Thursd 29
Frid 28** I have been here every day to see her **Sat 29** they send me word she
is dead **Sund** go to meeting get a letter from P G **Sund 30 Mond 31** I wrote
one to him one to Sylvia put them in the Office put 15 dollars cash into the
Poor fund and a cloak prised at [*blank space*] and a hat prised at

NOVEMBER 1853

Tuesd Nov 1 washed Sister Waylet helped me **wed 2** went to the counsel
Thursd ironed cut my cloak & sack **Frid 4 Sat 5** sent for to a sick man took him
through a course of medicine then I was sent for to go North 13 miles to Harry
Waltons wife she is sick called from there to another sick man then came home
then went to see another sick man **Tuesd** been to see if I could get him into a
house he is poor and in a poor place **Wed 9** husked corn **Thursd 10** husked
corn **Frid 11** caled to Ann Parrys babe **Satd 12** went again thought it would not
live **Sund 13** went to meeting again to the 14th ward school house in the
evening **Mond 14** set up a leach for soap two men gone for wood had two load
hawled last week & finished diging the vegatables Frid Br Waylot worked for us
10 days **Tuesd 15** washed **wed 16** went and washed & anointed a sister her
backbone out of place **Thursd 17** visited the sick Brs Moody & cocks [Orville
Southerland Cox, 1814–1888] ironed **Frid 18** made my quilted peticoat **Satd
19** went to the counsel of health **Sund 20** went to meeting **Mond 21** sewed
Tuesd 22 visited sick **Wed 23** we have had 5 load of wood holed four from
Brighams canyon 1 from red bute 5 in all **Satday 26** went up to P Gs Phebe had
a daughter [Sarah Phebe] born before I got there **Sund 27** I came home

DECEMBER 1853

Dec 3 went to the counse[l] of health **Sund 4** went to meeting **Tuesd 6** we
washed **Sund 11** went to meeting day before yesterday put Edward Wades
wife [Belinda Hickenlooper] to bed with a son born Dec 9 5 A M **Mond 12
Sat 17** went to the counsel of health **Sund 18** went to meeting **Mond 19** visited the sick last week set out Apple trees **Tuesd 20 wed 21** cut carpet rags
Thurs 22 kiled the pig weighed 226 lb **Friday** ^ 23^ put sister Radmal to bed
with a son [Alma] born 6 A M[19] came home cut my meat ma^ de^ my sasuges

---

19. Caroline Severn (1825–1883) was the wife of Henry Bullivant Radmall
(1814–1908).

Satd 24 gave sister Bouk [Euphronia Bouck] emetic the second one due me 5 dollars from Bouk **Sund 25** went meeting forenoon then went to cotton wood to Br Pews staid all night **Mond 26** went to Br Bunchs took diner went to a dance at Dr Richards in the evening **Tuesd 27** Mr Parry commenced a stable **wed 28** I wrote a letter to Sylvia yestarday let Enoch have it to finish commenced to double my carpet yarn **Thursd 29** wash and ironed **Frid 30** double yarn **sat 31** Mr Parry gone for the cow Enoch ^Tripps^ wife after us to go to P Gs to new years[20] ^I went to the counsel^

1854

that I may do good to my self and all others while I live this is my prayer

JANUARY 1854

Sund Jan - 1 1854 I go to meeting **Monday 2** put Elonor [Eleanor Houtz] wife of Lorenzo Snow to bed with a son born [*left blank*] A M **Tuesd 3** go to a dance at the school house[21] **wed 4 Thursd 5** went to the social Hall to a picnic party[22] **Frid 6 Sat 7 Sund 8** we went to meeting **Mond 9 Tuesd 10** put caleb Parrys wife to bed with a pair of twin sons [Arthur Evans and Llewelyn Evans] one born 15 minutes after 12 A M ^other 2 h after^ put Sophia Taylor [Sophia Whittaker] to bed with a ~~pair of~~ son [Hyrum Whittaker] born 7 2h

---

20. At this time Enoch Tripp had one wife, Roxanna Sophia Billings, whom he had married in 1846. In 1856 he married Phebe Peterson Eastman; in 1857 he married Jessie Eddins; in 1864 he married Kate Jane Allen; and in 1888 Mary Openshaw became his wife.

21. The casual manner in which Patty mentions community buildings shows how Zion was being built. As has been mentioned, Mary Jane Dilworth met with six pupils in her tent barely weeks after the first pioneers arrived. By 1850 bishops were in charge of education in their own wards. Some established schools in their meeting houses; others built schoolhouses. By 1851 each town was required to operate a public schoolhouse. To what schoolhouse Patty is referring is unclear (see John S. McCormick, *Salt Lake City: The Gathering Place* [Woodland Hills, Calif.: Windsor Publications, 1980], 16).

22. A sandstone and adobe brick hall, forty by sixty feet, with a capacity of 350 and said to be the first theater west of the Missouri River, had been erected at the west end of Social Hall Avenue where it joins State Street. On 1 January 1853 a program, a cotillion dance, and a supper celebrated the dedication. On 18 January two plays were presented, *Don Ceasar de Bazan* and *The Irish Lion*, beginning a new era in the development of a cultural climate in the valley of the Great Salt Lake. The Musical and Dramatic Company, under the direction of William Clayton, had been performing amateur theatricals as early as 6 October 1849 in the Bowery (see Dorothy Stowe, "A New Life Begins for the Old Social Hall," *Deseret News*, 19 July 1980, 31–33).

AM **wed** ^**11**^ visited sister Southworth with Enoch wife[23] then went to dancing school[24] **Thursd 12** gave Br Goff emetic **Frid** ^**13**^ he died I gave him a shirt to lay him out in I washed **Sat 14** went to the counsel of health a dreadful storm of wind and snow Wm= Parrys babe burried **Sund 15** do not go to meeting so much snow **Mond 16** put Mary Ann Taylor [Mary Ann Oakley] to bed with a daughter [Mary Elizabeth] born 5 minutes before 12 A M **Tuesd 17** twisted carpet yarn **wed 18** baked Jane and Wm Parry here **Thursd 19** caled to Mary Ann Taylor she has took cold a dreadful cold day went to prayer meeting **Frid 20** went to Br Climmans [John Clements][25] gave his sister a course of medicine then went to a dancing school **Sat 21** went to see Mary Ann again it has been the coldest time we have had since we came into the valley **Sund 22** went to meeting **Mond 23 Tuesd 24** carded & spun wool **wed 25** the same ~~wed 26~~ the same **Thursd 26** went to a party at the social hall[26] **Frid 27** wrote a letter **Sat 28** went went to the counsel of health **Sund 29** went to meeting **Mond 30** wrote letters to P G Sulvia & Mother **Tuesd 31** put them in the office then went to a mass meeting about the Railroad[27]

---

23. Chester Southworth (1793–1874) was married to Abigail Church and Mary Byington.

24. What constituted "dancing school" can only be imagined, but Richard F. Burton in *The City of the Saints and across the Rocky Mountains to California* wrote, "Dancing seems to be considered an edifying exercise. The Prophet dances, the Apostles dance, the Bishops dance. A professor of this branch of the fine arts would thrive in Zion . . . 'positions' are maintained, steps are elaborately executed, and a somewhat severe muscular exercise is the result. . . . Besides the grand fetes at the Social Hall and other subscription establishments, there are 'Ward Parties,' and 'Elders' Weekly Cotillon Parties,' where possibly the seniors dance together . . . in private . . ." ([New York: Harper & Brothers, 1862], 230). Another early settler stated, "The Mormons love dancing. Almost every third man is a fiddler, and every one must learn to dance. In the winter of 1854–1855, there were dancing schools in almost every one of the nineteen school houses, and necessarily so much more attention to dancing involved so much less attention to study. Just so much less education and just so much more injury" (John Hyde, an apostate, quoted in Andrew Love Neff, *History of Utah 1847 to 1869* [Salt Lake City: Deseret News Press, 1940], 599).

25. According to the bishop's list of 1852, John Clements would have been a member of Patty's ward.

26. The JH of 27 January 1854 describes the party: ". . . In the afternoon the Nauvoo Brass Band, the Military and Martial Band and the Tabernacle Choir met in a social picnic party in the Social Hall, G S L City. Pres B. Young and H. C. Kimball were also present." The reason for Patty attending this occasion was that John Parry, her husband, had been conductor of the Tabernacle Choir since 1849. Curiously, she never mentions that historical fact.

27. An article appearing in the *Deseret News* of Thursday, 2 February 1854, with the headline "Railroad Meeting" reported that thousands appeared in the Tabernacle on Temple Square on Tuesday, 31 January 1854. The article praised the

February 1854

Wed Feb= 1 put Wm Andersons wife to bed with a son ^born 9 A M^ **1854** then Higbees to a party **Thursd 2** card & spun **Thursd 2** spun went to ~~Higbees meeting in the evening~~ **Frid 3** ^dance school^ took sister Ormon through a course of medicine **Sat 4** my birthday 59 years old Mr Parry and I visited at Br Shirtliefs **Sund 5** went to meeting **Mond 6** card & spun **Tuesd 7** finished **wed 8** ^dancing school^ commenced some fringe for bed triming **Thursd 9** Mary came here **Sat 10** Phebe came here both staid **Sat 11** they are here Phebe went to her mothers ^dancing school^ Mary staid here **Sund 12** David came here all went home we went to meeting **Mond 13** snow & blow work on the bed fringe **Tuesd** dito **wed 15** made Mr Parry a cap **Thursd 16** put Harriet Snow [Harriet Amelia Squires] to bed with a pair of twins born daughter [Amelia Henrietta] 9 & 15 minutes son [Alonzo Henry] 9 3h A M ~~Thursd 19~~ **Frid 17** ^Wm= and Martha^ here went to dancing school **18** finished the fringe **sat 18 Sund 19** went to meeting **Mond 20** coulered my carpet yarn **tuesd 21** made fringe for a table cloth **wed 22** cut carpet rags went to dancing school **Thursd 23** spooled & warped my carpet sister Smoot & Martha Ann here **Frid 24** put in my carpet wove one yard & a half **Sat 25** wove two yards went to the counsel of health then to dancing school Mr Parry & Edward has gone after the cow[28] we here she is at Luke Jonsons[29]

---

music for the occasion rendered by the Nauvoo Brass Band and by Captain Ballo's Band and quoted a poem by Eliza R. Snow, written in two hours' time for the occasion. Finally, the resolution to Congress urging the railroad route to come through the territory was read. According to the last paragraph, "This meeting was got up on very short notice; and altho' the weather was cold, and much snow on the ground, and no fire in the Tabernacle yet that large place was filled; and so great was the interest felt upon this subject, that even the ladies would not remain at home. The first citizens of this place, both male and female, were present; and all noted with a spirit and resolution that said, they wanted the Railroad this way, and intended to have it, if possible." Nationally a movement for transcontinental railroads had been brewing since 1845, and the discovery of gold in California accelerated the process of surveying and promoting various routes to the Pacific. A young railroad man named Theodore Judah planned the route and guided through Congress the bill that brought the railroad through Utah. But Judah disapproved of the tactics of the financial investors he had wooed and was squeezed out of the process (Henry Sturgis, "The Iron Spine," *American Heritage* 20, no. 3 [April 1969]: 46–57).

28. Probably John Parry's nephew Edward (1798–1854), the son of his dead brother Edward (1769–1842).

29. Luke Johnson (b. 1807) had been one of the original members of the Quorum of the Twelve Apostles, ordained on 15 February 1835. In April of 1838 he had been excommunicated. At Nauvoo in 1846 he was baptized again. He died on 9 December 1861 in Salt Lake City.

Sund 26 Mr Parry did not get home it storms snows & blows hard and cold Oh Lord comfort and strenthen them to come home for they are gone 12 miles on foot it is bad I do not go to meeting 12 oclock ^they^ came home **Mond 27** wove on my carpet & wrote a letter to P G and one to Sylvia got one from P G **Tuesd 28** wove David down here brought a letter for P G I wrote in it

MARCH 1854

wed March 1 cold snowy I wove **Thursd 2** wove 2 yards went to fast meeting **Frid 3** wove **Sat** wove **Sund 5** went to meeting **Mond 6** wove **Tuesd 7** dito **wed 8** the same **Thursd 9** got my carpet out ~~Frid 10 washed~~ went to the store bought some linen for Mr Parry a robe **Frid 10** washed **Sat 11** went to the counsel of health Dr Richards died this morning **Sund 12** went to meeting he was buried **Mond 13** spooled & warped my blankets **Tuesd 14** put them in wove 1 yard **wed 15** had co Susannah sisters Pew Elizabeth & Tripp **Thursd 16** wove six yards **Frid 17** wove 3 4*h* & got them up made them up **Sat 18** washed them out Lucinia & Mary here **Sund 19** they staid all night we all went to meeting **Mond 20** David here got a letter from Sylvia cut Mr Parry some temple clothes and a pair of pants **Tuesd** fixed my pictures raked the weeds from the garden Naomi moved to sisters Risers yesterday **wend 22** Jane here help me make the temple clothes **Thursd** the same Finished them **Friday ^24^** visited at Edward Parrys **Sat 25** went to the counsel of health **Sund 26** went to meeting **Mond** sowed onions **Tuesd 29** Mr Parry saw Brigham **wed 27** told me what he said I felt bad that he did not tell me before Oh Lord help me to do right he is to have a woman sealed to him next sunday and this is the first I knew about and he has known it a long time but denied it to me **Thursd 30** wrote a letter to Sylvia with David or in his letter and one to P G **Frid 31** put them in the Office saw Susannah talked with her

APRIL 1854

Satd April 1 the Lord is my trust oh thatt he may help me to do right at all times and in all places that I may do good to my self and all others while I live this is my prayer all the time **Sund 2** we went to meeting they were sealed his wife was Hariet Parry[30] his children [Mary, John, William, Caleb] came home with us took supper **Mond 3 Tuesd 4 Wed 5** she is here still he has not said one word to me about her staying here but she told me she was acording

---

30. Harriet (1822–1901) should not be confused with Harriet Teeples, the wife of Patty's first husband, David, who was later married to Nathaniel Worden. This Harriet was the daughter of William Parry and Ellen Foulkes. They came to Utah in 1853. There was also Harriet Roberts Parry, who was the wife of John, a son of Patty's second husband.

to what he said to her it was his intent she has gone to work appears very kind to me she was a stranger to me ~~Mond 10~~ **Thursd 6** we went to conference Mary came here staid all night **Frid 7** went again Lucinia came staid all night **Sat 8** we went again David & Wm & Joseph Parry staid here allnight **Sund 9** Wordon [Nathaniel P. Worden] & J Parry staid confrence ajourned last night untill June 27 **Mond 10** Mr Parry gone to the high counsel **Tuesd 11** he took out his potatoes frose bad **Wed 12** plowed this lot I payed for it **Thursd 13** I have paid 16 dollars to John Taylor for wood 4.50 to Edw Wade 6-75 to Winegar [Alvin Winegar, 1816–1874] 6 to sister Walker this last winter total 33-25 **Frid 14** received a part of a letter from P G he is sick will start for home as soon as well enough to come I planted all the potatoes on this lot to day **Sat 15** then went to the counsel of health **Sund 16** went to meeting **Mond 17** sewed flower seeds peas beets carrots &c **Tuesd 18** planted corn took the potatoes out Lucinia down with the bishop **wed 19** rained sheled corn changed the beds **Thursd 20** rains put fringe on a table cloth nit some more wrote a letter to P G to send by O Spencer **Frid 21** went and see Br Spencer do not send the letter put my name in to give all I have to the church[31] then went to Mr Parrys lot planted beets **Sat 22** finished puting in my lot I have put in all the seeds corn & potatoes myself except a few redish & lettice & pepper grass seed **Sund 23** went to meeting **Mond 24** nitting fringe went to Cables [John Cable, 1810–1885] staid all night: **Tuesd 25** rained finished the fringe **wed 26** caled to Cables then went to Br Colmons [John Coleman] with sister Angel & Susannah washed and anointed his wife then came back to Cables staid most all night put her [Mary Ann Cornelius, 1823–1904] to bed with a son [John Cornelius] born 15 minutes past 12 A M **Thursd 27** went with sister Angel Susannah to see sister Abot went a foot she sent for us wished to see us befor she died as she does not expect to live long we had a good visit carried her some things for her comfort blesed her and was blesed we went all of 3 miles to see her **Friday 22** I feel none the worse this morning for my walk the Lord has strenthned me **Satd 29** been down to Mr Parrys lot planting corn finished it **Sund 30** went to meeting sent a letter to Sylvia 2 to P G

---

31. A law of consecration, instituted by revelation through Joseph Smith, had been announced in 1831, asking members to give their all for the Kingdom of God. The law of tithing superseded the law of consecration, although the latter was still considered to be a higher law. By 1854 demands on the church and the territory far exceeded the resources. So the original law was revived, and church members were asked to deed all their properties to the trustee in trust, after which inheritances would be assigned by the presiding bishop according to need (see *The Doctrine and Covenants*, Section 42, and Leonard Arrington, *Great Basin Kingdom* [Lincoln: University of Nebraska Press, 1958], 145–46.

MAY 1854

Mond May 1 made soap **Tuesd 2** finished then helped wash went to school to learn the new alphabet[32] **wed 3** went to see MarthaAnn **Thursd 4** she and I visited at Br Pecks **Frid 5** I came home **Sat 6** rainy some Hariet went to Edwards [probably Edward Parry] ^left Mr Pary he was bed^ when I was gone to Enochs [Tripp] **Sund 7** I was sick they went to meting I staid at home Sophia [Tripp] came staid with me **Mond 8** I am some better **Tuesd 9** Mr Parry has gone to work the first he has done this spring only on the lots I am quite well to day went to the school **May 9 1854**

[On the facing page appear the following accounts:]

John Hall Dr to John Parry

March wall tax	April 1	<u>1854</u>
	to 2 bushel potatoes -	2-00
	peas 2 qts	1-00
	1 cabbage & seeds	0-30
April 10		
	peas 1 pt 1 oz onion seed	050
School		
<u>Master</u>	1 qt molases most qt	070
15	to 2 qts peas	100
	to onion seed	020
May 2	Molasses 2 qts ——	150
May 4	to 1 bushel potatoes	100
	to 3 quts molasses ——	225
17	to 6 bushel potatoes	600
29	to 1 bush potatoes to	
	Br Welsh	100
25	to half bush potato	050
26	dito	050
Jun 1	to 3/4 bush potatoes	050
1	dito	050
1	to 1 quart molases	075
8	2*h* bush potatoes	050
	do 1 buhel potatoes -	100

---

32. Juanita Brooks states, "The Deseret alphabet was an attempt to simplify the writing of the English language. It was evidently designed to help European converts and to set up a common medium of communication. . . . Although two readers, the Book of Mormon, and excerpts from the Bible were printed, the system never came into general use" (*Hosea Stout*, 2:509, n. 9).

Sept 23 4 bushels
        onions   800 (2970
   1854

[upside down, at the bottom of the page:]
Honey lb   Food   April 15 *[and some other faded words]*

Wed May 10, 1854 I went to Roads [George Rhodes] bout some fringe then went with Enoch & wife to a party at Wilkins **Thursd 11** washed stuck the peas **Frid 12** bake pies and sweet cake went to social Hall to school Harriet carried her clothes away while I was gone Phebe came home with me **Sat 31** [13] Sister Foss Olive Tripps an wife here to dinner Hariet gone to Edwards the case of her leaving do not know we went to Tripps in the afternoon **Sund 14** went to meeting David and Phebe came here stay all night **Mond 15** rains they go home **Tuesd 16** fair I clean the house **wed 17** sick **Thursd 18** some better **Frid 19** went to the social Hall to school Mr Parry came after me I came home he took a bedstead carried it to Harriet **Satd 20** fixed my silk dres **Sund** went to meet gave Br Grant 25 dollars to bye wheat for the Public hands **Mond 22** Mr Parry has laid a bed all this forenoon feels bad in mind I staid alone last night **Tuesd 23** went to counsel of health **Wed 24** worked in the garden **Thursd 25** the same **Frid 26** the same in the morning rains I was pulling weeds for the pigs today and found a five dollar peice gold that I lost last year a wattering I thank the Lord for finding it I have set some cabbage **satd 27** Mr Pary went t[o] the High counsel in the after noon he was a planting corn where the beats did not come Vilate & Mary Kimb Sarah Geneat & Ellen all here to day **Sund 28** went to meeting **Mond 29** snowed I went to cotten wood to Br Pughs to a party **Tuesd 30** came home **Wed 31** go up to Enochs ^& to the store^ bought a pint of Osage orange seed

June 1854

Thursd June 1 planted them Wm= Smoot here yestarday & to day gone home **Frid 2** worked in the garden **Saturday 3** went to Calebs **Sund 4** went to meeting Jane [Vaughn (Parry)] came here staid allnight **Mond 5** she done me some caps up **Tuesd 6** she and I went to Enoch Tripps she then went home I went to meeting to the counsel of health **wed 7** I washed my dresses &c **Thursd 8** rains I set out some cabige baked sprouted potatoes ironed ~~Frid 9~~ ironed **Frid 9** hoed in the garden **Sat 10** went to the ward meeting of the sisters organised a benevolent society to clothe the Indians & squas I was put in Presidentes[33] I then went to the new school **Sund 11** went & put Elizabeth

33. At the 1853 October conference, President Young initiated missionary work to the Indians of the Great Basin. Parley P. Pratt took up the banner: ". . . we are

[Loomis] Shirtlief to bed miscarriage then went to meeting **Mond 12 Tuesd 13** hoed in the garden **wed 14** I washed rained **Thursd 15** sewed & hung out my clothes **Frd 16** ironed & baked **Satd 17** worked in the garden **Sund 18** went to meeting **Mond ^19^** had my lot plowed among the potatoes I hoed **Tuesd ^20^** hoed in the forenoon rained in the afternoon ^hailed^ **wed 21** rained **Third 22** rained **frd 23** & **Sat** finished hoing my lot two boys helped me went to the meeting of the sisters in the ward **Sund** went to meeting **Mond 26 Tuesd 27** confrence **wed 28** it ajorned the mail came in got a letter from P G **Thurd 29** I went up to P Gs with Wm= & Martha **Frd 30** ^wrote a letter to P G^ came home had green peas

July 1854

Sat July 1 Phebe Olive and Tripps wife here had peas & potatoes for supper **Sund 2** went to meeting **Mond** work in the garden I do work so hard I am almost tired out **Tuesd 4** went to the celibration to a ward party in the evening **Wed 5** worked in the garden **Thursd 6** Mr Parry went to work to Br chases **Frid 7** a man come and worked in the garden with me **Sat 8** the same I went to the benevolent society Mr Parry came home **Sund 9** went to meeting **Mond 10** Mr Parry went back again I wattered the garden **Tuesd 11** did the same in the forennoon in the afternoon went to the counsel of health **wed 12** went to the store to bye cloth for the indians got none it had not got in then watered garden **Thursd 13** Wm= Alred came to put new shingles on my kitchen[34] **Frid 14** he is here to day I have to work very hard get so tired I cannot sleep good **Sat 15** finished my roof Mr Parry came home **Sund 16** went to meeting **Mond 17** he went back **Tues18** he came home I have washed yestarday been to the store got two bolts of cloth for the indians & a dress for me **wed 19** cut out the indians clothes **Thursd 20** put Charlotte Baker [Charlotte Leavitt, b. 1820] to bed with a son [Wiear Leavitt] born five minutes past 7 A M[35] **Frid 21 Sat 22** went to the benevolent society **Sund ^23^** went to meeting **Mond 24** went to the aniversiary in the evening went to Wilkins to a party with E Tripp & wife **Tuesd 25** went to the counsel of health **wed 26 Thursd 27 Frid 28 Sat 29 Sund 30** went to meeting **Mond 31** washed ~~Tues Au~~ here from P G and Sylvia Lucinia David and Carlos came down here staid all night

---

able to feed and clothe the Indians, or at least, the women and children," he said. Without formal authorization, several women organized themselves into a "society for the purpose of makeing clothing for Indian women and children." This was in January and February of 1854 (see Richard L. Jensen, "Forgotten Relief Societies, 1844–67," *Dialogue* 16, no. 1 [Spring 1983]: 108–9.

34. William M. Allred was listed as a carpenter in the 1860 census.

35. Charlotte Leavitt married Simon Baker when he was a widower with eight children.

AUGUST 1854

Tuesd August 1 I went with them to meet P G and Sylvia camped that night alone beyond the big mountain I slept in an open waggon **Wed 2** went on crosed webber river went to the mouth of Ecko canyon there we met them and a happy meeting it was my son had been gone almost two years and been very sick the most of the time and I had not seen my daughter for over seven years we wept for joy and rejoiced exceedingly we then came crosed the river & camped **Thursd 3** we came and camped on kanyon creek [in what is now Parley's Canyon] **Frid 4** we camped ~~on the~~ between the mountains P G caled his co together and thanked them for their good conduct on the way and bore testimony to them of the truth of mormonism, as some of them were jentiles they then gave him a vote of thanks ~~for~~ as he was their captain **Satd 5** we then came home took dinner at Enoch Tripps. **Sund 6** did not go to meeting **Mond 7** Sylvia went to see Heber[36] **Tuesd** she washed I baked went to the counsel of health **wed 9** P G his wives & David come down Sylvia went home with them **Thursd 10** not well E R Snow here **Frid 11** I gathered onion seed sage & rasbery leaves **Sat 19** been to get a pickle tub hooped went to the benevolent society **Sunday 13** went to meeting P G & wives here & Sylvia **Mond 14** went to the store with sister Roundy got a bolt of hickery 26 yds calico for the squaws cut half of it out **Tuesd 15** made a dress of it wed made another ^**wed 16**^ went to the store got some cap stuff ~~Thugas~~ **Thursd 17** made more dreses **Frid 18** went 10 miles North to Lasles [Lasley] his wife sick [Elizabeth White, 1813–1884; *two letters scratched out*] put her to bed 11 & 8 minutes P M staid all night **Sat 19** went t[o] P Gs staid till after dinner David & Phebe came home with me **Sund** went to meeting **Mond 21** washed **Tuesd 22** sewed **wend** ^**23**^ visited at sister Foses **Thursd 24** ironed **Friday 25** visited at Tripps **Sat 26** went to the benevolent society **Sund 27** went to meeting **Mond 28** went to the store bought with Sister Roun^dy^ fifty five yards of hickery for the squaws cut 2*h* it out **Tuesd 29** had co sisters Foses & Lucijane **wed 30** coulered squaw dresses 6 **Thursd 31** sick

SEPTEMBER 1854

Frid Sept 1 not well last Sunday night put sister janes to bed with a daughter born August ^27^ 11 P M **Frid Sep 1** P G down here Phebe here has been almost this week made me a dres & Sylvia 1 she has now gone to her mothers **Satd 2** I am some better take care of the onions **Sund 3** went to meeting

---

36. According to Stanley Kimball, Sylvia Sessions had become a plural wife of Heber C. Kimball on 26 January 1846. As previously noted, nothing indicates they ever lived together (*Heber C. Kimball: Mormon Patriarch and Pioneer* [Urbana and Chicago: University of Illinois Press, 1981], 313).

Mond 4 washed Enoch started on his mission[37] **Tuesd 5** went to the counsel of health **wed 6** visited with Sylvia at Br Leonards then went and put sister Parks to bed with a son born 11-2h P M **Thursd 7** went with Sylvia & Dimic to find a stove & tub **Frid 8** we visited at Br Hydes Brighams Rockwoods **Sat 9** at home **Sund** Sylvia & Josephine ^re^ Baptised & Mr Parry **Sund 10** went to meeting then went and put my granddaughter [Martha Ann] to bed with daughter [Martha Ann] born 10 minutes before 11 P M **Mond 11** Sylvia moved away Dr Bernhisels wife here **Tuesd 12** made caps **Wed 13** took care of garden seeds **Thursd 14** have been to Jonzes to get my tray got it ^2-00^ caled to Mr Parry house he is plastering the roof **Fri 15** I went up to the store with Sophia Tripps in the afternoon went with P G & folks to see the two Indians hanged[38] **Satd 16** cut up my corn and husked it **Sund 17** went to meeting **Mond 18** been to see the sick **Tuesd 19** went to the counsel of health had a good meeting then caled to Bakers [Henry W. and Charlotte had a son] **Wed 20** put sister Jordan to bed with a daughter born 2 & 10 minutes A M then went to susannah met Pres Richards there & Caroline[39] came home noon **Thursd 21** washed baked & ironed **Frid 22** made preserves **Satd 23** visited sister Cates been confined Mr Parry cuting up his corn **Sund 24** went to meeting **Mond 25** went up to see Buells to get an order on the stove **Tuesd 26** went again got none **wed 27** visited at Dr Spragues **Thursd 28** visited at Br Haywood [Joseph L. Heywood, 1815–1910] **Frd 29** went to see Rhoda Richards boy[40] very sick **Sat 30** went to Doltans on the church farm miscariage then wrote a letter to my Brother Jonathan, and Mother put it in the Office

37. On the anniversary of Joseph Smith's martyrdom, 27 June 1854, Enoch was called on a mission to Texas. He took a bit of a detour, stopping in Wapello, Iowa, to look after his business, then visiting his parents in Maine since he hadn't seen them for nine years. On 15 January 1855 he set out for New York City, where John Taylor, mission president, made his headquarters. President Taylor reassigned Enoch Bartlett Tripp to Maine, where many of his relatives and friends lived.

38. On 8 August Allen Weeks, who lived in Cedar Valley, had sent his two sons, William F. and Warren D., to the canyon for a load of poles. A small group of Goshute Indians had separated from their tribe, intent on taking revenge for the killing of some of their friends and relatives a year before. They therefore waited at the mouth of the canyon for some inhabitants of the valley to go for wood. The Weeks boys, the first to pass by, were slain and scalped. Long Hair and Antelope were turned in by friendly Indians, a trial was held, and they were hanged two miles below the Jordan bridge on the other side of the river (Brooks, *Hosea Stout*, 2: 525–27).

39. Franklin Dewey Richards (1821–1899) was a member of the Quorum of the Twelve Apostles.

40. There were two Rhoda Richardses. The first Rhoda Richards (1784–1879) was a sister of Willard, Levi, and Phineas. She was one of the numerous women sealed on 31 January 1846 to the prophet Joseph Smith. Accounts of her marital

OCTOBER 1854

Sund Oct 1 went to meeting Harriet came in here the first time she has spoke to me since she left here she would not set down then **Mond 2** sister Orman here ^sick^ gave her Emetic **Tuesd 3** she went home last night better to day visited sister Robert in a waggon sick went to couns^el^ of health then went to see her again she is better then called to sister Galley [probably the wife of John Gailey] sister Amen [Ahman?] had been with her 24 hours hard labour I delivered her less than ^8 1*h* P M ^ half an hour child dead had laid in the birth 24 hours **Wed 4** put sister Wheeler to bed with a son born 3 3*h* P M **Thursd 5** caled to sister Morton she had a bad foot and leg baked **frid 6** went to confrence **Sat 7** there again **Sund 8** again visited the sick every day to day caled to Br Shirtleifs put Mary [Elizabeth Hadlock] to bed with a son [Brigham Young] born 2- 1*h* P M confrence ajourned **Mond 9** sister jones here gave her babe emetic **Tuesd 10** Brs Gally commenced diging my potatoes **wed 11** danish man dug beets **Thursd 12** dito **Frid 13** finished my potatoes 80 bushels sister Wardrope brought her babe here I gave it Emetic **Sat 14** I am sick afternoon better go and anoint sister Williams daughter **Sund 15** go to meeting went to Jane Taylor [Jane Ballantyne] miscariage then to meeting **Mond 16** wash and iron Mary Elen Kimbal here **Tuesd 17** visited sister Foss and Olive and sister Angel all sick then to the store bought ten lb sugar then to the counsel of health **wed 18** worked in the garden all day gathering ground cheries **Thursd 19** worked in the garden **Frid 20** dito **Sat 21** dito **Sund 22** went to meeting **Mond 23** worked in the garden diging beets **Tuesd 24 wed 25** finished the beets **Thursd 26** took care of my roots **Frid 27** had a man to mow the grass **Sat 28** did up a cap went to the benevolent society **Sund 29** went to meeting in the forenoon rained in the afternoon David Lucinia & Sylvia here let Sylvia have some cabage beets carrots & some pork **Mond 30** dug carrots **Tuesd 31** went to the Counsel of health bought eight yards flannel apron parasol cover

NOVEMBER 1854

wed Nov 1 1854 made me a sack and apron **Thursd 2** sewed carpet rags **Frd 3** the same **Sat 4** bought some mutton visited a sick woman in Bouks house **Sund 5** visited her again went to meeting caled to caleb Parrys babe [one of the twins] very sick dont think it will live see the woman again **Mond 6** washed went to Calebs again babe no better the other sick some better **Tuesd 7** there again that quite well but the other died about 4 P M **wed 8** went to the

---

status conflict. One source says she was a spinster; another that she was widowed; another that her fiance had died in 1812; still another that she was later sealed to Brigham Young. The second, Rhoda Harriet Foss, married Franklin Dewey Richards in 1857. The reference to "her boy," then, is confusing.

funeral **Thursd 9** cut me a dress **Frd 10** bought 11 lb of tallow tried it out
went to the store got an oil cloth for the table **Sat** molding candles have got 6
lb rags cut and sewed for the benevolent society and went there have visited
that sick woman every day **Sund 12** went to meeting **Mond 13** doubled carpet yarn for the benevolent society **Tuesd 14** finished it **wed 15** mended Mr
Parrys coat **Thursd 16** sewed on my dress went to the store bought more yarn
for the carpet sister Angel died 6 oclock P M[41] **Frid 17** she was buried **Sat 18**
finished my dress went to the benevolent society **Sund 19** went to meeting
again in the evening to the school house **Mond ^20^** have a man here geting
out manure **Tuesd 21** he is here to day again **Wed 22** in the forenoon afternoon cut wood for Harriet **Thurd** have a wheel I am spining **Frd 24** same
Satd 25 went to town found Sylvia there went to the counsel of health **Sund
26** put sister Tomlinson to bed with a daughter born [*blank space left*] A M then
went to meeting **Mond 27** put sister cawdee to bed with a daughter born 10
minutes before 10 A M Doubled 14 skeins of stocking yarn **Tuesd 28** caled to
sister Messor [Anna Barr Musser] **Wed 29** finished twisting my yarn **Thursd
30** wash iron ^commenced stockens^ went to waltons in the night

DECEMBER 1854

Frid Dec 1 visiited at P Gs then to Sylvias in the afternoon and evening went
to P Gs to sleep caled to waltons 11 2*h* P M put his wife to bed with a son born
3 1*h* A M **Sat ^Dec 2^** then came home went to the benevolent society **Sund
3** went to meeting ~~Mon~~ see P G & folks been to see Martha she came in with
them I see them **Mond 4** caled to sister Cooms she not well I stoped at wheel-
ers she let me have 10 1*h* yards of calico also been niting **Tues 5** to Cooms
again to Sister Risers red his imprissonment[42] **Wed 6** went to Cooms again
Thursd 7 niting for Mr Parry **Frd 8** nit him some mittins **Sat 9** went to town
and setled part of my tithing then to Calebs then to the store got some 1 2*h*
velvet on an order 3 lb sugar got me some alipaca for a cloak then to sussan-
nahs saw sister Pew she came to ask us to go there to christmas then to the
counsel of health **Sund 10** went to meeting ^Br Whittecor here^ **Mond 11**
sewed some went and see about ^~~making~~ weving^ the carpet for the tabernacle as this ward is to make 60 - 2*h* yards we that belong to the benevolent
society make it **Tuesd 12** made me a night dress **wed 13** been and setled up
my tithing paid this year [*space left blank*] and $10 into the emigrating fund to

---

41. Phebe Agnes Morton (1786–1854) and James W. Angell were the parents of
    Truman Osborn Angell, architect for many of the early church buildings.

42. While George C. Riser was on a mission in Germany, he was arrested for
    preaching and imprisoned. This was in August of 1854. He was released and
    arrived home in September 1855. (See Andrew Jenson, *L.D.S. Biographical
    Encyclopedia*, 4 vols. [Salt Lake City: Deseret News Press, 1936], 4:338.)

gather the poor[43] **Thursd 14** washed **Frd 15** reading the history of Mother Smith & niting **Sat 16** went to the B. society **Sund 17** went to meeting **Monday 18 Tuesd 19** caled to Br Flonys then to Br Coons [Abraham Coons] put his wife to bed with a daughter born 10 P M then to sister Flony again put her to bed with a pair of twins daughters born 1 $2h$ A M **wed 20** went to the counsel of health **Thursd 21** killed our pig **Frd ^22^** & salted it **Sat 23** mad[e] sasages caled to sister Tinga [Tingey?] she is very sick I do not think she will live **Sund 24** see her again go to meeting **Mond 25** see her again go to Br Pews to christmas he came after me **Tuesd 26** we went to Br Birchs [probably Francis Birch, b. 1808] danced and staid all night **Wed 27** came home had a good time see sister Tinga again is no better Charles Hyde came here and David Charles blesed Mr Parry and me **Thursd 28** went to a meeting of mid-wives **Frd 29** made half of the carpet for the tabnercle I was sick took emetic **Satd 30** better **Sund 31** went to meeting in the forenoon staid at home in the afternoon then Mr parry and me went up to P Gs

1855

I was apointed Presidentess over the females of that Counsel

JANUARY 1855

Monday Jan 1 1855 had a party there I was sick we danced I danced some had a good time **Tuesd 2** about 14 inches of snow had fallen still snowing we came home in the storm I took my bed set up no more untill Satd **wed 3** the wind blew very hard **Thursd 4 Frid 5** a little more moderate **Satd 6** fine I got out door I have been alone the most of the time Wm= & Martha came here staid all night **Sund 7** I do not go to meeting they go home **Mond 8 Tuesd 9** put Sophia Dimic Huntingtons wife to bed with a son [Joseph Smith] born 1-25 minutes A M **wed 10** worked on caps **Thursd 11** went to meeting of the midwives staid all night to sister Fosses then went to Calebs came home sister Colebrook came here cut me a cloak **Satd 13** made me a sack **sund 14** went to meeting **Mond 15** went to store got some buttons for my cloak fixed my dress sister Moss here **Tues 16** I washed **Wed 17** went to the President ^Br Richards^ of the counsel of health told me that I must go tomorrow and pre-side over the counsel as he could not be there also told me that I must take sis-ter Angels place and Susannah take mine and she and I must choose another counsellor **wed 17** I went to the counsel Br Deremus came I gave the charge of the meeting to him he being a member **Thursd 18** ironed and knit **Frid 19** I have been to see the Bishop he told me he would apoint a meeting for the

43. This is a reference to the Perpetual Emigrating Fund.

sisters next week as the Presd had caled on us to do somting for the poor said we had clothed the squaws ^and children^ firstrate we now must look after the poor in each ward David has been here to day I sent Sylvia some cabbage and also my ~~Andirons~~ handirons to have untill I caled for them **Satd 20** been to Sister Colbrooks got my cloak **Sund 21** went to meeting Harriet went with us set with us I came home then was called to Br Cowins his wife had a pair of twins one was born before I went Sister Harrington was there delivered her of the first the other more difficult she sent for me I delivered her of the other soon left them all comfortable **Mond 22** called and see her again found them all doing well Br Manson brought ~~us~~ a load of wood **Tuesd 23** I hired Br Moxon to put up some fence **Wed 24** nit me a pair of mits **Thursd 25** went to a meting of midwives **Frd 26** finished me two pair of stockins got sister Foster to coulour them black **Satd 27** done me up a cap went to the female society of benevolence Bishop Roundy there[44] had a good meeting received much good instruction from him **Sund 28** went to meeting **Mond 29** Mr Parry put down 2 fence posts very warm & pleasant **Tuesd 30** I commenced a hearth rug yestarday work on a frock for Mockson **Wed 31** went to the counsel of he[a]lth spoke much upon the subject of raising children

February 1855

Thursd Feb 1st went to Tripps on a visit with sisters Higbee & Dudley **Frid 2** worked on the rug **Sat 3** Phebe staid here last night sister Tomas sent for me she was sick **Sund 4** my birth day went to meeting Sylvia & David here at noon gave them some beets carrots cabbage & onions **Mond 5** called to Sister Gambel miscarriage I then went to dancing school **Tuesd 6** caled to sister Kamkin put her to bed with a son [George Campkin] born 20 minutes before 6 P M **wed 7** went round sister Tripps block for her to collect for the poor **Thursd 8** went to a meeting of the midwives **Frd 9** ~~Sat 10~~ ~~went to the be~~ went to Wordels to dancing school **Sat 10** went to the benevolent society **Sund 11** went to meeting **Mond 12** went to see a sick child in the 14 ward Br Cooms **Tues 13** worked on my rug **wed 14** went to the counsel of health had a good time much good counsel given good things spoke in toungues ~~Frd~~ **Thursd 15**~~Fri~~ worked on my rug baked pies Mr Parry put down 3 fence posts **Frid 16** sister Cross & daughter & Caleb & wife Hariet came here for the first time since she left she apeared Br Birch & wife was here this forenoon to have me go down there to a party next Mond **Satd 17** visited some poor in the ward found them kneedy I then saw Br Jackman and reported to him[45] he sent

---

44. Shadrach/Shadrack Roundy was bishop of the Salt Lake sixteenth ward from 1849 to 1856.

45. Levi Jackman was a counselor to Shadrach Roundy. He had helped to build wagons for the trek west.

me to visit those poor **sund 18** went to meeting my children all there then Lucinia came here staid all night **Mond 19** went to Br Birches to the party they sent a carriage after me we had a good dance a good spirit prevailed many speeches were spoke songs sung speaking in toungues interpretations and thus we spent the time good order and the Spirit of God which caused peace goverened the party and truly it was a good time **Tuesd 20** they brought me home Mr Parry ^and Hariet^ would not go but was wiling I should go **Wed 21** quite cold **Thursd 22** I went to a meeting of midwives then to Br Leonards with Lucinia staid all night **Frid 23** we then went to Dr Richardsons then home **Sat 24** old sister Wilson here went to the school to the benevolent society I gave her my muff and boea and a black lace veil and a pair of stockins **Sund 25** went to meeting wrote a letter E S Bartlett Maine **Mond 26** washed **Tuesd 27** put the letter in the office and I sent a Book of Mormon with it to E S Bartlett I visited sister Davis,s babe sick I then ironed then visited a sick man I had to get an interpretor to go with me they were french I found them destitute of food I boiled some flour potatoes & meat carried to them for thier supper **wed 28** I went to see Bishop Hickenloopers babe it is a criple & has a bunch on its back Susannah went with me we took dinner at Br Warcmans then went to the counsel of health I was then caled to go up north ten miles to see my son David he had hurt himself loading rock I left the counsel we found him very sick Br Kimbal was there I gave him Emetic and swet him set up a most all night

MARCH 1855

Thursd March 1 David is a litle better this morning but soon took a chill then a fever Br Kimbal preached in the school house last night talked here at P Gs to day good in the after noon I went to see H Waltons wife she is sick P G took sick to night very sick all night **Frd 2** gave him emetic afternoon came home not well myself **Satd 3** my sons worse they send for me again I went up in the stage found them quite sick I then went and see sister Duncan she was very sick gave her some medicine Set up part of the night with P G & David **Sund 4** went and see sister Duncan found her much better then went and see Waltons wife found her much better took dinner with Sylvia then came home with Wm Smoot & Martha they came up last night I found Sophia Tripp sick **Mond 5** put her to bed with a son [Arnal Ondree] born 12 & 12 A M **Tuesd 6** caled to Br Messengers babe sick gave it emetic then to Edward Waides wife Elen [Mary Ellen Page and Edward Davis Wade] staid all night **Wed 7** put her to bed with a son [Daniel] born 15 minutes before 11 A M **Thurs 8** went to counsel of midwives **Frd 9** I brought my molasses home 2 2h gallons **Sat 10** went to the benevolent society **Sund 11** went to meeting went to see Harriet took supper there **Mond 12** worked on my rug **Tuesd 13** carried my onions to the store got Mr Parry a neckstock gave $4 00 for it got me some things **wed 14** put John Bagers wife Ann to bed with a daughter [Electa Ann] born [*space* *left blank*] A M[46] then went to counsel of health caled to see sister Brown came back to the counsel I was apointed Presidentess over the females of that Counsel sister Susannah Richards & Judith Higbee my counselors all three by unanimous vote to be sustained ~~that~~ in their places **Thursd 15 Frid 16** David wife & Sylvia went to see Marthann wished me to go with them but I could not go **Sat 17** P G here to dinner Sylvia P G & children & Chester Lovlin staid here all night **Sund 18** went to meeting they went home **Mond 19** Josephine came down staid at Tripps **Tuesd 20** staid here **Wed 21** put sister Mcentire to bed with a son born 3 & 35 minutes A M then went & bought me a mahogany chest sugar bowl & tumbler gave $3=50 for all then went to Br Kimbals with Josephine stopt & see sister Birnhisel **Thursd 22** cut me a dress then went to a meeting of midwives Carline wife of Br Martindale [Caroline Smith, b. 1814] was there had been growing large for ten years she is now very large looks as though she would be confined every hour yet there is nothing of that kind the matter and Susannah R= and myself are a going to try to do something for her acording to Prs=d Youngs counsel my children came & caled for me and I left the meeting came home let them have garden seeds and roots let P G have 26 peach trees 50 cents each $13=00 **Frd 23** went and see sister Bagger Cate came here **Satd 24** I went last night took sister Bagger through a course of medisene to day ^Carline^ to then counsel of health sisters Pew Birch [probably Elizabeth Hardman, b. 1810, wife of Francis Birch] and Susanah came home with me staid all night **Sund 25** put sister Parker to bed this morning with a daughter born 5 & 5 minutes A M[47] then went to meeting Br Higbee & wife stopt here to supper **Mond 26** caled to sister Cowin she has got a bad breach **Tuesd 27** went and see Carline again then to the benevolent society had a good meeting **wed 28** caled to Hariet Taylor put her to bed with a son dead born–born 15 minutes before 2 P M **Thursd 29** worked on my dress **Frd 30** went to see sister Cowin and Harriet Taylor found them comfortable then to the store got me some ribband then to susannahs to see caroline Martde [Martindale] then to a party at Br Kenzys he came after us we had a good time feasted body & spirit **Satd 31** sewed ^on dress^

APRIL 1855

Sund to meeting **Mond 2** washed **Tuesd 3** ironed **wed 4** finished my dress **Thursd 5** covered my parisol went to meet the midwives **Frid 6** to confrence P G & Mary staid here P G plowed this lot sowed it with oats **Sat 7** to con= David & Phebe staid here **Sund** to con= Wm= and <confrese done> Martha ann & Harrit Sessions or ^Wordon^ staid here I gave Harrit a new dress delaine and

---

46.   Ann Haynes Kindness (1830–1929) was the wife of John Chamberlain Badger (1825–1888).

47.   Margaret Kittle (1826–1899) was the wife of William Knowlton Parker (b. 1809).

some other things **Mond 9** they all went home I went to the store with Martha Ann ^bought &^ gave her a ring gave 3-00 for it I have sowed some peas parsnips & clover seeds since **Tuesd 10** went to see sister Cowin carried my bonnet to Agatha Pratt to clean **wed 11 Thursd 12 Frd 13** went to Jane Blackest [Jane Hamilton Blackhurst, b. 1807] had a good time David came down Lucinia Sylvia came I let them have my keys he got ^some^ my potatoes <bush> **Sat 14** I went to sister Williams 13 ward she was salivated & had canker[48] to took her through a course of medicine then to the counsel of health sister Higbee apointed treasurer Br Bager came for me his wife is salivated she & sister williams have both had med= of the same Dr Vale William & Martha Phebee & Elizabeth all staid here all night **Sund 15** went to meeting **Mond 16** planted potatoes Br Bensons man worked here Mr Parry & I went to Lorenzo Snows to a philosophical meeting[49] **Tuesd 17** cold I nit **Wed 18** I nit **Thursd 19** Phebe & Olive here **Frd 20** Sylvia & Sophia here Sylvia staid all night **Satd 21** I Susanah & sister Higbee went to Br Wareham washed & anointed both of his wives Mary Watt Caroline Martindale & Julia a french girl then came home went to the benevolent society ^yesterday^ sold potatoes 8 bushels to Lorenzo Snow ^for a load of wood^ 3 to Sylvia I give sold 2 to Rhd [Richard?] Moris for 25 lb flour let David have 10 Sylvia 2 last week **Sund 22** went to meeting **Mond 23** planted beans & mellons cucumbers **Tuesd 24** went to see sister Cowin she is beter made me an apron watered the garden it rains a little to night **wed 25** wet down my leach & prepared to make soap Mr Parry went to the theologic society heard Brigham speak **Thursd 26** made soap four pails full **Frd 27** put sister Shaw to bed with a daughter born 20 minutes past 12 A M name Eliza I have paved around the kitchen door **Satd 28** went to the counsel of health **Sund 29** went to meeting **Mond 30** washed sister Moss helped me

May 1855

Tuesd May 1 she came & ironed I am not well **Wed 2** I have done up some caps went and joined the theological society **thursd 3** went to the midwives

---

48. Salivation produces an excess secretion, often accompanied by soreness of mouth and gums.

49. The *Deseret News* (14 March 1855, p. 7) announces under the heading "The Polysophical Academy" the following: "Will be opened next Monday in Lorenzo Snow's Building, East of Gov. Young's Residence. Reading, Spelling, Writing, Arithmetic, Grammar, Composition, History, and Declamation, together with such other Branches as may be required, will be taught in this Institution. During interval of School hours the Young Gentlemen will be taught Gymnastic and Military exercises. The Young Ladies also will have the advantages of classes in Music and Drawing. . . . Terms of Tuition, five dollars per quarter. . . ." The names at the bottom of the notice are "Lorenzo Snow, Wm. Edington, Saml. Cornaby, Instructors."

meeting **Frid 4 Sat 5** went to see sister cowin then to Dr Frances lectures[50]
Sund 6 went to meeting **Mond 6** went with Sister Smoot & Wm= & Martha
up to P Gs **Tuesd 7** came home this morning in the afternoon went to Tripps
with Br Heywood & wives[51] **Wed 8** went to the theological society Br Hyde
spoke on language **Thursd 9** visited Bishop Browns wife with Sister Vary or
Heywood caled and see sister cowin **Frd 10** watered the part of the garden
Satd 11 went to the counsel of health **Sund 12** went to meeting **Mond 13**
sprouted potatoes **Tuesd 14** cleaned the cellar then went to Dr France
Lectures **wed 15** making a smock for Moxen **Thursd 16** went to the midwives
meeting **Frid 17** made me a bonnet white one **Satd 18** went to France Lecture
Sund 19 went to ~~meeting~~ cottenwood **Mond [21** to sister] ^Pews she sick^
made me a calico bonnet **Tuesd 22** Mr Parry sick gave him emetic Sund I was
caled with Susanah to sister Pew she was very sick **wed 23** I watered some
Thursd 24 made me a cap done up some more I bought a load of wood I got
it paid with potatoes to day **Frd 25** sold 8 bushels potatoes for an other load of
wood **Satd 26** went to the counsel of health **Sund 27** went to sister Page she
had a pair of sons born before I got there one dead born went t[o] meeting in
the afternoon **Mond 28** washed & ironed **Tuesd 29 wed** garden afternoon
went to cotton wood to Br Pews with sisters Susannah Higbee & others they

---

50. On 18 April 1855 Dr. William France (1814–1860) advertised in the *Deseret News*
that he was beginning a series of lectures on "The Principles of Midwifery and
the Management of Women and Children." He would avoid "all unmeaning
technicalities, and speculative theories. Plain matter of fact and principles of
undoubted truth–drawn from an extensive experience in one of the most celebrated Lying-in Institutions in the world–which form the nucleus from whence,
guided by the light of Eternal Truth, it is hoped much useful Knowledge may be
developed" (p. 44). The cost was ten dollars for the midwife lectures and five
dollars for the mothers' lectures.

    Dr. France was born in Kidderminster, England, graduated from the
University of Glasgow, and practiced in Liverpool, England. After he converted
to Mormonism, he came to Salt Lake City in 1850 and set up practice. Upon his
death on 20 March 1860, Wilford Woodruff recorded in his journal, "Dr
[France] died this morning at 6 oclock with the pleurisy of the heart. He died
very suddenly. He has been one of the most skilful Surgeons of his generation"
(*Woodruff's Journal*, 5: 444).

51. Joseph Leland Heywood's first wife was Sarepta Maria Blodgett, to whom he
was married in 1841. His plural wives were Sarah Symonds, Martha Spence,
and Mary Bell. He managed a store for Joseph Smith, was a bishop in Nauvoo,
and was left behind with others to manage church affairs when Brigham Young
and his followers abandoned the city. Heywood joined church members in Utah
in 1848, made a number of trips to Washington, D. C. on behalf of the church,
and acted as postmaster and United States marshal. He was instrumental in
founding and settling several towns in San Pete and Utah's Dixie, moving finally to Panguitch, where he was a patriarch and lived out his life.

came after us had a good party there **Wed 30** went to Br Birches had a good party there **Thursd 31** came home then went to the midwives meeting

JUNE 1855

Frid June 1st painted my doors **Sat 2** cleaned & picked herbs went to Dr Fr= lectures **Sund 3** went to meeting Brigham preach the [law of] consecration **Mond 4** watered garden **Tuesd 5** went to Dr France lectures ^John heart here sister Higbee here^ **wed 6** went to the theological Lecture **Thusd 7** P G came here I went with him down to see Martha she was sick **Frd 8** came home he went to Fort Harriman came here staid all night **Satd 9** he went home I went to the counsel of health **Sund 10** we went to meeting **Mond 11** John Pulsiphers wife here[52] **Tuesd 12** sister Higbee here **Wed 13** Sister Higbee here **Thursd 14** went to the midwives meeting **Frid 15** wattered the garden then went to sister Higbees to the benevolent society **Sat 16** I am not well go to Frances lecture **Sund 17** went to meeting **Mond 18** sick **Tuesd 19** went to Frances lecture **wed 20** not well **Thursd 21** ~~went~~ watered the garden in the night **Frd 22** Lucy Smith and Sylvia here **Sat 23** went to the counsel of health **Sund 24** went to meeting Mr Parry did [not?] go **Mond 25** I washed Sisters Foss Elizabeth Rhoda Olive here on a visit **Tuesd 26** went to Frances lecture **wed 27** puled the peas planted potatoes **Thursd 28** sold peas 200 worth one to France one to Southworth **Frd 29** went to a pic nic ragcarpet party to Bishop Roundys **Satd 30** went to Dr Frances lecture Judge Shaver burried[53]

JULY 1855

Sund July 1st wrote a letter to E S Bartlett 29 and to Mother 29 [of June] **Mond 2** made a truss for sister Whipples child it has a breach **Tuesd 3** moved the stove into the kitchen cleaned the house **Wed 4** went to Br Southworths to see the prosesion in the afternoon went to the bowry north of the tabernacle to hear the oration and toasts **Thursd 5** carried peas to the tithing office Phebe & Elizabeth came here staid all night **Frd 6** David and Ezra here to Dinner Phebe and I went up to Tripps **Satd 7** went to the counsel of health Martha

---

52. John Pulsipher (1827–1891) was married to Rosella Huffaker (b. 1837) and Esther Minerva Murray.

53. Appointed by the federal government, "Judge Leonidas Shaver had arrived in Utah in October of 1852. . . . A Virginian and an affable bachelor, Judge Shaver had up to this time maintained cordial relations with President Brigham Young and the Mormons in general. Although there is no account of a definite or violent break, there is evidence of a growing coolness . . . " (Brooks, *Hosea Stout*, 2: 503, n. 1). The judge was found dead in his bed on 29 June. An inquest was called, according to Stout, that concluded death came from a disease of the ear and brain. There were those, however, who maintained the judge had been poisoned. At any rate he was accorded great honors at his funeral.

Ann here staid all night **Sund 8** I do not go to meeting in the forenoon Sister
Smoot here to dinner I went to meeting Brigham spoke forbid the feeding or
taking Soldiers sent here from the states into our houses we suffred enough
last winter by doing it **Mond 9** put our wood inside the lot bought a pound of
rols of sister Grow twisted some yarn at Br Foxes **Tuesd 10** P G here brought
me a cheese I went to Frances lecture **wed 11** packed down my chese **Thursd
12** ^watered garden^ I was niting **Frd 13** I went to the benevolent society
Satd 14 went to Dr Frances lecture **Sund 15** went to meeting went to Br
Eldridges took sick with colery marbus sick all night Mr Parry left me 2*h* past
2 A M to water his lot did not come again till 11 A M I was very sick did not
set up any I was all alone **Mond 16** after he came he staid here some **Tuesd 17**
I staid alone all night quite sick **Wed 18** I am some better so that I can work
Mr Parry has been here the most of the time yestarday and to day taking care
of the oats and hay watered the garden this morning **Thursd 19** made me a
cap nit **Frid 20** washed and ironed baked David here to dinner **Sat 21** went to
see sister Cowin she has been carless and the breach has come down again
very bad it has been doing well I then went to the counsel of health was caled
to cottonwood to Br Pews his wife was sick came home **Sund 22** went to meeting **Mond 23** nit **Tuesd 24** went to Br Shirtleifs and [Seth Millington] Blairs
with Sister Higbee **wed 25** nitting **Thursd 26** I went to Dr Spragues took dinner there Br Bullock was there sick I then went to Bishop Perkins to a midwife
meeting[54] Mr Parry went to Ogden in the Stage Sister Foss staid here all night
again **Frd 27** Lucinia and Sulvia here Lucinia staid all night **Sat 28** we went up
to Tripps she staid here all night again **Sund 29** I was called this morning to
Stepehen Mores wife put her to bed with a son born 4 - 3*h* A M premature
birth child lived 6 hours I then went to meeting P G and David down and
Emerett down brought me some sarvice berries Lucinia went home with them
Mond 30 got a load of wood of Alexander A Lemon for for Kanada worth 5
Dollars) I wrote a letter to Wm= Smoot and one to E Tripp the 24th **Tuesd 31**
went to Dr Frances lecture ^Mr Parry came home^

August 1855

wed ~~25~~ Aug 1 went up to P Gs with Lucy Jane Thurstin[55] staid all night
Thursd ~~26~~ ^2^ came home **Frd ~~37~~** [*a 2 has been changed to a* 3] cut peices for
a quilt **Sat ~~49~~** [*a 2 has been changed to a* 4] went to the counsel of health **Sund 5**
[*5 is written on top of* 29] put Mary Caroline More [Caroline Hawk, b. 1837,

---

54. Thomas Bullock (1816–1855) had been a member of the Pioneer Company.
     William G. Perkins (1801–1886) was bishop of the seventh ward from 1849 to
     1856.

55. Lucy Jane Leonard was a daughter of Lyman and Abigail Calkins Leonard. She
     was married to Moses Thurstin (1817–1873).

wife of Samuel Moore] to bed with a daughter [Mary Hawk] born [*left blank*]
Mond 6 [6 *is written on top of* 7] **Tuesd 7** [7 *is written on top of* 8] put Mary
Sessions to bed with a son [Cyril] born 20 minutes past 11 A M came home
Nancy came with me found my house broke open many things taken breast
pins needles pins hymb Book &c &c **Wed 8** Hariet sick she would not have
me with her I watered my garden in the night alone she had one son [Joseph
Hyrum] born 8 P M **Thursd 9** P M she sent for me after having Dr France
there twice ~~for twenty~~ twenty minutes past one ^**Frd 10**^ I delivered her of
another son [Bernard Llewelyn] a very difficult case as she had a blood vesel
broke when the first was born and was badly tore and injured she had a sister Frances with her I staid with her took care of her and the two babes till
Satd 11 9 oclock P M **Sund 12** went again till meeting time then went to
meeting ^then^ went again staid till 6 P M **Mond 13** went again the most of
the day **Tuesd 14** went in the morning as I have to wash and siringe her out
many times a day I then came home took sister Nancy Hickenbottom
[Higgenbotham?] through a course of medicine after noon went and aprised
sister Higbee ^and Tate^ things to put into the church then went staid all
night with Harriet **wend 15** came home Nancy went away I went to the
benevolent society then staid all night with Harriet came home got bread
went again staid all night made risen baked bread **Frid 17** ironed churned
took care of her and children came home staid all night then **Sat 18** morning
went anointed sister Higbee laid hands on her felt quite sick myself then went
to see Harriet staid till 9 A M then came home sick was sick all day could not
go to the counsel of health Mr Parry came administered to me I got better he
wanted me to go down said the babe [Bernard Llewelyn] was very sick he
went back came after me at 3 A M ^**sund 19**^ again said it was dying I went
he wished me to anoint and lay hands on it I did again it stoped crying but it
breathed very hard at 3 P M he wished me lay hands on it again said he was
to sick himself I did it went to sleep slept the most of the time untill 5 A M
Monday ^**20**^ it breathed its last we buried in the evening I came home
staid all night Mr Pary staid with me **Tuesd 21** several has been here for
counsel for themselves and children I gave both counsel & medicine **wed 22**
worked in the garden gather herbs & seeds P G Lucinia and her sister here
Thursd 23 went to setle up taxes then to a midwife meeting **Frd 24** baked)
garden taking care of things Ransom moed the grass **Sat 25** put Elizabeth
Shirtleif to bed with a daughter [Laura Celestia] born 1: 2*h* P M then came
home gave H. Waltons babe emetic she and Sylvia David & Ezra staid all
night **Sund 26** do not go to meeting sister Walton stays here with her babe
they all go home **Mond 27** got got county orders $4=50 gave sister Bauk
emetic **Tuesd 28** cut up my corn **Wed 29** setled and paid all the tax on both
lots $19=5 stoped at P P Pratts saw Elizabeth then to the benevolent society
Thursd 30 made cankor medicine and bitters for Harriet **Frd 31** gathered
herbs and seed

September 1855

Satd Sept 1 I went to the counsel of health **Sund 2** do not go to meeting stay at home to watch my peaches some ripe gave sister Ann Tomas child emetic and sister Elizabeth Taylors child one also **Mond 3** put in my peticoat to quilt visited the sick **Tuesd 4** quilted watched the peaches **Wed 5** got my peticoat out Mary & Sophia here **Thursd 5** did not go to the midwives meeting **Frd 7** sister Bouk here Worden and Sidney Teaples here[56] **Sat 8** they came back took supper went home Ralf Smith [1835–1914] came here to board to day David & Pheebee came here Staid all night **Sund 9** went away this morning I do not go to meeting stay at home to watch the peaches **Mond 10** baked went to see Caleb Parrys babe verry sick **Tuesd 11** Mr Parry work for J Gibs yestarday **wed 12** went to see Calebs babe it is dead Dr France tended on it sister Steed washed for me and Br Smith **Frd [Thurs] 13** cut peaches to dry **Frd 14** ironed Cate here **Sat 15** caled to Ann Cottom Jhons wife the child born the ~~string~~ cord tore from the placenta before sending for me sister [*left blank*] took the child & cord I took the placenta left her comfortable **Sund 16** do not go to meeting P G David Emerett here **Mond 17** many here the most of the day **Tuesd 18** cut peaches to dry ^Rolf Smith started south^ **Mond 17** put David Emeses [1826–1885] wife [Esther or Hester Cullen] to bed with a daughter [Catherine Mary Cullen] born 11-3*h* P M **wed 19** cut peaches to dry made pres[erves] **Thursd 20** cut peaches to dry caled to sister Whitehead[57] found her very sick Dr France has Drd her **Frd 21** cut Peaches **Satd 22** ~~the same~~ it rained sister Smoot & Martha here staid all night **Sund <23>** they go home I do not go to meeting **Mond <24>** cut peaches sisters Chase Whitne & Snow here **Tuesd 25** gathering & cut peaches **Wed 26** the same **Thursd 27** P G David & wives & Sylvia and sister Shirtlief here let P G have two bushels of peaches & a basket 2 dollars been to see Br [*corner torn off*] **Frid 28** cut peaches **Sat 29** the same **Sund 30** do not go to meeting had peaches stole near all that was not gathered

October 1855

Mond Oct 1 cut peaches Br Henry staid here last night Mary Re [*torn off*] here and Betsey **2** cut peaches **Tuesd 2** cut peaches **wed 3** finished cuting went to P Gs Lucinia sick **Thursd 4** came home [*torn off*] have an other bushel of peaches I got [*torn off*] feet of lumber for my fence wed bought all my winters wood & got it [*torn off*] **Frd 5 Satd 6** went to confrence **Sund 7** went again **Mond 8** went again it ajorned **Tuesd 9** dug carrots **wed 10** Mr

---

56. This would be Nathaniel Worden, husband of Harriet Teeples (Sessions), and Sydney Teeples (1838–1902), her brother.

57. William Whitehead (1816–1885) had been married to Jane Hardman, who had died in 1847; he later married Ann Spencer and Jane Taylor.

Parry sick I gave him Emetic he then went over to the other house took cold **Thursd 11** I went and see him dug carrots & beets **Frd 12** dug beets got Mr Parry brought here very sick **Sat 13** got my potatoes dug **Sund 14** do not go to meeting **Mond 15 Tuesd 16** Mr Parry still very sick **wed 17** got all my veg- itables took care of **Thurd 18 Frd 19 Satd 20 Sund 21** all I can do to take care of Mr Parry **Mond 22 Tuesd 23 wed 24** I was caled to P Gs to Emoret she had a daughter [Fanny Emorett] born **Thursd ^25^** 7 minutes past 2 A M came home Sylvia staid with Mr Parry while I was gone Sophia Tripps babe is very sick **Frd 26 Sat 27** bought 2:28 feet pickets I had nit a pair of stockens for Ralf Smith this week **Sund 28** did not go to meeting Mr Parry still sick **Mond ^29^** sister Peck wa[shed] for me **Tuesd 30** ironed Br Staynor [Charles Stayner] c[ame] here I gave him Emetic **wed 31** Sophias babe verry sick yet

NOVEMBER 1855

Thursd Ralf Smith came here to board **Nov 1 frd 2** Sophia Tripps babe [Arnal Ondree] died **Sat 3** buried **Sund 4** do not go to meeting **Mond 5** P G & David here bought me a cash of nails brought it here I must go and pay 30 dollars for them **Tuesd 6** I have been and paid for them got 15 lb Sugar **Wed 7** I have been to meeting the benevolent society P G & David brought me a peice of beaf [*torn off*] Mr Parry walked to his other house to day and back **Thursd 8** I went up to P Gs to see Julia she is sick Sylvia is here staid with Mr Parry while I gone **Frid** went to Bishop Stokers to[ok] his daughter through a course of medicine then come home found Mr Parry worse had a chill Sylvia went home with D[avid] I went up in town got some things of the store on order **Sund 11** do not go to meeting ^it stormed^ **Mond 12** quite a snow six in[ches] mostly gone before night **Tuesd 13** snows again **wed 14 Thursd 15** went to the midwives meeting **Frd 16** David here **Sat 17** gave Staner Emetic **Satd 17 Sund 18** do not go to meeting **Mod 19** visit C Stainer & Mary Daniels **Tuesd 20** visited them again **Wed 21** went to the benevolent society **Thursd 22** I visited them again Mr Parry is getting better **Frid 23** R Smith left here to go work on the canell[58] ~~Sat 24 Snowed~~David here went to get some Aple trees did not get any I gave him what I did not set out for P G **Sund 25** I did not go to meeting Mary here **Mond 26** I went to town **Tuesd <27>** washed **wed 28**

---

58. According to Leonard Arrington, ". . . a decision was made in 1855 to build the temple of granite from quarries in the Little Cottonwood Canyon twenty miles southeast of Salt Lake City. Using tithing labor, the public works devoted two years to building a canal from a point near the canyon to the Temple Block. This canal was intended to augment the supply of water for irrigation and for the operation of mills, as well as for boating granite rocks to the temple. The canal proved to be impractical as a means of transportation, however, and was largely abandoned . . ." (*Great Basin Kingdom*, 112).

went to town to the post Ofice spun and visited the sick **Thursd 29** Mr Parry worse had a chill last night **Frid 30**

DECEMBER 1855

Sat Dec 1 take care of him **Sund** ^2^ do not go to meeting he is a great deal worse Sylvia came here staid all night **Mond 3** he is better P G sent me a peice of pork David here **Tuesd 4** Mr Parry better R Smith left again to work on the canel I found him a weeks pro[visions] **wed 5** do not go to the benevolent society **Thursd 6** finished a pair of mittens for the poor **Frid 7** P G came after me Lucinia sick Mr Parry went down to the house **Sat 8** I put her to bed 20 minutes past 4 ^P M^ with a son [Keplar] sister Smoot & MarthaAnn came there just before the child was born **Sund 9** I came home with sister Smoot found Mr Parry comfortable **Mond 10** Sulvia staid here last night went home **Tuesd 11** R Smith came here again **wed 12 Thursd 13** Mr Parry went to his house I went to the midwives meeting **Frid** put Walter Thomsons wife to bed with a son born 7 A M lased [laced] the mittens and let R Smith have them **Sat 15** David brought me 2=00 cwt of flour **Sund 16** Ralf Smith left here at night David & Phebe came here staid all night **Mond 17** Mr Parry and I went home with them[59]

Tuesd 18 visited Sylvia **wed 19** we spent the evening there again Br Dible there both evenings **Thursd 20** we came home Mr [Parry] went down to his house staid all night I went to Wordles Hall to a party Mr Parry not able to go **Frd 21** I washed **Sat 22** ironed **Sund** do not go to meeting the snow has blowed into the chamber through the roof and it has melted yestard and much of the plastering fell off it is very cold let Br Dible have 5 peech stones **Mond 24** very cold **tuesd** ^25^ christmas Harriet here **wed 26** still cold **Thursd 27** the cellar freses **Frid 28** snows and blows ^R^ Smith came back again **Sat 29 Sund 30** more moderate I do not go to meeting I go and put John Nortons wife Becke [Rebecca Ann Hammer, b. 1827] to bed with a daughter [Rebecca Ann] born 5 minutes past 12 P M **Mond 31** R Smith cut me wood half days

[Records compose the covering pages]
April 4 1853 Carlos took the cow put her to Turnbows

Br Waylot work 10 days
had 2*h* bushel carots
do 2*h* do popatoes

---

59. This ends one page of Patty's diary. At the bottom three lines of strange characters appear, penciled in a kind of shorthand. According to Ron Watt, the expert in Deseret Alphabet, Patty was probably practicing the Deseret Alphabet in script, although some of the characters appear to be more like Pitman's phonography.

Isaac Moris 2/3 do carrots
  1 bushel potatoes   [*crosswise*]   Isaac Moris
  1 bushel carrots   Dr 85 cts
  2 bushel potatoes
  Day 1 bushel carrots   [*crosswise*]   Luis Forsith
  Waylet molasses——   250 $2=50 if Anns
  1 qt molasses——   075   is paid at the
  cabbage   80   tithing office
               if not 1=40
  Patty Sessions   Martha Blair
  1853–1856   Dr to me 250
               She quilted
               a peticoat 100

[vertical along the margin:]
Jan 1

[upside down, with the corner torn off:]
oon garden seeds   250
Hovey seeds   125
   settled this day
Jaobs seeds   120
   cabage plant
April 18 1855 350 Norton Jacobs

[on the other covering page:]
Jan 1 1853

[upside down at the bottom of the page:]
Isaac Littlehales wife
sister Higins

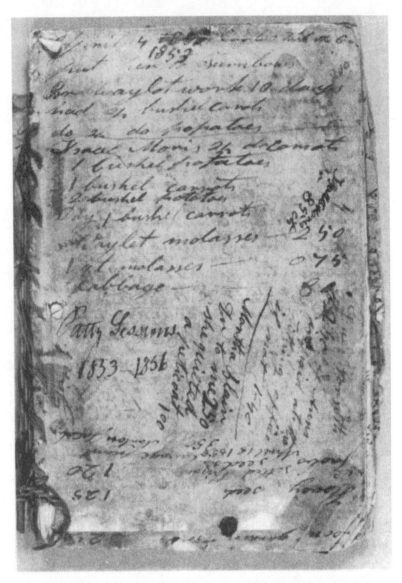

Diary four (1853–1855, titled 1853–1856), also handmade, has at least two
different colors and sizes of paper sewn together. The first part is written on
discolored white or beige paper and is 6¼ inches long and 4¼ inches wide. A
white section of the same size sheets follows. Light blue 5½ x 4¼ inch pages
begin on 10 May 1854 and are for the most part folded separately. Whereas
the first handmade diary was sewn together with three long stitches along the
middle pages, this one is overcast along the left edge. The white pages are
secured by gray thread and the blue by black thread. The thread looks handmade. The ink is brown. At the bottom of the next-to-last page, Patty practiced the Deseret alphabet; this was her only entry in pencil. Courtesy of LDS
Church Archives; photograph by J M Heslop.

DIARY FIVE, 1856–1862

During the years 1856 to 1862, Patty bent her back to her garden and plied her fingers to the needle and the loom in ever more intensive fashion. She continued to give care to the sick and needy through her expertise in midwifery and in mixing medicines, and she shared her hard-earned money and produce for worthy purposes.

But these years encompassed events of lasting historical importance: The Utah War drove the saints from their homes for a brief period. And in 1862 a ferocious flooding of City Creek threatened to destroy Patty's property. In all circumstances, she showed her grit in marshaling her own energies and recruiting help from others in order to survive these and other challenges.

Nor did she neglect her diary.

On 16 July 1862 the Deseret News ran a small article from the London Magazine entitled, "Keeping a Diary." It began, "If a man keeps no diary, the path crumbles away behind him as his feet leave it; and days gone by are but little more than a blank, broken by a few distorted shadows. His life is all confined within the limits of today. Who does not know how imperfect a thing memory is?"[1]

Although Patty's entries are cryptic, she knew what-of and where-of and whom-of she wrote and noted enough to encourage a reader to discover the details. Who knows how history may be enriched by exploring the shadows within the allusions she didn't trust to memory alone?

---

1. "Keeping a Diary," *Deseret News*, 16 July 1862, 12:22.

1856

I have been reading my journal and feel to thank the Lord
that I have passed through what I have

JANUARY 1856

Jan 1 1856   Patty Sessions
                                  1856

I spent the forenoon at home Mr Parry staid here last night took his brekfast
with me then went to his ^house^ to see Harriet came back to dinner we then
went with Br Pew to Cotten wood to his house he came after us had a party
there **Tuesd 2** [I] went to Br Birchs took dinner then came home **Thursd 3** I
went up to town took dinner at Tripps P G was there I then went to Samuel
Mores to see his wife Eunice she has a very bad sore I lanced it **Frd 4** at home
attending to my domestic conserns **Sat 5** the same **Sund 6** went and see sister
More again she is doing well then went and see Mary Daniels she is better
Mond 7 baked some mince pies **Tuesd 8** at home bought a load of Sage Brush
to burn **Wed 9** made me a cap **Thursd 10** bought more lumber for fence paid
$9:00 cash to store pay a dress pattern tea & socks $6:00 **Frid 11** I staid alone
last night the first time I staid alone since Mr Parry was sick three months since
he took sick I went up to town ^this morning^ got a blank for a consecration
deed Sister ^Joseph^ More visited here in the afternoon he came both staid
the evening **Satd 12** P G here got some dates from my Journal for his Journal
staid all night ^let Br Woodbury have $2.00 worth of peach pits^ **Sund 13** I
was called this morning to sister Townsens [Townsand] she was very sick I
gave her emetic left her better I came got breakfast P G went home I do not go
to meeting to day I am here alone I have been reading my Journal and feel to
thank the Lord that I have passed through what I have I have gained an experience that I could not have gained no other way **Mond 14** Sister Smoot came
after me to go there Martha Anns litle girl [Martha Ann] fell into a tub of hot
water scalded both of her hands very bad I went found ^her^ quite sick but
she soon began to get better and her hands began to heal **Tuesd 15** I went to
Br Carns to a party **Thursd 17** came home stopt at Br [. . .]mmers found sister
Kingston posesed with evil spirits Br Smoot and Eldridge and others administered to her I left with Br Smoot came home **Frd 18** wrote a line to P G sent
two pair of socks I have nit for his children **Satd 19** ^I caled with sister [Ann]
Booth found her very poor^ went round in the ward to find a place for sister
Booths two youngest children as the rest have got places **Sund 20** Mr Parry &
I went to meeting ^Erastus Snow preached^ the first time since confrence that
he has been able to go and sit in the cold in the evening we went to the ward
meeting **Mond 21** still cold frezing very hard **Tues 22** still cold I attend to my
domestic concerns ~~Wed 23 snow~~ I went to Bishop Roundys told him I could

not find any place for sister Booths children **Wed 23** snows I am at home sewing **Thursd 24** I am not well **Frid ^25^** no better Sylvia came here staid all night **Satd 26** ^I am quite well^ she and I went up to Heber C Kimbals then to Prsd Youngs then came home in the evening ^we^ went [to] A W Babbits she had buisiness with him[2] Mr Parry has been to a meeting in the Tabernacle to see about getting an express line from here to the states **Sund ^24^** Sylvia staid here slept with me went home this morning Mr Parry and I went to meeting Brigham Preached then Heber then Jedidiah [Grant] we went to the ward meeting in the evening **Mond 28** the Teacher has been here to day gave me good counsel said all was right found my tithing paid told me whom to setle with ^the Bishop^ Ralf Smith took his chest away from here to day paid me what he owed ^me^ with an order on the tithing **Tuesd 29** I went to the tithing office to get a ~~re~~ receipt. John Edwards here cutting wood I baked mince pies & bread &c **Wed 30** sewing in the evening went up to David Sessions, Phebe sick she had a daughter [Cardenia Estella Sessions] born before I got there **Thursd 31** gave Lucinia emetic

February 1856

Frid ^Feb= 1^ I went over to Sylvias took breakfast Phebe very poorly I stay all night again **Satd 2d** I came home **Sund 3** we went to meeting P P Pratt & Heber C. Kimbal preached went to ward meeting in the evening **Mond 4** my birthday 61 years old to day I have bought 12-00 feet of lumber today paid $24-50 cash $4-00 trade Sylvia here to dinner she said Phebe was no beter, I feel first rate in body and mind the Lord has blesed me and ^I^ desire to do right that I may enjoy his spirit and have wisdom to direct ^me^ in all I do or say **Tuesd 5** I went up to the tithing office got a receipt to setle with the Bishop John Hart & Br Tolmond [Tolman?] & Sylvia staid here all night **Wed 6** she has gone home I am at home alone my meditation is sweet feeling that the Lord will bless his saints ^in the afternoon setled all my tithing^ **Thursd 7** I went up to Susannahs she is not well **Frid 8** I valued my property 1347 and have been to the Judge E Smith acknoledged the deed[3] carried it to T[homas] Bullock to record paid Robery [Rowberry?] $4=40 for lumber hear from Phebe she is better **Satd 9** finished my workpacket Mr Parry told me that Hariet had but little

2. Almon Whiting Babbitt (1812–1856) had a stormy relationship with the church. He was tried by six church courts and disfellowshipped three times. In 1852 he was appointed secretary of Utah Territory and in 1856 made a trip to Washington, D.C., to purchase supplies for the new statehouse. On the return trip he was killed by Cheyenne Indians in Nebraska (see Lyndon W. Cook, *The Revelations of the Prophet Joseph Smith* [Salt Lake City: Deseret Book Co., 1985], 251–52).

3. Elias Smith (1804–1888) was a cousin of Joseph Smith and was at this time judge of probate; he became territorial judge in 1870.

beside cornbread to eat I told him not to let her suffer if she would come and live here she should fare [as] I did and if she would not come here to carry some from here to her as what I have here I have provided it myself I told him I thought we had better live together keep but one fire eat at one table and what we could save by doing so we could let those have that have none he made me no reply **Sund 10** we have been to meeting Orson Pratt preached Alen Huntington cut off from the church for taking the name of God in vain.[4] I am here alone Mr Parry has gone down to the other house to take [care] of ^cow & calf^ I feel well in body and mind I have been reading in the Book of mormon and the spirit of the Lord rests upon me although alone by myself I am happy **Mond 11** attend to my domestic concerns **tuesd 12** the same **Wed 13** bought 7.4 ^feet^ of lumber paid $18-40 for it Br Whitehead here sawing and spliting wood yesterday and today **Thursd 14** went to town then came home cut me a dress skirt worked on it ^David here^ Mr Parry commenced sharping pickets for the fence **Frid 15** Olive Foss here to dinner **Satd ^16^** went to town again to see if my consecration deed is recorded Clerk not there finished my dress **Sund 17** very warm days but cold nights we go to meeting Brigham preached **Mond 18 Tuesd ^19^** and **wed 20** I helped Mr Parry sharp pickets Br Whitehead here cutting wood finished all I had **Thursd 21** went to Susannahs Sister Higbee and I washed and anointed her then we went to the midwife meeting I then came to Br Nathan Davis,s took supper with Br P P Pratt Elizabeth and Mary Pratt I have enjoyed myself well to day **Frid 22** ^helped Mr Parry^ sharpn pickets **Satd 23** went to Sister Tomson took the names of the femeles that helped the poor then to ^sister^ Tripps took dinner visited sister Wolice [Wallace][5] **Sund 24** went to meeting Br Hovey [Joseph Grafton Hovey, 1812–1868] preached then Brigham gave Judge Snow the greatest whiping I ever herd from any bodys toungue[6] he spoke with power

4. Clark Allen Huntington (1831–1900) had been a member of the Mormon Battalion. He was a son of Fanny Marie Allen and Dimick Baker Huntington. Orson Pratt preached about everyday duties and said that "Allan Huntington, who was appointed a missionary to the Indians, had been guilty of using profane language a great deal, he had heard him." Parley P. Pratt said that "the three Nephites could not very well visit the Lamanites yet, and tell them to believe what the Mormon Missionaries said to them, lest there might be occasionally a wicked man . . . who would swear as Huntington did . . ." ("Journal History of The Church of Jesus Christ of Latter-day Saints," 10 February 1856, [hereafter cited as JH], Archives of the Historical Department, Church of Jesus Christ of Latter-day Saints, Salt Lake City).

5. Benjamin George Wallace (1817–1900) married Mary C. McMurphy, Melissa H. King, Lydia Davis, and Hannah Martha Davis.

6. Zerubbabel Snow (1809–1881) was an elder brother of Erastus Snow. On 24 February 1856 President Young praised Brother Joseph Hovey and scathingly reprimanded a lawyer, who the day before had appealed to the jury to witness

and authority he said he would be cursed and the people said Amen Sylvia came here staid all night **Mond 25** I went up to town with her and ~~deliver~~ got my deeds the transfer deed from P G Sessions to me and also my conscration deed paid three 3 dollars for recording then took the consecrations deed to the Govn= Office for the trustee in trust[7] came home ^Mr Parry brought me a spare^ **Tuesd 26** making a cap **Wed 27** got 4 lb nails of cottom **Thursd 28 Frd 29** attended to my domestic conserns

MARCH 1856

Satd March ^**March**^ **1** bought 5.77 feet of lumber P G staid here last night **Sund 2** We have been to meeting A Lymon & Brigham preached in the forenoon Heber & Jed^ed^idiah in the afternoon **Mond 3** Atended to my domestic **Tues 4** the same Oliver Paine staid here all night **Wed 5** he went away **Thursd 6** fast day we are requested to fast all that has enough to eat and give to those that have not I sent 6 lb of flour to the Bishop beleiving the Lord would bless me I washed ~~Fr~~ and before night a sister brought me 22 lb of flour for garden seeds **Frid 7** another sister sent me 34 lbs flour for dried peaches I

---

his honesty and then "threw dust in their eyes, that they might give an unrighteous decision." He further chastized those who out of curiosity frequented the courtroom—even those who sat on juries. "Keep away from court houses," he said, "no decent man will go there unless he goes as a witness, or is in some manner compelled to." He had sent Thomas Bullock to take the names of all who were in the courtroom. "I wanted to know the men who were coaxing hell into our midst, for I wish to send them to China, to the East Indies, or to where they cannot get back, at least for five years . . . we will send off the poor curses on a mission, and then the devil may have them, and we do not care how soon they apostatize, after they get as far as California" (Brigham Young et al., *Journal of Discourses*, 26 vols. [Los Angeles: General Printing and Lithograph, 1961], 236–41). Zerubbabel Snow was sent on a mission to Australia from 1856 to 1859; then he returned to Utah and continued his service in law as judge and city and county attorney.

7. Brigham Young was always anxious to promote the law of consecration, and members nagged at him: "When will we get around to living it?" This led to the consecration movement of the 1850s. People listed their property on a "deed of consecration" and gave this document to him as trustee in trust (there is no way he could have done this as territorial governor). Result? Nothing. After several thousand deeds had been turned in, the United States government failed to establish a land office in Utah, which had been expected in 1855 or 1856. Land laws were not enacted, which meant that people did not have clear title to their property. Then in 1857 came Johnston's Army. So the real significance of these deeds is simply to show the willingness of church members to consecrate their property (see Leonard Arrington, *Great Basin Kingdom* [Lincoln: University of Nebraska Press, 1958], 145–48; also see chapter 4 in Leonard Arrington, Feramoz Y. Fox, and Dean L. May, *Building the City of God* [Salt Lake City: Deseret Book Co., 1976]).

felt to thank the Lord **Satd 8** Oliver came here Thursday evening not well wished to stay all night last night I found he had the measles he is quite sick to day I keep him here as he has no home to go to and take as good care of him as I can **Sund 9** went to meeting **Mond 10** Mr Parry here sharping pickets **Tuesd 11** Oliver went away **wed 12** Br Pew brought me a load of posts I paid him $4:00 cash **Thursd 13** commenced spading my garden **Frid 14** have a man here spading **Sat 15** two men here spading Caleb Parry & Joseph Parry here to dinner I have set out some plumb trees bought 6 load of manure to put on my lot yestarday **Sund 16** Caleb & Joseph staid here last night we went to meeting much good counsel given **Mond 17** P G Caleb & Joseph staid here last night two men here to work one on the fence the other spading **Tuesd ^18^** Joseph & Caleb went home ~~Tuesd~~ **wed 19 Thursd 20** put Eliza Dykes to bed with a son born 2*h* past 11 A M **Frid 21** I have been to see Mary Shirtleif babe I gave it Emetic left medicine I then planted potatoes the weather is quite warm **Satd 23** Br Haywood made the two gates for my fence have had two and three men here to work all the week **Sund 23** the teacher has been here this morning to see how much breadstuff I have and found I was doing about right with it said he was glad I had so much and for the benefit of the poor and also that I had work for them to do to pay for it I have been to meeting Brigham said this people would go ^back^ to Jackson Co as shure as the Lord lived we had a good meeting I feel first rate he said there was life in our bodies that caused them to decay after the spirit left them **Mond 24** the Bishop came here told me I must not let my breadstuff go out of this ward so I dismised 3 men that was to work for me that lived in other wards and hired two more that lived in this ward. I have been to work in the garden sewing onion sets I winnoed up some oats **Tuesd 25** sewing beets onions potatoes **wed 26** ^the same^ **Thursd 27** my grand daughter here **Frid 28** ~~Frid~~ bought ^60 feet of lumber &^ 20 apple trees helped set them out **Satd** ^~~feet lumber~~^ **29** setled up with my work men paid them all off then went to the theater with Ralf Smith[8] he staid here all night ^**Sund 30**^ I went to meeting P G Lucinia David & Sylvia came here **Mond 31** the wind blew so hard the men could not work on the fence

APRIL 1856

1856 Tuesd April 1 the ~~wind~~ wind blows some to day but they work **wed 2** have a man here fixen the side walk **Thursd 3** ^I^ worked in the garden **[Frd 4** [*written over* Thursd] worked in the garden lost a pocket book an eight Dollar

8. Patty and "Ralf" Smith probably saw *Othello*, as a list of twelve plays presented during the season of 1856–1857 lists *She Stoops to Conquer* by Richard B. Sheridan and then *Othello*, followed by *Richard III* (see Myrtle E. Henderson, *A History of the Theatre in Salt Lake City From 1850 to 1870* [Evanston, Ill.: by author, 1934], 33–34).

order in it and a silver pencil and gold pen cash one Dollar and half or more needles &c **Satd 5** baked for confrence ^Joseph Parry came^ **Sund 6** I went to confrence P G called to go to ^Carson^ Carson Valley on a mission[9] he staid here all night & Josept Parry **Mond 7** went to confrence P G Joseph & Sylvia staid here all night **Tuesd 8** confrence closed we have had a good conferene Br Benson told to go home and turn over a new leaf in our Journals and not let a blot come upon it but keep it clean and obey counsel Heber told us if we would do as we were told from that stand we should never want we should always have bread I have sold Joseph Parry $15-00 worth of Powder & lead he paid $8-00 cash one in sugar $6=00 in a buckskin hunting shirt I feel well and thank the Lord for the blessings I enjoy both tempral & spiritual **Wed 9** worked in the garden had men at work on my fence **Thursd 10** I went to the midwives meeting **Frd** ^**11**^ the wind blows so hard the men could not work on the fence I went to town got 2 2*h* lb tallow & a spit box ^bought^ some currant slips brought home my wash boiler **Satd 12** worked very hard in the garden **Sund 13** went to meeting it rains we feel very thankful for the ground needs it very much **Mod 14** rains some **Tuesd 15** fair I work in the garden Mr Parry helped me plan^te^d a few English beans worked about 15 or 20 minutes all he has helped me plant or sow this spring **wed 16** I let him have 16 pounds of flour **Thursd 14** the men have used all the joice [joists] are ^waiting^ for more **Frid 18** the joice is come **Satd 19** they work on the fence again **Sund 20** we go to meeting rains again **Mond 21** Gibs sends ~~Fife~~ Br Fife to work on the fence **Tuesd 22** he came himself & David Emes [Eames or Ames?] came they finished the fence **Wed 23** I worked in the garden **Thursd 24** P G and wives down I went up to Tripps to see them **Frid 25** [*written over* Thurs] Harriet had her endowment Mr Parry went with her did not let me go altho I never have been sealed at the alter I felt bad about it yet I do not know but it is all right **Satd 26** I am not well **Sund 27** I am better go to meeting **Mond 28** work in the garden very hard Caleb Parrys wife came here from Ogdon she staid here all night **Tuesd 29** I went up to town got me a pair of shoes I was expecting to go up to P Gs to a party and when I went to get my fine shoes to

9. According to Leonard Arrington, Brigham Young called two hundred men to outlying settlements in 1856 in order to mitigate the suffering caused by unemployment—and to build up the kingdom at the same time. Arrington quotes from Heber C. Kimball: "There has been Courts in session here for weeks and weeks, and . . . one hundred and fifty or two hundred of the brethren have been hanging around . . . brother Brigham sent Thomas Bullock to take their names for the purpose of giving them missions, if they had not anything to do of more importance . . . for Los Vegas some thirty . . . forty-eight to go to Green River . . . some thirty-five or forty to go north to Salmon River . . . some thirty to go to Carson Valley . . . eight to go to the East Indies . . . eighteen called to Europe, and seven to Australia. . . . These are all good men but they need to learn a lesson" (*Great Basin Kingdom*, 155). Kimball's job was to make the assignments.

wear they were gone I know not where they are think they are stolen it snows and rains and is quite cold P G has come I go and Sophia Tripp goes up Selah Lovlin goes up with us get a short distance above the hot springs the waggon tire broke and come off of the wheel and we got out and went on a foot P G got some withs[10] put it on and fasened it on came on overtook us we then sisters took turns about riding and got there first rate had a good party Br Heber and Jediah was there **Wed 30** came home Wm Smoot got home yestarday[11] he and Martha and his Mother came to see me this afternoon P G and David came home with me and we were all here together they went home with P G

MAY 1856

Thursd May 1 worked in the garden **Frid 2** worked on my carpet making it **Satd 3** finished the carpet went to the store got me a muslin ^or laun^ dress & 2 padlocks took on an order **Sund 4** rained I went to meeting Brigham preached **Mond 5** I went to Dimic Huntingtons their child Sarah died this morning I came home Tomas Spiking helped me take up my old carpet and put down my new one put the old one down in the kitchen **Tuesd 6** ^sisters Elizabeth & Mary Pratt here^ commenced making soap **Wed 7 Thursd 8** P G Lucinia Mary & Sylvia here I went up to town with them then they came here took dinner went home P G made me his last visit before he goes to Carson valley ^on his mission^[12] he is to start next Satd **Frid 9** I finished my soap **Sat 10** finished planting my garden set out to matoes plants did up a cap the eastern mail has got in to day **Sund 11** went to meeting **Mond 12** washed **Tuesd 13** went to the Office got a letter for P G hear that he started yestarday for Carson as I came from the Office I stoped at the public workshop to get some shavings to kindle fire as I was tieing them in my handkerchief the wind blew the door too it hit my head I did not feel the hurt at first but before I got home it pained ^me^ bad at times I felt very sleepy but would not go to sleep for fear it would make it worse I was alone so I ironed my clothes and kept up all day **Wed 14** I feel worse have a woman to clean my dishes sister Ruff **Thurd 15** feel better went to weeding in the garden my head began to ache again I had to go to bed **Frid 16** set up but litle feel very bad alone the most of

---

10. Patty probably referred to withes, tough, supple willow twigs used to bind things together.

11. Martha Ann's husband, William C. A. Smoot, had served a year-long mission to the Indians in the Las Vegas area.

12. Brigham Young had sent settlers westward to Carson Valley in 1855. Orson Hyde, a member of the Quorum of the Twelve Apostles, was the leader of thirty-five men whose main objective was to trade with overland emigrants on their way to California. In 1856 more settlers, including Perrigrine Sessions, went to Carson Valley. They were recalled, as were all others from outlying areas, during the Utah War scare.

the time **Satd 17** I am better go to see Susanah yet my head is not well **Sund 18** go to meeting **Mond 19** worked in the garden hoing **Tuesd 20** hoing at times my head feels bad yet **Wed 21** my head feels worse Mr Parry has ~~had~~ hoed a little this week about an hour or two in a day I have a man here yestarday and to day has ^done^ one days work let Mr Parry have some corn meal **Thurs 22** have two men here half a day I go to town gave twenty $20 Dollars to the perpetual Emigrating fund then went to the midwives meeting **Frid 23** hoed in the garden **Satd 24** watered the garden Lucinia came here staid all night **Sund 25** Mr Parry brought his boy up here I then went to meeting we had much good teaching I feel well **Mond 26** work in the garden **Tuesd 27** the same **Wed 28** the same Calvin Foss [b. 1826] cut the hay **Thursd 29** visited Susannah Richards her birth had a good visit **Frid 30** stacked my hay watered the garden some **Satd 31** made vinegar and brewed some beer

JUNE 1856

Sund June 1st 1856 I have been to meeting Heber and Brigham proposed opening the cannall and bring the water from cottenwood to water our city lots rising of 3:00 volentered to go this week and open the ditch and get the water here after meeting I went to the baptising of the ward I then went to Bishop F Keslers[13] gave him five dollars cash to hire men to work on the canal for I feel that the Lord has coled on the brethren by his servants to open that canal and I wish to see all such calls responded to the Lord has given us the former rain and if we do right I beleive he will give us the later rain in its season and we shall have a good crop **Mon 2** watered the garden had the water 4 hours I then set out plants beets & cabage untill 4 P M was sick **Tuesd 3** cannot work to day ^have a mess of green peas^ hired Tomas Spiking to go and work on the canall for Mr Parry **Wed 4** I still feel sick **Thursd 5** Sulvia here I do not go to the midwives meeting **Frd 6** Br Peck set some posts for a yard for me yesterday to day I feel beter go to town bye me a pair of shoes **Satd 7** work a litle in the garden but have to quit and lay down get one coat of paint put on my gate and a good latch **Sund 8** I feel better go to meeting **Mond 9** Br Morris finished painting the gates ^paid 2 2h dollars for it^ I work in the garden **Tuesd 10** ^Rhoda Richards came here to Board^ Br Monteag [Montague?] commenced a back house for me ^I washed^ **Wed 11** he finished it I paid him 3 dollars for it I worked in the garden **Thursd 12** the same **Frid 13** Br ^Wm^ Lewis commenced white washing my fence **Satd 14** he finished it <paid him $3-00 for it> in afternoon Mary came after me to go up to David the horse had kicked him I went found him hurt bad I set up with him

---

13. Frederick Kesler (1816–1899) was the second bishop of the sixteenth ward in Salt Lake City. He served from 1856 to 1899. He was a builder, architect, surveyor, millwright, and engineer.

all night **Sund 15** I did not come home in the after noon he got better I gave
him an emetic and other things and releived him **Mond 16** I came home with
Br Duncan prepared my lot for watering ^Wm Smoot Martha & his Mother
here^ **Tuesd 17** had the water from 12 ^A M^ untill 4 hard watering in the
night I feel almost sick to day I am so fatigued with hard work received an
order of $9=00 Ralf Smith on the tithing office for the one I lost in the pocket
book on the 3d of April **Wed 18** I feel better work in the garden ^Sylvia
here^ **Thursd 19** go to Susannahs **Frid 20** go up to see David find quite low
Sat 21 came home with Brs Brigham & Chase & wives Brigham laid hands on
David before I came away calvin Foss has cut the grass again **Sund 22** went to
meeting **Mond 23** worked in the garden **Tuesd 24** the same **Wed 25** the same
Thursd 26 I have so many here to bye flour and I have so little to spare I hardly know who needs it most for they all tell the same story and it almost makes
me sick because I cannot suply their wants last Mond two sisters came here by
the name of Rogers & Taylor sister Rogers brought a work box here to sell
wished me to bye it said I should have it and all there was in it except two
rings for five Dollars I told her it was an old box & I did not want it but she
plead so hard said she had no bread and the money would help her to some
and also another family I then told her I would take it I paid her all but five
cents and I stept into the other room to get that for her and while I was gone
she took out two cards of ^steel^ pens that was in the box & carried them off
her sister Taylor came here after a few days I told her about it she said she
should fetch them back I told her if she did not I should think she meant to
steal them but she has not brought them yet **Frid 27** sisters Heywoods were
here on a visit yesterday **Sat 28** David Phebee & Sylvia here to dinner Sylvia
staid all night **Sund 29** she got letters from Cleark and Ethiel I go to meeting
Mond 30 work in the garden every day

July 1856

Tuesd July 1 the same **Wed 2** dito **Thurd 3** went to Susannahs she was gone
to Utah ~~Dr~~ Wm= Smoot and Martha came here staid all night **Frid 4** she
and I went to Br Roundys to see the celibration of the 4 of July[14] they went

---

14. In those early days in the Salt Lake Valley, the celebration of the Fourth of July
was a grand occasion. The flag of the United States, the Constitution, bands,
cannon rounds, bells, banners, and different sections of the army were all part of
the festivities. On 9 July 1856 the *Deseret News* carried a full account of Governor
Young's oration. Brigham said, ". . . None but sinister or pecuniary motives can
prompt those who are not of us abide in our midst. All other localities have more
tempting facilities. . . . The country suits us merely because no other well
informed people can covet its possession . . . let us remember that the perpetuity
of our free institutions, yea, the Constitution and Government itself, depends
upon the intelligence, virtue, integrity and patriotism of the people . . ."
("Celebration of July Fourth and Grand Military Review," 6:140).

home after super **Sat 6** [*written on top of* 5] **Sund 6** [*written on top of* 7] went to meeting in the forenoon put Marry Pratt to bed with a son born 5 and 1*h* P M **Mond 7** washed **Tuesd 8** ironed and baked watered the garden in the night **Wed 9** divided my flour with Mr Parry to carry to Harriet ~~Thursd went up to ... was gone to Provo~~ **Fri 11** put sister [Sophia] Riser to bed with a son [Orson] born [*left blank*] A M **Sat 12** worked in the garden ^puled the peas^ **Sund 13** went to meeting **Mond 14** ^**Tuesd 15**^ thrashed the peas ~~Da~~ David Phebe & Sylvia here I watered the garden in the night alone **Wed 16** ^John Winegar [1838–1914, son of Alvin and Mary Judd Winegar] cut my grass again^ worked in the garden **Thursd 17** went to town sister Babit [Babbitt] paid me 2 dollars cash I got 7 2*h* lb sugar got Rhoda R to cut my laun dress **Frid 18** raked & stacked the hay made my dress skirt **Sat 19** worked in the garden **Sund 20** went to meeting **mond 21** baked David Sylvia and Lucinia came here I went to Wm= Smoots with them it rained some staid there all night **Tuesd 22** went to Dr Lee's [Ezekial Lee, 1795–1879] to see if the Dr could do any thing for David he is not well of that kick of the horse I got a pint of brandy to make some medicine for Mr Parry at John Kimbals we came home they took dinner here then went home I went to see a sick woman ^thought she would not live^ then in the night I watered my garden **Wed 23** caled to see her again she was speechless **Thd 24** she died 7 oclock this morning I helped lay her out made her cap **Frid 25** she is buried I have made Mr Parry some bitters put a new back to his vest **Satd 26** attended to many things **Sund 27** went to meeting **Mond 28** baked bread & pies worked in the garden **Tuesd 29** worked in the garden watered in the night fell down could not get up alone lamed me came near braking my thigh **Wed 30 Thursd 31** quite lame

AUGUST 1856

Frd August 1 can hardly step Sister Townsends was here on a visit Rhoda finished her school **Satd 2** ^I gave two dollars to bye flour to meet the co^ I am better **Sund 3** quite well go to meeting go to sister Taylors take supper Harriet & Worden came here staid all night **Mond 4** I bake they are here ~~Tuesd 5~~ I bought 1=00 cwt flour of David & 50 cwt of Harriets father Teaples **Tuesd 5** they all went home I prepared to water **Wed 6** I watered then washed coulered yellow sister Woodruff here I gave her some roots[15] **Thursd 7** ironed baked **Frd 8** went to staineses got some Apricot buds Wm and Martha Smoot here to dinner I then put in the buds **Satd 9** got some Aple buds of G

---

15. Wilford Woodruff does not record what roots Patty gave to his wife. But on 6 August 1856 he writes, "I put into my trees about 50 buds of Carringtons large Early white & late white preserve peach" (*Wilford Woodruff's Journal*, ed. Scott G. Kenney, 9 vols. [Midvale, Utah: Signature Books, 1983], 4:434).

Nebeckar put them in **Sund 10** went to meeting stoped to Tripps to super **Mond 11** worked in the garden **Tuesd 12** the same **Wed 13** watered at 4 A M alone **Thursd 14** visited with Mr Parry and Sophia Tripp at Br Heywoods **Frd 15** ^E B^ Tripp came home from his mission ^**Satd**^ <16> took his wife and children and me and went out and met the company **Sund 17** went to meeting **Mond 18** worked in the garden **Tuesd 19** the same **Wed 20** watered took the water 2 A M **Thursd 21** worked in the garden buded some more ^commenced me a cap crocean^ ~~Frid 22~~ went to Trips David and Sylvia there last night **Frd 22** Josephine came down staid here all night **Sat 23** we went to many places in town I then went to the manufactory society[16] **Sund 24** went to meeting stoped at Tripps took supper **Mond** <25> went to the store got 10 lb nails Br <Pew & wife here made a truss for them> **Tuesd 26** croschan on my cap **wed 27 Thurs 28** got the grass cut again the 4th time this season **Frid 29** I raked it **Sat 30** put it up David here I went to town with him got 5 lb Nails & 10 lb sugar & 1 lb candy I then put in some Apricots buds **Sund 31** got news from P G all well went to meeting Brigham preached and prophesied in 26 years more every faithful elder in this church would be as much greater than the Kings of the earth as they were now greater than their subjects that they ruled over.

SEPTEMBER 1856

Mond Sept 1 sister M Hyde here on a visit **Tuesd 2** Sister M Hyde Violate Kimball Knight & Sylvia & Phebe Walton all here & Lucinia Marry had a good visit I watered the garden in the night **Wed 3** Sylvia myself Sister Foss Phebe & Sophia Tripp all went to Br Leonards on a visit **Thurd 4** let P Minor have thirty Dollars to bye wheet for me at one Dollar & half per bushel **frid 5** sisters Fosss ^and^ E[lizabeth] & R[hoda] Phebe Sophia Tripp **Sat 6** I went to the agricultural society carried some pye plant I then went to sister Fosses visited with sisters Leonard Lucy Jane and sister Bewel **Sund 4** went to meeting **Mond 8** sister Keeler washed for me **Tuesd 9** ironed & worked in the garden

16. In January of 1856 the Utah territorial legislature chartered the Deseret Agricultural and Manufacturing Society. Its purpose was to encourage church members to produce their own needs, all the while gathering and making use of advancements in the outside world (see Thomas G. Alexander, *Things in Heaven and Earth* [Salt Lake City: Signature Books, 1991], 207–8). The *Deseret News* of 6 September 1856 reported that "Sister Patty Sessions presented two very large stalks of rhubarb, known as the 'Victoria Rhubarb,' and raised from seed brought from England" (6:216; see also note 27 below). In 1856 the Deseret Agricultural and Manufacturing Society received appropriations for premiums and subsidies, gathered statistics, and received and distributed seeds. Because church members officered it and it served as a church agent, it met monthly in church meetinghouses throughout the territory. It published educational pamphlets and held an annual fair (Arrington, *Great Basin Kingdom*, 226).

taking care of corn **Wed 10** frost last night finished cuting my corn gathered a part of my plumbs **Thursd 11** cut me a dress that I bought with cucumbers of Tripp ^sister Spencer & Cumings and I visited there Trips **Frd 12** sewed on it **Sat 13** went to see about my wheet found it ready ~~but~~ got Br Stoker to bring it home for me I then made a bin emtied it **Sund 14** went to meeting **Mond 15** worked on my dress Wm= & Martha Ann staid here last night **Tuesd 16** David came after me to go to P Gs ^last night^ Byron had the waggon run over him[17] I went found him badly bruised came home to night left him better **Tuesd 17** went to town carried some plumbs sold them for 10 cents per doz bought six lb sugar with the money **Thursd 18** bought 12 lb flour with some more plumbs ~~Frd 19~~ sister [Mary Judd] Winegar & Hess here on a visit I finished my dress **Frd 19** dug potatoes **Sat 20** the same have dug overground enough to dug fifty bushels and I got but little over one **Sund 21** went to meeting **Mond 22** dug potatoes **Tuesd 23** the same **Wed 24** do **Thurd 25** finished diging potatoes got 1 2h bush **Frid 26** went to town saw the first hand cart co come in I came home got bread carried to them[18] **Sat 27** carried them some vegetables **Sund ^28^** went to meeting <then put sister Stophert to bed with twin girls> **Mond 29** sister Keeler washed for me Martha Ann came here and her children Wm= came with her but went home **Tuesd 30** Martha and I went up to Tripps in the forenoon in the afternoon we went to Gibses

OCTOBER 1856

Wed Oct 1 1856 ironed did me up a cap Martha is still here **Thursd 2** we all went to the fare ^went to Wilkins to a party gentiles there we came home 9 oclock did not stay^ Mr Parrys children came in with the hand cart co[19] **Frid 3** all here to supper **Satd 4** Worden came here to stay through confrence **Sund 5** ^went to meeting^ call for flour & clothing ^& teams^ to send back to the hand cart co yet behind I came home got a Jeans coat for a man shoes stockens sack shawl Mr Parry got a blanket we carried them to the tabernacle had a good meeting come home Wm= & Jane Parry came here staid all night **Mond 6** went to confrence **Mond 7** went again confrence ajorned until April

---

17. Byron Sessions (1851–1928) was the second child of Perrigrine and Mary Call.

18. During the years of 1855–1856, nature afflicted the struggling Mormons with grasshopper scourges, unusually high temperatures, and light water supply. By contrast the numbers of new settlers inflated. To continue to provide means for the saints to gather, Brigham Young conceived the idea of handcart companies. This company, having traveled fourteen hundred miles in nine weeks, was the first of five that set out that year.

19. John Parry and Mary Williams had seven children, all born in Wales. Not previously mentioned are Bernard, born in 1809; Elizabeth, born in 1811, Sarah, born in 1815, and John, born in 1817.

6 we have had a good time **Wed 8** I have had a good deal of co but I have enjoyed the confrence first rate I have had a great deal to do but work has been no burden I have had the good spirit thank the Lord and my desire is to do right that I may keep it ever with me **Thursd 9** I gave John Parrys wife material to make her a hood put sister Winegar to bed with a daughter born 7 P M **Frd 10** planted some plumb stones **Satd 11** caled to sister Kaighans babe very sick gave it emetic **Sund 12** went to meeting plain preaching in the evening to the school house Jedidiah Grant preached **mond 13** bought 1:00 20 cwt flour $4=00 per hundred visited the babe found it better **Tuesd 14** visited it again found it worse she had took it out doors and it took cold Phebe Walton came here made me a hood Sylvia came here went with me to see the babe before we went to bed found it beter we came home she went to bed I went to watering some ground to set out some fruit trees watered till midnight **wed 15** went to see the babe again found it better I then cleaned my house David came here got a scab to vaxinate with Sylvia went home with him **Thursd 16** went to the ward meeting in the evening **Frid 17** worked taking care of my cabages set out some plumb trees **Sat 18** attended to my domestic concerns **Sund 19** went to meeting ^all day & in the even^ **Mond 20** washed **Tuesd 21** snowed last night **wed 22** cold **Thursd 23** went to the ward meeting **Frid 24 Sat 25** bought 2:00 cwt of flour of David **Sund 26** went to meeting to the schoolhouse in the evening **Mond 27** carried up my tithing **Tuesd 28** went to the tinners spoke for some stove pipe **Wed 29** at home **Thursd 30** went to the tinners again paid for my stove pipe David Mary & Sylvia down went to the ward meeting in the evening Jediah spoke to us and others Spencer Richards **Frd 31** dug about my pye plant

November 1856

Sat Nov 1 the same **Sund 2** went to meeting hear from the co back 30 had died out of one co **Mond 3** work on a peticoat **Tuesd 4** go and try to collect some debts **wed 5** quilting my peticoat **Thursd 6** fast day have been to meeting visited Sister Newman she is sick **Frd 7 Sat 8** made up my crocia cap **Sund 9** went to meeting and in the evening **Mond 10** cleaned house **Tuesd 11** worked in the garden Ann & Jane with me **wed 12** took up my carpet Mr Parry plastered up some spots **Thursd 13** put down my carpet moved my stove **Frid 14 Sat 15** attended to my domestic concerns went to sister Roundys she being the treasurerys of the relief society drew about six dollars worth of clothing for Mary Williams and daughters one pair of shoes to small for them I gave her a calico dress for them I let her have 7 lb salt that belonged to the society let her have an old bed tick that was mine and some other things **sund 16** went to meeting caled to Eligah Tomas wife Ann she miscarried staid all night **Mond 17** caled to sister Williams her child had a breach **Tuesd 18 Wed 19** cleaned house **Thursd 20** I have felt the nessesety of this refformation and I am trying to reform and I truly feel thankful to my ^hevely^ Father that he has servants to call after us and teach us our duty[20] I went to meeting in the evening **Frid 21** I am home alone I feel well my meditation is sweet and my prayer is that the Holy ghost may be poured out upon the servants of God and that they may ferret out evil untill we may become a pure people I desire to do right and live my religion that I may enjoy that light to see as I am seen and know as I am known. Oh my Father help me to live my religion this is my greatest desire **Sat 22 Sund 23** went to meeting to ward meeting in the evening this morning Mr Parry request- ed me to go down and see Harriet he wished her to come to me but she was not willing so I went down she asked me to forgive her I did and told her if she had anything against me I wished her to forgive me she did I stoped and eat **Mond 24** ~~caled to Aaron Farrs wife~~ ^~~last night~~^ ~~she had a son born 3 A M~~ **Tuesd 25 wed 26** attended to my domestic conserns **Thursd 27** went to the ward meeting in the evening **Frid 28** croatied on my cap **Sat 29** put Lucretia [Barr Thorpe] Aaron Farrs wife to bed with a son [Charles Lyman] born 3 A M **Sund 30** went to meeting in the forenoon the last handcart co came in we had no meeting in the afternoon I came home the Bishop sent me a boy 17 years old that came in the hand cart co I wash and cleaned him up dresed his feet that were frozen

December 1856

Mond Dec 1st he was taken to provo I gave him a flanel shirt a new pair of socks &c **Tuesd 2** went to see Mr Parrys Daughters as I was agoing I heard that Br Jedidiah M Grant was Dead **Wed 3** I worked on my cap **Thursd 4** went to the funeral of Br Grant[21] ~~Frd 5 Sat 6~~ and to ward meeting in the evening **Frd 5 Sat 6** attended to many things **Sund 7** went to meeting to ward meeting in the eve **Mond 8 Tuesd 9 Wed 10** nitting and sewing **Thurd 11** E Tripp and wife and Sylvia here Sylvia staid all night we went to the ward meet- ing in the eve **Frid 12** it snows at night she went up to Tripps **Sat 13** she went

---

20. In an effort to cleanse the saints from being drawn into the secular world, Brigham Young decided to call church members to repentance. On 6 October 1856, during general conference, he organized the territory into six missionary districts and appointed home missionaries to lead the people. They answered directly to the Quorum of the Twelve Apostles. Secondly, he challenged the elders to preach in a manner that would "wake up" the people. Counselors Heber C. Kimball and Jedediah M. Grant responded to the challenge, and Grant in particular preached with unabated fervor. This movement became known as the "Reformation" (see Alexander, *Heaven and Earth*, 181–89).

21. On 3 December 1856 the *Deseret News* published the account of the death of Jedediah M. Grant, second counselor in the First Presidency and mayor of Salt Lake City: "The funeral will take place in the Tabernacle, at 10 A.M. of the 4th inst., when Prest. Brigham Young will address the assembly, if his health and the state of his feelings will permit. The demise of Prest. Grant has cast a deep gloom over our city; stores are closed and the ordinary avocations of business suspended . . ." ("A Mighty Man Has Gone to Rest," 4:309).

home I went to see Br Hyde he has got home from carson valley I got some news from Perrgrine my son there **Sund 14** went to meeting it snowed to ward meeting in the eve **Mond 15** to day the last of the cos have come in[22] Mr Parrys grand daughter Jane came to school to me to learn ^the^ English language **Tuesd 16** she did not come to day she learns fast I have made me a flanel under garment to day **Wed 17-18-19** I attended to my domestic conserns **Satd 20** the same **Sund 21** went to meeting to ward meeting in the evening **Mond ^22^** finished my cap it is very nice **Tuesd 23 Wed 24 Thursd 25** it is christmas spent the day with Sylvia at Tripps he preached good principles to us and we had a good dinner and a good time enjoyed much of the spirit Sylvia and Lucinia came home with me staid all night **Frid 26** I went with them David and Phebe took Dinner at Sister Fosses Phebe came home with me staid all night **Satd 27** Elizabeth & Olive [Foss] come here Calvin [Foss] came took super carried them home **Sund 28** went to meeting **Mond 29 Tuesd 30** I went and gave Thomas Blackam [Blackham] emetic at Br Bouks **Wed 31** wrote a letter to P G

1857

attended to my domestic concerns

JANUARY 1857

Thursd Jan 1 1857 fast day a nationall fast it snowed very fast I went to meeting enjoyed new years first rate went again in the evening **Friday 2** snow very deep **Satd 3** I went to Tripps to dinner Wm & Martha Smoot came home with me she staid all night **Sund 4** snows & so deep do not go to meeting she did not go home **Mond 5** he came & carried her home ^I setled my tithing^ the Bishop sent sister Williams here to stay with me a few days **Tuesd** wash **Wed 7** ironed **Thursd 8** ^went to meeting in the ward Lorenzo Snow there^ **Frid 9 Sat 10** we have attended to many things **Sund 11** went to meeting to the ward in the evening **Mond 12** sister Williams went away ^**Tuesd**^ **13** Sister Knight here staid all night **Wed <14>** sister Riser here sister Knight went home with her **Thursd 15** sister Higbee here snows I do not go to the ward meeting **Frid**

---

22. The last two handcart companies to arrive in 1856 were the ill-fated Willie and Martin companies. Unavoidable delays caused them to start too late in the season; the James G. Willie Company left Iowa City on 15 July and the Edward Martin Company on July 28. On the plains they were pelted with snow and suffered from frost and lack of food. Although Brigham Young, when informed of their approach, sent rescue parties, 67 of the 500 in the Willie Company perished, and 135 of the 576 persons in the Martin Company also died (see LeRoy Hafen and Ann W. Hafen, *Handcarts to Zion* [Glendale, Calif.: Arthur H. Clark, 1960]).

<16> the snow has fallen 16 or 18 inches and still fals fast **Sat 17** snow deep roads bad **Sund 18** go to meeting to the ward in the eve **Mond 19** Mary & Sylvia came here staid all night **Tuesd 20** I went with them to Br Leonards had good visit David & Phebe came home with me staid all night **Wed 21** I went up home with them ^The missionary here before I went catecised me^ [23] **Thursd 22** at the Bishops and at Sylvias went to meeting in the evening **Frid 23** visited Br Willey he was sick **Sat 24** see him again the sisters had a meeting at Perrigrines ^last evening^ Mary called them together to tell them what Br Kimbal told her to tell them this Morning visited sister Mixwell [Sylvia Smith, wife of John B. Maxwell] she talks of going to the states in the spring I told her to leave her son with me and I would be a mother to him untill she came back she said she would think of it I told her I was affraid she would lose him if she took him Br Carter then brought me home **Sund 25** went to meeting to the ward in the eve **Mod 26** went to sister Bouks funeral **Tuesd 27 wed 28 Thursd 29** attend to my domestic concerns went to the ward meeting in the eve **Frid 30** measured my wheet **Sat 31** went to sister grows in the eve he came the amount of provision I had 20 bushels wheat 3:00 flour 2 bushels corn 1 do potatoes

FEBRUARY 1857

Sund Feb 1 I went to meeting to the tabnacle Brigham Preached to the ward in the eve **Mond 2** Caleb Parry ~~took~~ took a wife [Winifred] yestarday they staid here last night went home this morning I am making chair cushions **Tuesd 3** I washed then went and visited Sister More Mr Parry went with me **Wed 4** my birthday Sixty two years old I went to see sister Susannah Richards then stoped at sister Fosses **Thursd 5** fast day I went to meeting had a good meeting it snowed all day went again in the evening **Frd 6** put my grand Daughter Martha Ann Smoot to bed with her 3 child [a son, Abraham Owen] born 35 minutes past 11 A M ^I^ staid with her **Satd 7 Sund 8** I still stay then go to the sugar house ward meeting in the evening **Mond 9** visited with sister Smoot And=r Smith his Mother also his Br Wm= Smith we took supper there **Tuesd 10** I came home found all well **Wed 11** I went up to Tripps had a good visit **Thursd 12** visited at sister Fosses Olive was married yestarday[24] came home went to the ward meet= in the evening David came here after me

---

23. Jedediah M. Grant had drafted a set of questions to test the faithfulness and obedience of members. The home missionaries were instructed to report the results of the catechism. (See Gene A. Sessions, *Mormon Thunder: A Documentary History of Jedediah Morgan Grant* [Chicago: University of Illinois Press, 1982], 219–21.)

24. Olive Foss married Franklin Benjamin Woolley (1834–1869). He was killed by Indians on the Mojave Desert. According to *Diary of Hosea Stout* (ed. Juanita Brooks, 2 vols. [Salt Lake City: University of Utah Press, 1964], 2:723, n. 26), an account of the murder is in James G. Bleak, "Annals of the Southern Utah Mission," Book A, 291–94, typescript, Brigham Young University.

to go home with him I told him I felt that I should be wanted at home and I had better not go **Frd 13** this morning before day I was called to Br Bouks to his child they thought it would choak to death with phlegm I gave it an emetic and it soon got better **Satd 14** I was caled to Br Parkers his boy had cut his big toe nearly off ^finished my cushions^ **Sund 15** I went to meeting Aropene the Indian chief spoke, the spirit revealed to me nearly all he said,[25] went to the ward meeting in the evening **Mond 16 Tuesd 17 Wed 18** I attended domestic conserns **Thursd 19** Sylvia & Tilda Ann Duncan [Matilda Ann, b. 1836] came got Dinner I went to the ward meeting **Frid 20** baked E Tripp and wife Sophia here in the eve **Satd 21** I visited at Dimic Huntingtons with Sylvia Precinda and Zina ^Sylvia told me what Heber told her to tell me to get wool and make me some flanel I said I shall= =get it now for I know he is a prophet of God^ [= *Patty indicates by this sign that this statement is sandwiched between lines of her diary*] Sylvia & Zina came home with me staid all night **Sund 22** we went to meeting to ward meeting in the eve **Mond 23** there was a sick child brought here I gave it some medicine **Tuesd 24** read much in the book of mormon I feel well I never read [that] book but I get the spirit of god, I have commenced to crocia the 3d cap this winter beside one last faul **Wed 25** David & Bishop Stoker here to dinner **thursd 26** went to the ward meeting David Cantlin Preached [David Candland, 1819–1902] had a good meeting **Frd 27** wrote a letter to my Mother went and put it in the office caled at Br Woodruffs spoke for some grape vines got me a pair of new shoes at Tripps on a debt that T Smith owed me **Sat 29** one week ago to day when Sylvia told what Heber said I claped my hands & said I shall get some wool ^or rolls^ now for he would not tell me to do any thing that I could not, for I knew he was a Prophet of God, & I have got three pound rolls now and am shure I shall get some more

MARCH 1857

Sund March 1 went to meeting ^John Parry & wife [Harriet Julia Roberts, b. 1829] came home with me^ to ward meeting in the eve **Mond 2** I have got two lb more ^wool^ rolls ~~to~~ have been with sist Precinda & Mary Elen Kimbal washed and anointed Susannah ^Richards^ she was sick **Tuesd 3 Wed 4 Thursd 5** atended to my domestic concerns went to ward meeting this eveng **Frid 6** I have got four lb more rolls I have now 9 lb all brought to me I think I will now go to spining soon the Bishop commenced baptising this ward[26] Sylvia here **Satd 7** Mr Parry and Harriet were baptised **Sund 8** went to

25. The JH for 15 February 1857 records, "Arapene, a Utah Indian Chief, delivered a powerful exhortation to the saints, telling them to follow their leaders and do right, not drink whisky or do wrong in anything."

26. Rebaptizing ward members reflected the bishop's effort to follow instructions and solidify the reformation in the lives of his parishioners.

meeting never heard such comforting preaching as Brigham gave us to ward meeting in the eve **Mond 9** I was Baptised I never felt so weel in my life I then commenced spining **Tuesd 10** spun 4 skeins **Wed 11** David came here took my wheet to mill 23 bushels Lucinia come here she and I went to sister Smoots she staid all night I came home **Thursd 12** Mr Parry & John worked in ~~the~~ my garden I with them went to ward meeting in the eve I feel well all the time I am happy **Frd 13** I went to sister Smots to see Martha and children then to sister Leonards on a visit **Sat 14** David and Phebee came brought my flour staid all night ^**Sund 15**^ went to meeting to ward in the eve **Mond 16** James Worden here I had manure haled onto my lot **Tuesd 17 Wed 18** spining **Thursd 19** went to the ward meeting in the [eve] **Frd 20** worked in the garden **Sat 21** James goes home I go up to P Gs with Tripp & wives **Sund 22** go to meeting up there came home went to the ward meeting in the eve **Mond 23** sent 1-10 peach trees to the office for tithing **tuesd 24** spun **wed 25** washed Br Crosleys Daughters came yestar **Thursd 26** spun went to ward meeting in the eve **Frid 27 Sat 28** spun **Sund 29** went to meeting rained hard went to meeting in the eve **Mond 30** wrote a letter to my sister Naamah Tripp **Tuesd 31** had pie plant for breakfast sent some to the Editor of the News with ~~a~~ peach blossoms[27] John Parry worked in the garden planted corn and potatoes Susan Hunter here

APRIL 1857

^**wed**^ **April 1st** ^1857^ spining **Thursd 2** fast day paid my fast in flour & carrots **Frid 3** spining Sylvia & Josephine staid here all night **Sat 4** they went up to town John Parry took up some Locust trees set them out side for shade trees round my lot **sund 5** went to meeting ward meeting in the evening Charles Foster staid here all night **Mond 6** went to confrence Lucinia staid here all night **Tuesd 7** went again Sylvia & Mary staid here all night **Wed 8** went again ~~sold J~~ Brigham caled for us to give him 1-25 Dollars money I gave all I had[28] come home sold John Ragen [Reagan?] ten dollars worth of peach trees **Thursd 9** went to meeting confrence adjourned at noon came home went and put sister Andrew Coltrin to bed with a pair of twins the daughter born about 5 P M the son about 10 P M **Frd 10 & Satd 11** finished spining my dresses Sat went to Tripps to dinner then took some rubarb to the tithing

27. The *Deseret News* for Wednesday, 8 April 1857, reported, "Sister Patty Sessions has our thanks for a liberal bunch of good sized pie plant stalks plucked on the 31st ult. A peach blossom accompanied the pie plant, and was the earliest that we have seen this season" (p. 37).

28. The JH for 8 April 1857 records, "Pres. Brigham Young made a call for a subscription to raise $125. Following this request James Blake, Sabra Savage and Polly Phelps handed in rings. Money has been and is still very scarce among the people." The entry fails to specify a purpose for the subscription.

office gave a small shaul 75 and pair of embroidered under sleeves $1=50 David Lucinia & Mary came down I went with them to the circus they came here staid all night **Sund 12** went to meeting **Mond 13** attended to my domestic concerns **Tuesd <14>** went to store took up the order Coltrin gave me for puting his wife to bed they have started for the states to day **Wed 15 Thursd 16** went to the ward meeting hear that Br Gays family have the small pox **Frid 17** they are moved over Jordon **Sat 18** went to Agatha Pratts got my bonnet **Sund 19** went to meeting **Mond 20** spining **Tuesd ^21^** went to see Martha Smoot with Tripps and wife had a good visit Mr Parry commenced work on the temple **Wed 22** spining Sylvia Mixwell Smith came here staid all night sister Smith was married to day **Thursd 23** went to town saw Mixwell [John B. Maxwell, assigned to Europe] and about 80 other Missionaries start off with thier hand carts[29] went to Lorenzo snows got a frame to put the likenesses of the first Presidncy & the twelve in ^then went to the ward meeting^ **Frd <24>** finished spining my rolls went to see E B Tripp start on his mission North with Presidency & many others **Sat 25** watered my garden some planted some beans **Sund 26** went to meeting **Mond 27** worked in the garden **Tuesd 28** the same **Wed 29** the same planted beans and corn **Thursd 30** ^baked^ pies and bread attended ward meeting Mr Parry has brought me ten and a half pounds flour and one pound of butter the first ~~of~~ he has brought me of his earnings for about t[w]o years

May 1857

May 1 ^1857^ I went and doubled carpet yarn for sister Tripp **Satd 2** cold dry winds **Sund 3** went to meeting **Mond ^4^** watered the garden some **Tuesd 5** visited Sister Cumings with sisters Tripps ~~Wed 6~~ came home found Wm= and Martha at the gate waiting for me they staid all night **Wed 6** we went to Tripps in the forenoon in the afternoon Sophia & Jessess [Jessie Smith Eddins, another wife of E. B. Tripp] came here Martha went home **Thursd 7** Mr Parry made me an arch to make soap I had to help him and did not go to fast meeting **Frd 8** wattered my garden **Sat 9** I am sick to day Mr Parry brought me 10 2*h* lb shorts 2 lb butter 4 eggs this week David & Marry down

---

29. The JH for 23 April 1857 reports, "Early on Thursday morning . . . those that had been selected at the Conference for missions, that were to cross the plains on the way to their various fields of labor in the states, in the British North American Provinces, in Europe, Africa, and other parts of the world, commenced assembling on Temple Block, preparatory to starting off together . . . with their hand-carts, the means of conveyance adopted instead of horses, mules and carriages, as hertofore. Most of the carts were well fitted up for the trip, with names and mottoes beautifully painted on some of them, to suit the taste and fancy of the owner, and which will no doubt greatly add to the pleasure that will be derived from rolling them up and down the mountains, and across the plains that intervene between this and the frontiers of Iowa and Missouri."

brought 2 letters from P G one from Carloss to me I was glad to hear from them they went to smoots staid all night **Sund 10** went to meeting **Mond 11** put in some apricot buds it rains Sylvia here staid all night **Tuesd 12)** ^**Wed**^ **13** I went up to the store with her she went to Martha Smoots I went to Brighams to sell some things for sister Mixwell ~~Wed~~ **Thursd 14** scoured [washed] my yarn & went to the ward meeting **Frid 15** Phebe here cutting and fixen a tight sack for me very cold **Sat 16** I transplanted many things in the garden we have had quite a rain this week still cold but fair to day **Sund 17** went to meeting **Mond 18** washed **Tuesd 19** ironed **wend 20** white washed Jesess helped me **Thursd 21** warped a carpet for Tripps wife[30] went to the ward meeting **Frid 22** Dr Williams wife and Sophia Tripp here visiting **Sat 23** worked in the garden watering **Sund 24** went to meeting **mond** ^**25**^ went to the tithing office got some butter **Tuesd 26** went to see Ralf Smith **wend 27** made soap Tripp got home last night **Thursd 28** went to the Machine got 4 lb rolls visited Martha came home went to see sister Higbee **Frd 29** went to see her again Tripp came home from his farm sick sent for me I went see him **Satd 30** went and see him again **Sund 31** went to meeting

JUNE 1857

Mond June 1 1857 commenced spining my rolls **Tuesd 2** the Bishop sent a man here for me to bord his name Richard Saden and I water the garden some **Wed 3** Elizabeth Pulspher Died I went and laid her out she was 70 years old lived with Zera Pulsipher I tried to have his wife Mary let Elizabeth have her robe to be laid out in she said she would not she should not have it[31] **Thursd 4** I went to see her buried **Frd 5** watered the garden **Satd 6** spining Mary came here staid all night **Sund 7** went to meeting saw David & Lucinia she brought me down a cheese Called to Nelson Whiple wife Rachel put her to bed with a daughter [Cynthia] born 10 minutes before 10 P M[32] **Mond 8** spining **Tuesd** ^to sister Hagen boy gave him emetic^ **Wed 10** visited sister whiple **Thursd 11** put Sophia Tripp to bed with a daughter [Roxana Sophia] *[At this point Patty inserts small white pages and begins to write crosswise.]* born **Thursd 11 1857** then went to ward meeting caled from there to sister Kegan now Simons miscarage **Frd 12** waterd the garden **Sat 13** Sylvia here **Sund 14** went to meeting **Mod 15** the man left here Seden by name I worked in the garden **Tuesd 16** I went up to Davids his babe sick **Wed 17** came home

30. Warping meant to arrange strands of yarn to run lengthwise in the carpet design.

31. Elizabeth Dutton and John Pulsipher were the parents of Zerah. "Her robe" probably refers to sacred clothing worn in the temple. It was also used for burial.

32. Nelson Wheeler Whipple (1818–1887) was a blacksmith, carpenter, lumberman, and policeman. He is said to have made the first shingles for the Tabernacle. Rachel Keeling (dates unknown) was his wife.

got Br Moss to cut my hay **Thursd 18** raked some female releif society organ-ised[33] **Sat 20** finished my hay got it stacked **Sund 21** went to meeting **Mond 22** work in the garden **Tuesd 23** ^hear that Br P P Pratt is dead^[34] finished spining my rolls **wed 24** went to town ^stoped to see Br P P Pratts family **Third 25** went to ward meeting **Frid** ^**26**^ went to the releif society **Sat 27** David Phebe sister Foss Liza Rhoda all here visiting after we visited Elizabeths school **Sund** ^**22**^ went to meeting **Mond 29** buded some apple trees and apricots **Tuesd 30**

July 1857

wed July 1 ^1857^ <1857> attended to my domestic conserns **Thursd 2** was at the ward meeting ^fast day^ **Frid 3** sister Clarry & sister Polly Vose here **Sat 4** legion musterd[35] I went to Br Roundys saw them on prade in the after-noon went to sister Fosses Mr Parry went with me I went from there with sis-ter Precinda Kimbal washed & changed sister F G Williams anointed and laid hands on her **Sund** ^**5**^ went to meeting **Mond 6** washed **Tuesd 7** worked in the garden **Wed 8** carry some currants to the tithing office then went to the releif society **Thursd 9** went to the ward meeting worked in the garden **Frid 10** watered p^u^led my flax tied it up[36] **Satd 11** cleaned went to the tithing office **Sund 12** went to meeting **Mond 13** Sylvia staid here last night we went to the store she gave me money ^50 cts^ to bye eggs 4 doz & 50 cts more to bye some tea she went home I bought 2 lb rolls **Tuesd** ^**14**^ worked in the garden **Wed 15** puled the peas took care of the flax **Thursd 16** sowed some

---

33. As a follow-up to the Indian Relief Society mentioned earlier, Bishop Roundy informed Patty Sessions in January 1855 that, according to Brigham Young, the "Benevolent Society now must look after the poor in each ward," ("Forgotten Relief Societies," *Dialogue* 6 [Spring 1983]: 105–125). This must refer to the reestablishing of the Female Relief Society as it had been organized in Nauvoo on 17 March 1842.

34. In Arkansas the jealous and estranged husband of Elenore J. McComb McLean shot at Parley P. Pratt seven times and then stabbed him to death. There were numbers of men with McLean, who claimed that Pratt had eloped with Elenore from San Francisco, an allegation that Elenore staunchly denied.

35. Probably the Nauvoo Legion paraded on this day to help celebrate the birth of the United States. By this date, however, rumors were astir that a federal army was being sent to Utah to control the Mormons.

36. "The flax had been used for medicinal purposes as well as to make cloth and it was due to the medicinal qualities that they brought the seed to Utah. . . . It took a full year to produce the flax plant's fibers and they had to be kept moist every step of the way–from the planting of the seed to the spinning of the thread" (see Shirley B. Paxman, "Early Mormon Family Life and Home Production" [lecture delivered at Harold B. Lee Library, Brigham Young University, Provo, Utah, 7 December 1979], 5). Whether Patty intended to use the flax for medicine or thread or both is unknown.

turnips went to the ward meeting then to Amanda Bungs put her to bed with a son born 20 minutes before 12 P M **Frd 17** spun Phebe Tripp here Mr Parry had a ticket to go to the kanyon to a picknic party Brigham gave it to him **Sat 18** made me a cap bought two hundred feet of boards to make a flourchest watered the garden stuck up the boards **Sund 19** went to meeting **Mond 20** washed **Tuesd** ironed baked got ready to go to the Kanyon **Wed 22** go with wilson Lund and Br Day & wife camped near the upper mill **Thursd 23** went onto the campground a splended place toungue cannot describe it I felt well and was happy Mr Parry did not go **Frd 24** spent the day very agreeable enjoyed the society of many of my old aquaintances went forth in the dance and enjoyed the party well[37] **Sat 25** at day light we started for home got home at 4 P M watered my garden **Sund ^26^** went to meeting **Mond ^27^** spun some went to town got some butts and screws and some sugar **Tuesd 28** finished spining **wed ^29^** scoured my yarn went to the sewing society **Thursd 30** had some of my grass cut cut me a dress **Frd 31** worked in the garden

August 1857

Sat August 1 1857 put Mary Wordrorbe to bed with a son 13 pounds born 4 P M **Sund 2** went to meeting watered my garden last night **Mond 3** raked my hay & stacked it went to the tithing office carried currants and cucumbers **Tuesd 4** worked in the garden **wed 5** went to the sewing society **Thursd 6** fast day went to meeting **Frid 7** went to town to see Morgan Phelps cast iron **Sat 8** Mercer Bessee now King came in[38] I went to Tripps to see her Wm= & Martha Ann came here staid all night I watered my garden in the night **Sund 9** went to meeting Br Taylor[39] and Erastas Snow[40] has got home both

37. The three-day party, attended by 2,587 persons, was held in Big Cottonwood Canyon to celebrate the tenth anniversary of the Mormon arrival in Salt Lake Valley. Contemporary accounts describe the beauty of the scenery, three large dance floors built of planks, a swing that could carry three or four persons, and good food. The nation's flag flew from the ridges of mountains around them. Ironically it was here that first definite word came that a federal expedition was actually en route to Utah, escorting Governor Alfred Cumming to establish control over the Mormons. This was the beginning of what was called the "Utah War."

38. Mercy Bessey (b. 1839) was a daughter of Anthony Bessey (1785–1856) and Thankful Stearns (1798–1865). Thankful Stearns was a daughter of Thankful Bartlett, Patty's sister, and Charles Stearns. Mercy was married to Thomas King (b. 1839).

39. John Taylor, George A. Smith, and John M. Bernhisel had been delegated to present a petition for statehood to the government in Washington (JH, 9 August 1857).

40. Erastus Snow's mission to St. Louis on 11 April 1856 included a variety of responsibilities: obtaining type for the English and Deseret alphabets; recommending settlements to support the migration to Utah; sending a steam engine

preached to day Sylvia came home with me she staid all night **Mond 10** she went home I have got my beet seed and flax seed took care of I have worked very hard to day **Tuesd 11** spun for sister Riser to fit him for any emergency **Wed ^12^** spun for sister grow to make a comforter for him to fit him in the evening I went up to Perrigrines **Thursd 13** visited at Sylvias sister carters Ruth was sick hear that P G is coming home tomorrow David is going to meet him **Frid 14** he came home from Carson Valley with his family all that was with him all well **Satd 15** I came home **Sund 16** went to meeting P G Lucinia & Mary came down to meeting I went to Smoots with them staid all night **Mond 17** they came home with me spent the afternoon & went home I finished Br Grows comforter[41] **Tuesd 18** worked in the garden **Wed 19** I went to the sewing society gave one dollar material for a quilt **Thursd 20** commence Elgriges comforter put Ann Br Eldridge wife [Ann Marie Peck, b. 1839, and Elnathan Eldridge] to bed with a son [Loring] Born 2 A M went to the ward meeting **Frd 21** finished the comforter **Satd 22** visited at Tripps with sisters Fosses **Sund <23>** went to meeting **Mond 24** worked in the garden **Tuesd** the same **Wed 25** went to town **Thursd 26** nitting Br grow a pair of double mittins **Frd 27** worked in the garden Br Elis commenced a grain chest for me I went to the ward meeting **Frd 28** had co **Sat ^29^** finished the mittens and commenced striking a harness[42] **Sund 30** went to meeting **Mond 31** Br Elis finished the chest

September 1857

Tues Sept 1 ^1857^ wed 2 finished my harne^(-ss^ **Thursd 3** fast I went to meeting **Frid ^4^** commenced a comforter for Br Eldriges boy **Sat ^5^** finished it Sister Higbee sick I have been there to day **Sund 6** went to meeting My Neice sister Bessee got in last night she came here to night[43] P G &

---

purchased the summer before to Utah; publishing the *Luminary*; and acting as agent for the Perpetual Emigration Company in St. Louis. Since he was in poor health, he was summoned home (see Andrew Karl Larson, *Erastus Snow: The Life of a Missionary and Pioneer for the Early Mormon Church* [Salt Lake City: University of Utah Press, 1971], 278–79).

41. Henry Grow (1817–1891) arrived in the valley in 1851. As an architect and builder, his work contributed to mills, bridges, the theatre, the old Tabernacle, Z. C. M. I., the Assembly Hall, the hoists and scaffolding for the Temple, and notably, the domed roof of the Tabernacle. He superintended church building and carpentry during the presidency of Brigham Young. He was married to Mary Moyer, Ann Elliott, and Julia Veach. Ann Elliott was the widow of William Veach (d. 2 November 1845) and the mother of Grow's wife, Julia Veach.

42. The harness is the part of the loom that raises and lowers the warp threads.

43. Anthony Bessey had died on 27 August 1856 at Wapella, Iowa. His widow was Thankful Stearns (see note 38).

David came here **Mond 7** commenced another comforter **Tuesd 8** finished it begun another had my grass cut **wed 9** went to the releif society **Thursd 10** went to the ward meeting **Frd 11** raked the hay & got it together spun 18 knots of yarn finished the 4th comforter for Eldridge it is good days I feel well in body and mind and the Lord prospers me in all I do I am trying to live my religion and I am happy **Sat 12 Sund ^13^** went to meeting **Mond 14** commenced a comfeter for Br Grow **Tuesd 15 wed 16** went to the releif society **Thursd 17** my peaches begin to get ripe sell some today **Frd 18** went to the ward meeting **Satd 19** Mary gibs put her to bed with a daughter [Euphemia Eliza] born 6 P M **Sund 20 Mond 21** went meeting **Tuesd 22** finished Br grows comfeter commenced one for the boys **Weds ^23^** put Harriet Mr Parry wife to bed with a daughter [Louisa Ellen] born 10 A M **Thursd 24 ^Frd 25^** atended to my domestic concerns **Sat 26** went to the releif society **Sund 27** sick did not go to meeting **Mond 28** taking care of my peaches **Tuesd 29 wed 30** dito

OCTOBER 1857

Thursd Oct 1 ^1857^ went to fast meeting **Frd 2 Sat 3** taking care of my peaches **Sund 4** sick at home **Mond 5 Tuesd 6** confrence I went **Wed 7** to home confrence closed **Thursd 8 Frd 9 Sat 10** worked at my peaches **Sund 11** it rains do not go to meeting **Mond 12** take care of my peaches **Tuesd 13** the same **wed 14** the same **Thursd 15** put Pheebe Tripp to bed with a son born 5 P M **Frd 16 Sat 17** taking care of my peaches **Sund 18** do not go to meeting the wind blew very hard last night I had a heavy bed comforter blow of of the roof of the house and I know not what is become of it it was over my dried peaches **Mond 19 Tuesd 20** worked at my peaches **wed 21** caled to Br Campkins put his wife to bed with a son 2 P M **Thursd 22** I have had many men to work for me this week **Frd 23** put sister Davis to bed with a daughter born 3 P M **Sat ^24^** finish harvesting and gathering all my peaches and all my vegatables got all my manure out and much of my lot spaded Mr Parry has not been here any days and only three times in the evenings for two weeks and I have been very unwell Just able to attend to oversee my buisnes **Sund 25** not able to go to meeting it rained last night P G & David and Calvin Foss here to Dinner **Mond 26** spooled some [yarn] not well **Tuesd 27** McArther & wife here[44] I went and got a reed[45] **wed 28** Josephine came down to stay with me untill I get well warped my dresses **Thursd 29 Frd 30** got my web in[46] **Sat 31**

---

44. Susan McKeen (1801–1866) was the wife of Duncan McArthur (1796–1865).

45. When making fabric, a reed goes into the beater on the front of the loom to push the thread down.

46. The web is created by the threads that run from back to front on a warp beam.

NOVEMBER 1857

^Nov 1^ **Sund** ^1857^ put sister Ash to bed with a daughter born 7 A M went to meeting **Mond 2 Tuesd 3** wove some I am not well **wed 4 Thursd 5** the same **Frd 6** got my web out 13 yards warped another web **Sat 7** drawed it in wove 3 yards finished sister grows comforter **Sund 8** went to meeting Calvin Foss started for california to day I am some better but not well **Mond 9** wove 10 2*h* yards **Tuesd 10** got my web out 16 yards took the loom down moved my stove cleaned up things &c **wed** ^11^ washed **Thursd** ^12^ ironed **Frd 13** nit Br grow a comforter **Sat 14** got my things ready to go up to Davids to have Phebee help me make my dresses **Sund 15** went to meeting in the forenoon in the afternoon went up home with David found sisters Foss and Vose there **Mond 16** worked on my dresses we all went to Sylvias in the afternoon I staid all night **Tuesd 17** we visited at Br carters **wed 18** Sisters Foss & Polly Vose came home **Thursd 19** we finished my dresses and a pair of mittens came down to stay with me untill **Frd 20** nit a pair of mitens for Sylvias boy Perry **Sat 21** visited at Silvias with Br cowley and wife[47] did up my caps **Sund 22** came home did not get home in season to go to meeting **Mond** ^23^ went and washed and anointed sister Higbee wrote a few lines to John Parry & sent him a pair of mittens he is out in the canyons watching the troops[48] **Tuesd 24** ~~wed 25~~ put John Parrys wife Harriet to bed with a daughter born 1 P M[49] then put Ann Grow to bed with a daughter born 10 P M **wed 25** visited them both **Thursd 26** commenced me a comforter **Frd 27** and **Satd 28** sewed at the school house on coats for the boys in the mountains **Sund 29** went to meeting **Mond** finished my comforter commenced one for Br Grow

DECEMBER 1857

Tuesd worked on it **wed Nov [Dec] 2 1857** the same **Thursd 3** fast day I went to meeting the boys came home from the mountain I went to see Tripp & John Parry **Frid 4** I have finished Br Grows comforter commenced a pair of fringed mittens **Sat 5** nit on them **sund 6** went to meeting **Mond 7 Tues 8 wed 9 Thurs 10** [*she corrects and writes on top of all these dates*] attend to my domestic concerns made up my blankets washed &c **Frd 11** spun shoe thread for David **Sat**

---

47. Sarah Elizabeth Foss married Matthias Cowley (1829–1864).

48. Twenty-five hundred Mormon volunteers wintered in Echo Canyon and other strategic locations, where they rocked up breastworks in the cliffs and prepared to flood the canyon to resist the approaching army. These preparations proved unnecessary. In effective guerilla tactics on the Wyoming plains, the Nauvoo Legion burned fifty-two wagons loaded with 150 tons of food and equipment– and drove off hundreds of oxen and beef cattle, forcing the army to winter near Fort Bridger.

49. This is Harriet Roberts, the wife of John Parry's son John (see note 30 to Diary 4).

12 finished the fringed mittens **Sund 13** put Mary More to bed with a son born 12 2 *h* A M went to meeting ^came home sick^ **Mond 14** P G here to dinner ^I am week^ I have had the good luck to get 15 lb sugar I have all things to make me comfortable for which I thank the Lord and enjoy myself first rate in trying to live my religion **Tuesd 15** baked mince pies **wed 16** went up to Tripps ~~Wed~~ **Thursd 17** I went up to P Gs with Tripp & wifes **Frd 18** visited Sylvia came home she came home with us I have nit a pair of mittens for Mr Parry **Sat** fixing my caps **Sund 20** went to meeting **Mond 21** worked on my quilt **Tuesd 22 wed 23 Thursd 24** the same **Frd 25** chrismas went to Tripps took dinner **Sat 26** prepared to go to Davids he came after me staid all night **Sund** ^27^ went to meeting in the forenoon then went up to Davids in the evening went to see Chester Lovlins child very sick stoped at Sylvias Perry had a whip struck into his eye hurt bad **Mond** ^28^ worked for Phebe fixing a peticoat for Jane **Tuesd** went to Br chisnels to a party **wed 30** viseted at Sylvias **Thursd 31** commenced a pair of mitens for P G

1858

I think I can take the spoiling of my things with joy

JANUARY 1858

Frid Jan 1–1858 spun for Phebe Wm= Smoot & wife & Mother & Anna came up to P Gs[50] **Sat 2** we all went to Sylvias Perrys eye quite well **Sund 3** Wm= & folks went home Elizabeth & her husband Cowley came to Davids I went over to Sylvias we went to meeting in the evening **Mond 4** we all went to Br Dibbles to a party had a good time **Tuesd 5** ^and **wed 6**^ I wound yarn moulded candles &c had a party at P Gs in the evening for the youth it could not easily be beat for good order and a good spirit was there **Thursd 7** finished P Gs mittens ^and went to fast meeting^ **Frid 8** another party at P Gs **Sat 9** I sold my fringed mittens and a pair of socks for two bushels of wheet, put Phebe Davids wife to bed 1 - 45 minutes P M [with a son, David] **Sund 10** she is comfortable **Mond 11** another party at P Gs **Tues 12** David has made me a pair of shoes since I have been here **wed 13** came home sister Foss went up **Thursd 14** put John Pulsipers wife Rosilla to bed with a daughter [Emily Sariah] born 7 P M **Frd 15 Satd 16** attending to my domestic conserns **Sund 17** went to meeting **Mond 18** went to a welsh party in the 15 ward **Tuesd** <19> washed **wed** <20> ironed **Thursd 21** visited sister Besseys **Frd 22 Sat**

---

50. William's mother was Margaret McMeans, and his father was Abraham Owen Smoot. His grandmother (Anna) was Ann Rowlett (1787–1871); George Washington Smoot was his grandfather.

23 worked on my quilt **Sund 24** went to meeting **Mond 25** setled up my tithing for last ^year^ found Due me seven Dollars five cents $7-05 after setling seventy three Dollars seventy six cents I have raised 2 -3*h* lb flax E B Tripp rotted broke and swingled it with his ~~I gave him~~ he asked me $3-50 for [*two words scratched out*] doing it **Tuesd 26** went out to Wm= smoots on a visit **wed 27** croachied Wm= a cap **Thursd 28** croached another cap **Frd 29** came home) **Sat 30** combed my flax moulded candles David came here he has made me a pair of gaters **Sund 31** went to meeting

FEBRUARY 1858

Mond Feb 1 attended to my domestic concerns **Tuesd 2** Tripp and wives here on a visit **wed 3** carded some tow [towse straw] **Thursd 4** my birthday sixty three years old, fast day I go to meeting, in the afternoon Mr Parrys boy[51] was lost we hunted for him till night found him about a mile from home **Frd 5** made a chair cusheon I have got a new rocking chair **Sat 6 Sund 7** went to meeting **Mond 8** went up in town to get some lumber for flour boxes found none got 5 lb sugar **Tuesd 9** visited at sister Foses with Tripp and wives **wed 10** caled to sister Creek miscarriage **Thursd 11** gave sister Vernon emetic **Frd 12** Phebee Tripp here on a visit **Sat 13** made me a cap not well **Sund 14** so unwell do not go to meeting Mr Parry has been here two days quite unwell he is better to day **Mond 15** Davids wife came here soon after she came here Perrigrine came told us David was sick she went home with him I am still sick **Tuesd 16 wed 17** no better Mr Parry sent for the Bishop [Kesler] he came they anointed and laid hands on me **Thursd 18** I am better to day **Frd 19 Satd 20** I am ~~still~~ getting better slowly I have some appetite to day I hear from David to day he is better **Sund 21** I am not so well to day David came down here to day **Mond** ^22^ I am no better my head is very bad in the afternoon a sore broke in my ear[52] I feel better **Tuesd 23** began to nit a little **wed 24** Lucinia came down to stay with me a few days **Thursd 25** she washed **Frd 26** I can work a little **Satd 27** Sophia Tripp here on a visit **Sund 28** I do not go to meeting I am not well enough David came down he and Lucinia went in the forenoon went home in the afternoon Col= Cane is here in town[53]

---

51. Probably Joseph Hyrum, the surviving twin boy who was born on 8 August 1855.

52. This illness may have contributed to Patty's extreme deafness later in life.

53. Colonel Thomas L. Kane, a longtime friend of the Mormons, on his own initiative came to negotiate a settlement of the difficulties with the government. As a result of his efforts, agreement was reached for the army to march peaceably through Salt Lake Valley and establish a camp in Cedar Valley, forty miles southwest of Salt Lake City.

MARCH 1858

Mond March 1 Susannah Marry & sister Franklin here on a visit **Tuesd 2** commenced to crocia me a cape **Wed 3** John Parrys wife here I am quite well and the Lord has heard the prayers of his servants and I can hear again after being deaf with one ear for over four months and I do rejoice in his goodness **Thursd 4** fast day I went to meeting **Frd 5** work on my cape finished it **Satd 6** Sisters Foss Olive Elizabeth sister Vose Emerett David Matthias cowly here on a visit I bought 400 cwt of flour **Sund 7** went to meeting **Mond 8** visited with Emerett at Br Sam= Mores **Tuesd 9** had co all day sisters came to me to comfort them I did comfort them and they went away feeling well thank the Lord **wed ^10^** Emerett went home P G here planted peas and potatoes & beets ~~Thu~~ bought ten bushels of wheat **Thursd 11** bought 1 more commenced spining **Frd 12** sold $11:00 worth of peach trees I have had a man to work in the garden all this week ~~Sat 13~~ sent 80 peach trees to the tithing office $20=00 and a bunch of peach blossoms to the editor the first we have seen **Satd 13** carded tow **Sund 14** snows I do not go to meeting **Mond 15 Tuesd 16 wed 17 and Thursd 18** I have been spining tow have finished it this morning the men were caled to go to Tooelee the Indians have been stealing catle there bought 3 2h bushels wheat **Frd 19** nit a purse **Satd 20** attended to my domestic concerns sent ten plumb trees to the tithing office $1-00 **Sund 21** went to meeting the word was for us all to go south as soon as we could that the United troops were determined to come in and kill us all[54] **Mond 22** buisiness al stoped as to springs work **Tuesd 23** all preparing to move P G was down yesterday he and David and Sylvia down again Sylvia P G & Sylvia staid here all night **Wed 24** P G had a talk with the Bishop & Mr Parry concluded that I should go with P G and the rest of my children **Thursd 25** I commenced preparing to pack my things **Frd 26 Sat 27** dito **Sund 28** went to meeting **Mond 29** finished making my soft soap into hard **Tuesd 30** P G came down told me that he would take all the flour that I could get sacked by 9 oclock next morning **Wed 31** he came I sent 18=50 ^hundred^ pounds by him

APRIL 1858

Thursd I commenced packing **Frd <April>** P G came back he had hired a storeroom & left it at American fork **Sat 2** the team came for Mr Parry **Sund**

---

54. On 18 March 1858 in a meeting of the First Presidency, eight of the twelve apostles, and the territory's leading military officers, the decision was reached to abandon the idea of armed resistance to the federal forces. The Mormons were prepared to abandon the city and burn it, however, if needed. Brigham Young sent an exploring expedition as far as the Muddy River in southern Nevada, seeking, but not finding, suitable places to settle in the desert. During much of the spring of 1858, roads to Provo and on to southern settlements were crowded with the wagons of Mormons leaving their homes.

3 Lucinia and Sylvia came here staid all night I sacked the rest of my flour yesterday Mr Parry started this morning ^took all the things that he brought here away from me^ I went to meeting G[eorge] A[lbert Smith] Br Vernon Brigham John Taylor & capt Hunt preached Susan Bessee came home with me we went to the ward meeting she staid with me all night **Mond 5** I have washed I feel first reate cheerful and happy I think I can take the spoiling of my things with joy Oh Lord help me so to do ~~Tuesd 6~~ P G David Lucinia came down took a load of wheet for me ^26 2*h* bus^ David has gone with it and a load for P G two men with him Lucinia and I went to making soap P G went home **Tuesd 6** the f[c]onference P G came down I did not go we were mak soap Wm= and Martha came here yesterday staid all night have gone home to day we finish the soap Lucinia went home with P G ~~wed~~ confrence ajorned till Oct= **Wed** P G down again he has to move into the city and the city to Utah co I have been packing David came back staid here all night **Thursd 8** they start home this morning two four horse teams I emt[y] my straw ticken & wash it boil out my tow yarn **Frd 9** take up my carpet have co the most of the day **Satd 10** finish packing **Sund 11** go to meeting went to the ward meeting in the evening **Mond 12** took up my other carpet Sulvia moved in with me I send 30 bushels more of wheat and a verry large flour box and 5-00 lb flour **tuesd 13** Sulvia washed **Wed 14** David & Carlos got back from American fork been to carry two load Mr Parry came with them **Thursd 15** Richard came to carry a load for him **Frd 16** they load up start to go back about 12 oclock we are making starch from potatoes **Sat 17** it rains hard **Sund 18** we go to meeting Mr Parry came back to meeting staid all night **Mond 19** he started again ^David moved down^ **Tuesd ^20^** Joseph Parry and wife came here **wed 21** John Parry came from ecko canyon **Thursd 22** I have finished planting my garden John Parry helped me **Frd 23** I went up to P Gs mended up their tin ware he loaded up a load of goods I came down with them **Sat 24** David came back brought Martha & children here Wm= came at night staid all night **Sund 25** David carried Sulvia & I Wm= and Martha up to Br Smoots we then came back to meeting Gov= Cumings was there[55] we had

---

55. Urged by Colonel Kane, Governor Cumming decided to leave the federal army at winter camp at Fort Bridger and travel unescorted to Salt Lake City. He and Colonel Kane traveled by night through Echo Canyon, where the Mormons saluted the governor from their fortifications and he formally addressed them. He arrived on 12 April to find the Mormons abandoning their homes and moving south. The next day he began a series of meetings with Brigham Young and others. His inspections convinced him the Mormons were loyal to the government. The meeting of 25 April overflowed the Tabernacle. Cumming affirmed the government's authority but said he would act in consultation with the Mormon leaders and declared, as Brigham Young recorded, that he "had nothing to do with our social and religious views; we had the right to serve God, in

all sorts of a meetings P G Mary came here to supper and John Stoker **Mond
26** sister Stoker here visiting **Tuesd 27** made me a ^sun^ bonnet **wed 28**
Sylvia washed I mended some braided some straw[56] **Thursd 29** rained P G
here David Ed & John Poorman staid all night **Frid 30** sewed Sylvias boy a hat
then went to Br Hydes Hebers & Bernhisels Sylvia went with me

MAY 1858

Satd May 1 bought 25 lb flour this week paid in pye plant ^spun Sylvia
some thread^ **Sund 2** went to meeting **Mond 3** Sylvia washed **Tuesd 4** made
soap sisters Foss & Vose here on a visit sister Vose staid all night **wed 5** she
went home **Thursd 6** David & Ed gone with another 2 loads think Sylvia and
I will go next time P Gs family are mostly gone **Frid 7** Sylvia and I went to
Tripps on a visit **Sat 8** we are packing up to go away to morrow David & Ed
came back ^Br Lasley is dead^ go up to P Gs and get a load and donot take
us untill next time **Sund 9** go to meeting Br Brigham talked to us so good my
heart rejoiced and I felt to praise God David and Ed came down with two
load stay all night **Mond 10** start early to go down Sylvia washes **Tuesd 11**
we bake and packed Sylvias things David and Ed came back & P G came
down the loaded up Sylvias things **wed 12** she starts they carry 25 bush
wheat for me I am left alone I clean up the house John Parry came back from
Summit where his wife is he takes care of my garden he is one of the gard
that stays here **Thursd 13** I braid straw and put in some beets and carrots
Frid 14 I sew my straw into a basket David and Ed came back here **Satd 15**
they go up home Eldriges child got scalded I was caled for I went and took
care of it **Sund 16** it is doing well I go to meeting ~~P G~~ Lucinia David down
Mond 17 I water my garden **Tuesd 18** P G and Ed came down took the last
of my wheet and a box to put it in 23 bushels 2*h* **wed ^19^** they go down
Thursd 20 came back P G after loading a load of boards went home **Frd 21**
Ed goes down with the boards John Parry is released from the gard starts this
morning to go to Sumit with a young man that started to go to the states John

---

any way we pleased." His favorable reports led to the army's peaceable passage
through Salt Lake City, the return of the Mormons to their homes, and, in June,
a presidential proclamation of pardon for any past rebellion (Brigham H.
Roberts, *A Comprehensive History of the Church*, 6 vols. [Provo, Utah: Brigham
Young University Press, 1965], 4:391).

56. Much later in Patty's diaries are accounts of a straw-braiding school in her
home. She doesn't say why they were braiding straw. Later she mentions sewing
a hat for a grandson and still later records that she made her straw into a basket.
Since this was in the spring, it is unlikely that she was using straw left over from
the harvest, although they evidently braided wheat and oat straw as well as
towse straw, a coarse, hollow plant grown especially for braiding (Paxman,
"Early Mormon Family Life," 6–7).

told him he was here and he had better stay here he concluded to do so and
has gone south with John I have boarded John since he came back and fited
him and the boy with provision to go three days Br Eldrige starts to go south
with the last of his family his child has [been] geting well fast I have dresed its
wound twice a day since it was scalded yestarday I gave sister Jones an emetic I have been up to Tripps to day **Sat 22** John Dalton came after me to go to
his wife at the church farm[57] when I got there she was better but his child had
a breach he wished me to do something for it so he brought me home to get
some medicine for the child Ed came back I got him some dinner he went
home I went back again made trusses for the child staid all night **Sund 23**
came home left his wife better the child breach did not come down any more
~~Mond~~ Wm= Smoot came here after I was a bed I got up got him some supper he staid all night **Mond 24** he went over my garden and orchard said he
never saw such a beautiful sight in his life so many trees so full of fruit so says
every one that has seen them. I wash make canker medicine pack up my
things once more to go south I think I shall go this time 6 oclock P M P G
and Ed came down loaded up my things stay all night **Tuesd 25** we start go
to the point of the mountain stopt to bait it rained I got wet some it soon stopt
raining we got to American fork $2h$ past 4 P M found them all well I helped
unload my things felt first rate **Tuesd 26** P G built me a shanty **Wed 27** he
finished it put my things into it **Thursd 27** [*written over* Wed 26] he and Ed
started back again **Frd 28** John and William Parry came here ^brought me a
letter from Mr Parry^ I made them some coffee Homer Call wife & Fany
Lovland came here Emerett went home with them[58] Sister Foss [*word obliterat-
ed*] & Mathias Cowley & wife came here staid all night **Satd 29** they go on in
the afternoon I went to the celibration of Susannah Richards birthday 40 or
50 persons there we had a good time table set under a bowry loaded with
very delisious food of which we partook in fulfilment of a prediction of Dr
Willard Richards to Susannah in my presance five years ago this day he told
her that in five years more she should have a plenty of room to set as big a
table as she wanted and plenty to put on it and room enough to acommodate
all that she wished to have presant her room then being rather small he also
said many more things which have been fulfiled **Sund 30** the wind blows
hard very cold do not go to meeting **Mond 31** wrote a letter to Mr Parry in
answer to one he sent me by John

---

57. The church farm was located where Sugar House is now situated.

58. Homer Call (1834–1908) was a brother to Anson Call and Mary and Lucina
    Sessions, Perrigrine's wives. At this time he had two wives: Maria Ferrin and
    Nancy Merrill. Fanny Call (1815–1899) was their sister. Her husband was
    Chester Loveland, and their daughter was Fanny Emorett, who also married
    Perrigrine.

JUNE 1858

Tuesd ^**June**^ **1** John came I sent the letter by him Wm Smoot came here
Staid all night **Wed 2** I went home with him **Thursd 3** I went to see Harriet
Mr Sessions wife **Frd 4** I visited sister Smoot & others **Satd 5** I came home
Wm & Marth came home with us I have knit a stocking since I went away I
carried some things to Harriet which she was verry thankful for **Sund 6** I
went to meeting **Mond 7** I visited the sick **Tuesd 8** ^**wed**^ **9** I made canker
medicine P G came down brought some pye plant **Thursd 10** I made pies had
co sisters ^Mary Elen^ Kimbal her Mother and Bishop Hunters wife Susan
Frid 12 P G went home Mary Elen staid with me last night she made me a
sack to day I have watered the garden here **Sat 12** Braided straw **Sund 13**
went to meeting Mon Brigham & Heber [Orson] Hyde preached in the afternoon gave us a synopsus of what they had done with the commissioners at the
city[59] **Monday 14** visited the sick Washed &c **Tuesd 15** carded wool **wed 16**
the same **Thursd 17** the same it rained my bed wet through the house leaked
bad **Frd 18** rained some in the afternoon ^it cleared^ we dried our things
^David came down here^ **Sat 19** finished carding spun some did me up a cap
it rained hard again house leaked bad things got wet **Sund 20** fair again we
put our things out to dry then went to meeting David & Ed here still
[The size of the paper changes here; she must have run out.]
Mond 21 David made Jim a pair of shoes[60] Mr Parry came here we went to
see Mary ^his daughter^ **Tuesd 22** he made us a shade David and Ed went
home **wed 23** I spun **Thursd 24** Mr Parry and I & Mary went to Lehi **Frd 25**

---

59. On 7 June a two-man Peace Commission (L. W. Powell and Ben McCulloch)
    sent by President Buchanan arrived in Salt Lake City. In meetings on 11 and 12
    June and in private conversations with Brigham Young, the Mormon leaders
    denied all allegations of sedition or rebellion in Buchanan's proclamation of par-
    don, except the charge that they had burned the army's wagons and driven off
    cattle in Wyoming. They accepted the president's pardon and agreed to the
    peaceable passage of the army through Salt Lake City. This was the official end
    of the Utah War (see JH, 11, 12, 13 June 1858).

60. She must be referring to Jim Indian. Descriptions in Sessions family histories
    vary in details about Jim "Injun." Evidently he came to Sessions Settlement in
    1852 at age eight as part of a group of Indians. At least one account says his par-
    ents died there and Perrigrine and David buried them and adopted Jim. Another
    records that because some of the Indians had died at Sessions Settlement, the boy
    had only his grandmother to care for him, and she sold him for a pony, saddle,
    blanket, and a little flour. One narrative claims that he was the first Indian to
    receive his endowments in the Logan Temple (1885) and that Wilford Woodruff
    preached his funeral sermon after his death on 12 July 1894. Another "Life
    Sketch" states that an uncle persuaded David and Perrigrine to "relieve him of
    the responsiblity of rearing his nephew." The accounts have no documentation

I spun **Sat 26** I washed Mr Parrys clothes P G came down **Sund 27** we went to Provo to meeting Mr Parry went home I went to Br grows staid all night ^**Mond 28**^ I visited round engaged ten lb rolls came up to Tripps staid all night **Tuesd 29** visited in the camp **wed 30** came to battle creek

July 1858

Thursd July 1 came home soon caled to go to Lehi to see Br Daltons sick child **Frd 2** finished shining my wool and have packed my things to go home many have gone the Prsd went night before last **Sat 3** Mary Emerett & Phebee Josephine all started home **Sund 4** I do not go to meeting **Mond 5** David & Carlos came after me **Tuesd 6** we start get to the point of the mountain meet the U S troops we sat there three three hours waiting for them to pass[61] one oclock we started got home at 6 unloaded **Tuesd 7** David & Carlos goes back after Lucinia & Sulvia **Thursd 8** they came got supper went home I have got my carpet down my bedsted set up my things mostly unpacked I have had a man to work for me in the garden **frid 9** I watered the garden **S** Mr Parry came back **Satd 10** ^I worked in the garden^ Caleb Parry worked for me in the forenoon another man in the afternoon Eldridges boys all day **Sunday 11 Mond 12** ann here David & Carlos here gone to Provo P G came took dinner Julia ^Sessions^ came here to stay with me a few days Br James Olcout [Olcott?] came here to Board last Thursday is here now has worked 1 2*h* days for me **Mond 12** worked in the garden made myself sick **Tuesd 13** do not set up much **wed 14** no better quite sick **Thursd 15** I am better Mr Parry came here Cate here **Frd 16** made me a cap **Sat 17** worked in the garden **Sund 18** no meeting David & wife & children & Sister foss here **Mond 19** called to Br Mosesleys[62] put Wm= Robinsons [1831–1903] wife [Susannah Grimshaw] to bed with a

---

and some are unsigned. However, Olive Cordelia Sessions, the daughter of David and Phebe Foss Sessions, wrote at least one history filed by the Daughters of Utah Pioneers. It seems clear that Jim for the most part lived with David and Phebe and she, being a teacher, gave him whatever education he obtained.

61. The army, under the command of General Albert Johnston, broke camp at Fort Bridger on 13 June and in twelve days reached the mouth of Emigration Canyon. Entering early on the morning of 26 June, the army marched through the deserted city to camp on the west bank of the Jordan River. An article in *Atlantic Monthly* described, "All day long, from dawn till after sunset, the troops and trains poured through the city, the utter silence of the streets being broken only by the music of the military bands, the monotonous tramp of the regiments, and the rattle of the baggage wagons" (quoted in Roberts, *Comprehensive History*, 4:445). In succeeding days the army moved south along the Jordan to the Point of the Mountain, where they met the returning Mormons, then southwest to Cedar Valley, where they established Camp Floyd, remaining there until ordered back East at the outbreak of the Civil War.

62. Probably George W. Mousley, a member of Patty's ward.

son [Jesse Benjamin] born 20 minutes before 2 P M I have washed to day Br James Aulcot left here to day to work on the miletary road[63] **Tuesd 20** Ironed put down my carpet in the bedroom had my grass cut Sister Higbee here on a visit **Wed 21** put Jesse Martins wife Sophronia to bed with a daughter [Eunice Sophronia] born 20 minutes past 4 A M I got some buds of Br More put them in put down my carpet in the kitchen **Thursd 22** commenceed spining got my grass cut **Frd 23** spun **Sat 24** got my hay raked and stacked ^John Parry did it Sylvia here^ **Sund 25** no meeting I went up to Tripps **Mond 26** spun **Tuesd 27** spun sister Polly Vose here **Wed 28** put sister [Sophia] Riser to bed with a daughter [Emma] born 5 minutes before one P M **Thursd 29** finished spining **Frd 30** scoured out my yarn & washed **Satd 31** not well

AUGUST 1858

Sund ^August 1^ no meeting P G & David & Chester Lovlin here **Mond 2** spooled my web ^visited John Cottoms child^ **Tuesd 3** warped it P G Mary & Emeret here to dinner I went home with them ~~stai~~ the wind blew verry hard going up I staid all night with Sylvia **Wed 4** I came home **Thursd 5** watered my garden **Frd 6** took care of my peas & picked two pails full of currants to make wine of Br Filawry came here a week ago with a verry bad hand it was poisoned by skining a cow that died did not know what ailed her he had a small place on his finger where the skin was scrat[c]hed off and it swelled verry bad & made him sick all over, to day he is better I have took care of his hand polticed it with catnip & Lobelia mostly put in salt & soap and molasses his finger turned black & the flesh dead ~~when the~~ but it begins to come to its feeling a little now **Sat 7** carried ten quarts of currants to the tithing office went to the store got a bunch of cotten yarn No 11 went to sister Smoots **Sund 8** no meeting staid at home alone **Mond 9** sized my web and spooled it put the other web a colouring blue **Tuesd 10** warped my web stoped at Tripps to dinner P G went bye while I was there going south after a load of flour ^Martha^ came here **Wed 11** set up the loom the irons at provo yet **Thursd 12** while eating my dinner was taken verry sleepey and quite unwell Wm= Smoot came here he staid all night **Frd 13** he & Martha started home I still ^am^ quite unwell P G returned from the south I got him some vituals eat a little with him Sylvia & Alma Stoker came after me to go and see sister Stoker she is sick they thought it would do me good to ride I went the ride did me good and I got quite well I found her very sick I gave her a Lobelia emetic she soon got better I also found

---

63. Soon after the army arrived in Cedar Valley, General A. S. Johnston ordered his chief topographical engineer to survey Timpanogas Canyon east of Lehi for a wagon road to connect Camp Floyd with the army supply depot at Fort Bridger without going through the Mormon capitol. The Mormons had already roughed out the road. Perhaps the army hired Mormons to work on it again.

my sons babe very sick I staid with that all night **Sat 14** child no better sister Stoker better I came home went right back again found the child very bad thought it would not live through the night I gave that Lobelia it soon got easey **Sund 15** I stay all day **Mond 16** we think the child is better I came home Lucinia gave me a cheese I pack that down **Tuesd 17** I wash **wed 18** iron & draw in my web **Thursd 19** gave Caleb Parrys babe an emetic then put his second wife [Winifred, b. 1838] to bed with a son [Gronway] born 15 minutes before 11 A M then went home with P G his child is wor[s]e stay all night hope it is a litle better I came home ^**Frd 20**^ wove one yard visit Calebs folks &c David and wife came here stay all night **Satd 21** visit calebs again came home wove 2 yards caled to T Cottoms child watter my garden to night we have had a shower wet the potatoes so that it is bad going among them **Sund 22** I have wattered my garden got wet my self it rained a little **Mond** ^**23**^ wove a little went up to P Gs his child is worse thought it was dying I stay all night came home **Tuesd 24 wed 25 Thursd 26 Frd 27** wove **Satd 28** got my second web out **Sund 29** went up to P Gs again Davids children sick came home **Mond 30** pooled my 3d web **Tuesd 31** worped it and drawed it in

SEPTEMBER 1858

wed Sept 1 Sylvia here David gone after a load of salt got back & went home I wove 1 yard **Thurd 2** spun & couloured red David here again going after salt I have made some more wine ~~Frd 3 wove Sat 4~~ caled to George Wallice,s put Hann^ah^ [Davis] his wife to bed with a pair of twins sons born between 11 & 12 P M **Frid 3** wove **Sat 4** wove some had co[64] **Sund 5** P Gs child died name Alice Emeretts child[65] **Mond 6** Mr Parry and I went up to the funerel with Wm= & Martha Smoot Sister Parrish burried the same time **Tuesd 7** we came home **wed 8** I wove **Thursd 9** carried a 2½ bushel apples to the tithing office got my web out took down the loom **Frid 10** made me a skirt & watered my garden **Sat 11** gathered peaches sold Br Dopp $40-25 forty Dollars & twenty five cents worth of peaches & Apples & plumbs[66] peaches 25 Dollars Aples 10 Dollars plumbs 5-25 **Sund 12** No meeting **Mond 13** washed **Tuesd 14** ironed and baked **wed 15** sewed on my aprons and sack **Thurss 16** cut peaches to dry **Frd 17** had a place fixed to spread my peaches **Sat 18** picked peaches sister Vose came here staid all night **Sund 19** David and Carlos and Lucinia & Byron came down & Br Dopp staid all night I sold Br Dopp eight bushels of peaches $68-00 & eight doz Apples $4-00 and Plumbs $13-76 total

64. According to the JH (4 September 1858, p. 1), "George A. Smith called on Mother Sessions to examine her orchard. She gave him some fruit." Uncharacteristically, Patty fails to give his name.

65. This daughter was born on 16 June 1857 in Carson, Nevada.

66. In the 1860 census, Peter Dopp, age sixty-three, was living in Bountiful.

amount eighty one dollars & seventy six cents **Mond 20** cut peaches **Tuesd 21 wed 22** the same I carried my tithing plumbs to the office six quarts P G here Lucinia hes been here ever since sunday helping me **Thursd 23** cut peaches David & Carlos came back from the camp **Frd 24** they went home Lucinia went home with them Byron [her grandson] staid with me I let them have 2 bushels of peaches **Sat 25** Sylvia came down **Sund 26** Wm= & Martha here & Tripps folks here to eat peaches David came down **Mond 27** David went south for wheet Dopp came back let him have three bushels more of peaches ^$13=50^ sold one more to Br Ed Pace [Edwin Pace, 1829–1917] **Tuesd 28** let Br Diamon have five bushels for 20=00 Dollars David came back **Wed 29** he went home P G with him bought a mule gave $1=50 for it cash **Thursd 30** worked at my peaches Br Dopp came let him have 3 bushels more for 12 Dollars

OCTOBER 1858

Frd Oct 1 sold 2 bushels for 8 Dollars ~~Sat 2~~ Oct 2 I put Martha Wallice [Martha Davis, b. 1836] to bed with son born 20 minutes before 12 **Sat 2** Worden & Harriet & James came here he went south left her & children here Sylvia & Byron went home it rains **Sund 3** has rained all night very wet this morning ^~~Emerett came down~~^ rainy weather ^ (all day^ ~~again~~ **Mond 4** wet **Tuesd 5** ^Emerett came here^ fair **wed 6 Thursd 7 Frid 8 Sat 9** good weather **Sund 10** P G came down Harriet went home with him Warden came back staid here all night David here staid all night **Mond 11** they went home **Tuesd 12 Wed 13 Thurd 14** I have sold sold a good many peaches cut and dried a good many more for this last two weeks Martha Ann had a daughter [Margaret Esther] born last satd 9 day born 4 A M it looks likely to rain P G is down here I have sent ~~2000~~ twenty Dollars by him to the store to get groceries **Frd ^15^** Sylvia and Wm= Smoot came here brought my groceries 25 lb sugar 5 lb coffee 1 lb tea David came brought 2=000 lb flour and my big flour bin they went home **Satd 16** it rained last night then snowed this morning every tree and srub is loaded down with snow and some broke down snows to day **Sund 17** still snows this afternoon the sun shines a part of the time I have many peaches not gathered **Mond 18** Thornton brought the last of my flour and things from American Fork got here last night P G and David and Josephine come here gathered peaches staid all night **^Tuesd 19^** gathered again this morning took away 15 bushels they are frost bitten Emerett went home with them I have paid all my tithing ~~20000~~ in 20 or 21 bushels sold 15 bushels to day besides what P G took away **Wed 20** sold some **Thursd 21** sold many **Frid 22** Josephine started for home **Satd 23** David came down she went home with him **Sund 24** Carlos and Jimy here **Mond 25** sister Foss here on a visit Charles Grow here[67] geting out manure ^I^ boutgh some rolls paid

---

67. Charles Moyer Grow (1840–1904) was the son of Henry Grow and Mary Moyer.

in pea^(ches^ **Tuesd 26 wed 27** taking care of my peaches **Thursd 28**
Charles Grow here to work I bought 5 2*h* gallons molasses **Frd 29** bought one
gallon more sold nearly all my peaches but few dozen left **Satd 30** been and
paid up my taxes P G here Sold five dollars of Apples six dozen I have paid 20
△3 *h*△ bushels ^3 *h*^ of peaches 17 2 *h* quarts plumbs half bushel Apples ten
quarts of currants for tithing **Sund 31** went up to ^E^ Tripp

NOVEMBER 1858

Mond Nov 1 I washed **Tuesd 2** charles Grow finished paying me in work
which his Father owed me **wed 3** P G here to breakfast Wm= Smoot here I
ironed took care of my dried peaches **Thursd 4** made me an under garment
Br Birch paid me twenty Dollars fifty cents owes me eight Dollars more **Frd 5**
attended to my domestic concerns **Satd 6** went up to the store got ten lb sugar
and half yard green silk for an apron[68] **Sund 4** no meeting yet **Mond 8** coul-
loured my yellow made me two flanel night dresses colloured them **Tuesd 9** to
day sold fifty peach trees some plumb & Apple trees 15 Dollars cash sold trees
last week 7=2*h* Dollars **wed 10** ^sold 9 Dollars more^ **Thurs 11 Frid 12**
Tripp and sophia here on a visit **Sat 13** I have attended to my domestic concerns this week John & Caleb Parry came back from ft Briger to day is conference **Sund 14** it closed **Mond 15** Wm= & Martha Smoot here six peach trees
paid me $1=50 Ben Jonson bought forty more paid me ten dollars **Tuesd 16**
Br church here to work for some more I have had forty three Dollars cash for
trees **wed 17** sold $2=25 more **Tursd 18** ^Frd^ **Sat 20 Sund 21** I have been
sewing this past week **Mond 22** quite dull weather some snow **Tuesd 23** the
same **wed 24** I wash **Thursd 25** John Parry starts for Summit for his family
Frd 26 snows all day **Satd 27** clars off **Sund 28** fine weather I have sold $7:00
more trees last week gave away eight trees I enjoy myself well the Lord blesses me with his spirit to comfort my heart I am alone the most of my time but
my meditation is sweet and I feel to thank the Lord all the time **Mond 29**
Tuesd 3d attending to my domestic concerns

DECEMBER 1858

Wed Dec 1 I have moulded candles went up to ^S M^ Blairs **Thursd 2** finished my peiceing my bed quilt went to the store got $6=00 of Blair with his
order ^got a dress for Harriet Sessions now Wordens wife^ **Frid 3** quite cold
froze very hard last night I have wrote a letter to Joseph Knapp finished it last
night I have sold fifty two ^Dollars^ 25 ^cts^ worth of trees this faul got all
my pay **Satd 4** went up to P Gs put Mary his wife to bed with a daughter
[Zina] born near 5 P M **Sund 5** south wind blew so hard they could not have

---

68. Patty was planning to make an apron to use with other sacred clothing in the
temple.

any fire in Marys room all day only a ketle of coals I went and staid with Sylvia all night **Mond 6** gave Mary and Phebe both an Emetic **Tuesd 7** I came home left them quite comfortable Josepine [her granddaughter] came home with me staid all night **wed 8** she & David went home it is very cold yet **Thursd 9** ^I^ went up to town with 50 lb dried peaches sold them for 30 Dollars cash then went to see John Parrys wife they got back last Mond I then ^came^ back home baked some mince pies **Frd 10** very cold **Satd 11** made me a cap the watter runs over the ice and has flowed up the road made it very bad crossing the street **Sund 12** many got in some waist deep **Mond 13** the men turned out cut a chanel for the water in the midle of the street and fixed crossing places I went and showed sister Grow about her web **Tuesd 14** went there & spun 42 knots of yard to crocia for myself **Wed 15** cut and sewed carpet rags **Thursd 16** a very pleasant day warped sister grows web **frd** ^17^ drawed some of it in and showed her how to draw it in **Satd 18** mended my comforters **Sund 19** Wm= and Martha here I went to Brother Smoots with them **Mond 20** scoured out some yarn washed **Tuesd 21** I was caled to see a sick child then to Br [Zera] Pulsipers wife Martha [Ann Hughes] **Wed 22** put her to bed with a daughter born 15 minutes before one A M commenced crociaing **Thursd 23** went to John Parrys **Frd 24** went to town bought 65 lb Pork paid 25 cents per pound ^$16-25^ **Satd 25** christmas John Parry & wife here and P G to dinner I have knit two pair of stockings for sister Grow this last week David here s[t]aid all night **Sun 26** he went away I went up to Tripps Mr Parry came we spent the evening **Mond 27** I crociaed on a comforter **Tuesd 28** prepared some yarn for Mr Parry some mittens I have lent William Smoot one hundred and fifty Dollars cash to go to Callifornia after goods for Chrisman[69] the weather is warm and pleasant has been for some days I feel well in body and mind the Lord blesses me all the time **Wed 29** sisters Foss & Phebe & Olive here came before breakfast staid untill night **Thursd 30** I helped sister Grow put in a web showed her how to weave **Frd 31** I went there again spun for myself

1859

I pray . . . that I may enjoy the use of all my senses and live to a good old age

JANUARY 1859

Sat Jan= 1–1859 Carlos Sessions Jimmy & Frank Higins here to dinner and supper went to the [*word omitted*] Carlos staid here all night **Sund 2** we went to meeting ^in the tabernacle^ carlos came here staid all night **Mond 3** P G

---

69. Charles Crisman operated a chopping mill, the first in the valley, according to Juanita Brooks (*Hosea Stout*, 2:343, n. 15).

brought me a load of wood **Tuesd 4** Mr Parry went up to P Gs **wed 5** came home Sylvia & David came down with him Sylvia staid here all night she and I went up to Tripps in the evening **Thursd 6** David and wife came here all here to dinner it is fast day the first we have had since we went south I paid my fast in fish they have all gone home I went and setled up my tithing for 1857 paid one hundred eight Dollars and sixty cents **Frid 7** finished Mr Parry mittens **Sat 8** I am knitting for sister Grow **Sund 9** went to meeting **Mond 10** Martha Smoot & Wm= Pearce [1833–1908] here to dinner **Tuesd 11** I have knit three pair more stockins for sister Grow put Julia [Melville] wife of Henry Grow to bed with a son [Theodore Melvin] born about 5 P M **Wed 12** doubled and twisted yarn **Thursd 13** crociaing a chair cover **Frd 14** ^dito^ **Sat 15** finished my chair cover ^lent P G sessions 25 Dollars ^~~let him~~^ ^let him have 25 more to send to the states for me^ **sund 16** went to meeting **Mond 17** spun John Parry & wife here **Tuesd 18** Mr Parry went up North to P Gs **Wed 19** he came home **Thursd 20** I went up to town **Frid 21** I am crociaing on my bed cover **Sat 22** the same **Sund 23** went to meeting Lucinia came down here **Mond 24** we worked on her quilt **tuesd 25** the same Tripp and wives here on a visit **wed 26** put in my quilt **Thursd 27** got it out **Frd 28** we went up to Tripps Lucinia went home Emorre^tt^ was down **Sat 29** I went down to John Parrys **Sund 30** went to meeting **Mond 31** Harriet Kimball & sister Higbee ~~B~~ & Br Grow and wife here on a visit sister Kimball staid all night

FEBRUARY 1859

Tuesd Feb 1 very warm I have sold some peach trees eight Dollars worth cash Worden & family came here staid all night **Wed 2** they are moving to Provo they gave me Alzinia [Alzina, b. 1852] the oldest daughter to raise as my own she is sick **Thursd 3** crociaing **Frid 4** my birthday sixty four years old I am in good spirits feel well and thank the Lord that it is as well with me as it is **Sat 5** David staid here last night I sent 75 cent by him to get me medicine for Alzinia he got it P G came here paid me the 25 Dollars I lent him **Sund 6** went to meeting, in the evening I was called to sister Marry Wordrop it rained hard very muddy **Mond 7** put her to bed with a daughter born 5 and 1*h* P M **Tuesd 8** I washed **Wed 9** ironed Alzinia is better got almost well I have nit her a pair of stockings and made her an apron **Thursd 10** Mr Parrys birth day he is 70 years old **Frid 11** I have been up to town got some lace for caps I have sold one hundred and eight pounds of dried peaches for sixty four Dollars 85 cts cash also ten lbs more for six Dollars cash **Sat 12** Carlos Sessions came here I went home with him Alzinia went with me very muddy roads **Sund 13** snows I stay all night **Mond 14** make Alzinia a dress ^flannel^ and bonnet and pantalets Pheebe ^& Sylvia^ has helped me **Tuesd 15** came home P G David and Sylvia came with me I lent David $15 00 money let Sylvia have $2 2*h* to get some callico to make Alzinia some aprons **Wed 16** while I was at P Gs I mised my gold ring I thought it was in those dried peaches I sold on Frid last so this morning I started went to the man told him I beleived my ring was in those peaches I sold him they were packed up ready to go to camp Floid he did not like to open them but I felt so sure it was there I went the second time he opened the box and in less than two minutes I found my ring with out emting the box the man was Br George Godard [Goddard] I went to the store bought 6 2*h* yards of callico for Alzinia dresses **Thursd 17** I am crociaing **Frid 18** the same **Sat 19** made Alzinia a white peti-coat and pantalets I am learning her to read and knit she learns fast **Sund 20** caled to Br Smoots put his wife Emily [Hill Harris] to bed with a daughter born [*left blank*] P M came home I was not well all night **Mond 21** sold 5 lb peaches Br Holmes came here got dinner cut me some wood **Tuesd 22** he came here again trimed some peach trees I finished crociaing my bed spread **Wed 23** John Parrys wife came and helped me wash **Thursd 27** Br holmes went home he charged me $1=50 for triming trees I made Alzinia an apron **Frid 25 Sat 26** attended to my domestic concerns **Sund 27** I was called to Jesse Martins wife Ann [Clark, b. 1835] put her to bed with a daughter [Elizabeth] Born 3 ^oclock^ and 6 minutes P M **Mond 28**

MARCH 1859

Tuesd March 1st 1859 we have had a very deep snow fall yesterday ^E B^ Tripp spent the evening here last night laid hands on Mr Parry he is better this morning **wed 2** he is better I have done up some caps **Thursd 3** cut me some undergarments **Frd 4** sewed some **Satd 5** marked some for Elizabeth Veach [b. 1836] Carlos came here went to see Martha [Ann] his sister **Sund 6** ^I^ went to meeting Alzina went with me carlos went home **Mond 7** I went down to see Martha **Tuesd 8** I cut and made Alzinia an apron **Wed 9** came home **Thursd 10 Frd 11 Sat 12** I have made her a dress **Sund 13** did not go to meeting David & Br Holmes came here **Mond <14>** they both work pruning my trees **Tuesd 15** they both went away **Wed 16** I have been sewing **Thursd 17** Br Holmes came back he is pruning **Frid 18** he is still pruning ^I^ gave Br Wilson holmes some dried peaches Mr Parry has gone up to P Gs to see James Bucland [Buckland] and get his Pay of him **Satd 19** it snows very fast 4 oclock P M clears of snow fell over a foot **Sund 20** I do not go to meeting Br Holmes went as he was agoing along the side walk a harrow lay there buried up under snow with the teeth up he steped on one of the teeth it went through his foot he had on an india rubber boot I dressed it as well as I could Mr Parry has just returned from P Gs rode home one of P Gs mules for Br Holmes to ride back so he started off I feel affraid he will be laid up with it Mr Parry eat dinner here went down to his ^other^ house took sick **Mond 21** early in the morning sent for me I went he is very sick at night I went again no better **Tuesd 22** went again no better at night I went again found him some better **Wed 23** went again he is still better I am in hopes he will get well I have done all I could for him with works and faith mixed together if he was here I could do more for him **Thursd 24** I went again to see him found him quite well Br Holmes came here his foot is much better he is at work for me **Frd 25** went to see Mr Parry again found he had been out door **Satd 26** he came up here I gathered up the trimings of my trees and Br Holmes brought them to the house **Sund 27** snows I do not go to meeting in the afternoon I was taken sick in the evening I sent for John Parrys wife she staid with me untill I was better **Mond 28** I can set up a very little **Tuesd 22** I am still better Br Holmes has cut up the limbs he cut off of my trees for the stove yestarday and to day **wed 30** he has gone away **Thursd 31** very cold ground covered with snow froze very hard last night and will again to night

APRIL 1859

Frd April 1 weather cold **Sat 2** clean **Sund 3** go to meeting **Mond 4 Tuesd 5** attend to my domestick concerns **Wed 6** went to confrence **Thursd 7** went again confrence ajorned ^I went and put Margret Wardrope to bed with a daughter [Jane] born 6 A M^ I think as good a confrence as we have ever had **Frid 8** Martha & Margret and children here **Sat 9** Br Birch here got fifty two trees Carlos here has gone to see Martha I have put in some peas lettice redishes &c **R sund 10** I down to Br Foxes his child sick **Mond 11** worked in the garden **Tuesd 12 Wed 13 Thursd 14 Frid 15 Satd 16** Attended to my domestic concerns **Sund 17** Morn put Marry Ann Terry to bed with a daughter [Wilhelmina] born 15 minutes past twelve A M[70] then went to meeting **Mond 18 Tuesd 19** P G and Pheebe down here got some fruit trees **Wed 20** planted some potatoes **Thursd 21 Frd ^22^** finished planting potatoes ^John Parry worked for me^ **Sat 23** aired my dried peaches **Sund 24** went to meeting it rained **Mond 25 Tuesd 26 wed 27** worked in the garden **Thursd 28** put sister Mellon to bed with a dead child a daughter it had been dead some weeks born 4 P M I cut Alzinia a dress **Frd 29** worked in the garden and on her dress **Satd 30** dito

MAY 1859

Sund May 1 rained do not go to meeting **Mond 2** I put in some beans and posy seeds **Tuesd 3** John Parry worked for me **wed 4** I was sewing **Thursd 5** fast day **Frd 6 Sat 7** finished Alzinias dress **Sund 8** went to meeting **Mond 9 Tuesd 10** made soap **Wed 11** worked in the garden **Thursd 12** went to town **Frd 13** John Parrys wife made me a bonnet **Satd 14** made me a cap **Sund 15** went to meeting **Mond 16 Tuesd 17 wed 18** ~~attended to my domestic conserns Thursd 18~~ very heavy thunder storm Joseph Abbot[t, b. 1840, son of Lewis Abbott and Ann Marsh] killed with the lightning and Wm= Harris hurt

---

70. Mary Ann Pulsipher (b. 1833) was the wife of Thomas Sirls Terry (1825–1920).

bad[71] **Thursd 19** I went and see them **Frd 20** I sewed ^straw^ baskets made three **Satd 21** Sylvia came here staid all night **Sund 22** went to meeting in the forenoon Brigham was here spoke it made our hearts glad to see and hear him in the afternoon Wm= Smoot and Martha here their son Wm= was very sick with the cramp in his stomach for a while got better they started for home but he got worse again and they did not go any farther than their Fathers **Mond 23** David and two others came here last night about twelve oclock found the water runing into my lot I got up got the lantern we went and turned it off they stay till morning had been to Toolee the men have turned out to turn the water it is overflowing the road and many lots **Tuesd 24** the same **Wed 25** still at work turning the water I have been at work in my garden **Thursd 26** the same **Frid 27 Satd 28** worked in my garden **Sund 29** put Emerett wife of P G= Sessions to bed with a son [Chester] born 15 minutes before 5 I came home ^Sylvia came staid here all night^ David and Phebee came here she staid all night **Mond 30** we went up to Tripps **Tuesd 31** worked in my garden

June 1859

Wed June 1 John Parry worked for me hoeing and fixing gate post **Thursd 2 Frid 3** Sylvia staid here last night **Sat 4** watered **Sund 5** went to meeting **Mond 6** been looking up material for fixing my house **Tuesd 7** worked in my garden **Wed 8** the same **Thursd 9** got clay and sand hauled **Frid 10** had 12 load hauled 3 of clay 9 of sand gave 2=00 cwt of flour for hauling and 3 load of stone gave 1-00 cwt of flour for hauling them **Sat 11** had adobes hauled **Sund 12** do not go to meeting Carlos & Jimy here I was caled Br Wollaces put his wife Lydia [Davis, b. 1836] to bed with son [Joseph Bates] born 11 P M **Mond 13** went to P Gs ^Sessions^ put Lucinia to bed with a son [Harvey] born 15 minutes before three P M Tuesd 15 came home found all the adobes ho^u^lled **Wed 15** paid for them and the hauling mostly cash I have worked in the garden **Thursd 16** the same **Frid 17** ~~Sat~~ ^washed^ **Sat 18** ironed and watered **Sund 19** Wm= and martha staid here last night we went to meeting ^Episcopalian^ preached **Mond 20** cleaned my cellar ^got^ my stone houled and **Tuesd 21** commenced repairing my house[72] **wed 22** I worked in the garden **Thursd 23** watered my garden **Frid 24** I have been and bought some sleepers [wooden structural supports] for my house I have made me a

71. On 18 May 1859 the JH noted: "At half past five this city was visited by a heavy thunder storm. Bro. Joseph Abbot was then killed by lightning, while planting corn in the old Fort field. Wm. Harris was also injured while plowing in the same field, at the same time."

72. As previously mentioned, Patty's house was on the southwest corner of North Temple and Fourth West. She may have been adding an extension, or storeroom, or a granary to her home, but she was also giving it a major cleaning and repairing.

cap commenced my apron finished it **Sat 25** Joseph Parry staid here last night
P G and Mary here to dinner gone home bought 11 lb tallow **Sund 26** went
to meeting **Mond 27 Tuesd 28 Wed 29** got my sleepers in paid for it **Thursd
30** John White came down cut my grass

JULY 1859

Frd July 1 he went home ^put Betsey Bouk [Elizabeth Howells, b. 1827] to
bed with a daughter [Louise] born 9 P M **Sat 2 Sund 3** did not go to meeting
Mond 4 raked and stacked my hay **Tuesd 5** I went up to the store **Wed 6** John
Staniford [John Henry Standiford, 1831–1924] and David came down
brought my rafters & some boards **Thursd 7** ^Sylvia & Ed Cutler here I put
George Hales [1822–1907] wife [Louisa Ann Eddins, b. 1834] to bed a daughter [Louisa Serena] born 8 A M^ put the roof on **Frid 8** commenced shingling
Satd 9 finished shingling **Sund 10** do not go to meeting **Mond 11** worked in
the garden **Tuesd 12** the same Lucinia here **Wed 13** a Joiner here to work ~~Br
Gibs here to work~~ **Thursd 14 Frid 15 Sat 16** worked in the garden **Sund 17**
do not go to meeting **Mond 18** Br Gibs here to work Joinering **Tuesd 19** Mr
Parry cut a hearth stone **Wedn 20** made me a cap **Thursd 21** been puting
^in^ bushes Br Leonard and wife here **Frid 22 Satd 23 Sund** ^24^ go to
meeting **Mond** ^25^ Wm= & Martha here **Tuesd 26** Br Gibs finish **wed**
^27^ I go up to P Gs settle with him for my lumber pay him fifty Dollars
Thursd 28 I came home **Frid 29 Satd 30** clean a little **Sund 31** do not go to
meeting

AUGUST 1859

Mond August 1 go to the store bought 30 lights of glass **Tuesd 2** ^washed^
wed 3 Thursd 4 been puting my things in place preparing to white wash **Frd
5** white wash **Satd 6** clean **Sund 7** go to meeting **Mond** ^8^ go to the store
bought puty [putty] one bolt of ^brown^ cloth one bolt of bleached cloth one
bunch of cotten yarn one bolt of calico David & Sylvia down went with me
Tuesd 9 attended to my Domestic concerns let Sylvia have the calico all but 9
yards **wed 10** ~~Thursday~~ attended to many things **Thursd** ^12^ [11] set the
glass and put in the windows ^my house is now finished^ **Frd 12** [*written over*
Satd] carried my wheet in to my store room **sat 13** white washed my bed
room cleaned up and went up to P Gs with Wm=& Martha to eat Mellons
Sund 14 came home **Mond** ^15^ got my flour into my storeroom John Parry
helped me **Tuesd 16** whitewashed the kitchen & cleaned up **wed 17** went up to
town **Thursd 18** took care of my beans **Frd 19** made my wine **Sat 20** wattered
my garden washed some went up to town boug^ht^ two bolts of calico **sund
21** went to meeting **Mond 22** went up to town bought some thread hooks &
eyes carpet tax &c **Tuesd 23** ~~wed 24~~ went to the office put in twenty Dollars
into the petual emigrating fund carried my stuff to E R Snow to make me a
temple apron **wed 24** carried my currants to the tithing office **Thursd 25** went

to the stores bought two bunches of cotton yarn one bolt calico two lawn dress patterns ^one for me^ ^one for Alzinia^ thread combs &c **Frid 26** made me an apron and Alzina a chimee P G sent me 4 mellons **Satd 27** bought 5 lb cotton batting & Alzina a pair of shoes **Sund 28** went to meeting ^**Mond 29**^ fixed my cellar **Tuesd 30** went to town bought two sacks of sugar one chest of tea fifty lb coffee 5 bunches cotton yarn me a pair of shoes &c **wed 31**

SEPTEMBER 1859

Thursd Sept 1 Frid 2 Sat 3 attend to my domestic concerns **Sund 4** went to meeting in the afternoon **Mond 5** got a wheel spun some **Tuesd 6** went to town got my sugar coffee & tea that I sent to the states for by Br Lemon **wed 7** spun **Thursd 8** did many things **Frd 9** washed scoured my yarn P G & David here to dinner **Sat 10** ironed **Sund 11** do not go to meeting ^David & Carlos here^ **Mond** ^**12**^ cut me a bonnet ^sold my blue seedling plumb for $29:05 **Tuesd 13** sisters Jane Kesler [plural wife of Bishop Frederick Kesler] Olivia Pratt here on a visit[73] **Wed 14** ^carried some plumbs to Br Brighum got my apron from sister E R Snow^ Sylvia came down with Parry to send him to the states[74] **Thursd 15** he starts she goes home **Frid 16** I gather apples ~~Sat 17~~ gather more White cut a part of my grass Mary came down her babe is sick **Satd 17** she is here Lucinia is gone see Martha **Sund 18** I do not go to meeting they all go home **Mond 19** collour with bark **Tuesd 20** finish my bonnet **Wed** got my hay raked and the rest cut sold $35-50 cts worth of Aples peaches & plumbs it rains hard this afternoon **Thursd 22** sister Mores child Died it rains yet ^David here been to the camp bought a waggon^ **Frd 23** cloudy **Satd 24** carlos & Josephine here gone to see Martha ann **Sund 25** they come here started for home broke the waggon came back staid all night **Mond 26** gone home it is fair weather **Tuesd** ^**27**^ I washed **wed 28 Thursd 29 Frd 30** sold $7:00 of Fruit

OCTOBER 1859

Sat 1 ^oct^ gathered Fruit **Sund 2** do not go to meeting **Mond 3** went to the Fare[75] **Tuesd 4** sold $18:00 more Fruit have been cuting peaches to drye David and Pheebe here **Wed 5** Alzinia went to the fare **Thursd 6** confrence

---

73. Olivia Pratt (b. 1841) was the second child of Parley P. Pratt and Mary Ann Frost.

74. Perry Ezekiel Clark was born in Iowa City on 4 February 1851, the first child of Sylvia Sessions and Ezekiel Clark. When Sylvia left Iowa City to rejoin the Mormons in Utah, she promised to send Perry back to Iowa for an education when he turned nine. Perry returned to Utah as a young man and died in Bountiful on 8 April 1919. He did not marry.

75. The JH (9 October 1859) lists awards at the fair. Patty Sessions received a first place for the "Best Knit Cape" and one for "Crochet Bed Spread (woolen)." Edward Hunter, president of the Deseret Agricultural and Manufacturing

commenced **Frid 7** bought 5 bushels of potatoes paid in peaches **Satd 8** sold
$15 00 peaches Sylvia & David staid here last night Byron came down to help
me pick peaches & Aples **Sund 9** ^P G^ Sylvia Wm= Martha Carlos ~~P G &c~~
here **Mond 10** gathered and sold peaches ^8 bushels^ **Tuesd 11** the same
sold 17 2*h* bushels **wed 12** sold 1 **Thursd 13** Julia came down to help me **Frd
14 Sat 15** sold Br Ludington 12 bushels of peaches[76] he agreed to give me 28
bushels of good clean wheat next week Julia and I gathered nearly all my
peaches P G came here staid all night **Sund 16** he and Julia went home it
rains **mond 17** froze peaches last night the coldest night we have had this faul
Tuesd 18 sold 7 2*h* ^bushels^ made preserves **Wed 19 Thursd 20** sold 3
bush bought 18 pound ^wool^ rolls David & wife & Sylvia here gone home
Frid 21 sold 8 bushels to Br Birch $4:00 per bushel **Satd 22** gathered the last
of my peaches **Sund 23** went to meeting partook of the sacrement **Mond
^24^** coulored my worp yarn **Tuesd 25** sold the last of my peaches by the
bushel I have a few doz left yet and one bushel reserved for Mr Parry **Wed
26** P G sent me 2 gallons molasses I made preserves 2 gallons **Thursd 27**
partley made me a sack then Mr Parry and I went to Br Brighams to a party
by James Works [1822–1888] and wife Phebe **Frid 28** Furgeson hung[77] I have
finished my sack Phebe ^Works^ and Sally the Indian girl here gone to John
Parrys **Satd 29** I went to see the horse race **Sund 30** went to meeting **Mond
31** went to the store bought me a ~~shall~~ ^shaul^ gave 12-50 a bolt of calico 19
to cts per yd delain[78] dress pattern 3=60

Society, called the exhibition "abundant testimony for habits of industry and
happy homes. . . . To our ladies, mothers, wives and daughters we would say,
continue . . . and improve . . . whether you knit, nett or crochet . . . throw the
shuttle or wield the pencil and pen . . . the music of the wheel . . . your household treasures . . . of the piano . . . let it be . . . your highest ambition, to throw
around you the 'spirit of gladness,' the 'spirit of love,' the 'spirit of industry,' the
'spirit of truth. . . .'" Surely statements such as these must account somewhat for
Patty's zealous, almost frenzied, productive activities.

76. Elam Luddington (1806–1893) had been a member of the Mormon Battalion,
was city marshal in 1850, and was listed as a gardener in 1869.

77. Thomas H. Ferguson, age twenty-seven, was tried for murder and found guilty.
Although the account, "Execution of Thomas H. Ferguson," in the *Deseret News*
of 27 October 1859 does not give the details, a statement from Ferguson asserts
that he had never before committed a crime and he had been angered by an
Indian who "goes trading with white people, who gets credit at the stores kept
by white people, and I cannot get my money when I am without money. . . ." He
further states that he would not have committed the crime except for too much
drink and even then, the murder took place in self-defense. He claims that the
judge, Sinclair, had had too much whiskey on the day of sentencing and then left
the territory. The execution took place with an elaborate procession and fanfare
(9:280).

78. Delaine was a light dress fabric of wool or wool and cotton.

NOVEMBER 1859

Tuesd Nov 1 washed **wed 2** ironed went and put Marry wife of Ezra Bullard to bed with a son [William Austin] born 2*h* past 11 A M[79] **Thursd 3** went to fast meeting then up to P Gs his children sick Mary & Emoretts Lucinia not well **Fri 4** she had a chill last night **Satd 5** she is worse children better **Sund 6** all better I came home **Mond 7** cut Alzinias lindsey dress **Tuesd 8** sewed on it **wed 9** finished it **Thursd 10** finished Byrons comforter **Frid 11** made me a cap took care of my dried peaches put my Aples down cellar **Sat 12** I was sick all day **Sund 13** a litle better do not go to meeting **mond 14** worped a web or showed Jessess how P G here to dinner **Tuesd 15** went up to Tripps helped beam the web on **Wed 16** repairing my quilts **Thursd 17** made some covers for my comforters **Frid 18** David & Carlos here to dinner made canker medicine **Sat 19** Gave John Winegars child an Emetic **Sund 20** put John Pulcipers wife Rosilla to bed with a daughter [Mary Elizabeth] Born 3 1*h* A M came home and went to meeting **Mond ^21^** washed **Tuesd 22** sewed **Wed 23** the same **Thursd 24** sewed carpet rags **Frid 25** made me a cap **Sat 26** made another P G sent me a peice of beaf **Sund 27** do not go to meeting it is so bad under foot read the book of mormon I thank the Lord that I can read, and I pray the Father in the name of his son Jesus christ that I may enjoy the use of all my senses and live to a good old age and have good health that I may enjoy life and spend it to his honor and glory **Mond 28** sewing **Tuesd 29** the same **Wed 30** made Alzinia a quilted peticoat

DECEMBER 1859

Thursd Dec 1st cut me a dress Alzinas Mother came here going to Ogdon staid all night Alzina stays with me I go and worp a web fo[r] sister Grow Julia was here this evening **Frd 2** I work on my dress ~~Sat~~ Alzinias Mother gone to Ogden I gave her a dress and apron and some dried peaches **Satd 3** finish my dress **Sund ^4^** go to meeting **Mond 5** ~~wash~~ **Tuesd 6 wed 7 Thursd 8 frid 9 Sat 10** this week I have been to town bought me some cap stuff made me some caps and done many things P G sent me a good peice of beaf been at sister Grows several times showing a woman there about weaving **Sund 11** do not go to meeting **Mond 12** ~~put in a~~ quilt a peticoat **Tuesd 13** quilted a small quilt **wed 14** made made them up **Thursd ^15^** quilted another peticoat **Frd 16** and **Satd 17** knit Br Winegar a pair of double mittens P G Mary and Sylvia here Mary brought some yarn to knit 3 pair of double mittens **Sund 18** went to meeting **Mond 19** I knit P Gs mittens **Tuesd 20** knit carlos **Wed ^21^** knit Byrons Wm= ^Smoot^ and Martha and Sister Smoot here **Thud 22** made me a hood **Frid ^23^** did many things **Sat 24** went to collect some money to

---

79. Mary Harriet Burgess (b. 1842) was the wife of Ezra Nelson Bullard (b. 1833).

Br Palmers and Ludingtons got none came home cut and ^made^ Alzinia an
apron with sleeves **Sund 25** went to meeting Br Amasa Lyman spoke & gave
us a good Christmas presant **Mond 26** I went up to town get some things out
of the store coffee pot pail candle snuffers &c came back bougt a pig ready
killed weighing 107 lbs 14 cts per lb **Tuesd 27** cut and salted my meat P G
Lucina Mary Bishop Stoker & wife came here Just as I got it done P G went
after Mr Parry got him and we all went to a party at Pres John Youngs **Wed 28**
we all got back here 4 oclock this morning P G and the Bishop & wives went
home this afternoon I commenced a pair of mittens for Mr Parry **Thursd 29** I
went to a ward party at Wardles Hall[80] **Frd 30** prepared some corn for the mill
knit some **Sat 31** wash a little & clean for new year

1860

*I am Sixty five years old and my prayer is that I may keep the spirit of
God which will lead me to do right*

JANUARY 1860

Sund Jan= 1st 1860 I went to meeting **Mond 2** went up to Tripps spun
some stocking yarn **tuesd 3** knit another pair of mittens **wed 4** doubled some
yarn for a carpet **Thurd 5** the same and knit another pair of mittens **Frid 6**
Brs Leonard & Thurstin [Thomas Jefferson Thurston, 1805–1885] & wives
here on a visit P G Lucina & Carlos here to dinner **Sat 7** finished my carpet
yarn and spooled it went up to town got P G to attend a sale and bid of a
house and lot for me at two hundred Dollars **Sund 8** it snows do not go to
meeting **Mond 9** go & pay the money & get the Deed bought me a pair of spec-
tacles ^& Alzina a dress^ worked my web **Tuesd 10** put in carpet web wove
some **wed 11** wove **Thursd 12** wove **Frd 13** got it out I have wove it at Br
Grows **Sat 14** made it up and put it down on the floor **Sund 15** went to meeting Precinda Kimb^al^ and Zina Young here to supper **Mond 16** put in ^a^
comforter **Tuesd 17** got it out & made it up **Wed 18 Thursd 19** I washed **Frid
20** have been and setled up my tithing for last year 1859 paid $62:23 ~~Frid~~
Satd 21 I have carded bats [quilt batting] for sister Grow **Sund 22** went to
meeting then went and put Maria William Burges' wife to bed with a son
[William Harrison] born 7 2*h* P M[81] **Mond 23** ironed did me up a cap **tuesd**

---

80. "In 1851 a dance hall was built by George Wardle on the west side of 2nd West
Street, between North and South Temple Streets, which was a social center for Salt
Lake City for some years" (Andrew Jenson, *Encyclopedic History of the Church of Jesus
Christ of Latter-day Saints* [Salt Lake City: Deseret News Publishing Co., 1941], 751).
This would have been within the boundaries of Patty's ward, the sixteenth.

81. Mariah Pulsipher (1822–1892) was the wife of William Burgess (b. 1822).

24 carded more bats for sister Grow **Wed 25** cut and sewed carpet rags for sister Grow **Thursd 26** Brs Tripp & Bishop Kesler and wives here on a visit **Frd <27>** made Alzina a bonnet ^P G & David here^ put Phebe [Phebe Peterson Eastman, b. 1819] wife of E B Tripp to bed with a son [Paschal Morrill] born 7 2*h* P M **Satd ^28^** attended to many things **Sund 29** went to meeting **mond ^30^** picked wool sister Pulcifr here on a visit **Tuesd 31** cut carpet rags & made a chair cushion I have been reading the fifth volume of the ^Journal^ of discourses lately they are a rich treat

FEBRUARY 1860

wed Feb 1 sewed **Thursd 2** fast day I went to meeting **Frid 3** sister Foss here to dinner I put Cathrine Wm= Birges wife [Katherine Chamberlain, b. 1839] to bed with a son [Joseph Chamberlain] born 20 minutes past 3 P M **Satd 4** my birth day I am Sixty five years old and my prayer is that I may keep the spirit of God which will lead me to do right **Sund ^5^** went to meeting **Mond 6** commenced spining I have 20 lb ^rolls^ to spin **Tuesd 7** P G and Sylvia here I went up to P Gs with Sylvia **Wed 8** Phebe cut me a dress I went to Sylvias **Thursd 9** we worked on my dress **Frid 10** I came home Mr Parrys birth day he is seventy one years old finished my dress **Satd 11** I spun **Sund 12** went to meeting then went out to Wm= Smoots David staid here last night he went with me **Mond 13** I came home **Tuesd 14** spun **Wed 15** went to the tithing Office to settle **Thurd 16** I went to a party at the seventys Hall[82] **Frd 17** spun **Satd 18** spun **Sund 19** went to meeting **Mond 20** washed called to Br Parkers **Tuesd 21** called there again **Wed ^22^** spun **Thursd 23** called there again **Frid 24** spun **Satd 25** spun **Sund 26** been to meeting P G brought me a load of wood yestar^day^ put Br Parkers wife [probably Jane Flemming and William Knowlton Parker] to bed with a son [William Knowlton] born 5 1*h* P M **mond 27** spun **Tuesd ^28^** spun then went to the social hall to a lecture delivered by capt- [Walter M.] Gibson[83] **Wed 29** put her that was Mary [Ann] Pettet wife of Joseph Emily [Joseph Johnson Imlay, b. 1838] to bed with a daughter [Mary Elizabeth] born 8 1*h* P M

82. Joseph Young had been ordained president of the First Quorum of Seventy on 1 March 1835. He served in this position until 1881. The Seventy's Council Hall was built on his property at First South and State Street. The Promised Valley Playhouse now occupies some of that land. Joseph Young also owned another lot in that block, on Second South between Main and State streets.

83. Captain Walter Murray Gibson also appears in the journal of Wilford Woodruff. The first entry is on 11 January 1860. The event mentioned by Patty is expanded by Woodruff as he writes, "I attended the Lecture of Capt Walter M. Gibson delivered in the Social Hall upon the geography of the Indian Archipeligo. . . . His lecture was vary interesting." Captain Gibson joined the

MARCH 1860

Thursd March 1st not well **Frid 2** spun **Satd 3** spun **Sund 4** went to meeting **Mond 5** Elizabeth [Foss] Cowley here on a visit **Tuesd 6** P G had come after me to go up there to a blesing meeting I went had a good meeting **wed 7** came home went to a lecture delivered by capt Gibson **Thursd 8** ~~spun~~ worped a web and drawed it in **Frid 9** wove **Sat 10** wove **Sund 11** went to meeting **Mond 12** wove **Tuesd 13** finished weaving mine **wed 14** spun **15** spun **Frid 16 Sat 17** spun **Sund 18** went to meeting **Mond ^19^** spun **Tuesd 20** ^had a man to^ set out apple trees **wed 21** the same **Thursd ^22^** John Parry worked for me fixing my fence **Frid 23 Sat 24** Spun **Sund 25** put Rebeca wife of [*left blank*] Lee to bed with a daughter born 4 A M[84] went to meeting **Mond 26** spun **Tuesd 27** finished my rolls planted some peas **wed 28** Sylvia here **Thursd 29** Br Waterson worked for me I set out some strawbery vines **Frd 30** I washed **Satd 31** worked in the darden

APRIL 1860

Sund April 1 went to meeting **mond 2** cut carpet rags went to a lecture delivered by Capt Gibson **Tuesd 3 Wed 4** cleaned and cooked for confrence **Thursd 5** fast I went to meeting **Frid 6** conference be[g]an I went also **Sat 7 ^&^ Sund 8** it ajourened the best conference I have ever had **Mond 9** I have washed and scoured my yarn Carlos [*word blotted out*] ^Sessions^ my grand son came here to board he is going to the acadamy it commenced to day[85]

---

church and stayed around for some time, lecturing and being generally admired. He served a number of missions for the church. However, on Sunday, 17 January 1864, Woodruff's journal reports, "After Prayers President Young informed us He had a letter from Brethren on the Sandwich Islands which was read informing us that Capt Gibson Had ordained on the Island A Quorum of Twelve Apostles & Seventies & Bishops & High Priests &c. He Charged $100 for Ordaining the 12 each & $50 for 70, $5 for a Bishop $2.50 for a Bishops Counceller &c And he had Claimed all the Island. . . . He has taken possession of the Island & takes from the Saints all that they raise & is playing the Tyrant over all the Saints on those Island . . ." (*Woodruff's Journal*, 6:153). Accordingly, Ezra Taft Benson and Lorenzo Snow were dispatched to the islands to check the allegations, which they confirmed. On 29 January 1846 they reported that Gibson had been cut off from the church.

84. Alfred Lee's wife, Rebecca Orme, gave birth to a daughter Carolina on 6 April 1860, according to some records. This could be the same birth.

85. On 20 February 1860 the JH reported that "Pres Young announced his intention of hiring Orson Pratt, Jr & James Cobb as teachers of a Free High School . . . to be called The Union Academy . . . to be sustained from the tithing, if . . . approved . . ." The *Deseret News* for 9 April 1960 announced the opening of the Union Academy under the supervision of Orson Pratt, Sr. The school opened its doors on the southwest corner of First North and Second West, a short walk

doubled harness yarn for Lucinia **Tuesd 10** twisted it **wed 11** worked in the garden **Thursd 12** set out strawberry vines **Frd 13** attended to many things **Sat 14** Br Joseph Heywood and his three wives here on a visit **Sund 15** went to meeting in the forenoon went to Br Smoots to dinner then came home P G was here **Mond 16** carried 46 peach trees to the tithing Ofice planted some potatoes and carrots **Tuesd 17** cut carpet rags **Wed 18** the same **Thursd 19** the same it rains **Frid 20 Sat 21** attended to my domestic concerns P G Lucinia & Sulvia here yestard **Sund 22** went to meeting Wm= ~~Attch~~tchson came here to Board **Mond 23** ^washed^ sewing **tuesd 24** Br Tomas Jeremy plowed my east lot ~~On~~ **wed 25** he furrowed it Carlos & Wm= planted it with corn **Thursd 26** I went to see Martha Ann with Tripps & wife **Frid ^27^** coul-dord~~bled~~ my carpet yarn **Sat 28** doubled it **Sund 29** went to meeting **Mond 30** made soap

MAY 1860

Tuesd ^May 1^ went to town **Wed 2** worked in the garden **Thursd 3** twisted my carpet yarn **^Frid 4^** finished it **Sat 5** worped my carpet and sister Grows 65 yards **Sund 6** do not go to meeting not well **Mond 7** spining **Tuesd 8** put the carpet into the Loom sister Grow is weaving hers **Wed 9 Thursd 10** spining Wm= & Mrartha & sister Smoot here went home **Frid 11** finished spining **Satd 12** scoured my yarn and washed my bed blankets it snowed last night and this morning **Sund 13** frose very hard last night snows fast this morning clears away the sun comes out I go to meeting this forenoon no meeting in the afternoon on the bottom the ground is covered with snow some say it has fell two feet some say more **Mond 14** washed **Tuesd ^15^** ironed **wed 16 Thursd 17** ^put Mary Gibs to bed with a son born 3 P M^[86] worked in the garden **Frd 18** couloured red & yellow then went home with P G came home **Sund 20 Mond 21** washed out my yarn **Tuesd 22** cut carpet rags **Wed 23 Thursd 24** the same **Frd 25** sized and spooled my dreses **Sat 26** worped them then wove on my carpet **Sund 27** put sister Forman to bed with a son

from Patty Sessions's home. No fee was charged for those studying algebra, surveying, astronomy, chemistry, mineralogy, geology, and modern languages. Earlier the building had been the Union Hotel. George C. Lambert said the building had been the old Winkings Hall, later became the Deseret Hospital, and eventually turned into the Salt Lake Knitting Factory. ("Journal of George Cannon Lambert" in *Heart Throbs of The West*, ed. Kate B. Carter [Salt Lake City: Daughters of Utah Pioneers, 1948], 9:290–91.) The JH said the school was "to be kept in the Wilkin House on Union Square . . ." The Union Academy evolved into the University of Deseret.

86. Gideon Hayden Carter Gibbs (1821–1901) and Mary Ellen (or Elizabeth) Frederick (1830–1907) had a daughter, Sarah Ann (Sadie), on 17 May 1860. The text almost looks as if Patty has written "dauter" over the word "son."

[Leander] born 9 A M[87] did not go to meeting **Mond 28** ^carlos brought the cow^ **Tuesd 29 wed 30** been weaven **Thurd 31**

JUNE 1860

Frid Sat 1-2 ^**June**^ weaving **sund 3** went to meeting **mond 4** ^Lucinia here staid all night^ **Tuesd 5 Wed 6** weaving **Thursd 7** got my carpet out put in my dresses **Frd 8** wove 3 yds **Sat 9** went to Br Heywoods on a visit went to the ~~store~~ tin shop bought me a tin bucket ana pan David and Pheebe come home with me staid all night **Sund 10** went to meeting **Mond 11** ^A M put Harriet Mr Parrys wife to bed with a son^ [Edwin Francis] **Tuesd 12 Wend 13** wove got my dresses out **Thursd 14** sised and spooled my blankets **Frd 15** worped sister Grows web **Sat 16**

[On the center pages of this diary, the following information appears in Patty's handwriting:]
Patty Bartlett daughter of Enoch and Anne Bartlett was born February 4 1795 ^Bethel Mane^ and was married to David Sessions June 28th 1812 who was the son of David and Rachel Sessions, he was born April the 4th 1790 Veshire Vermont I was Baptised into the church of Jesus christ ^of later day saints^ July 2 1834 Mr Sessions was Baptised Aug<st> 1835 ~~we received our~~ we received our endowment Dec 16 1845 in Nauvoo Rosilla Cowin was sealed to Mr Sessions Oct= 3 1845 by Brigham Young Nauvoo Harriet Teaples was sealed to him Jan= 13 1850 ^by Brigham Young^ G S L he died August 11 1850 G S L City
I was sealed to Joseph Smith by Willard Richards March 9 1842 in Newel K Whitneys chamber Nauvoo for ^time and all eternity^ Eternity ~~and I~~ and if I do not live to attend to it myself when there is a place prepared I want some one to attend to it for me according to order Sylvia ^my daughter^ was presant when I was sealed to Joseph Smith. I was after Mr Sessions death sealed to John Parry senior for time on the 27 of March 1852 G S L City

[Three daubs of wax attach a buff-colored, lined piece of paper to the bottom of the blue sheet. It folds in within the above pages. Opened, it extends approximately three inches below the diary and reveals the following information in Patty's hand:]
G. S. L. City. July. 3d 1867
I was sealed to Joseph F Smith for time and all eternity and had my second anointing. He Joseph F. Smith acting for and in behalf of his Uncle Joseph. Smith. The Prophet. Who was Martired June 27,th 1844. in carthage Jail with his Br Hyram. Joseph Fs Father.

Patty Sessions

---

87. Margaret Jane Mousley (1819–1888) was the wife of Joseph Foreman (1822–1902).

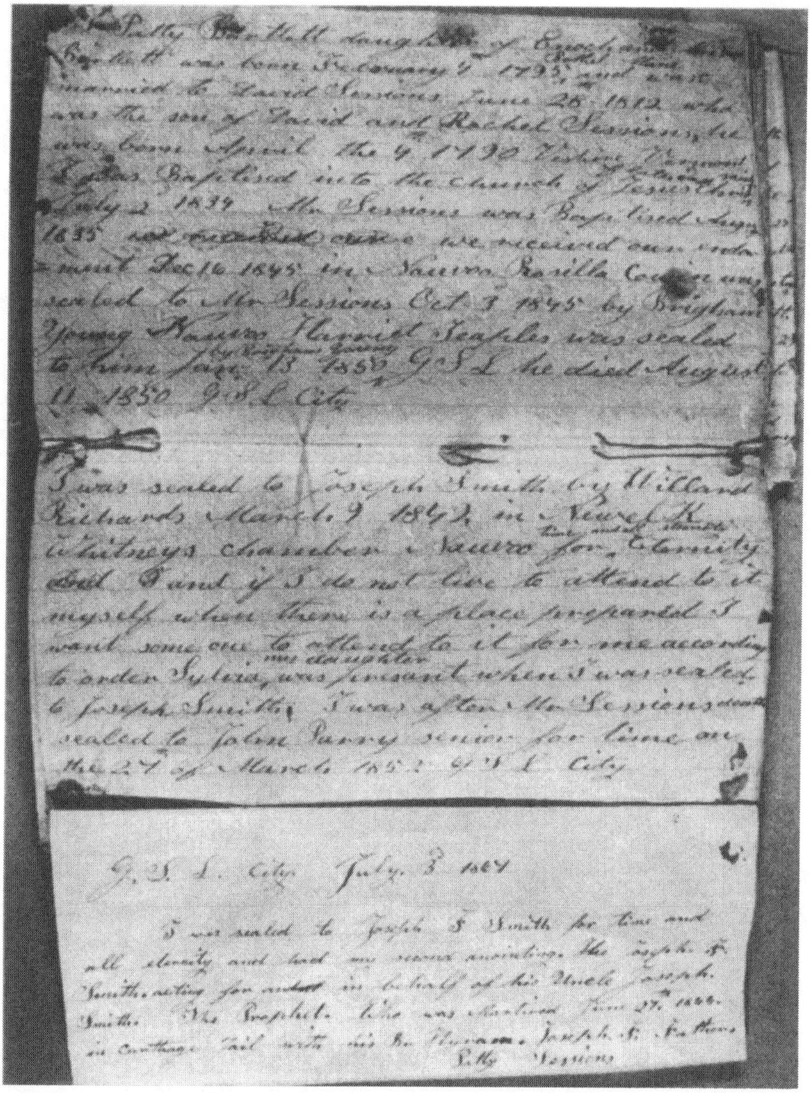

Diary five (1856–1862) is in two handmade parts. The first is 8 inches long by 5 inches wide on faintly-lined blue paper, except for a few pages of discolored white, which are attached to the blue but read from top to bottom instead of left to right. They are folded from 8 x 6½ inches sheets to make 6½ by 4 inch pages. Patty started writing on the outside, or the cover has been lost. There are only two large stitches to hold the pages together. The second section begins on 6 July 1857 in the middle of the move back to Salt Lake City after the flight south to escape from Johnston's Army. The pages shown here regarding Patty's sealing are in the middle of the diary. The diary is written in brown ink. Patty ends this diary on 17 February 1862. Courtesy of LDS Church Archives; photograph by J M Heslop.

[The diary continues:]

warped mine **Sund 17** went to meeting **Mond 18** got my corn plowed **Tuesd 19 Wend 20** got it hoed **Thursd 21** had my fence finished **Frid 22** I have made Alzina a dress this week wash **Sat 23** ironed finished making up my carpet Sylvia called here **Sund 24** went to meeting **mond 25 Tuesd 26 Wed 27** worked in the garden **Thurd ^28^** put in my web for blankets[88] **Frd 29** wove **Sat 30** wove

July 1860

Sund July 1st went to meeting in the afternoon **Mond July 2 Tuesd 3 wed 4** went up to the Taberncle to celebrate the 4th went to a theatre at Br Mousleys[89] **Thursd ^5^** fast visited at sister Grows with sisters Newman & Yates **Frd 6** got my web out 33 yds **Sat 7** worked in the garden **Sund 8** do not go to meeting ^not well^ **Mond 9 Tuesd 10 wed 11 Thursd 12** I have not been well this week Hannah Conklin washed for me[90] Br Grow has cut my grass on shares he has one third in the stack sister Teaples has been here[91] **Frd 13** I am kniting for sister grow **Satd 14** ^got my hay stacked^ Sylvia & Br Williams staid here all knight **Sund 15** went to meeting **Mond 16** cut carpet rags for Martha Ann **Tuesd 17** the same **Wed 18** finish the the rags P G has sent word down to have me get ready to go up into big cotton wood Canyon to celibrarte the 24 he will take me up there **Thursd 19** made me a skirt **Frd 20** washed **Satd 21** cooked **Sund 22** started for the canyon with P G Carlos Lucinia and Emerett & Josephine camped at the gate **Mond 23** got there got dinner soon after it began to rain we had quite a shower **Wed 24** we spent in dancing fishing and various other kinds of amusement **Wed ^25^** we came home **Thursd** *[written on top of* Wed*]* 26 I watered my lots **Frid 27 Satd 28** worked very hard **Sund 29** do not go to meeting **Mond 30** sister Woodruff here **Tuesd 31** E R Snow Zina D[iantha] & Harriet Young,s & capt= Gibsons daughter [Leulah] here on a visit

---

88. Here Patty changes from brown to faded blue ink—for four lines only. Since she made her own ink, perhaps she found blue unsatisfactory.

89. The *Deseret Evening News* of 10 May 1919 records that "George Washington Mousley established the old Salt Lake City Academy, the first school of its kind in the community. The building which housed it [was] . . . on Fourth West between North Temple and First North street. . . . He was an early promoter of the drama, and an association that he fathered and instructed gave frequent performances in the academy as well as in various meetinghouses of the city . . ." ("Leaves From Old Albums," vol. 52, sec. 3:7).

90. Hannah Conklin was listed in the census of 1860 as fifty-four years old.

91. Huldah Clarinda Colby (1812–1881) was the mother of Harriet Teaples, the plural wife of Patty's first husband David.

AUGUST 1860

Wed August 1st Thursd 2 wattered my lots **Frd 3** have been and gave Br
Oens babe an Emetic it rained this evening **Sat 4** I washed with the rain water
Sund 5 went up to P Gs and put Mary his wife to bed with a son [Perry] born
4 and 1*h* P M Charles Stodard came after me with P Gs horses and one of
them died ten oclock that night the other is spoil ^ (=ed ^ if she lives **Mond 6** I
do not come home **Tuesd 7** the mare is a litle better but can hardly walk I
came home **Wed 8** I have been preparing to water Alzina s Father came here
to see her while I was gone the first time he has seen her since she came here I
left her at Br Gibses I commenced kniting for sister Grow **Wed 8 Thursd 9** I
water Mr Parry helped me **Frd 10 Sat 11** ^went & setled my taxes^ & kniting
Sund 12 I went to meeting **Mond 13** not very well **Tuesd 14** washed **Wed 15**
ironed **thursd 16** kniting **Frd 17** the same I am not very well my arms are
lame pulling weeds for the cow and calf **Sat 18** kniting **Sund 19** do not go to
meeting **Mond 20 Tuesd 21 Wed 22** kniting **Thursd 23** watered ~~Frd~~ Mr
Parry has gone up North with P G he staid here last night **Frd 24** Mr Parry
came home **Sat 25** put down my carpet in my new room **Sund 26** do not go
to meeting not well **Mond 27** kniting Wm= Smoot here took Marthas carpet
rags home that I have sewed for her **Tuesd 28** I went to town got some couler-
ing stuff P G here **Wed 29** I coulered yellow **Thursd 30** made my ^currant^
wine **Frid 31** put sister Reed [Margaret Pettit, wife of Ira Beckwith Reed,
1835–1892] to bed with a daughter [Margaret Ann] born 10 A M Sylvia here

SEPTEMBER 1860

Sat Sept 1st made Alzina a dress **Sund 2** went to meeting **Mond 3** pulled my
beans **Tuesd 4** kniting **Wed 5** got my beans in aired my dried fruit **Thursd** [*written on top of* Sat] **6 Frd 7 Sat 8** kniting **Sund 9** went to meeting **Mond 10** Br Gibs
commenced cuting my corn **Tuesd 11** I washed **wed 12** Lucinia here I commenced striking a harness for her **Thursd 13** got one half done done up some
caps **Frid 14** P G David & Carlos came here **Satd 15** went got a load of salt I finished the harness and went home with them **Sund 16** staid with Sylvia **Mond 17**
strung the loom and harness put in a web and set it work wove half yard **Tuesd
18** came home **wed 19** David and Jimme came down last night have got a load
of salt to day stay all night **Thursd 20** go home **Frd 21** I have put in five Dollars
[*word scratched out*] cash for the missionaries gave it to Bishop Kesler **Satd 22** I
have been to see sister Higbee an hour or two we had a good visit together the
spirit of the Lord was poured out upon us I have been kniting the most of the
week for sister ~~Grow~~ **Sund 23** I went to meeting **Mond 24** ~~Tuesd 25~~ I gave John
Winegars babe an emetic **Tuesd 25** strung sister Winegrs harness and loom
Wed ^26^ put in her web then went and see sisters Foss & Voce before they go
to the east **Thursd 27** they start with the missionaries I go and give Ezra Bullards
babe [William Austin] an Emetic **Frd 28 Sat 29** kniting **Sund 30** I go to meeting

OCTOBER 1860

Mond Oct= 1 make medicine for rheumatism **Tuesd 2** wash & iron **Wed 3** do up our bonnets **Thursd 4** cut out Alzinias cloak we go to the Fair **Frd 5** I make her cloak **satd 6** do not go to confrence it rains **Sund 7** go **Mond 8** conference ajourned we have had the best conference ever I was to[92] P G here to dinner & Mary Wm= **Tuesd 9** washed **Wed 10** did many things ^got my corn all into the chamber^ **Thurs 11** cut me a flanel dress **Frd 12 Sat 13** worked on my my dress **Sund 14** went to meeting **Mond 15** gave Phebe Tripps babe an Emetic **Tuesd 16** finished my dress David Phebe & the children here gone home **Wed 17** kniting **Thursd 18 Frid 19 Satd 20** the same **Sund 21** went to meeting **Mond 22** finish sister Grows kniting **Tuesd 23** went to Br Tripps spun some stocking yarn 30 knotts **Wed 24** I went up to P Gs **Thursd 25** set her web to work **Frid 26** wove **Satd 27** sold Br Williams a pair of mittens for potatoes came home went away to the 11 ward to get some one to go and weave for P Gs folks did not get any one **Sund 28** went to meeting **Mond 29** kniting for P Gs folks **Tuesd 30** the same **Wed 31** striking harness for sister Coon

NOVEMBER 1860

Thursd Nov= 1 kniting **Frd 2** finished the harness **Sat 3** helped sister Pulsipher strike a harness **Sund 4** went to meeting ^Sulvia staid here^ **Mond 5** ~~Tues 6~~ finished Carlos and Jimys socks **Tuesd 6** Abigail Kesler here on a visit **Wed 7 Thursd 8 Frd 9 Sat 10** kniting **Sund 11** went to meeting **Mond 12** finished Br Grows mittens **Tuesd 13** ~~spining~~ put Sophia ^E B^ Tripps wife to bed with a daughter [Sarah/Sadie/Ann] born 3 & 5 minutes A M commenced spining for sister grow **Wed <14>** **Thurd 15 Frid 16** I have spun 5 lb rolls this week carried home sister Keslers two pair of socks I have [been] kniting **Sat 17** been cleaning moved my stove piled up my corn Br Gibs commenced plowing my East lot he is going to sow it with wheat gives me one half of the wheat ^delivered^ in my house and he has the straw for thrashing and cleaning he finds the seed **Sund ^18^** go to meeting then put sister [Sophia] Riser to bed with a daughter [Celestia Christiana] born 11 1*h* P M **Mond 19** two men to work for me **Tuesd 20** spining Br Gibs finish plowing my lot **Wed 21** John Winegar works for me again take up some currant bushes & set them out **Thursd 22** spin in the afternoon I am not well Josepine came here staid all

---

92. In conference 8 October 1860, Brigham Young urged the saints to give gold and silver and their best in-kind offerings to the tithing fund and keep the worst for themselves so he could pay the debts of the church. He spoke of being in "the midst of eternity and in the presence of holy beings." He said that beauty is found in women and men who have accepted the gospel and the love of God. And he declared that all should be devoted to the building of the kingdom (*Deseret News* 10:305).

night **Frd 23** she made Alzina a hood I am quite sick **Sat 24** she starts home loose the team stay all night at Tripps David & Williams stay here **Sund 25** I am not well enough to go to meeting **Mond 26** fix a web in for Tripps folks **Tuesd 27** kniting mittens for Byron **Wed 28** sent for to go to sister Angel she was very sick I was not well and I had to walk home and I could scarcely reach my home **Thursd 29** I am quite sick again to day **Frd 30** better

DECEMBER 1860

Sat Dec= 1 quite well **Sund 2** go to meeting **Mond 3** spin for sister Grow **Tuesd 4** finish spining for her **Wed 5** knit me some over shoes I have knit P G a pair of mitens last week **Thursd 6** washed rained **Frid 7** washed and ironed **Sat 8** Alzina starts for Ogden to day to see her Mother her uncle Henry [Alanson Teaples, 1842–1904] & John Duel and wife staid here last night she has gone with them I sent her Mother Harriet Sessions $20 Dollars in orders for her own use **Sund 9** I do not go to meeting it snowed last night it is bad walking **Mond 10** caled to sister Foremans babe [Leander] it sick prepare some medicine for it **Tuesd 11** it better **Wed 10** bake pies &c **Thursd 13 Frid 14 Satd 15** I have ^been^ knitting the most of the time this week for sister Grow Alzina came home to night **Sund 16** she is almost sick She is quite lame I do not go to meeting **Mond 17** kniting **Tuesd 18 wed 19 Thursd 20** ^the same^ **Frd 21** wash **Satd 22** iron bake **Sund 23** go to meeting **Mond 24** knitt a pair of Double mittens **Tuesd 25** christmas day went up to E B Tripp to dinner **Wed 26** Jesess Tripps wife here on a visit **Thursd 27** Julia Grow here on a visit **Frd 28** kniting **Sat 29** the same P G here Sylvia & Williams here stay all night **Sund 30** go to meeting **Mond 31** go over the river put Br Scows wife to bed with a daughter born about 9 A M

1861

stay at home watch my fruit and keep it from being stole

JANUARY 1861

Tuesd Jan= 1st new year ^we^ go to Br E B Tripps with Bishop Kesler Br Riser Derr & Mcentire with their wives[93] **Wed 2 Thursd 3** preparing for a party **Frd 4** Carlos & Josephine my grand children came down here took me to the party we had a good time **Satd 5** they went home **Sund 6** do not go to meeting it is so bad walking **Mond 7** make me a comforter **Tuesd 8** wash **wed 9** peice a quilt **Thursd 10** quilt a peticoat for Julia Grow **Frd 11** quilt for

---

93. William Derr, a comb maker, was listed in the 1860 census as living in Salt Lake City. He was forty-six.

myself **Sat 12** quilt a peticoat for Alzina and made it up **Sund 13** snow hinders
me from going to meeting **Mond 14** P G and Chester Lovlin here to dinner
Tuesd 15 ^put Jane Winegar [Jane Grace Mellon, b. 1840, wife of John
Winegar] to bed with a daughter^ [Lucinda Elizabeth] ^born 9 P M^ **Wed
16** kniting Julia Grow here in the evening **Thursd 17** Sylvia Williams &
Staniford here I went to a party with them in the evening at Ballos Hall[94] **Frid
18** making a chair cushion cover **Sat 19** had co sisters Grow Yates and
Newman were here **Sund 20** went to meeting **mond 21 Tuesd 22** P G Sylvia
here she paid $19-50 she had borrowed of me **Wed 23 Thursd 24 Frd 25** put
Jessess wife of E B Tripp to bed with a son born 4 A M then worped a web for
sister grow P G & Bishop Stoker came here and thier wives took me to a party
at the seventys Hall **Sat 26** they went home **Sund 27** went to meeting **Mond
28** Carlos here to dinner I finished a comforter for Br Grow **Tuesd 29 Wed 30
Thursd 31** Kniting

FEBRUARY 1861

Frid Feb 1 I have the toothache very bad the Bishop & Br Riser came in laid
hands on me & the ^pain^ left me instantly and I fell asleep **Satd 2** put
Martha [Matilda Jane Nease] Br Hunts wife to bed with a daughter born 8 A
M **Sund 3** do not go to meeting **Mond 4** my birthday sixty six years old to
day go to a party with Mr Parry at the 14 ward hall Br Giles a blind man made
the Party **Tuesd 5** kniting **Wed 6 Thursd 7** sewing making night caps. I feel to
praise the Lord for his goodness and mercy unto me I am blessed all the day
long. **Frid 8** P G and wives came down Wms & Sylvia & Jimme took me to a
party at Br John Youngs we staid untill daylight they came here took breakfast
then went home we had a splendid party **Sat 9 Sund 10** it snowed last night I
do not go to meeting **Mond 11** sewing **Tuesd 12** I washed **Wed 13** I ironed
did me up some caps **Thursd 14** sewing **Frd 15** I have had a man cuting up
my wood it is all cut and piled up **Sat 16** crociaed me a neck tie **Sund 17** go to
meeting **Mond 18** went up to Tripps and spun stocking yarn **Tuesd 19** Sister
Kesler here on a visit **Wed 20** put John Cottoms [Jr., b. 1823] wife to bed with
a son [Hyrum] born 8 A M P G Lucinia Sylvia & Sarah Crosley[95] here ^to
dinner^ I went to Br Brighams school house to hear Br Hyde lecture[96]
Thursd 21 went up to Br Brighams Office gave him two Hundred Dollars

---

94. Ballo's Hall was located at First South between First and Second West. It was
    also called Ballo's Music Hall. The JH entry for 27 June 1855 refers to Captain
    Delmonico Ballo's band as the foundation for Ballo's Hall (p. 1).

95. Sarah Crossley (1843–1906) married Perrigrine Sessions on 2 March 1861.
    Oddly Patty never mentions the marriage.

96. An historical plaque now stands at the northeast corner of State Street and South
    Temple. It reads in part, "A private schoolhouse built by Brigham Young for his
    own children stood on this corner lot 1860–1903. . . ."

^cash^ As a deposit for him to use for the gathering of the poor untill I call ~~call~~ for it and I do not mean to call for it unless I need it, **Frd 22** David and Phebe here to dinner went up to a party **Satd 23** David come and carried me down to Wm= Smoots to see them came home with me staid staid all night they carried me up to meeting in **Sund ^24^** morning went home in the afternoon **Mond 25** I commence a pair of stockings for Phebe **Tuesd 26** washed David came after me to go to a party at the seventys hall I did not go **Wed 27 Thursd 28**

MARCH 1861

Frd March 1 I have been kniting **Sat 2** sold the old house on my other lot for 26 dollars ^to Br Winegar^ took for pay a set of grave stones to put up at Mr Sessions grave $20 00 and the Deserett News $6.00 I also bought me a Lounge paid in trees gave $14-00 bought 3-00 feet of lumber $13-50 paid in dried peaches **Sund 3** it snows I do not go to meeting **Mond 4** called to M Cowleys babe it had the croop **Tuesd 5** went to Bishop Keslers to show her how to coulor black **Wed 6** Sisters grow and Phebe Tripp here **Thursd 7** went to get my News[97] and Settled my half of the mountaineer[98] then commenced a comforter for Phebe Tripps boy **Frid 8** have sold $6.00 worth of trees this morning[99] **Sat 9** sold $150 more finished the comforter **Sun 10** go to meeting **Mond ^11^** Sold $43=50 worth of trees P G here bording he is ^one of the^ juror on the grand Jury **Tuesd 12** very fine weather **Wed 13** P G went home and I went and put Martha wife of Zera Pulsiphe [Martha Ann Hughes, b. 1843, wife of Zera Pulsipher] to bed with a daughter [Mary Elizabeth] born 4 2*h* A M **Thursd 14** worked in the garden sewed peas set out some trees **Frid 15** the same **Satd 16** worped and beemed on a web for sister Grow **Sund 17** went to meeting **Mond 18** Lucinia here staid all night **Tuesd 19** she went to see Martha Ann came back here we then went to see sister Precinda Kimball

---

97. What Patty would have read in her *Deseret News* of 7 March 1861 were remarks by President Brigham Young from 17 February 1861, the report of a meeting of the Deseret Agricultural and Manufacturing Society, news stories on the impending Civil War and President Lincoln, as well as articles about Napoleon and Queen Victoria. There were articles about a repeater pistol, about men subscribing to *Godey's Lady's Book*, and about Indians raising hemp in Tooele and, of course, a variety of advertisements.

98. These few words demonstrate just how curious Patty's mind was. The *Mountaineer* was an early newspaper published in Salt Lake City by Hosea Stout, Seth M. Blair, and James Ferguson. It was intended to refute another paper, *Kirk Anderson's Valley Tan*, designed specifically to attack Mormonism and its leaders (see Wendell J. Ashton, *Voice in the West* [New York: Duell, Sloan and Pearce, 1950], 97–100).

99. Wilford Woodruff writes on 8 March 1861, "I bought 4 plums trees of Mrs Sessions and set them out . . ." (*Woodruff's Journal*, vol. 9, p. 230).

in the evening she staid here all night again ^**Wed 20**^ I went with her up to sister Pratts in the forenoon I came home sister Zina Young here in the evening went and put Hannah wife of David Daniels to bed with a daughter born 9 P M[100] **Thursd 21** P G Lucinia & J Staniford here went home it snowed fast I have commenced some fringe and also a chair cover **Frd 22 Satd 23** finished the fringe **Sund 24** went to meeting it rained **Mond 25** called to P Gs Emerett sick **Tuesday 26** Phebe cut and fitted a dress for me I then put Emorett to bed with a daughter [Agnes Emoret] born 6- 3*h* P M **Wed 27** came home P G John Staniford came down with me staid all night **Thursd 28** they ^took^ seventy five peach trees to the Office for tithing for me Aple trees 14 wild plumb trees 9 t.m..o [tomato?] 10 got a letter from my Br Elisha my Mother alive and well Feb 13[101] **Frid 29** ^washed^ **Satd 30** ironed did up some caps **Sund 31** wrote a letter to my Br

April 1861

Mond April the 1st had co all day Syvia here Elisabeth Pratt here **Tuesd 2** sister Blair here with a babe that had a breach for me to cure **Wed 3** I worked in the garden in the forenoon went to sister Grows in the afternoon with Phebe & Jesess Tripp **Thurd 4** wrote a letter to Mother went and put them in the Office then went and put Betsey Bouk to bed with a son [Alexander] born about 4 P M **Frd 5** worked in the garden **Satd 6** the same it is conference but I stay at home to give place to those from the country **Sund 7** I go have a good meeting it was ajourned **Mond 8** I feel sick Mr Parry administered to me in the evening **Tuesd 9** I am quite well sister Higbee was here to see me took dinner we had a good visit **Wed 10** I went down to Br Piggets took his wife through a course of medicine came home then went and put sister Pettit to bed with a son born 10 P M[102] **Thurs 11** been making medicine for Sister Piggot Sister Granger here on a visit **Frd 12** Josephine here P G & David Wm= Smoot also Br Pew he is going on a mission to England it has been a general cattle drive to day, they ^have^ gone home now **Sat 13** went to Br Leonards on a visit with Mary she came here staid all night and Josephine **Sund 14** I gave her Josephine a new dress pattern went to meeting **Mond 15** embroidering a collar for myself **Tuesd 16** sewed on a waggon cover for the boys to go back with after the poor **wed 17** work on my collar **Thursd 18** ~~the e~~ commenced a chair cover for sister grow **Frd 19** sewed on another waggon cover Alzina ran away up to Sylvias **Satd 20** I went to Br Piggets took his wife

---

100. Hannah Thomas (b. 1842) was the wife of David Daniels (b. 1835).
101. Undoubtedly this was the date Elisha wrote the letter.
102. Catherine Allen Howland (1812–1887) was married to George Washington Piggot (1809–1882). Catherine (1822–1874) was the wife of Richard R. Pettit (1822–1870).

through a course of medicine it rained the most of the day **Sund 21** Alzina came home very humble I went to meeting she promised very fair that she would be a good girl if I would let her stay with me **Mond 22** still rainy **Tuesd 23** I washed ~~Thursd 24~~ ironed worked in the garden **Thurd 25** worked on the chair cover **Frid 26** took up my carpet made my new one up **Satd 27** worked on the chair cover **sund 28** went to meeting **Mond 29** prepared for white-washing **Tuesd 30** whitewashed

May 1861

wed May 1 put my things in place again **Thursd 2** went down to MarthaAnns **Frd 3** worked in the garden **Sat 4** P G & carlos here to dinner Carlos went down to see Martha Ann **Sund 5** went to meeting carlos here to Supper rained Frid night **Mond 6** I washed **Tuesd 7** ironed Jesess ^Tripp^ here on a visit **Wed 8** I was called to see Winnefords child sick with a sore throught **Thursd 9** better **Frd 10** made med for sister Pigot **Sat 11** worked on the chair cover **Sund 12** went to meeting **Mond 13** worked in the garden planted my corn beans squashes cucumbers &c **tuesd 14** ^Mary Pratt here^ ~~some~~ in the afternoon went to see that child again found it bet-ter **Wed <15>** P G Lucinia & David here we went to the grave yard to find Mr Sessions grave to put some stones down when I get them lettered **Thursd 16** cut me some undergarments made me one **Frid 17** David here I let him have 16 lb dried peaches to get nails with to put the rough of his house on it was taken of yesterday by a whirlwind and smashed all to peices but nobody hurt **Sat 18** worked garden **Sund 19** went to meeting **Mond 20** worked on the chair cover **Tuesd 21** the same **Wed 22** finished the chair cover twisted me some yarn to make me one **Thursd 23** commenced it **Frid 24** made me a cover for my Lounge **Sat 25** made me two more under gar-ments **Sund <26>** went to meeting came home David came after me to go up to P Gs his son Syrril was sick[103] I went got there about 11 clock P M found him very sick **Mond 27** had the Dr no better **Tuesd 28** no better **wed 29** I came home see to my things then went back again found him worse he died **Thursd 30** at 2 oclock A M he mortified he was buried 5 P M I did not come home staid all night undressed for the first time since I have been here I stood over him and did all I could for him P G his father ordained him an Elder on Tuesday evening Brs J L Heywood & Jerimiah Willey laid on hands with him **Frd <31>** I came home I have bought 27 lbs butter ^at 15 cts per lb^ to day also some pottery $2=50 worth worked over my butter and laid it down

---

103. Cyril Sessions, son of Perrigrine and Mary Call, was born on 7 August 1855 in Bountiful. He would have been only six years old when he died, so it was unusual for him to be ordained an elder.

JUNE 1861

Satd June 1 ^**1861**^ I washed and watered my garden **Sund 2** called to a sick child Br Joneses do not go to meeting **Mond 3** Mr Parry is engraving the stone for Mr Sessions grave **tuesd 4** the same I am crociaing at knight went to sister Tomases to get some caster oil to give to Alzinia and when I steped out of the door to come home I fell hurt my foot and ancle very bad **Wed 5** I slept but little it pains me very much **Thursd 6** no better **Frd 7** It has made me quite sick **Satd 8** it does not pain me quite so bad and I feel better P G and David came down here David wanted me to go home with him his boy was sick but I could not I am so lame **Sund 9** I feel better and can move my foot but cannot bear my weight on it yet. Brigham has been south got home last night **Mond 10** Williams and Sylvia here[104] brought me some vituals cooked **Tuesd 11** finish my chair cover. Sarah P Gs wife came here about 11 P M from Filmore, appeared **Wed 12** David here his boy no better **Thursd 13** Marry here, Sarah went home with her P G made me some crutches, David brought them down yestarday, I can walk a little with them, I am very glad that I am no worse. **Frid 14** making cushion cover. **Satd 15** P G down here ^said Harvy was sick^[105] staid all night. Smoots Negro drowned. named Jerry. I am very lame yet, Davids boy is better. **Sund 16** P G goes home after meeting Martha Ann and her children here to see me. **Mond 17** P G sends me word his boy no better Henry Teaples here [Henry Alanson Teaples, 1842/47–1904]. **Tuesd 18** I get the water turned on to my lot, my foot is so I have been on my crutches & turned the water got it watered very well, thank the Lord that I can get about as well as I can finished cushion cover, and been kniting some suspenders for Williams. **wed 18** mending and fixing chair cushions **Thursd 19** embroidering a colar William Martha & Margret here **Frid 20** Mary here made me a loaf of bread ^brought me a cheese^ **Satd 22** finished my collar and apron **Sund 23** Carlos & Josephine Wollace Willey & Elizabeth Simmons [Simmonds, b. 1819, wife of Silas, b. 1810] here **Mond 24** put down my cheese made some oil of egg **Tuesd 25** made me some ristlets and embroidered them David here said Carlos was going to Rubey Valley[106] Carlos came here eat supper started about dark and David went home **Wed 26** cut and made me a night cap **Thursd 27** Williams

104. This is the third mention of Joshua P. Williams, who, from this date throughout Patty's diaries, is mentioned regularly with Sylvia. Finding his full name proved to be very difficult until an obscure entry in Patty's accounts mentioned that he had borrowed money that he never paid back. See 25 October and 29 December.

105. Harvey was the two-year-old son of Perrigrine and Lucina Call.

106. Why Carlos went to the Ruby Valley in Nevada is not clear. Perhaps he was freighting.

Sylvia & Emerett came here he is cuting my grass I made a truss for Emeretts girl Fany cut some ristletts & a collar for me and commenced embroidering **Frd 28** went with them up to ^Br^ Tripps he finished cutting the grass brought me home as I am yet lame then they all went home **Sat 29** finished another collar bought 1 2*h* lb rolls **Sund 30**

July 1861

Mond July 1st 1861 work on my ristlets finish them **tuesd 2** made me another collar transfered the work from another it was french work **wed 3** prepared Alzinas clothes to go to the fourth made her a scarf and rozett **Thursd 4** she went in Br Mousleye school I went with David in the waggon had a good prospect although I am yet lame I can walk a litle without crutches **Frd 5** I am getting better Josephine staid here last night she went to a party with Br Jesse Fox at the essembly rooms has gone home to day I have cut Alzina a skirt and apron Br Hunt here from Ogden has been at Provo **Satd 6** made her skirt and apron **Sund 7** Joseph Parry here in the evening he and wife here **Mond 8** David and Lucinia here I have been weeding my garden some and embroidiring some ristlets **Tuesd 9** been triming my nursery a little my ancle is geting better I have laid my crutches bye but do not wear a shoe yet **Wed 10** wattered my garden finished my ristlets **Thursd 11** mendind **Frid 12** embroidered **Sat 13** made me a cap Sister Pulsifer came cooked for a family feast & blesing meeting I am yet lame do not wear a shoe yet but can walk a little **Sund 14 mond 15** Selah Lovlin came here washed for me[107] as I had commenced expecting another woman but she did not come John Staniford and Jo= Hyde came here after Selah after dinner I went up to P Gs with them **Tuesd 16** went to Davids Phebe fixed my dress and fitted another lining **wed 17** went over to Sylvias David not able to work **Thursd 18** he is better he came home with me I gave him some ^10 lb dried^ peaches 1 lb coffee 1*h* tea one old dress one pair of old pants 1 dollar cash sent Sylvia 1*h* ^lb^ tea **Frd 19** ironed **Sat 20** finished my dress **Sund 21** lame yet. have to stay at home from meeting I do hope I shall get so I can go next Sund **Mond 22** worked on another dress **Tuesd ^23^** work some in the garden **Wed 24** finished my dress **Thursd 25** put a curtain on my chair cusheon **Frid 26** ~~went up to p Gs with~~ worked in the garden **Satd 27** did up some caps **Sund 28** go to meeting for the first time for over two months I can walk and wear a shoe **Mond 29** went to Br Nebecars got some buds came home put them in **Tuesd 30** ^went to Joseph Risers funeral^ worked in the garden watered **Wed 31** the same went to Br Cannons got more buds put them in

---

107. Celia Lenora Simmons was a plural wife of Chester Loveland (1817–1886).

AUGUST 1861

Thursd August ^the^ 1st Alzinia Baptised went to fast meeting she was confirmed commenced a comforter for sister Tripp **Frd 2** went to Phebe Tripps with sister Grow and sister Riser on a visit **Sat 3** worked on the comforter **Sund 4** went to meeting **Mond 5** David ^Sessions^ Wm= & Martha Smoot Sylvia & Wilims here it rained very hard after the rain they all went home **Tuesd 6** I washed **wed 7** ironed **Thursd 8** went and setled my taxes got a botle of sweet oil **Frid 9** did up my caps and crotiaed on the comforter **Sat 10** baked pies and cake and worked the com=t **Sund 11** went to meeting P G Lu: Em= & Sarah down came here to supper Tripp came home his Brother Bartlett [Bartlett Tripp, 1839–1911] with him he has been out on the road to meet him I went up there to see him **Mond 12** they all came down here to see me had a good visit **Tuesd 13** finished the comforter commenced spining my foot is lame yet **Wed 14** Dr Richardsons wife here to see me **Thursd 15** watered my garden **Frd 16** finished my rolls what I have got cleaned my storeroom to store away my wheet **Sat 17** went to Br Nebecars and got some buds put them in then went up to P Gs with Tripp wife & his Br Bartlett to eat mellons **Sund <18>** came home **Mond 19** get some more rolls spun **Tuesd 20** the same **wed 21** finished them carried the wheel home Bartlett Tripp here took supper he is my Nephew **Thursd 22** prepared green corn for winter worked in the garden some wrote a letter to my sister Tripp **Frd 23** wrote a letter to my grandson Carlos Sessions washed some **Sat 24** carried my letter to the Office Bartlett came here to watch my fruit staid all night ^William & Martha here going up to her fathers P G Sessions^ **Sunday 25** go to meeting Bartlett here **Mond 26** he staid here all night P G here **Tuesd 27** ~~Bartlett staid all night again~~ baked pies worked in the garden **Wed 28** John ^Cottam^ or Young here making a wheet bin for me **Thursd 29** I worped a web for sister Grow **Frd 30** beamed it on for her **Satd 31** Young has finished my wheet bin

SEPTEMBER 1861

Sund Sept 1 ^1861^ do not go to meeting stay at home watch my fruit and keep it from being stole **Mond 2** bought twenty-five lb sugar gave eight dollars for it cash **Tuesd 3** spining **wed 4 Thursd 5 Frd 6** finished spining what rolls I have, I have not been very well P G & Selah Lovlin here **Sat 7** attended to my domestic conserns **Sunday 8** Wm= & Martha here **Mond 9** P G sent a man here for me to board while he works on the tabernacle or theater **Tuesd 10** cut Alzina a dress **Wed 11** finished making it **Thursd 12** water my garden **Frd 13** paired apples & strung to drye **Satd 14** washed Bart= here made me a ladder the man that P G sent here has finished and gone home **Sund 15** do not go to meeting **Mond 16** gathered my big plumbs **tuesd 17** cut apples to dry **Wed <18>** the same **Thurs 19** took my big plumb tithing up to ^Br^ Brigham Young ^got a letter from Carlos^ cut Alzinia a chimea **Frd ^20^**

Bartlett fixed a place for me to dry peaches **Satd 20** Wms Sylvia & Julia here Sylvia gone to Wm= Smoots **Sund 22** Wm= Martha & children & Sylvia came here **Mond 23** Wms= Sylvia & Julia gone home he has cut my hay put Phebe wife of E B Tripp to bed with a daughter Born 10- 3*h* **Tues 24** gave Sophia Tripps babe emetic then cut peaches to drye **Wed 25** the same **Thursd 26** washed **Frid 27** ironed **Sat 28** cut peaches bought a load of wood **Sund 29** do not go to meeting **Mond 30** Harriet Alzinas Mother came here ^brought me 10 lbs butter^

OCTOBER 1861

Tuesd Oct 1 1861 cut peaches **Wed 2** sold 13 bushels to James ^Dimond^ four bushels Aples Wms Sylvia here gone home it rains **Wed ^2^** cut peaches **Thursd 3** the same **Frid 4** washed **Sat 5** got my wood cut **Sund 6** confrence I do not go I have plenty of co **Mond 7** do not go **Tues 8** confrence ajourned **Wed 9 Thursd 10** Harriet has gone home Alzina has gone with her I have clothed her up well she has enough to last her more than one year I have kept her almost three years she is now almost nine years old now but I do not want her any longer **Fri 11** gathered some aples Bartlett Tripp helped me Elizabeth Tomas came here to help me **Sat 12 ^Sund 13^** do not go to meeting **Mond 14** work at my peaches gathering cuting and drying **Tuesd 15** the same **Wed 16** sold 20 bushels took 27 bushels wheet 60 lbs flour &c **Thursd 17 Fri 18** David wife & John Staniford here **Satd 19** seling peaches **Sund 20** do not go to meeting David Sylvia & Mary here ~~go~~ they go to meeting ^Wm=^ Martha Ann & children here yestday **Mond 21** have got my peaches gathered & the most of my aples **Tuesd 22 Wed 23** sold the most of my peaches Phebe here staid all night **Thursd 24** she has gone to Olives **Fri 25** my Aples all gathered I have bought three cord ^& half^ of wood ^2*h*^ this week **Satd 26** Mr [Edmund Lovell] Elsworth here doing some writing here **Sund 27** do not go to meeting **Mond 28** Mr Elsworth here again wrting I have made preserves he has done his writing and gone. my granery has overflowed and I have now to put it on my kitchen floor ~~Dav~~ David here his horse sick he staid all night **Tues 29** he has gone to big Cotten wood after lumber his horse well **Wed 30** I went & helped Sop[h]ia Tripp worp a web **Thursd 31** made preserves

NOVEMBER 1861

Frd Nov 1 1861 the same **Satd 2** finished gathered my fruit **Sund 3** I went to meeting **Mond 4** I have peaches yet **Tuesd 5** williams here g[a]thered my corn foder carried home the hayseed **wed 6** preparing for winter **Thursd ^7^** baked mince pies **Frd 8** Julia grow here visiting **Sat 9** the most of the neighbors have gone south that are going this faul **Sund 10** it snows the first we have had this faul I go to meeting **Mond 11** Bartlett Tripp commenced his school he came after school and fixed a place in the cellar to put my Aples

David came here staid all night **Tuesd 12** I put 16 bushels of Aples in the cellar Br Grow and wife here in the evening **wed 13** put 12 more in **Thursd 14** finished Br Gibs mittins **Frid 15** went up to town **Sat 16** had company Sister bessee Anthony Bessy & wife Tripp & wife & Bartlett **Sund 17** went to meeting **Mond 18** washed **Tuesd 19** (ironed <& did up my caps>) **wed 20** prepared many things for winter gave Mr Parry a bushel of Aples **Thud 21** mended and fixed my dresses **Frid 22** gave David a half a bushel Aples & Sylvia half a bushel **Satd 23** coullored red & blue Wm= & Martha here gave them half bushel Aples **Sund 24** they staid all night carried me up to meeting **Mond 25** I was kniting **Tuesd 26** it rained last night I wash to day ~~Joseph~~ sent two bushels more Aples up for tithing **wed 27** ironed worped a web for sister Grow **Thursd 28** drawed it in P G & Sarah here stay all night Emerett here **Frd 29** this morning they have gone up to town came back I went home with them it rained we hear from carlos he has froze his feet two more boys froze to death Carlos staid with his teams untill six of the oxen froze to death he then ran for life **Satd 30** still raining I went over to Davids wrote a letter to carlos with David & sent it by mail saw a letter from carlos in which he said if he had had to gone half a mile further he never could a got in

December 1861

Sund Dec= 1st it rains I staid last night with Sylvia John Young & wife & L[yman] O[mer] Littlefield [1819–1893] came up had a meetting in the afternoon in the evening had a meeting to P Gs I went over there staid all night **mond 2** I came home Wms & David & Josephine came home with me they went home she staid with me **Tuesd 3** I couloured some yarn to nit me a hood **Wed 4** went up to Tripps Josephine went with me it rained we came home it then snowed **Thursd 5** a heavy snow she went up to Tripps again to day I finished my hood **Frid 6** cold froze hard last night the snow covers the trees yet, the limbs are weighed down with it it sticks tight to them I went with Josephine and got our liknesses taken I gave her mine **Satd 7** she went home I moulded candles crotiaed me a neck tie **sund 8** went to meeting **Mond 9** finished moulding candles washed **Tuesd 10** ironed spining **Wed 11** Sylvia & the two litle girls here[108] Phebe staid with me **Thursd <12>** Davids wife & Elizya Cowly [Sarah Elizabeth Foss, wife of Mathias Cowley] here on a visit **Frd 13 Sat 14** I have been spining the most of this week **Sund 15** I went to meeting Phebe went with me **Mond 16** Sylvia here & P G Phebe did not want to go home **Tuesd 17** worped a web for sister Grow yestarday **wed 18** finished spining Phebe went home with David I commenced a muff for me **Thursd 19**

---

108. Phebe Jane Clark (b. 1852) and Martha Sylvia Clark (b. 1854) were Sylvia Sessions's daughters from her second marriage and they were, of course, Patty's grandchildren.

work on my muff it is such a one as I never saw before **Frid 20** finish my muff
Sat 21 sewing **Sund 22** went to meeting sister Nebicar here in the evening Mr
Parry and I went home with her **Mond 23** been sewing on Sylvias quilts got
one ready to quilt got some more rolls today **Tuesd 24** spining **wed 25** christmas I finish my rolls **Thursd 26** sewing **Frd 27** cuting carpet rags niting on Mr
Parrys mitings [mittens] **Satd 28** finished them Br Jenkins Williams and
Rachel Vaughn came here in the evening at seven P M Mr Parry married
them after they went away I was called to Br Gideon Gibs & wife mary put her
to bed with a daughter [Mary Isabella] born 10 minutes to 9 P M **Sund 29** I
went to meeting **Mond 30** sewing **Tuesd 31** the same

1862

sewed and did other things nessessary

JANUARY 1862

Wed Jan= 1 1862 Mr Parry here the most of the day **Thursd 2** called to
William Burges put his wife Cathrine to bed with a son [William Riley
Chamberlain] born 6 P M his wife Mariah also was put to bed by sister
Harrington 6 2*h* P M the same evening with a daughter **Frd 3** I was sewing
Satd 4 the same Bartlett Tripp here all day he staid all night **Sund 5** it has
snowed so much I do not go to meeting many sleighs runing **Mond 6** a mass
meeting held in tabernacle **Tues 7** I was sewing **Wed 8** the same **Thursd 9** the
snow is gone its very warm the ground not froze **Frd 10** washed worped a web
for sister Grow ^went to a lecture on grammer^ **Satd 11** ironed in the evening
the wind blew very hard rained and hailed thundered and lightened **Sund 12**
the ground covered with snow I do not go to meeting **Mond 13 Tuesd 14** cutting out peices for a quilt for Sylvia **wed 15** P G Mary, Emerett and Sarah and
Julia came down took me to a party at John Youngs we had a splendid supper
a good party came home in the morning they went home and in the evening I
hear that Lot Huntington is shot dead refusing to be taken prisoner[109] I was

---

109. Lot Elisha Huntington (b. 1834) was the second child of Dimick Baker
Huntington and Fannie Marie Allen. His death was related to Governor John
W. Dawson's leaving of Great Salt Lake City on 4 January 1862, earlier than his
planned departure at the close of the legislative session. A note stated simply,
"My health is such that my return to Indiana for the time being is imperatively
demanded; hence, I start this day" (see *History of Brigham Young 1847–1867*
[Berkeley, Calif.: MassCall Associates, 1964; second printing, 1966], 325).
Because he had alienated many Mormons, he hired a number of bodyguards to
accompany him. At Hanks Station he was beaten and robbed by nine or ten persons. Other passengers were robbed of clothes, blankets and other items important to their comfort while crossing the plains. On 8 January 1862 the *Deseret*

then sent for to go to Wm= Smoots I there put Martha Ann to bed with a daughter [Josephine] born Jan=17 1862 12 1h A M she was very poorly and I staid untill towards night when I was coming home I heard that 2 more were shot in trying to make their escape after they were taken prisoners and brought to the city viz Moroni Clwson & John Smith **Satd 18** I go and see Lot at his Fathers it is very warm and wet underfoot I have bought more lumber in all fifty five dollars worth paid for it in Aples **Sund 19** it is so wet underfoot I do not go to meeting Julia has been here ever since the party Bartlett staid here last night has gone to meeting **Mond 20** I have washed and been at the Bishops and setled my tithing $81=85 for last year **Tuesd 21 Wed 22** Sylvia and williams here to dinner Weston fixed my fence I bake mince pies **Thursd 23** sewed and did other things nessesary **Frid 24** set up the loom sized my web **Satd 25** spooled my web **sund 26** went to meeting **mond 27** worped my web and one for Sophia Tripp beemed mine on **Tuesd 28** drawed it in wove 1 -2h yard then Sulvia came here and we tied a comforter **Wed 29** she staid all night and I went home with her staid all night at P Gs **Thursd 30** went to Davids Phebe cut me a dress then went to P Gs put Lucinia to bed with a daughter [Lucina] born [*left blank*] to 12 **Frid 31** came home went and put Ezra Bullards wife Mary to bed with a daughter [Mary Ellen] born 11- 3h P M

FEBRUARY 1862

Satd Feb= 1st wove 1 2h yards and attended to other concerns **Sund 2** went to meeting **Mond 3** weaving **Tuesd 4** my birthday sixty seven years old **wed 5 Thursd 6** went to a pic nic party of high priests at the social hall Brigham Heber & Danil were there we had a good party **Frd 7** I have been weaving **Satd 8** sister Buel here cut out a part of my web for Mr Parry I have made him some cloth for pants & drawers **Sund 9** went to meeting **Mond 10** Weaving **Tuesd 11** put Harriet [Mr. Parry's wife] to bed with a son [Henry Edward] born 5 & 20 mints A M **Wed 12** Bartlett Tripp came here to board last satd 8 **Thursd 13 Frd 14 Sat 15** Birch paid me 21 bushels wheat 2 corn got my web out 50 yards gave Mr Parry 5 yards **Sund 16** went to meeting **Mond 17** Sewing

News reported, "We are informed that a communication from Governor Dawson has been received by a gentleman residing in this city, in which he states that there were nine or ten persons in the gang, and among the names of the assaulting party as given by him, are some of the individuals who were in his retinue when he left the city, and reported to have been hired by him as guards," ("Disgraceful Outrage," 11:221). Among those arrested in connection with the crime were Lot Huntington, Moroni Clawson, and John P. Smith. In Rush Valley, while trying to escape, Huntington drew his gun and was shot dead. The other two were killed as they attempted to escape from police officers who had taken them into custody in Salt Lake City. Moroni Clawson (b. 1839) was the oldest child of Moses Clawson and Cornelia Brown.

DIARY SIX, 1862–1880

This diary covers the time period from 18 February 1862 through 1866 and a short period in 1880. Patty's life moves along at its accustomed rate with its accustomed activities. She does illuminate a few important events during this period. For the most part, however, she focuses on what she is doing.

Alice James recognized the same characteristics in herself when she wrote,

> *You must remember that a woman, by nature needs much less to feed upon than a man, a few emotions and she is satisfied: so when I am gone, pray don't think of me simply as a creature who might have been something else. . . . Notwithstanding . . . my outside experience, I have always had a significance for myself, and every chance to stumble along my straight and narrow little path, and to worship at the feet of my Deity, and what more can a human soul ask for?[1]*

Of course, Alice became an invalid at a very young age so her life does not parallel Patty's in any way. But Patty was largely concerned with herself and her own doings. Although she cared enough about other people to name them in her diaries, it was their impact on her environment and personal well-being that she generally described. Nevertheless, Patty's own "doings" continued to impact the community and individuals whose lives mingled with hers. Despite the fact that her profession of midwifery was winding down, she continued to contribute to the welfare of others with her fruit farming, land development, support of education, and activity in the benevolent Relief Society. Unquestionably Patty's life, as told in her diaries, reflected, chronicled, and contributed to the growing economic and social life of the community.

---

1. Alice James, quoted in Mary Jane Moffat and Charlotte Painter, *Revelations: Diaries of Women* (New York: Vintage Books, 1975), 194.

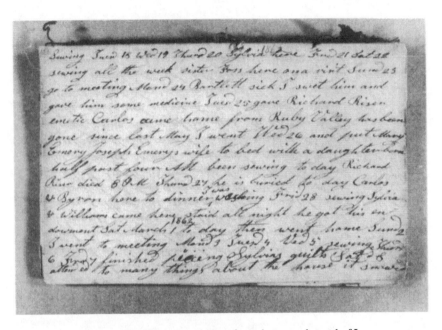

Diary six picks up at 18 February 1862 and continues to the end of January 1866. This is again a homemade diary of white, lined paper, folded over and stitched together. It had a cardboard cover of deep purple (almost black), but the front is missing, and the back is tattered. The size is roughly 8 x 5 inches. Patty used more punctuation marks during these years, probably due to her attendance at "Grammar School." There are four sections of folded paper, each one stitched in the middle; then they have all been tacked together in the middle. The remaining back cover is tacked on as well. The entries from 4 July 1880 to 24 August 1880 appear on a separate sheet of paper, slightly larger than those in Diary 6. The ink is brown. Courtesy of LDS Church Archives; photograph by J M Heslop.

1862

The watter is in my cellar and keeps gaining

FEBRUARY 1862

Sewing **Tuesd 18 Wed 19 Thursd 20** Sylvia here **Frd 21 Sat 22** sewing all the week sister Foss here on a visit **Sund 23** go to meeting **Mond 24** Bartlett sick I swet him and gave him some medicine **Tuesd 25** gave Richard Riser emetic[2] Carlos came home from Ruby Valley has been gone since last May I went **Wed 26** and put Mary Emery Joseph Emerys wife to bed with a daughter born half past four A M been sewing to day Richard Riser died 8 P M **Thursd 27** he is buried to day Carlos & Byron here to dinner ^I was washing^ **Frid 28** sewing Sylvia & Williams came here staid all night he got his endowment

MARCH 1862

Sat March 1 ^1862^ to day then went home **Sund 2** I went to meeting **Mond 3 Tuesd 4 Wed 5** sewing **Thursd 6 Frd 7** finished piecing Sylvias quilts **Sat 8** attended to many things about the house it snowd last night and it is very bad walking to day **Sund 9** do not go to meeting to day **Mond 10** sewing **Tuesd 11** put in a quilt for Sylvia **Wed 12** got it out **Thursd 13** sewing **Frid 14** washed **Satd 15** ironed carded some cotton it snowed last night warm to day very bad traveling mud and watter plenty Bartlett Tripp wished me to go to the theatre but the roads are so bad I cannot go[3] **sund 16** I went to meeting **Mond 17** carded cotten **Tuesd 18** finished carding David came down after me to go up there his babe was sick, I went up found very sick. **Wed 19** went to Sylvias and P Gs went back to Davids again staid all night. **Thursd 20** the child appears better I came home. **Frd 21** knitting Mr Parry a comforter and some wristers. **Satd** ^22^ baked Carlos here he went to the Theater, I went with Bartlett.[4] **Sund 23** went to meeting, saw Martha and Wm=. **Mond 24** I have been writing a piece to carry to the Grammar school went to the school the school closed this evening. **Tuesd, 25** I was called to go and give sister Russell an emetic I went and gave it to her **Wed. 26.** my tooth aches very bad, ^I^ hear from sister Russell she is better. Last Mond. the 25 1862 I went up

---

2. Richard Riser was the son of George C. and Sophia Christiana Kull Riser. He was born in 1852.
3. The Salt Lake Theatre, situated on the corner of State Street and First South, was begun on 1 July 1861 and opened for temporary use on 5 March 1862. Its capacity was fifteen hundred and its cost more than $100,000.
4. The first shows were *Pride of the Market* and *State Secrets*.

to Prs-d. Youngs. Office. Gave him one hundred and seventy five dollars cash for him to use until I called for it. ~~He went to the last Grammar school Tuesd 25 sewed carpets~~ **Thursd 27** my tooth still aches **Frd 28** do not sit up but little **Satd 29** I am quite sick Martha and William here last Thusd wanted me to go to P Gs with them I was so feble I could not go William here again to day Bartlett has gone up to P Gs **Sund 30** P G Mary & John Staniford came here Mary gave me a sweat and an emetic **Mond 31** I am better P G & John commences my granery

APRIL 1862

Tuesd April 1 1862 Wed 2 P G goes home it has snowed the most of the time since they came down Wms Sylvia and Josephine came down went to the theater went home John has gone home with David to day ^**thurd**^ **3** the weather is so bad he cannot work Mary has gone up to E B Tripps Mary came back tonight **Frd 4 Satd 5** Mary has washed and ironed yestarday and to day **Sund 6** I went and put George Russells wife to bed with a son born 5 A M confrence Mary sick I not well enough to go **Mond 7 Tuesd 8 wed 9** conference ajourned **Thurd 10** P G Lucina & Carlos here got some trees **Frd 11** Williams and Sylvia here got trees Bartlett Tripp closed his school to day **Satd 12** I set out some big strawbery vines John [probably Parry] came yestarday noon worked in the afternoon and to day **Sund 13** he went to meeting I did not go it rained **Mond** ^**14**^ I commenced roping my cotton rolls **Tuesd th 14** I washed then went to the theater **wed 16** finished roping my rolls **Thursd 17** commenced spining I had company my class mates in grammar spent the evening here Phebe Tripp here and a sister Gardner from Payson **Frd 18** she left here **Satd 19** I am spining **Sund 20** I went to meeting **Mond 21** John Stanifird finished my granery and went home **Tuesd 22** I finished spining my cotten **Wed 23** I put in a quilt for Sylvia **Thursd 14** quilted it out **Frd 25** Sophia and Jesess Tripp here visiting **Satd 26** I worked in the garden **Sund 27** went to meeting **Mond 28** made Bartlett an overshirt **Tued 29** worked in the garden **Wed 30** went to see Martha Ann Smoot went to the paper mill saw make paper

MAY 1862

Thursd May ^**1st**^ **1862** I worked in the garden **Frd 2** made Bartlett another overshirt **Satd 3** worked in the garden got my wheet out of the kitchen in to my granery cleaned the kitchen &c. **Sund 4** I went to meeting **Mond 5** I worked in the garden **Tuesd 6** Bartlett went up to P G's to day **wed 7** he helped me put down some layers round my Apple trees. **Thurd 8** Sister Higbee here had a good visit **Frid 9 Satd 10** worked in the garden **Sund 11** I went to meeting **Mond 12** put in a quilt for Sylvia **Tuesd 13** P G & David came after me to go up there thier children sick Perry was very sick **Wed 14** I was caled to sister Cooks ^her^ child very sick **Thursd 15** rained think Perry better I came home **Frd 16** I gave the boys that are going to the states after the poor 13 lb dried peaches and two quarts of beans[5] got the quilt out **Satd 17** made me some caps **Sund 18** went to meeting **Mond 19** washed **Tuesd 20** ironed cut Bartlet some shirts **Wed 21** worked on them **Thursd 22** finished them got him a pair of pants made Martha here yestarday Wm= and his Mother here P G here to day **Frd 23** ^Josepine came here^ spining **Satd 24** the same **Sund 25** went to meeting in the afternoon **Mond 26** Br Gibs here fixing my granery **Tuesd 27** watered a little Josepine went home I went up to E[noch] B[artlett]s **wed 28** the water is so high we are afraid we shall be all washed away[6] **Thurd 29** I was up the most of the night watching it **Frd 30** I did not go to bed last night this morning it came within one inch of runing to my door I hired a man to work and bank up my fence and build an embankment across the side walk to keep the water from washing my ^house^ away Davids wife came here **Sat 31** watched all all night again Phebe went home I have got the embankment done but we are none of us safe on neither side of the street there has been a great many men at work night and day all this week to keep the water from washing our houses and lots away it is higher than my floor in the street and is rising

JUNE 1862

Sund June ^1862^ 1st I do not go to meeting the men work all day banking up to keep the water in the street **Mond 2** I did not go to bed last night **Tuesd 3** the same **wed 4** no better **Thursd 5** I have not had my clothes of since Mond night we think the water is faling a little I undress and go to bed **Frd 6** I had a good sleep lie in bed the most of the night **Sat 7** rains hard untill noon then the sun

---

5. By 1861 it was decided to send "church trains" east to bring back immigrants and goods. In 1862, 262 wagons carrying 143,315 pounds of flour, 2,880 oxen, and 293 men made the round trip, bringing approximately three thousand immigrants, as well as an undetermined amount of machinery (see Leonard Arrington, *Great Basin Kingdom* [Lincoln: University of Nebraska Press, 1958], 206, 211).

6. On 26 May 1862 the "Journal History of The Church of Jesus Christ of Latter-day Saints" reported, "The Jordan overflowed its banks and the water reached up to the Warm Springs Lakes. The ground which was now covered with water had been dry for many years" ([hereafter cited as JH], Archives of the Historical Department, Church of Jesus Christ of Latter-day Saints, Salt Lake City). On 28 May the JH quoted from the *History of Brigham Young: 1847–1867* (Berkeley, CA: MassCall Associates, 1964 and 1966): "The 4th, 6th and 7th Wards turned out all hands to save the upper bridge over Jordan; by which bridge many herds go out. The herds in coming home by Jordan bridge (on North Temple Street) have all had to swim in consequence of the little bridge 1/4 mile from the Jordan being submerged." On 4 June, "President Young was having some of the Temple foundation taken up. The water in City Creek had washed under President Heber C. Kimball's bridge to his mill. The water from the creek had also washed out the

came out the water high the men are still at work opening the chanel and it keeps filing up I have spun all my rolls **Sun** [*written over* at] 8 I do not go to meeting fighting the watter all day **Mond 9** the same Bartlett has gone up north to P Gs **Tuesd 10** I staid alone last night I slept but litle **Wed 11** staid alone again P G here yestarday David here to day water rising T Cottom has moved out of his house and Wm= Morse is moving Bartlett has got home Mr Parry cannot get here the watter is so high **Thursd 12** I undresed last night and went to bed but was up many times slept but little **Frid 19** it ^is^ very cold and it rains on the mountains allmost all the time **Satd 14** it rains very fast David came after me to go to P Gs wife Sarah she is sick put her to to bed with a son [James Crossley] born 5 P M I then came home it rained all the way up there and back **Sund 15** the water very high **Sund 22** we all upon this street have done but litle else the past ^3^ weeks but fight water my lots have been all nearly under water the past week and some other lots the same this morning I sent for P G & David they came Carlos and Jim with them they brought two load of brush and have done a good job P G and Carlos have gone home David and Jim stay all night ^get another load of brush^ **Mond 23** [*written twice, once smeared*] the water higher than ever David and Jim gone home this after noon they think I will be safe a few days and they say they will come again if I send for them **Tuesd 24** I send for them again they four came again brought two load of brush they all work untill after dark and before they all went to bed it burst out again and they all worked and all night Bartlett worked with them night and day they get two load more brush to day **wed 25** they work night and day Wms Sylvia and Joseph^ (ine^ came down he helped move my wheet to the tithing Office 1-69-bushels 20 lbs lent him seven bushels ^wheet^ untill faul **Thursd 26** ^get two load brush^ begin to think I need not move out my things are all packed to move, to night P G carlos & Jim go home David stays with me gets another load of brush ~~cut~~ I have a man beside to work for me yesterday and to day **Frd 27** Mr Parry sick sends for me David carries me down to see him he came home with us feels some better David has gone home to night Bartlett stays with me all the time I have paid out $16 Dollars beside what my boys have done and Bartlett and I have worked and watched all the time night and day found candles lumber and logs and poles and I am still in fear that my house will fall down the watter is in my cellar and keeps gaining **Satd 28** Mr Parry better the watter high yet we have to watch it yet **Sund 29** do not go to meeting the water gaining in my

street nearly to Albert Carrington's house on the northeast side of the Temple Block. The people were trying to save the street by building dams." And on 9 June, "The water sects in the city were booming; most of the bridges had to be taken up to let the flood wood pass. The Jordan River was still rising rapidly. Brother John Pulsipher's house, one and half stories high, had been washed down."

cellar **Mond 30** three of Brighams men came here this morning work almost all day here in front of my house on the side walk

JULY 1862

Tuesd July 1 ^st^ **1862** the water is falling I think it is setled one inch in my cellar Mr Parry has gone home on Sund night [Oscar] Winters [1825–1903] & wife she that was P P Pratts wife [Mary Ann Frost (Stearns)] came here from Sandpete staid all night **Wed 2** the water rises in the cellar **Thursd 3** I have put in a quilt and got it out the first work I have done of the like for six weeks it is more than six weeks since I have lain in my bed all night, and many nights that I have not undresed me at all but sit up and watched the water all night last night we thought it would break over the levee in spite of us but it did not and the water is faling again in the cellar **Frid 4** last night is the first night I have lain all night in bed for more than six weeks the water is high this morning I go up to the bowery to the celebration of the independance of America[7] I went with Bartlett spent the time very agreeablely it caused me to think of the past and to reflect upon the presant scenery before us war and bloodshed in the states [the Civil War] but peace in Deseret **Satd 5** the water is faling a little **Sund 6** I went to meeting **Mond 7** the water is still in my cellar **Tuesd 8** I wash **Wed 9** iron bake &c **Thurd 10** making me a dress **Frd 11 Satd 12** finish my dress **Sund 13** go to meeting **Mond** ^14^ work in my garden Bartlett has been to American fork got home last night sold his horse to day **Tuesd 15** work in the garden **Wed 16** hear that Bartletts Sister Susan [Tripp, b. 1836] will be in this evening or in the morning Bartlett has gone to meet her he missed her she got in this evening **Thurd 17** he got back rode about 20 miles and came back I went up to E Bs saw her they all came down here staid all day E B wife Bartlett Susan and husband [Charles Flanagan] and teamster I was glad to see them but feel sorry that they are going to callifornia **Frd 18** they brought their horses here E B has nothing to feed them with I have a plenty Flanigan Susan's husband has been here to day twise Susan has been here this evening **Satd 19** they have taken the horses to day all four of them over Jordon to recruit them a little I have knit Mr Parry a pair of gallosis this week **Sund 20** I went to meeting **Mond 21** baked and worked in the garden Susan and Husband here stay all night **Tuesd 22** they ^stay^ all day and all night

---

7. The celebration included artillery fire at sunrise, flags flying and bands playing at different locations, and a promenade through the principal streets to the Bowery. After Ballo's Band played "The Star-Spangled Banner," John Taylor offered the invocation, followed by the reading of the Declaration of Independence. More band music preceded a lengthy oration, a poem by Eliza R. Snow, a historical address, and two other short addresses, one of them by President Brigham Young. Invited guests attended a luncheon. In the evening a ball was held at the Social Hall.

again I go up to Davids he came after me his wife is sick **Wed 23** I do not come home she has a son [Fabyan Carter] born yestard 3 oclock P M **Thurd 24** I came home went to the aniversary 15 years ago today that the Pioneers came to this Valley[8] **Frid 25** I have washed ironed and baked to day Bartlett and Flanigan is puting up my hay **Satd 26** I have been cooking Susan came here staid all night P G and Mary here stay all night and James is going home to Ogdon he staid all night **Sund 27** I do not go to meeting Susan stays with me her husband came here **Mond 28** I pull weeds in the garden P G here Susan gone home with him her husband and Bartlett was going up there but one of Bartletts Mules got loose and went over Jordon **Tuesd 29** they went up this morning I pull weeds the most of the day **Wed 30** the same **Thursd 31** the same

August 1862

Frd August 1st 1862 Bartlett Flanigan and wife all came home **Sat 2** I go up to ^E B^ Tripps **Sund 3** I went to meeting took dinner at E B Tripps Bartlett went to meeting with me in the afternoon ~~Mond 4~~ they get up thier horses to start for Callifornia **Mond 4** got them shod **Tuesd 5** they all start for Callifornia Flanigan and wife and Bartlett I went over Jordon with them Bartlett has been here with me six Months lacking three days I gave him his board and horse keeping he gave me some few things did some little work fore but no charge made by Either of us, he said I had been a mother to him and it was hard parting I felt bad to see them go but ^I^ feel that my garments are clear if they never come back or I never see them again they talk of coming back in the spring, **Wed 6** I have prepared to quilt to quilt **Thurd 7** I went up in town **Frd 8** quilted the quilt for Sylvia **Satd 9** set out some strawbery vines **Sund 10** went to meeting hear that Bartlett was Baptised before he left on sund 3d inst **Mond 11** make me a peticoat and air my ~~things~~ clothes **Tued 12** put in some buds **Wed 13** wash Uncle J Young here lent him 3 Bushl wheet and 1- ^lb^ 100 flour **Thusd 14** ironed made me a cap Carlos and J Poorman here to dinner Dimics wife [Fanny Maria Allen (Huntington)] here **Frid 15** sewing **Satd 16** the same ^got a yard made^ **Sund 17** went to meeting **Mond 18** worked in the garden **Tuesd 19** went to Dimics put Namas [Naomi Gibson] ^Huntington^ Lots ^Huntington^ wife to bed with a daughter born 12 minutes past one P M **Wed 20** visited her again **Thursd 21** went up to ^E B^ Tripps to see Susannah Richards **Frd 22** Sisters Buel

---

8. This celebration to some degree resembled that of Independence Day. However, church authorities led the procession, and all of the wards were represented with marchers and banners. According to the report in the *Deseret News,* five thousand people were assembled in the Bowery, and many others, who could not find shade, moved about outside. President Brigham Young was the concluding speaker.

Susannah and Jesess Tripp here **Satd 23** I have been to see Nomas again she is smart **Sund 24** I went to meeting ~~Mond 15~~ Nomas is worse is worse again **Mond <25>** she is better **Tuesd 26** she is quite smart **wed 24** I went to sister Gibs to a quilting **Thurd 28** I went and paid my taxes then helped her quilt again **Frd 29** put in some rose buds **Satd 30** got some lumber and shingles **Sund 31** do not go to meeting David and Phebe and children sister Foss and Olive all here after meeting

September 1862

Mond Sept 1st 1862 cut some Aples to dry **Tuesd 2 Wed 3** Harriet Kimball here <I made me a black cap> **Thursd 4** I went up to town carried some Aples & plumbs to sister Ruff got some Nails **Frd 5** Wms Sylvia & David here to dinner I had washed **Satd 6** starched & ironed did me up a cap **Sund 7** do not go to meeting have to watch my fruit the pickets get tore off of my fence and my fruit stole if I am gone away I have been in to see sister Pace she has a cancer I carried her some of my big plumbs and gave her Wm and Martha Ann here **Mond 8** ~~had~~ ^having^ a new roof put on my house **Tuesd 9** mary Elen Kimbal here I have been to sister Russels **Wed 10** Mary Elen staid all night to night she has gone to her sisters **Thursd 11** Br Gibs works on the house **Frd 12** sent more plumbs to sister Ruff **Sat 13** finish my house Sent for to go to Tomas Winegars I put his wife to bed with a son [Samuel Thomas][9] **Sund 14** do not go to meeting Carlos here to eat fruit Sisters Nebecar and Fitsgurl [Fitzgerald?] here **Mond 15** went to sister Buels she anointed my arm and laid hands on me it was very lame **Tuesd 16** to work preparing to dry my fruit **wed ^17^** Sylvia ^&^ Martha Ann here and many others **Thursd 18** commenced drying peaches **Frd 19** worked on a harness for sister Spencer **Satd 20** finished it **Sund 21** do not go to meeting **Mond 22** Harriet Sessions here and [*At this point there are five lines of text scratched out:*] ~~Worse Mon 25 she is better Tuesd 26 she is better Thursd 28 I go up to town settle my taxes Wed 27 went to a quilting at Br Gibs Thusd 28 went again helped her quilt Fri 29 put in some rose buds Sat 30 got some lumber and shingles Sat 30 bake and clean~~ her Father stay all night **Tuesd 23** ^he is^ gone home she has gone to P Gs **Wed 24** cuting peaches to dry **Thursd 25** the same **Frd 26** I took 13 qts of the honey plumbs up to the Brigham Young for tithing I gave the first Presdcy ^Pres^ a qt each beside **Sat 27** drying fruit and making preserves **Sund ^28^** do not go to meeting Wm= and Martha here left Anna with me[10] **Mond 29** cuting peaches **Tuesd 30** the same

---

9. Rachel Jane Kilfoyle (1843–1892) was the wife of Samuel Thomas Winegar (1840–1874).

10. Probably Martha Ann, born on 10 September 1854.

October 1862

wed Oct 1 1862 Thursd 2 Frid 3 Satd 4 attending to my fruit **Sund 5** ^Anne went home^ do not go to meeting Carlos here yestarday helped me gather some Aples I have gathered many of them through the week **Mond 6** conference I do not go I am taking care of my fruit **Tuesd 7** the same P G & Emerett staid here last night **Wed 8** conference ajourned **Thurd 9** seling peaches **frid 10 Satd 11** the same **Sund 12** do not go to meeting **Mond 13** bye fifty pound butter and about the same of cheese **Tuesd 14 Wed 15 Thurd 16 Frd 17** I have worked very hard gathering and seling my peaches. **Satd. 18** got up well eat breakfast well and while washing my dishes I was taken with the cramp in my stomack I was alone but I saw a little girl in the street I called to her and sent her for sister Russell she came and soon many more. The Elders administered to me again and again but the destroyer would not let go his hold untill evening. John Parry came in took me by the hands I beged of him to pray for me and exercise mig^h^ty faith if my work was done that I might die easy, if it was not done that the Lord would heal me. He said I should get well see many good days and do much good, And when he said that I should do much good I began to revive and soon spoke loud. He told me to be anointed all over and have a number of Elders come in and lay hands on me and I would be better Zina Young was here she washed and anointed me she said I should get up in the morning well the Elders laid hands on me I slept good all night got up in the morning well with the exception of weakness and soreness. **Sund 19** I have set up the most of the time to day. many that saw me yestarday are astonished to see me so well and go out doors & in as usual. David and Carlos here gathered some Aples. **Mond 20** Brs Leonard & Thurston [Moses, husband of Lucy Jane Leonard] and their wives here to see me they expected to find me but just alive but they found me in the garden. **Tuesd 21 Wed 22 Thurd 23 Frd 24** I have attended to my domestic concerns finished gathering my peaches and sold them all out. The Lord has healed me and blessed be his name, I desire so to live that I may do good and gloryfy my Father which is in heaven **Sat 25** attend to my concerns **Sund 26** do not go to meeting **Mond 27 Tuesd 28 wend 29** I do not feel strong yet but I am able to attend to my work and I feel thankful for that **Thurd 30** get my washing done out of the house **Frd 31** taking care of my dried peaches

November 1862

Satd Nov= 1 ^1862^ I go with sister Buel wash and anoint sister Gray at Sister Russells **Sund 2** ^William & Martha here^ do not go to meeting **Mond 3** knitting some little socks for Julia Grow **Tued 4 Wed 5** finish 5 pair **Thurd 6** David here stay all night Carlos has been here **Frd 7** puting in a web for sister Winegar **Satd 8** finish puting it in and go and help Sophia Tripp worp a web sell $2500 worth of trees to George Peacock **Sund 9** do not go to meeting **Mond 10** Anna Alen came here to stay a week with me I told her Mother I would give her a weeks board **Tuesday 11 Wed 12 Thurd 13** she goes to Find another place but came back again **Frd 14** I wash **Satd 15** I have been preparing for winter I have put a part of my Aples down cellar **Sund 16** go to meeting **Mond 17** sewing **Tuesd 18** spining **wed 19** fix sister Spencers loom and harness Br Pulsipher starts for the cotton country Br Grow has moved away **Thurd 20** plant Aple seeds Mr Parry helped me **Frd 21** went up to town **Satd 22** worped sister Spencers web and beamed it on and David & wife Carlos and Josephine came here and I came home got dinner then went up to the grave-yard took the grave stone and put them up to Mr Sessions grave carried 2 bushels Aples up to town sold them to sister Ruff for eight Dollars Anne has gone to her Mothers sais she does not want to go away from me to live she wants to come back and live with me **Sund 23** I do go to meeting **Mond 24** Anne came back last night **Tuesd 25 wed 26** I have put sister Spencers web in set it to work strung the loom and harness got it to work good **Thurd 27** prepared some yarn for Mr Parry some mittens **Frd 28 Sat 29** niting **Sund 30** I go to meeting

December 1862

Mond Dec ^1st 1862^ Finish Mr Parrys mittens **Tuesd 2 Wed 3** baking pies ^Tripp paid me 12 dollars^ **Thurd 4** Sylvia brought down some yarn for Wms= some mittins **Frd 5** nitting **Satd 6** P G & Lucinia came down wished me to go down to Wm Smoots with them I went **Sund 7** I wen we came home **Mond 8** finished Br Williams mittens. Nit Martha Anns babe some socks **Tuesd 9** finished them three pair Wms & Sylvia here to supper Mr Parry and I went up to the concert in the tabernacle **Wed 10** a little snow this morning then some rain I have mended some Attended to many things **Thurd 11** the same **Frd 12** snows **Satd 13** I went to meeting it snowed in the afternoon ^**Sund 14**^ **Mond 15** crotiaing a cusheon curtain **Tuesd 16** I went home with P G staid there all night **Wed 17** went to Davids then to Sylvias took dinner there spent the Evening to Davids staid all night to P Gs came home **Thurd 18** with Br Williams & Sylvia went up to town they came here staid all night I went up to town with him to day ^**Frd 19**^ carried up 3 bushels of Aples sold them to Sister Ruff they are gone home **Satd 20** finished my chair curtain baked mince pies. **Sund 21** I went to meeting this evening wrote a letter to Bartlett **Mond 22** he came home **Tuesd 23** he came here **Wed 24** I prepared my yarn for weaving scoured it **Thurd 25** christmas Bartlett and Mr Parry here to dinner Bartlett and Br Green staid here all night **Frid 26** Bartl= and I went to see Br Gibs he has been sick a long [time] I went to sister Buels got a reed to weave my web in came home sized my web **Satd ^27^** spooled and warped it. David and Bartl= staid here all night **Sund 28** it snows I do not go to meeting they are gone **Mond 29** drawed in my web **Tuesd 30** wove **Wed 31** went up to P Gs with Williams and Sylvia Bartlett went up with us staid all night to P Gs it snows

1863

have been taking care of my fruit the most of the time

JANUARY 1863

Jan ^1st^ 1863 new year P G invited a house full we had a good party **Frd 2** we came home **Satd 3** I wove 3 yards **Sund 4** went to meeting **Mond 4 Tuesd 5** weaving went and put Julia Grow to bed with a daughter [Mary Ann] born 2 1*h* A M **Wed 7 Thursd 8** got my web out **Frid 9** washed **Satd 10** baked went up to town carried 4 bushels Aples to sister Ruff went with P G **Sund 11** went to meeting **Mond 12** ^**Tuesd 13**^ P G & Warner here to dinner then they went to ^hear^ O Pratt lecture on Astronomoy ^P G^ staid here all night I went home with him **Wensd 14** I went to Sylvias staid all night to P Gs **Thursd 15** I went to Davids with P G Lucinia & Emerett and Sylvia & Williams staid all night at P Gs **Frid 16** went to Sylvias Mary & Sarah there staid all night at P Gs **Satd 17** came home with Carlos and Josephine they go to the Theatre then to Wm= Smoots **Sund 18** I do not go to meeting it is to snoey last week I knit a pair of double mitins for Br Cole I have bought a calveskin of him gave three Dollars for it let him have two pair of socks and one pair of mittens the rest in Barley Carlos and Josephine gone home. **Mond 19** I have been and setled my tithing found due me seven Dollars Paid $87=52 **Tuesd 20** made some aprons **Wed 21** did many things in the evening Carlos came after me to go up there to ^see^ Emorett she is not well **Thursd 22** it snows in the evening 1=00 soldiers came there to P Gs ^going to fight the Indians^ stoped over night got supper and breakfast for sixty or seventy ~~at~~ of them[11] Emerett was sick all day. **Thursd 22** I put her to bed with a son

---

11. On 29 January 1863 a detachment of soldiers from Fort Douglas under the command of Colonel Patrick Connor attacked Indians camped on the Bear River fifteen miles north of Franklin, Idaho. Reports of the number of Indians killed vary greatly. Some ninety Indian women alone were killed during or after the battle, some of them, according to contemporary accounts, while resisting or after rape. Fourteen soldiers died in battle, and two later succumbed from wounds. What modern historians call the "Bear River Massacre" largely stopped depredations of the Bannocks and Snakes on emigrants in northern Utah. Colonel Connor's official report that "in my march from this post no assitance was rendered by the Mormons . . ." is contradicted by Patty Sessions's diary, as well as other contemporary records (see Brigham H. Roberts, *A Comprehensive History of the Church,* 6 vols. [Provo, Utah: Brigham Young University Press, 1965], 5:31–35 and JH, 26 and 29 January 1863).

  Brigham D. Madsen's account of the massacre adds up-to-date information in "Encounter with the Northwestern Shoshoni at Bear River in 1863: Battle or Massacre?" (Dello G. Dayton Memorial Lecture at Weber State College, Ogden, Utah, 11 May 1983). Madsen gives even more details in *The Shoshoni Frontier and the*

[Sylvanus] born 11 P M **Frd 23** I came home **Sat 24** crotiaed me a neck tie **Sund 25** it snows I do not go to meeting **Mond 26** went up to town got several things out of the store **Tuesd 27** quilting Sylvias quilt ^Bart[lett] here staid all night^ **Wed 28** got it out commenced Mr Parry a pair of socks **Thursd 29** washed and went and warped a web for sister Spencer **Frd 30** David here brought me a pair boots he had made for me **Satd 31** ^I went to town got many things^ have been piecing a quilt for Sylvia she and Williams and Lucinia here to supper then went home

FEBRUARY 1863

Feb= 1 ^**1863**^ **Sund** I went to meeting Bartlett here staid all night **Mond 2** Jesess here I show her how to plad her dress and how to spool it I work on Sylvias quilt **Tuesd 3** the same **Wed 4** my birthday sixty eight years old Bartlett here staid all night **Thursd 5** Lucinia David & Byron here to supper then went home P G came here eat supper staid all night To day they have burried the soldiers that was killed by the Indians in the war **Frd 6** P G has gone to Barnards trial **Satd 7** I have been to work on Sylvias quilt all this week I go up to town get some dyestufs **Sund 8** go to meeting then go with Joseph Parry and wife to John Parrys. **Mond 9** finish Peicing the quilt **Tuesd 10** work on my cap border **wed <11>** the same **wed Thursd 12** attend to many things **Frid <13>** snows **Satd 14** Josephine here and Bartlett they go to the theatre **Sund 15** we go to meeting Josephine went up to Prsd Youngs after meeting **Mond 16** I wash Julia here we went up to Bartletts school in the evening[12] P G & the Bishop here to dinner **Tuesd 17** it snows I iron Julia went up to Phebe Tripps came back here staid all

---

Bear River Massacre (Salt Lake City: University of Utah Press, 1985). Controversy still swirls about the place where the massacre occurred. An Associated Press story from Preston, Idaho, noted in early December 1995 that the National Park Service was suggesting National Historic Site designation for roughly 144 acres of the 1,600 acres that encompass the site, a move staunchly opposed by many of the twenty-eight different property holders. Giving the number of Shoshoni Indians massacred as from 250 to 400, the press release says, "It was the largest single-day loss of American Indian life in the frontier West." In 1990 the area was designated a National Historic Landmark ("Landowners Don't Want Site to Get National Historic Status," *Deseret News*, 17 December 1995, B8.)

12. According to the "Autobiography of Joseph F. Horne," "About the year 1863 and 1864 Bartlet Tripp, who was among the best educators we had in those times, taught what was termed an 'Advance School,' being ahead of the ordinary Ward Schools in the several Wards of the City. This school was popular and much appreciated. . . . He had been teaching in the 14th Ward School House where we had previously been school boys, and where we wanted to attend school–being residents of that ward. He informed us that he had decided to remove his school to another and smaller building and would have only the higher grades; he feared there would not be room for us" (pp. 3–4, mimeographed copy, #331Ms93, Western Americana Division, University of Utah Library, Salt Lake City).

night again **wed 18** she went up to sister Pratts **Thurd 19** P G came down after her she went home I went up to town. I went to see a child of Hugh Evens it was dying **Frd 20** I went there again Josepine came here again went to Bartletts school again in the evening she staid here all night **Satd 21** Sylvia and Williams came here took Josephine home **Sund 22** it snows I do not go to meeting **Mond 23** I go and see Sister Grow came home then went and showed sister Spencer how to spool and warp their carpet then went up to P Gs ^with Br Williams^ staid there all night then went to Sylvias in the afternoon we went to Davids in the evening I went home with Sylvia Phebe went with us I staid there all night. P G brought me home on **Wend 25 Thursd 26** went to sister Spencers to see about her carpet she was doing first rate **Frid ^27^** put Sylvias quilt ~~Sat~~ Jesess and Bartlet here on a visit **Satd 28** I got the quilt out David here I let him have two chairs he and Carlos eat dinner here sister Teaples here staid all night

MARCH 1863

Sund March 1 ^st^ -1863 she went to meeting I did [not] go it was so muddy ^Br^ Williams and Sylvia came down and brought Josephine here to board and go to school this quarter Bartlett commences to morrow to keep school **Mond 2 ^d^** sister Teaples starts home this morning **Tuesd 3 ^d^** I was caled to John Winegars put his wife Jane to bed with a daughter [Alice] born about $2h$ past 12 P M **Wed 4** crotiaing on my cap ~~went to the~~ **Thurd 5** picking wool **Frd 6** the same ^Phebe Jane [Clark, Sylvia's daughter] here^ **Sat 7** worked on my cap went to the Theatre in the evening with Bartlett and Josephine[13] **Sund 8** went to meeting came home went to the 14 ward in the evening **Mond 9** picking wool **Tuesd 10 Wed 11 Thursd 12** the same **Frid 13** finished picking wool and went up to Sylvias staid all night **Satd 14** went to the dedication of the tabernacle in the city ɉ Bountiful.[14] **Sund 15** went again staid last night to P Gs eat dinner at Davids staid at P Gs all night P G had about fifty there four meals **Mond 16** I came home Williams & Sylvia came home with me **Tuesd 17** David came down brought word that P Gs & Lucinias daughter [Lucina] was dead that she died in ten minutes after they knew that any thing ailed her I went up with David staid there all night ^**Wed 18**^ attended the funerel came home after **Thursd 19** cleaned the nessesary things had co

---

13. They would have seen *Pizarro* and *Artful Dodger* by T. A. Lyne.

14. The Bountiful Tabernacle was begun in February 1857 and finished in six years, construction being suspended during the Utah War. The dedication was a big event with many out-of-town visitors and general authorities. "After the meetinghouse was completed it became the religious, political and social center of village life. The building stands today and is the oldest chapel in continuous use in Utah and in Mormondom" (Leslie T. Foy, *The City Bountiful* [Bountiful, Utah: Horizon Publishers, 1975], 106). The Sessions family held a reunion at the Bountiful Tabernacle in August of 1992.

Sisters Nebecar Sophia Tripp & Crisse Parsons **Frid** ^**20**^ I greased my wool Sylvia & Williams came down after dinner I went up to town with them got some bonnet lining and a green veil **Satd 21** finished my wool for the machine. **Sund 22** I am not well do not go to meeting **Mond 23** I washed David here after some trees brought me eight gallons molasses he said Sarah P Gs wife was very sick with lung fever **Tuesd 24** I carried my bonnet to Agatha to clean and trim **Wed 25** iron and work in the garden **Thurd 26** & **Frid 27** the same Sedenia has been here [perhaps Cardenia Estella, David's daughter] she and Josephine has gone home this week I have had some shade trees set out buy the inside of my fence to protect the fence had plumb trees set out acros the end of my lot to make a hedge when the fence is done I gave the trees Br Stokes set them out **Satd 28** I have had co= all day Bart= David Br Cole & ^Jack Jonson^ here to dinner William Smoot Martha & Frank Armstrong here to supper **Sund 29** I went to meeting **Mond 30** I worked in the garden **Tuesd 31** Sam= Russell worked for me triming trees

APRIL 1863

Wed April 1st ^**1863**^ Sam= here half of to day **Thursd 2** Sam= here all day **Frid 3** worked in the garden **Satd 4** I have got my trees trimed and the most of the brush cut up for the fire **Sund 5** I went to meeting **Mond 6** Conference I went **Tuesd 7 Wed 8** I have been all the time to the conference it has ajourned **Thurd 9** I have been selling fruit trees **Frid** the same and had about 75 th-taken up and set out by my fence it snowed this fore noon it lay on the ground two inches deep beside what melted as it came, at noon cleared away warm and find fruit blossoms covered with snow this morning made a fine scenery in my lot as it was warm enough to stick to the trees **Satd 11** I washed **Sund 12** I went to meeting **Mond 13** ironed **Tuesd 14** I worked in the garden **Wed 15** I went up to Presd Youngs Office gave him seventy five Dollars ^cash^ for the missionaries I have put in five dollars cash before and twenty five ^lb^ peaches for them,–and ten lb of peaches and 3 2*h* yards of sheeting for those that go after the saints to the Missouri River **Thursd 16** put Sophia ^wife of E B^ Tripp to bed with a son [Ernest Alonzo] born 20 minutes before 9 A M **Frid 17** washed Williams Sylvia and Phebe Jane here Josephine and Bartlett went home with them **Satd 18** Carlos here to dinner P G Mary David and Jim here to supper. I then went and see sister Grow she was very bad I do not think she can live long **Sund 19** I went to meeting ^Brigham went south^ **Mond 20** ^Josephine here^ I put Betsey wife of John Bouk to bed with a son [Hiram] born 9 P M **Tuesd 21** sent my wool to the carding machine by John Nebecar **Wed 22** braided straw **Thursd 23** made me a straw ^sun^ bonnet it rained and snowed **Frd 24** I washed Ed Parry worked for me for J Cottom **Satd 25** ironed Josephine went home last night **Sund 26** I went to meeting **Mond 27** ^got my rolls^ carded some wool **Tuesd 28** spun it for a comforter for me **Wed 29** worked in the garden **Thurd 30** commenced spining my rolls

May 1863

Frd May 1st 1863 the same **Satd 2** Sarah stoped here she has started on a visit to her Fathers for her health P G Lucinia here with her **Sund 3** I went to meeting **Mond 4** spining **Tued 5** P G & Lucinia called here as they went home **Wed 6 Thursd 7 Frd 8 Sat 9** I have been spining all the week **Sund 10** I went to meeting in the evening I put Phebe wife of E B Trip to bed with a son [Charles Albert] born eight oclock P M **Mond 11 Tuesd 12** ^hear from Carlos all well^ have been in to Br Winegars to see a young man I think he will die before morning **Wesd 13** he is dead **Thurd 14 Frd 15 Satd 16** I have been spining the most of the week **Sund ^16^** I have been to meeting **Mond 17 Tuesd 18 wed 19 Thursd 20** I have been spining finish to day **Frid 21** carded **Satd 22** spun finished all and went to the Examination of Bart- Tripps school then went ~~af~~ up North to Sylvias staid there all night went **Sund ^23^** to Davids went to P Gs in the evening staid all night came home in the morning on **Mond 24 Tuesd 25 wed 26 Thursd 27 Frid 28** I have washed scoured and ~~and~~ coloured my yarn **Sat 29** spooled it **Sund 30** <th> went to meeting

June 1863

Mond 31 warped my web **Tuesd ^2^** ~~June 1~~ ^st^ 1863 put it in Sister Spencers loom **Wed 3** was sick **Thursd 4 Frid** <5> I wove **Sat 6** William and Martha here and Byron **Sund 7** do not go to meeting water my lot **Mond 8 Tuesd 9 Wed 10** been weaving got my web out 15 yards for dresses **Thursd 11** washed **Frid 12** Spooled another web **Sat 13** warped it **Sund 14** do not go to meeting **Mond 15** put my web in weave 1-2*h* yd **^Tuesd 16^ wed 17 Thursd 18 Frid 19** Josephine went home **Satd 20** I have been weaving the the most of the week **Sund 21** I went to meeting **Mond 22 Tuesd 23 Wed 24** got my web out ^for blanket & undergarments^ 28 yds I do feel thankful to my heavenly Father that he gives me health and strenth and a dispostion to work and make cloth and other things for my comfort now in the sixty ninth year of my age. And I also feel thankful that I had a mother that put me to work when I was young and learned me how. Br Green came here to board with me. **Thursd 25 Frid 26 Satd 27** been cleaning. ~~the~~ and watering my lot **Sund 28** I went and see sister Grow in the forenoon in the afternoon I went to meeting I think sister Grow is dying **Mond 29** She is dead I go to her funeral **Tuesd 30**

July 1863

Wed July 1 - 1863 Br Green moved his things here **Thusd 2** this ~~day~~ ^week^ I have sold 1 -95 - 2*h* lb dried peaches And took my pay out of the store **Frd 3 Satd 4** Josephine here has concluded not to go to school any more **Sund 5** I went to meeting **Mond 6** Sylvia here **Tuesd 7 Wed 8 Thursd 9** I have been pulling weeds in the garden **Frid 10** wattered I have crocheted a tidy for my chair commenced a comforter for myself **Satd 11 Sund 12** went to meeting

Mond 13 Tuesd 14 Wed 15 Frid 16 ^**Frd 17**^ I have worked in the garden the most of the time **Satd 18** P G and Lucinia here **Sund 19** I went to meeting **Mond 20** ^Br Art Green^ paid my taxes for me eight Dollars fifty cents **Tuesd 21** Sister Russell is sick I went and steamed her and anointed her Br Jena Cole laid hands on her **Wed 22** we have some green corn to day **Thursd 23** I go up to P Gs to celebrate the 24th tomorrow **Frid 24** it is 16 years to day since the Pioneers came into this valley[15] **Satd 25** I came home **Suntd 26** I do not go to meeting I have a sick man here he is an emigrant bound for Carson California he has gone on this evening **Mond 27** work on my comforter **Tuesd 28 Wed 29** finished it **Thursd 30** commenced a chair tidy **Friday 31** worked in the garden the wind blew very hard this evening blew off many Aples

August 1863

Satd August 1st 1863 I picked them up cut some up to dry Sister Holmes came here staid all night **Sund 2** we went to meeting **Mond 3d** I went to a lecture delivered by ~~James~~ John F Kenny deligate to congress[16] then I went with sister Holmes to Prd B Youngs visited sisters Marg^a^ret [Pierce (Young)] & Snow and Zina then to sisters Cob and Chase I then came home **Tuesd 4** cut more Aples to day **Wed 5** I was sent for to go to Br D Huntingtons to a funeral of Lots [Lot Huntington] child. In the evening I was sent for to go to George Nebecars his child sick died I think it was dying when I got there **Wed 6** sister Holmes here again **Thurd 6** cut me three pair of flannel garments spun and wove myself **Frid 7** Sister Holmes came here staid all night **Satd 8** she has gone home to Farmington Sister Wilson here made me a good visit Sylvia and Williams here **Sund 9** do not go to meeting **Mond** ^**10**^ bought half bushel potatoes **Tuesd 11** Br Green has gone to American Fork Brs Hill and Kingsbury here after flour that I donated for the building of the new tabernacle 23-50 ^lbs^ two thousand three hundred and fifty pounds **Wed 12** paired and cut apples to dry **Thursd 13** work on my chair cover **Frd 14** I went to town went to see Phebe Tripps babe it is very sick **Satd** ^**15**^ finished my chair cover did many other things **Sund 16** I went to meeting saw Sister Vose

---

15. Even at this early time, it appears that the celebration for Independence Day was less important, because Pioneer Day took the spotlight. Patty does not even mention Independence Day in 1863.

16. John F. Kinney had been appointed chief justice for Utah in 1860. The *Deseret News* article "For Delegate to Congress, John F. Kinney" was extravagant in praise of his speech as ". . . containing more of truth and less of political twaddle, than any harangue of an M. C. in prospective, we have heard within the last thirty years . . ." (22 July 1863, 13:23–24). On 31 August the Honorable John F. Kinney received every vote cast for delegate to Congress. He had been released from his judgeship earlier.

she has returned from the states with Br Staines he preached P G & Emeret
here to supper **Mond 17** pared and cut Aples to day **Tuesd ^18^** I did the
same **Wed 19 Thursd 20 Frid 21 Satd 22** have been taking care of my fruit
the most of the time[17] made my undergarments David and Phebe here she ^&
children^ staid all night **Sund 23** William and Martha Smoot and children
here Br Green came home this morning I do not go to meeting **Mond 24** P G
& Mary here to dinner and David P G brought me a peice of veal **Tuesd 25**
Wms= and Sylvia here **Wed 26** taking care of my fruit **Thursd 27** Phebe
Tripps babe is dead I go to the funeral John Fisher and Josephine here[18] I gave
them some Aples and sold them a peck of plumbs **Frid 28** I was sick all night
not well this morning Wms & Sylvia here and many others **Satd 29** I have sold
to James White one ^bsh^ 3 pecks of Aples and 27 qts plumbs this week to
day sold 12 - 2*h* bush Aples and 14 lbs ^dried^ peaches & six & half of Aples.
I have taken eighty Dollars green backs this week called money[19] **Sund 30** I
do not go to meeting to day. I have a bad cough and do not feel well. I have
wrote a letter to my Br Jon.= B David Sylvia here after meeting. **Mond 31**
took care of my fruit

---

17. Patty's obsession with her fruit began very early as her diaries indicate. But
Elizabeth Ellis Lund, "a relative" reported in a brief history of David Sessions,
Jr., that he "secured apple, peach, apricot, plumb, pears and prune trees also
some berries, he wrapped these in burlap in small bundles, whenever he heard
of a company of Saints leaving for the West, he would get permission of the driver to tie the bundles of trees on the wagon and then pay the driver to pour
water on them each time they came to a watering place to keep them from drying out on the long trip. By the time David and his wife Phebe came to the
Valley in 1850, he had sent trees enough to start one of the first orchards in Salt
Lake City Utah." David was not married when he first came to the valley, but he
might well have sent fruit trees to his parents (family tradition, as written personal history "Biography of David Sessions, Jr.," by Ellis Lund, photocopy in
possession of Donna T. Smart).

18. John Fisher (1842–1905) and Josephine Rosetta Lyon (1844–1924) were married on 15 August 1863.

19. In a press release from Iowa City on 29 June 1898 concerning the death of the
eighty-one-year-old Honorable Ezekiel Clark, a second husband of Patty's
daughter Sylvia, Clark was called a "History Maker and Neoplism of Finance."
After giving a flowery summary of the life and contributions of the deceased, the
author wrote, "It is stated that he is in reality, the father of the greenback. One
night long ago he awakened at his hotel in New York City, springing up, paced
the floor until dawn, his mind filled with a great idea. Then after a consultation
with his associates on the trip, the representative of the governor of Indiana, as
Mr. Clark was governor Kirkwoods representative, he went to Secretary
Soloman P. Chase before whom he laid his plan. The cabinet officer adopted the
giant idea, carried it into execution and the greenback was born" (Sessions family records provided to the editor). Obviously Patty could not have known about
the ironic relationship she herself had with the greenback "called money."

SEPTEMBER 1863

Tuesd Sept 1 ^**1863**^ worked drying fruit. ^my peaches are ripe some of them^ **Wed 2** Br Green came home a Mr Acord with him went back that night **Thurd 3 Frd 4** gathering fruit **Satd 5** gathered many of my big plumbs in the afternoon a very heavy wind quite a hurricane broke down a big cottonwood tree at the corner of my lot and broke some limbs from my Apple trees and blew of much fruit **Sund 6** I do not go to meeting **Mond 7** cuting peaches David and Jim came down after salt they carried ~~ten~~ 9 bushel of Apples and thre and half peaches up for tithing for me **Tuesd 8** I have let David have one hundred and fifty Dollars to bye a waggon witt he is to let me have a good breede mare worth $1-00.) And fifty Dollars cash **Wed 9** cuting peaches **Thurd 10** I am not well Atending to my fruit **Frid 11** sold 15 -1*h* Apples took 61=00 Dollars greenback **Satd 12** Cut many peaches to drye **Sund 13** do not go to meeting Elsie Fullers Boy came here this morning is going to work for me a week if well enough to work he is not well now he has got worse and gone to his Uncles **Tuesd 15** ~~Br grene has gone out to meet the Train with Bartlett and~~ he came back and gone North ^Br grene has gone out to meet the Train and get Bart's girl^ his mother [Elsie Fuller] has worked here this afternoon David and Phebe here took 4 - 3*h* ^B^ peache to the tithing Office for me **Wed 16** ~~P~~ Sister Fuller has concluded to work for me untill my fruit is gathered **Thursd 17** she took twenty quarts of my blue plumbs to Brigham for tithing, Yestarday. ~~and~~ 23 qt of Red ones to the tithing Ofice to day. **Frd 18** ^2 bushel more peaches for tithing^ we are gathering and drying fruit as fast as we can **Satd 19** the same P G and Kepler here to dinner **Sund 20** I do not go to meeting Elsie went **Mond 21** Br Grene came back ^to night^ Bartlett found his girl ~~and~~ Was married and brought her home **Tuesd 22** Elsie left me said she could not work she had a pain in her side so I am alone she left 10 oclock to day **Wed 23** Bartlett and wife here to see me **Thursd 24 Frd 25** I get along ^alone^ very well **Satd 26** P G Lucinia and Mary here **Sund 27** I do not go to meeting **Mond 28** Sold fruit $14 - 50 let sister Coon have 6 B peaches to dry on shares. Bought a cow of Mr Parry ^gave 30-00 dollars for her^ **Tuesd 29** let sister Coon have 6 B more **Wed 30** let her have 2 B more

OCTOBER 1863

Thurd Oct 1 1863 bought a colt of G Gibs gave $ 40 - 00 for it **Frid 2** Sarah P Gs wife here **Sat 3 Sund 4** do not go to meeting **Mond 5** hire Sam Rollins he commences work 4 Oclock P M **Tuesd 6** Conference P G & Lucinia here stay all night **Wed 7** P G & Mary Julia & Parks [Thompson Parke] here stay ^all night^ ~~stay~~ **Thursd 8** Br Green goes to American Fork P G & Mary here stay all night again **Frid 9** Conference ajourned **Sat 10** P G and Fanny [Fanny Emorett, her granddaughter] came here he went down to see Martha Ann she

is sick Fanny stays with me Sam goes away has done gathering my Aples
Sund 11 I do not go to meeting I am not well P G came back Fanny goes
home with him **Tuesd 13** I am taking care of my dried Fruit Aples and peaches **Wed 14 Thursd 15 Frid 16 Satd 17** I have been attending to my domestick
concerns **Sund 18** I do not go to meeting **Mond 19 Tuesd 20** Prescot came
here to board at four Dollars per week I spin yarn for him some socks **Wed 21
Thurd 22 Frd 23 Satd 24** I have been knitting them **Sund 25** I go to meeting
Mond 26 finish the socks **Tuesd 27** ~~wed 28~~ Josephine has been here almost a
week Williams and Sylvia and David here she went home with them **Wed 28
Thursd 29** I have knit Br Grene a pair of mittins and a pair of socks **Frid 30
Sat 31**

NOVEMBER 1863

Sund Nov 1 ^st^ 1863 do not go to meeting **Mond 2 Tuesd 3 Wed ^Nov^ 4
Thursd 5 Frid 6** ~~Satd 6~~ **Sat 7** I went to the Theatre with Br Grene **Sund 8** I
went to meeting **Mond 9 Tuesd 10 Wed 11 Thursd 12** I have been attending
to my domestic concerns **Frid 13** Br Edgar Debenham died Satd he was buried
^Sund 15^ Mond <16> his sister Naomi came here to board ^and rest^ I
had never seen her before and did not know she was sick untill she came here
she then said she only wanted rest **Tuesd 17 Wed 18 Thursd 19 Frid 20** she
gets no better **Satd 21** her Friends have sent Dr Morgan here to see her she has
not been up to day to have her bed made **Sund 22** I have got her up to day. I
have to work very hard to do my work and take care of her. And ^I^ fear I
shall give out **Mond 23** she grows worse Sister Mercy Banks came here to help
take [care] of her Dr Morgan here again he says it is very doubtfull if she gets
well again **Tuesd 24** she is no better **Wed 25** she is worse the Dr comes every
day but says she is no better **Thursds 26** he has come again ^says^ her liver is
sweling and will burst and she will drop off quick Br Stains told Mercy to not
give her any more of his Medicine but try the Preisthood to go and get Br
Teasdale, that he would come himself if he was well she went. And when she
came back, Naomi looked like death we thought she could live but a short time
but ^we^ ~~P G~~ gave her no more of the Medicine Br Teasdale administered to
her. she had been before administered to **Frid** ~~G~~ **27** Br Teasdale came again
Brought Dr Hovey along they gave an Emetic **Satd 28** she apears a ^litle^ better Zina Young came washed and anointed her and she is desidedly better
Sund 29 she is still better we now think she will get well **Mond 30**

DECEMBER 1863

Tuesd Dec 1 ^1863^ she is gaining fast **wed 2** ^David took my colt home
with him^ **Thursd 3 Frd 4** she begins to set up **Satd 5** I had company Sisters
Cole Daughter ^Annie^ and Newman **Sund 7** I do not go to meeting I cannot leave Naomi yet. **Mond 7 Tuesd 8** ^Naomi walks out^ **Wed 9 Thursd
10 Frid 11 Satd 12** She goes to Br Teasdales to live **Sund 13** I do not go to

meeting I have a bad cold cough bad **Mond 14** wash **Tuesd 15 Wed 16 Thursd 17** I make soap. **Frid 18 Satd 19 Sund 20** I do not go to meeting **Mond 21 Tuesd 22 Wed 23** have got me a flannel dress made this week ~~Thurs 24~~ Prescot leaves here he has been here 5 weeks come Frd. **Thurd 24** Carlos here P G wishes me ^and Mr Parry^ to come up there next Tuesd Julia is to be married. **Frid 25** Christmas a very deep heavy snow fell last night and yestarad. Fair to day and warm **Satd 26 Sund 27** I do not go to meeting **Mond 28** I prepare to go up North to P Gs **Tuesd 29** P G and Lucinia came after me took dinner here and we started it snowed very fast. Mr Parry did not go. **Wed 30** fair and fine they were Married by her Father P G Sessions[20] **Thursd 31** we went over to Davids took dinner then I came home with Wm= and Martha Smoot rode in a sleigh

1864

*I have a good deal of co[mpany] but I have stood it first rate
and feel quite well in body and mind*

JANUARY 1864

Frid Jan= ^**1st**^ **1864** more snow fell last night **Satd 2** I visited with sister Leonard at sister Russells **Sund 3** more snow I do not go to meeting **Mond 4 Tuesd 5** it is very cold **Wed 6** colder **Thursd 7** still colder I carried fire into the cellar to keep it from freezing **Frid 8** more moderate **Satd 9** more comfort able Wms and Sylvia here Julia here Parks was with her **Sund 10** more snow last night I do not go to meeting I have been reading to day Sermons that was ten years ago preached and many predictions that were then made are now being fulfiled. It makes my heart rejoice **Mond 11** plenty of snow **Tuesd 12** Jason Luce was shot to day[21] we scraped the snow off of the house for fear the roof would break in **Wed 13 Thursd 14** I have been knitting **Frid 15**

20. Julia Sessions, the daughter of Perrigrine and Mary Call, married Thompson Parke on 30 December 1863.

21. Jason Luce, a father of five children, who, according to Wilford Woodruff's entry of 11 January 1864, had "gotten a woman with a child who was not his wife . . . ," was executed for the murder of Samuel F. Burton. In 1860 he had killed Joe Rhodes, who was attempting to enter a house where W. A. Hickman was confined because of a gunshot wound. Hickman was a brother-in-law of Jason Luce. Luce expected clemency, but a letter from Bannock City, Idaho, where the murder had occurred, was never delivered. The letter pleaded for the court to deal lightly with Luce because his victim, Burton, was himself a murderer who was to be hanged anyway, and both killings were in self-defense. More information is available in "The Execution of Jason R. Luce," *Deseret News,* 9 March 1864, 13:182.

Gleason & Hudson came here to board **Satd 16** Carlos here **Sund 17** he and Wm= and Martha here **Mond 18** I was sick all night Sister Russell came and staid with me **Tuesd 19** she is here still **Wed 20** Sally came and staid with me **Thursd <21>** I am a little better **Frid 22** quite sick yet **Satd 23 Sund 24** not able to go to meeting **Mond 25** I can hardly sit up **Tuesd 26** had a sore broke that came on my Jaw I feel some better David has been down and took my cow home to keep. my hay is gone **Wed 27 Thursd 28** I am very feble yet **Frid 29** ~~Harriet Sessions and all her family came here last night seven of them I waited on them it has made me quite sick again She went on again to night up to P Gs Satd~~ **Satd 30** I am quite unwell yet **Sund 31** do not go to meeting

FEBRUARY 1864

Mond Feb 1 - 1864 Tuesd 2 Wed 3 Thursd 4 my birthday sixty nine years old to day Harriet Sessions and all her family came here stay all night **Frd 5** they stay untill after dinner then go up to P G **Satd 6** Mr Parry sent for me to come and see him he had been sick all night I went before sunrise it was very cold. I came home sick and have been sick all day Sylvia Josephine and David here I sold Josephine a bushel of aples Mr Parry is better **Sund 7** I am very unwel Martha Ann sent for me I am so sick I dare not go and I feel bad about it **Mond 8** Martha Ann has sent little Willey [her oldest son, William Cochran Adkinson Smoot, Jr.] up to tell me that she has a daughter [Lucina] born yestarday one oclock and she is quite smart. And I feel better about her Sylvia and Wms ^l^= here to dinner I am getting some better I have no fever this afternoon. **Tuesd 9 Wed 10 Thurs 11** Mr Parry is quite well ~~Frid 12~~ very pleasant here but a dreadful storm of wind north and south it was so bad that they could not travel north the stage coach turned back. One woman and child froze to death we have not heard the particulars **Frd 12 Satd 13** I have got quite smart Homer Hughins came here to board yesterday I have four men boarding here now **Sund 14** I do not go to meeting **Mond 15** hear that the storm on last Thursd buried up many cattle and sheep they say that the ^snow^ has drifted fifteen feet deep in some of their yards and sheep are under it yet. **Mond 15 Tuesd 16** Charles Kimballs child was burnt to death in the bed two years old last night the bed caught fire from the candle ~~We~~ Sister Kesler here she told me that Mariette and Joseph were both Married Naomi she was here said she was married **Wed 17 Thursd 18 Frid 19 Satd 20 Sund 21** do not go to meeting **Mond 22 Tuesd 23 Wed 24** Peter Gleason came here **Thursd 25 Frid 26** I have five men here boarding now I have been sewing this week what time I can get **Satd 27** Carlos came after me to go up to P Gs I went up **Sund 28** I put Sarah P Gs wife to bed this morning with a daughter [Elvira] born five oclock and five minutes I then came home before breakfast sister Gibs staid here while I was gone **Mond 29** Peter Gleason starts for the East in the stage

MARCH 1864

Tuesd March 1 1864 Wed 2 Thursd 3 M. V. Gleason and Homer Hewins start for the North for their team **Frid 4** Julia Parks here to diner. In the evening Mr Lyne here[22] **Satd 5** ^P G here^ **Sund 6** I went to meeting the first time I have been this winter **Mond 7 Tuesd 8** Wms= and Sylvia David and Phebe all here to dinner it is very cold the wind blows very hard **Wed 9** more moderate **Thursd 10 Frid 11 Sat 12 Sund 13** I do not go to meeting Wm= Smoot here said Martha was at his Fathers. She was coming here but the babe was sick and she could not bring it out. **Mond 14 Tuesd 15 Wed 16** the children came down and told the babe was very sick and their Mother wished me to come and see it. I told them I would go after supper they went home and got the team and came after me I found it very sick I staid untill 9 oclock and they took me home **Thursd 17 Frid 18** Wille caled and tole me his Mother thought the babe was a little better I was glad to hear Gleason and Homer got back from the North in the evening **Satd 19** I have been cooking for them all day. **Sund 20** Gleason starts for the States and Homer and Hudson start for the mine. And I go to meeting At and noon I went up to see Marthas babe it is better **Mond 21** I have men her[e] to work in my garden. **Tuesd 22. Wed 23** a man here to work again **Thursd 24 Frid. 25** David.- Parks.- and Julia here to Dinner. Let Wm= Newman have four bushels wheat to sow **Satd 26** let E Eldridge have 5 bushels to sow John Boyce two to sow **Sund 27** I do not go to meeting it snowed yesterday and it is very bad going **Mond 28** I washed **Tuesd 29** P G Mary and Carlos down here Sylvia and Wms= ^all^ here to dinner Br Grene went over to the west mountain. **Wed 30** he came home I have been peiceing a quilt. **Thursd 31**

APRIL 1864

Frid April 1st 1864 Sister Eldridge here **Satd 2 P G** came down Brought Lucinia. Carlos and his girl Elizabeth Wintal [Elizabeth Wintle 1848–1909] came down with them got their Endowment and was sealed. They wanted me to go home with them but it was very cold and snowing S I did not go **Sund**

---

22. T. A. Lyne (1806–1891) was the first significant teacher of speech in Utah. He produced plays and trained stock companies in Nauvoo and Salt Lake City. He was a popular actor, who had been converted in Philadelphia and given responsibility for theatrical productions in Nauvoo. After the saints left Nauvoo, he drifted away from the church and returned to the stage in New York City. In 1863 Hyrum Clawson hired Lyne to coach and instruct the company at the Salt Lake Theatre. Several plays between 1862 and 1864 featured Lyne. In 1865 he formed a theatrical company—which failed—with John S. Potter to compete with the Salt Lake Playhouse (see Myrtle E. Henderson, *A History of the Theatre in Salt Lake City from 1850 to 1870* [Evanston, Il.: by author, c. 1934, 1936]).

3 I do not go to meeting **Mond 4** I have washed George Russel has a cow here they took her here ^satd^ to get her under cover she ~~got~~ lay down as soon after she came here has not been up since she is so poor I think they will lose her and calf too **Tuesd 5** they have got her up she can walk **Wed 6** they take her away I go to conference **Thursd 7 Frid 8 Satd 9 Sund 10** I have been to all the conference it is ajourned I have a good deal of co but I have stood it first rate and feel quite well in body and mind **Mond 11** I work in the Orchard **Tuesd 12** I have a man to work here **Wed 13** he is here to day at work I have got Mary Eldridge here to whitewash **Thurd 14 Frid 15 Satd 16** we have got done **Sund 17** I do not go to meeting **Mond 18** Br Grene starts for Virginia City **Tuesd 19** I go over Gorden [Jordan] Mr Parry with me and his little Boy in a carriage with Peter Shirts to look at his farm he wanted me to bye it but we found no chance to watter it naturally and I did not bye it And when we were coming home we were all thrown out of the carriage by the horse taking a fright broke the carriage bad. But we all escaped very fortunately without any serious injury **wed. 20** David here **Thurd 21** Tomas Lyne came here to board **Frid 22 Satd 23** I have been washing some carpet and taking care of my dried peaches **Sund <24>** I do not go to meeting. **Mond 25 Tuesd 26 Wed 27 Thurs 28** I have been attending to my domestic concerns Julia came here staid all night gone home this Morning in the stage David came down here **Frid 29** Carlos Sessions here I bought a peice of [property] of him gave him fifty Dollars ^25 down^ for it ^25 in the faul^ I have bought a yoke of oxen to send to the states to bring on the poor saints gave one hundred and thirty Dollars for them cash ^**Satd 30**^ Got them branded this morning ready to start. I then went with sister Buel washed and anointed sister Russell she is very sick. After ^-noon^ she is no better

May 1864

Sund May 1st 1864 she is no better David came after me to go up home with him. In the afternoon I went to see sister Russell again before I went she said she was a little better. I went but she was no better and grew worse fast Died **Mond** ^12 oclock^ noon I came home **Tuesd 3** I came home called to see her found her dead she was buried in the afternoon I went to the funeral. Br Brigham was there spoke good **Wed 4** the wind blows very hard I have been to look at a house and lot of Stephen Winegars [1830–1903] he wishes me to bye it **Thursd 5** I have bought it and paid for it gave two hundred seventy five Dollars for it P G Lucinia and Carlos's wife came down here I went up to town with them **Frid 6** I have watered a little but the water is turned off and I cannot do any more **Satd 7 Sund 8** Bartlet came after me to go and see his wife she is sick I staid all day with her she is better **Mond 9** I been looking at a house and lot I did not buy it the oner asked too much for it **Tuesd 10** Wm= S Jones came here offered me two lots in City Bountiful for two hundred Dollars I told him I would take them **Tuesd 10** he came again I took the

the Deed gave him $2-00 then bought some lumber in a shanty and other things gave him thirty five Dollars for it **Wed 11** Joanna Olson came here to work for me Tomas Lyne has gone away from here I did not wish to board him any longer **Thurd 12** cutting carpet rags **Frid 13 Satd 14** the same **Sund 15** go to meeting **Mond 16** Brigham starts for the North I go and look of a peice of land a ten acre lot did not bye it it was to Dear **Tuesd 17** wrote a letter to my Br Jon= **Wed 18** Cut carpetrags ^and watered my lot Carlos here gone to Provo^ P G & Sarah & C Lovlin and wife here Joanna washed **Thursd 19** cut rags again **Frid 20** the same **Satd 21** P G here eat dinner soon after David and his two girls[23] and Sylvia here and sister Willie all here to Dinner I went home with them Staid all night with Sylvia. Then went over to Davids. Came home. ^**Sund 22**^ **Mond 23** cut rags ^finished^ **Tuesd 24** Mary ~~Gay~~ Grey cut me a dress I wattered my lot and made the skirt. ^~~it rained~~^ **Wed 25** ^Mary finished my dress^ it rains hard all the forenoon has wattered the earth well about here. **Thursd 26** ^Joanna^ washed my quilts **Frid 27 Satd 28** ^Sylvia and John and Josephine here^ finished sewing carpet rags. **Sund 29** I went to meeting **Mond 30** I went up to town bought a bunch of yarn **Tuesd 31** doubled a part of it then went to the funeral of Jesess boy it died last night[24] **Wed**

JUNE 1864

Wed June 1 ^1864^ finished doubling my carpet yarn **Thursd 2** Joanna finished twisting it. I coulored it she wen to spining **Frid 3 Satd 4** Wms Sylvia David Phebe here I went up to town with them bought 16 ^yds^ cloth sheeting sixty cents per yd they went home **Sund 5** I went to meeting in the forenoon heard that Mathias Cowley was drowned I went there and staid with his wife in the afternoon. came home he was not found **Mond 6** David and Phebe here stay all night **Tuesd 7** they went home the people have given up looking for Br Cowley they think it no use **Wesd 8** Joanna carded bats for her quilt. **Thursd 9** she goes to E B Tripps to work. Wms= and Sylvia came here last night near midnight I went up in town with them let him have four hundred Dollars in green backs he is to give me the same amount in gold coin in one year I stopt at Bartlett Tripps with Julia made them a visit **Frid 10** she went home I quilted Joannas peticoat **Satd 11** William Smoot here Br Cowley is not found yet. He is found this Afternoon **Sund 12** he is buried this forenoon. I went to the funeral In the afternoon I went to meeting hear that Br Grene is coming home **Mond 13** Br Hoit came

---

23. David had three daughters at this time: Sarah Phebe (1853–1933), Cardenia Estella (1856–1933), and Olive Cordelia (1859–1932).

24. Bartlett Tripp, son of Enoch Bartlett Tripp and Jesse Ann Eddins, was born on 18 October 1862.

here to board Br Grene came home **Tuesd 14** I went up to E B Tripps spooled and worped my carpet **Wed 15** commenced making a harness **Thursd 16** ^bought a mare of George Grant^ finished the harness Br Formans daughter ^Annie^ died **Frid 17** she was buried. <I gave [*word scratched out*] $2:25 two hundred twenty five dollars for her> [the mare] I have been up to Tripps drawed in my web wove two yards 1*h* **Satd 18** mended Grene,s Clothes and helped him sack the peaches 4-60 ^lbs^ 50 ^ct^ per pound **Sund ^19^** I went to meeting then I went to Isabelle and Lorin Gutherys weding supper **Mond 20** I helped Grene off he starts 3 oclock in the afternoon I then went up to weaving **Tuesd 21** wove 5 yards **wed 22 Thursd 23 Frid 24** got my carpet out Hoit went away I got my pay for his board in ^an^ order **Satd ^25^** I went up to town got some things. Acord brou^ght^ them home for me **Sund 26** I went to meeting **Mon 27 28** ^~~I had a man~~ here to work cuting trees^ Sylvia & Ed Cutler & his sister and another man & wife here to dinner ~~Tuesd 28~~ **Wed 29 Thursd 30** <Wiliams> =trimed trees cut up parsnips on the other lot

JULY 1864

Frid July 1st 1864 I put in a quilt Carlos & wife here to dinner **Sat 2** got my quilt out and made it up **Sund ^3^** I went to meeting **Mond 4** P G & Sarah Fanny David & his two girls Byron Kepler & Jim all here to eat after dinner P G Sarah and I went up to ^Br^ Smoots to see Martha we took supper there then came home I then went up to see the fire works **Tuesd 5** I watered **Wed 6 Thursd 7 Frd 8** I have attended to my domestick concerns **Satd 9** I put Nellie [Ellen A. Jennings, b. 1839] wife of Bartlett Tripp to bed with a daughter born 8 & 16 minutes A M **Sund 10** I went to meeting **Mond ^11^** washed & ironed **Tuesd 12** watered then went to a wool picking at Phebe Tripps **Wed 13** worked in the garden **Thursd 14** had my grass cut in the afternoon I was taken sick I was very sick and in the evening the Elders came in laid hands on me I was better but very weak **Frid <15>** no pain but very weak could not set up **Satd 16** I can set up David and Jim came down here stacked my hay **Sund 17** I am quite well to day. I do not go to meeting **Mond 18 Tuesd 19** watered got my currants picked in the other lot over a bushel **Wed 20** prepared them to dry **Thursd 21** picked more on this lot spread them then went up to P Gs with him staid all night there **Frd 22** I went to see Carloses wife in the forenoon to David in afternoon Lucinia went with me Sylvia came there I went home with her staid all night **Satd 23** she and I went and see Josephine John brought me home I feel quite well it has done me good riding and changing the air and resting **Sund 24** I went to meeting **Mond 25** I went up to town ^sold some Apricots^ saw David Carlos and Wm- Smoot **Tuesd 26** Wattered **Wed ^27^** quilted me a petticoat **Thurd 28** coulored yellow **Frd 29** Cut up weeds it is very warm **Satd 30** very warm **Sund 31** I go to meeting

AUGUST 1864

^1864^ **Mond 1** preparing to quilt **Tuesd 2** wattered put in a quilt and then went up to Sylvias with her Wms and David **Wed 3** went to Davids then to P Gs staid all night **Thursd 4** came home Lucinia came with me staid all night **Frd 5** she went home afer helping me get out my quilt **Satd 6** made up my quilts **Sund 7** I went to meeting ^**Mond 8**^ Setled with E B Tripp **Tuesd 9** I wattered **Wed 10** I have been and worped a web for Phebe Tripp for dresses I am knitting ^litle^ soks for Julia Grow **Thurd 11 Frd 12** finish them **Satd 13** made me a cap **Sund 14** I am quite sick **Mond** ^**15**^ I am worse cannot sit up **Tuesd 16** no better **Wed 17** some better **Thursd 18** I can work worp a web for sister Winegar **Frid 19** Br Grene came back from the mines P Gleason came ^back^ from ^the^ states his Br and their families are near bye P G & Lucinia here to dinner I then went & worped a web for her between 60 & 70 yds long I then went up to P Gs did not get there untill after 11 oclock in the evening **Satd 20** we beamed it on I drawed it in and got a half yard wove **Sund 21** I came home Br Wms brought me home **Mond 22** Mr Parry came to see if I had got home and was well it rains this morning a litle **Tuesd 23** Gleason & families have got in **wed 24 Thursd 25** I attend to my domestic concerns **Frid 26** the Gleasons and families came down here **Satd 27 Sund 28** I do not go to meeting **Mond 29 Tuesd 30**

SEPTEMBER 1864

Wed 1 ^**Sept**^ **1864** I went up to John Fishers Josephine was very sick has got a pair of twins both boys [Irvin Frederick and Ivan John] one born last night 6 oclock the other this morning 3 oclock. I ~~get~~ left her comfortable and came home got here 10 oclock[25] **Thursd 2** ^**Sept** [2 *changed to*] **1 1864**^ **1864** Gleasons start to go to Origon **Frid 2** Wms and Sylvia came here I went up to town with them bought me a peice of delaine for a dress. at night Phebe Davids wife came here staid all night. **Satd 4** [*a number of dates are written over here; she first put 4 and then 3 on top, etc.*] Mary Grey sent for me she is very sick I gave her an emetic came home Sisters Foss and Olive Wooley here with Phebe they stay untill night **Sund 4** I do not go to meeting **Mond 5 Tuesd 6 Wed 7** I went up to town to a sale of stoves I did not buy one **Thursd 8** I have got my hay all in the stack good **Frid 9** Br Grene starts for the mines again Sylvia here **Satd 10 Sund 11** I do not go to meeting it rains. We think a cloud has burst City Creek has come down by here like a flood this afternoon **Mond 12** I wash Wms= & Sylvia here I go to town with them **tuesd 13** I water my lot ~~city~~ Wm= and Martha and all her children 7 here **Wed 14** taking care of my fruit **Thursd**

---

25. It appears that the Fisher twins would have been born on 30 and 31 of August, since Patty omits that date and corrects 2 to 1 September.

15 the same gather some Aples **Frid 16** gather all my tame plumbs and sell all but the tithing **Satd 17** carry the tithing up to Brighams Davids girls here and Phebe Jane go up with me **Sund 18** I do not go to meeting ~~go and put Betsey Whiticar to bed with a son~~ **Mond 19** Ruth Mitchel helped me gather apples in the forenoon Carlos wife came down she helped me **Tuesd 20 Wed 21 Thurs 22** the same In the afternoon she went home **Frid 23** I work alone **Sat 24** Jim came here staid last night this morning he gather ^(ed^ some Aples **Sund 25** I do not go to meeting go and put Betsey Whitecar [Betsey Gallant, wife of Andrew Isaac Whittaker, 1812–1874] to bed with a son [Joseph] born 6 minutes before one **Mond 26** Sarah came down her Father with her she staid all night Mary Mitchel helped me to day **Tuesd 27** David & Phebe came down took my tithing fruit up to the Ofice Sarah went home with Byron **Thursd 29** I am alone I work very hard gathering fruit **Frid 30**

October 1864

Satd Oct= 1 ^1864^ the same **Sund 2** I do not go to meeting **Mond 3** Sister Wintal came down she is helping me[26] **Tuesd 4 Wed 5** Elizabeth came down her Mother has done me two good days work they both went home **Thursd 6** conferrence Commenced I went P G & Mary came home with me staid all night P G gathered Aples for me **Frid 7** we all went to meeting P G & Lucina came home with me staid all night he gathered Aples again **Satd ^8^** we all went to meeting again Mary came home with me aga[i]n staid all night **Sund 9** we went to meeting again conference ajourened I came home alone **Mond 10** I was taking care of my fruit **Tuesd 11 Wed 12 Thursd 13** the same I have worked very hard this week I have felt well **Frid 14** I have had a man here sawing wood he has sawed a cord lacking 8 feet and split some of it he is almost blind P G & David here to supper then went home **Satd ^15^** he has split the rest of the wood and piled it up in the forenoon. Mary Williams helped me gather~~ed~~ aples. I have got them nearly all gathered. This after noon I have gathered some plumbs **Sund ^16^** I do not go to meeting **Mond 17** I have made preserves got my fruit nearly all took care of I put Sister Beard to bed with a daughter born half past eleven P M **Tuesday 18 Wed 19 Thursd 20** taking care of fruit **Frid 21** got my hay seed thrashed **Satd 22** Jim Sessions after me for Davids wife last night did not find me David here to day said she had a son [Darius] all right I have my hay seed took care of **Sund ^23^** I do not go to meeting it rains **Mond 24** I wash go to town buy me a stove pay 1=85 Dollars for it **Tuesd 25 Wed 26 Thurd 27** I have been preparing for winter **Frid ^28^** David Wms and ~~Sylvia here I went home with them staid all night with Sylvia Satd 29 I went see Josephine then went and see Julia Park~~

---

26. Elizabeth Sewell Wintle (1814–1882) was the mother of Elizabeth Wintle, who was married to Carlos Sessions.

~~Wms and Sylvia went with me and Sylvia went with me brought me back to P Gs Lucinia and I went over to Davids spent the evening then back to P Gs staid all night it rains I stay there all day Sund 30 and all night again Mond 31 I went over to Sylvias took breakfast. Wms brought me home P G & Carlos~~ <P G came and> ~~came here and~~ staid all night

NOVEMBER 1864

Tuesd Nov= ^1st^ 1864 he put up my stove pipe this morning then ^went home^ ~~went home~~ **Wed 2 Thursd 3 Frid 4** I went up with Wms David & Sylvia staid all night with her **Satd 5** visited Josephine Julia and David staid all night at P Gs **Sund 6** staid there all day it rained **Mond 7** went over to Sylvias then came home P G & Carlos came here staid all night I let Carlos have my old stove they took it away this morning it is **Tuesd 8** they soon found me a load of Coal sent it to me I paid $35= per ton **Wed 9 Thursd 10 Frid 11** I went up to Parks to ~~put~~ ^see^ Julia she is sick **Sat 12** put her to bed with a daughter born 3 3*h* in the P M **Sund 13** I came home went up to Bartlett Tripps **Mond 14** I have made some preparations for winter **Tuesd 15** Wms= & Sylvia & David here I went up to town with them bought a quarter of beaf 1=80 lbs gave 13 ^cts^ per lb $23:40 ^cts^ Wms brought home for me they went home it rained **Wed 16** it has snowned about 3 or 4 inches I commenced some muffs for Sylvias girls ~~P G~~ **Thursd 17** P G came here staid all night told us about the wind blowing down some buildings and unroofing many more the taberncle is injured very much & much hay and straw is blown away it commenced blowing about 10 A M yestarday continued until this morning up there there was but little here **Frid 18 Satd 19** the ground is still covered with snow **Sund 20** I do not go to meeting it wet underfoot the snow has melted some **Mond 21** Wms & Sylvia here I went up in town with them bought ten pound of suet **Tuesd 22** tried out my suet ~~Wed~~ 23. I put Julia Grow to bed with a daghter [Julia Ellen] Born 5 A M ~~yesterday~~ <Monday> morning the 21 **Thursday 24** ~~put~~ put Mary Gibs to bed with a son born 4 A M **Frid 25 Satd 26 Sund 27** I went to meeting Joseph Mitchel was maried to day **Mond 28 Tuesd 29 Wed 30**

DECEMBER 1864

Thurd Dec 1st ^1864^ I have been knitting for Sylvia **Frid 2** I have finished two muffs two pair of gloves & one pair of mittens P G staid here last night he was down to the cattle drive **Satd 3** Wms Sylvia & her two Girls here we all went to the Theatre [saw *Richard III*] they staid here all night **Sund 4** it rains all day they went home in the rain **Mond 5** it rained all day Sarah P G,s wife came here in the stage from her Fathers **Tuesd 6** she went home **Wed 7 Thursd 8 Frid 9 Satd 10** ^I have been kniting^ P G Wms & Sylvia here I went to town with them got material for me a bonnot they went home I finished sister Greys socks for her child **Sund 11** I went to meeting **Mond 12**

went to town to see about making my Bonnot **Tuesd 13** washed **Wed 14**
made me a black cap **Thursd 15** went and got my Bonnot **Frid 16** made me a
cap to wear with it P G & Br Crosley here to Dinner I sold Br C some Aples
Satd 17 Carlos & wife and her Mother Mary & Emeret here to dinner **Sund
18** I went to meeting **Mond 19** I washed **Tuesd 20** I went to town with Wms
& Sylvia **Wed 21** made me a cap ~~fo~~ **Thurd 22** have knit P G a pair of mittens
Frid 23 attended to many things **Satd ^24^** P G & Chester Lovlin here to
dinner I went home with them **Sund 25** christmass it rains P G had quite a
number there to dinner of his own connection ^had a good meeting in the
evening^ **Mond ^26^** it rained I went with Carlos my grand son to a party
in the evening **Tuesd 27** it snowed last night such bad going I do not go home
P G went with his carriage and took L, M and me over to Sylvia,s we had a
good visit ~~Tuesd 27~~ I ^**wed 28**^ came home Wm,s & Sylvia came with me
~~wed 28~~ **Thurd 29** quilted Sylvias Peticoat **Frid 30** got it out **Satd 31** knit two
pair of mittens for P Gs children Sund

1865

*I enjoy health and activity can go and assotiate with my children
and their children and thier children,s children*

JANUARY 1865

Jan- 1st 1865 I went to meeting **Mond 2d** baked pies **Tuesd 3** P G here staid
all night told me that Phebe ^Tripps^ son Pascal [Morrill] was very sick he
did not think it would live **Wed 4** I went up and see it Found it very sick
Thurd 5 I washed sisters Buel & Durphe here on a visit **Frid 6** I went up to see
~~P~~ E B's child again found it dead P G and wives Lucinia and Emeret were here
I went with them down to Wm= Smoots staid all night **Satd 7** came back went
to the buriel of Br E B Tripps son with three more of his sons that was burried
in his garden he had ^them^ taken up and all ^4^ buried in one grave in the
grave yard **Sund 8** I went to meeting noon ^went^ home with Mary Elen
Kimball came back to meeting and then home **Mond 9** fixing a skirt I had of
Sylvia **Tuesd 10** P G sent for me to go up there Mary was sick with a sore
throat I went up with Wms and Phebe Jane & Martha Syvia. Mary was better
when I got there a sore had broke and she could speak quite plain. I went
down to see Josepine with Wms & Sylvia in the evening & back to P Gs staid
all night **Wed 11** I went over to Carlos,s staid all night at P Gs **Thurd 12** I
came home Carlos,s wife and her Mother came down I put in a quilt for
Lizebeth **Frid 13** we got it out I went to a ward party in the evening They
staid here **Satd 14** they went home ^I made me a cape^ **Sund 15** I do not go
to meeting it is very cold and looks like snowing **Mond 16** fixing my dress
Tuesd 17 finished it **Wed 18** I visited at Br Grows with Sister Buel **Thurd 19**

I put in a comforter for Carlos,s wife tied it and got it out **Frid 20** been fixing my ^merino^ skirt. **Satd 21** sewing **Sund 22** I went to meeting sister Gunbar here in the evening **Mond 23** knit a pair of stockins for a child **Tuesd 24** kniting a pair of mittens for Mr Parry **Wed 25** finished them. Then went and setled my tithing found due me fifty Dollars **Thursd 26** finished making a pair of sheets commenced a pair gloves for Mr Parry **Frd 27** Marry Grey here **Satd 28** finished the gloves gave some wood to a sick man by the name of Frost **Sund ^29^** I went to meeting **Mond 30** P G Br Wm's Lucinia & Sylvia came here got dinner Lucinia stoped here the others went home **Tuesd 31**

FEBRUARY 1865

Wed Feb 1-1865 I was kniting comforters for Lucinia,s boys **Thursd 2** Mary Grey here making me a dress **Frid 3** she finished the dress & Lucinia and I went to see Sister Buel (**Satd 4** ^finished the comforter^ Lucinia went home ^**Satd 4** my birth day being 70 years old^! **Sund 5** she and I went to meeting in the forenoon **Mond 6** I washed **Tuesd 7 Wed 8** I have been making me a sack **Thursd 9** finished it **Frid 10** P̶ ̶G̶ Wm,s & David here to dinner **Satd 11** attend to many things **Sund 12** I go to meeting **Mond 13** finish a pair of mittens **Tuesd 14** I go up to Sylvias ^with E B. & Bartlett Tripp & wives^ to a family Party P G David & Carlos T Park & J Fisher with their families were there we had a good time enjoyed ourselves well. There I saw my Sons grand Sons & great grand Sons, Also my Daudhter grand Daughters & great grand Daughter [Eunice Parke] **Wed 15** we came home. I feel to thank the Lord that I have lived to see and enjoy what I enjoy that I enjoy health and activity ^can^ go and assotiate with my children and their children and thier children,s children and can dance with them with as much ease as when I was young. And the Lord be thanked for all his blessings to me **Thursd 16** Tomson Park and Julia were here went to see Martin the Wizard play came back staid here all night **Frid 17** it snows hard they do not go home untill near noon Carlos and Wallice Willey [William Wallace Willey] here to dinner I gave Carlos some Aples and dried Peaches and some tea to carry home **Satd 18** I have been piling up my corn and cleaning my chambers **Sund 19** it snows very fast the snow is geting very deep fell about ten inches last night and has snowed all day I get a man to shovel the snow off of my house for fear it will break the roof in **Mond 20** I am knitting **Tuesd 21** the same **Wed 22** P G and Wms came after me to go up to Carlos,s wife she was sick I went up found her better when I got there. I staid all night to P Gs Presd John Young & wife was there **Thursd 23** they came home I went over to Br Willeys with P G & Lucinia he was very sick Br Dible Br Wms & Sylvia came there we staid there untill after dinner talked with him P G said many good things to him reminded him of the blessing that had been sealed upon him and his washings and annointings also the position he ocopied in this Kingdom he began to feel better soon spoke loud and caled for his clothes got up and dresed him ate dinner with us said he was well we left him seting up we went over to Carloses staid untill night then went to Davids spent the evening I went home with Lucinia staid all night in the morning heard from Br Willey he was up said he felt first rate I came home **Frid 24** rode down with Br Dible found all well **Satd 25** finished my mittens and ristlets **Sund 26** it is so snowy and cold I do not go to meeting Bartlett & Nelley came here in the evening **Mond 27** molded candles **Tuesd 28 Wed 29**

MARCH 1865

March ^the^ 1st 1865 Thurd 2 very cold and snowey very deep **Frid 3** Joseph Parry here from Ogdon staid all night **Satd 4** I with sisters Smith and Buel were called to administer to sister Riser she is very lame cannot bear any weight on one foot and her Daughter Mary Ann [b. 1844] has the Iresipelis is very sick we administered to them both **Sund 5** Sister Smoot came wished me to go and ^see^ Wm. & Martha Anns children they are sick I could not leave home It is more pleasant to day it has thawed a good deal to day **Mond 6 Tuesd 7** Wms and Sylvia here to dinner **Wed 8** made me an apron **Thursd 9** made another Mary Gr^e^y here finished my satin dress **Frid 10 Satd** cleaning the snow away from the house and reading the Vedette a paper published at Camp Duglas a great deal of falsehood and but litle truth **Sund 12** I do not go to meeting it is so wet under foot the snow is melting away fast **Mond 13** look over my Aples **Tuesd 14** ^cow came^ the same **Wed 15** wash The cow came home ^the 14^ **Thursd 16** iron **Frid 17** sold 21 & 2*h* bushels Aples of my own ^&^ 2 bushels ^for^ Mr Parry. sold them to Coolley & Co Sold 1 2*h* to to a Frenchman mine had 24 Dollars for them Received of Coolley $305=50 pay Mr Parry 25 Dollars out of it Sylvia & ^Br^ Wms here to dinner **Satd 18** attend to my domestic concerns **Sund 19** not well do not go to meeting **Mond 20** sift over some flour **Tuesd 21** P G came here staid all night **Wed 22** knit a pair of suspenders for Br Grey **Thursd 23** I have had co all this week **Frid 24** I went up to Carlos,s wife she was sick put her to bed with a daughter [Patty Bartlett] born ^March^ **Satd 25 ^1865^** 3 oclock and 10 mints ^A M^ I then came home it snowd very hard P G & Mary & Emerett & Bishop Stoker Elizabeth Birdeno [Elizabeth Gabriell Birdenow, 1827–1903] Elizabeth got her endowment and was sealed to P G they came here staid all night **Sund 26** we all went to meeting they went home at noon **Mond 27** P G moved her ^Elizabeth^ down to live with me he is not willing that I should live alone any longer **Tuesday 28** I put sister [Sophia] Riser to bed with a son [Alma Christopher] born 2 oclock 10 mints P M **Wed 29 Thursd 30 Frid 31**

APRIL 1865

Satd April 1st 1865 I have Delivered those Aples I sold on the 17 of March last to Cooley and co= and they have taken them away but have not given me the receipt **Sund 2** I went to meeting **Mond 3 Tues 4 Wed 5** been preparing for conference P G Sarah and her Father came here went to the Theater P G came back sick **Thursd 6** he is no better is not able to go to confrence I went I come home found him worse I went for the Elders they administered to him the pain soon left him but he is very feble ^&^ sore **Frid 7** he cannot set up any **Satd 8** he has not had his clothes on yet **Sund 9** a litle stronger conference closed **Mond 10** they have come down with his carriage he has got his clothes on for the first time since wednesday night he starts for home **Tuesd 11** hear from him he is better **Wed 12** I wrote a letter to my Br Jon= Bartlett **Thursd 13 Fri 14** P G Lucinia David Phebe & Carlos here to dinner got some trees Sister Wilson was here [*crosswise in the margin:* I sold on the 17 of last March to Cooley and co= and they have taken them away but have not given me the receipt] **Satd 14** she ^sister Wilson^ came here again it being her birthday eighty three years old very smart and spry she brought me the news that Presd. Lincon was dead shot last night[27] **Sund 16** we went to meeting much said about about him and Seward s being assasinated **Mond 17** Dic= Pettit worked for me took up trees spaded I set ^strawbery^ vines sowed peas & carrotseed **Tuesd 18** he is here fixing my hencoop **Wed 19 Thursd 20 Frid 21 Satd 22** P G here staid all night **Sund 23** he went to meeting ^with us^ David Phebe & Carlos down **Mond 24** P G sent Br Fisher down to work for me Got here noon **Thursd 25 Wed 26 Thursd 27** noon he ^Fisher^ went home ^P G^ Carlos David Phebe & Jim came down here staid all night David Carlos and Jim started **Frid 28** for the Colorado[28] **Satd 29 Sund 30** we went to meeting

---

27. The news came by telegraph, as specified in the *Deseret News*. On 14 April the headline read, "By Telegraph–Assassination of President Lincoln." The wires were connected to Salt Lake City in October of 1861, and by 1865, "Pres. Brigham Young . . . introduced the subject of erecting a telegraphic line through our territory. . . . On motion of Delegate Maughan it was voted unanimously that a telegraph wire be erected through the settlements" (JH, 10 April 1865).

28. In October 1864 Brigham Young sent fifty or sixty families to the Muddy River near its confluence with the Colorado–an area now flooded by Lake Mead. Their purpose was primarily to supplement the cotton production in the St. George area, and indeed most of the cotton grown in Utah's Dixie between 1866 and 1870 came from the Muddy River colony. Another purpose was to establish a way station for freight and passengers brought up the Colorado by steamer to Call's Landing (named for Anson Call, a major leader of the pioneering effort), then by wagon to the Muddy, St. George, and on to Salt Lake City. Heat, crickets, alkali soil, and uncertain water bedeviled the colony. The end of the Civil War and arrival of the railroad made cotton available from the East, and prices plummeted. As a final blow, an official survey showed the colony was in Nevada, which demanded payment of back taxes that had been going to Utah. Brigham Young authorized abandonment of the area in 1871, and most of the colonists settled in Long Valley, where they established the United Order that gave Orderville its name (see Arrington, *Great Basin Kingdom*, 217–18, 221).

MAY 1865

Mond May 1st 1865 ~~Tuesd 2~~ <I went to a> ~~wed 3 Thursd 4~~ Missionary Party with Mr Pary & Hariet **Tuesd 2 Wed 3 Thursd 4** been preparing to white wash **Frid 5** Hannah Conklin came and whitewashed for me did it well **Sat 6** we cleaned up **Sund 7** I went to meeting **Mond 8 Tuesd 9** Wms Sylvia here I went home with them **Wed 10** We ^Sylvia and I^ went to see Josephine then to P Gs then to Carlos-s to see his wife then I went up to see Julia I staid there all night **Thursd 11** I came home **frid 12 Sat 13** I worked on my fringe **Sund 14** I went to meeting **Mond 15** finished my fringe washed it **Tuesd 16** ^we^ sewed it to the curtains put them up **Wed 17** I have hoed my peas **Thursd 18** worked in the garden **Frid 19** put my peticoat in & quilted it hoed my potatoes ^planted some corn^ **Satd 20** Betsey got the quilt out made it up I watered my lot P G & Sarah came here Wm= Smoot has been here to day **Sund 21** P G & Betsey went to meeting in the forenoon went home in the after noon Betsey went home with them The water is very high yestarday it ran through the Wm= Morse house the men have worked all day to day to keep the water in the street **Mond 22** ^John Pary came bade me farewel^ the water very high **Tuesd 23** ^this morning he starts on his mission to Wales^ P G sent Br Fisher down he is puting an embankment against my fence Wms= came down the water is over Br Foxes lot and Sister Daniels lot I send by him for P G. he said he would send Millard down **Wed 24** P G this morning came John Poorman and Millard Mary & Betsey (Millard fixed my cellar By bracing the wall the water came in to it last night Br Fisher took the potatoes out this morning they cut my shade trees banked up on the side walk in front of both my lots **Thursd 25** they have all four worked yesterday & to day & it looks as though it would be safe they go home **Frid 26** still riseing on Br Foxes lot and against his house the families have all moved out **Satd 27** I ~~star~~ make soap **Sund 28** Nellie is sick Bartlett came after me I went there **Mond 29** Mr Parry came here the water has been so high he has not been here for more than a week ^Sarah Sessions here^ **Tuesd 30** the water looks as though it would be on to us every hour **Wed 31** it broke out last night ran over every lot but one on Cottoms block it looks very bad this morning

JUNE 1865

Thursd June 1st 1865 it still looks bad **Frid 2** the water begins to look clearer **Satd 3** it is falling **Sund 4** I do not go to the meeting **Mond 5** I go up in town bought me an oil cloth for my table watered my lot **Tuesd 6** finish watering **Wed 7** Mr Parry came here he has not been here for 3 weeks ^but once^ the water has been so high he could not cross safely **Thursd 8** I spooled a web for Mr Parrys wife I am agoing to weave it for her I go to Br Winegars to weave it **Frid 9** P G & Lucinia came down I go up in town with them see about my bonnet bought me a Parisoll we then went down to Wm= Smoots to see

Martha Ann We also went to Brighams factory to see that[29] come home ~~They~~ P G & Lucinia staid here all night **Satd 10** they went home I warp the web **Sund 11** P G Emorett & Sarah came down carried me up to meeting and back went home **Mond 12** I put my web in **Tuesd** ^13^ wove 6 yards **Wed 14** Sylvia here with Wms= and her two girls [Phebe and Martha] **Thursd 15** weaving **Frid 16** I have got it out 21 yds ^a part of it Harriets for Mr Parry^ **Satd 17** I went up to town with Harriet picked out a bunch of yarn for her P G came here staid all night **Sund 18** went to meeting **Mond 19** I made me a cap **tuesd 20** Wms & Sylvia & P G came here I went home with them staid all night to Davids **Wed 21** Phebe & I went to P G I staid there all night **Thursd 22** I went to Sylvias came back to P Gs staid all night **Frid 23** came home Carlos,s wife came home with me **Satd 24** I went up to town my bonnet not done I took it to Agatha Pratt **Sund 25** I do not go to meeting **Mond 26** Libys Mother [Elizabeth Wintle] & Grandmother [Sarah Stevens Sewell, b. 1797] came here her Mother staid here all night **Tuesday** ^27^ she went up to town came back they all went home Lyby got a letter from carlos while she was here all well **Wed 28** Sylvia here and Wms= **Thursd 29** spun two skeins for Margret Winegar **Frid 30** made me a cap

July 1865

Satd July 1st 1865 I have sised a web for Mr Parry I am a going to weave it as soon as I can get a loom **Sund 2** I went to meeting **Mond 3** spooled and warped the web **Tuesd 4** went up to town to the celibration[30] P Gs folks were here Tomson and Julia staid here last night **Wed 5** ^went up to town with Agatha Pratt^ **Thursd 6 Frid 7** atended to my domestic concerns **Satd 8** picked currants I went and got my Bonnet **Sund 9** I went to meeting **Mond 10** I went up to P Gs staid there all night ^**Tuesd 11**^ went over to Davids see Phebe she went with me to Sylvias Liby was there with us after dinner I came home with P G he staid here all night ^got Sylvia some yarn^ **Wed 12** I dou-

---

29. Patty is referring to a cotton factory that was located in Parley's Canyon. It operated for two years, after which it was moved to St. George to bolster a flagging economy. In the celebration of Independence Day, "several young ladies from President Young's Cotton Factory neatly dressed in uniform" walked in the parade (JH, 4 July 1865).

30. The attitude of the pioneers toward the Independence Day celebration is expressed in a quotation from "Celebration of the Fourth" in the *Deseret News*, 5 July 1865, 316: "No other people can enter so fully as we can into a participation of the Spirit which animated the Revolutionary Fathers, for no others profess or possess such a breadth of faith in the inspiration that moved upon them. . . . We look upon the work which the Fathers of our country consummated as directed throughout by the Almighty, to prepare the way, by the framing of a government, free and liberal over all others, for the ushering in of the last dispensation, laden with blessings above every other that has preceded it."

bled it **Thursd 13** ~~Frd 14~~ I got two letters one from David the other from Carlos **Frid 14** [*written on top of* Thursd] I wrote to David and Carlos finished twisting the yarn for Sylvia **Satd 15** [*written on top of* Frid] **Sund 16** went to meeting **Mond 17 Tuesd 18** attended to my domestic concerns **Wed 19** evening got a loom set it up **Thursd 20** drawed in Mr ^Parrys^ web wove two yds **Frid 21** do 6 yds **Satd 22** wove 7 yds **Sund 23** went to meeting **Mond 24** wove 3 yds went up to town **Tuesd 25** wove 7 yds **Wed 26** wove 5 yds got the web out soon after I got it out I was taken very sick the Elders came & administered to me and I soon got better ~~Frid~~ **Thurd 27** I am so weak I can do but litle **Frid 28** I put in Sylvias carpet wove 4 yds **Sat 29** I wove 11 yds <Sund 30> do not go to meeting **Mond 31** wove 11 yds

AUGUST 1865

Tuesd ^**Aug 1st 1865**^ I put Nelly to bed with a Daughter^ ^Bartlett Tripps wife born 4 A M^ wove 6 -1*h* yds got it out took down the loom I have wove forty one yds for Mr Parry thirty 32 yds for Sylvia ten for myself ~~Thursd~~ **Wed 2 Thursd 3 Frid 4** we have been picking currants and drying **Satd 5** P G down & Phebe I went up to town got 9 ^lb^ sugar on an order **Sund 6** I went home with P G & Phebe ^&^ Henry Millard they put up my hay last night I went over to Sylvias Lucinia went with me I came back there staid all night **Mond 7** helped Lucinia put in a web went over to carlos,s then to Davids then back to P Gs staid all night ^**Tuesd 8th**^ set her web to work wove 2*h* yd then went up to Farmington ^with Wms & Sylvia^ to sister Franklin she is very sick then back to Father Parks to dinner ^stoped at Tomson Parks^ then to Sylvias staid all night came home with Sylvia & Wms. **Thursd 10 Frid 11** attended to my domestic concerns **Satd 12** watered my lot Bishop Stoker here & Jane[31] **Sund** ^**13**^ do not go to meeting **Mond 14 Tuesd 15 Wed 16** made a chese **Thursd 17 Frid 18** atended to many things bought 12 hundred of cole gave $15 for it **Satd 19** watered my lot went up to town ^with Sylvia & Wm,s^ bought some sugar on an order P G broug^ht^ me home he staid here all night ^~~Lewis~~ Lew with^ **Sund 20** do not go to meeting **Mond 21 Tuesd 22 Wed 23 Thurd 24 Frid 25** Father Parks and wife here to dinner[32] I sold them peck of Aples ^$1:25^ 8 qts of plumbs ^$2-00^ ~~under~~ **Satd 26** Cut Aples to drye P G here **Sund 27** he went home Henry and Jim went home with him I do not go to meeting **Mond 28** take care of my fruit I bought two cord of wood last Satd pay for it to day **Tuesd 29** P G & Lucinia down ~~He~~ he fixed my scaffold to drye fruit on I then went up to town with him got me a Sickle got 7 yds of cloth let Betsey have it **Wed**

---

31. Jane McDaniel or Jane Allen. Both of them were wives of Stoker.
32. Thomas Harris Parke (b. 1803) and Huldah Jane Curtis (b. 1805) were the parents of Julia's husband Thompson.

30 I bought a pair of stairs to go up on the scaffold with my fruit **Thursd 31** pairing and cuting Aples to drye

SEPTEMBER 1865

Frid Sept ^1st 1865^ went up to Sylvias ~~to~~ with Wm & Martha Smoot. To a party Phebe Janes birthday 14 years old **Satd 2** ^I sent David ten Dollars down to mudy^ I came home with Tripps boys I then watered my lot P G & Sarah & sister Mills here stay all night Gibs & wives go to Farmington I take care of thier things & milk **Sund 3** Sarah has gone home with her Father Carlos has come back from the Collorado Jim got home last Frid David is there yet I did not go to meeting to day **Mond 4 Tuesd 5 Wed 6** I have made me another Chese **Thursd 7** ^the wind blows very hard a great deal of my fruit down^ **Frid 8** I have been cuting and drying Aples **Satd 9** this morning the ground is covered with snow the trees bent to the ground and some of them broken sugar cane snarled every way still snowing and raining it is very cold Sylvia & Wms= come down she was very much chiled in the afternoon it cleared off they went home I fixed my cellar to put my Aples in **Sund 10** hard frost last night my other peach Orchard the trees are broken bad a great deal worse than either of these lots **Mond 11** I sent David fifty Dollars more **Tuesd 12 Wed 13 Thursd 14 & Frid 15 Satd 16** I have worked at my fruit all this week **Sund 17** I do not go to meeting **Mond 18 Tuesd 19 Wed 20 Thursd 21 Frid 22 Satd 23** I have worked at my fruit all this week. **Sund ^24** do not go to meeting P G here had a mare stole last night^ I was called to Br Greys to see Grace Wilsons babe very sick **Mond 25 Tuesd 26 Wed 27 Thursd 28 Frid 29 Satd 3[0]** I have done but litle this week beside work at my fruit Betsey and I have worked very hard all this month gathering and drying

OCTOBER 1865

Sund Oct 1-1865 Put Betsey Bouk to bed with a daughter [Mary] born 15 minutes before 5 A M I do not go to meeting **Mond 2 Tuesd 3 Wed 4** P G came after me to go up there Emeret sick put her to bed 7 P M [with a daughter, Lucina] **Thursd 5** came home gathered Peaches for tithing sister Willey dries them **Frid 6** Conference I go in the Afternoon **Satd 7** I go again **Sund 8** Betsey goes I go in the afternoon P G hears from his mare that was stole got the thief in jail P G & Wm= Smoot starts this evening after the mare at the head of Eco Canyon **Mond 9** It has rained hard most of the night rains hard this morning I go to the conference all day it has ajourned untill the 6 of Oct. next **Tuesd 10** it still rains P G has got back with his mare **Wed 11 Thursd 12** I still work with the fruit ^all the time **13-14-15-16-17-18-19^** have sold 33 = 2*h* bushels of Aples we gather them to day ^~~Frid 20~~^ **Frid 19** ^put Ann Eldrige to bed with a daughter [Margaret Jane] born 10 A M^ they have come to pack them P G came after me to go up there Mary is very sick he thinks she is dying I go and leave the men to measure and pack them **Satd 21** I come home **Sund 22** P G came after sister ^E R^ Snow to go up and wash and anoint Mary I went with her came home that night ^ met David got back from the mudy^ P G staid here all night **Mond 23** they took the Aples away **Tuesd 24** Tomson and Julia here she helped me gather Aples I let them have a bushel **Wed 25 Thursd 26 Frid 27** I have been gathering Aples ~~Satd 28~~ I have sold 57 qts of plumbs and 12 bushels of Aples and 3 bushels peaches it rains this evening John Boice has dug the potaoes put mine in the cellar and in a hole to burry **Satd 28** gathering Aples **Sund 29** do go to meeting **Mond 30 Tuesd 31** gathering Aples

NOVEMBER 1865

Wed ^1865^ Nov ^1st^ Thursd 2 Frid 3 finish gathering my Aples Sarah has got back here–her Father with her Sister Wintle here staid all night **Satd 4** I dug my carots **Sund 5** do not go to meeting **Mond 6** Betsey is spining get the manure hauled out **Tuesday 7 Wed 8 Thursd 9 Frid 10 Sat 11** Mary is still no better Lavinia has sent m[e] a web to finish spooling and to worp **Sund 12** do not go to meeting **Mond 13** spool and worp 39 yds **Tuesd ^14^** worp 19 yards more **wed 15** made me a cap **Thursd 16** I went up to P Gs **Frid 17** put in the web found Mary no better and Harvy sick I went over to Davids in the evening **Satd 18** I came home put my potatoes down cellar the wind blew very hard blew one pannel of my fence down **Sund 19** P G helped me put it up then went home I do not go to meeting **Mond 20** P G came down again said Mary was worse **Tuesd 21 wed 22** attend to my domestic concerns **Thursd 23** have a man to help me he took down my old stab[l]e cleared away the lumber **Frid 24** carlos here ^on^ **Satd 25 Sund 26** P G came down said Marry was Dead wished me and Betsey to to go up there we went **Mond 27** we helped make her clothes and helped put her in her coffin **Tuesd 28** she was buried we came home with E B Tripp **Wed 29 Thursd 30** Br Oostead here to work

DECEMBER 1865

Frid Dec 1st 1865 it rains and snows all day **Satd 2 Sund 3** do not go to meeting **Mond 4** P G and David came down here brought some lumber I went up town bought some nails **Tuesd 5** they built me a place for my cow P G went home I was caled to sister Marsden she was sick **Wed 6** David finished the cowhouse went home **Thursd 7** Thanksgiving day **Frid 8** I was caled to sister Marsden again P G and David came down again to build me a place for hay **Satd 9** I came home they have built me a good stable for my cow and hay went home I went to bed early not having any sleep the night before and working hard after I came home went to sleep woke up very sick with colery morbus and in great distress Mr Parry administered to me and I was made well imediately **Sund 10** I feel quite well only sore & weak it rains and snows to day in the evening Br Marsden came after me his wife sick again I told him I was not able to go on foot if he had a wagon I would try to go but he had none I told him who to get and he went after her **Mond 11** he sent me word that she had a pair of twins a son and a daughter **Tuesd 12 Wed 13 Thursd 14** the first day I have felt like work **Frid 15** David and Phebe came down a very cold day brought me some yarn to knit Carlos some mittens **Satd 16** I finished them **Sund 17** they came here again took the mittens and went home the snow fell last night and night before about 1 ft and 2*h* thawed some to day. I have shoveled snow untill I am very tired **Mond 18 Tuesd 19 Wed 20 Thursd 21 Frid 22** I have got my hay into the stable **Satd 23** it has snowed almost every day this week **Sund 24** get the snow shoveled of the roof of my house still snowing **Mond 25** Christmas I go up to E B Tripps he sent for me **Tuesd 26 Wed 27** more snow it is very deep roads bad **Thursd 28** P G here staid last night here again to day with Wm,s and Sylvia gone home **Frid 29** Betsey finishes spining Sylvias Rolls **Satd 30** Blacks the stove I bake mince pies we straiten up for New year **Sund 31** pleasant but bad walking I do not go to meeting ^Bartlett & Nelly here gave me a can of oisters^

1866

Br Greys . . . carried me across the water on his back put his wife to bed with a daughter

JANUARY 1866

Mond Jan= 1 ^1866^ new year Mr Parry and Hariet here to supper ^David Phebe P G Sarah P Gs wife here^ **Tuesd 2** I am not well **Wed 3** I feel better **Thursd** ^4^ cut me a dress **Frd 5** worked on my dress **Satd 6** P G & David Carlos & J Wintle here to dinner Carlos & Wintle staid all night **Sund 7** more pleasant has been very cold thaws a litle to day Carlos took me up to town yesterday in a sleigh I went to Brighams and to the store got some Nails and a fork & Betsey a pair of sh[o]es they go home to day **Mond 8 Tuesd 9 Wed 10** Bishop Stoker here to dinner with P G and David **Thursd 11** P G & Lucinia here take me with them down to Wm= Smoots they were gone we come back they staid here all night **Frid 12** they took me up to town I bought a quarter of beaf they brought it home for me then they went home ~~Satd 13~~ Sedenia [Cardenia Estella] Davids Girl came here to see me **Satd 13 Sund 14** I go and see Br Kesler he is badly hurt his hip broke **Mond 15** I crotiaing Betsey a net P G and Lucinia came here took ^me^ down to Wm Smoots we staid all night Sedenia went up to her Grandmother Foss,s [Sarah Brackett Carter Foss] **Tuesday 16** we came back Lucinia brought down some yarn For me to knit for Zina [daughter of Mary and Perrigrine] and Agnes [daughter of Fanny Emorett and Perrigrine] some mittins I have knit them I have brought home some more yarn for Wille and

Abe some mittins[33] **Wed 17 Thursday 18 Frid** finished them all **Satd 20** work on Betseys net **Sund 21** do not go to meeting **Mond 22 Tuesd 23 Wed 24** Wm= and Martha Ann here stay all night **Thurd 25** they went home P G came here **Frid 26 Satd 27** finished Betseys net P G here staid all night **Sund 28** Carlos and Libe here she staid all night he and P G went home **Mond ^29^** Sylvia and Wms here we had an oister soup **Tuesd 30** Libe went home **Wed 31** work on Phebes carpet rags

February 1866

Thursd Feb 1st 1866 Frid 2 Satd 3 Sund 4 I go to meeting the first time I have been since conference it is my birth day seventy one years old **Mond 5** John Fisher and Josephine with her twin boys Sylvia and Wms all here I went to the Theatre with them[34] **Tuesd 6** they took me up to town I had my likeness taken Photograph 12 of them then they went home it rains **Wed 7 Thursd 8** David and Ezra Foss [1833–1919, brother of David's wife, Phebe] staid here all night **Frid 9 Satd 10** we finish Phebes carpet rags **Sund 11** we go to meeting **Mond 12** we wash **Tuesd 13** P G & David here to dinner P G staid all night **^Wed 14^** let him have 35 Dollars for David **Thursd 15 Frid 16** Wms, and Sylvia here I went up to town with them then staid here all night **Satd 17** I went home with them stoped at P Gs took dinner then went over to Davids came back to P Gs staid all night **Sund 18** Wms= came over with the team took David and Phebe and Lize and me over to Sylvias Tomson Parks and Julia John Fisher and Josephine all there P G came over in the eve **Mond 19** Wms= brought me home Sylvia came I commenced Wms= a pair of mittens **Tuesd 20 Wed 21** David here to dinner **Thursd 22** finished Wm,s mittens commenced a pair for Carlos **Frd 23 Satd 24** finished making me a dress **Sund 25** do not go to meeting it is so mudy **Mond 26 Tuesd 27 Wed 28** finished writing a letter to my Br Jon= Bartlett

March 1866

Thursd March 1st 1866 Frid ^2^ Satd ^3^ finished crotiaing me a cap. Sent the letter to the Ofice with my likeness in it to go to my Br and Mother, Br stoker staid here last night. P G. here to day **Sund 4** I go to meeting **Mond 5 Tuesd 6** finished Carlos mittens **Wed 7 Thursd 8** work in the garden **Frid**

---

33. William Cochran Adkinson Smoot, Jr., and his brother Abraham Owen Smoot were the two sons of Martha Ann and William Smoot.

34. On 5 February 1866, the JH records, "A benefit was given in the Salt Lake Theatre for John T. Caine, on which occasion Edward W. Tullidge's historic play 'Eleanor Devere' or 'The Queen's Secret' was played for the first time. Bro. Tullidge was called before the curtain and received the vociferous plaudage of the house; John T. Caine was also called before the curtain and delivered a very appropriate but short speech. Miss Hayne, as usual was called before the curtain."

9 Carlos here got 49 trees Aple and plumb trees fixed up my stairs on the side of the stable **Satd 10** David Phebe & Lucinia here Wm= Smoot & Martha all here to dinner Martha took sick she was agoing up to her Fathers but she could not go David started back with them she got to Br Smoots could not go any forther David wife and Lucinia staid here all night **Sund 11** we went to see Martha she was a litle better but could not set up I then went to meeting **Mond 12** work on some fringe for Julia Grow **Tuesd 13 Wed 14** the same **Thurd 15** wash some of my wool Carlos came here to work for me **Frid 26** he put up fence on my lot acros the street **Satd 17** John Fisher & Josephine and their Mothers and the twins they got their likenesses taken David Phebe & P G here Carlos went home with them **Sund 18** I do not go to meeting I do not feel well **Mond 19** sorting my Aples **Tuesd 20** Wms & Sylvia here got some trees 60 Dollars worth **Wed 21 Thursd 22 Frid 23 Satd 24 Sund 25** ^P G here^ do not go to meeting David and Phebe here **Mond 26** Sarah here **Tuesd 27 Wed 28 Thursd 29 Frid 30** I went up to P Gs put ^**Satd 31**^ Sarah to bed with a daughter [Mary] born 2 2*h* P M

April 1866

Sund April ^1st^ **1866** snowed and rained hard **Mond 2** still snowing and raining all day **Tuesd 3** I came home found all well **Wed 4** A two days meeting commenced to day ~~Thur~~ I do not go **Thursd 5** I go to day **Frd 6** Conference commenced I do not go Betsey went **Satd 7** I go **Sund 8** We both go the conference ajourned **Mond 9** Convention P G & Bishop Stoker staid here last night here to day after meeting Byron & Cam brought me two load of lumber from my old Jones house lot P G ^helped me make a chicken coop^ have 40 Aple trees **Tuesd 10 Wed 11 Thursd 12** went up to E B Tripps got a tidy to crotia one for Julia Grow I have got her fringe done E B was taken very sick while I was there had the Doctor **Frid** ^13^ he is some better **Satd 14** Sylvia down **Sund 15** I go to meeting come back to Bartlett Tripps took supper **Mond 16** I was very sick last night feel very bad to day **Tuesd 17** Mr Pary is very sick sent for me **Wed 18** he came up here **Thursd 19 Frd 20 Satd 21** been at work on Julias tidy **Sund 22** do not go to meeting hear that Sarah P Gs wife is very sick **Mond 23 Tuesd 24** I go up to see Sarah find her a little better **Tuesd 25** I came home went with Ezra Foss he got my rolls for me **Thursd 26** Betsey began to spin **Frid 27** I went up to E Bs he is worse **Sat 28** some better **Sund 29** Mr Parry is sick sent for me again **Mond 30** he is better I go and see Bartlett and Nelle start for the East E B Sophia and I go with them to the canyon came back by the camp Sedenia came here

May 1866

Tuesd May 1 ^ts^ **1866** I went up to Davids with Ezra and Sedenia she went a May walking it rained went to P Gs staid all night **Wed 2** went to Davids again Sylvia came there we all worked for Phebe **Thursd 3** I came home went and see Mr Parry ^better^ **Frid 4 Satd 5** Wms & Sylvia P G & David and Br Crosley here **Sund 6** been to see Mr Parry again found him out door **Mond 7** he came here **Tuesd 8** we wash **Wed 9** I iron **Thursd 10 Frid 11** work on Julia Grows Tidy **Satd <12>** Wms & Sulvia here I went home with them stay untill **Mond 14** Sedenia S Sessions came home with me she wants to live with me she is my grand daughter Mr Parry is quite smart came here last night **Tuesd 15** Betsey has got her a bonnet **Wed 16 Thursd 17 Frid ^18^** P G David Byron & a man from calyfornia all here to dinner **Satd 19** the water is very high the men are hauling brush & banking up **Sund 20** very high the men work all day on the street **Mond 21** Water still rising **Tuesd 22** ^Sylvia & Wms= here I went to town with them got some indigo^ Commence coloring blue **Wed 23** Carlos here fixed my cellar the water came into it a foot deep put some brush and gravel on the side of the street for me I gave him a pair of flannel shirts for it He brought me a load of straw to put in if needed **Thursd 24 Frid 25** it rained last night **Satd 26** ^P G here lost money came by stage last night~~ **Sund 27** rains ~~Mr Parry~~ **Mond 28** ~~P G David Phebe** and Sarah came Sarah staid here P G & David went to meeting then went home ^Betsey went with them^ **Mond 28** Sarah and I went up to Tripps on a visit **Tuesd ^29^** went to see Mary Elen Kimball she was not at home we called on sister Hyde **Wed 30 Thurd 31** P G Lucinia Phebe Davids wife ^and Betsey^ came down Sarah went home with them

JUNE 1866

Frid June ^1st^ 1866 **Satd 2** P G came here in the night came in the stage lost some money **Sund ^3^** it rains I do not go to meeting **Mond 4** we wash I go up to town get my watch ^put a letter in the office for E B Bartlett^ it has been there since conference **Tuesd 5** Liby ^Carlos s wife^ came here could not get home staid all night **Wed 6** rains ^David came here staid^ **Thursd 7** rains very hard Phebe Clark came here could not get home **Frid 8** ^fair^ they all started for home **Satd 9** cloudy **Sund 10** rains hard this morning the water higher in my cellar than ever has been I do not go to meeting **Mond 11** I wash a litle scour some yarn Wms & Sylvia and Martha here all go home **Tuesd 12 Wed 13** Davids wife came here staid all night **Thursd 14** Cedenia went with her home **Frid 15** ~~fany~~ Fanny came here **Satd 16** she went up to town with Betsey **Sund 17** Wm,s Sylvia Phebee Jane ^&^ Martha all here & David they all went to meeting Betsey went with them they all came back here took dinner then went home took Fanny with them **Mond 18** Collor my yarn black the water very high runing into my lots my cellar full up to the adobes **Tuesd 19** Color Red the water s[t]ill runing onto my lots **Wed 20** size my yarn **Thursd 21 Frid 22 Satd 23** attend to my domestick concerns got the water stopt off of my lots **Sund <24>** it is broke over again evening get it stoped again **Mond 25** broke over again runing into both lots untill evening get it turned off again we think the water has began to fall David came down brought Cedenia down **Tuesd 26 Wed 27 Thursd 28** I have got my web spooled and worped **Frid 29 Satd 30** I went last night to Br Greys [John C. Gray] his wife sick he carried me across the water on his back put his wife to bed with a daughter born half past Seven A M

July 1866

Sund July 1 ^**1866**^ do not go to meeting I am lame **Mond 2** I have sold 34 quarts of strawberrys to day David staid here last night **Tuesd 3 Wed 4 Thursd 5 Frid 6 Satd 7** I have Taken ~~sold~~ over fifty Dollars for strawberrys this week money **Sund 8** I go to meeting hear a cambelite preacher[35] **Mond 9** put my web in **Tuesd 10 Wed 11 Thurs 12** ^David got his mares that was stole^ **Frid 13 Satd 14** I have been weaving **Sund 15** I do not go to meeting Betsey & Cedenia goes **Mond 16 Tuesd 17 wed 18 Thursd 19 Frid 20 Satd 21** got my web out ^37^ put the other in 37 ^yds^ more drawed it through the harness then went up to Sylvias with Tripps folks **Sund** ^**22**^ came home **Mond 23** I am waiting for a reed to put my web in **Tuesd 24** I went over to Salt Lake with E B Tripps and family went into the Lake and bathed came home **Wed 25** still waiting for the reed get the read draw in the web **Thursd 26** have got my grass cut **Frid 27** We have spread it **Satd 28** we put some of it up in bunches **Sund 29** I do not go to meeting it rains Bishop Stoker here to dinner **Mond 30** we have to open the hay **Tuesd 31** it is not dry enough to put up

August 1866

Wed August 1^**st**^ **1866** we put the hay up good **Thursd 2 Frid 3 Sat 4** I have been weaving when I could I got my hay into the Stable drye P G here ^and Sarah^ staid all night **Sund 5** I do not go to meeting it rains **Mond 6 Tuesd 7** I get my web out 37 yds took the loom down **Wed 8 Thursd 9** double some yarn commence a pair of mittens **Frid 10** ^it rains very hard^ **Satd 11 Sund 12** I do not go to meeting the ground is wet in the Bowery Betsey ^and D[enia]^ goes **Mond 13 Tuesd 14 Wed 15** ^put Amanda [Elizabeth Conrad Mitchell, b. 1849] wife of Robert [Mathias] Harmon [b. 1844] to bed with a son [Robert Joshua] born 11 P M^ **Thursd 16** David staid here last night gone for cole [coal] Denia [Cardenia] gone to Martha Anns I commence a pair of mittens for Wallase Tripp **Frid 17** put in a web for sister Riser **Satd 18** finished Walase mittens **Sund 19** I go to meeting **Mond 20 Tuesd 21**

35. At the time the Mormon Church was organized, other religions were forming. One such was founded by Thomas and Alexander Campbell. Thomas Campbell is reputed to have said, "where the Scriptures speak, we speak, where the Scriptures are silent, we are silent." Many early Campbellites converted to Mormonism (John Henry Evans, *Joseph Smith An American Prophet* [New York: The Macmillan Co., 1946], 214).

David & Sedenia got back she and I went home with him then we went to P
Gs staid all night ^**Wed 22**^ I then went and see Carlos wife then went to
Sylvias she had a quilting went to P Gs staid all night **Thursd** ^**23**^ came
home got some lime I had three load of hay from my farm **Frid 24** another
load P G came down he stacked it **Satd 25** I white washed and put down my
new carpet **Sund 26** I do not go to meeting Betsey and Sedenia goes **Mond 27**
~~Thud~~ **Tuesd 28 Wed 29 Thurd 30** ~~Fr~~ Make soap **Frid 31**

SEPTEMBER 1866

Satd Sept 1st 1866 we wash **Sund 2** I go to meeting **Mond 3** I com to dry
Aples **Tuesd 4** Carlos,s wife here **Wed 5** Sylvia here **Thursd 6** Drying Aples
Frid 7 ^Mr Parry is sick I go and see him^ Martha Clark here **Sat 8** she is
here we are cuting Aples I have aired my fruit got it all put up **Sund 9** I do not
go to meeting Betsey Cedenia and Martha goes **Mond 10** Wms Sylvia here
Martha goes home with them **Tuesd 11 Wed 12 Thursd 13 Frid 14 Satd 15** I
have been tak care of my fruit and dring Aples & plumbs **Sund 16** I go to meeting **Mond 17** commence dring peaches **Tuesd 18 Wed 19 Thursd 20 Frid 21**
Satad 22 worked very hard gathering and drying my fruit **Sund 23** I have put
Betsey Whitecar to bed with a daughter [Rachel] born 4: $2h$ A M I do not go to
meeting it is very cold looks likely to rain snow on the bench land Cedenia
gone up to her Fathers she came home **Mond 24 Tuesd 25 Wed 26 Thurd 27**
Frid 28 I have been to work with my fruit all the week **Satd 29** I carried my
plums tithing up to Brighams P G took another wife [Sarah Ann Bryson,
1849/50–1934] to day they came here to dinner Lucinia and Sarah with them.
Sund 30 I have been to meeting to day wrote a letter to Bartlett Tripp

OCTOBER 1866

Mond Oct= 1^**st**^ **1866** Sent it to the Office **Tuesd 2 Wed 3 Thursd 4 Frid**
5 Satd 6 Conference ^to day Sylvia & he [probably Joshua P. Williams] came
here^ Betsey goes I stay at home take care of my fruit we have worked with it
all the week **Sund 7** We all go to meeting **Mond 8** We all go again Conference
Ajourned **Tuesd 9 Wed 10 Thursd 11 Frid 12** gathering fruit all the time
Satd 13 rains and snows **Sund 14** do not go to meeting **Mond 15** wash **Tuesd**
16 Wed 17 Thursd 18 Frid 19 It has been wet and cold all the week it rains
this afternoon I have sliped and fell and hurt my Ankle and foot that I could
scarcely get up **Satd 20** it has pained very much last night I cannot walk on it
but I can sit up and put it in a chair and feel quite well that it is no worse **Sund**
21 it is a litle better to day **Mond 22** Mr Parry said this morning it would be
well before night. It began to feel better and grew stronger from that moment
before night I laid by my croutches and walked with ease **Tuesd 23** been on it
all day with out hurting me any at all **Wed 24** the same **Thursd 25 Frid 26**
Satd 27 I have worked hard all the time gathering and taking care of my fruit
felt no inconvenance from my lameness. Thank the Lord for faith and the

power of the Preisthood **Sund 28** I do not go to meeting Betsey went **Mond 29 Tuesd 30** Margaret Winegar staid here last night I gave her some peaches for preserves **Wed 31**

NOVEMBER 1866

^**Thurd**^ **Nov= 1 - 1866 Frid** ^**2**^ David Byron Carlos Kepler and Perry here to dinner **Satd 3** Sylvia here I went up to E Bs= with her found Josephine there **Sund 4** I went to meeting **Mond 5** I went up to P Gs with him and Sarah Cedenia went with me We went over to Davids got her dress cut I staid all night to P Gs **Tues 6** went to Davids again Phebe and I almost mad[e] Cedenias dress staid all night at P Gs **Wed 7** David brought us home we stoped a few minutes at Carlos-s **Thursd 8 Frid 9 Satd 10** put sister Wood to bed with a daughter born ^ten^ 10 minutes before two P M **Sund 11** we do not go to meeting snow 5 or six inches deep fell last night still snoing **Mond 12 Tuesd 13** let Wm= Newmam have ten Dollars ~~M~~ Money to get ^wood to boil^ my part of the cane Juice. After he had promised to get it boiled ^and^ deliver my molasses at my house. He demanded the money said my part of the cane might rot on the ground if I did not let him have the ten dollars. I let him have [it] saying in my heart the Lord would prosper me as well without it as he would him with it **Wed 14 Thursd 15** P G and David here **Frid 16** P G and Lucinia here went [to] Wm= Smoots wished me to go with them I did not go **Satd 17** they came back stopted here to dinner **Sund 18** I do not go to meeting Betsey and Cedenia goes **Mond 19** had a man here cutting wood **Tuesd 20 Wed 21 Thursd 22** I have been preparing for winter **Frid 23** made me a cap **Satd 24** Carlos and Libe here took supper [t]hey had a new bedsted **Sund 25** We do not do [go] to meeting it rains I got my molasses home yestarday about twenty 1 or 2 galons **Mond 26 Tuesd 27** we wash **Wed 28 Thursd 29 Frid 30** I have knit P G a pair of mittens Sylvia here & Martha & Perry

DECEMBER 1866

Satd Dec 1st 1866 Carlos & Perry here gone to Wm= Smoots **Sund 2** it snows we do not go to meeting Mr Parry here I give him a pair of flanel drawers **Mond 3** I am knitting **Tuesd 4 Wed 5 Thursd 6 Frid 7** ~~Satd 8~~ I have been kniting the most of the time this week **Satd 8** Mr Parry was very sick last night in the night he sent for me thought he would not live until morning I went he wished me to lay hands on him I anointed him Harriet and I laid hands on him he was healed instantly ~~Satd~~ At night I went home with David Phebe was sick got better before I got there **Sund 9** John Fisher came after me his boy was sick I stayed all night with Sylvia **Mond 10** I went with her to see Julia she has a babe 3 days old [Mary Effie Parke] **Tuesd 11** I came home. went back again untill **Sund 16** came home **Mond 17 Tuesd 18 Wed 19** I have knit a pair of mittens since I came home **Thursd 20** commenced another pair **Frid 21** finished them **Satd 22** P G sent me 20 bushels of wheat and ten bushels of

potatoes toward my part for the use of my farm **Sund 23** I went to meeting
Mr Parry came home took very sick got better about 12 at night **Mond 24**
David sent for me his wife sick she had a son [Calvin Foss] born before I got
there I came home Sedenia went up with her Father **Tuesd 25** christmas I
went up to E B Tripps **Wed 26 Thursd 27** Cedenia came home Betsey went
up **Frid 28** Mr Parry sick he sent for me I went and see him **Satd 29** he is better **Sund 30** I do not go to meeting it snows **Mond Ɠ 31** the Last day of this
year I feel thankful to the Lord for the preservation of my life thus far and I
desire to live the remainder ^of my life^ in his service And among his saints
Which may he grant in the name of Jesus Christ Amen

*[Here there is an inexplicable gap in the diaries. Little is known of Patty's life during the
missing years, although her chronological overview in Diary 7 fills some of the gaps. Perhaps
she wrote other diaries that have disappeared or are yet to be found. When her diaries
picked up her story later, she was eighty-five and still doing "many things," although her
medical work and midwifery had largely ceased. During the interim she had temporarily
kept a cooperative store.]*

July 1880

July 1880 Sund 4 we went to meeting **Mond 5** we went to the celabratiuon of
[Independence Day] enjoyed the time firstrate **tuesd 6** I went to the R S [Relief
Society] and to the store got some calico for Betsey a dress caried some tithing
peas and fast Donations **wed 7** put on a rug as I have finished the other and
made it up **Thud 8** work on it **Frid 9 Satd 10** work on the rug **Sund 11** we
went to meeting **Mond 12 Tuesd 13** work on the rug **Wend 14** watter the lot
& work on the rug **Thursd 15** got it done and made up and put another on
Frid 16 conference R S Liza and Zina Young up I go to meeting Primary and
all **Satd 17** work on the rug all day got my hay into the barn good **Sund 18**
dry and warm weather we went to meeting **Mond 19 Tuesd 20** got my rug
out and made up **wend 21** cut out Blocks for a quilt **Thursd 22** sewed 15 of
them **Frid 23** sewed five Blocks got ready went to the city staid all night to E
B Tripps **Satd 24** went to the celibration of the day we entered the valley 33
years ago a grand time staid all night to Tripps and went to meeting then went
to se[e] a family was burnt by the explosion of a can of oil the man and his
wife and two children burnt bad the little girl is dead[36] I then went again to

---

36. The *Deseret News* for 29 July 1880 reported that Mr. Julius Selander of the 16th
   ward took a can from his woodshed to fill with coal oil from a five-gallon can. As
   he poured from the large can to the smaller, it exploded, severely burning him,
   his two children, and his wife, who rushed to their aid. Mr. Selander's teeth were
   driven up into his nose and he sustained a broken jaw. He experienced profuse
   bleeding, as well. Immediately following the news item was information on safe
   handling of coal oil and how to tell high quality oil.

Trips staid all night **Mond 26** went up in town got me a rocking chair and some other things and came home on the cars[37] **Tuesd 27** wattered my lot and sewed peices for a quilt **wed 28** cut out blocks for a quilt sewed on them Teachers meeting here **thd 29 Frid 29 Frid 30 Satd 31** finished peicing my quilt commenced another

AUGUST 1880

Sund August 1–1880 warm Days & cool nights I take 3 papers Deseret News Juvinelle Instructo[r] & Womans Exponant. I read them all we went to meeting **Mond 2 Tuesd 3 Wed 4 Thursd 5** fast day went to meeting went to R S Tuesd **Frid 6** put in my quilt got it out **Satd 7** made it up put in rug **Sund 8** went to meeting **Mond 9 Tuesd 10 Wed 11 Thursd 12** got me a dress cut **Frid 13** made it and Bask **Satd 14** have got my Lucern cut and in the Barn the rest of my time I have worked on my rug Got a letter from W C A Smoot yestarday **Sund 15** I have wrote a letter Wm C A Smoot went to meting **Mond 16** worked on my rug **Tuesd 17** Wallace W Bartlett came here yestarday this morning wished me to go to E B Tripps with him and P G I went had a good visit **Thursd 19** came home **Frid 20** finished my rug **Satd 21** did many things got a letter from W C A Smoot Jun **Sund 22** all well went to meting **Mond 23 1880 Tuesd 24** got ready to go to cash valley we went **Wend**

---

37. The first public transportation in Salt Lake City was mule-drawn trolley cars that began operation in 1872. The fare was ten cents for about a half-hour ride (see John S. McCormick, *Salt Lake City: The Gathering Place* [Woodland Hills, Calif.: Windsor Publications, 1980]).

Diary seven covers the years from 1884 to 1888 and measures about 8 x 12½ inches. It is well preserved, with a marbled tan and brown cover and black-watermarked paper. This diary is a more recent addition to Patty's records, generously donated to the LDS Church Historical Department by a descendant of Perrigrine, who had become its custodian. Courtesy of LDS Church Archives; photograph by J M Heslop.

DIARY SEVEN, 1884–1888

Patty Sessions must have possessed an unusual sense of history and the importance of one life. She began yet another record book, perhaps in 1884, since that is when her diary entries begin, but she included many other records, as well. She logged the dates of her reminiscences patriarchal blessings, numerous pages of genealogical information, and minutes of the Benevolent Society of the sixteenth ward, and wrote everything carefully in her own hand. Perhaps she realized some of her diaries were missing and wanted to fill in the gap. Her daily inscriptions had become such a habit that she continued at her advanced age to write a few words when she really didn't have anything to say, except repetitious accounts of what handiwork she was diligently accomplishing.

Nevertheless, there is something compelling about such persistence. She persisted well into her nineties. She made scores of rugs, cleaned snow off her house, cleared trees from her orchard, knitted, colored fabric, dug sage, weeded and worked the ground, and cut and dried fruit. But she gradually declined in health, dexterity, and mental acuity. We witness the winding down of a life in dramatic and touching ways. Readers may not be prepared for that experience, even as human beings are seldom prepared for the slowing of their own lives, a universal condition that makes Patty's heroic efforts to maintain productiveness particularly touching.

Will and Ariel Durant expressed a thought that may further explain Patty's painstaking record keeping:

If a man is fortunate he will, before he dies, gather up as much as he can of his civilized heritage and transmit it to his children. And to his final breath he will be grateful for this inexhaustible legacy, knowing that it is our nourishing mother and our lasting life. If progress is real . . . it is not because we are born any healthier, better, or wiser than infants were in the past, but because we are born to a richer heritage[1]

---

1. Will Durant and Ariel Durant, "Is Progress Real?" *The Lessons of History* (New York: Simon and Schuster, 1968), chap. 13, pp. 101–2.

Retrospective Chronology and Financial Record

[Inside the front cover, Patty instructed what should become of this diary, and then wrote a retrospective account and chronology of her life, which became primarily a record of important financial transactions. The chronology helps fill in the gaps in Patty's earlier diaries. In this section many end marks appear, a number of which have been deleted. She must have touched her pen to the paper as she pondered.]

This Book when I Patty Sessions have done with it is to be given to Perrigrine Sessions My Son=

When we came into this valley I had one five cent peice which I picked up on the red Bute and since Mr Sessions died I have took care of myself and have laid up considerable [*scratched out, indecipherable*] I have always paid my tithing my fasts my taxes and all other demands. And have donated when called upon For Public purposes. And some donations when not called upon I gave liberaly. I have done these things with a willing heart and hand and the Lord has blessed me in basket and in my store. He has blessed me with the enjoyment of his holy spirit which has comforted my heart in every time of need. And I have to say to my Grand children and Great Grand children. Be faithful in paying your tithing your fasts donations. And responding to every call made by the Authorities of the Church be punctual in fulfilling all your contracts. Be faithful in your Prayers in your families. And elsewhere. Do right let the result follow. And the Lord will bless you with wisdom, knowledge. and inteligence. Riches, Honor, and every good thing that your hearts can desire in righteousness. Teach your litle ones to pray as soon as they can lispe a prayer. And they will call down blessings upon your heads The blessings of health when you are sick. and long life for this is what a child most desires for thier parents. Pray with them continually And they will be more obedient to you. I have kept up family prayer in my house ever since Mr Sessions died. And when I had but one beside myself and that a litle girl I have knelt and prayed with and for her. And I do know that I have been blesed and prospered a great deal better than if I had not done it

I Patty Sessions Daughter of Enoch & Anna [Hall] ^Bartlett^ Was Born Feb: 4th. 1795. in the Town of Bethel, County, of Oxford, State. of Maine. – Married. to David Sessions. **June 28.th** ^**1812**^. I bore him Eight children. Four Sons and Four. daughters. Three of them are still living. Perrigrine [1814–1893]. Sylvia [Porter, 1818–1882]. and David [1823–1896].

I buried Four of them in Maine [Sylvanus, Anna, Anna B., and Bartlett] and one ^in Nauvoo^ [Amanda] I was Baptised. into the church of Jesus Christ of Latter Day. Saints In Maine. **July 2^d^. 1834.** ^by Elder Daniel Bean^ Moved to Missouri in **1837** with my husband and three children. Gave birth to a daughter soon after I got there. Perrigrine had a wife and one child. ~~Sylvia~~ Sylvia was married to Windsor. P. Lyon. [in] Mo.

We we were all driven out in the winter of **1839** We started **Feb. 15** I brought my child, all the way ^sick^ in my arms. We arived in Ilinois. **April 2^d^.1839**. Staid on Bear creek one year. Moved to Nauvoo **May 2^d^1840**. My child that was born in Mosouri, ^she^ Died **May 15 1841** in Nauvoo–We were driven from Nauvoo in the winter of **1846**. My husband, and I. We left our children There Crossed the Missisippi river **Feb. 12** with Many of the Brethren. Went to Sugar Creek camped two weeks without a tent very cold the river froze over. After this we had a tent the most of the way. We arived at winter ^quarters^ now Florance **Sept= 25** Perrigrine And family overtook us at the Bluffs **June 22^d^** he and his Father built a house at Winter quarters. we staid there untill **June 5th.1847** Then we started for a resting place we knew not where Arived in this Valley **Sept. 24th. 1847**. I drove A four ox team all the way. In the fifty third year of my age.–**June. 26 1850** David my son Arived here.–**August 11** ^**1850**^ Mr Sessions my husband died. After his death I built me a house where I now ^live^ in Salt Lake City moved into it the **3^d^** **of Dec 1850**. **Sept=-17-1851** I was apointed first counselser for sister [Phoebe] Angel[l] she was Presidentes of the counsel of health

Dec 14–1851. I was Married to John Parry seni[or] **March 27–1852** I was sealed to him for time When the Perpetual emigration ^Fund^ was organised I put in five Dollars. The next I put in was ten dollars more I did not make a minute of any more that I paid in untill **Nov 1^st^1853** I put in fifteen Dollars cash. And a **13** ^**Nov**^ cloak apprised at ten Dollars. And a hat two Dollars

May 21–1854 gave Br Jedidiah Grant twenty five Dollars to bye wheat for the Public hands

June 10–1854 The sisters was caled to gether by Bishop Rowndy to organise a benevolent society to clothe the Indians. I was put in Presidentes over the society

August 5–1854 My son Perrigrine with my daughter Sylvia Arived in this vally My son had been gone almost two years on a mission to Europe. And had been sick the most of the time. And I had not seen my Daughter for more than seven years We met each other with tears of joy.

Dec. 13.–1854. I gave ten Dollars into the Perpetual Emigration Fund, cash.

March. 14. 1855. I was appointed Presidentes over the females of the counsel of health. And sister Susannah Richards My first And Judith Higbee my second councelers. All three of us by a unanimous vote. To be sustained in our places. Much good done in both societies over which I presided The squaws were cloked the sick and the poor were visitet and administered to and their wants releived.

Feb. 25 1856 I have been and got my Deed of consecration from the recorders Office. And delivered it to the Govns Office For the Trusttee in

Trust I have been to a good deal of trouble and have had many journeys up in town to get the Deed filed out And to acknowledge it and get it recorded. But it is all done now; and I feel very thankful for it. I am happy

April 22 ^1856^ I have built a picket fence round my lot finished & paid for it ^ (myself six feet high^

May 22–1856 I gave twenty Dollars to the Perpetual Emigration Fund. About this time F[rederick] Kesler became Bishop ^ (in place of^ S[hadrack] Roundy

June 1 ^st^–1856 gave Bishop Kesler five dollars to hire men to work on the cannel to bring the water to our ^ (lots^

June 3. I h^i^red a man to work on the cannel.

August 2.^d^1856. I gave two Dollars to bye flour to carry to the emigration Co.=

Oct 5. [*written over* Sep] A call for clothing and flour to send back to the hand cart Co.= I carried some clothing a mans coat. shoes, stockings, sack shawl &c to the Taberna^=cle^

Nov. 30.–1856 The last handcart Co. came in. the Bishop sent me one of the boys 17 years old I cleaned him up dresed his feet which were froze bad I gave him a new pair of socks and a flanel shirt a cap and comforter & pants ^ (&c^ The next day the Bishop sent for him to go to Provo. I gave him the clothes for his was not fit to put ^ (on^

Jan. 4.1857 The Bishop sent one of the same company A woman to stay here untill she could get another place she staid about two weeks

April 8 1857 Brigham caled for one hundred and twe^n^ty five Dollars money. I gave all I had.

March 9.–1857 I was rebaptised with the rest of the saints[2] I have donated for the boys to go & meet the emigration & when when they came in I made no minute of it it was in 1857

May 25. 1858 I moved south stoped at American fork untill **July 6th 1858** then I came back with the rest of the saints.

Oct= 18–1858 I got the last of things from American fork and I felt very thankful

June 6 1859 I commence to gather material to build an addition to my house

---

2. Joseph Fielding Smith in *Doctrines of Salvation* explains why rebaptism was established in the day of the Prophet Joseph Smith and continued for a number of years in Utah under Brigham Young. He states that some members who had transgressed were rebaptized; others renewed their covenants as evidence of their gratitude for deliverance from enemies; and members whose records had been lost or destroyed were baptized to obtain certificates. For these reasons and others, all Mormons who entered the valley were baptized—and settlers obviously joined them (comp. Bruce R. McConkie [Salt Lake City: Bookcraft, 1955], 2: 332–35).

June 21 1859 I commenced worked on my house

August 11–1859 my house is finished and paid for material and all ^cost^ over $700=00 over sevenen hundred dollars

August 23 1859 I put twenty Dollars into the perpetual emigration Fund

Jan= 7 1860 I got P G my son to attend a sale and bid of a lot adjoining the one I live on at two hundred dollars. the next monday I went paid the money and got the Deed.

Sep= ^t^ 21–1860 I gave Bishop Kesler five dollars cash for the missionaries

Feb= 21–1861 I gave Presd= Brigham Young two hundred Dollars gold as a deposit untill I call for it

Sep=^t^ 9 1861 I boarded a man a week to work on the tabernacle gave the board

March 24–1862. I gave Presd= Brigham Young One hundred and Seventy five Dollars For him to use untill I call for it gold

March 31 1862 I have my granery commenced building to day

^April^ ~~March~~ <April> **21 1862** I got my granery built finished Cost me five hundred Dollars paid for

May 16 1862 I gave dried peaches and beans to the Bishop for the boys that go to the states after the poor seven Dollars worth 7.00

June 25 1862 I had my wheat all moved to the tithing office The water was so high we was afraid it would all be washed away house and all it flowed over both my lots. and for six weeks I did not lay in bed one night there was one hundred sixty nine bushels ^(20 lb^ and **July 1st 1862** the water began to fall

Sep-^t^ 13 1862 I have had the roof of my house ^new^ shingled cost me over one hundred Dollars it is paid for

April 15 1863 I gave him ^Presd= Young^ seventy five Dollars for the missionaries. I have put in five Dollars before ^all^ befere gold and silver. <u>And twenty five pounds dried peaches.</u> And ten pounds dried peaches and three and a half yards of sheeting To those that go after the saints to the Missouri River

1863 August 11 I gave two thousand three hundred and fifty pounds of flour for the building of the new tabernacle

Sept= 28 I bought a cow of Mr Parry. gave thirty five dollars for her

1863 Oct= 1 ^st^ I bought a colt of G[ideon] Gib[b]s gave forty Dollars 1863 for it

Nov= 16 1863 Naomi debenham came here to stay a few days to rest her. she was a stranger to me I never saw her before she said she was tired out and full of grief she had buried her Brother the day before. she took very sick the Doctors were here to see her one said she could not live. but by the faith of the saints and the power of the priesthood and good nursing she got well

Dec= 12= 1863. She left here but not able to pay any thing for her trouble she was here four weeks lacking two days.

April 29 1864. I bought a piece of land of Carlos Sessions up the canyon gave him fifty Dollars for it

April 30 1864 I Paid one hundred and thirty Dollars cash for a yoke of oxen to send to the states to bring the poor saints on.

1864 May 5 I have bought a house and a part of a lot of. Step^h^en Winegar gave him two hundred and seventy five Dollars for it. It is acros the street south West from me.

1864 May 10 I bought two lots in city Bountif^ul^ of William Jones gave him two hundred dollars for them. and I bought some lumber in a shanty and other things gave him thirty five Dollars for it

1864 June 9 5 I lent four hundred Dollars green backs to to Joshua P Williams <never Paid one cent of it> [*the words below the line are in different ink, as if added later*]

June 17 I bought a mare of George Grant gave two hundred and twenty five dollars for her

Oct 24 1864 I bought me a stove gave one hundred and eighty five dollars for it and gave my other one to my grand son Carlos Sessions boudht a load of coal paid paid forty two dollars and fifty cents over a ton of it two dollars worth

Jan 1866 <May> I bought a farm of my son David Sessions paid him eightteen hundred and sixty Dollars for it

1867 June 1st I got a kitchen built on the backside of my other house that I bought of Stephen Winegar cost me fifty Dollars.

1867 June 13 got ^me^ a cupboard worth sixty Dollars made of boxelder the tree was set out at the corner of my house in the spring of fifty two. not more than eightten inches high. cut down in the spring of sixty six Made into the cupboard June 1867

1867 Sept. 2 I have sent to the states got a cider mill gave forty seven Dollars thirty cents for it delivered here

Sept. <3d>1867 I have had a room put onto my house cost five hundred sixty dollars.

1867 Sept 28 I have donated thirty bushels of Aples for the tabernacle & ten bushels for labour ^on the^ temple

1868 Jan= 13 Mr Parry died he has been sick over a year Suffered more than toungue can tell. in all his sickness he was patient more so than any person I ever saw. I never heard a murmur from his lips. Died without a strugle or a groan A good man A kind husband a tender Father and a good Latter day Saint

1868 Jan= 23 I went to the ^female^ relief society and joined Betsey [Elizabeth Birdenow] ^Sessions^ and I

Feb 22 1868 Cedenia E Sesions [Cardenia Estella, daughter of David and Phebe] joins

1868 June 20 I bought me a Parlor stove gave twenty four Dollars and fifty cents for it

June 22 The releif society finished the organisation Appointed me as an appriser of the propperty put into that society Sisters Minkly & Tomson [Mercy Rachel Fielding Thompson] the other two

Jan= 2 1869 I was chosen and voted in as one of the committee on block No 10 on which I live[3]

Nov= 5 1868 I went and put fifteen hundred Dollars into Zions Co opporative Mercantile Institution[4]

April 13th I Put one share Twenty ^20^ Dollars into the ~~Ward~~16 Ward coopperative Store

May 1869 I gave Bishop ^F^ Kesler forty Dollars to Put in to the ~~Petu~~ Perpetual Emigration Fund to gather the Poor

Aug 4^th^1869–I Paid Fifty Dollars for A Bureau

In the ^A D^ **1867** I gave Bishop F. Kesler three hundred Dollars to put into the Perpetual Emigration Fund to gather the Poor

July 7th 1869 I Paid fifteen Dollars for the School ^New^ house on an Order given on me By Theodore McKean[5]

Nov= 1868 Paid six Dollars for fencing in the School house

July 8 1869 Paid forty Dollars for finishing a room in my house

March 25 1870 Paid nine Dollars ^50 cts^ to get a Deed of my two Lots in City Bountiful

Frid= May 13 1870 I with my son P G Sessions And many more of the Elders of the church of Jesus Christ of Latter day saints and several Sisters Started on the cars some for a visit in the States and some on a Mission to the old country P G and I went to Maine on a visit to see my rellatives that I had not seen for 34 years we traveled near 7-000 miles by Railroad. stage and carriages.

---

3. Soon after the Relief Society was organized in Nauvoo, members were assigned other members or sisters to visit on a regular basis. These visits sought to fulfill the charitable purpose of the society to look after the needs of others. Often in the early days, the visitors were called "block teachers." Today the program is called "visiting teaching."

4. After October conference in 1868, a group of business leaders met to establish a cooperative store (a move designed to sustain themselves against outside influences that would enter the valley as a result of the railroad). Small investors could buy a single share for five dollars; shares were available for money or produce. Within a few days of the first meeting, the project was a reality. Dividends began to flow to investors as early as 1869 (see Martha Sonntag Bradley, *ZCMI: America's First Department Store* [Salt Lake City: ZCMI, 1991], 15–26).

5. Ward meeting houses were often used as schools, too. Theodore McKean (1829–1879) became a counselor to Bishop Kesler in 1871, and a new chapel was built in 1872. Since these entries seem to be written in retrospect, perhaps Patty does not remember the precise dates.

May 13 1870 We started. for our visit. had a pleasant journey not sick one day while we were gone. and I neve[r] tasted tea nor coffee while I was gone I drank cold water And it was my meat and my drink and I know it is good for me to let those things alone that we are told is not good for us [Word of Wisdom, *Doctrine and Covenants* 89] We got home

Aug= 7 1870 I being 75 years old last Feb 4th This journey cost ^me^ over 500=00 ^$^ Dollars but I do not Regret going I have seen my friends and Bore a faithful testimony to them wherever I went of ^the^ truth of the Latter day work caled mormonism

Oct= 20 ^1870^ Paid 500 ^$dollars^ [*The word* dollars *is in different ink*] five Dollars for the Weekly News to send to my Br Enoch Bartlett his wife was Baptised into the church of L.D.S= the day we left by P G my son

Oct= 1870 I have lett Br William Clayton have three hundred and fifty Dollars for 1 per ^ct^ per month untill Paid [*written across at a slant*] it is paid[6]

1871 Wed= April 5 1871

April 5 I Donated ten Dollars for the P.E. Fund To gather the poor saints from the old country

April 17 1871 I have setled with the Treasurer of Zions coopperative ^mercantile^ Institution drew a part of the Divident put the rest to the main stock which make it now twenty three hundred Dollars or twenty three Shares).

April ^1871^ 29 gave ten Dollars to the Y.L.R.S .[Young Ladies Retrenchment Society][7]

May 15 1871 I have put two hundred ten Dollars more into the P E fund

May 9 1871 I have moved my Barn Cost ^me^ sixty Dollars cash beside some other things

June 3-1872 I I put fifty Dollars into the Perpetual Emigration Fund for to help Richard Wilson here

June 5 1872 My stock in ZCMI is now $3:300 three thousand three hundred Dollars

Oct 12 1872 Donated twelve hundred Dollars cash. for Tithing—1200 H K Whitney Clerk

---

6. William Clayton (1814–1879) made the trek west with the Pioneer Company. His journal accurately chronicles that historic trip. He authored the famous hymn "Come, Come, Ye Saints."

7. In November of 1869 Brigham Young organized his family into a society in order "to retrench from their extravagance in dress, in eating, and even in speech . . . to set an example before the people of the world worthy of imitation . . ." Eliza R. Snow, ever at the forefront of exemplary behavior, worked out a full program with constitution, bylaws, and regular meetings. Thus began the present Young Women organization of the church.

[Written crosswise under Oct 12 is the note] **March 1872** I have Sold my two lots here in the City for twelve thoussand Dollars

Oct 29. 1872 I have setled up my Dividend with the Tresurer of Z. C. M.I. and aded to the main stock which now amounts to twelve Thousand Dollars in that Institution. Credited to my Name Patty Sessions

May *[smudged]* **1873 Oct= 1st** I have now twelve thousand six hundred dollars in that Institution 12=600 Credited to my Name Patty Sessions

Dec 4 1872 I left the S L city and moved to Bountiful where I am having a house built I move my things into it but it is not finished <u>when</u>

Dec 19 1873 my house is finished cost me three thousand five hundred dollars 3500 and all paid for I owe no one anything But love & goodwill I bought a wire Matress gave twenty ^Dollars^

May 1874 Bought furniture one hundred Dollars Gave seventy five Dollars for puting my water pipes up on my house

July 15 1874 I put three hundred and ~~fift~~ twenty five Dollars—3.25 int[o] the P E Fund built a corn crib cost fifty Dollars

1875 May the First I put five Dollars into the agrecultural instutution

July Gave ten Dollars for the printing of the book of mormon in the spanish language to Br Jones[8]

Nov 18 1875 Gave ten Dolars to Wm= Smoot Jun ^or^ to go on his mission to Europe [Patty's great grandson, son of Martha Ann Sessions and William Cochran Adkinson Smoot]

Dec 1875 I have paid thirty three Dollars for the building of the school house

March 1 I bought a house and lot 1 2*h* acre of William Tripp[9] Paid three hundred and ninty Dollars for it

1876 March 5 I have put in fifty ^cents^ per month since *[in margin on an angle]*1874

Dec 1 1875 1874 for building the temple at st George

Nov 1876 I have put in fifty cts Monthly to date **Dec 3 1876**

~~Feb 24~~ **1876 Feb= 24** let My Br Enoch Bartlett [b. 1811] have Ninty eight Dollars to go home to Maine

1876 Oct= I gave James Brown ten Dollars 10-00 <cash>

Nov= 9 Charles Hyde patriarch said he had A blessing for me he laid his hands upon my head blesed me and to my surprise ordained me to lay hands on the sick Prophesied many things to me for which I feel thankful

---

8. The Book of Mormon had been translated into Danish (1851), German (1852), French (1852), Italian (1852), Welsh (1852), and Hawaiian (1855). This was the first translation of selections into Spanish.

9. Probably Patty's nephew, son of her sister Naamah Bartlett and Reverend William Tripp. William would have been a brother of Enoch Bartlett Tripp.

Nov= 20 1876 I here say to all my children and my grand children and great grandchildren &c-&c and to all others I have been punctual to my word I never have given my note to any one ~~one~~ Neither have I had any acounts on any Books in any Store I have kept out of debt Paid my taxes my fasts my donations. and my tithing willingly of the best I have and the Lord has blesed me and Prospered me in all I have done for which I feel very thankful. hoping he will continue to bless me while I live both Spiritually and temporially, with all that shall be for my good and his Glory to give unto me I am now Almost eighty two years old february next ^th^ 4 ^th^ I drink no tea nor coffee nor spirutous liquors I dont smoke nor take snuff nor any poisonous medicine. I use consecrated oil for my complaints. Now I say to ^you^ do as I have done and as much better as you can and the Lord will bless you as he has me Patty Sessions

Jan= ^1st^ 1877 I have Paid in fifty cents into the hands of Anson V Call monthly for two years for the st George temple.–1875–& 1876- $12-00

April 15-1877 I have this day paid in to Anson V Calls hand forty Dollars for the Salt Lake City Temple to be put on to the right Books 1877

1877

May 2 let Br [William] Pullin have one bushel ^seed^ corn 1-50 I waited on Pullins wife to turn [in] on the ^temple^ 3-00 in Satt [Salt] Lake temple

1878

Feb=18 I let Br Pullin have 28 yds carpet 75 ^cts^ per yd $21-00

twenty one Dollars to apply on the Salt Lake temple to be put to my Name[10]

Patty Sessions

July 1st 1878 I gave James Weight ^receiver^ fifty Dollars to 50 00 subscription in cash to the temple ^Salt Lake^ Fund got a receipt from him

August 23 I also put in one quilt six 6 Dollars and $6:00 one Rug five Dollars eighteen yards ~~5-00~~ ^5^ Carpet thirteen Dollars and fifty cents 13.50 and gave to James Weight receiver all to go as subscription in Salt Lake City Temple I got a receipt for that I also paid seven yards carpet for Elizabeh G[abriel Birdenow] Sessions five Dollars 25 ^cts^ got a receipt for her 5:25

Sept 5 1878 I have sent one hundrend and twenty five Dollars to my Br Enochs sons to bring them here. by so doing in hopes it will be the means of bringing thier Father and Mother here as they both belong to this church but the sons do not

---

10. William Pullen fell and was killed while working on the temple. The citizens of Bountiful and his fellow workers raised four hundred dollars for a good house for his widow and small children and for a monument made of the same granite as the temple (see Leslie T. Foy, *The City Bountiful* [Bountiful, Utah: Horizon Publishers, 1975] 143).

Home of Patty Sessions in Bountiful, Utah. Left to right: Betsy Birdenow, Perrigrine, and Patty Sessions. Courtesy of Irene S. Poulson.

Family portrait of Patty with Perrigrine Sessions family, September or October 1885. *Top row, left to right:* Alice, Esther Mabey holding Linnie, Thomas, Sarah Crossley, Sylvanus or Samuel, Perrigrine, Joseph, Betsy Birdenow. *Third row:* Sarah Ann Bryson holding Heber, Patty, Fanny Emorett Loveland. *Second row:* Jed, Lillis, Hyrum, unknown, Perrigrine, Samantha, Wallace, David. *First row:* Patty, Chauncey, Olive, Olivia, Parley, Sadie, Susan, Ezra, Eliza. Courtesy of Irene S. Poulson.

Oct 4 1878 My two Nephews Worington and Herbert Bartlett Arived here safe. thier Parrents did not ^(come^ we feel much pleased they both went to confrence[11]

Nov 5 1878 they have both been Baptised and confirmed into the church of Jesus Christ of latter day saints to day, I thank the Lord.

March 23 1878 [9 *is written on top of the* 8] they are both trying to live their religion attending to thier duties in public and private. they take thier turns praying in the families and asking a blessing to the table Warrington lives with me ever since they came. Herbert lives with James Beard has hired out for a year Both good Boys, so far as I know.

March 29 I have got a letter, from my Brother Enochs wife, with a slip from a paper in it stating that my Brother Jonathan Bartletts widow is Dead died ^feb= 18~1879^ Stoneham Oxford Maine aged eighty four years nine months. 84 ye 9 month Born near the same place Name Tryphenia, died feb= 18 1879

April 30 1879 Warington A Bartlett my Nephew has startet for Ogdan for work

May 8th 1879 I Patty Sessions have this day let James Weight have one hundred and fifty Dollars ^$1:50^ cash Subscription to the Salt Lake Temple Fund. he James Weight receiver and got his receipt for the same

Sept 1879 I have paid my fasts donated when caled upon by the releif society or the ward to pay for an organ or for keeping the tabernacle clean and in order and also for the poor in small amounts. And also for building school houses

Oct 9 1879 I have got News that my Grand sons are burnt out thier all is gone Byron and Keplers houses both burnt and every thing else but thier clothes on thier backs and also Harveys & Perrys things all burnt by leaving the Lamp burning and it exploded. it was in the night[12]

Oct 11–1879 I have sent them one comforter and one quilt both woolen one cape two pair stockings calico 14 2*h* yds And money $15.00 the other things about 15 Dolars15 00 I have built me a Barn of rock cost me ^three^ hundred fifty Dolars $350 00 all paid for done it this last summer

May 6 1880 I Paty Sessions have donated of my own freewill two shares of ZCMI Stock to the P E Fund 200 for gathering the poor one hundred dollars each share [*in the margin, she has written*] from this page I carry over to page [*but has not completed her note and the next page has been cut out*]

---

11. Warinton A. Bartlett (b. 1850) and Herbert Bartlett (b. 1859) were sons of Patty's brother Enoch Bartlett and Sarah Hinkson.

12. Byron, Keplar, Harvey, and Perry were all sons of Perrigrine.

East Bountiful, I patty Sessions have put into S L City Temple the following ^(sum^

July 1st 1878 fifty Dollars paid to James Weight	^$^50(00 receiver
August 29 1878 Twenty four dollars fifty cents	24:50
May 8 1879 one hundred fifty dollars	1-50.00
Jan=^y^ 6 1880 fifty Dollars cash	50.00
May 15 1880 one hundred Dollars cash	1-00-00
June 3 1880 quilt 5.00 ^$^ rug 5.00	1:0.00-
Nov 17 1880 stockings two dollars	2.00
- 17 1880 two hundred Dollars cash	2-00.00
Feb 28 1881 stockings four Dollars	4-00
April 16 1881 stockings two dollar forty cts	2-40
June 2 1881 stockings two dollars Sixty cts	2.60
/ 2 1881 two hundred dollars cash	2-00-00
July 11–1881 one quilt 3 pairs stockins	7-35
Oct 12 1881 two hundred dollars cash	200-00
^Nov^21 1881 three hundred Dollars cash	300-00
Dec 20 1881 two hundred Dollars cash	200-00
Feb 17th 1882 ^one^hundred dollars cash	100-00
and nine pairs children stockins	5-00
April 29 1882 7 pairs childrens stockins	3-00
April 29 same date cash fifty Dollars	50-00
May 27 1882 cash three hundred Dollars	300-00
childrens stockins	3-00
Nov 20 1882 cash 1 hundred Dollars	1-00 00
Nov. 30 1882 7 pairs of childrens stockins	3-00
July 5. 1883 ~~cash 3 hundred dolars~~ ^150.00^	150 00
cash one hundred fifty dollars	150-00
March 13 1883 children Stockins 13 pair	6-00
July 5 1883 cash one hundred fifty Dollars	150 00
Oct 20 1883 8 pair children stockins	8 50
Jan 29 1884 stockings & cash 1 hundred	110 00
May 14 1884 stockings five dollars	
cash one hundred	100 5.00
August 26 1880 I have put ten Dollars	
into the Logan temple	$10 00
Oct–9 put in ninty Dollars more	$ 90 00
April 14–1881 put one hundred Dollars more	
in to the Logan Temple	$ 100-00
I have C O cards receit for the above amount	
~~April 14= 1881 put into Logan temple one hundred more $100 0~~	
~~I have C O cards receit for the above amount~~	
Nov 18th 1881 three hundred more	300-00

May 25 1882 three hundred Dollars cash	300 00
Nov 18 1882 the sum of one hundred Dollars	
^cash	^100 00
March 12 1883 the sum of one hundred dollars	100 00
Jan= 27 1884 one hundred more	100 00
May 17 1884 one hundred more	100 00

January

    Jan-27-1885 I have put two hundred dollars cash and 28 pair children stockins 14 Dollars more into the Salt Lake Temple gave it to James Waight got his receipt for it two hundred Dollars cash and 14 Dollars for the Stockins

[At this point, Patty recorded her patriarchal blessings (special blessings that designated church patriarchs officially confer on individual members). Her diary reflects how her actions relied to a great extent on her faith in those who directed the affairs of the church. She depended on her patriarchal blessings as well.]

I commence here again

Perry Sessions is down at Salt GSL city his eyes is bad I hear that the Dr will do no more for him without pay as he goes along & Perry has no more money I send him 26 Dollars by Wallace W Bartlett [b. 1842] to day. **26 of March 1882**

    April 14 1882 I send twenty Dollars more by the hand of Enoch B Tripp to Perry got receits for the above of Perry Sessions

    May 26-1882 I let David Sessions have twenty-five Dollars to ^wards^ ~~build~~ building his house to commence with I calculate to let him have 75 more   25 00

    June 3 1882 I let him have thirty more to day   30 00

    July 14 I let him have ten more   10 00

    August 15 I let David have ten more   10-00

    Sept 9 I let David have ten more   10-00

    Oct 10 I let him have twenty five more   25-00

    1883 April 23 I lent him ~~trade~~ have ten Dollars more   10-00

    July 13 1883 I have let Perry Sessions have three hundred Dollars cash to let William Wallace Bartlett have to get Carlos Sessions house & lot here in East Bountiful as Perry had not enough to get it he is nearly blind

    July <1883> I have given Perry a lot which I bought of Wm Tripp known as the Walton lot I gave Tripp 3-90 00 Dollars for it. I also have given him my cook stove that I gave 1.85.00 for it one hundred eighty five Dollars for it **Oct 24 1864** when I bought it

    Nov 24 1884 I Patty Sessions have let Elvira Brigs ^Elvira Brigs^ have twenty Dollars cash to be paid as soon as she can get it for me the above is paid in full Patty Sessions *[This entry is crossed out.]*

[Next Patty gave more genealogical information:]
I Paty Sessions was Born Feb= 4th 1795 Bethel^Oxford co Maine^ the Daughter of Enoch Bartlett who was the son of Ebenezar Bartlett [1711–1788] My Father was Born Newtown Mass Sep=15–1741 died August 20 [1825] Newry Oxford ^co^ Maine My Mothers Name Anna Hall Born April 28 1768–Standish Maine Died August 27 1868 Stoneham Maine Being more than one hundred years old My Father had been Married to Eliza Seagar and ^she bore^ him ten children names Anna. Reuben. Releif. Submit. Thankful. Betsey. Burruh. Olive. Lucy. And a son died when Born. his wife Eliza died when Lucy was nine year old. And when she was twelve years old he Married my mother. She bore him nine children I being the Eldest. Names Patty. Elisha. Nomah. Jonathan. Polly. Apphia. Lydia. Lorania. she died when two years and a half old. Enoch. the youngest~I was Marrid to David Sessions who was the son of David Sessions and Rachel Stevens I bore him eig[h]t children Names. Perrigrine. Born June 15.–1814. Sylvanus. Born June 3d 1816 [*splotched, and someone has written in pencil* 1818] Sylvia. P. Born July 31 [*splotched, and* 1818. *written in a different pen*] Anna. B. Born March 21 [11?]–1820. David. ju^n^ Born May 9, 1823. Anna. B. 2d. Anna. Born March 16, 1825 Bartlett. Born August 1st 1827 Amanda D. Born Nov. 14 1837 in Missouri. their Father, David Sessions was Born in Fairly Vermont. April 4, 1790. Died August 11, 1850. Salt, Lake, City I sold my place in Salt La city in March 1872 for Twelve thousand Dollars paid twelve hundred Dollars tithing Built me a ^Brick^ house in ^eat^ Bountiful moved into it Dec= 20 1873 it is not finished April ^1873^ house plastered and Painted & clea^n^d where I still live East Bountiful March 10 1878 Patty Sessions

I Patty Sessions have borne eight children names follows
Perrigrine Sessions–Born June 15–1814
Sylvanus Sessions–Born June 3–1816–died Sept 15 1832
Sylvia P-Sessions–Born July 31–1818–died April 13 1882
Anna–Sessions–Born March11 [21?] 1820–died Sept 20 1823
David–Sessions–Jun Born May 9 1823
Anna–Sessions–Born March 16–1825–died August 10 1832
Bartlett–Sessions–Born August 1–1827–died Feb 15–1828
Amanda–Sessions–Born–Nov 14–1837–died May 15 1841
The above are my childrens Names I will now put down my Brs and sisters names My Brother Elisha Born Dec–7 1796 Bethel
My Sister Naamah Born oct 13 1796 [8?] Bethe[l] oxford Maine
Jonathan Born July ^31^ 1800 Newry oxford Maine
Polly Born May 8 1802 Newry Maine
~~Aphia~~ Born
Appia Born April 28 1804 Newr oxford Maine
Lydia–––Nov. 15 1806
Lorania Newry Maine

Enoch Born July 5 1811 Newry oxford Me
these are my Brs & Sisters Names all dead but Br Enoch

[After more genealogical records, Patty turns the book over and begins again from the back, adding more financial accounts.]
Received of Patty Sessions in full of all Demands up to this date **July 16 1884**
  [*signed*] James Neville
This the **4 day of Sept 1884** I paid five Dollars for cleaning & diging the cellar to David Dilles wife Emily Dille
Sept 17 1884 I let Nailor have seven Dollars cash to get laths with Patty Sessions
Sept 20 1884 I let Aurther Nailor [Arthur Naylor?] have five dollars to get lime with for his Father to plaster my house Patty Sessions
Sept 24 1884 Paid James Sessions three Dollars & fifty cts for holling lumber for flooring & windows Patty Sessions[13]
Feb 22 1886 I lent Phebe Jane Elis ten Dollars cash to be paid in one month she Promised to pay to me Patty Sessions[14]
Jan 31 ^ 1885 ^ I Patty Sessions let P G Sessions have thirty Dollars for John Weight for for keeping School to be paid to me again after they draw the dividen April next[15]
[*written at an angle across entry:*] ~~Paid May 16 1885~~ **Jan 27 1885** I Patty Sessions let Perrigrine Sessions have thirty Dollars for John Weight for keeping School to be paid to me again after they draw the dividend April next [*the preceding crossed out with a big* X]
March 24 I Patty Sessions let Perrigrine Sessions have seven Dollars to get wire to fence the two lots where Sallys house is Patty Sessions[16]
I Patty Sessions have let Chester Call the bishop have twenty Dollars gold to pay for land in old Mexico. for the church in East Bountiful Patty Sessions date **Feb 26 1885**
March 9 1885 I Patty Sessions have let George Linkon have five Dollars cash for the church—5 00 <in East Bountiful>
I Patty Sessions let John Weight have five 5 00 Dollars for keeping school ~~**March 27 1885**~~ [*written at an angle:*] paid **May 16 1885**

---

13. James Crossley Sessions (1862–1952) was the oldest child of Perrigrine and Sarah Crossley. Sarah had come west with the Willey Handcart Company.

14. Phebe Jane Clark (1852–1912) was the daughter of Sylvia and Ezekial Clark. She married John Henry Ellis on 31 January 1870.

15. John Anson Waite, Jr. (1863–1932) married Lucina Sessions (1865–1929), sixth child of Perrigrine and Fanny Emorett Loveland.

16. Carlos Lyon Sessions married Sally Lavina Hill on 20 January 1882 in the Endowment House. This was a polygamous marriage.

I let P G Sessions have twenty dollars to bye wheat at mill **March 28 1885** Patty Sessions

I let Elvira Brigs have twenty Dollars=I let her have twelve Dollars more this **29 day of August 1885**

Sept Tuesd 29 1885 I have let the Thomas Wardrope & Holbroke have four Dollars for the ward in East Bountiful the expences Patty Sessions

Nov 6 1885 I Patty Sessions let Perrigrine Sessions have ten Dollars to go & see his Boy to pay his expences on the cars

May 8 1886 I Patty Sessions let Sylvanus Sessions have one hundred & fiftem pounds of seed corn to plant[17]

May 20 1886 I Patty Sessions let Fayben Sessions have one bushel and a half of seed corn well shook together in a sack[18]

Oct 7 1886 ^I Patty Sessions^ let James Sessions have one hundred Dollars ^in^ cash Sent it to him for a few days or two months [*a large cross covers the entry; written at an angle:*] Paid in full

I Patty Sessions let Sara Ann ^Sessions^ have one hundred Dollar cash to finish her house this the **16 of Oct 1886** (I gave it to her as a presant to finish her house & as a free gift

May 5 1885 I let P G have a half bushel seed corn Patty Sessions

May 8 1885 I let P G have half bushel seed corn Patty Sessions

July 20 1887 I Patty Sessions let Ester [Mabey] have one hundred Dollars money for Sarah C Sessions. to finish her house with

Sept 24 1887 Sarah has paid twenty Dollars of the above sum[19]

[The next entries were minutes of the Benevolent Society of the sixteenth ward. The society was organized on "Saturday June 10th [1854] for the purposes of clothing the Lamanite Women and children." Patty is listed as "presidentess," Mary Pulsipher and Judith H. Higbee as "councilors," Betsy Roundy as treasurer, and Mercy K. Thompson as clerk. The handwriting is not Patty's. The interesting feature about the minutes is that Patty usually gave at least one of the prayers and made remarks as well. In the beginning the society met three times a month, but gradually the meetings were less frequent. Attendance waned, and finally, perhaps because the immediate need had been met, the society ceased to function. Between the minutes and the lists of donations of each member to the society, Patty again recorded some of her business dealings:]

17. Sylvanus Sessions was the son of Perrigrine and Fanny Emorett Loveland.

18. Fabian Carter Sessions was a grandson, the fifth child of David Sessions and Phoebe Carter Foss.

19. Sarah Ann Sessions was Perrigrine's wife, Sarah Ann Bryson. Sarah C. Sessions was Sarah Crossley, another of Perrigrine's wives (see note 13). Evidently the wives had their own houses, which was often the case in polygamous marriages.

June 3–1886 ^I^ let Chester Sessions have ten Dollars cash to get lime & lumber with for my granery[20] **June 4 1886** he paid me ~~300~~ three dollars & five cents after getting the lumber and lime worked on the granery **Sat 5** puting down the foundation.

Mond 7 ^1886^ Jim Indian worked to day & Chester on the foundation

June Mond 7-1886 I let Chester have Twenty five Dollars gold to get lumber **Tuesd 8** Chester has been to day & got the lumber all paid for Jim Indian worked half day **Wed 9** been to the store got Nails one dollar fifty cents

wed 9 1886 let Chester Session have cash to get lumber forty Dollars cash to get lumber

Thursd 10 put ^it^ on to the granery

Frid 11 let Chester ^have^ 32 Dollars more cash

Satd 13 Chester has been & got the lumber ^(13-25 Brought me back 1800 75 cents

Mond 14-1886 I let Chester Sessions ^have 14-00^ dollars & 75 cts to get the shingles with **Tuesd 15** has got them **Wed 16** put some of them on **Thursd 17** has got them mostly on **Frid** got them all on Finished the granery & have paid them all up forty eight Dollars and fifty cts Chester & Jim [*signed in another hand*] Chester and Jim 3rd Sessions

[*The following entries are in another hand.*]

January 29–1887 this is to Cirtify tht Henry Jones has received 10 Dollars from Miss Patty Sessions as Borrowed money with intres to Be Paid on

July–1887 Witness my Hand Henry Jones Paid 5 Dollars of the above on the **4 of July 1887** Henry Jones

Paid 5 Dollars on the **30 of August 1887** wich Settles all in full Henry Jones

[*After a number of blank pages and the alphabetical lists of Relief Society donations and more blank pages, Patty began writing the minutes of a straw-braiding school held at her home (see Appendix 3). She was in charge and offered the opening and closing prayers. The minutes are chiefly interesting in showing her personality and the types of songs the group sang on such occasions. After the minutes Patty continued writing her diary.*]

---

20. Chester Sessions was another son of Perrigrine and Fanny Emorett Loveland.

1884

I am getting ready to go to Logan to administer for the dead

APRIL 1884

Tuesd April 1 1884 I commence here in this Book to write. I went to Mary Scots Birthday Party the 31 day of March 1884 we had a good time enjoyed ourselves well **Tuesd April 1 1884** I commence here to write **wed 2 Thursd 3** I have worked on the rug[21] **Frid 4** I went to conference staid all night at E B Tripps **Satd 5** came home found all well. **Sund 6** Betsey went I stay at home she came home all right. **Mond 7** I put on a rug **Tuesd 8 wed 9** work on it. **Thursd 10** got my lot plowed and harrowed Chester did it **Frid 11 Satd 12** got the rug out I went up to Jonny ^Fishers^ he carrid me up & brought me home she gave me rags to make her a rug.[22] **Sund 13** I go to meeting **Mond 14** I cut the rags **Tuesd 15 wed 16** put on the rug worked on it **Thursd 17 Frid 18 Satd 19** I have worked on it all the time I could get **Sund 20** went to meeting **Mond 21 Tuesd 22 Wed 23** got the rug out **Thursd 24 Frid 25 Satd 26** I have done many things out door & in knit one pair stockings. **Sund 27** I was caled to go & see Mary Carter she is sick. Sister Brison & Esther Sessions went with me[23] we washed and anointed her & laid hands on her. we then laid hands on sister Reighnolds. then came home. P G

---

21. Patty has written before about making rugs, but this part of her diaries is replete with allusions to the process. It was lengthy and complicated. Preparing the wool and winding it on a shuttle were only the first steps. The looms were made of a large framework of wood with a high beam to hold the harness, through which the warp was threaded, and another beam for beating the threads together. At the back of the loom was the warp beam. It was as wide as the loom, and its end was attached to an upright beam with a pivot in each end. On the other side of the loom was a cloth beam on which the finished material was wound. The harness was a large frame hanging from above on which heavy twisted threads were placed.
    In the case of rag rugs, mentioned so often by Patty, the woof is the rag sewed together and wound on shuttles. These rags had to be washed, dyed, torn, or cut into strips varying from a half inch to an inch in width. According to the Daughters of Utah Pioneers, sometimes a group of friends would gather around a large basket of prepared rags and sew and wind "while their tongues kept time to their flying needles." For a more detailed and fascinating description of pioneer rug making, see Kate B. Carter, ed., *Heart Throbs of the West,* vol. 2 (Salt Lake City: Daughters of Utah Pioneers, 1940), 479–81.
22. John Fisher, the husband of Josephine Rosetta Lyon, had married Harriet Knighton on 2 February 1881 in Bountiful.
23. Sarah Ann Connery (Bryson) was the mother of Sarah Ann Bryson, Perrigrine's wife. Esther Mabey was another of Perrigrine's wives.

here. he read a letter to me four pages large paper that he had writen to
Hyrum Bartletts daughter Mary **Sund 27** we then went to meeting **Mond 28**
put on a rug worked on it **Tuesd 29 wed 30**.

MAY 1884

Thursd May 1:1884 Frid 2 Satd 3 got got it out & made up. A sister came
here Br Thurgoods Aunt wished me & Betsey to anoint & lay hand on her. we
did so as she had been sick for some time & grew worse. we then planted some
peach pits. I done before dark but it rained & I got wet. **Sund 4** I feel well
today think I shall go to meeting if it dont rain. we went to meeting. **Mond 5**
cut and made me some undergarments. **Tuesdy 6** put on a rug **wed 7** work on
it **Thursd 8 Frid 9 Satd 10** got it out & made up. I have worked hard all the
^time^ **Sund 11** I feel well think I shall go to meeting got a letter from
Carlos. Woringtons wife has started for **May 11 1884** Eagle Rock to go to her
husband. [*Obviously paper was not as scarce as in earlier years. When Patty began a new
page, she now often wrote the full date of the first full or partial entry on a separate line.
These have been deleted for the sake of easier reading.*] **Sund 11** go to meeting **Mond
12** picked my pyeplant for tithing 35 ~~lbs~~ pounds carried to the store. **Tuesd 13**
I went to the city. Br George Q Cannon sent me letter of invitation to go to the
Dedication of the Logan Temple[24] ^President^ Br Taylor gave me a invitation ^2^ cards. 1 for me & one for P G to to go we went **wed 14** I got ready
Thursd 15 P G and I & Emorett **Frid 16** went to the temple to meeting. **Satd
17** to the dedication of the temple a good time.[25] **Sund 18** went to the tabernacle to meeting **Mond 19** we came home all well & safe Mary Elen Kimbal
came home with us staid all night. **Tuesd 20** I have been kniting **Wed 21** fin-

---

24. George Quayle Cannon (1827–1901) was ordained a member of the Quorum of
the Twelve Apostles on 26 August 1860 and sustained as counselor to President
Brigham Young on 9 May 1874. On 18 October 1880 Cannon was sustained as
first counselor to President Wilford Woodruff, and on 7 April 1889 he was sustained as first counselor to President Lorenzo Snow.

25. The building of the Logan Temple was prophesied by Wilford Woodruff on 21
August 1863, although the site was not dedicated until 17 May 1877. The cor-
nerstone was laid on 17 September 1877 with President John Taylor in charge,
since Brigham Young had died on 29 August 1877. The temple was dedicated on
17 May 1884 by President John Taylor (see N. B. Lundwell, comp., *Temples of the
Most High* [Salt Lake City: Bookcraft, 22nd printing, 1975], 87–101). Nolan
Porter Olsen recorded in *Logan Temple: The First 100 Years,* "Sister Patty Bartlett
Sessions Parry was perhaps the largest single contributor to the building of the
Logan Temple outside of the temple district. On [one] occasion she wrote a
check for $500, and made many other donations. She was a strong character,
thrifty almost to the point of stinginess, and yet generous to the superlative
degree when it came to a worthy church cause. She was . . . the grandmother of
Logan's Harvey Sessions" ([Providence, Utah: Keith W. Watkins, 1978], 211).

ished 2 pair of stockins **Thursd 22** went to a surprise party at Sarah Anns her Birthday [her daughter-in-law] **Frid 23** kniting & weeding garden &c&c **Satd 24** commenced a pair of stockins fo^r^ my self to wear to the Logan temple as I expect to go there in a short time to work for my dead relatives **Sund 25** went to meeting John Fisher wished me to go to his Fathers I went had had a good ride it did me good he brought me home **Mond 26** put on a rug **Tuesd 27 Wed 28 Thursd 29 Frid 30** I have got the rug out & made up **Satd 31** I am geting ready to go to Logan to administer for the dead so I keep buisy P G and Betsey will go with me

JUNE 1884

Sund June 1 1884 we went up to Logan staid all night to Betseys Brs Birdeninos **Mond 2** went to the temple was Baptised for some of my relatives &c &c at night went to John Parrys staid all night **Tuesd 3 Wed 4 Thursd 5 Frid 6** I have done all I can at presant **Satd 7** we came home found all well **Sund 8** went to Centerville to conference had a good meeting **Mond 9** I feel better than before I went **Tuesd 10** work in the garden a part of the time **wed 11** the same **Thursd 12** I went to Josepine Fishers she came after me a man there Name Works wished to see me I staid all day **Frid 13** trimed some trees **Satd 14** Jimma cut some of my Lucern was sick went home **Sund 15** P Gs birth day we gave him a surprise Party we then went to meeting **Mond 16** Jimy cut the rest of my Lucern. I spread it **Tuesd 17** I got it into the Barn **wed 18** I went to Salt Lake City got som money paid Robbert Tripp for doing some writing for me he took twenty Dollars for it all wright I paid it[26] **Thursd 19** hear that hear that David Brigs my grand son in law got his foot almost cut off with a moing machine the Dr came and took his foot off[27] I put a rug on and work on it **Frid 20** I went & see David Brigs I went up a foot. I found him bad enough Jonny Thurgood brought me home **Satd 21** got the rug out **Sund 22** we went to meeting **mond 23** put in a rug **Tuesd 24 Wed 25 thursd 26** teachers meeting here ^we got the rug out it is Phebes girls Izabelells Zobells^[28] **Frid 27** 40 years to day since Joseph & Hyram Smith were murdred in Carthage jail **Satd 28** hear that David Brigs is dead ^died^ 8 oclock last night we got up P G went up there in the night **Satd 28** I went up there to see him with P G to day he looks bad **Sund 29** he is to be buried to day Chester Lovlin

26. Robert Tripp was a son of Enoch Bartlett Tripp.

27. David Briggs (1858–1884) was married to Elvira Sessions (1864–1933) on 4 April 1881. Elvira was the second child of Perrigrine and Sarah Crossley. David and Elvira had two children, Sarah and Laura, who was only five months old when her father died.

28. Phebe Jane Clark and John Henry Ellis had a daughter, Isabelle Jane (b. 27 February 1873).

[Loveland, father of Fanny Emorett] here to see us to day I go to the funeral of David Brigs to day I went up to his house P G went and all his family Betsey and I rode in P G wagon we follwed him to the Tabernacle a great gathering Br Penrose spoke[29] and several more then went to the grave saw him buried this is **Sunday 29 ^of June^ 1884 Mond 30 1884** put on a rug worked on it

JULY 1884

[*written in the margin:* **July 2d 1884** Sallys house] **Tuesd July1 1884** worked on the rug **wed=2d** worked on the rug got it out **Thursd 3** put on an other worked steady all the time on it. Commenced work on Sallys house yesterday **July 2 1884 Frid 4** worked on the rug steady in the fore noon in the after noon I went to a meeting in the tabnercle to celebrate the 4th had a good time came home worked on the rug Byron came down I went over to the Big house to see him **Satd 5** he went to town early I did not see him. I worked on the rug got it out Betsey made it up Phebe sent me some peices to make one for her. **Sund 6** fair I have not seen Byron he has gone home. I saw him when he first came I have been to meeting to day. Sarah Ann is quite sick has been for two or three days ^could not set up^ **Mond 7** I was sent for to go and administer to Sarah Ann Sister Rainon^l^ds ^or Barlow^ came after me I went washed her face and neck & anointed her & laid hands on her gave her some oil to take first & formost as she had taken almost every thing else she could get I staid with her some time she appeared better and I came home. worked on Phebes rug. I went over again to see Sarah Ann she is still seting up quite smart I came home went ^to^ work again. **Tuesd 8** I went over to see her again found ^her^ up & quite smart I work on the rug **wed 9** she is still better is at work is quite well out doors and in as well as ever. **Thursd 10** got the rug out **Frid 11** work on it **Satd 12** work on it do not get it done. **Sund 13** fair weather. we went to meeting. **Mond 14** got the rug out & made up **Tuesd 15** we went to the releif society. **wed. 16** I went up to sister Brisans she asked me to go with her to see sister Wood she has a cansor I went with her saw the cansor it looked bad three large bunches runing & bleeding I looked at it they washed it. it bled a stream into the bason. the blood stoped they prepared a cloth wet with linement. I told sister Brison to hold on I felt very curious I feel as though I must lay hands on her. I never felt so before without being caled on to do it. she said well do it I knew I had ^been^ ordained to to lay hands on the sick & set apart to do that. she had been washed clean & I anointed her gave her some oil to take & then laid hands on her. I told her she would get well ~~well~~ if she would beleive & not

---

29. Charles William Penrose (1832–1925) later became a member of the Quorum of the Twelve Apostles in 1904, second counselor to President Joseph F. Smith in 1911, second counselor to President Heber J. Grant in 1918, and first counselor to Grant in 1921.

daught it we put on a cloth wet in oil. she got up & went out door said there was no pain in it at all she did not come in while I staid. I came home it was in the forenoon heard the next day she had no more pain in it all night. she got up in the morning put on some salve & it soon began to pain her bad. has continued to pain her ever since. I hear from her often **Thursd 17** I put another rug <in> **Frid 18 satd 19** got it out I have worked hard got my hay cut & put up in bunches Betsey & I put it up **Sund 20** fair weather we go to meeting after meeting I go & see Sister Wood she is no better puts on the old medicine but no consecrated oil **Mond 21** hear from her again no better **Tuesd 22** got another rug on work on it got went to the releif Socity my hay in the barn all right & have paid my tithing on it all. **wed 23 Thursd 24** ^went^ to the celebration of our coming in to valley. it brought many things to my mind as I drove a four ox team all the way and landed here safe no road only what we made as we came along or bridges. & some of the way no timber to make a bridge & we mowed grass & put in & came over on that & some times waided the creeks & som[e]times unloaded our waggonons & brought them over by hand then load up again & push on the best we could & when ^we^ got here we put up a liberity pole & hoisted our flag on it as we had brought a flag with us & we dedicated the day to the Lord as best we could. I was thank[ful] to the Lord that we had found a resting place. we could set down on the ground eat what little we had brought with us & have our meeting & was happy & contented & I remain so to this day & can say thank the Lord that I am as well of as I am at this day **July 24 1884 Frid 25** I went to the school in my school house as Phebe Sessions has been keeping it[30] she now has a vacation. I then ~~home~~ went to see what was done on a house I am building for Sally to live in she is here without a home Carlos has not come to look after her **Satd 26** work on the rug. in the evening went to the circus see many curiositys walking the rope riging & horses dancing &c &c came home all well **Sund 27** fair go to meeting **Mond 28** ^got my rug out^ **Tuesd 29** put on a rug work on it steady **wed 30** work on the rug ^another rug^ **Thursd 31** I went to John Fishers had a good visit

August 1884

Frid August 1 1884 work on the rug **Satd 2** got it out **Sund 3** fair we went to meeting Br Anson Call come & said to we sisters five or six of us stop to the high priest meeting so we stoped they ordained 8 or 10 had a good meeting[31]

---

30. In 1884 Patty built a schoolhouse in Bountiful for her grandchildren and the children of the poor. It was called the Patty Sessions Academy.

31. Anson Call (1810–1890) had moved into Sessions Settlement in 1848 and became its second bishop the same year. He served many settlement missions throughout the West and was assigned the responsibility for finishing the Bountiful Tabernacle in 1861.

Mond 4 Josepine gave me some Rags I cut them up **Tuesd 5** cuting rags finished **wed 6** commenced another rug **Thursd 7** work on the rug **Frid 8** work on the rug **Satd 9** got it out **Sund 10** P Gs horse got a bad cut on her thigh do not know how it was done fair think I shall go to meeting I went to meeting Br Gill preached I then went and see ~~Br~~ Scoot [Scott] he is Better eat ice cream rode there with Josephine Fisher. rode home with Thomas Sessions.[32] **Mond 11** work on the rug. **Tuesd 12 wed 13** got it out **Thursd 14** Put on another **Frid 15** worked in the rug ^then^ went over to Br Brisons to a surprise Party his birth day 69 years old. we had a very good time **Satd 16** worked on the rug do not get it out **Sund 17** we have been to meeting. I have read the exponent through.[33] **Mond 18** got the rug out. **Tuesd 19** did many things. **wed 20** went over to Sister Pullins she let me have some peaces for my rug. **Tursday 21** she sent them to me I sent her some sugar fore them. there was a teachers meeting at our house this after noon. **frid 22** did many things cut up some pie plant to dry and spread on the racks. **Satd 23** did many things. read a letter from Chester Sessions he has lost his horses expe^ts^ they are stole as he & Br Birtino has hunted four weeks for them & no sings [signs] of them. I feel as though I would like to help him some to get another team as he is ^called^ on a mission & is away off almost to Sunset so called. **Sund 24** fair weather P G has gone to Malad to fix some machinery for thrashing has not got home yet we do not go to meeting as I have no way to go the meeting is at Farmington a funeral over the bodys of the Mishonaries that were murdered.[34] it was a great

---

32. Thomas Mabey Sessions (1870–1955) was the first child of Perrigrine and Esther Mabey. Purportedly Thomas owned a cane made from the same wood as Joseph Smith's casket.

33. The 15 August 1884 issue of the *Woman's Exponent* contained a "very ably written address by Mrs. Lu Dalton delivered on the 24th of July in Beaver. So much space is occupied by the publication of this address that we are unable to commence the Biography of Sister Patty Sessions in this number, but intend doing so in September 1st" (p. 44). The address was about the last dispensation, Joseph Smith, persecution, and the accomplishments of the saints in establishing Zion. Included were the instructions given by the prophet to the Relief Society in Nauvoo–their right to the privileges, blessings, and gifts of the priesthood. The article said that "the signs should follow them, such as healing the sick, casting out devils, etc., and that they might attain unto these blessings by a virtuous life and conversation, and diligence in keeping all the commandments . . ." (44). The paper also included an article on marriage and cultivating love, a letter from a new convert on how truth had come to her, and "A Day Dream" by M. Elizabeth Little about suffering and wickedness.

34. The *Deseret News* of 20 August 1884 reported, "The following dispatch from Elder B. H. Roberts was received this afternoon. . . . We publish herewith the news items: Elders J. H. Gibbs and W. S. Berry were murdered by a mob on Can Creek [Tennessee] August 10th. . . . The Elders were buried by the Saints on the 11th. . . . We are making efforts to get the bodies. . . . Let the friends be

gathering. it was a long day to me. **Mond** ^25^ Emerett wrote a letter to
Chester as he is her son she & Lucinia put five ^$5 00^ dollars. I put in twen-
ty five dollars in a letter to send to him $25 00. ~~Tuesday ^26^ we send it to him
I work on a rug. wed 27 work on the rug Thursd 28 I got it out Teachers meeting here ^frid 29^ Satd 30 Sun 31~~ **Tuesd 26 Wed 27 Thursd <28>** ~~Teachers~~
I have worked on a rug Sarah Ann sent me some peices to make a rug. I work
on them cuting them up **frid 29** got my rug out **Satd 30** made S Ann one braided it & sewed it together. cut some Aples spread them &c &c **Sund 31** fair the
skies look very red P G has got ^home^ last week we go to meeting

SEPTEMBER 1884

Mond ^**Sept 1 1884**^ cut rags to make a rug **Tuesd** ^**2**^ the same **Wed 3** put
on a rug **Thursd 4** fast day ~~we~~ I went to meeting **Frid 5** I work on the rug
Satd 6 the same **Sund 7** I went over to meeting but as there was a conferance
at farmington there was no meeting. I went & see Br & Sister Hibert **Mond 8** I
work on the rug **Tuesday 9** I cut Plumbs & sprea^d^ them **wed 10** the same
Thursd 11 got the rug out & put another on finished cuting the plumbs **Frid
12** worked on the rug **Satd 13** work on the rug & spread Aples & took care of
the fruit **Sund 14** it rains we bring the fruit into the house we go to meeting
Mond 15 got the rug out **Tuesd 16** put in another rug ^worked on it^ **wed 17**
work on it **Thursd 18** the Teachers meeting here **Frid 19** I went to the Primary
fair[35] **Satd 20** went to the Primary Conference had a good time do not get the
rug out **Sund 21** fair we have cut ^& paired^ Aples last week **Mond 22** got
the rug out **Tuesday 23 wed 24 Thursd 25 Frid 26 Satd 27** we have worked
with the fruit all this week got a good deal cut & dried rains to day we have to
cover it up & bring it into the house & work with it hard all day **Sund 28** we go
to meeting **Mond 29** put in a rug & work with the fruit **Tuesd 30**

OCTOBER 1884

Wed Oct 1 1884 Thursd 2 Frid 3 Satd 4 got the rug out & have worked with
Aples & peaches very hard this week **Sund 5** Conferance commences to day at
the city P G and his folks goes I cannot go no meeting here it is a lonesome
day to me. yestarday I Bought a Bible very large print gave it to Betsey when

---

assured we shall get the bodies" (p. 1; see also the *Deseret News* of 27 August
1884, p. 1).

35. In the summer of 1878, Aurelia Spencer Rogers approached Eliza R. Snow with
an idea for an organization to train little boys to become better men. Eliza presented the idea to President John Taylor, who authorized its establishment on 11
August 1878 with Aurelia Rogers as president. At the first meeting on 25 August
1878, 224 boys and girls met to be taught obedience, faith in God, prayer, punc-
tuality, and good manners (see Naomi Shumway, "Primary," in *Encyclopedia of
Mormonism,* ed. Daniel H. Ludlow [New York City: Macmillan, 1992], 3:1146).

I have done with it my old one is so fine print we can hardly see to read in it & hers is just the same. this is verry large print & good so we can read to day. I have read the Book of Geneses through **Mond 6** I went to conference P G caried me in his carriage **Tuesday 6** cut ^& spread^ peaches **wed 7** the same **Thursd 8 Frid 9 Satd 10** I have cut & spread peaches & took care of them Betsey has gathered them we have worked very hard all the week **Sund 11** we went to funeral of Br Naillors child William Tripp has been here from ~~fo~~ Richmond went home to day or to the city & home tomorrow. two Sisters from Logan here yestar & to day Sister Andrews [*left blank*] **Mond 12** I cut peaches & spread them Betsey gathers them **Tuesd 13** the same **Wed 14** the same **Thursd 15** gathering and cuting & spreading peaches untill 2 oclock Teachers meeting here **Frid 16** ~~the Satd 17~~ Betsey gathering peaches I cut & spread them work very hard it looks likly to rain we fetch them into house on the racks with the lanterns ^as I have been to the city to day^ work untill almost midnight ^**Satd 17**^ we got them all into the house in almost every room up stairs & down & it rained soon after we got them in[36] **Sund oct 19 1884** it has rained hard to to day some of the time & some of the time the sun shines yestarday **Satd 18** I went to the city drew my dividen-eight hundred Dollars & intrest on two notes forty three Dollars 87 cts **Monday 20** we have worked in the peach trees in my fence and orchard a peach tree fence gathering the dry limbs and twigs I have cut them up to burn Betsey cuts them off I carry them to the house & cut them up **Tuesd 21 wed 22 Thursd 23 Frid 24** ~~I~~ we went to meeting female confrence **Satd 25** we have worked cleaning the dead brush out of the fence & cuting it up to burn **Sund 26** fair & nice weather my fruit is doing well almost dry we go to meeting **Mond 27** ^P G has got hurt by a horse bad he is so lame he can hardly move^ still work cleaning the brush out **Tuesd 28 wed 29** the same finish it put in a rug **Frid 31** we have been husking corn and taking care of it & the foder have done but litle else

November 1884

Satd Nov 1 1884 ~~Sund 2 Cloudy~~ P G has gone to the city I let him have one hundred Dollars to get shingles for his barn **Sund <2>** he is very lame and sore he can neither dress nor undress himself we have been to meeting I

---

36. From her earliest days in the Salt Lake Valley, Patty spent many weeks every year gathering, cutting, and drying her fruit. Leslie T. Foy, in *The City Bountiful,* describes fruit drying as one of the early industries of Bountiful. Foy quotes Angus Smedley's account: ". . . The job lasts for several weeks in the fall of the year. Enough fruit was gathered each morning to last for the whole days cutting. It was brought to the house. . . . The cutting consisted of cutting the fruit in halves, removing the stone or pit, and spreading the halves right side up on the homemade wooden trays. The trays were then placed in a good position in the sun to be sun dryed . . ." ([Bountiful, Utah: Horizon Publishers, 1975], 91–92).

could hear the most that was said **Mond 3** we husked corn **Tuesd 4** fair husking corn **wed 5** husking good weather **Thursday 6 Friday 7 Satd 8** have been husking all the week **Sund 9** fine weather have been to meeting **Mond 10** husking **Tuesd 11** the same **wed 12 Thursd 13** got it all husked & took care of the foder & all teachers meeting here in the afternoon then put on a rug got the other out this morning **Frid 14** work on the rug **Satd 15** Jim Indian mowed my Lucern cut down two Aple trees cut up the bodies for wood and split it we have cut up the limbs all cleaned up good **Sund 16** fair weather we go to meeting **Mond 17** got the rug out & put another on work on it to ^ **19** ^ day the funeral of a child Br Days was run over with a wagon & [*in margin*] kiled **Tuesd 25** the same **wed 26** I went to Perrys she had a sewing Bee had a good time[37] **Thursd 27** I went to Davids to dinner Sarah was there with her twins[38] **Frid** ^ **28** ^ work on the rug **Satd <29>** the same got it out I have worked hard **Sund 30** fine weather we have been to the funeral of John Harison [Harrison] died in the Hospittle in Salt Lake ^ city ^ brought up home to bury his folks live up here

DECEMBER 1884

^ **Dec** ^ **Mond 1-1884** get the Locust & Boxelder cut down that were among my peach trees **Tuesd 2** the same **wed 3d Thur 4 Frid 5 Satd 6** we have worked all the week piling up the wood & brush & cleaning up the lot **Sund 4** I do not go to meeting to day it is very cold ^ **Dec** ^ **Mond 1 1884** finish cleaning up the Lot **Tuesd 2** put in a rug **wed 3** work on it **Thursd 4 Frid 5 Satd 6** got it done and made up **Sund 7** it is cold wind has blown hard it snowed yestarday & is still snowing to day and is cold & windy **Mond 8** put in a rug ~~for myself~~ work **tuesd 9 wed 10** ~~John & Agnes Stodard~~ ^ Phebe Janes girl Iisabell ^ here to see me and their three children **thursd 11 Frid 12 Satd 13** I have got the rug out and made up **Sund 14** ~~A~~ it is so stormy we do not go to meeting **Mond <15>** I put another rug this for myself work on it **Tuesd 16** the same **wed 17** the same **Thursd <18>** 1 work on it very stormy all the time John Stodard & Agnes and all thre of their children here to see me **Frd 19 Satd 20** got the rug out and made up it mine **Sund 21** it snows all day wet and cold **Mond 22** put on another rug for myself work on it **Tuesday 23** the same **Wend 24** the same **Thursd 25** Chrismas Jony Fisher came after me I went up there his folks there Father & wives & child<ren> & Hariet [Knighton, a plural wife] & her children there & we had a good time He

---

37. Perry Sessions (1860–1895) was the fifth child of Perrigrine and Mary Call. He was married to Esther Jane Tolman, the "she" who is mentioned, on 6 January 1881.

38. Sarah Phebe Sessions was a daughter of David and Phebe Carter Foss Sessions. She was married to Joseph Moss.

brought me home in the evening **Frid 26** work on the rug got it out put on a
foot rug to give to Betseys sister Stoker. **Satd 27** made that. I was then sent
for Br Jones came after me & Lucina P Gs wife & Phebe Davids wife to go &
wash & anoint his wife she has the Dropsy[39] sweled all over they washed I
anointed her we all laid hands on her. we then came home ~~P~~ Found P G &
Chester Lovlin here both staid all night. **Sund 28** I have read some of my
journal to chester some of my donations to the Temples Logan & Salt Lake
Temples. I dont know as I can go to meeting to day it so bad going I went to
meeting ^one of^ the boys took me over in the Buggy **Mond 29** got my rugs
made up **Tuesd 30** I went to town carr[i]ed my fruit **wed 31** attended to
many things

1885

independance [day] . . . the Band came & seranaded us this morning

JANUARY 1885

Thursd Jan1 1885 New years we went to P Gs a big gathering **Frid 2** we went
to Sarahs. had a good time **Satd–3** Betsey we^n^t over to ~~the~~ see her sister
Stoker I staid here alone **Sund 4** I went to meeting it was a conferance of the
young gentlemen & Ladies a good meeting. John Stodard & Agness starts for
home this afternoon **Monday 5** I have cut a few peices for a rug **Tuesd 6** put
on another rug **wed 7** worked on it a litle **Thursd 8** work on my rug **Frid 9**
cut up peices for a rug for Sarah Moss **Satd 10** got the rug out **Sund 11** went
to meeting **Mond 12** put on another rug **Tuesd 13** work on the rug **wed 14** E
B Tripp and Phebe here staid all night **Thursd 15** we went to Lucinias had a
good time **Frid 16** we went to Sarah Anns **Satd 17** went to Davids **Sund 18**
went to meeting **Mond 19** E B & Phebe went home I have got Sarah Moss
Rug on done considerable to it **Tuesd 20** got it out. the snow is the deepest
that I have seen for a long time about18 inches deep warm and pleasant **wed
21** I went to the city with P G in a sleigh got some things for me & Betsey got
her two dress patterns one flanel & one calico & linings &c got many things
Thursd 22 put on a rug worked on it **Frid <23> Satd 24** worked on the rug.
It has snowed almost every day this week the most snow on the ground that I
have seen this year. **Sund 25** P G told me the Boys would carry me to meeting
in the Sleigh to day we are all well as common. the boys came after us we rode
in a sleigh had a good meeting I rode home last week when I went to town I
bought Betsey a black Alapacka dress she has made it up & wore it to day. I
feel pleased that I can get her something that suits her **Mond 26** got my rug

---

39. Dropsy was an accumulation of diluted fluid in tissues and body cavities.

out **Tuesd 27** Betsey went releif coiety I am cuting rags that Mary ^Scot^ brought here for a woman wishes me to make it for her I have been cuting the rags to day **Wed 28** I went up to Jony Fishers Josephine came after me he brought me home **Thursd 29** I went to Sarahs to a surprise party her birth day. **Frid 30** I went to John Weights [John Anson Waite, Jr.]. [He is] Lucinias [daughter of Perrigrine and Fanny Emorett] Husbands & put on the Rug for Sister Forbes that Mary brught here **Satd 31** I worked on the rug.

FEBRUARY 1885

Sund Feb 1 1885 pleasant sun shines but cold. I went to meeting **Mond 2** worked on the rug **Tuesd 3** got it out & made up & put on another **Wend 4** my birthday 90 years old. four of my grand children came in here brought me a birth day presant that they bought with their own money it was David & Jedidiaha & Samantha & Anna Davids girl[40] it is a nice litle Box and I think much of it ~~Frid~~ **Thursd 5** William Smoots Boys here to see me[41] have gone to the big house I work on the rug **Frid 6** work on the rug **Satd 7** got it out & made up done many other things **Sund 8 1885** it has snowd I clean the snow off the house it has cleard of a litle Smoots Boys started home yesterday caled and bid me good bye we went to meeting the boys took me over in the Buggy. **Mond 9** put on a rug **tuesday 10** worked on the rug **wed 11** the same got it out ~~Thursd 12~~ & put on another **Thursd 12** work on it **Frid 13** got it out **Satd 14** put on another ~~Sund 15~~ we have had the deepest snow I have seen since I have lived here I have been to see Sarah she is sick the boys have been to see if I wish them to cary me to meeting Zina & babe has been here two weeks went home yestard[42] **Sund 15** the boys did not come after me so I did not go to meeting E B Tripp came here to Night staid all night John Fisher came with him & went home again **Mond 16** Tripp staid here all day untill after dark then started to go to Jony Fishers. I did ^not^ work on the rug any to day **Tuesd 17** I am to work on the rug to day **wed 18** The same **Thursd 19** I have got it out and put another on and worked some on it. **Frid 20** work on the rug **Satd 21** P G came home from Logan caled to see me this morning he has done some work in the Temple I have not got the rug out **Sund 22** I do not go to meeting Betsey went

40. David (b. 1858) and Annie Sophia (b. 1875) were children of David and Phebe Carter Foss Sessions; Jedidiah (b. 1875) was a son of Perrigrine and Sarah Ann Bryson; while Samantha (b. 1874) was a daughter of Perrigrine and Fanny Emorett Loveland.

41. William Cochran Adkinson Smoot and Martha Ann Sessions were parents of five sons: William, Jr. (b. 1853); Abraham Owen (1857–1876); Albert Carlos (b. 1865); Perrigrine (b. 1872); and Parley Wilson (b. 1875). In addition they had four daughters.

42. Zina Sessions (1859–1951) was the fourth child of Perrigrine and Mary Call. She married Thomas Burningham on 15 April 1880.

Mond 23 got the rug out **Tuesday** ^24^ cut up ~~carpet~~ rags for Perrys wife a rug **Wed 25** made a braided rug round one **Thursday** ^26^ Josephine Fisher came after me I went up there staid all day they brought me home **Frid 27** got another rug in work on it **Satd 28** work on it do not get it out put it by

MARCH 1885

Sund March 1-1885 fair weather we went to meting **Mond-2** got the rug out & put on another & worked on that **Tuesd 3-** I am at work on the rug Betsey has gone round teaching as she is a teacher & I am here alone **wed 4** I work on the rug Betsey is washing & Ironing **Thursd 5** fast day we fast but do not go to meeting Sister Barlow came here to see me[43] in the afternoon the Teachers met here about forty the Bishop Chester Call & Br Camton here I could not hear much I am so hard of hearing I have got my rug out & made up & am kniting **Frid 6** fair weather I coloured red for my rug Analine Sara Ann came & helped me **Satd 7** it is conferance for the Females fair weather. I went to meeting had a good seat heard allmost all that was said had a good time sister Miller ^from Farmington^ came here staid all night. **Sund 8** fair weather I go to meeting again to day all day went a foot Betsey took me by the arm there and back had a good seat & heard the most that was said see many old friends **Monday 9** I put on another rug and cut many peaces for it **Tuesday** ^10^ work on it. **Wends11** We went to John Waits Lucinia had a quilting got it out and made up. **Thursday** ^10^ we went to see Olive Corbrige ~~saw~~ Davids daughter had a good time[44] Emma corbrige came home from the Sandride [Sandridge] ^we^ had a good visit **Frid 13** I worked on the rug **Satd 14** got the rug out Betsey has gone over to see her sister Stoker. I am here alone. the sun shines warm got a letter to day from my cousin in maine **Sund 15** fair & pleasant we go to meeting **Mond 16** the sun is Eclipsed almost entirely this morning I cut rags for a rug for Liza Davids daughter to make a rug for her[45] **Tuesd 17** still cuting rags I have worked hard to day **Wed 18** put the rug on the frames to work on it **Thursd 19** work the rug steady **Frid 20** work on the rug steady. I got a letter yesterday from my Nephew Elisha Bartlett. I want to answer it but my hand trembles so I cannot write. I get P G to answer it. he has wrote a long letter to him. **Satd 21-1885**. I have worked on the rug all day steady **Sund 22** fair I go to meeting **Mond: 23** I have worked on the rug **Tuesd 24**. I went to Salt lake City went in

---

43. Probably Elizabeth Haven Barlow (1811–1888), who had been present at the organization of the Female Relief Society in Nauvoo. She became the first president of the Relief Society in Bountiful, called by Brigham Young, who was her cousin.

44. Olive Cordelia Sessions was the seventh child of David and Phebe Foss Sessions. Her husband was William Henry Corbridge.

45. Elizabeth (b. 1868), daughter of David and Phebe Foss Sessions, was married to William Lewis.

the Bugy with P G got home all well **wed 25** we went to Sarah & Esthers to a sewing bee[46] had a good time **Thursd 26** I have got the rug out to day have cut some rags for another fair weather. **Friday ^24^** cut rags for Fanny Beards rug **Satd 28** fair weather have ^finished^ cutting Fannys rags. **Sund 29** fair I went to meeting Betsey did not go ~~W~~ **Mond 30** I cut rags for myself ^had Corbage wife^ **Tuesd 31** coulered green & yellow & cut them up

April 1885

Wed April 1 it rains this morning we went up to David Brigs house to a bee sewing carpet rags has cleared of fair the sun shines warm **Thursd 2** fast day I put on a rug I have worked on it this forenoon in the afternoon the releif Society met here had a good meting **Frid 3** I have sent a letter to Patty Bittern my Great Grand Daughter[47] **Satd: ^4^** fair worked on the rug ~~yestarday~~ ^yestarday^ and to day **Sund 5** I have been to meeting to day **Mond 6** I have got the rug ready to put the lining on Betsey & I have took the sage roots up & dug the ground over set them out again **Tuesday 7** put on another rug & worked on it **wed 8** worked on the rug again **Thursd 9** got itout **Friday 10** I have cut rags for another rug **Satd 11** finished a pair of stockins for a poor girl **Sund ^12^** we have been to meeting **Mond 13** put on rug worked on it **Tuesd 14** worked on it **wed 15** the same **Thursd 16** got the rug out I have cut a few peices for another rug Frederic Keslor here to diner Sarah & Esthers youngest children both sick **Frid 17** I have been to Salt Lake City to day ^got^ my dividen got some other things got home all well **Satd 18** I have put on a rug for sister Ramtons girl **Sund 19** fair weather **Mond 20** work on the rug **Tuesd 21 wed 22** the same **Thursd 23** got it out **Frid 24** cut rags **Satd 25** got another rug on Wallace Bartlett & Vene & E B. ~~Trit~~ Trips wife here went over to P Gs in after[noon] they went home in the evening Linkon was there making out some writings for me **Sund** [April *written on top of*] ^~~May~~ April^ **26** 1885 I went to meeting **Mond 27** George Lincoln here doing some writing for me making me will of my stock in the Zions commercial institution **Tuesd 28** I went to Salt Lake City got it finished up[48] **wed 29** worked on the rug got it done ^the releif Society met here^ **Thursd 30** put in another rug worked on it

46. Probably Sarah Ann Bryson and Esther Mabey, wives of Perrigrine.

47. Patty Bartlett Sessions (1865–1895), a daughter of Carlos Lyon Sessions and Elizabeth Wintle, was married to William Barney Bitton on 5 January 1882.

48. No will is on file in Davis County. Patty died on 14 December 1892. On 9 November 1898 the probate process began. On 28 February 1900 it was completed. At that time the total estate was $6,079.25, which, when divided among Patty's children, provided each one with approximately $2,026. Sylvia, David, and Perrigrine were all deceased, but their descendants split the inheritance. This meant that Sylvia's descendants, who were fewer, received $506.60 each, whereas Perrigrine's children (and living wives) received $47.12. Grandchildren

MAY 1885

Frid May 1 I work on it **Satd 2** worked on it **Sund 3** we went to meeting **Mond 4** got the rug out put another in **Tuesd 5** worked on it **wed 6** the same **Wed** [*written on top of* Thursd] **7** worked on it **Frid 8** got it out & made up cut rags for another **Satd 9**. I went up to Br Winns to the funeral of John they had just finished burring one before we got there **Sund 10** we have been to meeting to day **Mond 11** I put on another rug worked on it **Tuesd:12** I have worked on the rug to day steady **wed:13** I have got it out I am very tired **Thursd 14** put on another Josephine Fisher came after me to go up there I went up staid all day had a good time John brought me home and I found that Eliza Snow had been here I felt sorry that I was not at home **Satd** [*written on top of* Frid] **15** I found that Eliza was down at Br Nobles P G said one ^of the^ boys might take me in the bugy to see her I went had a good visit with her & others staid all day Lucinia Weight came after me & brought me home **Satd 16** I have worked on the rug Chester ^Sessions^ came here to see me he has come back from Arizonia **Sund**:fair this morning it rains we do not go to meeting. **Mond 18** work on the rug **Tuesd 19** I got it out and are moving our things we are going to have our rooms white washed **Wed 20** the man did not come to white wash **Thursd 21** he has come is white washing has done it good I paid him two Dollars for it he done it well **Frid** ^**22**^ we are cleaning Esther & Elis came & helped Betsey clean **Satd 23** Still cleaning ^&^ puting down carpets ^Br whiple here to see me staid a good while 3 hours or more^ **Sund 24** we went to meeting **Mond 25** cleaning the walls **Tuesd 26** got on Josehine rug worked on that **wend 27** worked on it **Thursd 28 Friday 29** got it out and another in Chester Sessions here triming my shade trees **Satd 30** he came & did more triming **Sund 31** we went to meeting

JUNE 1885

Mond June 1 1885 Chester & Harison here fixing the tops of my chimney Chesters wife [Isabelle Jane Corbridge, 1862–1950] here all day to see me **Tuesd 2** worked on the rug **wed 3** worked on the rug **Thursd 4 Frid 5** got the rug out **Satd 6** cut rags **Sund 7** rains do go to meeting **Mond 8** put on another rug **tuesd 9** I went up to Elvirys [*unreadable word written in margin*] house & lots ^went^ in the Bugey stoped at Hariets & Josephines **wed 10** worked on the rug **Thursd 11** got it out put on another **Frid 12** worked on it **Satd 13** moved my corn some of it into the cellar the crib leaked Chester cut

---

received $3.92. At the filing of probate, Patty's possessions were listed as property worth $147.50; 40 shares of ZCMI stock, worth $5,000; one organ worth $25.00; one stove and pipe and 24 benches and a map, worth $2.50. No doubt some of her belongings were given away while she was still living. Perhaps some were sold to help pay for her care—but that, of course, is speculation.

my Lucern frid turned it over last night **Sund 14** it rained last night Libby came down last night after Sally to go up there to live **Mond 15** put on another rug Sally wants my advice about her going up to Carloses I do not like to give her any advice about it let her do as she pleases.[49] Chester put my hay in the barn today **Tuesday16** Lybbee stays with me nights and visits round days **Wed 17** P G carried me in the buggy to the store I have contracted for one hundred bushels ^of^ wheat to lay up I bought one [*in margin*] **Thurs<day>18** hundred ^weight^ of flour got it home to night gave $1-00 80 cents for it **Frid 19** worked on my rug **Satd 20** got my rug out cut some rags for another rug ^coulered yellow yestarday for another rug^ I have done many things to day am very tiered p̶ Phebe Janes Father Mr [Ezekiel] Clark he was here to see me last Tuesday has gone home gave her 2̶0̶0̶ considerable money and is going to build her a house[50] **Sund 21** I have not been to meeting to day **Mond 22** put on a rug worked on it **Tuesday 23** worked on the rug **wed 24** went to a sewing bee at Lucinias **Thursd 25** got the rug out put on another **Frid 26** worked on it **Satd <27>** worked on it & did many other things Mr Clark ^Phebe Janes Father^ and wife daughter & son here **Sund fair 28** we go to meeting **Mond 29** Got the rug out & put another on **Tuesd 30** worked on it

JULY 1885

wed July the 1 1885 worked on the rug ^I was caled to se a child that had a breach I fixed a twin Pad for it^ **Thursd 2** the same **Satd 4** independance we stay here alone Betsey & I the Band came & seranaded us this morning. that woman that had the child with a breach came down to day I see it I told her

49. Patty had mentioned building a house for Sally Lavina Hill, the second wife of Carlos Lyon Sessions. His first wife was Elizabeth Wintle.

50. Ezekiel Clark (1817–1898) married Sylvia on 1 January 1850, about a year after Windsor Palmer Lyon died in Iowa City, Iowa. They were parents of three children: Perry (b. 4 February 1851), Phoebe (b. 1 September 1852), and Martha (b. 20 January 1854). Josephine, a daughter by an earlier marriage, said later, "Patty had never stopped praying that her daughter Sylvia might join the saints in Utah, and the heart of Sylvia seemed to be turned this way in spite of her worldly comforts. When Perrigrine finished his English mission, he stopped at Iowa City. Sylvia decided to come west with him. Mr. Clark was not a Latter-day Saint. He would not come himself, but he outfitted Sylvia in the best possible manner, with two wagons and two teams of oxen and three cows, and everything deemed necessary. Martha was only three months old. Josephine was ten years old. She drove part of the way. It took courage to make that long, wearisome journey of three months" (told to Josephine Eckman Fisher by her mother-in-law, Josephine Lyon Fisher). Ezekiel Clark, successful businessman, banker, and state legislator, evidently provided generous support to Sylvia and their children through the years. Sylvia was his second wife; his first had been Susan Urina Dyer; his third was Mary Dewey.

how to fix it and how to make the pad she said she would call at our house next week and have me fix it I let her have some oil of egg to put on it **Sund 5** we went to meeting **Mond 6** I went to the store let David Stoker have Sixty Dollars he is to let me have one hundred bushels of wheat for it I have cut rags & knit to day **Tuesd 7** cut rags **wed 8** put on a rug **Thursd 9** Libby Carlos wife has been here the most of the time for a long time she stayes here nights mostly **Thursd 9** I work on the rug P G has got burnt in the night with the lamp burnt his hands bad both of them and a narrow escape for life & house & all they had. I have got my rug out **Sund 12** P Gs hands are both bad we go to meeting **Mond 13** did many things P Gs hands are very bad **Tuesd 14** put another rug on **wed 15** work on the rug **Thursd 16** work on the rug **Frid 17** got it done P Gs hands look a little better. **Satd 18** cut rags for Esthers girl Geneva a rug. Last Monday Sarah Ann had a son [Heber John Sessions] born P Gs fiftyeth child[51] Born July 13 1885 all doing well. P Gs hands looks better **Sund 19 1885** healing fast we went to meeting **Mond 20** I put on a rug for Geneva **Tuesd 21 Wend 22** worked on it **Thursd 23** got it out & made up P Gs hands gets better fast Lucinia Weight came here to day **Frid 24** we had a celebration to day we both went to the Tabernacle & to the grove saw many old aquaintances **Satd 25** I have cut apricots to dry & also cut some peaces for another rug **Sund 26** went to meeting **Mond 27** put on another rug **Tuesd: 28** worked on the rug **wed 29** worked on the rug & cut fruit & spread it **thursd 30** gave fifty cents to the teachers for the poor cash I have been cuting fruit & got my rug out & made up ^**Friday 31**^

AUGUST 1885

Satd August 1 1885 cut fruit & spread it **Sund 2** we went to meeting **Mond 3** Election day I went & put in my vote then cut & spread fruit Apricots **Tuesd 4** cut & spread fruit **wed: 5** done the same **Thursd 6 Frid 7 Satd 8** the same at night I went over to Br Weights carried 20 pairs of stockens to put into the Temple ten dollars got a receit **Sund 9** I did not go to meeting Betsey went **Mond 10** cut fruit & spread it **Tuesd 11** took care of my fruit **Wed 12** went up to John Fishers **Thursd 13** put on a rug **Frid 14** worked on it **Satd 15** worked on it then went to the Funeral of Chester Sessions babe–died[52] ^got the rug out^ **Sund 16** ~~Mon~~ fair Went to meeting **Mond 17** put on another rug **Tuesd 18** worked on the rug **wed 19 Thursd 20** got the rug out **Frid 21** cut rags for another **Satd 22** I have cut fruit & took ^care^ of it **Sund 23** I did not go to meeting Betsey went **Mond 24** put on another rug & worked on it **tuesd 25**

---

51. According to the list of children in Appendix 2, Heber John was actually Perrigrine's forty-ninth child.

52. Chester's daughter, Laura Bell, was born on 4 January 1885 in Arizona and died on 13 August.

worked on it ~~tues~~ ^wed^ 26 the same **Thursd 27** got the rug out. cut ~~frut~~ fruit **Frid: 28** cut rags & in the morning then cut fruit & spread it ~~plumbs~~ worked at it all day cut & spread a good deal **Satd 29** did the same I have cut and spread a good deal to day **Sund 30** I do not go to meeting Betsey goes **Mond 31 1885** cut fruit

SEPTEMBER 1885

^Sept^ [*word scratched out*] <1 1885> I have cut fruit the most of the time **wed 2** ^Sept^ **1885** ^I^ cut fruit **Thursd 3 Frid 4 Satd 5** have cut fruit **Sund 6** I stay at home Betsey goes to Farmington to confrence **Mond: 7** I have cut plumbs & spread them **Tuesd 8** done the same ~~Thursday~~ ^wed 9^ cut & spre^a^d plumbs old Sister Fackeral died yestarday is to be buried to morrow 1 P M **Thursday 10** I went to the funeral I have cut and spread fruit all I could **Frid** it rained I brought my fruit into the house last night & night before to day got it up chamber it rains by spels not fair it is **Satd 12** at noon rains by showers cut some plumbs &c **Sund 13** ^Betsey &^ I went to meeting fair weather **Mond 14** cut plumbs **Tuesd** <15> the same **wed 16 Thursd 17** finished cuting plumbs cut peaches **Frid 18** hear that Zinnas babe is dead cut peaches **Satd 19** cut peaches & took care of my fruit at 4 oclock went to the funeral of Zinas babe **Sund 20** fair weather Betsey goes to meeting I stay at home have read a good deal in the book of Mormon **Mond 21** P G has pulled three teeth for me to day all right **Mond 21** cut peaches **Tuesd 22** the same ~~Wed~~ **Wed 23 Thursd 24** cut and spread peaches **Frid 25 Satd 26** done the same. it rains to day **Sund 27** fair the sun shines Betsey goes to meeting I stay at home finished reading the Book of Mormon through [*illegible word above line*] sinse last ~~s~~ June let Thomas Wardrope have four Dollars for the Ward Expenceses **Wed 30** work with the fruit ~~Thursd cut the fruit again~~

OCTOBER 1885

Oct Thursd 1 1885 Satd 3 work with the fruit cuting taking up & spreading work hard my racks all full going to put some on the corn crib sprerad some there **Sund 4** fair work at the fruit finished spreading fruit on the corn crib covered it all over I have worked very hard **Tuesd 6** cuting fruit and spreading **Wed 7 Thursd 8** the same **Friday 9 Satd 10** cuting & spreading fruit the most of the time Carlos has been down here took Sallys things home with him I gave him five Dollars cash & ^sent^ Sally a rug too as she sent me some peices to make one in part he started for home this morning I have worked very hard all this week it has rained a good deal to day cold **Sund 11** fair this morning froze hard last night Betsy went to meeting I did not go **Monday 12** I work with the fruit **Tuesday 13.** I still work with the fruit **wed 14** the same **Thursday 15** taking care of my fruit **Frid 16 Satd 17** my fruit all cut & drying I have worked hard all day **Sund 18** fair weather Betsey goes to meeting I stay at home have read a good deal to day **Mond 19 1885** work with the fruit

Tuesd 20 work with the fruit **wed 21** the same **Thursd 22** have finished cutting my peaches **friday 23** takeing care of my fruit **Satd 24** cut & paired my Aples got them all spread Enoch Tripp & wife came down here yestarday all well. it is now fair weather and we have got our fruit all in the chamber in good condition. I feel well but very tired **Sund 25** I do not go to meeting Betsey went **Mond 26** James has been triming my ^fruit^ trees & we have been clearing the Brush away & cuting it up to burn **Tuesday 27 Wed 28 Thursd 29** P G has got home all well he has been to see Kepler & many of the rest of his children **Friday 30** been taking care of my drided Fruit it has rained a litle this morning I have piled up my Fruit put some in sacks **Satd 31** piled up the brush

NOVEMBER 1885

Sunday the first of Nov 1885 I went to meeting with Betsey **Mond 2 Tuesd 3 Wed 4 Thursd 5** I have been puting on a rug **Frid 6** I went up to John Fishers he and Josephine came after me then they sent a boy ^& team^ took me to Br Holts to a weding supper of James Sessions ^&^ Holts daughlter [Selma Selena Holt] Betsey went. Br Holt came home with us. **Satd 7** worked on my rug **Sund 8** fair weather we had a deep snow last week about eight inches ^it is^ mostly gone now I think I shal go to meeting to day we went had a good meeting **Mond 9** I have worked on the rug **Tuesd 10** finishe it **wed 11** I have put on another rug. **thursd. 12** work on it **Frid 13** work on it **Satd 14** dont get it quite done. **Sund 15** we go to meeting Betsey & I. the rest of the ol friends David & Phebe all the family went to the city. to Sister Woodruffs funeral she was Davids wifes Aunt.[53] **Mond 16** I have got my rug out and another on worked some on it **Tuesd 17 wed: 18 Thursd 19 Frid 20 Satd 21** got my rug out **Sund 22** go to meeting **Mond 23** put on another rug **Tuesd 24** work on it **wed 25** I am making this rug out of an old shall shaul I bought of a poor man when we first came into the valey he had lost his wife before he got into the valley his children had nothing to eat I let him have a litle of what I had as we had but litle of any thing to eat only what we had

---

53. Phebe Whittemore Carter (1807–1885) was Wilford Woodruff's first wife; she had married him in 1837. As a result of the 1882 Edmunds Tucker Act prohibiting unlawful cohabitation, Woodruff went into partial hiding at St. George in 1884. In November 1885, however, he returned to Salt Lake City to meet with the Quorum of the Twelve Apostles to deliberate on the membership status of Albert Carrington and John W. Young. Phebe, already ill when Woodruff went to St. George, fell and split her scalp about a month before his return to Salt Lake City. On 9 November her husband visited her secretly and "anointed her for burial." She died soon thereafter (see Thomas G. Alexander, *Things in Heaven and Earth* [Salt Lake City: Signature Books, 1991], 241). David Sessions was married to Phebe Carter Foss, daughter of Calvin and Sarah Brakett Carter (Foss), who was a sister of Phebe Whittemore Carter Woodruff.

brought with us & I have made the shaul into a rug after wearing it as long as I could utill it droped all to holes I now have the rug ~~ly~~ by the side of my bed to think of & how I got it **Thursd 26 Frid 27 Satd 28 Sund 29-1885** rains some to day I do not go to meeting **Mond Nov 30 1885** put on a rug

DECEMBER 1885

Tuesday Dec 1–1885 work on the rug **wed 2 Thursd 3 Frid 4** I have worked on the rug **Satd 5** Chester Sessions worked for me got me a load of coal and fixed my fence round my lot cut down some fruit trees &c &c **Sund 6** very cloudy and wet P G has got home has been to see the children has been gone a good while for him to be gone I was glad to see him **Mond 7** work on the rug **Tuesd 8 wed 9** ~~Thursd 10~~ got the ^rug^ out Betsey has gone round for the releif society I gave 25 cents the ground is covered with snow I put in five Dollars a short time ago I have made no munite of but litle that I have given a good deal **Tuesd 8** put on a rug **wed 9** worked on it **thursd <10>** ~~th~~ the same **Frid ~~9~~ 11** I went to the city Salt Lake City & home all right **Satd 12** worked on my rug **Sund 13** Betsey has gone to Center ville to meeting I am here alone quite well think I shall go to meeting this after noon I went to meeting **Mond 14** got my rug out **Tuesday 15** put on another rug **wed 16** work on the rug **Thursday 17** work on the rug **Friday^18^** Christmas Betsey & I went to Davids had a good time with many others relatives **Satd 19** finished my rug it rained some **Sund 20** cloudy we went to meeting **Mond 21** put on another rug **Tuesday 22** work on the rug **wed 23** the same **Thursd 24 Frid 25** got the rug out **Satd 26** did many things **Sund 27 Mon 28 Tuesd 29** got another rug on work it **Wed 30** work on the rug **Thursd 31**

1886

got the lining on the rug ready to to quilt it on
I cannot do that my hands and arms is so lame

JANUARY 1886

Frid January 1 New years went to Scots My Grand sons had a good time many others there **Satd 2** worked on the rug **Sund 3** cold **Mond 4** put on another rug **Tuesd 5 wed 6 Thursd 7 Frid 8** got the rug out **Satd 9** cut rags for another **Sund 10** P G came here this morning bid us good bye has gone away I let him have 30 Dollars cash to bear his expences we went to meeting **Mond 11** I have got another rug on **Tuesd 12** I work on it **wed 13** work on the rug **Thursd 14** The same **Frid 15** got it out we have had a deep snow **satd 16** the sun shines cut some rags got some gunysack **Sund-17** we went to meeting **Mond 18** I put another rug & worked on it **Tuesd 19 wed 20 Thursd 21 Frid 22** got it out doubled some factory yarn for thread & twine and many did many other things wound 2 lb kniting yarn **Satd 23** I have been doing got a letter from P G all well **Sund 24** I do not go to meeting bad going **mond 25** put put on another rug **Tuesday 26** work on the rug **Wed 27** the same **Thursd 28** work on the rug **Frid 29** went up to James Beards to a sewing Bee **Satd 30** work on the rug got it done **Sund 31** we do not go to meeting

FEBRUARY 1886

Mond Febuary 1-1886 I have got my rug out & cut some rags for another ^rug^ **Tuesd 2** I have put on another have been over to the store Esther went with me carried five pound of ^5^ butter and 2 doz eggs for tithing **wed 3** I then went up to Jonny Fishers he sent for me a waggon & brought me home **Thursd 4** my birth day 91 years old to day. **Frid 5 Satd 6** I work on the rug **Sund 7** we went to meeting **Mond 8** got it done ready to take it off **Tuesd 9** put on another **Wed 10 Thursd 11 Frid 12 Satd 13** got it out went to the store got some guny sack Zina brought it home for me **Sund 14** Betsey has gone to meeting I stay at home P G has been here to see us took dinner with us **Mond: 15** I put on a rug & work on it **Tuesd 16** work on the rug **wed: 17 Thursd 18** ^work on the rug^ go to Davids to a party **Frid ^19^** got the rug ~~out~~ done cut some more peices for another **Satd 20** Paid to James Weight one hundred Dollars cash & twenty two pair of children stockins Eleven Dollars to go to the Salt Lake temple got his Receit I I have cut rags for another rug **Sunday 21** fair weather we have been to meeting **Mond 22** I have put on a rug & worked on it **Tuesd 23** Mary Scot came in here to bid me good bye she is going to her husband Walter Scot to Ophir she is gone I have worked on the rug all day **Wed 24** work on the rug **Thursday 25** ~~Frid~~ work on the rug **Friday 26** work on the rug in the forenoon in afternoon go to the school the last day. Irvine Fisher has kept the school sent for me to come to the [s]chool I went had a good time. **Sate^r^day 27** I finished my rug. got it made up cut some rags for ~~f~~ another for Sarah Anns [Bryson] girls Eliza [Tryphena, 1877–1943] & Patty [Orilla, 1879–1983] **Sunday 28** it has snowed a litle Betsey went to meeting I stayed at home ~~Mond 29~~

MARCH 1886

March the first day Mond 1 1886 I put on Eliza & Pattys rug **Tuesday 2** work on the rug **wed 3** work on it **Thursday 4** fast day I do not work female meeting here in the afternoon **Frid ^5^** work on the rug **Satd 6** got it done all but lining Betsey has gone to see her sister Stoker I have been to the store Chester took me there with his waggon I got some yarn to knit carried some ~~Thi~~ Tithing fifteen dozen & eight eggs & four pound of butter. I have got the lining on the rug ready to to quilt it on I cannot do that my hands ^(and^ arms is so lame Betsey has come got the rug out **Sund 7** I do not go to meeting **Mond 8** I put on another rug & work on it **Tuesd: 9** work on the rug **wed 10** work on the rug **Thursd 11** work on the rug **Frid 12** got it ready for lining

P G came home yestarday we were glad to see him Betsey has come put the Lining on & finished it **Satd 13** we went to conference P G sent the waggon after us carried us over had a good meeting **Sund 14** it has snowed more roads is bad P G sent the waggons after us we rode over to the meeting had a good meeting **Mond 15** I have cut some rags for a rug ready to put in got it on have worked on it **Tuesd 16** worked on the rug **wed 17** worked on the rug steady. **Thursday ^18^** got it done & made up. I have worked hard & steady it has snowed the most of the time to day & is still snowing **Frid 19** Jony Fisher come after me I went up there Josephine came home with me to see P G he was over to Davids she went over there **Satd 20** P G starts this morning to go & get geanoliges of our dead relatives so that he can do a work for them he came here & bid us goodbye I feel very sober for to have him go away and I do not know when he will come back[54] soon after Jane Holbrook sent for me & some others to go & wash and ~~anond~~ anoint & lay hands on her she fell some time ago & broke her hip & is very bad I went Lucinia & Phebe & sister Carter went with me we administerd to her & came home. I feel lonesome and solemn not knowing when he will come back. **March 21 first 1886** we go to meeting I went a foot **Mond 22** I put on a rug & work on it **Tuesd 23** work on it **wed 24 ^again^** got the rug done and I have cut some rags for another **Thursd 25** worked gathering up brush trimings from the trees **Frid 26** the same got my lot plowed Chester did it **Satd <27>** it snowed last night cold to day got a letter from P G he was in Boston paid Chester all ^up^ we are square now. I am knitting the most of the time this morning I have done many things to day **Sund: 28** we go to meeting **Mond 29** I have been kniting the most of the time phebe Jane here to diner **Tuesd 30** got a rug on ready to work **Wed 31** worked on the rug

April 1886

Thursd April 1 fast day we have been to meeting in the fore noon then to a funeral & then female releif society at my house and the bishop was here ~~to~~ with us **Frid 2** worked on the ^rug^ got it done **Satd 3** done many things knit a good deal **Sund 4** it has snowed some we have ~~to~~ got another letter from P G sent him one yestarday **Mond 5** put on another rug worked on it all day **Tuesd 6** work on the rug I have got it ~~done~~ done and made up this is the second one I have made in two days each one. I got a letter to day from P G **wed 7** put on another rug work on it **Thursd 8** work on it **Frid 9** work on the rug got it done & made up Betseys Brother N Birdeno came here to day has gone over to his

---

54. Perrigrine traveled by rail to Maine, where he collected genealogical data. According to his diary, he returned on 14 July 1886 (p. H-33, Archives of the Historical Department, Church of Jesus Christ of Latter-day Saints, Salt Lake City). He was quite ill at the time.

Sister Stokers he came back staid here all night **Sat 10** he has gone started for home ~~I have cut rags cut rags knit and~~ ^I have been to town to day in a wagon and done^ (many other things **Sund 11** we have been to meeting and to a funeral came home wrote a part of a letter to P G **Mond 12** my house leaks the shingles are cracked & warped up. I went & got George Linkon to come & fix it he has fixed it it rained in the night but did not leak only in one place. I had some new Pipe put on **Tuesd 13** I have got a rug on and work on that to day **Wed: 14** work on the rug got it done **Thursd 15** it has rained & snowed it looks like fair weather now. I have been doubling factory yarn cloudy again looks like rain again **Frid 16** I fell to day My litle grandson got ~~hung~~ hung on the wire fence I see him hanging there I hurried to get to him and fell my whole wheight on my right hand hurt me bad I got him off ^the fence^ my hand is very bad **Satd 17** my hand is sweled bad I cannot work any I cannot write much **Sund 18** we went to meeting I had the Elders ~~lay~~ Administer to me after meeting & my hand is better **Monday 19** the swelling has gone down a good deal. I can knit some to day ^it is^ **Tuesday 20** yestarday & last night the ^wind^ blew very hard blew all the pipe off of the East side of my house that I had it put on last week By Lincon it is very pleasant this afternoon the wind has gone down & Lincoln says he will come & put the pipe on again day after tomorrow **wendsday 21** rains some to day **Thursday 22** it has rained the most of the day & Lincoln did not come **Friday 23** Betsey has gone to meeting Conferance I am here alone my hand is beter but not well it is purple yet & very lame & weak I can just hold the pen in it as it is my right hand **Satd 24** no better I can knit a very little **Sund 25** I went to meeting then to Sister Reighnolds then home my hand is very lame **Mond 26** no better **Tuesd 27** it is about the same **wed 28** I think it is a litle better we are fixing round the door Betsey has gone as teacher on this block **Thursd 28** she is gone to finish up this morning I have finished another Pair of stockins the Releif Society met here today they had a good meeting speaking in toungues & proffcing &c &c **Friday 30** we have been doing many things fixing round the house

May 1886

Satd 1 day of May Same my hand is very lame yet **Sund 2** we went to meeting E B Tripps wife ^Jesess^ here carried me over in her carriag & Brought me back **Mond 3** I have put a rug on work on it **Tuesday 4** have worked on the rug I am very lame yet **Wed 5** got the rug out ~~yestarday~~ **Thursday 6** fast day I am going to meeting we got a letter from P G he was well got it yestarday **Frid 7** Knitting **Satd 8** the same **Sund 9** we have been to meeting my hand is getting better but is lame yet **Mond 10** I have collored some Green & blue & cut it up to work into a rug **Tuesday 11** I have done many things have been over Br Weights ^wed 12^ carried 13 pair of stockins got his receit I keep kniting stockins & giving them to the poor & putting them in the temples &c &c **Thursd 13 -1886** I have been knitting cleaning up the brush & burning it &c &c **Friday 14** I have been to work on a rug **Satd: 15** finished it **sund 16** we went to meeting **Mond 17** put on a rug **Tuesd 18** finished it **wed 19** worked on kniting ~~I~~ and put on another rug **Thursd 20** work on it then ~~Frid 21~~ I went up to John Fishers had a good visit Hariet was there ~~Satd~~ **Frid 21** finished my rug **Satd 22** I have many things to do **Sund ^23^** we went to meeting & a funeral of Sister Lovland **Mond 24** I have put another rug on ^&^ have worked on it some Sylvanus has trimed some limbs of my shade trees I put the limbs under the wier fence to keep the hens out of the lot & have done many things worked on the rug in the afternoon **Tuesday 25** worked on the rug the most of the time **Wed 26** I have finished it ready for the lining got that on Betsey has gone to visit the society I am here alone she will quilt the lining on when she comes home she has come **Thursd 27** the Releif society met here had a very good meeting **Frid 28** Chester worked for me laid down a floor for ^me^ took down the hen coop & also the old corn crib and I helped all I could **Satd 29** Betsey & I have cleaned up the rubish & the peices of boards & have got all cleaned away & she has gone to see sister Stoker her sister & I have knitt we had a shower of hail the largest I ever saw the hail stones were as large as ounce balls **Sund 30** we have been to meeting all well Br Crosley Sarahs Father is down & her Brother they came here **Mond 31** I have knit the most of the time

June 1886

Tuesd June 1 1886 I have put on a rug ready to work I worked on it **Wed 2** worked on the rug some **Thursd 3** Chester commenced work on my granyry I have worked some on the rug **Frid 4** finished it. **Satd 5** Chester worked on the foundation of the granery **Sund 6 -1886** I went to Farmington to meeting to Conferance. **Mond 7** I have worked kniting & doing many things **Tuesd 8** I have done many things **wed 9** they have worked on the granery Jim Indian has worked on it all the time ^**Thursd 10 Frid 11 Satd 12** I have waited on them^ He & Chester he goes to town to get lumber **Sund 13** we go to meeting **Mond 14** I have Put on a rug worked on it some Jim & Chester has worked on the granery I let Chester ~~Tuesd~~ have $13-75 ^cts^ to get shingles he got the shingles **Tuesday 15** I work on the rug **wed 16** got the rug done **Thursd 17** I have worked on the granery waiting ^on^ Chester & Jim **Friday <18>** finished the granery and paid for it all material and labour) Chester has trimed my chade trees I have cut up the brush **Satd 19** Chester has come and cuting of some more limbs **Sund 20** we went to meeting **Mond 21** I have been cutting up the limbs Chester and Jim Indian has cut of some more limbs & Betsey and I have cut the limbs all up **Tuesd 22** & **Wed 23** we have got the limbs all cut up & pretty well cleaned up **Thursd 24** put on a rug worked **Frid 25** I visited Phebees School **Satd ~~25~~ ^6^** finished the rug cut some more rags **Sund 27** we went to meeting ^then^ wrote a few lines to P G got a letter from him **Mond 28** I have put on a rug this morning I have got the border done &

the midle laid out ready to work on **tuesday 29** worked on the rug **wed 30** I have finished the rug

July 1886

Thursd July 1 day Frid 2 Satd 3 Sund 4 Mond 5 ~~Tuesd 6 wed 7~~ I have <went to the celabra>-tion ^made another rug^ **Tuesd 6 wed 7** got another rug don & cut more rags for another **Thursd 8 Frid 9** had my shade trees trimed picked up the brush knit finish another pair stockens **Satd 10** took care of my rugs put on shure pop to keep the moths out **Sund 11** I do not go to meeting Betsey goes **Mond 12** knit some and did many things cut some rags **Tuesd 13** done many things **Wed 14** knit the most of the time P G came home he is quite feeble went round and see us all but had to go to bed before it was dark he did not sleep much **Thursd 15** he is quite sick Afternoon some better he has been here ~~went~~ has set up but litle I have put on a rug worked a litle on it **Frid 16** I have worked on the rug P G is better **Satd 17** P G is not so well finish the rug got it out **Sund ^18^** I do not go to meeting Betsey went **Mond 19** I have knit the most of the time P G is quite unwell I have been over to see him three or four times **Tuesday 20** P G has come over here to stay **wed 21** he is some better **Thursd ^22^** he is quite feble we have a releif cociety meeting here I am cuting some rags for Elis a rug[55] **Friday 23** P G is quite feeble **Satd 24** he is quite feeble Dr Murphy came to see him staid all night I am not well at all but keep up and knitt the most of the time to day **Sund 25** I am very feeble but keep up P G about the same sets up but litle **Mond 26** he is better **Tuesd 27** he is still better so he has had his clothes on for the first time since he came here ~~Wend 28~~ he went over to Saryanns staid all night **Wed 28** David ^took^ us out riding we had a good ride we both feel better I feel quite well P G gave me some birch Bark & leaves that grew in the cellar under the house where we was Born he is now [*left blank*] years old **Thursd 29** I have worked in the garden some to day **Friday 30** I have cut rags for Elis a rug **Saturday 31** worked in the fence triming the brush out of the shade trees & bring it to the house

August 1886

Sund August 1 I do not go to meting Betsey goes **Mond 2** I put on a rug for Elis worked on it the most of the day **Tuesd 3** went to town ~~to go~~ **wed 4** ~~got~~ work on the rug **Thursday 5** fast day got the rug mostly done **Frid 6** finished the rug **Satd 7** Betsey is puting the lining on I have cut some more rags for another rug Emorett has ~~A~~ got home and I hear from P G he is well **Sund 8** Betsey goes to meeting I stay at home **Mond 9** I put on another rug & work on it **Tuesd 10** I I work on the rug **Wed 11** got it off and done Betsey will make

---

55. Patty may mean Lillis (b. 1875), a daughter of Perrigrine and Sarah Crossley.

it up I cut some rags for another **Thursd 12** I cut some more rags **Frid 13** I have cut some more rags and knit some & read a good <deal> **Satd 14** Cut some more rags that Liza Brought over to me cut some limbs of my shade trees & knit a good deal **Sund 15** I have read the News this morning we went to meeting **Mond 16** put on another rug & worked on it Josephine came after me to go up there Bartlet Tripp & his folks came there we had a good visit **Tuesd 17** we went over Davids we had a good visit **wed 18** worked on my rug **Thursd 19** got it out **Frid 20** got it made up have knit almost two Pair of stockins ^P G came home well^ **Satd 21** I am kniting & doing many other things the Teacher came here I gave him fifty ~~to~~ cents to give to Br Brigs for fast offering **Sund 22** I dont go to meeting I have read a good Deal to day **Mond 23** I put on a rug & worked on it **Tuesday 24** worked on the rug **Wed: 25** got it done it is a large & prety one a fine horse on it **Thursday ^26^** done many things to day knit a goodeal **Frid 27** done many things kniting a goodeal **Satday 28** finished another pair of stockins ^&^ comence another pair of stockins taking care of many things out door & in **Sunday 29** I have been to the funeral of Harriet Fishers Babe Jony took me to the graveya^r^d then to his house to super then brought me home all right **Mond 30** I put on a rug & worked on it **Tuesday 31** I worked on it

September 1886

~~Wenday~~ ^Sept Wed 1^ got it out & made up cut rags & knit **Sept the 1 - 1886** I have done many things **Thursday 2** put on another rug worked on it **Friday 3d** worked on the rug **Satday 4** got the Rug out and mad[e] up so you see that I have made two this week **Sund 5** I do [not] go to meeting Betsey goes **Monday 6** I have been to the store got some differant co^u^llars of cloth 5 cents a yard to make more rugs have cut it up ready to work **Tuesday 7** put on a rug worked on it **Wednesday 8 - 1886** I am ready to work go to work Sister handshet [Handchett?] Lucinias Sister is to be buried to day she came here to see her sister & rellatives took sick & died I went to the Funeral then worked on the rug **Thursday 9** I have got it done **Friday 10** have cut rags for another and done many things **Satday 11** cut more rags & done many things finished another pair or stockins. making ten pair I have knit since I sold the last **Sunday 12** Betsey goes to meeting I dont go **Monday 13** put on another rug work on it **Tuesday 14** work on the rug **Wed: 15** finish the rug got it out and put away my frames David my son has bought me a cow I found the money ~~100~~ fifty Dollars **Thursday <16>** teachers meeting here **Friday 17** do many things cut peaches & spead them & knit **Satday 18** done many things **Sund 19** do not go to meeting Betsey goes **Mond 20** I think of going to town to day. I do not go I do many things I have cut some peaches & spread them **Tuesd 21** ~~done~~ go to town to day get some money ~~120~~ ^100^ Dollars for James Sessions ^& lent it to him^ **Wendsday 22** cut & spread peaches **Thursd 23** the same **Frid 24 Satd 25** the same **Sund 26** do not go to meeting Betsey goes I have read a good deal

Monday 27 cut & spread peaches **Tuesday 28** the same got my peaches all gathered cut and spread **wed 29** ~~I~~ we have got the peaches now to take up that are spread it rains some & the sun shines some we have got them all into the house

OCTOBER 1886

^**Thesdy**^ **Oct 5** on the racks w**ed 6 Thursd 7 Friday 8 Satad 9** we have got the corn hauled here & stacked **Sund 10** do not go to meeting it rains some **Mond 11 Tuesd 12** we have husked some **Wednesday 13 Thursd 14 Frid 15** got it all husked **Satd 16** and took care of **Sund 17** I do not go to meeting **Mond 18** took care of the corn & knitt some **Tuesd 19** I took care of many things **wed 20** spread the corn in the chamber **Thursd 21** I have knit the most of the time **Frid 22** kniting again **Sat 23** I have done many things **Sunday** ^**October**^ **24** Cloudy. the ground wet & cold I do not go to meeting **Mond 25** I put on a rug & work on it some **Tuesday** ^**26**^ worked the most of the time on the rug **Wed 27** worked on it the most of the time **Thursd 28** I have got it out ready to make up **Friday 29** made it up **Satday 30** ~~Sat~~ **Sunday 31**

NOVEMBER 1886

Nov. ^**1886**^ **Monday 1 Tuesday 2 wed 3** put on a rug worked on it **Thursd 4** made rug finished it **Frid 5 Satd 6** worked on a rug **Sund 7 Mond 8** put on a rug **Tuesd 9 Wed 01 [10] Thursd 11 Frrid 12** I have made the rug finished the stockins **Satd 13** ^**1886**^ got my rug done & another pair of stockins done **Sund 14** I dont go to meeting Betsey goes I have read the most of the time **Mond 15** I have cut rags for a rug & knit some **Tuesday 16** took my dried fruit to the store paid my tithing took the rest out of the store **wed 17** I have knit the most of the time cut up some 5 cent calico for a rug P G is here up stairs has not been down since Sunday is quite sick has been the most of the time I have had some brush cut up for the fire & some of the trees trimed ~~Josp~~ Joseph did it I let him a rasor for pay **Thursday 18** put ^on^ another rug & worked on it ^some^ **Frid 19** worked on the rug some ~~some~~ and did other things **Satd 20** worked on the rug but did not finish it **Sunday 21** it snows hard this Afternoon we do not go to meeting **Monday 22** finish the rug **Tuesday 23** put on another **wed 24** worked on it **Thursd 25** finished it & put on another ^& worked on it^ **Frid 26** worked on it **Satday 27** finished that have knit a good deal besides. P G is here sick yet sits up a good deal but is quite feeble yet **Sunday 28** he stays up chamber all the time we keep a fire there all the time and I stay there the most of the time & work on my rugs & knit & keep him company **Mond 29** the same put on a rug & work on it some **Tuesday 30** work on the rug

DECEMBER 1886

^**Dec the 1**^ **wed** ~~31~~ the same **Thursd 2** finished my rug have knit a good deal **Friday 3 Satd 4 of Dec** I have many things to do stay up stairs with P G the most of the time **Sunday 5** he came down to day **Sunday December 5**

1886 I ~~ex~~ do not go to meeting to day **Monday 6 Tuesday 7** I have put on another rug & finished it to day this week **wed 8** put on another **Thursday 9 / Frid 10 / Satd 11** I have finished ~~that that~~ that and knit another pair of stockins **Sunday 12** I do not go to meeting P G is about the same has gone over to Davids to night **Mond 13** put on another rug have many kinds of work to do **Tuesday 14** work on the rug some **wed 15** & **thursd 16** got the rug almost done **Friday 17** finished it have knit a good deal. cut some more rags for another rug P G is at Davids **Satd 18** finished it I have knit a pair of stockins about every week & made a rug besides **Sund 19** do not go to meeting read a good deal **Mond 20** & **Tuesday 21** have knit a pair of stockins **wed 22** I am taking care of things **Thursday 23** we went to Davids to a party had a good time **Friday 24** put 27 pair of stockins into the store for tithing **Satd 25** finished another pair of stockins then went over to Licinias to a party **Sunday 26** do not go to meeting I have read a good deal to day **Mond 27** I have knit & done many other things **Tuesday 28** I have been many things to day Think I will put on another rug this afternoon I did good deal ^on it^ **wed 29 Thursday 30 Friday 31** got it done & have knit 4 pair of stockins

1887

I don't go to meeting I cannot hear but litle. . . .
I am so deaf & I am so feeble I can hardly walk there . . .

January 1887

Satd January 1 new years I have done many things **Sund 2** do not go to meeting

[At the bottom of the page a line is drawn; upside down under the line is written in green ink:]
March 2 1884 I gave fifty dollars to Zina D H S to ~~at~~ pay at Washington 50-00[56]
March 10 1884 let george Linkon have 1:50 one Dollar fifty cents

---

56. The *Woman's Exponent* published a "Memorial" on 1 April 1886 (14:164). It appealed for protection from insults and wrongs to Mormon women because of polygamy and was signed by six prominent women. On 1 May 1886 in "Notes From Washington" the *Exponent* (14:180–81) reported how the memorial had been expanded on before the United States president and Congress, how they were lobbying against the attempt to disfranchise women of the Territory of Utah and against banishment of husbands. They appealed for the protection of their rights as women. This communication was signed by Emmeline B. Wells, editor of the *Woman's Exponent*. The memorial was entered into the Congressional Record of the Senate on 6 April 1886.

January the first day New years I have done many things to day
Sat^ur^day the first day of the ^year^ Sund 2 do not go to meeting
Mond 3 put a rug **tuesday 4** & worked on it have knit a goodeal **wednesday
5** work on the rug **Thursday 6** finish the rug & knit **Frid 7** & **Satd 8** finished
the <rug> cut some rags done many things finished 3 pair of stockins **Sund 9**
read a good deal Betsey has gone to meeting. **Monday ^10^** put on another
rug **Tuesday ^11^** work on it **wednesday 12 thursday 13 Friday 14** finished
the rug & another pair of stockins commenced another pair yestarday ~~Frid 14~~
I have knit & cut rags **Sattarday 15** I have been over to see Esther she is sick
had the Elders there she is verry bad I have got the peices of new cloth that I
bought cut up allmost all of them ~~Je~~ Betsey is over there now with Esther
Sund 16 she is quite sick now this this morning she has been sick all day
Mond 17 she is a litle Better this morning is worse again I have put on another rug work on it **Tuesd 18** she is better this morning **Wed 12 Thursd 20 Frid
21** [*Patty's underlining*] ~~Satd 22~~ **Satd <1> January 1** New years **Sund ^2d^**
Betsey has gone to meeting I stay at home ~~put on a rug~~ **Mond 3** put on a rug
& work on it **Tuesd 4 ^the same^ Wed 5** John Fisher came after me to go up
there I went had a good visit **Thursd 6** got my rug out **Friday 7** cut rags **Satd
8** cut more ready to work and have cut and sewed & knit all the time that I
could get it is now January 30 and I have made rugs & knit all the time that I
could get **Sunday January 30** I do not go to meeting Betsey goes I stay here
alone **Monday 31** [*She draws another line underneath these entries.*]

FEBRUARY 1887

Febuary Tuesday the first Wend the 2nd I have made a rug & knit a pair of
childrens stockins & done many other things ~~Frid 4th M~~ **(Febuary the fourth
Frid 4th** my Birth day 92 years old to day and I am well & feel well in body &
mind **Sat^tur^day the 5** work a knitting the most of the time **Sund 6** I have
read the exponant through to day Harvy Lucinia & P Gs son from goose creek
came here to see me to day it is now noon I keep reading I have read the
Juvinill through[57] ~~Monday 8~~ **Monday 7** I have put on a rug & worked on it
Tuesday 8 the wed 9 finishe it **Thursd 10** kniting **Friday 11** kniting ~~Satd~~ finish 3 pair of of stockins & did many other things **Satd 12** commenced two Pair
of stockins and done many other things **Sunday 13** do not go to meeting a
good deal of snow & keeps snowing I have read a good deal. **Monday 14** put
on a rug & worked on it **Tuesday 15** worked on it **Wednesday ^16^** finished
it **Thursday 17** have knit the most of the time **Friday 18** I have knit the most
of the time to day **Satd 19** I have cut rags & knit the most of the time have knit

---

57. The *Juvenile Instructor* was a children's magazine that was first published in
January 1866 to help prepare children of the church for future responsibilities
(see Ruel A. Allred, "Juvenile Instructor," in *Encyclopedia of Mormonism*, 2: 777).

two pair of Stockins & cut rags **Sunday 20** I have read a goodeal to day. it snows the most of the time but it does not lay on the ground it melts **Mond 21** I have knit the most of the time **Tuesd 22** I have been kniting the most of the time yestarday & to day I have just heard that Sister Dunkin is dead died this fornoon **wed 23 Thursd 24 Frid 25 Satd 26** have been kniting the most of the time I have put on a rug have not got it done **Sund 27** I go to meeting Lorenzo Snow preached **Mond 28** the last day of Feb I have been kniting the most of the time

MARCH 1887

Tuesday March the first I have been to the store got some yarn for stockins & other uses[58] **wed 2** have knit a good deal & done many other things **Thursd 3** we have been up to Chesters to a sewing bee **Frid 4 Satd 5** I have put on a rug & finished all but making it up **Sunday 6** it is clouday & has been for weeks ~~the~~ is mudy all the time we went to meeting had a good meeting **Mond 7** the sun shines this morning but was soon cloudy I put on a rug worked on it **Tuesday 8** worked on worked it again **Wed 9** finished it **Thursday 10** I went with Zina over to see Phebee Jane she has a young babe found her not very smart **Frid (^11^ (<11> finished another pair of stockins done many things went to conferance on **Satturday 12** let P G have a hundred dollars cash to bye a bugga **Sund 13** I rode in the bugga to meeting to day **Mond 14** put in rug & worked on it **Tuesday 15** worked on the rug **wed 16** finished it I knit & cut rags **Thursd 17** worked in the garden & did many things ~~Frig~~ went over and [see] Phebe jane she is sick & carried some butter & tarts to her &c **March Frid 18** finished Another pair of stockins &c **Satday 19** I went to Salt lake City got my Dividen & I have got home all safe & feeling well **Sund 20** I have been out riding as I have found money in part to bye a buggy to ride in and I am so Deaf I can hear but little any how if I go to meeting I have rode a good ^deal^ to day I have been to see many of my friends and came home & read a good deal the life of Lydia Knight especially it was very good & I enjoyed it first rate[59] **Monday 21** I put on a rug & worked on it the most of the time **Tuesday 23** I have worked steady on the rug yestarday & to day have got it done Betsey is puting the lining on to it now as I cannot sew my hand is lame so I cannot sew any scarcely. but I can knit & make rugs **Wed ^24^**

---

58. Note that Patty is adapting to the use of ready-made materials. She produces less and consumes somewhat more.

59. Lydia Goldthwait Knight was born in 1812 in Massachusetts, the daughter of Jesse Goldthwait and Sally Burt. She divorced Calvin Baely and was remarried to Newel Knight. She died in 1884. Susa Young Gates and Amelia Young wrote Lydia Knight's history for the Noble Women's Lives series (see "Homespun," [pseudonym] *Lydia Knight's History* [Salt Lake City: Juvenile Instructor Office, 1883]).

<24> ~~I have~~ I have been out riding today have rode a good deal to day have seen many of my friends & relatives **Thursday 25** I have knit a gooddeal this week **Frid 26 & Satd 27** I have knit two pair of stockins this week for children it is now 4 P M **Sattarday <27>** P G is here sick has been all the week **Sund 27** I have been out riding **Mond 28** I have ^kniting^ **Tuesday 29 Wed 30** I have been knitting the most of the time **Thursd 31** ^meeting at our ho house^ been kniting the time

April 1887

Friday April 1 cut some rags & knit & done many other things **Satd 2** cut rags done many things P G still sick **Sund 3** all about the same this morning **Mond 4** cut & sewed rags **Tuesday <5>** the same **wed 6 Thursd 7** Sent Isac Jonson 16 Dollars untill july 7 I have been to see Br Carter he is very sick he cant speak I dont think he will live long **Friday ^8th^** I have cut rags & knit the most of the time **Satday 9** I have done the same I have rode out to day in my Buggy & feel a gooddeal better **Sund 10** I do not go to meeting stay at home with P G he is still a bed the most of the time Betsey goes to meeting **Mond 11** I put on a rug and work on it **Tuesday 12** I work on it & finish it wrode rode out besides **wednesday 13** I am knitting the most of the time **Thursday 14** I have knit the most of the time had a good ride in my Buggy **Friday15** I have knit the most of the time look after P G & wait on him Betsey is gone to a sewing Bee she has just got home **Satd 16** I have knit the most of the time **Sund 17** Betsey goes to meeting **Mond 18** I have knit quite a number of pairs of stockins ~~got~~ **Tuesd 19 Wed 20** got a rug on **Thursday 21 Frid 22** got the rug out & made up **Satd 23** I went up to John Fishers staid there most of the day have knit another pair of stockins **Sunday 24** I have read the most of the time Betsey went to meeting I rode out after meeting with Fayben. **Monday 25** put on a rug & worked on it **Tuesday 26** I have got the rug done I have worked hard and steady Betsey has waited on P G he is quite feeble yet I am quite hard to hear what is said **wed 27** I have knit a good deal **Thursd 28** the Females have ^a^ meeting here to day I have knit a gooddeal I cannot hear but little **Frid 29 and Satd 30** I have made a rug & knit two pair of Stockins this week. P G is about the same quite feble

June 1887 [May 1887]

^**Sunday first day of June**^ it is quite stormy some of the time & sun shine some of the time the wind blows hard and cold **Sunday June the first** and has all day it is quite cold P G is about the same **June the first 1887 Sunday 1** I have read a good deal to day Betsey went to meeting I staid at home with P G **Mond 2** I have knit a good deal to day one pair of stockins **Tuesd 3** I have knit another pair of stockins to day beside doing many other things P G is about the same we have had a good deal of co to day. **wednesday 4** I have put on another rug **thursday 5** worked on it & finished it **Friday 6** have knit a good deal to day **Satd 7** finished two pair of stockins & almost knit another pair **Sunday 8** I have read a good deal to day Beside riding out I have rode out a good deal this ^last^ week **Mond 9** I have knit another pair of stockins to day **wednesday 11** I have I have knit another pair to day **Thursday 12** I have got another pair almost done P G is some better finished the stockins **Frid 13** commenced another pair **Satd 14** finished them Sarah Ann Collared some red for me to night **Sund 15** I feel well I rode out with my son David in my carriage down to Dell Burnams they wlere just going away so we did not stop **Monday 16** cut the peices Sary coulered for me **Tuesday ^17^** put on a rug & worked on it some **wed 18** worked on it **Thursday ^19^** finished it Enoch Tripp here this morning staid here all day & all night **Friday 20** I have knit the most of the time cut some rags E B is here all day to day **Satd 21** I have done many things he is here still I rode out to day **Sund 22** I rode out to day again went to Dell Burnams staid there Longer than I expected the boys went to the river with the Buggy E B has gone to Lucinias he has not come back **Mond 23** I have cut some rags for a rug ~~Mond~~ Tuesday 24 I have put on a rug a rode out again ~~Tuesd~~ **wednesday ^25^** I rode out with P G up to James Beards we had a good visit came home worked on the rug **Thursday 26** got the rug done put the lining on but have not sewed it I cannot sew it on my hands are so old & lame Sarah has gone up to her Father Crosleys went yestarday Expect she will be gone a good while two or three months **Friday 27** cut rags rode out with P G ~~Satd~~ yestarday **28** I have cut rags rode with Davids Daughter down to Mosses had a good ride yesterday I have got my rags cut **Satd 28** finished them this morning have knit have knit & rode out today and almost every day it does me good to ride out **Sunday 29** I have read good deal to day **Monday 30** cut rags & ~~knit~~ knit a dood deal to day & rode out **Tuesday 31** put on a rug

JUNE 1887

Wednesday The first 1 day of June finished my rug **Thursday 2** knit a gooddeal **Friday 3** I have rode out every day this week P G has got so he can ride out I go with him I have made a rug knit one pair stockins & cut a good many rags. **Satday ^(4^ 4** I have done a good many things to day cleaned the brush up that was cut off of the trees **Sunday 5** fair weather Betsey went to meeting **Monday 6** I have knit a good deal **Tuesday 7** put on a rug & worked on it P G has gone to Ogdon **Wednesday 8** finished my rug **Thursday 9** have knit the most of the time **Friday 10** have knit a goodeal to day **Satd 11** have knit the most of the time puled many weeds in the garden when not kniting **Sunday 12** I feel feeble I am expecting P G home this forenoon he has come P G has come home feels quite well Betsey has been to meeting to day I have staid alone **Monday 13** I have knit the most of the time **Tuesday 14** I have put on a rug **Wed 15** have worked and finished it this morning I have knit the most of the day **Thursday 16** I have commenced another pair of stockens & knit the most of the time I prepared myself to go to town to day but David sent me word he could not go so I am at home knit-ing **Friday 17** I went to town with David got my dividend did some other buisiness come home & went over & see sister Stoker she is sick **Satd 18** I have knit the most of the time today Sister stoker is some better Betsey has been over to see her I have done all that I could **Sund 19** fair weather I feel prety well **Mond 20** I have knit the most of the time **Tuesday 21** I have cut rags the most of the time **wedns 22** put on a rug ~~Wed 22~~ got it out **Thursday 23 Friday 24 Satd 25** I have been up to Joepines all day cut rags she gave ^me^ a good many I have knit near three pairs of stockins I have rode out every day this week **Sunday 26** I have read a good deal to day I dont go to meeting I cannot hear but litle I am so deaf & I am so feeble I can hardly walk there & I stay at home **Monday 27** I have cut rags for a rug to day and knit P G has gone to see Byron they came home up to ~~Slires Ashdown~~ was I have been to work on a rug to day **Tuesday 28** work on the rug **wed 29** finished the rug **Thursday 30** cuting rags for another rug.

JULY 1887

Friday July the first I put on a rug got the border almost done **Satday 2** fin-ished the rug have done many more things **Sunday 3** I have rode out with David & let him have ~~one nity~~ Ninty Dollars to Bye a horse with 90 Dollars cash

[*A line is drawn between the last entry and the following*] Lent Joseph Sessions five Dollars this **third day of July 1887** it is paid this the **5 day Febuary 1888** & setled up ^all^ right

^**Monday**^ **July 4 1887** I have been out riding up to Elviras caried her rug up to her went to the children & groan peoples celibration ^gave^ me some ice cream &c I then had a good ride I put on a rug & worked on it **Tuesday 5** got it out & made up **Wed 6** all well I put on another rug got the border done. have got it done & made up **Thursday 7** put on another ~~Frid~~ got it done **Frid 8** ~~Fr~~ put on another **Sat 9** got it done ~~Sat 9~~ & made up **Sund 10** I have read a goodeal to day **Mond 11 Tuesd 12 Tued 13 Thursd 14 Frid 15 Satd 16** I have made two rugs & knit a pair of stockins this week beside doing many other things **Monday 18** work on another rug & knit some **Tuesday** ^**19**^ finished the rug **Wednesday 20** have done many things took up a pair of stockins **Thursd 21** commenced a rug **Frid 22** worked on the rug **Satd 23** finished it finished the stockins & the rug & ~~took~~ commenced another pair of stockins **Sund 24** I have read a good deal **Mond 25** com-menced another rug **Tuesday 26** I finished it **wed: 27** I have cut fruit Apricots to dry I have rode out in my carriage every day almost. sometimes P G and sometimes ~~Dav~~ David goes with me I have knit a goodeal **Thursday 28** I have knit the most of the time to day **Friday 29** I have done a good deal to this month **Satd 30** I work with the fruit I have done a good deal with the fruit and other things

SEPTEMBER 1887

Sept 1887 Sept I have worked with the ^fruit^ all most all the time it is now the **7 day of** ~~October~~ **October 1887**

OCTOBER 1887

I have done many things this last month have got my fruit the most of it took care of. it is now **october the 7 day Friday** & I can do but litle of anything I have took care of many things have knit some and took care of my fruit it looks like rain it does rain some sprinkles some litle on ^the^ mountins **Saturday the 8th of october** I have done many things I have let Perry Sessions have one hundred dollars cash gave it to him to get his eys Doctered to let the Docter have it I have done many things to day have rode out to day with my Grand son Fayben had a good time **Sunday 9** Betsey has gone to the city to conferance I am here alone I have rode out ^with^ Sara Ann went up to Brigses come home come home all well Betsey has come home all well **Mond 10** finished a rug & done many other things Betsey has husked out the last of our corn **Tuesday 11** cut some peaches done many things **Wendnesday 12** finished cuting my peaches now are geting dry I have got some more peaches have cut them got them spred **Thursd 13** have done many things **Friday 14** & **Satd** ~~14~~ **[15] Sund 15 [16]** I have read a good deal I have read a good deal & done many things knit [*some letters scratched out—illegible*] & sewed read a good deal it is now ~~Satd 21~~ f **Friday the 21 of October** & I have done a good deal made a rug this week finished it to day & finished much more finished a pair of stockins **Satday 22** done a good deal to day rode out & done ~~a~~ many things **Sund 23** have rode out to day to see the sick I have knit a pair of stockins & done many other things ^I have knit a pair of stockins^ it is now **Oct 26 1887** & I have done a good deal of many things. I have lent P G Sessions money one hundred ninty ~~five Dollars~~ & 100:95 50 cents five dollars fifty cents cash I have knit a goodeal & done many other things **Thursday 27** I have sold my fruit to day 81 dollars fifty cents ^eighty one dollars^ I have knit three pairs of stockins this last week & done many other ~~thngs~~ things **Sunday 30 of october** all well. **Monday Oct 31 Monday October 31** I have knit the most of the time had many other things to do

NOVEMBER 1887

Tuesday the first day of Nov I have put on a rug **wed the 2d** worked on the rug & have rode out **Thursday 3** I have worked on the rug **Frid 4** the same **Satd 5** finished the rug I have also knit a gooddeal besides **Sunday 6** red a good deal **Monday 7** I have knit a good deal finishe two pair stockins

Tuesday 8 commenced a rug **wednesday 9** worked on it **Thursday 10** worked on it I have **Friday 11** I have finished my rug and knit a good deal & done many other things have rode out almost every day besides. **Satday 12** I have knit a good deal to day done many ^things^ **Sunday 13** all well **Monday 14** I put on a rug ~~Monday~~ ^Tuesday^ (15) worked on the rug & knit some **Wednesday** ~~28~~ ^16^ did the same I have knit a good deal & worked a good deal at things kniting & many other things **Thursday 17 Friday 18 Satay 19** finished the rug & knit a goodeal done many things knit & done many things **Sunday 27** I have done a good many things this last week it is Now **Nov 27 day Sunday** I have read a good deal **monday 28** I have worked on my kniting work &c **Tuesday 29** I have put on a rug & worked on it ~~Tued~~ **Wensday 30** worked on the rug

DECEMBER 1887

Thursday fast day the first day of ~~December~~ ^January^ **1 Friday** it snows fast and I am going to work on my rug ^Jan^ ~~Decemb~~ ^December^ thursday 1 **first day of December** I am going to work on my rug **Friday 2d** finished my rug **Satd 3** ~~we~~ knit the most of the time **Sunday 4** have read the most of the time **Monday 5 Tuesday 6** Knit the most of the time **Wed 7. Thursday 8** have worked on the rug & finished it **Friday 9** am kniting the most of the time **Saturday 10** kniting the most of the time **Sunday 11** reading the most of the time **Monday 12** kniting the most of the time **Tuesday 13** worked on a rug & knit some w**ed 14** cut up some rags & knit a gooddeal **Thursday 15** I have knit a good (^deal^ **Friday 16 Satd 17** I have worked a good deal kniting & Sewing **Sunday 18** ~~kniting~~ reading most of the time **Monday 19** kniting **Tuesday 20 Wends 21** I have knit a good deal **Thursday 22 Friday 23 Satd 24** I have knit the most of the time **Sund 25** I have read the most of the time to day **Mond 26 Tuesday 27 wensday 28** I have knit the most of the time & done many other things **Thursday 29** I have knit two pair stockins this week **Friday 30** I have got a peice of cloth fixed to put on my chamber stairs **Satday 31** I have done many things to day

1888

I have knit & rode out almost every day . . .
have knit a goodeal to day I have rode out a goodeal

JANUARY 1888

Sunday the first day of January I have read a good deal to day **Mond the 2d of January** I have done many things to day rode (<out in a slay> **Tuesday the 3d** the wind blows hard & cold I have knit a good deal to day beside doing many other things **wednesday 4** I have knit a good deal to day cleaned the snow off the house **Thursday 5** fast day[60] a deep snow fell last night we have cleaned it off the windows & doors & round the house this morning I am very tired ~~this morning~~ I will now try to read some I have read a good deal to day **Friday 6** I knit a goodeal today **Satd 7** the same ~~8~~ **Sunday 8 Mond 9 Tuesday 10 wed 11** I have knit ~~two~~ **thursday 12** I ~~read~~ have knit two pair of stockins this week childrens **Friday ~~18~~ 13 Satday 14 Sunday 15 Tuesday 16 ^mondy 16^ wednesnesday 17 Thursday 18 Friday 20 Satdarday 21 January Satday Saturday 21** I have knit a good deal this week **Sunday January 22 1888** I have read a good deal to day **Monday 23 Tuesday 24** I have knit two pair of stockins **wednesday 25 Thursday 26 Frid 27 Satd 28** I have knit a goodeal this week **Sundd 29** I have rode out a good deal last week **Monday 30** I have knit a good deal **Tuesday <31>** I have knit & rode out almost every day rode out with P G to day & have knit a goodeal to day I have rode out a goodeal ~~to~~

FEBRUARY 1888

Febuary the first wensday 1 Thusday 2 ~~Thursday~~ **friday 3 Satday 4 Sunday 5 Mond 6** I have knit a good deal **Tuesday 7 Wendsy & Thursday 9 Friday 10 Satday 11** I have knit a goodeal this week **Sunday 12** I am so hard of hearing that I do not go to meeting **Monday 13 Tuesday 14 wensday 15 thursd 16 Friday 17 Saturday 18** I have knit and sewed a goodeal **Sunday 19** I have knit & sewed a goodeal this last week & done many othe[r] things **Monday 20 Tuesday 21 wed 22 Thursday 23 Friday 24 Satd 25 Sunday 26** I have read a good to day **Monday 27 Tuesday 28 Wenday 29**

MARCH 1888

March the first of March thursday 1 Friday the 2 Satday 3 Sunday 4 Monday 5 Tuesday 6 Wed 7 Thursday 8 Friday 9 Satday 10 Sunday 11 fair this morning I have knit a good deal this last week & done many other things **Monday 12 Tuesd 13 wed 14 Thursd 15 Frid 16 Satd 17 Sund 18 Mond 19 Tuesday 20 wed 21: Thursday 22 Friday 23 Satday 24 Sunday 25 ^Mond 26^ Tuesday 27 wed 28 Thursday 29 Friday 30 Satday 31**

APRIL 1888

April the the first day of April <the first> ~~^April 1^~~ the first day Sunday the first day I have done a goodeal this last week to day is **the first day of April** I do not go to meeting **Monday the 2 day of April Tuesday the 3 day of April wednesday 4 Thursday 5 Friday 6 Satd 7 Sunday & Mond 9**

---

60. Patty has consistently mentioned "fast day." In the early days, the first Thursday of each month was designated as a day to forgo two meals and donate the value of the meals for the poor. Today, the first Sunday of each month is dedicated to similar purposes.

Tuesday 10 I have knit six pair of stockins **wendnesday 11 Thursd 12 Frid 13 Sat 14 Sund 15 Mond 16 Tuesd 17 wed 18 Thursday 19 Friday 20** I have knit the most of the time for a long time I have done many things **21.22.23.** I have worked all the time this month it is now

May 1888

May I will begin with the Month **Tuesday the first day wensday the 2d day Thursd the 3d Friday the 4th** I have knit & the most of the time three pair of stockins this week it is now **friday the 4th**

[Upside down on the next page in Perrigrine's writing is information about ordinance work for the dead performed in the Logan Temple.]

Loose crossstitch sheet found in Patty's medical book, *W. Beach's The Family Physician.* Courtesy of Norma A. Earl.

EPILOGUE

As far as we know, Patty Bartlett Sessions's sketchy May 1888 entries were her last written words. According to her diary, she wrote many letters throughout the years. Probably few survive. The Daughters of Utah Pioneers have one damaged photocopy of a letter she wrote from "Camp of Isriel Winter Quarters" to daughter Sylvia and her husband Windsor Lyon and son David Sessions, Jr., in Nauvoo. It was dated 12 December 1846 and recounted some of the events mentioned in her diary, as well as urging Windsor to move his store to Winter Quarters since, she reported, people had to make three or four trips to the one church store to get waited on. She quoted some prices, such as "molasses one dollar per gallon sugar six pound for a dollar salt 1-75 per barel groceries are high dry goods but litle higher than in Nauvoo sheeting from 12 1h to 16 cts per yd. . . ."

Other information about her comes from secondary contemporary accounts. The name Patty Sessions appears in the 9 October 1859 "Journal History of the Church of Jesus Christ of Latter-day Saints" among the winners of premium awards at the exhibition of the Deseret Agricultural and Manufacturing Society: Best Knit Cape and Crochet Bed Spread (woolen), achievements she failed to note in her diaries. The *Deseret Almanac for the Year of our Lord 1852*, compiled by W. W. Phelps, lists her name on the same page with "Officers in the Priesthood of the Church"–the presidency and other general authorities. Names of officers of the Council of Health include Brigham Young, Heber C. Kimball, and Willard Richards as "Ex-officio Presidents," with W. A. Morse as "President," P. Richards as "Recorder," and P. Meeks as "Pres.t, p.t." Phebe Angel is named as "Presidentess" and Patty (Sessions) Parry and Susanna S. Richards as "Counsellors." On the death of Phebe Angel, Patty was chosen as "presidentess."

Samuel W. Taylor gives Patty credit for a letter to the editor of Nauvoo's newspaper, *Times and Seasons*, of 15 September 1843. "It was signed 'P—–S,'" he wrote, "but everyone knew the author was Patty Sessions, for the midwife had been frank in expressing her views about doctors." He relates her story about a Revolutionary patriot who lived to be ninety-nine. "He took no medicine until after he was eighty years old. From this fact alone," P——S railed, "it is possible that if he had taken no medicine at all, he might have lived to be as old as Moses, one hundred and twenty years."[1] It's doubtful Patty wrote the letter attributed to her; if she did, the editor took great license with her content and style. But now the reader of her diaries is free to make judgment based on an acquaintance with what we *know* she wrote.

As a matter of fact, she has been quoted, misquoted, extolled, and misrepresented numerous times by well-meaning people who have rightly wanted to give her her due. Many other persons have also been the beneficiaries of such efforts. For years filling in the gaps has been an elusive goal for historians and families.

Patty sometimes adds to the mysteries about herself by omitting information. For example her diaries mention only briefly the school she built for her grandchildren and other children whose parents were unable to afford the expenses of education. An article, "Patty Sessions' School" in the *Deseret Evening News* of 20 December 1883 gives more details. The dedication was held on 15 December, the meeting was called to order by Brother Henry Rampton, and the dedicatory prayer was offered by P. G. Sessions. As she addressed the meeting, Patty named a board of directors: P. G. Sessions; John Fisher, who was married to her granddaughter Josephine; and Lemonia Holbrook.[2] Patty explained that she had "$16,000 invested in ZCMI at Salt Lake City. The school committee were to see that a sufficient portion of the dividends was kept out to pay the expenses of the school." The *Deseret News* described the schoolhouse as "a brick building 18x36, with a twelve-foot ceiling and well finished and furnished."

The "Journal History" quotes frequently from Patty's diary in 1847. David Sessions is mentioned occasionally, as are many of the persons whose names appear in Patty's writings.

Although she wrote in a kind of outline style, Patty daily shared consistent and dependable information. She sketched a remarkable portrait of one pioneering woman caught up in the often dramatic historical events that were swirling around everyday Mormon life during the last half of the nineteenth century.

It would be nice to conclude her story with details of her last years, neatly packaged. But so far there is no clue as to what those last four and a half

1. Samuel W. Taylor, *Nightfall at Nauvoo* (New York: Avon, 1971), 190.

2. This was probably Joseph Lamoni Holbrook, who became the first mayor of Bountiful upon its incorporation in 1894. As the reader has undoubtedly noticed, Patty had a tendency to add *ia* to names that ended in *a*. The most obvious example is substituting "Lucinia" for the name of Perrigrine's wife Lucina.

years were like—her health, her caregivers, her mental and emotional condition. Perhaps her final years were much like all the others, except marked by
poorer health and increasing infirmity. Perhaps Perrigrine's wife Betsey
nursed her to the end. The obituary "Almost a Hundred" in the *Deseret Evening
News* of 14 December 1892 states simply that she died at her home "at 6:30
o'clock this (Wednesday) morning of old age."

Some years later in 1898, her daughter-in-law, Phebe C. Sessions, wrote
a rather sentimental biographical sketch of Patty, which was published in the
Woman's Exponent (27:6). It acknowledged some of Patty's many accomplishments but didn't discuss her life after the diaries ended.

On 14 December 1892 the "Journal History" published a life sketch that
included the numbers of her posterity. "She lived to see her fourth generation
and has left two sons, thirty-three grandchildren, one hundred and thirty-
seven great grandchildren, and twenty-two great great grandchildren. Total
posterity, 214. She was ever a true and faithful Latter-day Saint, diligent and
persevering, her whole soul, and all she possessed being devoted to the
Church and the welfare of mankind. She has gone to her grave ripe in years,
loved and respected by all that knew her."[3]

For one who kept such copious records as Patty, it is strange that a will
is not on file in the county recorder's office. Perhaps because of that, Patty's
estate was not settled until 28 February 1900. A. L. Burnham, Carlos L.
Sessions, and Fabyan C. Sessions, grandsons, acted as administrators. The
belongings were sold, consisting of stock in ZCMI, an organ, stove and pipe,
twenty-four wooden benches, and a map (most of which probably came from
the school). Her real estate was sold as well. The amount to be distributed
after all expenses were paid totaled $6,079.25. It was equally allocated among
the families of Perrigrine, Sylvia, and David, by then all deceased; each family
inherited approximately $2,026.40. Since Perrigrine had fathered the most
children, the dollars were thin by the time his children and grandchildren
claimed their shares, but all received something.

Although her diligent labor and business acumen allowed Patty to
amass a small fortune for her day, her legacy is worth more than dollars and
cents. She left an example of sacrifice, determination, industriousness, austeri-
ty, dedication, drive—all these and more—sharply etched in her diaries. That
legacy lives on for her posterity and all who gain any degree of personal or
historical insight through what she recorded. At the very least, those records
confirm that Patty Sessions was a valuable cog in building the Salt Lake
Valley.

---

3. "Journal History of the Church of Jesus Christ of Latter-day Saints," Archives of
the Historical Department, Church of Jesus Christ of Latter-day Saints, Salt
Lake City.

Salt Lake City was the subject of a syndicated column by Georgie Anne Geyer, published in the *Salt Lake Tribune* on 30 May 1996.[4] Geyer's present perception also fits the place Patty Sessions described 150 years ago. Geyer writes

> And so, of all the interesting things about the "Mormon state," perhaps the part that would be most wisely attended to by the rest of the nation is this public propensity—and this unstated inner passion—for cooperativeness in place of competitiveness, for harmony instead of adversariness, and for connectedness in lieu of disconnectedness.

Patty knew about being cooperative and harmonious. She maintained strong connections with her family, her church, and her community. Patty also provides a connection for us. Her moments in time as chronicled in her diaries could be our own in their ordinariness and significance; in their transience and permanence.

Geyer continues her column by quoting from her own 1996 commencement address at Westminster College in Salt Lake City.

> If you don't know history . . . you are a prisoner of your time and place; you don't know what came before, so you can never know what will come next. You've lost the knowledge of the origins of things. You're frozen in "me," and most often in "now," when it should be "we" and "forever."

Patty valued her origins and looked toward "forever" with optimism. Because her capable hands dealt daily with life and death as midwife and medical provider for the community, she lived with a serious sense of urgency and preparation. Her contributions to the well-being of her contemporaries cannot be overemphasized. But she did not neglect other important aspects of daily living. As she took care of her "domestic concerns," she also shared her skills and the fruits of her labors with her immediate family circle and with the larger community. She thrived on work and freely expressed satisfaction in work done well enough to satisfy her own high standards. When she realized a profit from her medical skills and from the fruits of her gardens and orchards, a necessity if she was to be self-sufficient, she valued her accomplishment. And being an astute businesswoman, she invested any surplus wisely.

Patty gave much simply out of an innate goodness and a desire to use her considerable talents and means to serve others. She earned a place as a leader among women in spiritual and practical ways. Called by her bishop to

---

4. "Good Example Found in Salt Lake City," *Salt Lake Tribune*, 30 May 1996, A13.

be a leader in providing relief for Indian women and children, she enthusiastically responded. She was a charter officer in the remarkably foresighted Council of Health. Being naturally good-hearted, she helped others with time as well as with material goods.

Despite these obvious accomplishments and others that could be cited, however, Patty's greatest contributions are still her diaries, on-the-spot chronicles of the Mormon trail experience and of life in early Utah. She was no prisoner of time and place. She kept track of her origins and never wavered from her firm belief in the here and now and the future hereafter. She leaves much to ponder, to admire, and, yes, to emulate.

APPENDIX ONE:
Account Book

Soiled from age and handling, a well-preserved tan leather-bound book contains a detailed record of Patty's financial dealings. On the upper left corner of the cover is written in her handwriting:

1864
1862
Patty Sessions

On the bottom of the page, upside down, is written Sept 74, and on the back, upside down, are the words:

Jan 1864
<u>Patty Sessions</u>
<u>Her Book</u>

April 29–1864
I gave one hundred & thirty Dollars to the Bishop F Kesler to send back to bye a yoke of oxen to bring up the poor from the frontiers he bought the oxen here and will send them back they are well matched both red. The off one has a small white spot between the horns another over the left eye and one on the right jaw very small spots an underbit under the left ear. Crop off the right ear left horn a littly stuby flesh brand on left hip Illegible [*this is Patty's word*] nigh ox all red flesh brand on left hip Illegible both oxen branded on the left horns G. Gibs with Gideon Gibs brand. Done by Samuel Russell for me
Patty Sessions

The remaining pages of Patty's account book contain financial records between the years 1862 and 1877. Many of the figures deal with loans to her immediate family, but she also itemized transactions with others in the community. When accounts were settled, she crossed out the entries. Most individual transactions were separated by a line. These accounts would be interesting to someone researching costs in those days. For example, an entry of special interest in the diaries is one made on 13 May 1864 concerning J[oshua] Williams, who is mentioned very frequently in connection with Sylvia. Mr. Williams rented a house from Patty for $6.00 a month. He was to build a corral and pigpen to leave and "keep the fence up–" Williams paid with a $4.00 order, worked two days for $4.50, stacked hay for a part of a day for 50 cents, and paid $15.00 with wood and $1.00 by threshing.

On 10 May 1869 Patty began keeping a cooperative store. What she sold and for what amount are recorded until the end of December 1869. The figures are, of course, very revealing of the times.

Patty also recorded her tithing settlements. On 9 January 1868 she "found Due me" $30.00. On 26 January 1869 the amount due was $25.00. On 20 January 1871 it was $33.00. On 5 February 1872, "Settled my tithing for 1871 found due me $33-00 the Bishop Balanced the Book would not allow me anything–" And on 10 January 1873, "Setled my tithing for 1872 found Due me thirty dollars and 13 bushels Aples 13 got a certifacate to Bishop Stoker from Bishop F Kesler–"

The archive box of Patty Sessions's diaries held by the Historical Department of the Church of Jesus Christ of Latter-day Saints contains another small handmade book, approximately three inches by five inches. The paper is blue and lined. The book contains for the most part more than ninety midwife accounts and payments from 1858 to 1866, although there are a few other records of medical dealings. The actual deliveries were also noted in her daily diaries.

Several scraps of paper detail other business dealings, including various payments totaling $270.00 to John Parry for his building Patty's house in Bountiful in 1872.

APPENDIX TWO:
Children's Families

WIVES OF PERRIGRINE SESSIONS

Julia Ann Kilgore (JA)	md:	21 Sept. 1834
Mary Call (M)		28 June 1845
Lucina Call (L)		28 June 1845
Fanny Emorett Loveland (FE)		13 Sept. 1852
Sarah Crossley (S)		2 Mar. 1861
Elizabeth Birdenow (B)		25 Mar. 1865
Sarah Ann Bryson (SA)		29 Sept. 1866
Esther Mabey (E)		22 Nov. 1868

CHILDREN OF PERRIGRINE SESSIONS

1. Martha Ann (Smoot)	birth:	22 Sept. 1835	JA
2. Carlos Lyon		16 July 1842	JA
3. Julia (Parke)		25 Apr. 1848	M
4. Perrigrine		14 Oct. 1848	L
5. Byron		7 Nov. 1851	M
6. Cyril		7 Aug. 1855	M
7. Fanny Emorett (Baird)		25 Oct. 1855	FE
8. Keplar		8 Dec. 1855	L
9. Alice (b. in Carson, Nev)		16 June 1857	FE
10. Zina (Burningham)		4 Dec. 1858	M
11. Chester		29 May 1859	FE
12. Harvey		13 June 1859	L
13. Perry		5 Aug. 1860	M
14. Agnes (Stoddard)		26 Mar. 1861	FE
15. Lucina		30 Jan. 1862	L
16. James Crossley		14 June 1862	S
[17. Sylvanus		22 Jan. 1863	FE

18. Elvira (Briggs, Ashdown)	28 Feb. 1864	S
19. Lucina (Waite)	4 Oct. 1865	FE
20. Mary (Scott)	31 Mar. 1866	S
21. Samuel	23 Oct. 1867	SA
22. daughter (died at birth)	date uncertain	B
23. Joseph	27 May 1868	S
24. Sylvia	29 July 1869	FE
25. Thomas	9 June 1870	E
26. Wallace Orlando	25 Nov. 1870	S
27. Alice (Freestone)	13 Dec. 1870	SA
28. Orson	8 Aug. 1871	FE
29. David Albert	5 Mar. 1872	E
30. William Westley	28 Feb. 1873	S
31. Hyrum	2 May 1873	SA
32. Samantha (Smith)	9 Feb. 1874	FE
33. Jane M.	8 Mar. 1874	E
34. Jedediah	2 Mar. 1875	SA
35. Lillis Cordelia (Egan)	10 Nov. 1875	S
36. Presley	18 Feb. 1876	E
37. Perrigrine	18 Feb. 1877	FE
38. Eliza Thriphena (Armstrong)	7 Sept. 1877	SA
39. Parley Pratt	5 Dec. 1877	E
40. Patty Orilla (Hatch, Scott, Mann)	23 July 1879	SA
41. Susan Geneva (Neath)	18 Dec. 1879	E
42. Hannah Ann	25 July 1880	S
43. Chauncey	8 Sept. 1880	FE
44. Sarah Ann (Sadie Clark)	4 Oct. 1881	SA
45. Ezra T.	26 Dec. 1881	E
46. Phoebe Olive (Loll Howells)	7 Mar. 1883	S
47. Olivia (Waddoups)	21 Sept. 1883	SA
48. Linnie (Hepworth)	12 Feb. 1885	E
49. Heber John	13 July 1885	SA
50. Hannah L. (Burningham)	25 July 1886	S
51. Walter	2 June 1887	E
52. stillborn	date unknown	S
53. LeRoy	14 Sept. 1888	SA
54. Alvin	15 Feb. 1890	E
55. Calvin	28 Apr. 1890	SA

HUSBANDS OF SYLVIA SESSIONS LYON CLARK

Windsor Palmer Lyon (WPL)	md:	1838
Joseph Smith (JS)		date uncertain
Heber C. Kimball		1846?

Ezekial Clark (EC)   1850

CHILDREN OF SYLVIA SESSIONS LYON CLARK

1.	Marian	birth–death:	1839–1842	WPL
2.	Philafreen		1841–1844	WPL
3.	Asa Windsor		1842–1842	WPL
4.	Josephine Rosetta (Fisher)		1844–1924	WPL or JS
5.	Byron Windsor		1847–1851	WPL
6.	David Carlos		1848–1850	WPL
7.	Perry Ezekial		1851–1919	EC
8.	Phebe Jane (Ellis)		1852–1912	EC
9.	Martha Sylvia		1854–1952	EC

CHILDREN OF DAVID SESSIONS, JR.

Married to Phebe Carter Foss, 30 December 1852

1.	Jim Madover (Jim Indian, adopted)	about 1843–1894
2.	Sarah Phebe (Moss)	26 Nov. 1853–1933
3.	Cardenia Estella (Burnham)	30 Jan. 1856–1933
4.	David Sessions	9 Jan. 1858–1915
5.	Olive Cordelia (Corbridge)	26 Dec. 1859–1932
6.	Fabyan Carter	22 July 1862–1934
7.	Darius	22 Oct. 1864–1935
8.	Calvin Foss	24 Dec. 1866–1868
9.	Elizabeth(Lewis)	19 May 1868–1919
10.	Rhoda Harriett	3 Oct. 1871–1873
11.	Annie Sophia (Neville)	30 Apr. 1875–1965

Appendix Three:
Braiding School Minutes

The following minutes are sandwiched between Patty's recollections and the last years of her diary entries in Diary 7.

Oct.-24–1868 Patty Sessions I have been to find some one to braid straw

Nov= 9 sister Ruth Free came and commenced a school at my house.–Ten scholars.

Nov= 18 Sister Free finished her school. The girls have learnt well

19 Sisters [Olive H.] Walker [Adah] Phipin and [Sophia] Tripp[1] came to my house wished me to take charge of the braiding school and continue it at my house as long as I Felt willing to ^do^ so. And also to take care of the braid and straw.

Nov= 20 I have been to many stores to find some s[t]raw spliters found none that would do. I then engaged a man to make some ten. I bought a box to keep the braid and straw ^in^

Nov= 25 I have been to the releif society. Sister Walker motioned that I presided over the S[t]raw Braiding, and that the school remained At my house. It was seconded. and a vote taken which was unanimus.

Dec 3 1868 1 oclock P M the ^school^ opened agreable to apointment prayer by Mrs Patty Sessions spent the time in braiding then ajourned at 4. P M to meet again on satd 19 Singing Lo the gentile chain is broken prayer by Mrs. Patty Sessions.

Dec 9 We went to the releif society I was caled on to go round as a commite on this block.-Caled Betsey [Birdenow] to teach the straw Braiding a vote taken which was unanimus

---

1. Olive Walker, Roxana Sophia Tripp, and Julia Phippen were the presidency of the sixteenth ward Relief Society from 1868 to 1873.

Mond. Dec 14.–1868

Dec=

14.–1868 I went round on this block to see the sisters

16 we quilted a quilt a quilt for Cordelia Ziderland

30 I went round the block again saw the sisters found them feeling well

Jan 2= 1867 I attended the releif society they ^voted^ me in as one of the commitee to attend the block No 10 on which I live

Dec 19 ^1868^ School met agreable to appointment. opened by singing Now we,ll sing with one acord & Prayer by Mrs Patty Ses= the minutes of the last school read and excepted adjourned untill next Satd Dec. 26 Singing hark ye mortals Prayer by Mrs Patty Sessions

Dec 26 School opened agreable to appointment singing Farewell all earthly honor &c prayer by Mrs P Sessions. minutes of the last school read and excepted spent the time in braiding adjourned untill Jan= 7 1869 on satd. singing an angel from on high prayer by P S

Jan, 7–1869 School opened agreeable to apointment singing Farewell all earthly honor prayer by P S but few presant read the minutes of the last school they were excepted spent the time braiding ajourned untill Jan-16 1869 singing Lo the gentile chain is broken Prayer by Mrs Patty Sessions

Jan.-16

1869 School met agreable to apointment Opened by singing Lo the gentile chain is broken. Prayer Mrs P Sessions The minutes of the last school was read and excepted spent the time in braiding very agreable. Ajourned to meet again at the same place at 1-oclock sat^ur^day next Singing Arise my soul arise &c

Jan 23 School met agreable to apointment I was not Presant but few there they spent the time braiding.

1869

Feb= 4th School met again ^I not presant^ spent the time in braiding untill I came home I closed by prayer and singing Lo the gentile chain is broken

Feb= 13 School met agreable to appointment singing Arise my soul Arise &c ^Prayer by Patty Sessions^ spent the time very agreable in braiding and singing Ajourned to meet again on Satd next 1 oclock P M singing Away with our fears &c Prayer by Patty Sessions

Feb 20 ^1869^ school met agreeable to apointment singing Hark ye Mortals List be still &c Prayer by Sister P Sessions spent the time in braiding ajourned to meet Feb= 27–1869 by singing Farewell all earthly honors &c Prayer by sist Patty Sessions

Feb= 27 ^1869^ I was gone School met but four presant braided and ajourned to meet March 4th

1869

March 4th School met agreable to apointment quite a number presant they felt well braided good and seemed enerjectic ajourned to meet again March 13 I was presant but feeble and sick

March 13–1869 School met agreable to appointment a good turnout four that never had been before the school was opened by singing Hark ye mortals List be still prayer by Patty Sessions sisters Free and Mousley presant we spent the time very agreable in braiding &c ajourened by singing Arise my soul arise &c Prayer by sister P Sessions to meet again March 20th

March 20 ^1869^ School met agreeable to apointment Opened by singing Now weel sing with one accord Prayer by Patty Sessions singing We thank the Oh God for a Prophet &c quite a number presant spent the time in braiding the minutes of the last meeting read and accepted by a unanimous vote ajo^u^rned by singing Oh ye mountains high &c prayer by Mrs Patty Sessions. to meet again March 27

March

27 1869 school met agreeable to appointment singing Arise oh Glorious Zion &c Prayer by sister P Sessions Singing Now well sing with one acord &c the minutes of the last meeting read & accepted ajourned to meet again April 10 singing Come let us anew &c Prayer by sister P Sessions

April 10

~~**March**~~ **10**

1869 School met agreeable to the apointment opned ^by singing come come ye saints &c prayer by Patty Sessions spent the time in braiding very agreeable the minutes of the last school was read and accepted ajourned to meet again next satd April 17 singing Arise my soul arise &c prayer by Patty Sessions

Unaccountably the minutes end, and Patty begins the last years of her diaries.

BIBLIOGRAPHY

BOOKS AND PAMPHLETS

Alexander, Thomas G. *Things in Heaven and Earth: The Life and Times of Wilford Woodruff, a Mormon Prophet*. Salt Lake City: Signature Books, 1991.

Andover: The First 175 Years. Andover, Maine: The Writing Club (The Friday Club), 1979.

Arrington, Leonard. *Brigham Young: American Moses*. New York: Alfred A. Knopf, 1985.

——. *Charles C. Rich: Mormon General and Western Frontiersman*. Provo, Utah: Brigham Young University Press, 1974.

——. *Great Basin Kingdom: An Economic History of the Latter-day Saints*. Lincoln: University of Nebraska Press, 1958.

Arrington, Leonard, Feramoz Y. Fox, and Dean L. May. *Building the City of God: Community and Cooperation among the Mormons*. Salt Lake City: Deseret Book Co., 1976.

Ashton, Wendell J. *Voice in the West*. New York: Duell, Sloan and Pearce, 1950.

Barrett, Ivan. *Mary Fielding Smith*. N.p.: RIC Publishing Co., 1984.

Beach, W. *The Family Physician. Reformed System of Medicine*. New York: by author, 1842.

Bean, Eva. *East Bethel Road*. Bethel, Maine: Bethel Historical Society, 1984.

Beecher, Maureen Ursenbach, and Lavina Fielding Anderson, eds. *Sisters in Spirit*. Urbana and Chicago: University of Illinois Press, 1987.

Bitton, Davis. *Guide to Mormon Diaries and Autobiographies*. Provo, Utah: Brigham Young University Press, 1977.

Black, Susan Ward Easton. *Membership of the Church of Jesus Christ of Latter-day Saints 1830–1848*. 50 vols. Provo, Utah: Brigham Young University Religious Studies Center, 1984.

——. *Pioneers of 1847: A Sesquicentennial Remembrance*. Provo, Utah: Brigham Young University College of Family Living, 1980.

Book of Remembrance of Sixteenth Ward, Riverside Stake of the Church of Jesus Christ of Latter-day Saints, First Century. Salt Lake City: The Sixteenth Ward Book of Remembrance Committee, 1945.

Bountiful Area Historic Sites. Bicentennial edition. Bountiful, Utah: Bountiful Area Historic Sites Committee, 1976.

Bradley, Martha Sonntag. *ZCMI: America's First Department Store*. Salt Lake City: ZCMI, 1991.

Brodie, Fawn M. *No Man Knows My History: The Life of Joseph Smith, the Mormon Prophet*. New York: Alfred A. Knopf, 1963.

Brooks, Juanita, ed. *Diary of Hosea Stout*. 2 vols. Salt Lake City: University of Utah Press, 1964.

Brown, Leroy W., ed. *History of Patty Bartlett Sessions: Mother of Mormon Midwifery*. North Glenn, Col.: self published, 1975.

Bryson, Conrey. *Winter Quarters*. Salt Lake City: Deseret Book Co., 1986.

Burgess-Olson, Vickey, ed. *Sister Saints*. Provo: Brigham Young University, 1978.

Burton, Richard F. *The City of the Saints and across the Rocky Mountains to California*. New York: Harper and Brothers, 1862.

Carr, Elmer J., ed. *Honorable Remembrance: The San Diego Master List of the Mormon Battalion*. San Diego: Mormon Battalion Visitors Center, 1978.

Carter, Kate B., ed. *An Enduring Legacy*. Vol. 10. Salt Lake City: Daughters of Utah Pioneers, 1987.

——,ed. *Heart Throbs of the West*. Vol. 2. Salt Lake City: Daughters of Utah Pioneers, 1940.

——. "They Came in '47." *Heart Throbs of the West*. Vol. 8. Salt Lake City: Daughters of Utah Pioneers, 1947.

——,ed. *Heart Throbs of the West*. Vol. 9. Salt Lake City: Daughters of Utah Pioneers, 1948.

——,ed. *Our Pioneer Heritage*. Vol. 2. Salt Lake City: Daughters of Utah Pioneers, 1959.

Carvalho, David N. *Forty Centuries of Ink*. New York: Burt Franklin, 1971.

Coleman, Arthur D., comp. *Wives and Daughters of the Pratt Pioneers of Utah*. Salt Lake City: N.p., 1969.

Cook, Lyndon W. *The Revelations of the Prophet Joseph Smith*. Salt Lake City: Deseret Book Co., 1985.

De Platt, Lyman. *Nauvoo 1839–1845*. Vol. 1. Highland, Utah: n.p., 1980.

Derr, Jill Mulvay, Janeth Russell Cannon, and Maureen Ursenbach Beecher. *Women of Covenant*. Salt Lake City: Deseret Book Co., 1992.

Dewey, Richard Lloyd. *Porter Rockwell: The Definitive Biography*. New York: Paramount Books, 1986.

The Doctrine and Covenants. Salt Lake City: The Church of Jesus Christ of Latter-day Saints, 1986.

Durant, Will, and Ariel Durant. "Is Progress Real?" Chap. 13 in *The Lessons of History*. New York: Simon and Schuster, 1968.

Esshom, Frank. *Pioneers and Prominent Men of Utah*. Salt Lake City: Utah Pioneers Book Publishing Co., 1913.

Evans, John Henry. *Joseph Smith: An American Prophet*. New York: Macmillan Co., 1946.

Ferris, Mrs. B.G. *Mormons at Home with Some Incidents of Travel from Missouri to California, 1852–53*. New York, AMS Press, 1971.

Foy, Leslie T. *The City Bountiful*. Bountiful, Utah: Horizon Publishers, 1975.

Gabbott, Mabel Jones, comp. *A Tabernacle in the Land Bountiful*. Bountiful, Utah: Bountiful Area Centennial Committee, 1992.

Gates, Susa Amelia Young (pseudonym "Homespun"). *Lydia Knight's History*. Salt Lake City: Juvenile Instructor Office, 1883.

Gates, Susa Young, and Leah D. Widtsoe. *The Life Story of Brigham Young*. New York: Macmillan, 1930.

Gibbons, Francis M. *John Taylor, Mormon Philosopher: Prophet of God*. Salt Lake City: Deseret Book Co., 1985.

——. *Wilford Woodruff, Wondrous Worker, Prophet of God*. Salt Lake City: Deseret Book Co., 1988.

Godfrey, Kenneth W., Audrey M. Godfrey, and Jill Mulvay Derr. *Women's Voices: An Untold History of the Latter-day Saints*. Salt Lake City: Deseret Book Co., 1982.

Grow, Stewart L. *A Tabernacle in the Desert*. Salt Lake City: Deseret Book Co., 1958.

Hafen, LeRoy, and Ann W. Hafen. *Handcarts to Zion: The Story of a Unique Western Migration, 1856–1860*. Glendale, Calif.: Arthur H. Clark, 1960.

Henderson, Myrtle E. *A History of the Theatre in Salt Lake City from 1850 to 1870*. Evanston, Ill.: by author, c. 1934, 1936.

History of Brigham Young, 1847–1867. Berkeley, Calif.: MassCall Associates, 1964. Second printing, 1966.

Holmes, Kenneth L., ed. and comp. *Covered Wagon Women: Diaries and Letters from the Western Trails 1840–1890*. Vol. 1. Glendale, Calif.: Arthur H. Clark, 1983.

Holzapfel, Richard N., and Jeffery Cottle. *Old Mormon Nauvoo 1839–1846*. Provo, Utah: Grandin Book Co., 1990.

Jessee, Dean C., ed. *The Papers of Joseph Smith*. 2 vols. Salt Lake City: Deseret Book Co., 1989.

Jenson, Andrew. *Encyclopedic History of the Church of Jesus Christ of Latter-day Saints*. Salt Lake City: Deseret News Pub. Co., 1941.

———. *Latter-day Saint Biographical Encyclopedia*. 4 vols. 1901. Reprint, Salt Lake City: Western Epics, 1971.

Johnson, Clark. *Mormon Redress Petitions: Documents of the 1833–1838 Missouri Conflict*. Provo, Utah: Religious Studies Center, Brigham Young University, 1992.

Kearl, J.R., Clayne L. Pope, and Larry T. Wimmer, comps. *Index to the 1850, 1860, and 1870 Census of Utah: Heads of Households*. Baltimore: Genealogical Publishing Co., 1981.

Kimball, Stanley B. *Heber C. Kimball: Mormon Patriarch and Pioneer*. Urbana and Chicago: University of Illinois Press, 1981.

———. *Historic Resource Study: Mormon Pioneer National Historic Trail*. Washington, D.C.: U.S. Department of Interior/National Park Service, 1991.

———, ed. *On the Potter's Wheel: The Diaries of Heber C. Kimball*. Salt Lake City: Signature Books, 1987.

Kline, Mary-Jo. *A Guide to Documentary Editing*. Baltimore: The Johns Hopkins University Press, 1988.

Knight, Hal, and Stanley B. Kimball. *111 Days to Zion*. Salt Lake City: Deseret News Press, 1978.

Lapham, W.B. *History of Bethel 1768–1890*. Augusta, Maine: n.p, 1991.

Larson, Andrew Karl. *Erastus Snow: The Life of a Missionary and Pioneer for the Early Mormon Church*. Salt Lake City: University of Utah Press, 1971.

Larson, Carl V., ed. and comp. *A Data Base of the Mormon Battalion: An Identification of the Original Members of the Mormon Battalion*. Providence, Utah: Keith W. Watkins, 1987.

Ludlow, Daniel H., ed. *Encyclopedia of Mormonism*. 5 vols. New York: Macmillan, 1992.

Lundwall, N.B., comp. *Temples of the Most High*. Salt Lake City: Bookcraft, 22nd printing, 1975.

Madsen, Brigham D. *The Shoshoni Frontier and the Bear River Massacre*. Salt Lake City: University of Utah Press, 1985.

Maughan, Ila Fisher. *Pioneer Theatre in the Desert*. Salt Lake City: Deseret Book Company, 1961.

McCormick, John S. *Salt Lake City: The Gathering Place*. Woodland Hills, Calif.: Windsor Publications, 1980.

Moffat, Mary Jane, and Charlotte Painter. *Revelations: Diaries of Women*. New York: Vintage Books, 1975.

Mulder, William, and A. Russell Mortensen, eds. *Among the Mormons: Historic Accounts by Contemporary Observers*. New York: Alfred A Knopf, 1958.

Neff, Andrew Love. *History of Utah 1847 to 1869*. Salt Lake City: Deseret News Press, 1940.

1993–1994 Church Almanac. Salt Lake City: Deseret News Press, 1992.

Noall, Claire. *Guardians of the Hearth: Utah's Pioneer Midwives and Women Doctors*. Bountiful, Utah: Horizon Publishers, 1974.

Olsen, Nolan Porter. *Logan Temple: The First 100 Years*. Providence, Utah: Keith W. Watkins, 1978.

Parker, Jimmy B., comp. *Pottawattamie County, Iowa Index to 1850 Census*. Salt Lake City: Research Department of the Genealogical Society, 1964.

Peterson, Janet, and LaRene Gaunt. *Elect Ladies*. 1946. Reprint, Salt Lake City: Deseret Book Co., 1990.

Phelps, W.W., comp. *Deseret Almanac for the Year of Our Lord 1852*. Salt Lake City: W. Richards, 1852.

Plenk, Henry, ed. *Medicine in the Beehive State*. Salt Lake City: University of Utah Press, 1992.

Powell, Allen Kent, ed. *Utah History Encyclopedia*. Salt Lake City: University of Utah Press, 1994.

Pratt, Parley P. *Autobiography of Parley P. Pratt*. 1938. Reprint, Salt Lake City: Deseret Book Co., 1985.

Reeder, C. A., Jr. *The History of Utah's Railroads 1869–1883*. Ann Arbor, Mich.: University Microfilms Limited, 1970.

Richards, Ralph T. *Of Medicine, Hospitals, and Doctors*. Salt Lake City: University of Utah Press, 1953.

Roberts, Brigham H. *A Comprehensive History of the Church*. 6 vols. Provo, Utah: Brigham Young University Press, 1965.

——. *The Life of John Taylor*. Salt Lake City: George Q. Cannon and Sons, 1892.

Sessions, Gene A. *Mormon Thunder: A Documentary History of Jedediah Morgan Grant*. Chicago: University of Illinois Press, 1982.

Sloan, E.L., comp. *The Salt Lake City Directory and Business Guide for 1869*. Salt Lake City: E.L. Sloan and Co., 1869.

Smith, Joseph. *History of the Church of Jesus Christ of Latter-day Saints*. 7 vols. and index. Salt Lake City: Deseret Book Co., 1932–1970.

Smith, Joseph Fielding. *Doctines of Salvation*. Vol. 2. Compiled by Bruce R. McConkie. Salt Lake City: Bookcraft, 1955.

——, comp. *The Teachings of the Prophet Joseph Smith*. Salt Lake City: Deseret Book Co., 1977.

Snow, Eliza R. *Biography and Family Record of Lorenzo Snow*. Salt Lake City: Deseret News Press, 1884.

Stanley, Reva. *The Archer of Paradise*. Caldwell, Idaho: Caxton Printers, 1937.

Taylor, Samuel W. *Nightfall at Nauvoo*. New York: Avon, 1971.

Tullidge, Edward W. *History of Salt Lake City and Its Founders*. Salt Lake City: Star Printing, 1883.

Ward, Maurine Carr, ed. *Winter Quarters: The 1846–1848 Life Writings of Mary Haskins Parker Richards*. Logan, Utah: Utah State University Press, 1996.

Widtsoe, John A. *Joseph Smith: Seeker after Truth, Prophet of God*. Salt Lake City: Bookcraft, 1957.

Wight, Carrie. *[A History of] Newry, Maine 1805–1855*. Bethel, Maine: self-published, 1955. Reprint, Town of Bethel, 1990.

Wight, Paula M. *Newry Profiles 1805–1980*. Bethel, Maine: Town of Newry, 1980. Reprint, Town of Bethel, 1990.

Wilkins, Martha Fifield. *Sunday River Sketches: A New England Chronicle*. Rumford, Maine: n.p., 1977.

Woodruff, Wilford. *Wilford Woodruff's Journal*. Edited by Scott G. Kenney. 9 vols. Midvale,Utah: Signature Books, 1983.

Young, Brigham. *Manuscript History of Brigham Young, 1846–1847*. Edited by Elden J. Watson. Salt Lake City: by editor, 1971.

Young, Brigham, et al. *Journal of Discourses*. 26 vols. Los Angeles: General Printing and Lithograph, 1961.

ARTICLES AND PERIODICALS

"Anniversary Gathering." *Woman's Exponent* 9 (1 January 1881): 116.

Bennett, Richard E. "Mormon Renegade: James Emmett at the Vermillion, 1846." *South Dakota History* 15, no. 3 (Fall 1985): 217–33.

Bountiful Historical Society. *Bountiful Centennial Quarterly* (Winter 1990).

Compton, Todd. "A Trajectory of Plurality: An Overview of Joseph Smith's Thirty-three Plural Wives." *Dialogue* (Summer 1996): 1.

Deseret News 6 (6 September 1856): 216; 7 (8 April 1857): 37.

Dockstader, Julie A. "Angels of Mercy: Pioneer Midwives in Utah." *Pioneer Magazine* (Winter 1995): 13–15.

Hendrix, Roger A. "I Have a Question." *Ensign* (December 1992): 28.

Jensen, Richard L. "Forgotten Relief Societies, 1844–67." *Dialogue* 16, no. 1 (Spring 1983): 105–25.

Lobrot, Gertrude R. "Bell, bout and cannons trekked west together." *Church News* (14 July 1985): 5, 13.

"Memorial" *Woman's Exponent* 14 (1 April 1886): 164, 166–67.

Noall, Claire. "Mormon Midwives." *Utah Historical Quarterly* 10 (1942): 84–144.

——. "Superstitutions, Customs, and Prescriptions of Mormon Midwives." *California Folklore Quarterly* 3, no. 2 (April 1944): 102–114.

"Notes from Washington," *Woman's Exponent* 14 (1 May 1886): 180–81.

"Patty Sessions." Parts 1–8. *Woman's Exponent* 13 (1 September 1884): 51; 13 (15 September 1884): 63; 13 (1 November 1884): 86; 13 (15 November 1884): 94–95; 13 (1 February 1885): 134–35; 13 (1 March 1885): 150–51; 14 (1 June 1885): 2; 14 (15 November 1885): 85–86, 94–95.

Perrin, Kathleen. "Year of Church in Tahiti." *Church News* (7 May 1994): 12.

"Railroad Meeting." *Deseret News* (14 January 1854).

Sessions, Phebe C. "Biographical Sketch: Patty Sessions." *Woman's Exponent* 27 (1 and 15 June 1898): 6.

Smith, Norman Lee. "Why Are Mormons So Susceptible to Medical and Nutritional Quackery?" *The Journal of Collegium Aesculapium* 1, no. 1 (December 1983): 29–43.

Sturgis, Henry. "The Iron Spine." *American Heritage* 20, no. 3 (April 1969): 46–57.

Wanger, Joyce. "19th Century Medicine in Bethel, Maine." *The Bethel Courier* 14 (Fall 1990): 1–2.

Watson, Jeanne H. "Women's Travails and Triumphs on the Overland Trails." *Overland Journal* 9, no. 4 (Winter 1991).

Wilcox, Howard D. "Deseret's First Hospital." *Utah Medical Bulletin* (December 1976): 2–3.

Willis, Elizabeth. "Voice in the Wilderness: The Diaries of Patty Sessions." *The Journal of American Folklore* 101 (January–March 1988): 46–47.

Woodruff, Wilford. "The Temple." *Deseret News* 3 (19 February 1853): 26.

Manuscripts and Other Unpublished Material

Bachman, Daniel W. "Plural Marriage before the Death of Joseph Smith." Master's thesis, Purdue University, 1975.

Berlin, C. Elliott. "Abraham Owen Smoot, Pioneer Mormon Pioneer Leader" Master's thesis, Brigham Young University, 1955.

Bigler, Henry W. "Diary of Henry W. Bigler" (copy of typescript in Brigham Young University Library; obtained in 1937). Photocopy CHD.

Bountiful Cemetery Centennial Historical Walking Tour. Presented by the Bountiful Area Centennial Committee, 25 and 26 September 1992.

Cannon, Angus M. "Interview with Joseph Smith III." 1905, typescript. Archives of the Historical Department, Church of Jesus Christ of Latter-day Saints, Salt Lake City.

Dibble, Edwin S. "Genealogy of Philo Dibble." 1973, typescript. Copy in possession of Donna T. Smart.

Horne, Joseph F. "Autobiography." Mimeographed copy, #331Ms93, Western Americana Division, University of Utah Library, Salt Lake City.

Jackman, Golden L., and Teton Hanks, comps. "Descendants of Ephraim Knowlton Hanks and His Wives." Typescript. Archives of the Historical Department, Church of Jesus Christ of Latter-day Saints, Salt Lake City.

Jones, Gerald E. "Some Forgotten Pioneers: The Emmett Company of 1844." Paper presented at the Sperry Symposium, Brigham Young University, Provo, Utah, 26 January 1980; typescript in the Archives of the Historical Department.

"Journal History of the Church of Jesus Christ of Latter-day Saints." Chronological collection of clippings and other information. Typescript and microfilm. Archives of the Historical Department, Church of Jesus Christ of Latter-day Saints, Salt Lake City.

Kraut, Ogden W. "Pioneer Journals: Life History of Philo Dibble, Sr." Typescript. Archives of the Historical Department, Church of Jesus Christ of Latter-day Saints, Salt Lake City.

Madsen, Brigham D. "Encounter with the Northwestern Shoshoni at Bear River in 1863: Battle or Massacre?" Dello G. Dayton Memorial Lecture, Weber State College, Ogden, Utah, 11 May 1983.

Meeks, Priddy. "Journal." Typescript. #15941, Utah State Historical Society, Salt Lake City.

"Nauvoo Temple Endowment Register," 10 December 1845 to 8 February 1846. Bound typescript. Salt Lake City: Temple Index Bureau, 1974.

Paxman, Shirley B. "Early Mormon Family Life and Home Production." Lecture delivered at Harold B. Lee Library, Brigham Young University, Provo, Utah, 7 December 1979. Copy in Archives of Historical Department, Church of Jesus Christ of Latter-day Saints, Salt Lake City.

Sessions, Perrigrine. "Diaries." Original Holograph, Archives of the Historical Department, Church of Jesus Christ of Latter-day Saints, Salt Lake City. Photocopy in possession of Donna T. Smart.

Snow, Eliza R. "Journal. Winter Quarters of the Camp of Israel." 1 vol. Holograph, HM27522, Huntington Library, San Marino, Calif.

Thornwell, Emily. *The Lady's Guide to Perfect Gentility*. Duplicated copy of 1856 original, Huntington Library, San Marino, Calif.

Tripp, Enoch Bartlett. "Autobiography." Microfilm. Archives of the Historical Department, Church of Jesus Christ of Latter-day Saints, Salt Lake City.

Wolfinger, Henry J. "A Test of Faith: Jane Elizabeth James and the Origins of the Black Community." Typescript. Archives of the Historical Department, Church of Jesus Christ of Latter-day Saints, Salt Lake City.

MAPS

Map of Bountiful, 1900. Researched and compiled by Florence Tuttle Fog. Cartographer, Ronald L. Chowen.

Map of Nauvoo, compiled from the records of Hancock County. Photocopy obtained from Nauvoo Visitors Center, Church of Jesus Christ of Latter-day Saints, Nauvoo, Illinois.

The Old Maps of Oxford County, Maine, in 1858. Fryeburg, Maine: Saco Valley Printing, 1972–1984.

Pioneer Map: Great Salt Lake City, Great Basin, North America, comp. and copyrighted by Nicholas G. Morgan; map work by J. B. Ireland. [S.I.: s.n. 195-?]

Pioneer Map Showing Lot Locations of First Pioneer Owners in the Five-Acre Plat, A Portion of the Big Field Survey, Great Salt Lake City. Compiled for and copyrighted by Nicholas G. Morgan, Sr.; drawn by J. B. Ireland [S.I.: s.n. 1955].

INDEX

Civil War, 283n97, 299
Clark, Brother, 39, 170
Clark, Caroline. *See* Huntington, Caroline Clark
Clark, Cedenia O.. *See* Young, Cedenia O. Clark
Clark, Daniel, 42, 63n111
Clark, David W., 63
Clark, Ezekiel, 147, 234, 269n74, 310, 356n14, 373
Clark, Frances Jessie Swan Kimball, 78, 129, 136, 161
Clark, Martha Sylvia, 290n108, 327, 336, 337, 373n50
Clark, Mary Dewey, 373
Clark, Perry Ezekiel, 234, 251, 255, 269, 296–97, 337, 373n50
Clark, Phebe Jane. *See* Ellis, Phebe Jane Clark
Clark, Sarah E., 63
Clark, Sister, 148, 152, 161
Clark, Susan Urina Dyer, 373n50
Clark, Sylvia Porter Sessions Lyon, 13, 14, 17, 19, 20–21, 23, 25, 32, 33, 39, 40, 45, 46, 52, 55, 56, 59, 60, 63, 68, 72, 73, 77, 78, 79, 80, 81, 84, 85, 93, 96, 100, 109, 117, 118, 119, 120, 129, 133, 134, 136n38, 137, 153, 161, 163, 166, 169, 170, 171, 172, 174, 175, 176, 177, 178, 179, 181, 193, 195, 196, 197, 198, 199, 200, 202, 203, 206, 207, 209, 210, 212, 213, 214, 215, 219, 220, 221, 222, 227, 229, 230, 231, 232, 234, 235, 236, 238, 239–40, 241, 242, 243, 245, 246, 248, 250, 251, 253, 254, 255, 258, 259, 260, 261, 263, 264, 267, 268, 269, 273, 274, 275, 276, 278, 279, 280, 281, 282, 284, 287, 288, 289, 290, 290n108, 291, 292, 295, 296, 298, 300, 303, 304, 305, 306, 307, 308, 309, 310, 312, 313, 314, 315, 317, 318, 319, 321, 322, 323, 324, 326, 327, 328, 331, 332, 333, 334, 335, 336, 337, 342, 343, 355, 356n14
Clarke, Harriet Teeples Wixom Sessions Worden, 25, 70, 139, 142, 143, 144, 145, 147, 148, 149, 151, 152, 153, 154, 162, 163, 165, 172, 189n7, 194, 195, 202n30, 214, 220, 235, 257, 261, 262, 264, 271, 276, 278n91, 281, 289, 301, 314

Clary, Sister, 166, 167
Clawson, Cornelia Brown, 292n109
Clawson, Moroni, 292
Clawson, Moses, 292n109
Clayton, William, 45n48, 348
Clements, Alpheus G., 71
Clements, Alvin, 43, 71
Clements, John, 200
Clements, Rhoda Gifford, 71
Clements, Sister, 183
Clinton, Jeter (Dr.), 169
Clothier, Andrew Jackson, 138n45, 141
Clothier, Sister, 138
Cluff, Brother and Sister, 167
Clyde, Cynthia Davis, 51
Clyde, George Washington, 51n67
Cobb, Charlotte. *See* Drake, Charlotte Cobb
Cobb, Sister, 309
Colby, Alanson, 119
Colby, Fanny Knight, 119
Cole, Annie, 312
Cole, Brother, 304, 307
Cole, Jena, 309
Cole, Mary Eliza. *See* Bliss, Mary Eliza Cole
Cole, Sister, 312
Colebrook, Sister (Mrs. Charles), 211, 212
Coleman, John, 203
Collidge, Elizabeth Buchanan, 55, 63
Collidge, Joseph Wellington, 56
Collins, Sister, 150, 160
Colorado, 325, 329
Coltrin, Andrew, 243, 244
Coltrin, Graham, 164
Coltrin, Sister (Mrs. Andrew), 243
Columbus, Nebr., 89
Commerce, Ill., 23
Compton, Allen, 129, 136, 137
Compton, Todd: on Mormon marriages, 19
Conklin, Hannah. *See* Graybill, Hannah Conklin
Connor, Patrick, 304n11
Consecration, law of, 203n31, 217, 229n7
Consecration deed, 226, 228, 229n7, 343
Consumption, 73n164, 75n171, 111, 132
Cook, Ann Eliza Howland, 63

Murray, Sister, 172
Murray, Vilate. *See* Kimball, Vilate Murray
Musser, Anna Barr, 139, 142, 210
Musser, Susanna. *See* Sheets, Susanna Musser

N

National Party, 193
Nauvoo, Ill., 7, 14, 18, 32, 35, 39n38, 41, 44, 45, 45n48, 46, 49, 50, 54n78, 56, 61, 65, 67, 142, 276, 342, 343, 347, 370n43
Nauvoo Brass Band, 200n26
Nauvoo Expositor, 23
Nauvoo Legion, 23, 130, 246, 250
Nauvoo Temple, 21, 23, 60n96, 64n112
Nauvoo Temple Bell, 88, 133n27
Naylor, Arthur, 356
Naylor, Brother, 366
Nease, Matilda. *See* Hunt, Matilda Nease
Nebeker, Ammon, 109
Nebeker, Brother, 287
Nebeker, Elizabeth Davis, 111, 114
Nebeker, George, 235–36, 309
Nebeker, Harriet Ann Van Wagoner, 109
Nebeker, Henry, 109
Nebeker, John Sr., 108, 114, 178
Nebeker, Lurenia Fitzgerald, 108n276, 114, 178
Nebeker, Peter, 111
Nebeker, Sister, 291, 301, 307
Nebeker, Susannah Elizabeth, 111
Neff, John, 95n216
Neff, John II, 102n241
Neff, Mary Barr, 102
Neff's Mill, 121
Neville, James, 356
Newman, Sister, 238, 278, 312
Newman, William, 315, 337
Newry, Maine, 3, 12, 33n10, 34n15, 355
Newtown, Mass., 355
New York, 17
Niobara River, 79n183
Nishnabotna River, Iowa, 54
Noble, Bates, 43, 104
Noble, Brother, 372
Noble, Hyrum B., 69n137

Noble, Joseph Bates, 42, 69n137, 73n165, 95n216
Noble, Joseph H., 35n17
Noble, Joseph (son of Joseph Bates), 69n137
Noble, Mary Adeline Beman, 69n137, 73n165, 104, 162
Noble, Mary Ann Washburn, 73, 132, 135
Noble, Mary Elizabeth, 73
Noble, Sarah B. Alley, 69, 132
Noble, Sister, 78, 102
Nodoway River, Iowa, 54
Nolon, Mary, 112
No Man Knows My History, 20
Noon, Sarah Peak, 79
North Platte River, Wyo., 95n216
Norton, John, 222
Norton, Rebecca Ann (daughter of John and Ann), 222
Norton, Rebecca Ann Hammer, 167, 168, 222
Nowlin, Amanda Thomas, 109
Nowlin, Jabez Townsend, 109n279

O

Oakey, John, 109
Oakley, Elizabeth DeGroat, 33
Oakley, Ezra Hemstead Nassau, 33
Oakley, John Degroat, 43, 72n163
Oakley, Mary Ann. *See* Taylor, Mary Ann Oakley
Oakley, Mary Elizabeth, 73
Oakley, Mary McCormall Patterson, 72
Ockett, Molly, 7
O'Conner, Mrs., 188
Odell, Phebe. *See* Brown, Phebe Narcissa Odell
Ogden, Harriet. *See* Taft, Harriet Ogden
Ogden, Phoebe. *See* Chase, Phoebe Ogden
Ogden, Utah, 87n201, 110n288, 218, 231, 271, 281, 287, 300, 324, 352, 389
Olcott, James, 258
Old Bishop (Indian), 143n65
Old Elk (Indian), 143n67
Olson, Joanna, 317
Omaha Indians, 68n130
Oose, definition of term, 75n173
Oostead, Brother, 330

of David's illness, 252; tells Rosilla
to hold her tongue, 64; took PBS to
store, 373; on the trail in Nebraska,
93, 94; travels west, 52, 53; trial of,
131–32; at Tripp home, 226; visitors
to, 296; visits Byron, 390; visits
James Buckland, 265; visits PBS,
103, 127, 130, 131, 154, 163, 164,
165, 166, 167, 169, 170, 171, 172,
173, 177, 180, 217, 218, 219, 220,
230, 249, 251, 258, 259, 261, 262,
268, 270, 272, 273, 275, 280, 282,
283, 285, 286, 288, 291, 292, 297,
300, 302, 303, 308, 309, 310, 311,
312, 316, 317, 318, 320, 321, 322,
323, 324, 327, 329, 331, 332, 334,
335, 359–60; wagon of turned over,
96; wagon wheel ran over foot of,
90; walks with Rosilla and David,
60; was captain over fifty, 46n49;
went home, 254, 376; went hunting,
72, 89, 95; went to conference, 366;
went to conference of the seventies,
161; went to David's, 295; went to
farm, 112, 150; went to funeral, 362;
went to meeting, 149; went to Salt
Lake City with PBS, 370–71; went to
see children, 377; went to theater,
325; wife of is sick, 61; wives of,
44n44, 284, 368; writes letter for
PBS, 370
Sessions, Perry (son of PG and Mary),
279, 337, 352, 354, 367, 391
Sessions, Phebe Carter Foss, 7, 28, 123,
163, 167, 170, 179, 183, 185, 188,
189, 194, 196, 197, 198, 201, 206,
207, 212, 214, 215, 217, 227, 234,
235, 236, 238, 240, 241, 243, 245,
246, 250, 251, 258, 258n61, 263,
264, 266, 267, 269, 273, 276, 283,
284, 287, 288, 289, 297, 300, 303,
306, 310, 311, 315, 319, 320, 325,
327, 328, 331, 332, 333, 334, 337,
338, 346, 357n18, 363, 367, 368,
369n40, 370n44, 376, 379, 381
Sessions, Rachel Stevens, 6, 13, 276, 355
Sessions, Rosilla Cowan, 24, 25, 34n16,
38, 40, 56, 57, 59, 60, 61, 62–63,
64–66, 142, 276
Sessions, Sally Lavina Hill, 356, 362,
363, 373, 375
Sessions, Samantha, 369

Sessions, Sarah Ann Bryson, 336, 357,
359n23, 361, 362, 365, 368, 369n40,
370, 371, 374, 378, 382, 389, 391
Sessions, Sarah Crossley, 282, 286, 288,
290, 291, 298, 304, 307, 308, 311,
314, 317, 318, 320, 321, 325, 326,
327, 329, 330, 331, 333, 334, 335,
336, 337, 356n13, 357, 361n27, 368,
369, 381, 382n55, 389
Sessions, Sarah Phebe, 198, 317n23
Sessions, Selma Selena Holt, 376
Sessions, Susan Geneva, 374
Sessions, Sylvanus, 13, 14, 305, 342,
355, 357, 381
Sessions, Sylvia. *See* Clark, Sylvia Porter
Sessions Lyon
Sessions, Thomas Mabey, 364
Sessions, Zina (daughter of PG and
Mary), 262, 331
Sessions Settlement. *See* Bountiful, Utah
Seventy, Quorum of, 191
Seventy's Council Hall (Salt Lake City),
273, 282, 283
Seward, Brother, 325
Sewell, Sarah Stevens, 327
Shaver, Leonidas, 217
Shaw, Eliza, 215
Shaw, James B., 86, 101
Shaw, Laura Almira, 86, 89
Shaw, Laura Ann Gibbs, 86, 89,
101n236, 167, 215
Shearer, Sister, 189, 190, 192
Sheets, Elijah Funk, 43, 68n136, 89,
106n265
Sheets, Margaret Hutchinson, 68
Sheets, Susanna Musser, 106n265, 112
Shefflin, Mary Ann. *See* Kimball, Mary
Ann Shefflin
Shelton, Sebert C., 99
Sherwood, Henry Garlie, 40, 45–46, 47,
51, 55, 98, 100n234
Shimer, Laura Alvina. *See* Hunter, Laura
Alvina Shimer
Shirtlief. *See* Shurtlief
Shirts, Peter, 316
Shoal Creek, Iowa, 40, 44
Shockley, Mary, 108, 109
Shoshoni Indians, 305n11
Shumway, Charles, 66n121, 117,
162n11
Shumway, Charles M. (son of Charles),
117

Tripp, Robert, 361
Tripp, Roxana Sophia (daughter of
   Enoch and Sophia), 245
Tripp, Roxanna Sophia Billings,
   199n20, 202, 204, 205, 206, 207,
   208, 212, 213, 215, 216, 217, 220,
   221, 226, 228, 231, 232, 236, 237,
   239, 240, 242, 243, 244, 245, 248,
   250, 251, 252, 255, 256, 258, 261,
   262, 263, 264, 267, 271, 272n80, 275,
   280, 281, 282n94, 289, 290, 292,
   296, 302, 307, 308, 310, 333
Tripp, Sarah, 280
Tripp, Susan. *See* Flanagan, Susan Tripp
Tripp, Wallace, 335
Tripp, William, 34n15, 195n15, 349,
   349n9, 354, 366
True, N.T., 7
Tubbs, Sophia, 118
Tubbs, William, 118n320
Tubman, David, 198
Tubman, Jane, 198
Turnbow, Margaret Ann, 86, 88
Turnbow, Samuel, 86
Turnbow, Samuel Joseph, 148
Turnbow, Sylvira Caroline Hart, 86, 88,
   109, 148
Twist, Jane Anne, 135
Tyler, Abigail Abbott, 117, 140, 143,
   144, 151, 154, 161, 188, 197, 203
Tyler, Albert, 117n315
Tyler, Albert Peck, 138
Typhoid fever, 135
Typhus fever, 13

U

Union Academy, 274
U.S. Army, 253, 257n59, 258, 304
U.S. Soldiers, 304, 305
Utah County, 194n14
Utah Valley, 153, 254
Utah Valley War, 143, 144, 149
Utah War, 232n12, 247n37, 257n59,
   306n14
Ute Indians, 112

V

Vale, Dr., 215
Vance, John, 100n234
Van Cott, John, 86, 89n205

Van Cott, Losee, 86, 89n205, 96
Van Cott, Lucy Lavinia Sackett, 86,
   89n205, 96
Van Cott, Martha, 89
Van Dyke, Carolyn. *See* Grant, Carolyn
   Van Dyke
Vannorton, Sister, 43
Van Orden, Julia Ann. *See* Haight, Julia
   Ann Van Orden
Van Waggoner, Sister, 79
Van Wagoner, Harriet Ann. *See*
   Nebeker, Harriet Ann Van
   Wagoner
Vary, Sister, 216
Vasquez, Louis, 135n34
Vaughn, Jane. *See* Parry, Jane Vaughn
Vaughn, J.M. (Dr.), 149, 150, 151, 161,
   189
Vaughn, Rachel, 291
Veach, Elizabeth, 265
Vedette (newspaper), 324
Vernon, Brother, 254
Veshire, Vt., 276
Visiting teaching, 347
Vose, Polly, 246, 253, 259, 260, 279,
   309
Voting, 128, 374

W

Wade, Belinda Hickenlooper, 137–38,
   172, 198
Wade, Daniel, 213
Wade, Edward Davis, 138–39, 174, 198,
   203, 213
Wade, Edward William, 137
Wade, Mary Ellen Page, 213
Waggoner, Brother and Sister, 77
Waite, John Anson Jr., 356, 369, 370,
   374
Waite, Lucina Sessions, 292, 306,
   356n15, 369, 370, 372, 374
Wales, 326
Walker, Ann Agatha. *See* Pratt, Ann
   Agatha Walker
Walker, Chief, 195n14
Walker, Dionethia. *See* Lyman,
   Dionethia Walker
Walker, Elizabeth Foutz, 154, 203
Walker, Henson Jr., 154n95
Walker, Lucy. *See* Kimball, Lucy Walker
   Smith

Grover, 68n131; and Thomas Kane, 254n55; took dinner with PBS, 57, 121; took supper with PBS, 119; on the trail in Iowa, 44, 46, 50; treated by PBS, 44; visits PBS, 38, 70; wanted to buy PBS's stove, 53; and Willard Richards, 45n47; wives of, 8, 32n2, 35n17, 38n34, 50n60, 84n194, 86n200

Young, Brigham Hamilton, 42, 65

Young, Cedenia O. Clark, 65

Young, Clarissa Decker, 64, 86n200, 102, 140

Young, Delecta Adalia, 67

Young, Emily Dow Partridge Smith, 84n194

Young, George W., 73n164

Young, Harriet Elizabeth Cook, 32

Young, Harriet Page Wheeler, 8, 59, 86, 99, 120, 278

Young, Hyrum (son of Brigham and Louisa), 62n103

Young, J., 300

Young, Jane, 73

Young, John, 72, 100n234, 177, 272, 282, 290, 291, 323

Young, John Jr., 39, 40

Young, John W., 376n53

Young, Joseph, 273n82

Young, Joseph (brother of Brigham), 52n70, 99

Young, Joseph (son of Brigham and Louisa), 62n103

Young, Joseph Watson, 96n218

Young, Kimball: PBS visits office of, 307

Young, Leah Smith, 131

Young, Lorenzo Dow Jr., 99, 110

Young, Lorenzo Dow Sr., 8, 59, 86, 86n200, 96n218, 99, 110, 161n8

Young, Louisa Beaman, 35, 43, 45, 62, 69, 73, 80, 81, 119, 120, 133, 134, 138, 139, 140, 146

Young, Margaret Pierce, 309

Young, Mary Harvey Pierce, 75, 78n179, 127n7

Young, Miriam, 45n46

Young, Miriam Works, 45n46, 55n81

Young, Moroni, 69n142

Young, Persis Goodall, 96n218, 161

Young, Phineas Howe, 65n118, 95

Young, Sarah (daughter of Brigham H.), 65

Young, Sister, 60, 61, 78, 79, 82, 161

Young, Susannah. *See* Little, Susannah Young

Young, Theodosia Kimball, 72

Young, Vilate. *See* Decker, Vilate Young

Young, William G., 43, 46, 54, 67, 131

Young, Zina Diantha Huntington Jacobs, 20, 38, 39, 49, 50n60, 53, 66, 69, 72, 73, 76, 81, 84, 120, 128, 132, 151, 154, 161, 163, 165, 166, 242, 272, 278, 284, 302, 309, 312, 338

Young Ladies Retrenchment Society, 348

Z

Zions Cooperative Mercantile Institution, 26, 347, 348, 349, 352, 371